The Handbook of
magazine
Publishing

Fourth edition
Compiled by
the Editors of

Folio:
magazine

The Handbook of
magazine Publishing

Editors: RAMA RAMASWAMI, TONY SILBER
Designer: TOM ERNST
Production Coordinator: PETER GIRARD
Contributing Editors: LISA E. PHILLIPS, ANNE M. RUSSELL
Editorial Administrator: ROLF MAURER
Editor in Chief, FOLIO: ANNE M. RUSSELL
Executive Editor, FOLIO: TONY SILBER
Product Development Manager: RAMA RAMASWAMI

COWLES
Business Media

President and CEO: CAROLYN WALL; Sr. VP/CFO and COO: DOUGLAS J. MANONI; Sr. VP/Group
Publisher: PETER M. GOLDSTONE; Sr. VP/Strategic Planning and Marketing: DANIEL MCCARTHY;
President/Cowles Event Management: JOEL DAVIS; VP/SIMBA Information Inc.: CHRIS ELWELL;
VP/Human Resources: DIANNE HENNESSY; VP/Marketing: JUDY KRUEGLER LEE; VP/Production
and Information Systems: PATRICK M. PAGANO; VP and Publisher: ROBERTA THOMAS;
Corporate Editorial Director: THOMAS P. SOUTHWICK; Corporate Promotion and Communications
Director: JOEL J. BLATTSTEIN; General Editor/Educational/Training Products: BARBARA LOVE.

ISBN 0-918-110-21-1

Cowles Business Media, Inc.
11 River Bend Drive South, Box 4949
Stamford, CT 06907-4949

Printed in the United States of America

a Folio: book

table of contents

*Dates in parentheses indicate when the article originally appeared in FOLIO:.
Note: No attempt has been made to update titles and company affiliations of people named in the articles included in this book beyond the time the article originally appeared in FOLIO:. The biographies of all contributing authors are current as of May 1996.

Table of contents

section two
strategic focus
137

section three
editorial
173

Table of contents

section four
circulation

section five

ad sales   265

Issues and ideas

section six

promotion   293

Issues and ideas

section seven

design and production   307

Issues and ideas

Table of contents

introduction

■ If you've been listening to the debate about the much-vaunted information superhighway, chances are much of what you've heard concerns "the future." You've probably been cautioned that "the future is now," warned that it "awaits" you, or exhorted to "be prepared for it."

But for magazine publishers, there's no doubt about the status of the future—it has already arrived, and it's already revolutionizing the industry. Like other industries in the 1990s, magazines have experienced change at an unprecedented pace. We've faced an economic recession, downsizing, spiraling costs, fast and furious mergers and acquisitions, and the spectacular growth of new media. Zines and Web sites are now a part of our vocabulary. As we enter the 21st century wired for sound and video, the death of print media—prophesied for years—may seem inevitable.

Yet, to use a cliché, the more things change, the more they stay the same. The best and brightest minds in the business believe that magazines are here to stay. As always, the keys to survival are strong editorial, wise management, and a commitment to serving your readers. To prosper in the next decade, however, you must go beyond the basics and develop strategies to exploit the many exciting publishing opportunities that will come your way. This fourth edition of FOLIO:'s *Handbook of Magazine Publishing*

offers the tools you need to do what you've always done—only better.

The *Handbook* has long been considered the definitive reference work for the magazine industry's decision makers. This completely revised and expanded edition contains over 100 articles representing the best of FOLIO: from 1991 to early 1996.

The selections run the gamut from ad sales to zines. Whether you are a novice or a veteran, you'll find valuable advice from industry pundits on all aspects of magazine management, from launches to acquisitions to succeeding in cyberspace.

We've included hundreds of tips for efficient magazine management in all areas. Besides the traditional editorial, circulation, advertising, and production functions, areas covered in this book include legal and personnel issues, which are of great concern to the publishing industry in light of recent employment legislation and the increasing focus on diversity in the workplace. There's also a completely new section on electronic publishing in its various forms: CD-ROMs, fax delivery, cable TV, and online services. In addition, the *Handbook* provides a resource directory that lists dozens of valuable information sources.

The editors hope that with this *Handbook*, your travels on the information superhighway will be challenging, rewarding—and profitable.

section one

management

❝Managing without a strategic plan is **like driving only using the rear-view mirror:** You can see where you've been, but not where you're going."—p. 2

❝I don't want to make a million dollars. I want to make **readers rowdy."**—p. 12

❝Magazines can **consume money** like people consume air."—p. 24

❝The **best time to sell** your magazine is when you don't have to."—p. 50

Strategic Planning: A Six-Step Road Map to Your Company's Future

BY REED PHILLIPS III

Where creativity is king, management jargon is the language of serfs. The magazine industry, of course, is not alone in this belief. Dawn Steel, the former president of Columbia Pictures, observes in her memoir, *They Can Kill You—But They Can't Eat You,* that when Sony was acquiring Columbia, the Sony executives "would refer to the studios as 'suppliers of software' even though we thought of ourselves as 'creators of culture.'"

To bridge the gap between management and creativity, I have created a six-step, jargon-free guide to strategic planning for magazine executives. But before we start putting together a plan, let's answer a few of publishers' most commonly asked questions:

What is strategic planning? One senior executive recently challenged me to define—"in five words or less"—what, precisely, strategic planning is. Using just *six* words, I replied that it is the "road map to a company's future": It defines where a company has been and where it is going.

Managing a magazine company without a strategic plan in place is like driving a car by looking only in the rear-view mirror: You can see where you've been, but not where you are going. A strategic plan will give you the directions you need to get where you want to go.

Isn't that an operational plan? No. A strategic plan is like a map that shows you how to get from one city to the next; an operational plan is like a map that shows every street, park and public building. In fact, the task of developing an operational plan becomes much easier once the strategic thinking is done.

Why don't more publishers have strategic plans? There are a number of reasons, I think. First, many publishing companies are still run by brilliant entrepreneurs who have succeeded by following their *own* instincts, and who are therefore dubious about planning, which is a collective process.

Second, for small publishing companies that are struggling just to survive, there is no time for planning.

Conversely, if things are going well, the CEO may consider the business impervious to change and see no need to plan.

And finally, a reason many magazine companies do not do strategic planning is that it's easier to see results from operational planning. With strategic planning, you often have to wait years to see the plan's full impact.

Why should I have a plan? The magazine industry is changing so fast right now that publishers who do not adapt to technological and market changes risk losing marketshare to their competitors. In my experience, companies without strategic plans are usually companies with flat or declining growth.

Okay, so how do I put together a plan? I use the six following steps:

1. Define the purpose of your organization.

The statement of purpose, or mission statement, should be no longer than one sentence. It should say who you are today and who you want to be in the future. And, except for minor refinements, it should not change much from year to year unless a significant change in direction is warranted.

> The industry is changing so fast that publishers who don't adapt to technological and market changes usually have flat or declining growth.

Multi-title publishers, in particular, need strong, clear mission statements to focus the efforts of their companies. John Griffin, president of the magazine division at Rodale Press, told me that his company wants to be the number-one publisher of health and active-sports magazines in the United States and eventually in the world. With a single sentence Griffin tells us where he wants his titles to rank in marketshare, which markets he is in, and that Rodale has international aspirations.

Today, I see more and more publishers grappling with the question: "Are we in the magazine publishing business or in the information business?" This is precisely the type of issue the mission statement should address.

2. Decide on the planning process.

What should your company's planning style be? The following checklist will help guide you to the answer:

• Who should be in charge? The CEO may not be, but I believe he or she should actively participate; otherwise the process will not be taken seriously by the rest of the staff. Will you hire someone specifically as your planning director or give the assignment to one of your senior managers?

• Should you use consultants? If you don't have the internal resources, this may be your best option. In my own experience, I have found that we as consultants are able to inject fresh thinking and, sometimes, a more aggressive approach into the process.

• Who should participate? I worked with one West Coast publisher who had each department head write the section of the plan that he or she would ultimately become responsible for. This worked well because each of those managers became highly committed to the plan he or she helped create.

• Should you do top-down or bottom-up planning? Top-down planning usually works best in centralized companies where top management determines direction. Bottom-up planning is a decentralized approach that asks each division and department to do its own plan. For example, at International Data Group (IDG), more than 100 divisions prepare plans, which are then submitted to IDG's Boston headquarters. According to Susan Petrie, IDG's vice president of financial planning, these are merged to develop an overall corporate plan.

• Over what time period should you plan? Three years is probably the norm and makes sense for most companies. Plans can be extended to five years for publishers in more stable markets.

• How often should you plan? Obviously, publishers in fast-changing industries should do it more frequently. IDG creates new strategic plans every year. Other companies may choose to plan every two years, with interim updates.

3. Assess where you are now.

Look at how your company fits into the world as a whole and what factors will influence your future prospects. In planning jargon this is called the "situation analysis." Examine the internal and external factors

---

■ Gather information to prepare a situation analysis

To assess where your magazine stands in its market, you may find it helpful to collect information from the following sources:

• Interview securities analysts about the market you serve.

• Use the Dow Jones News/Retrieval service to do keyword searches of relevant topics.

• Conduct blind interviews with your advertisers and their agencies.

• If you are a member of the Magazine Publishers of America, compare your operating statistics with those from MPA's annual Price Waterhouse financial survey.

• Contact the trade associations in the industry your magazine covers.

• If you publish a consumer magazine, read copies of the trade magazines that cover your market. If you are a business-to-business magazine, do the same thing with consumer titles.

---

that will shape your future. External influences include:

• Macro factors: What is happening nationally and internationally that affects your business? If you are a publisher of a health-related magazine, for example, will President Clinton's new health plan help or hurt your business?

• Market factors: Define what markets you are in and how big they are. How are your markets changing? What are the industry forecasts for the future of your markets: growing, emerging, mature, stable or declining?

• Magazine-industry factors: After reviewing macro and market trends, turn the spotlight on what is happening with magazines. Are publishers downsizing? Are advertising pages up or down?

• Competitive factors: Do an objective assessment of all media competitors within your markets. Do you compete primarily with magazines or also with other forms of media?

You should do an even more detailed analysis of internal factors. These include:

• What are the strengths and weaknesses of your company? What are you good at and what are you not good at? Can you start new products effectively? It's important to do an accurate assessment of past performance here.

• What resources are available in terms of staff expertise, capital to invest in acquisitions, and so on?

• How are you doing compared to the competition? Are you increasing market share? Are you investing for the future? Are your competitors?

• Identify opportunities and threats. Are there any publishers in similar markets in the United States and/or internationally that you should acquire or do a joint venture with? What are the barriers to entry in your markets?

• One of the most helpful exercises is to do an analysis of your magazine's customers and markets. Who are the largest advertisers? How do they perceive the quality of the magazine and its pricing structure vs. competitors? We typically do blind interviews with advertisers and agencies to answer these questions.

4. Determine where you want to go.

Now that you can see the big picture and where your company fits, the next question to answer is which way to take your company. To determine direction, you need to set objectives. Objectives are broad statements, such as, "We want to increase marketshare."

For each objective, I develop one or more goals that support it. Goals are more specific and measurable than objectives. For example, if our objective is to increase marketshare, we may set goals of increasing advertising pages by 10 percent and circulation by 5 percent to reach that objective.

5. Develop a plan for how to get there.

Figuring out how you are going to achieve your goals and objectives and how much reaching them is going to cost is operational planning. It requires concrete plans for each area of the business that describe what needs to get done and who is going to do it. Most of us are quite familiar with this part of the process already.

The following checklist highlights the components of the operational plan:

• Editorial plans
• Marketing plans for advertising and circulation efforts
• Manufacturing plans
• Ancillary product plans
• Plans for new-product introductions
• Potential merger, acquisition and/or divestiture activity
• Staffing and resource plans
• Financial budgets

A secret weapon: Wherever possible, study existing paradigms to help you crystallize your thinking about how to accomplish different aspects of the plan. For example, if one of your objectives is to build strong ancillary businesses, you should look for clues in how Reader's Digest Association and Rodale Press have done it. It's easier when you follow the trails others have already blazed.

6. Review how you did.

Congratulations, the plan is finished. But our work is not done. As the plan is put into action, we constantly need to compare it with the actual results. You should think of this step as keeping score. What worked and what didn't? Did you get to where you wanted to go? If not, revisions need to be made to keep you on course.

Strategic planning is not at cross-purposes with the creative process. Strategic planning is itself a creative process. Done right, a proactive strategic plan is easy to put into action, and one that will stimulate creativity. □

How to Win a Magazine War

BY CATHERINE FREDMAN

"Don't look back," baseball great Satchel Paige once said. "Something might be gaining on you." Success breeds success in magazine publishing as in any other business: The maxim applies to advertising pages, circulation numbers, promotional efforts and editorial quality—and, ultimately, to competition. Discover a market and prove it viable and you virtually guarantee competitors will jump in.

Despite Paige's advice, we managed to halt a handful of editors, publishers and pundits in their race to out-distance the competition and ask for their considered advice on how magazines protect their turf in high-pressure, high-stakes competition. No matter whether the book was a newcomer or a familiar face, a pretender to the throne or a defender of the faith, certain fundamental rules applied:

1. Define your market.

When you're the first in a market, work immediately to define your editorial mission in a way that pre-empts others from easily establishing a foothold.

Even though there are now several magazines covering the booming software market for Microsoft's Windows operating system, Manhasset, New York-based CMP Publications' *Windows* was able to box potential competitors into a corner even before they appeared. Why? Because when it was launched in 1990 (the title was acquired by CMP in 1991), it was the first publication daring enough to risk the market, and therefore was able to develop a broad-based editorial lineup.

Designed to appeal to both the high-intermediate and low-expert reader, *Windows* also nods to novices with specific advice columns. It's an umbrella publication, covering everything from emerging technologies to product use. By contrast, the competition was squeezed into sub-niches right from the start: Ziff-Davis' *Windows Sources*, which launched in February 1993, focuses on the buying process, and Wandsworth Publishing's *Windows User*, which launched in the fall of 1992, concentrates on what to do with what's been purchased.

Getting to a market first also pays off in terms of learning which newsstands produce sales and which aren't worth stocking. That information provides an invaluable edge in the battle for circulation and influence among advertisers.

If you are entering a market where competition already exists, you can still make one aspect of this rule work for you: Deliver sharply targeted editorial.

2. Profit from your competitors' hype.

One would think that market pioneers would dread the entry of deep-pocketed competition. But that isn't always the case. Remember that heavy hitters like Ziff-Davis, Time Warner, Fidelity Investments and Hearst/Dow Jones, all of which have challenged smaller competitors with launches into special-interest categories, can serve to legitimize a new market. That means they expand the market rather than co-opting existing readers and advertisers.

In the personal finance category, more editorial products swept in a broader spectrum of readers, and advertising followed suit, says Knight Kiplinger, editor in chief and publisher of Washington, D.C.-based *Kiplinger's Personal Finance Magazine*, which saw its advertising pages grow 23 percent in 1992, despite two strong newcomers.

David Mays, publisher of New York City-based *The Source*, the hip-hop magazine that established the category, has masterfully developed a David vs. Goliath strategy. Since Time Warner's much-publicized development and introduction in 1992 of *Vibe*, which is more loosely devoted to hip-hop, total advertising revenues for *The Source* have doubled and advertising pages have increased by 75 percent (that's 35 paid pages in the 84-page April 1993 issue), Mays says. His strategy is to define his magazine as the scrappy, street-smart title that really understands the hip-hop sensibility, as opposed to corporate giant Time Warner, or its partner in the *Vibe* venture, the music impresario Quincy Jones.

Even established markets can continue to benefit from the presence of new competition. "We had some of our biggest months in 1992 because the entire category expanded," says Elizabeth Crow, president of

Gruner + Jahr, which owns *Parents,* the 67-year-old category leader in the booming market for parenting magazines. "We are better off because [Time Warner's seven-year-old] *Parenting* and [The New York Times Co.'s Women's Magazines' five-year-old] *Child* exist."

3. Seek legitimacy with big-name endorsements.

By being first out of the gate, *Windows* was able to sign up prominent names in this branch of computer publishing, whose tacit endorsement legitimized the magazine in advertising circles as well as endowing it with industry authority among the readers. This, in turn, led to an embarrassing moment in Ziff's rollout of *Windows Sources.* Ziff was so sure that it could lure well-known *Windows* columnists Jesse Berst and Brian Livingston over to its new publication that their names were used in early promotions of *Windows Sources* without prior approval. Both Berst and Livingston are still with *Windows.* Ziff was forced to issue an apology.

4. Learn from your competitors.

Having the right people on your masthead and a secure statement of purpose doesn't mean you can't learn from the competition. When the Fidelity Investments-backed *Worth* and *Smart Money,* the joint Hearst/Dow Jones & Co. project, began to move in on *Money*'s and *Kiplinger's Personal Finance Magazine*'s turf, *KPF* changed its name from the ambiguous *Changing Times* to reflect its renewed focus on personal finance. That and the increased attention being paid to the market by consumers has paid off, says Kiplinger, pointing to 1992's solid performance.

Even K-III Magazines' *Seventeen,* the market leader among magazines for teenage girls, has incorporated elements of the style of competitors *Sassy* and *YM. Seventeen* may not be wholeheartedly embracing grunge editorial, but a fashion pictorial of a hairy-legged male model nuzzling an underwear-clad female model seems to owe a debt of gratitude to its competitors' influence.

5. Create an unbreakable bond with readers.

The ace in the hole, argues New York City-based magazine consultant Leo E. Scullin, is the strong relationship that a market leader forges with its reader. If that partnership has been cobbled together through a cheap subscription rate or an agency discount, it can easily break apart when someone else offers greater savings. And if a magazine's fundamental idea isn't crystal clear and on target, then the competition can do it better. Flashing a corporate checkbook isn't always the answer, according to Scullin. Again, consider *KPF,* doing better than ever after the big-money launches of *Smart Money* and *Worth* in 1991. Scullin's conclusion: "If you have a strong relationship with the reader, no one with deep pockets can undo it."

It's vital to stand out in the crowd—both the crowd of potential readers and that of potential advertisers. In the me-too world of publishing, it's always tempting to imitate the competition, which itself imitates the innovator, leading to an exercise in tail-chasing. And that tendency is especially pronounced when a new magazine grabs a couple of hundred-thousand readers.

> The greatest strength a title has in the fight against newcomers is the numbers, namely on circulation and reader research.

6. Tout your readers' involvement.

Both *KPF* and *Seventeen* quote high reader response as another stone in their citadels. *Seventeen* editor Midge Richardson says she gets between 5,000 and 7,000 letters a month, a phenomenal number compared to 100 or so apiece for some competitors. As a barometer of audience opinion, letters can't be beat—and are used to show advertisers that editorial is right on track.

7. Win the numbers race.

Obviously, one of the most bitter battles will be fought in media planners' offices. The greatest danger for any front-runner is to take itself for granted. "You want to appear scrappy and aggressive and full of vigor, and never forget to thank people for their business even if they've been with you for 67 years," says Bill Hogue, vice president of promotion and communications at Magazine Publishers of America, and former corporate promotions director at Gruner + Jahr and *Glamour.* "You need to be as excited about your product as the competition is about theirs."

And in the process, says Hogue, you need to figure out how to counter the competition's pitch for the advertiser's dollar. "They'll damn you with faint praise. One of the most savage things they will say is, 'You're not contemporary.' They'll say they've found a new reader, a new marketplace, a new approach that you missed." There are two comebacks: past issues and numbers. Established magazines can sell their longevity by saying that the only way to last 40 or 50 years is to be contemporary every year, and then back that up with illustrative tear sheets.

But the greatest strength any magazine has in the battle against a newcomer is its numbers, namely its circulation and reader-research figures. Until a magazine has its audience researched by industry standard-bearers Simmons Market Research Bureau or Mediamark Research Inc., the numbers it is selling are not syndicated; the income, the age of the reader and any other demographic figures are a product of private research—and while those figures may sound good, they're not very convincing to advertisers.

Windows' publisher Drake Lundell cites his own experience: "We fully expected from the beginning that other people would enter the market and we were amazed that we had a full year of operation before anyone else jumped in." That year was critical to *Windows'* success, ensuring it not only a track record, but an official reader survey a year before the competition could marshal their numbers.

Kiplinger's measure of reader involvement is *KPF*'s subscription and renewal rates, which he prizes over any market research firm's readership surveys. "It's more important to observe how people are actually behaving than asking them how they are going to behave," he says. "Watch your newsstand sales closely to see which cover stories and which mix of stories sold most strongly. Watch subscription copies generated by insert cards in newsstand copies. Watch first-time renewal rates. Only then, survey your non-renewers. Your renewal rates are a rolling referendum on whether people like your magazine."

8. Make your rate card sacrosanct.
In the fight for advertisers, it's tempting to consider trying an end run around the competition by offering cheaper rates or special discounts. But industry observers widely agree that negotiating advertising rates or cutting special deals signals weakness rather than strength. Not that advertisers would agree. "No matter how well you explain it, someone will say, 'Where do you get off not negotiating your rates?'" says Hogue. "When they say that your competitors are giving them three for two and 50 percent off, look 'em right in the eye and say, 'The person I saw before you today and the person I see after are getting the exact same deal as you. I hope you get the best deal you could get from [the competition].'"

9. Employ premiums as part of a strategic plan.
Another weapon in the war for readers is reader benefits, which even relatively shallow-pocketed publications can offer once they achieve a critical mass of editorial staff and reputation. *KPF* includes querying privileges as part of the subscription cost. Any reader can call or write for financial advice and the staff will research the question at no extra cost. Other multimedia services that cement the relationship include a Kiplinger videotape on retirement planning, a nationally syndicated television program and an alliance with Prodigy, the interactive database. "None of this requires a lot of money, just some ingenuity and strategic planning," says Kiplinger. And such efforts pay off in related promotional advertising.

Tying it together
All of this translates to one simple formula: Don't do anything that might shake your reader's loyalty. Be very careful to assess reader attitudes before reducing the paper stock, or tampering with the trim size, among other things. "The reader doesn't often notice the competition," says Scullin. "But if you distract the reader, you've screwed it up." At that point, you might as well toss away the keys to the kingdom. □

Creativity Won't Flourish Unless Managers Nurture It

BY PATRICIA G. CAMPBELL

The single greatest hindrance to the creative process is management itself. Challenging assumptions and looking at information in new ways takes time and patience—not things management typically has lots of. And although fostering creativity and teamwork is basically easy, making it a priority is extremely hard. Without a major commitment by senior-level management, new ideas are highly unlikely to surface.

Every business's growth hinges on innovation. Unfortunately, creativity—the activity that leads to innovation—is one of the first things to take a back seat in a downsized environment. People aren't inherently less creative when they're working hard; they simply have less time to indulge their creative energies.

With this in mind, I offer four ingredients for fostering the creative process:

Make the time. Creativity can't be a hobby: It requires serious attention. Management's role must be to *force* the time to let it happen. Designate one day a month for the entire company to engage in some sort of creative activity, such as brainstorming sessions. For example, tell your employees to scour the press for creative ideas in other industries. The monthly "creative day" can then be used to identify the principles behind those creative successes and to see how they might be applied to your own business. I have found that the very best ideas for our industry often come from observing what works in other fields. We need not reinvent the wheel. Pairing things that have seemingly little in common often leads to new revelations.

There are a dozen ways to use the day effectively—the key for managers is to provide the structure to let employees take the time. People are not inherently motivated to structure themselves in teams—it takes effort, organization and a willingness to be flexible.

> Creativity—the activity that leads to innovation— takes a back seat in a downsized environment. Managers must make the time.

Make it fun. Creativity can't be simply another office task. Take off the ties, the jackets, the high heels. Develop entertaining procedures for engaging people in the process. For example, the entire Times Mirror circulation department spent a week thinking of ways to increase profitability by looking beyond the traditional ways of cutting costs and increasing revenues. To get the creative juices flowing, the department was divided into groups of eight people, and each group was assigned a certain task. One group was sent to the grocery store to buy boxes of cereal that caught their attention, with the idea that the cereal shelf is similar to a newsstand. When the group met and discussed their decision-making processes, the results were related to how consumers buy at the newsstand, which led to several new, very creative thoughts about magazine cover design.

Another group was told to purchase the most valuable item they could find (other than a magazine subscription) for $10. The group discussed what they bought and what they found valuable in the items they purchased. As a result of this exercise, a number of very creative copy platforms were developed for direct mail. There were several other similar activities that were fun to do; as a result, people became willingly engaged in the process.

Make it everyone's job. Some of the very best ideas can come from the people who sit quietly in their cubicles, typing away all day. You must figure out a way to unlock creative thinking at all levels of your company. We have a program called "Plant-a-Seed" that encourages employees to submit written ideas for improving the company. Once a month, a group of managers evaluates the ideas and moves forward on those with potential. Those ideas that are chosen are publicized, and the responsible individual receives a bonus.

Another approach is to include employees from all levels of the company in brainstorming sessions, and to mix people from different departments. I find that those who are inexperienced or just beginning their careers often have more open minds compared to those of us who have already developed our perspectives and set our minds on a certain course of action. Naiveté can be the best medicine for creative thinking.

Make it happen. A serious hindrance to the creative process is a company's inability to execute good ideas. Lack of follow-through leads to skepticism and inertia among employees. Nothing breeds success more than success itself. Set priorities, focus on two ideas, make those happen—and people will begin to believe in the process. Reward people financially and psychologically in a substantial way for the successful execution of a new idea.

Creativity can be learned, but it often requires training. But just as there are tools to train sales and management staffs, there are many practical tools and proven methods for nurturing creativity. For instance, several companies specialize in facilitating brainstorming sessions. Almost always, I find that a third-party perspective fosters our ability to think outside the boundaries of business. Synectics, Inc., in Cambridge, Massachusetts, is one company I have found particularly helpful.

For computer fans, there is the software program IdeaFisher. The computer helps you make unobvious connections as you fill out an on-screen survey form. Times Mirror's marketing communications department uses it regularly for creative tasks such as naming products and developing tag lines.

The best practical guide to idea-generating techniques that I have come across is *Thinkertoys: A Handbook of Business Creativity for the 90's*, by Michael Michalko, published by Ten Speed Press in Berkeley, California. It's full of very specific, mind-stretching exercises and many, many inspirational examples of companies that have achieved incredible success through seemingly small observations. For instance, Lenox China started the concept of bridal registries when the company realized few people could afford to buy an entire set of china at once.

These are a few of the tools. More important, you must make fostering creativity a top priority for you and your staff. Although creativity requires the same type of training that salespeople receive, in a down-sized environment, it's 10 times more important because people will not make the time to do it on their own. When we most need to be on the cutting edge, we can ill afford to have the backbone of our business—new ideas—be an afterthought. □

10 Ways to Abolish Power Struggles

BY FRANK FINN

The single biggest obstacle to success in magazine publishing today has nothing to do with ad spending or circulation renewals or postage costs. It is the power struggle that typically rages among the three core departments: Editorial, advertising and circulation. If the energy wasted on disagreements among these factions were devoted to creating better content, increasing ad sales and improving circulation results, the average magazine would be much healthier and more successful.

Most magazines still operate under the mistaken notion that editorial should be entirely divorced from goings-on in advertising and circulation. As a result, the three departments often pull in three different directions. Here are 10 ways to end the divisiveness and promote teamwork among editorial, advertising and circulation.

Form a magazine management team. Appoint the editor, advertising director and circulation director as equal partners on a management team with responsibility for the magazine's success. As teammates, the three department heads will have a mandate to share information, reconcile disagreements and reach a consensus on important decisions. Each member of the management team gains access to the same information about the magazine's performance. The team should meet at least once a month to review the current numbers relative to the magazine's performance: ad sales status, circulation reports, production expenses and financial results.

The usual conflicts between editorial, advertising and circulation will still erupt. But because team members now share responsibility for the magazine's success, the teammates have an incentive to resolve those conflicts. When the team members can't agree, the majority does *not* rule. The team should always work toward a consensus. Only as a last resort should the publisher (or whoever has ultimate authority) be asked to make the call.

Reach a consensus on the magazine's target audience. When editorial, advertising and circulation operate in complete isolation, they often have conflicting views on the magazine's target audience. This causes no end of trouble because the target audience is the basis for every decision each department makes. It's up to the management team to agree on a target audience and stick to it.

Here's how:
• Establish who your current readers are by conducting audience research. A statistically valid mail survey is the most reliable way of doing this.
• Decide whether the magazine can achieve its financial goals serving the current audience. Are there sufficient readers willing to pay to receive the magazine? Are there enough advertisers willing to pay your rates?
• If the answer to the last question is no, you need to consider whether you would do any better by pursuing a different target audience.

Agree on positioning. If all three departments can agree on where the magazine fits in its market, dozens of arguments will be resolved. One useful tool for analyzing a magazine's position is the pyramid. In amateur photography, for example, most photographers are just casual "shutterbugs" who have basic knowledge and prefer to use inexpensive "point-and-shoot" cameras. They form the base of the pyramid. The higher up the pyramid you go, the greater the sophistication of the readers and the smaller their numbers. At the very peak are the most elite amateur photographers, who spend lots of time and money on their hobby. Any magazine that hopes to serve the amateur photography market must decide where to position itself on this pyramid.

Develop a written strategic plan. Once positioning and a target audience are resolved, the management team has the foundation for creating a strategic plan for the magazine. Each team member contributes a section:
• Editorial: The editor should draft a mission statement that answers the following question in 25 words or less: "What is our magazine about?" The balance of the editorial plan should explain how the magazine fulfills that mission, including the function of each department; categories that will run in every issue, such as profiles, how-to stories, feature articles and so on; and an editorial calendar that outlines articles scheduled for the coming year.
• Ad sales: The ad director should list the categories of advertisers the magazine should attract and why, and the individual companies that are good prospects. There should also be a plan for selling to them.
• Circulation: This section explains how circulation will

sell subscriptions to the target audience or, in the case of controlled-circulation titles, obtain lists of qualified readers. For paid-circulation titles sold on newsstands, specifics on reaching the target audience are also needed.

When the three parts of the plan are drafted, the team should sit down to evaluate whether they are consistent with the target audience and the magazine's positioning.

Develop a cover strategy. Every magazine, whether it is sold on the newsstand or not, needs to have a clear cover strategy. It is the editor's job to articulate the magazine's cover strategy. Will the cover feature a photograph or an illustration? Should there be portraits of real people, or models portraying a concept? What kinds of coverlines will be featured? Will there be sell lines above the logo?

The editor's business-side teammates must agree on the strategy. Circulation has a direct stake in the cover, particularly if the magazine is sold on the newsstand. And advertising also has a stake, since advertisers often judge the magazine, quite literally, by its cover.

Establish a cover-selection process. On many magazines, the editor makes the final decision on the cover. But it's wise at least to solicit the opinions of advertising and circulation. Here is a useful procedure to follow: (1) Editorial prepares two or three preliminary covers for each issue. (2) The circulation director and advertising director provide their input. (3) The team works to reach a consensus. If that isn't possible, at least the editor and circulation director must agree.

For newsstand magazines, the team should try to discover which kinds of covers sell well and which do not. An effective way to do that is to post the last year's covers on a wall in order by sell-through percent. The team then analyzes what the best-sellers have in common, such as a combination of colors or a type of photograph.

The point of this exercise, however, is not to try to duplicate those elements on every cover, but to discover a mix of cover approaches that will maximize sales while at the same time giving editorial flexibility.

Give the editor and circulation director incentive compensation. All three members of the management team should have a financial stake in the magazine's success. Advertising directors usually prosper when sales go up through commissions. But circulation directors and editors seldom have such compensation arrangements. Without a stake, however, editors and circulation directors have little direct incentive to cooperate in the effort to make a magazine a financial success. Their mix of base and incentive compensation should have enough incentive compensation to encourage them to help their teammates succeed.

Critique advertising and circulation promotion. Just as the editor should give his or her business-side colleagues a say in cover selection and overall editorial strategy, the ad director should welcome input on the magazine's advertising sales materials. Every sales letter, promotion mailing and presentation script should get a thorough review by the management team.

The team should also discuss the categories of advertisers that ad sales is concentrating on, as well as individual prospects. The editor might be able to suggest potential advertisers, and the circulation director may have learned of companies interested in the magazine's audience through list-rental activity. By the same token, the circulation director should give the other members of the management team an in-depth review of the promotion materials going to potential subscribers. Both the editor and advertising director may find inconsistencies between the subscription packages and the target audience and magazine positioning strategy.

Even more important is a review of the lists the circulation department mails to. The team should discuss the "winners and losers," as well as new lists for testing.

Develop written policy statements. Too much time and energy is wasted on magazine staffs arguing issues that should be resolved by the management team running the magazine. These may be editorial or business questions. Some of the common ones include: Should the magazine publish negative reviews of products? Are advertisers entitled to coverage in articles? Are staff members permitted to accept gifts? Does editorial accept expenses-paid trips?

Develop a painless ad-close plan. The greatest friction between editorial and advertising often arises at closing. Production and editorial are anxious to stick to the schedule and avoid extra hours and late charges. But advertising doesn't care about the schedule if there's a chance that one more ad page might come in. Here are three suggestions for resolving closing conflicts:

• Build a "false close" into the schedule. Advertising promotes this date as its official close on the rate card and its other materials, but the actual close is a few days later.

• Build flexibility into the book imposition. Allow advertising to reserve extra space that it may sell or release at the last minute. Editorial prepares material to take up the space if it goes unsold, or a public-service ad fills the hole. This allows production to proceed while advertising continues with last-minute selling.

• Commit to a range of acceptable ad:edit ratios. At close, the book size is set according to that range. This ends arguments over adding more editorial pages. □

How to Launch a Magazine: Four Case Studies

COMPILED BY THE FOLIO: STAFF

■ SHANKEN'S FOLLY

Some rules are made to be broken. But when maverick New York City-based editor and publisher Marvin R. Shanken launched *Cigar Aficionado* in September 1992, he broke all of them. "When I announced what I was doing, most people thought I'd lost my mind," says Shanken. "I did the magazine because I love cigars; I had no expectation that it would be successful. I expected to lose money each year for the rest of my life. The secret was no budget, no research, no business plan.

"In fact," he continues, "when I talked to people about the idea of a men's lifestyle magazine centered around cigars—with travel, collecting, etc.—most said, 'If I want to read about travel, I'll read *Condé Nast Traveler*. If I want to read about art and antiques, I'll read *Art & Antiques*. Why would anyone pick up your magazine when the subjects are being very comprehensively covered by other magazines that specialize in these fields?' So the idea was that there was a lot of resistance at first."

Market saturation, lack of demographics and projected negative revenues were just the beginning. Add to those warning signs the declining cigar industry (Shanken says that at the time of the launch, sales were at an all-time low; in 30 years they had gone from $8 billion to $2 billion), the growing anti-smoking climate in America, and the end of eighties-style conspicuous consumption. What have you got? A list of all the reasons *not* to launch a magazine like *Cigar Aficionado*.

Despite the odds, *Cigar Aficionado* surpassed everyone's expectations, including Shanken's. The quarterly has turned a profit since its debut. Of the launch issue's 154 pages, 53 were ads. Some were endemic—spirits and cigars, for example—and others non-endemic—Barney's New York, Cartier and General Motors among others. The title recently closed its biggest issue to date. The Winter 1995 issue is thick with 404 total pages and 186 ads.

Although advertising synergy exists today between *Cigar Aficionado* and M. Shanken Communications' flag-ship publication, the 16-year-old *Wine Spectator*, Shanken says that *Wine Spectator* didn't have much to do with the launch of *Cigar*. "When we launched *Cigar, Wine Spectator* was essentially a wine magazine. It had not taken on its current posture of a lifestyle magazine, so there were only a few advertisers that would be in both."

Still, *Wine Spectator* deserves some credit for making a reality out of "a folly of an idea" that came to Shanken when he was returning from a trip to Cuba. (Shanken breaks another rule by writing about contraband Cuban cigars in his magazine.) He may not have leveraged ads from *Wine Spectator* in the beginning, but Shanken did use clout, credibility and cash from his company to generate a buzz about *Cigar Aficionado* and distribute 100,000 copies of the first issue in cigar shops, on newsstands and to *Spectator* readers who requested a complimentary copy.

Should other publishers take his cue and discount naysayers to follow their publishing passions? Says Shanken: "You can't always make decisions based on traditional research. You have to listen to your inner

> "You can't always make decisions based on traditional research. You have to listen to your inner brain, your soul. You have to be willing to take chances," says Shanken.

brain, your soul. You have to be willing to take chances. Then again, you shouldn't do this forever, unless you're in a position where you can afford to do it forever. I was very lucky. People give me credit. I probably don't deserve all the credit that I get. I'm a lucky guy."—*Jennifer Sucov*

■ HEALTHY START

When *Men's Health* was launched in 1986, people said it wouldn't work: They said that men didn't want general-interest lifestyle information. They said men didn't read magazines. They said the name was boring. Ten years later, with a circulation of nearly 1.4 million and an enviable status as one of the leading men's magazines in this country, *Men's Health* is proving everybody wrong.

In an ongoing effort to be the leading provider of health and fitness information, Emmaus, Pennsylvania-based Rodale Press launched *Men's Health* on the newsstand as an experiment. Executive editor Michael Lafavore, who produced the first issue with a staff of three, says the magazine was conceived by Rodale president and COO Robert Teufel. Lafavore bandied about the idea for under a year, held many casual focus groups with friends and Rodale employees, and came to the conclusion that men really would read a lifestyle/service publication. He was right: The first issue sold 90,000 copies on the newsstand.

"The two things that are key to a successful launch are being relevant to your readers, and being unique," says publisher Jeff Morgan, who joined *Men's Health* four years ago after serving as national sales director for *Playboy*. "If a magazine is a low-fat, low-sodium version of somebody else's title, it's really risky."

With its focus on health and relationships, sex and work, *Men's Health* was the first magazine to bring service journalism to the men's market. After three trial issues, it became a full-fledged quarterly in 1988. Lafavore says he didn't start a direct-mail program until 1988, when roughly 150,000 subscription offers were mailed to names on outside lists as well as to Rodale's in-house newsletter and book-buyer lists.

Lafavore says he tested numerous lists from both inside and outside the obvious men's and health categories. "Some of the men's magazines didn't work for us, but some general-interest magazines did," says Lafavore, who stresses that publishers should test a sampling of names from each list to measure its viability before renting or buying whole lists. Today, *Men's Health* comes out 10 times a year, and the circulation has been doubling every year (currently it's at 1.4 million). Newsstand sales have also maintained their strength: *Men's Health* sold an average of 294,000 copies per issue on the newsstand in the first half of 1995, according to the Audit Bureau of Circulations, up 36 percent from the same period in 1994.

Lafavore acknowledges the benefits of having Rodale's corporate backing. "I never worried about having to put my furniture on the lawn. But had it been my money, I probably would not have done it." Being an in-house launch is certainly easier than going it

---

■ The business of a business plan

Bruce Sheiman, managing director at The Jordan Edmiston Group, Inc., in New York City, likens a business plan to DNA. "The plan is a blueprint that provides all the instructions. When implemented, it results in a fully developed publication." Here, some pointers.

Can the hyperbole. "In one plan, revenues were projected at around $200 million year five," Sheiman says. "There's no magazine in the last 25 years that was able to reach that, much less exceed it."

Make it your business to know the business. One of the most common mistakes in magazine start-up plans is that they read as if they could just as well be about starting up a pickle plant. "You can talk about units of sale and production, but you must know your PIBs, your ABCs, your CPMs," Sheiman says.

Make a short story long. "A 12-page plan won't work. At 30 pages you're just starting to address the many questions that need to be answered. A good average length is 50 pages."

For whom should the plan work? Creating a business plan is not just for those seeking investors. The entrepreneur also does it for him- or herself. Notes Sheiman, "[It] demands that you clarify and articulate goals and strategies in every discipline."

---

alone. But the launch of *Men's Health* was not entirely worry-free. Lafavore says it was initially a tough sell because advertisers had never seen anything like it. Consequently, Rodale was compelled to offer a few deals during the title's start-up phase.

Deals or no deals, however, Lafavore advises entrepreneurs who have limited funds to invest their start-up money in building circulation rather than spending a lot of time, energy and money on getting ads. The reason is that many advertisers won't even look at a magazine until it can show significant circulation figures. Now, with the strongest circulation in the market and a rate of $66,175 for a full-page, four-color ad, *Men's Health* is doing fine on the advertising side. In 1995, ad sales grew 25 percent, and for the year, the magazine had 646 ad pages.—*Cris Beam*

■ NO GUTS. NO GLORY.

In hindsight, this adage probably best describes the start-up philosophy of publishers Stephen Osborne and Mike Bradley.

■ Pointers

Don't skimp. When you're launching, Osborne and Bradley say, the desire to cut corners may be strong. But that would be penny-wise and pound-foolish. Your title is the only thing you have to sell with.

Know who your bellwether accounts are before you make a commitment to your brilliant idea. Before launching *PMPN*, Osborne and Bradley identified 200 potential advertisers; their first issue carried 44 ads.

Apportion tasks. In a start-up, there's something to be said for doing nearly everything yourself. You get a better feel for the whole operation. But you need to be realistic: "We would never dream of writing and editing and laying out the magazine. It's not our strength," Osborne says.

Go with a local printer. You can save money by going out of state, but you lose control over the process. "We paid $2,000 more to stay local, but we get an excellent product. We've never had a makegood," says Bradley.

Don't count your ad revenues until they're in. With the new launch, the pair say they will factor in the long turnaround time for payments.

A little more than two years ago—with understandable trepidation—the former advertising-sales reps left the security of their full-time jobs at Cahners Publishing Co., cashed in their IRAs, took out second mortgages on their homes, and risked $200,000 of their own money to launch *Pharmaceutical & Medical Packaging News*. The 20,000-controlled-circulation title aimed at engineers and other packaging decision-makers, which was launched in November 1993, is already in the black: Ad revenues for 1995 exceeded $1 million dollars—and Osborne predicts a 16 percent growth for 1996.

Using profits from *PMPN*, the team is set to launch its second start-up in March 1996, the bimonthly *Cosmetic/Personal Care Packaging*, which will reach 8,000 packaging decision-makers in those industries.

"The one reason we hit the ground running," says Bradley, is that "there was truly a need for the magazine. We weren't just putting a different face on the same product."

Unlike Summit Publishing Company's *Packaging World*, Cahners' *Packaging Digest* and Independent Publishing Company's *Food & Drug Packaging*, contends Osborne, a former regional sales manager for Cahners' *Packaging Magazine*, "we're not horizontal or vertical: We're diagonal. We are for a specific job function—healthcare packaging. No one is doing what we're doing." The existing broad-based packaging titles touch on pharmaceutical and medical packaging about twice a year, he says. The vertical books that talk about pharmaceutical and medical issues touch on the packaging issues once or twice a year.

Putting their life savings on the line was not the pair's original plan. Their first strategy was to apply for a loan from the Small Business Administration. That didn't pan out, says Osborne, because bylaws, they learned, prohibit the funding of publishing ventures. Next, they sought the financial assistance of local banks. "They would not give us the time of day, because we had no publishing history," he recalls. The would-be publishers then explored the possibility of financing from two private investors "who were ready to write the checks," but they didn't like the deal. "They wanted a controlling interest in the magazine, and we didn't want that. If we could have gotten a deal where we could have bought out the investors, that would have been okay," recalls Osborne.

In hindsight, however, both Osborne and Bradley are thankful that they decided to sink or swim. "Looking back, we're pleased we did it on our own," says Bradley, adding that the approach may not be right for everybody. It depends, he says, on how much risk you're willing or able to take.

Turning the kind of profit they have in the short time they did it is unquestionably impressive. But the key to continued prosperity for any up-and-coming launch, the well-heeled entrepreneurs caution, is to be vigilant: "We're still watching our pennies," they say. "We're not on Easy Street yet."—*Lorraine Calvacca*

■ NURSING A NICHE

A common dilemma for trade magazines is how to provide objective coverage of the industry they depend on for advertising. As if the name weren't evidence enough, *Revolution—The Journal of Nurse Empowerment* is not a typical trade magazine.

In 1991, after a year of publishing material with a decided opinion about the rights and legalities of the nursing profession, the four-year-old, Staten Island, New York-based quarterly refused to accept hospital advertising, a staple of nursing magazines. "Hospitals that advertised with us called and said, 'Why are you printing this? It's making nurses mouthy and rebellious,'" publisher Laura Gasparis Vonfrolio recalls. "We decided we're not gonna sell ourselves."

Editorial integrity is what first inspired *Revolution*. Because their article ideas had been rejected by most of the nursing-category titles as too controversial, nurses-turned-authors Vonfrolio and editor Joan Swirsky thought up a magazine of their own in the summer of 1991. Through Vonfrolio's consulting and seminar business, they had an instant list of 150,000 names, as well as the $250,000 needed for the first issue. By December, A.D. Von Publishers, Inc., and its lone title were launched featuring information not discussed elsewhere: Unsafe nurse/patient ratios, mandated over-time and what Vonfrolio calls the "raping of the American health system and the country" by pharmaceutical companies and their prices.

Such strong opinions may have resulted in a sharp ad decline, but they clearly distinguished *Revolution* from the competition and attracted a loyal, subscription-based readership that grows by leaps of 2,000 each year. Although ad revenue fell from around $20,000 for the first issue to $2,000 for the Fall 1995 edition, the unaudited circulation has risen from an initial 1,700 to 10,000, Vonfrolio says. Its overhead low (a staff of four produces the title from the basement of Vonfrolio's mother-in-law's Staten Island home), one of the world's few politicized trade magazines has become a success, mainly because of its $24.95 subscription rate. The title turned a profit of $90,000 in 1994 while maintaining its independent voice. *Revolution* was initially audited by the BPA, but dropped out after a year. "It doesn't pay, because we're not going after ads," Vonfrolio explains.

During the course of the launch, Vonfrolio and company had to learn the ropes—sometimes the hard way.

For example, when funding the launch, the *Revolution* team valued its independence to such a degree that they did not seek outside investment. "I did not want to have people telling us what to do," Vonfrolio recalls. Similarly, she opted not to have a prototype. "Maybe if I did one, I would have gotten knocked down and given up," she explains.

Another eye-opener: Too much of Vonfrolio's $250,000 start-up costs was wasted, in the publisher's opinion. Printing a 150,000-piece direct-mail package cost her $32,000 and drew only 1,700 subscriptions, "which is absurd. I can get that done now for $6,000." She says she felt "ripped off" when she had the magazine printed. The initial print run of 10,000 copies set her back $50,000. "I didn't have a clue about prices. I got that down to $13,000 later." She writes off her losses as a learning experience. "I wasted the amount of money you pay to get a bachelor's degree."

From the start, however, growing circulation was the company's goal, although Swirsky says reaching a larger readership with *Revolution*'s material is difficult because nursing has traditionally been something of a downtrodden occupation. "When you take a group of people who have been associated with a subservient role and who aren't famous for considering themselves empowered, you have a lot of work cut out for you," she says. To attract this reluctant readership, The Best of Rev, a 150-page collection of every feature to appear in the magazine, is offered free to potential subscribers.

At the end of the day, the concerns of *Revolution* are different from those of most trade magazines: "I don't want to make a million dollars," Vonfrolio says. "I want to make readers rowdy."—*Steve Wilson* □

Did You Downsize Right?

BY STEPHEN BARR

Jim M., art director at a major trade publishing company, was exasperated. His magazine was in the process of converting its prepress and typesetting operations to desktop in late 1991 when company-wide downsizing hit. Jim's staff was reduced by half, and though the desktop equipment was already in place, the art director had to fall back on conventional means to get the magazine out on time.

"As soon as we were off desktop, we began to incur a lot more prep fees," he says, adding, however, that he does not think those increased fees negated the savings achieved in the downsizing.

What happened at Jim's company has happened all over the magazine industry over the last three years, and indeed, all over corporate America. There are few publishing companies that have not reorganized, eliminated positions and cut staff. In the process, the magazine industry became a leaner and perhaps meaner business. It hasn't been a fun time to be a manager.

Now, the industry is struggling with what's left—asking whether downsizing was done right, whether it went too far, coming to grips with the bitterness remaining when things went bad, and discussing how best to move ahead.

"We know we're in a period of change," says Kate Wendleton, a career development consultant. "But we don't know where we're going."

'The whole deal sucked'

The discussion of downsizing is going on throughout the industry and in management think-tanks across America. "There's been skillful downsizing and not-so-skillful downsizing," says John Emery, president of the American Business Press. "Showing care for people, helping those laid off, spelling out the responsibilities of those who remain—it should be done with great forethought, which is not how it has been done in all cases."

Adds Robert Boucher, former chief at New York-based Gralla Publications who was responsible for the 1989 reorganization at that company and for its 1991 merger with Miller Freeman Inc., both of which involved sizable staff reductions, "No matter what gestures were made—

any company program, memo or speech—the reality was that the whole deal sucked."

Indeed. According to the U.S. Bureau of Labor Statistics, periodical employment stood at 124,400 at the end of 1992, down from an all-time high of 130,800 in November 1990. There were more than 600 layoffs at Time Inc. in the fall of 1991, 200 at Cahners that spring, about 100 at Hachette in late 1990—and those are just the larger publishing companies.

Of course, the total number of jobs lost in the magazine business is dwarfed by the recently announced cuts at AT&T, or IBM or GM, or any other troubled titan. The smaller scale has even been an advantage when it comes to taking corrective action, in that the problems seem more manageable. "We're a pimple on the rear-end of an elephant, which means we can move quickly and react subtly," says Sal Marino, chairman of Penton Publishing. The Cleveland-based company laid off 35 people in 1991; factoring in the attrition of 35 more jobs, it is operating with 20 percent fewer employees than three years ago. "I don't envy the chief executive of IBM," Marino notes.

And yet, the disruptions in terms of morale, productivity and quality have been no less severe—and they may not be over. "The challenge to publishers is to remain strategic in their outlook," says Paul F. McPherson, a senior advisor at AdMedia Corporate Advisors, who expects an increase in merger and acquisition activity in the industry to trim job opportunities further.

With no slackening of the vigilance with which executives manage the bottom line, the effects of downsizing will continue to reverberate through the magazine industry. Headhunters report an increase in business, but are filling new positions only about 25 percent of the time. And even as advertising revenues start to pick up, the need to learn from several years of downsizing has not diminished.

"The real question is whether companies are just cutting people to cut costs, or if they are thinking about how they can concentrate resources and deciding what they want the company to be," says one magazine executive who asked not to be named. "Those losing their jobs never feel things were handled well, but has the process been done in a way that the people who remain don't feel victimized?"

By most accounts, downsizing has had the desired effect on company balance sheets—helping maintain profitability even as revenues tumble. Marino would not say how much has been saved by cutting staff, but notes that even with flat revenues, profitability increased significantly after downsizing.

Did the industry overreact?

It's inevitable, however, that layoffs will dent opera-tions, at least initially, because fewer resources are avail-able. "There's no question there has been a diminution of quality," says Marshall Freeman, chairman of San Francisco-based trade and consumer publisher Miller Freeman Inc., which has gone through a series of lay-offs in recent years. "The management challenge is to maintain quality—the depth of research or interpreta-tion, the number of edit pages—at less expense, and that takes some care."

Unfortunately, as employees have been asked to work longer and harder, the frustrations of Jim, the art direc-tor, are increasingly common. Over the past year he has converted back to desktop slowly, with the addition of

---

■ How to survive a downsizing debacle

Six good ideas for managers

If you're counting on economic recovery to undo the effects of downsizing and cutbacks, you're being unrealis-tic, warn management experts.

"The return of advertising may have a big impact, but telling people that everything is outside our locus of control can also be demoralizing," says John J. Parkington, direc-tor of organization research and development in the San Francisco office of the Wyatt Company, a consulting firm. "People like to feel they have some measure of control, and they want to know that top management has an idea of where things are going. That requires leadership."

So although it's true that ad revenue increases will repair the bottom line, they will do little to rebuild employ-ee morale or to boost productivity.

Instead, Parkington suggests publishers take the follow-ing steps to heal the rifts caused by layoffs and reinvigo-rate their staffs.

• **Start revitalizing before downsizing.** Treat non-survivors with dignity and respect; say something nice about their work; provide them with adequate bridges to new employ-ment. That sends a message to survivors and helps defuse some of the anger. Otherwise, those left behind after ruthless firings will go job hunting because they figure they're next.

• **Get managers' support.** Because managers often do not agree with the decision of top executives to downsize, make sure they understand what needs to be done and make them feel part of the equation. Provide managers with an explanation of the process and goals so that they can be agents of change.

• **Maintain an "open door" policy.** Rather than hide in the executive offices and delegate, senior management should be more visible with hands-on supervision. Hold "town meetings" in large and small groups; include employees in problem-solving committees; make the staff feel "we're all in this together." Employees need to have a feeling that someone is at the helm guiding the ship, setting and exe-cuting a clear policy.

• **Reward success.** Managers should focus on near-term accomplishments, on the here-and-now. A pat on the back goes a long way, and when management celebrates small achievements, not just things that save the company money, employees will be motivated to be more productive.

• **Be up front about changes.** Communication is always key, but be cautious about what you communicate. Executive silence exacerbates the pain, but making promises that can't be kept—no more layoffs, for instance—can destroy man-agement credibility. Deal openly with tough questions from employees; if you don't know the whole answer, say so.

• **Question basic business assumptions and outline a clear vision for the company that you share with the entire staff.** If the future holds a profound shift in profit levels, cost structures, product array—it's time to explain that. A 1992 Wyatt study of 1,000 corporate executives found that 86 percent had downsized, but only 43 percent had examined the way they do business. If you give employees a context for understanding change, they will find ways to add value to the company.

Remember, however, these steps are just that: steps in a much longer-term process. "It takes a while for employees to recover from the psychological effects of downsizing," says Parkington. "It's hard to say what the window is. But if layoffs become an annual event, a constant mode of corporate dieting, people never recover from that."

a recent college graduate and the training of a copy editor to double as editorial production manager. "We're back to 90 percent desktop after we already achieved it once," he says in an exasperated tone.

Like others who have managed to adapt under similar circumstances, the art director says he understands the logic of his company's layoffs, and he realizes there will be more savings as the desktop technology affords greater efficiencies. But too often there's little effort to measure the indirect costs of layoffs—the late fees, new recruiting costs and retraining expenses.

"The clear message is eliminate the work before you eliminate the people," says Vijay Kumar, a consultant at Coopers & Lybrand. "Downsizing can be favorable to the bottom line, but unless you change the way the work is done, people get overworked, morale is eroded and the compact with employees will be broken."

Time Inc. tried to cut workload first in its 1991 restructuring. Toward that end, the company outsourced its prepress operations. It then let go more than 100 people from that department. Similarly, New York City-based Times Mirror Magazines spent much of 1990 gathering input from throughout the company before it restructured departments, eliminated unnecessary work and cut about 30 jobs.

"Downsizing is needed to survive, but the mistake is that many publishers have not looked at layoffs as a last resort," says Allan Halcrow, editor of Costa Mesa, California-based *Personnel Journal*. More typical is that the re-examination process is a by-product of the layoffs; the layoffs are the engine that drives a restructuring as it becomes clear that the work simply cannot get done as it was when there were more people.

Reassuring the survivors

One publishing company president learned that the hard way. He describes an initial round of staff cuts in 1991 as "good medicine for creating a more efficient operation," but concedes that the effort was not planned well. "We found we couldn't work in advance." He speaks more favorably of the experience last year when his company centralized circulation, took fulfillment to an outside vendor, and laid off some data-entry personnel. "We were able to emphasize that this was not a performance issue," the executive explains. "We communicated that the company was changing direction, we were centralizing functions." He says the placement rate for this group was higher than for the first layoffs.

As downsizing becomes a familiar part of today's business culture, employees have a keener sense of when the business is in trouble and their jobs are at risk. Consultants warn that one of the most destructive downsizing mistakes is to leave people hanging. Management cannot ignore rumors, and when there are going to be layoffs, they should be done all in one shot.

"Because it's hard to keep decisions confidential, it's best to move quickly before rumors abound," says Jim Adler, vice president, human resources, of Cleveland-based Advanstar Communications. "It's also important to do all your changes at one time, so there's no waiting for the other shoe to drop." Adler concedes that Advanstar recognized the wisdom of these lessons only after it had trimmed about 100 jobs in two waves in late 1991 and early 1992.

After three waves of layoffs at Miller Freeman, "people lost confidence that their jobs were secure," says technical systems manager Ralph O'Brien. Only now, he adds, after more than a year without another major round of staff cuts, has some calm been restored.

When carrying out layoffs, says Coopers & Lybrand's Kumar, employers have a "moral responsibility" to provide a comfortable level of severance and a continuation of benefits, as well as to offer outplacement counseling, and even arrange interviews. "It's worth spending the money," he says. "You want to say good-bye in a way that those leaving won't say they got screwed."

Adds Boucher, now president of a new publishing company, suburban Philadelphia-based Cardinal Business Media, "One side of the brain can look at the financial imperatives and understand downsizing intellectually. But when friends are losing their jobs, it's hard to understand emotionally."

O'Brien says that morale was so damaged at Miller Freeman that a task force was formed in mid-1991 to give employees a chance to talk about what was wrong with the company. Management was not represented on the task force, but the group's recommendations were heeded.

Moving ahead

Such moves help convince those employees who remain that a company has a future. But even if the worst of the downsizing is behind the industry, the ensuing management problems won't be easily overcome. One participant in a Magazine Publishers of America seminar on downsizing half-jokingly asked consultant Wendleton to "let us know" when she finds the silver bullet to surviving layoffs. Her response: "I'm not here to give you the answers except that you have to manage change in a humane way." □

Finance

How to Talk to Your Banker

BY L. MARK STONE

It is ironic that so many magazine owners and publishers whose stock-in-trade is effective communication seem to suffer communication breakdowns when it comes to talking with their bankers. Bank debt, after all, should help one manage the business more productively. If the opposite is true, something is wrong with the communication between lender and borrower.

How is it that relations between magazine publishers and their bankers go so wrong? The primary reason publishers and bankers fail to communicate effectively is that publishers too often don't take the time to cultivate a close and friendly working relationship with their bankers. A solid banking relationship can be as valuable an asset as the subscriber list.

Even if you have no current need for financing, it can be worthwhile to meet with several banks. Presenting your business to a bank forces you to take an objective view of your company's strengths and weaknesses. The banker to whom you present your company may spot problems you've overlooked, or may offer some advice and counsel that a consultant would have charged dearly for. Additionally, good bankers are always looking for new borrowers, and the best borrower prospects are businesses that do not have a pressing need for money.

The first step in maximizing one's banking relationship is to have a clear understanding of how bankers think. Bankers see themselves as lenders, not investors. Smart investors will demand to know a lot more about how magazines are published than a lender will. We have all heard publishers complain that their otherwise bright bankers seem to understand little about publishing. But you can be very sure that your banker knows a great deal about the *business* of publishing.

Bankers only reluctantly find themselves in the investing business when a loan goes bad. "Investors" in the traditional sense take on a particular level of risk expecting to earn a commensurate financial return. Bankers, on the other hand, want to avoid risk and be absolutely sure that they will get all of their principal back. To satisfy themselves as to a borrower's creditworthiness, bankers will ask for reams of financial reports, ratio analyses and budget-vs.-actual charts.

Nonetheless, bankers recognize that the world doesn't always turn out as one would like, so they examine what would happen if your magazine were not able to meet its debt-service obligations. The bank wants to know that the magazine could be sold for more than the bank's loan exposure: That's why bankers are interested in valuations and comparable transactions.

There are no hard rules of thumb here, but a stable magazine producing cashflow margins of some 15 percent can reasonably expect to borrow a maximum of two to four times cashflow, in part on the presumption that the magazine could be sold for (conservatively) five to seven times cashflow. "Cashflow" is defined as pre-tax profit plus depreciation, amortization and excess owner benefits, and less capital expenditures.

Finally, bankers are extremely concerned about who the borrower is. They will ask for and check personal references because they will be relying on the moral commitment of the borrower to pay back the debt.

How to ask for—and get—more

Once you've secured a loan, you will send monthly or quarterly reports to the bank. You will be wise, as well, to arrange some face-to-face meetings with your banker(s) to give the bank some familiarity with your business. But if you are current in your payments, your bankers won't feel compelled to second-guess you and will probably leave you pretty much alone.

When you make it known that you are going to be seeking additional funds, however, you will undergo fresh scrutiny almost as excruciating as when you applied for your initial loan. Typically, you will be asked to make a formal presentation to several of the bank's officers.

Prior to that meeting, the bank will ask you to produce volumes of information. At the meeting, though, you may quickly conclude that the bankers haven't read any of it. And you may very well be right. Don't take it personally, however. One purpose in asking for the information is to recheck that you have good financial oversight of your magazine.

You'd be surprised at how many publishers do not take the same care in producing their financial reports that they do creating their magazines. It may sound obvious, but the reports you send to the bank say a lot about who you are. They should be legible, with line items labeled clearly. All numbers in the various reports should agree with one another. Unusual items should be explained in footnotes. The detail pages backing up summary pages should be clearly labeled and easy to find.

At the meeting, you may be introduced to a few new faces because it is at this point in the lending relationship that the greatest potential exists for collusion and fraud between the borrower and the lending officer. These "fresh faces" will often play "good cop/bad cop"—at your expense. Resist the urge to defend yourself. Focus instead on how you have managed the business proactively over the past few years. Fess up to the odd failure and what you learned from it.

In short, sell the fresh faces on you and your management team's abilities. Don't merely report that "Last year the magazine's advertising yield per page increased." Instead, take credit that your management team " enacted an adjusted commission plan that helped to increase advertising yield per page by 6 percent." Remember that these bankers are not interested in the magazine as a magazine; they are interested in the magazine as a business and your demonstrated ability to run it.

Assuming that you survive the grilling, the subsequent meetings and the numerous requests for more financial information, your application for additional funds may be approved. You will then be presented with a new loan agreement, which you should read carefully. It will probably have been completed by a junior member of the lending team, and may not reflect all of the covenants and ratios that you fought for and won during your negotiations in the first loan.

Finally, your CFO or your accountant should take your financial projections and layer underneath them the new repayment schedule and ratio and covenant tests. Make absolutely sure that you will meet all of the loan agreement's covenants and ratio tests throughout the life of the loan. If not, talk to your lending officer, because a seemingly ludicrous covenant could very well be just the result of an oversight.

> You'd be surprised at how many publishers don't take the same care with financial reports as they do creating their magazine.

How to break bad news

Bankers fear two things. First, an unforeseen disaster that results in a great financial loss. I recall a client whose entire printrun disappeared when distributor/wholesaler Select Magazines shut its doors a few years ago. Bankers typically are very accommodating in these situations and are often willing to postpone or extend payments.

The second fear is that management will miss a series of projections, where no one variant is important, but where the cumulative effect over a few quarters is that the company has trouble meeting payments. Here, the bank's inclination would be to declare you in technical default. The bank will be concerned that the magazine's value may deteriorate to a level near or below the bank's loan amount. To avoid having your loan called, you, the borrower, should bring the bank into the picture as soon as it's clear that you're going to miss your goals.

Take, for example, the situation where a magazine faces an aggressive competitor nipping at its advertising share. To avoid losing share, the borrower chooses to match the competitor's page-rate cuts, resulting in lower yields per page as well as less cashflow available to service the outstanding debt.

In this situation, we recommend to clients that they make their bankers partners in the solution by bringing the banker up to date immediately, *before* the impact on cashflow is felt. The magazine's budget should be revised to reflect the costs of combating the competitor, the net effect of which may require you to postpone one or more loan payments.

The next step is to explain to the bank how your ability to make payments will be affected by the new competitor. Bear in mind that banks are much more willing to postpone principal payments than interest payments. If you can get by with a short delay of a principal payment, the bank may simply agree to your suggested delay. The bank may or may not issue a formal waiver of covenant compliance, but you will have a clear understanding of the bank's expectations.

If instead you wait to inform the bank until just before your payment is due, on the presumption that it is too late for the bank to say "no," you risk having your loan called in full.

Similarly, even if you can make all of your payments as originally scheduled, you should still inform the bank of the situation as early as possible so that the bank will have tangible proof that you have their interests and concerns at heart.

The best rule for breaking bad news is that your banker should understand all the reasons behind the budget-vs.-actual variances long before the financial reports land on his or her desk.

How to restructure debt

When the bank has lost confidence in your ability to fully repay its loan on or close to schedule, a complete bank-debt-restructuring is necessary.

No borrower should go through a restructuring like this without good legal, tax and accounting advice. At this point, relations between lender and borrower are typically poor, and it is hard to be objective about negotiating a settlement that is both acceptable to the bank and that does not force a sale of the business. But having taken the time previously to cultivate a good relationship with your bank will increase the likelihood of a successful restructuring.

A typical restructuring goes like this:

Your loan will be taken out of the lending department and placed in the workout department. Your original lending officer will become scarce, and your new workout officer may not be cordial. Workout officers are required to make a confidential, for-internal-use-only estimate as to the bank's ability to recover its principal and interest. Consequently, it is in the workout officer's best interest to paint as bleak a picture as possible so that he can negotiate a settlement that exceeds the bank's expectations.

Should the bank not force a sale of your magazine, its officers will work to make the loan as secure as possible. One way to do this is to break the original loan into two parts.

The first part will look like a smaller version of the original. It will be a senior secured-debt instrument, and the amount of principal assigned to this loan will be small. This loan's principal will be set so that, under the worst circumstances, you will have no difficulty making regular interest and principal payments. A loan that is set up in this way can still be classified by the bank as "performing."

The remaining part of the original loan principal will become a subordinated debt instrument. Interest is not expected to be paid on schedule, and principal may not be paid back at all until the end of the loan. Interest that is due but that the magazine cannot afford to pay is converted to principal. (The bank effectively lends you new money to pay current interest.) Any excess cash produced by the magazine is "swept" out to pay past-due interest. The interest rate charged on this loan will be high because the bank sees this portion of your loan as a risky investment, and so deserving of a venture capital-type rate of return. Indeed, the interest-on-interest feature of this debt effectively results in the bank becoming your equity partner, whether or not warrants or other equity conversion features are attached to this subordinated debt.

To complete the restructuring, the bank may ask the shareholders to contribute additional equity capital, or to raise more equity from new sources. New loan agreements are prepared, and the shareholders must decide whether to sell the magazine now, or work a few years to rebuild the value of their equity.

As bad as a workout sounds, it is an opportunity that publishers who haven't made the effort to cultivate their bankers' trust would most likely be denied. That's why even if your magazines are so profitable right now that you do not need to borrow money, the time taken to craft a solid working relationship with your bank is a worthwhile investment. □

Finance

How to Bring Your Financials Into Focus

BY STEPHEN A. SOCHA

Small magazines, good marriages and wooden floors are exactly the same in several respects: All can be charming, interesting and a joy to have, and all require constant vigilance to keep them in good shape. Fearing repercussions from floor refurbishers and marriage counselors alike, this article will focus only on small magazines.

Small, established books tend to operate quite differently from their larger cousins; regardless of their type or subject area, small magazines are typically run as expense-driven entities. Profitability, therefore, depends on adequately controlling expenses while meeting market demands. As a result, it's necessary to be vigilant and watch every penny. A simple way to do this is to implement a three-step system of ratios that allows you to measure magazine performance accurately.

The ratios are simple to calculate and will show you either where you need to fine tune, or where you are not making the numbers. Small misses in one or two areas can be made up by borrowing from other categories. Large misses—or, more insidious, small misses in every category—will require immediate action to stop the bleeding.

Average issue revenue. The first step is to establish your average issue revenue (AIR). On controlled titles, this consists of display and classified net ad revenues, along with any predictable ancillary income. It is best to take as long an average as possible. Most companies try to do an annual average to compensate for minor seasonal variations. Exclude any abnormally large issues (such as a special anniversary issue or trade-show issue) and treat them as separate entities. The resulting calculation is as follows:

$$\frac{annual\ net\ ad\ revenue + ancillary\ income}{number\ of\ issues} = AIR$$

If a significant amount of paid circulation exists, circulation revenue should be included. In the case of subscriptions, all monies received—minus the replacement cost of lost or non-renewed subscriptions and fulfillment costs—should be added to the equation.

The cost of replacing lost circulation varies greatly. As a general guideline, most magazines today are thrilled with a 2 percent paid conversion on a campaign. If a mail offer is used, a cost of $0.40 per piece is reasonable. Thus, a magazine with a subscription price of $19.95, a circulation of 20,000 and a predictable renewal rate of 70 percent will need to replace 6,000 subscriptions each year. To accomplish this by mail, the magazine will have to send 300,000 pieces at a cost of $120,000.

The total subscription revenue for this magazine is $399,000 ($19.95 times 20,000). When the replacement cost of $120,000 and the fulfillment cost of $0.50 per piece ($10,000) are subtracted, $269,000 remains to be added to issue revenue. If newsstand sales are part of the picture, only historically proven distributor remits should be included.

If we make our sample publication a 10-times-per-year trade magazine with a print run of 30,000, the above paid subscription base of 20,000, controlled distribution of 8,000, and $700,000 in total ad revenue, the resulting AIR is $969,000 in annual operating revenues and $1,099,000 in annual gross revenues.

It is vital that revenue projections be conservative. The most dangerous thing a publisher can do is overestimate performance. Precious few small magazines succeed at selling themselves out of a tight spot, and Divine Intervention is notoriously unpredictable.

Expense categories. Once revenue streams have been established, you need to turn your attention to expenses. A simple and accurate way to monitor and control expenses is to divide them into four major categories: issue, sales, non-sales and overhead expenses.

Issue expenses are all the things you would save if you never produced a given issue. This includes printing, binding, paper, pre-press, separations, issue postage and labels, and freelance art, editorial and photographs. Together, the cost for the above items should be 37.5 percent of AIR—or, in the above example, $36,337 per issue. The total cost for the year based on 10 issues should equal $363,375.

Sales expenses (including support) run at 20 percent for most books. In our example, this equals $19,380 per issue. Some magazines with an in-house sales force can do a bit better. If sales are handled in-house by salaried employees, the total annual sales allotment is $193,800 (20 percent of annual operating revenue), or $16,150 if paid on a monthly basis.

Non-sales expenses are calculated on an annual basis and include full and part-time salaried personnel. The current industry average is about five people per million of sales. Non-sales expenses should run at 12.5 percent of your annual operating revenues. In the example given, this amounts to $121,125 per year, or $10,093 per month.

Overhead includes office rent, utilities, phone/fax, equipment leases, employer-contributed FICA, pens, pencils and a long laundry list of other necessities. These expenses shouldn't exceed 12 percent of annual operating revenues, or $116,280 per year in our sample magazine.

If our sample title hits the numbers, the above set of ratios produce a profit of 15.87 percent on gross revenues of $1,099,000. That translates to 18 percent on operating revenues of $996,000, with a $130,000 fund reserved for circulation maintenance.

An operating profit margin of at least 15 percent is essential, due to the nature of the magazine business. It is standard for a magazine to collect between 40 and 42 percent of its outstanding receivables per month. This means that a book will usually have an average of 18 to 20 percent of its net ad revenue out at any given time. And while in a steady-state situation future receivables are interchangeable with collections on past issues, it doesn't take much of a glitch to produce a real cashflow crisis.

Problem solving. Because most publishers are intimately familiar with their magazines' numbers, it should take only a few minutes to calculate these ratios. The art (if any) comes in drawing the right conclusions from the data and taking the appropriate actions.

If the overall picture is good, you might want to use the formulas to fine tune your book's performance. If it is less than splendid, begin by looking at the category that most misses the target numbers. Because issue costs represent the greatest expense, they are often the culprit. If issue costs are out, start with this calculation: AIR x .075, divided by the cost to mail a single issue.

This number will produce the ideal print run for your revenue. In the sample magazine, the run was 30,000. Its target run could have been as high as 33,034 copies. If you're running a controlled book and are printing too many copies, look at your ad rates and adjust the run length immediately. Find a way to add some other (less expensive) value for your advertisers. If you have a heavily mixed or paid book and are printing too many copies, look at your advertising rates and increase subscription prices. The increased prices are likely to result in a slight drop in subscribers (which is part of your goal) and substantially increased revenues from the rate hike.

If your print run is good but your issue costs are still out, look at your editorial color percentage and costs and your ad:edit ratio to make the needed adjustments. Also, you should take a hard look at your suppliers. Today, many suppliers are actively seeking new business, and good deals abound.

If sales expenses are high and you have an in-house operation, try a different compensation structure. One idea is to assume that repeat business is a direct result of proven reader responses to past ads. Offer your sales staff a reduced commission rate on repeat business and an increased rate on new business. Your sales force won't turn down the easy ad (even at reduced commission) and will push a bit harder for new customers. If you are dissatisfied with your rep firm's compensation schedule, re-negotiate or find a new firm.

If your overhead is high, work diligently to cut it down. This is usually easier than it first appears. Just remember, your presence in the market is reflected in the pages of your magazine, not in the size of your office or overnight courier bill. Similarly, non-sales staff expenses need to be in line with the revenues of the magazine. Although it is difficult to decrease staff, you should not allow excesses here to endanger the magazine or the livelihood of all those whom it supports.

When all is said and done, markets pay for what they demand, and little else. The market will tell an established title what it will and will not support. Listen carefully. Base your operations on the real world. You can be assured of profitability only by properly meeting—not wildly exceeding—market demands. Reasonable service at a fair price works every time. □

 Finance

Rock-Bottom Publishing

BY RICHARD P. FRIEDMAN

I've had the luxury of working in large, plush, well-funded magazine environments where substantial budgets were allocated to various departments. Because money there was plentiful if you could reasonably justify the expense, there wasn't much need or motivation for rock-bottom publishing tactics.

In 1988, however, the entrepreneurial bug bit me and I struck out on my own. I must confess, it was culture shock! From my basement, I launched a niche computer magazine about an up-and-coming software technology (object-oriented programming) on $1,500 that I had scrimped from savings. By using the techniques revealed in this article, I've "organically grown" SIGS Publications into a highly profitable, $6 million company with four magazines, one newsletter, books and conferences. With readers in more than 80 countries, we have operations in the United Kingdom and Germany.

But I haven't forgotten the warning Malcolm Forbes gave me six years ago when I sought his advice on my magazine launch—that is, that magazines can consume money like people consume air. My experiences to date convince me that he was—unfortunately—absolutely correct. But successful small publishers quickly learn that the formula for increasing profits is straightforward—either increase revenue or reduce expenses. Here are some of the cost-conscious tactics that work for us.

A dollar saved is a dollar earned

It's important to create a unified mindset that all employees live by. Here are the two basic credos of the SIGS staff:

Assume you can always buy it for less. From printing to shipping to office supplies, magazine vendors are competitive. Although loyalty is important, that doesn't mean you shouldn't aggressively shop your suppliers on an ongoing basis. This may sound obvious, but it's a challenge to instill this mindset in staffers of all levels—from VP to receptionist—for all projects. Knowing where vendors make their profits is extremely helpful in price negotiations. It also helps in learning how to prepare projects to achieve optimum savings.

You don't ask, you don't get. Never be embarrassed to ask for discounts—for volume, prepayment, remnant rates or for supplying materials in a cost-effective manner. Our fulfillment house provides a discount per subscriber as our database grows. Printing bind-in cards ganged together in large volumes has earned us sizable discounts. Providing film to the printer on time in an easily usable format results in cost savings on printing jobs.

Miserly management techniques

Involve all staffers in the cost-cutting mindset by rewarding them for savings achieved (perhaps a percent of annual savings). At SIGS, although we are still a young company, we have implemented a profit-sharing plan for all full-time employees. The more we save, the larger the profit pie.

Get what you pay for. If a vendor makes a mistake, promptly ask for an explanation and restitution. Put your grievance in writing, carefully explaining how the error was damaging both financially and strategically. Be flexible but firm in restitution negotiations.

Negotiate lower rates for prompt payment. In dealing

> Being scrappy and demanding quality and service for your hard-earned money doesn't mean being chintzy.

with vendors, ask for "prompt payment" terms, such as a 2 percent discount for paying within 10 days. On paper and printing, 2 percent can mean sizable annual savings.

Save on recruitment. Although executive recruiters generally provide excellent candidates—quickly—their fees can be quite high, frequently 15 to 25 percent of a job candidate's starting salary. If you have time, I advise that you instead ask staff members, vendors, associations and colleagues for recommendations. Try running a help-wanted ad in a local newspaper or trade magazine. Frequently, you'll reach the same candidates as the recruiter—just a little later.

Even if you don't need staff now, continue to conduct exploratory interviews. And don't overlook in-house potential: Promoting from within builds morale and motivates the staff. It also makes financial sense. Outside candidates frequently want more because they are taking a risk in "jumping ship." A grow-your-own policy, though, necessitates careful recruiting. At SIGS we expect all our "hand-picked rookies to make the big club," so we take the time to interview more than 30 candidates for every spot.

Cost-effective circulation building

Building and maintaining quality circulation on a tight budget is almost a contradiction in terms. Conventional wisdom says that building quality circulation costs millions, and that direct-mail-acquired subscriptions don't break even until year two, at best. That's not necessarily true. Here are some tips to keep subscription-acquisition costs down.

Swap mailing lists whenever possible. List rentals can account for as much as 25 percent of a direct-mail package's total cost. Eliminate this cost by aggressively offering your list in exchange. After all, your list generation costs are nominal. Negotiate exchanges with both other magazines and your advertisers. We've found that advertiser lists, whether customer or prospect files, are often top performers in direct-mail campaigns. But if advertisers do use your list, be sure to encourage them to take a two-pronged approach. The direct-mail message aimed at readers should complement—not substitute for—an ad. An increasing number of our advertisers are successfully using this multi-marketing mix in the software fields.

Encourage advertisers to use your magazine as a premium. Advertisers like to be associated with a magazine because it makes it clear that they are interested in keeping customers informed. (Offering a magazine also encourages customers to return warranty cards.) Get advertisers to include your magazine cover in their ads in other publications or in direct-mail offers.

Sell advertisers these "gift" subscriptions at a discount. Even if it's less than the price needed to qualify as BPA paid (*i.e.*, more than half the basic rate), it's still more cost-effective than acquiring paid subscribers yourself. We've found that these gift subscribers convert at an impressively high 25 to 30 percent rate—and you still have the names for future front-end re-solicitation.

Insert trial subscription cards into advertisers' products. Purchasers of your advertisers' products are the readers you want. By putting SIGS subscription offers in the software boxes of Microsoft and Borland, we've generated thousands of fresh and targeted trial leads annually, which flow in on an ongoing basis. In fact, we currently have trial subscription cards in the boxes of more than 10 software companies, totaling over 200,000 trial-offer subscription cards. This subscriber source generally provides your ad rep a great sales story for advertisers who want to reach active buyers. And this subscription source consistently pays up at an acceptable 15 to 22 percent.

Bargain with copywriters. Good copywriting for direct mail, space ads and back-end promotions can be expensive. Costs of $8,000 to $10,000—or more—for a direct-mail package are common. So negotiate a smaller up-front fee and a bonus structure based on the performance of the copy. That way, you've covered your fixed expense, and if the campaign is successful, you can afford to pay a little more.

Or write and design in-house. Nobody should know the nuances of your magazine better than your editor, circulation manager or art director/designer. They are frequently eager to participate in an advertising/promotion campaign. At SIGS, we do all promotion work in-house.

Buy late; buy remnants. For advertising, we've found that buying ads and card decks just after the close date can bring discounts of as much as 50 percent off published rates. You might also consider using a less expensive paper grade for your direct mail/promotion materials. Try buying remnant paper stock (either slightly damaged, leftovers or odd-size lots) that the printer is eager to get rid of.

Seek advice from your vendors. When you are creating or designing direct mail and promotion materials, it's best to ask the printer for optimal sizes and color based on his press. We found that printers have been able to "batch" jobs and eliminate paper waste, saving us thousands of dollars. Everybody wins.

Penny-wise production

The best advice here is to make sure you're using desktop capabilities to the fullest. Keep up with the latest upgrades for your software (a nominal cost), and make certain the staff has the dexterity to use the software and hardware. Money for training is well spent.

Buy used hardware. There are several brokers (such as the Boston Computer Exchange) that sell used, but current, computer equipment for a fraction of the list cost. Generally speaking, it's less expensive to upgrade memory (or get a Syquest disk) than to buy brand-new PCs or Macs.

Design with type. Keep illustration costs down by using desktop design software to its fullest. Such software offers the option of many different typefaces and graphic treatments.

Scan your own images. If you do use illustration and photography, edit both color and black-and-white images after scanning them digitally. When the scans are satisfactory, place them in desktop layouts to eliminate separation and stripping costs at the printer. For intermediate color proofs, use a laser printer instead of a Matchprint or similar commercial proof. It's very close in quality and is one-fourth the cost. When possible, give the printer composed film to cut prep costs.

Plan ahead. Plan your layout so that you make the most efficient use of color forms when printing. Ask your printer for advice. Try to use black-and-white or two-color forms wherever possible. Check quality control early in the production cycle. Revisions get more expensive as you get closer to your print date.

Trade-show savings strategies

Exhibiting at trade shows worldwide is a good circulation and advertising strategy. But shows can be prohibitively expensive unless you watch costs.

Hold out for the best events. Keep exact records of ad sales and circulation-building performance from each show so that you can select the shows that work best for you. Then try to limit the number of participants you send; perhaps your sales rep can do double duty at the booth by distributing magazines.

For additional visibility, ask your advertisers—who attend many more shows—to distribute copies of your magazines (and even collect names) at their booths. If they like your magazine, they are usually happy to help. This piggybacking method gets SIGS Publications "presence" at 15 extra shows worldwide, just for the cost of shipping.

Or you may be able to trade booth space for ad space where you plan to exhibit. To really benefit the show organizer, this must be arranged at least four months prior to the show.

Book early. Conference organizers often offer lower early-bird booth and drayage rates. Airlines also offer substantial discounts for early booking. Allow adequate time for shipping (say, five to eight days) and send any packages by ground service. When you're ready for post-show shipping, it's frequently cheaper to arrange pick-up by your own freight carrier than to use the official show carrier. Quality and service may also be better with your regular shipper.

Choose hotels carefully. The "official" conference hotel won't always offer the best rates, as commissions may have been added on for show organizers. Carefully establish a T&E budget and limits in advance for all those who are trade-show bound. Double-up on rooms, cabs and car rentals wherever possible.

Assemble your booth yourself. If you *must* use union staff (expensive), inform them that you are on a budget. Monitor their time and activity, or Parkinson's Law sets in. They may even charge you for time they spend lunching.

Never just give away magazines. Increase your database of prospects by collecting business cards in exchange for your magazine. We found that well-attended trade show floors can produce 1,500 hot subscriber leads in three days. In Europe, many publishers even charge attendees a nominal fee for magazines at their booth (to cover costs).

In summary, being scrappy and demanding of quality and service for your hard-earned money doesn't mean being chintzy. After all, your readers are unforgiving: They want a well-written and nicely designed magazine, on time, at a price they can afford. At the same time, though, magazine profit margins are very tight. But if you manage all your costs using these rock-bottom publishing techniques, you'll find a reasonable profit is within reach. □

Franchise building

Franchise Fever

Franchise building

BY THE FOLIO: STAFF

The 1991-1992 advertising *slump and the emergence of highly effective database marketing helped redefine the magazine industry. It's now a mainstream objective to leverage your title (your "brand") into as many different markets as possible, with the dual purposes of establishing new revenue sources and strengthening the core product. No longer are we magazine publishers—we're information providers. And no longer are ancillary revenues ancillary: The word that used to conjure images of sleepy little side businesses now has the same dimensional importance as advertising and circulation—and it can insulate against market fluctuations, advertising downturns and attacks from competitors.*

How do you determine what's right for your business? How should you work with partners? Where will you find your target audience? Following are case studies of six magazines—trade and consumer, large and small—that have built their magazines into extended franchises. Their experiences will give you valuable insights as you extend your own franchise.—Tony Silber

■ *The Blood-Horse* jockeys for a winning position

If you were going to gamble on any horse in 1986, you probably wouldn't have picked *The Blood-Horse*, the 24,000 paid-circulation weekly covering thoroughbred racing since 1916. Nine years ago, the Lexington, Kentucky-based title found itself crushed by the Tax Reform Act of 1986, which reduced tax benefits for investors in thoroughbred racing. As a result, fewer investors bid on mares and foals, thereby squeezing the advertising base. Advertising levels have yet to bounce back to the pre-1986 peak of nearly 10,000 pages annually, and this year, the magazine will hit about 4,000 ad pages.

To further shake the category, in 1989, *The Blood-Horse*'s century-old competitor, *The Thoroughbred Record*, closed, as did another industry title. There are now four contenders remaining, including *The Thoroughbred Times, Daily Racing Forum* and *The Pacemaker*. Charles B. Dowdy III, associate publisher of *The Blood-Horse*, says the thoroughbred racing market is stable, but has declined somewhat because of the

increasing popularity of casinos and riverboat gambling.

For *The Blood-Horse* to survive on its own, given the changed circumstances and a shrinking market, the company had to develop cash-producing spin-offs. "Everyone was waiting for the market to improve, but year after year it got worse," says Stacy V. Bearse, president and CEO of The Blood-Horse, Inc., who came to the company in 1990. "We realized we had to reduce our dependency on advertising as a major revenue source."

Five years ago, *The Blood-Horse* represented 82 percent of the company's total revenue. And Bearse admits that when the market first began declining, supplementary products were seen more as market enhancements than money-makers. But today the company takes in over $7 million a year through its ancillary businesses, representing about 30 percent of total revenue. Its other products, most launched in the last five years, have become mainstays. They include the following:

• "The Daily Dispatch," a newsletter officially launched in 1989 and distributed to The Jockey Club, which then distributes it online or by fax to any of 1,500 paying members. The newsletter contributes $25,000 in profit to the company's bottom line after expenses, says Dowdy.

• *Modern Horse Breeding* (renamed *The Horse* in March), a national paid monthly on equine health acquired from Round Table Publishing in November 1993 with a circulation of 14,000.

• The National Stakes Condition Book, published quarterly and polybagged with *The Blood-Horse*.

• Five annual reference editions, including The Stallion Register, a six-pound catalog with gross ad billings of nearly $1 million and 1,000 paid ad pages; The Source, an industry directory; Auctions Review; Stakes Review; and Sires Review, which ranks stallion performance.

• Instructional videos that sell for nearly $100 each.

• Books, including Royal Blood, a $75 art book introduced in November that has already resulted in sales of over $400,000.

• Custom-publishing projects, including the official Kentucky Derby souvenir magazine. The company is under contract to produce, publish and market the annual $5 Derby edition through August 1997, and plans to distribute 65,000 copies this year through ESPN and at racing tracks, newsstands and off-track betting sites. The company will share the sales proceeds with the Derby organizers.

"We had to push the envelope," Bearse says. "It's a dangerous strategy to focus on advertising and circulation to the exclusion of everything else." The numbers have taken a turn along with that philosophy. In 1987, the company derived 75 percent of its revenue from advertising, 19 percent from circulation and 6 percent from other sources. Today advertising contributes 52 percent in revenue, circulation contributes 26 percent, and 22 percent comes from other sources. Bearse says the company is now cash-positive, with strong operating margins, a healthy balance sheet and a marketshare that has risen 15 points.

The moral? "Find out what your audience needs and look for synergies," Bearse says. "If you choose these projects wisely, they add more dimension to your core product."—*Lambeth Hochwald*

> Side businesses can insulate you against market fluctuations, advertising slumps and competitors.

■ Big hits generated by *Billboard*'s ancillary ventures

When you think of Billboard, you might think of top-40 music countdowns and the voice of Casey Kasem that made them famous. But the 101-year-old magazine is merely the center of an empire that produces everything from contests to conferences, books to bars.

Billboard, published by New York City-based BPI Communications, is among the biggest moneymakers for BPI's $1.5 billion parent company, the Dutch conglomerate VNU, and that's due increasingly to *Billboard*'s ancillary products and services. In November 1993, the various music directories, contests, conferences and books, the research department, and the newly-created online services were united with *Billboard* and the other music weeklies under one name—the Billboard Music Group—and now ancillary products account for 15 percent of the group's total sales. "We're taking advantage of a natural synergy," says *Billboard* publisher Howard Lander, who is also the group's president.

The franchise is growing. Just 10 years ago, the magazine's ancillary revenues hovered around 5 percent, but Lander says he expects this figure to increase to 25 percent by the end of the decade. He notes that the push for ancillary product development is fueled in

part by rising paper and postage prices: "We have to find other avenues of revenue if we're going to survive these cost increases," he says.

Billboard's electronic ventures

Among the music group's newest initiatives are online services. There are three: the Billboard Information Network, the BPI Entertainment News Wire, and Billboard Online. All were launched within the past eight years and have just gotten out of the red. The oldest, Billboard Information Network (BIN), was launched in the early eighties and provides about 150 subscribers with the newest music charts before the magazine is published. The BPI Entertainment News Wire, which sells music news to other media, is in its sixth year and, according to John Morgan, general manager of the service, has 300 to 400 subscribers. Billboard Online, the newest service, was launched in April 1994. It allows subscribers to browse in five databases, in addition to giving them access to *Billboard* articles published since March 1991. It has grown from 10 or 20 subscribers to 350 in less than a year, says its manager of sales and customer support, Vince Beese. Each subscriber pays $79 for initial start-up software, and then $1.29 per minute online.

Voluminous directories

When clients prefer printed information, they can purchase any of *Billboard*'s seven directories—which cover everything from recording equipment to booking agents—or its 27 books. The directories cost anywhere from $50 to $135 and attract anywhere from 500 to several thousand subscribers, according to Ron Willman, publisher/directories. Lander says these directories, along with 12 others in the group, bring in over $2 million dollars. And, if you prefer to have someone else do your research for you, you can call Billboard Chart Programming Research, which receives an average of 20 calls per day from people requesting research information at a rate of $80 per hour with a $20 minimum.

Then there are *Billboard*'s five annual music conferences and award ceremonies, which bring in half a million dollars every year. The conferences attract anywhere from 250 to 700 participants each.

In the end, though, *Billboard*'s most successful ancillary product has always been its charts. Lander says many of its chart licensing deals are in the six-figure range, with one of the biggest being the Fox Network's five-year-old Billboard Music Awards. In addition to the money is the name recognition. "The countdown shows can be heard all over the world," Lander says.—*Cris Beam*

■ *National Geographic*'s world of ancillary success

National Geographic, published by the Washington, D.C.-based National Geographic Society, is perhaps the most venerable example of a magazine leveraging its name. The 107-year-old title with its familiar yellow border is one of the most recognizable brands of any kind in the country. To support that brand, the society, over the past 30 years, has expanded into a vast array of products—including television programs, books, videos, maps, atlases, CD-ROMs, games and more. In the process, it has developed a powerful line-extension business, with ancillary products generating $136 million of the society's overall revenue of $424 million in 1993.

The linchpin of this success is the National Geographic Society's high level of consumer-perceived quality and recognition. (The society has more than nine million members—dues of $24 include a subscription—and the magazine has a better than 80 percent renewal rate.) In 1994, *National Geographic* won two Equitrend awards: one for having a high level of quality measured against all U.S. companies; and another for reader satisfaction.

There are two spin-off magazines: *National Geographic Traveler*, launched in 1984, has more than 270,000 subscribers; and *World*, a 19-year-old magazine for children that carries no advertising and has more than one million subscribers.

The largest and most visible non-print extension has been television. Only the British Broadcasting Corporation has produced more documentaries than *NG*. Although Chevron, *National Geographic*'s corporate sponsor for periodic PBS specials, recently pulled its support for financial reasons, *NG* continues to produce the shows. In January, one of every four American households tuned in to NBC to watch *National Geographic*'s 30-year anniversary special. And "National Geographic Explorer," a weekly show on TBS, has not only proven successful in ratings, but is also selling well as a series of videos. This fall, a *National Geographic* children's television show will debut on one of the networks.

Robert Sims, senior vice president at the society, says that the television has become a solid revenue stream. "TV is not new, but it's booming for us now," he says.

Because the National Geographic Society is a non-profit organization, making money is not a motive. In fact, in 1993, the society operated at a net loss of $44 million because of one-time costs of voluntary early retirement programs as the society underwent a major restructuring. Member dues and contributions accounted for $222 million of the Society's revenues in 1993, the latest year for which figures are available. Advertising brought in $48 million, and educational programming and materials, in which television and other ancillary revenues are included, accounted for $136 million.

The museum shop on the first floor of *NG*'s headquarters does $1 million in sales by itself. And last fall, Random House published the Society's National Geographic: The Photographs, which sold out its first printing of 220,000 copies. Members bought 170,000 of those at $34.95 a copy, and 50,000 copies sold in bookstores at $50 a copy. A second printing of 50,000 copies is in progress, and a third printing is planned.

The society is also exploring opportunities in electronic publishing. *NG* is already on America Online. Sims says the board of trustees is looking for a senior-level person to head up the society's electronic efforts, but "like everyone else in publishing, we don't quite know where this is going."

In the meantime, the society is focusing on the April launch of *National Geographic* in Japan, its first foreign-language edition. With its joint venture partner, Tokyo-based Nikkei Business Publications, *National Geographic* will launch with a prepaid circulation of almost 100,000.— *Tim Bogardus*

■ *Industry Week* retools for new era

When Carl Marino became publisher of Penton Publishing's *Industry Week* three years ago, he understood that as one of the leading titles covering American industrial management, the 233,000-controlled-circulation biweekly had a unique position of influence. That position, combined with the rapidly changing face of media, compelled Marino to try to "build a multimedia organization around *Industry Week*." This means putting *IW*'s brand name and content, not the physical magazine, at center stage. His mission, then, has been to define and serve *IW*'s audience in as many other ways as possible. It's working. Non-advertising revenue is at 20 percent of *IW*'s total revenue, up from 7 percent three years ago. Marino's plan is to increase that number even more, to 40 percent of *IW*'s total revenue within four years.

Seminars pay off

The first brand extension from the Cleveland-based title was a series of short management conferences aimed at leaders in manufacturing. Since 1991, the conferences, whose topics have included "America's Best Plants" and this March's "Managing for Innovation," have had over 5,000 attendees at around $600 a head, producing revenues of more than $3 million, and have grown to account for 10 percent of *IW*'s total revenue. The conferences vary in cost, but the average is $75,000 to $100,000. Nine are scheduled for this year.

Other projects have recently burgeoned. In early 1994, in partnership with CRM Films, a former McGraw-Hill unit that specializes in training videos, *IW* released the first of a series of educational videos on strategic and management issues. The videos—four so far, sell for $179.95 each. Under the terms of the deal, CRM produces the videos and *IW* does the marketing; revenues are split 50/50.

IW's most high-tech spin-off, Industry Week Interactive, launched in December. Available on CompuServe, the venture includes an area called "Virtual Organization Inc." This interactive forum is set up as a hypothetical corporation, divided into departments such as accounting and research and development. Everyone who logs on becomes an associate. A case study is extracted from the magazine every two weeks and uploaded as a "marketing challenge," with discussion topics seeded throughout by the magazine's editors.

"We're setting up a place where executives around the world can interact with one another," says Marino. So far, says executive editor John Brandt, over 21,000 people have joined the forum. Marino says *IW* has had to dedicate 2.5 staffers to the project. He notes that it is producing revenue, but the terms of the deal prohibit saying how much.

February marked the launch of the newest franchise extension, *Industry Week*'s "Management Today," a half-hour television show broadcast on (and produced and owned by) CNBC. It airs Saturday and Sunday mornings. The 26-part show is still too new to have produced any tangible returns, but *IW* has high hopes for this feature-format program focusing on ways to increase productivity and better manage your workplace.

Under the terms of the deal, *IW* pays CNBC to get the show made, and is free to cut its best deals with advertisers. Full sponsorship of "Management Today," for example, includes 26 30-second commercials, 26 10-second billboards, and 24 full-page and 13 two-thirds page, four-color ads in *IW*. All that goes for $442,560—the same price as on the rate card for the ad pages alone. "Ancillary products help fuel advertising space in the magazine, that helps fund ancillary products," Marino says, adding that the show is making money for *Industry Week*.

Future franchise plans include a "Best Plants" newsletter and possibly a Penton World Wide Web site.—*Debby Patz*

■ *Penthouse* finds sex sells and sells and sells

Everybody knows that sex sells. But General Media Inc. knows firsthand that it sells and sells and sells and sells. *Penthouse*, the company's 25-year-old flagship title, has been the undisputed breadwinner of the 14-title company, regularly selling just over 60 percent of its newsstand draw.

In the last three and a half years, New York City-based General Media has taken the well-recognized name of the 1.7 million-circulation title—and in many cases, its content—and entered a variety of new markets, from print spin-offs to videocassettes to CD-ROMs. The line-extension efforts have paid off: Penthouse had $120 million in revenue last year, and 10 percent of the total came from ancillary ventures, up

> The linchpin of *National Geographic*'s success, and that of its spin-offs, is its high level of consumer-perceived quality and recognition.

from virtually zero three years ago. "Of course, we always want to protect our franchise, but we are also interested in product extensions that can enhance our position in the marketplace and find new consumers," says General Media COO and President Kathy Keeton.

Beyond seven related magazines, the foundation of the *Penthouse* spin-off franchise is its adult videocassettes, which produce more than half the magazine's ancillary revenue. The company's three-year old Santa Monica, California-based entertainment division releases 10 to 12 videos a year, and ships between 50,000 and 75,000 of each tape to national retail outlets that carry adult titles.

A 60-minute video sells for $19.95; a 90-minute video is $29.95. Most tapes average sales of about

60,000 copies, according to vice president of circulation James B. Martise. That translates into a gross revenue of $1.2 million for each hour-long video and $1.8 million for the 90-minute versions.

General Media has also found its erotic material well suited to the interactive realm. The first edition of The Virtual Photo Shoot, a CD-ROM that simulates a *Penthouse* photo session, sold an estimated 30,000 copies at $99.95 per copy five months after it was introduced in January 1994. Versions II and III were released in late December and sell for $69.95.

Created in partnership with ICFX, a multimedia firm in Fairfax, California, the first CD-ROM cost about $500,000 to create, according to Martise, but costs were amortized and covered through sales in about eight months. Martise says the CD-ROMs are so successful that eight more interactive CD-ROM games of a similar ilk will be released before year's end.

General Media's foray into new media also includes Penthouse Online, a two-and-a-half-year old service. Run by VideoTex of America in San Diego, Penthouse Online now has about 6,000 users—up 4,500 from November 1992. Subscribers pay $9.95 to sign up for the service, a monthly fee of $5.95, and 20 cents a minute to download photos and graphics. General Media and the online provider split the revenues. *Penthouse* also launched an Internet site in March.

General Media is also seeking to expand its franchise on the small screen. In an arrangement with SPICE, an adult pay-per-view channel, the magazine aired three three-hour specials last year. About 28,000 households ordered the $5.95 special, and revenues were split between the New York-based Graff Pay-Per-View Inc. and General Media. This year, SPICE has scheduled one special to air in May.—*Lorraine Calvacca*

■ Fast-growing companies get a lot of *Inc.*

Inc. these days is more than just the magazine for growing companies. It truly is *Inc.* Inc. It has spread throughout the world of small- to mid-size companies, offering an array of conferences, publishing services and educational products.

Although the 16-year-old title published by the privately held Boston-based Goldhirsh Group is tight-lipped about its earnings, the payoff from this franchise extension is strongly implied: *Inc.* made $58.5 million in ad revenues last year, according to PIB figures, up

$20 million since it started its ancillary operations unit in earnest in 1985.

That year, *Inc.* Business Resources was formed as a subsidiary of the 650,000-circulation monthly, primarily to sell reprints. In the late eighties, when Inc. began to invest in the division and make it responsible for all ancillary activities, IBR generated 5 percent of the magazine's total revenue. Now the division brings in 20 percent. "We realized the need for *Inc.* to address the needs of the small-business owner in a more in-depth fashion by taking advantage of the different media available," says IBR president Bob LaPointe.

Booming business conferences

Each year, *Inc.* hosts six national shows, 30 to 50 regional conferences, and five executive programs, all under the direction of the IBR conference group. National shows last three days and bring in anywhere from $250 to $1,500 per head. Attendance ranges from 200 to 1,500, meaning that a show attracting 1,500 people at $1,500 per person brings in $2.25 million. The national shows will typically have multiple sponsors, each paying between $30,000 and $150,000. The regional shows attract local companies that single-sponsor the events for a fee of up to $15,000.

IBR's product unit is responsible for various line extensions as well as for reprints and custom publishing. Its 11 book titles, which offer such advice as how to start a business and grow it, fetch anywhere from $12.95 to $15.95. IBR offers marketing partnerships that allow companies to attach their logos to existing *Inc.* books for fees that vary depending on what other IBR services are used in the partnership. It has had 10 such deals in the past four years.

IBR also has five guides (workbook versions of its books) and an audiotape, each of which sells for $59.95. In addition, there are 37 videos covering subjects similar to the books, which sell for an average $99. IBR is also dabbling in new media, having produced a $49.95 CD-ROM version of the video, "How to Really Start Your Own Business." Other projects include a presence on Apple's eWorld online service. An America Online site is slated to open in June, and an Internet locale will follow in 1996, says LaPointe.

The product group has also published six quarterly, 250,0000- to 300,000-circulation custom newsletters for corporations for the past four years. —*Steve Wilson* □

New-Market Smarts for Publishers

BY BARRIE J. ATKIN

Success in launching a new publication or entering a new market depends on many factors, including effective market analysis, hard work, good luck, smart timing and sufficient capital. But it also depends on avoiding common mistakes that have hampered—and sometimes torpedoed—other magazine launches.

Since you can't control every aspect of a start-up, it only makes sense to limit your risk where you can.

Choosing the wrong editor. The choice of editor is a critically important decision—and therefore one where a mistake can be devastating. Far too often, an editor is hired because the new magazine concept was that person's idea, or because that person was persistent in his efforts or support of the idea. Neither is sufficient reason to assign the title of editor to anyone.

How to avoid: Write a job description for the editor's position. Is your in-house "champion" a good match? If not, search for the right person. It can be difficult to turn down someone who has put a lot of time and energy into the magazine concept. But if he does not have the vision and leadership to attract and keep readers, a different editor is needed.

The fantasy model mistake. A detailed, three- to five-year financial model is part of a solid launch plan. But too often, the model is designed to reach specific corporate goals even though the assumptions to get to those goals may not be realistic. This can happen when modeling starts with the end point, such as a specific return on investment or break-even within a set number of years.

How to avoid: Document the reasoning behind all key assumptions. Are they reasonable and realistic? Is there any experience to back them up? Do some "what if" testing: What are the key assumptions and how confident are you that you can achieve them? Once you are satisfied with the model, have it and the assumptions reviewed by a relatively disinterested party.

> By avoiding others' mistakes, you'll have more breathing room and, hopefully, more resources to apply, to other challenges that arise.

Assuming effort is equal to size. Some publishers assume that a small-circulation or small-revenue magazine takes proportionately less effort to launch and manage than does a large one. In truth, it takes almost as much effort and oversight to plan and start a small magazine (though usually less investment) as it does to launch a large one.

How to avoid: Identify how much time will be required for any venture. Recognize that there is a minimum amount of time needed to manage even small ventures. Then evaluate whether the potential return (or perhaps the experience gained) from the smaller venture can justify the required investment of time, talent and money.

Doing too much that's new. By definition, a magazine launch is something new. But sometimes, the enthusiasm of the launch leads to doing too many new things at once—for example, depending on new channels of distribution, new advertisers and new readers—and then compounding that by hiring new staff who have not held similar positions in the past.

How to avoid: Established companies can reduce their risk by limiting the new components and building on existing strengths. Independent new ventures can limit risk by using proven people with knowledge of and relationships in the new market.

Overconfidence based on past success. Success with previous launches can provide useful experience that is helpful to future new ventures. But it's no guarantee of success. Sometimes previous success leads to too much confidence and clouds a company's vision. People start to feel invincible and may lose touch with reality.

How to avoid: Identify the steps that made previous launches successful. Where appropriate, make sure that those steps are incorporated into the new project. Also, identify the factors that led to previous failures and take steps to avoid repeating them. Consider incorporating the same amount of analysis that you would demand if this new venture were being proposed by an outside source.

'The arrow is always up' mistake. Almost all financial modeling presumes steady increases in revenue from year to year. But the world works more on economic cycles, as well as sudden shifts. Suppose, for example, that you had launched a magazine on international travel in July 1990 (the month before Saddam Hussein invaded Kuwait). Your steadily increasing model would have been woefully wrong.

How to avoid: Identify any factors that could have a significant impact on your business, and estimate the likelihood that they will happen. Ask industry experts to assess where the industry is in the "business cycle." Be sure to include a worst-case scenario, go/no-go points and contingency options in your business plan.

Too high a frequency. This is probably the most disastrous launch error after "Wrong choice of editor." Startups often take time to define their voice, establish readerships and build advertising pages. Too high a frequency puts pressure on the staff to produce the next issues, without time to consider feedback, read results or correct results.

How to avoid: Luckily, this is easy. Start with a six-times-a-year frequency, or some other frequency suitable to the magazine and its market. This allows time to recover from mistakes. Many successful monthly magazines were launched with a lower frequency.

The 'marginal cost' mistake. Companies often don't account for all the costs in a new venture, assuming that the new venture can utilize existing capacity or staff. This may be true—up to a point. But at some time, a successful venture will need its own staff and additional resources in its own right.

How to avoid: In financial modeling, evaluate the cost of the enterprise fully loaded—*i.e.*, the same way that the company's existing properties are evaluated.

Latching on to the first idea. New ideas can take on a life of their own. Be wary of latching on to an idea and running with it without adequate analysis or consideration of other ideas.

How to avoid: Establish a rigorous analytical process for new ventures—and use it. Apply that process to several good ideas, not just to the first idea or the one championed by the most vocal or the most successful individual.

Believing there's no competition. Some magazines think they have no competition. Others see competition, but downplay its relevance. It's important to recognize that there's always competition—if not with another magazine, then for people's time and money.

How to avoid: Identify all direct and indirect competitors in your subject area, including non-print competitors. Identify your magazine's compelling advantage: Why should people buy and read your magazine? Then carry out a similar analysis for advertising competition: Why should advertisers put money into your magazine over their existing schedules?

Avoiding these 10 mistakes does not guarantee a successful launch. But by avoiding others' mistakes, you'll have more breathing room and, hopefully, more resources to apply to other challenges that arise. □

Spin-offs Mean Spiraling Profits

BY ELIZABETH CROW

Spin-offs are an easy and efficient way to expand a magazine publishing company's profits. Properly managed, spin-offs—in the form of new magazines, special issues or newsstand-only editions—make excellent use of your existing staff, involve limited additional costs and are a natural form of phased, sustainable growth. Best of all, a good spin-off adds to your core business's strength and reputation, while making money and serving readers' needs.

Some years ago, Gruner + Jahr USA had three fine magazines: *Parents, YM* and *Expecting*. Today, without spending a ton of money (or buying someone else's headache), we have seven. Creating these four new publications (*BabyCare, Ser Padres, Una Nueva Vida* and *Embarazo*) wasn't hard to do because each was a logical extension of our existing magazine franchises.

There are no hard rules for creating spin-offs, but over the years, we've defined a few basic principles:

It's easier to spin new products off a powerful magazine than a weak one. A magazine with a clear mission and a well-defined market niche usually has strength to spare. The more profound your readers' loyalty to that magazine and the hungrier they are for the information your editors provide, the more likely it is that you will be able to define special-interest areas that will either serve your existing readers' specialized needs, or attract new readers into the fold.

Certainly a spin-off's ad strength (at first, anyway) is going to be in some measure a reflection of the flagship publication's reputation with the advertisers who already run in its pages. Yes, a successful spin-off will certainly attract new advertisers, but many of its pages will be bought by advertisers who already know the strength and effectiveness of the bond between their customers and your parent magazine's readers.

Keep the spin-off from cannibalizing the parent for ads. In addition to making money the old-fashioned way (through traditional ad sales and circulation efforts), spin-offs stand a good chance of helping advertisers with their promotional efforts. If you can serve these advertisers' promotional needs by getting their messages to customers either in a nontraditional setting (at

point of purchase, say) or at a critical moment in their lives (right after childbirth, for example), you're likely to have your spin-off supported by promotional dollars. This strategy will result in saving regular print-ad budgets for your other magazines, and will prevent cannibalization of your flagship's pages, which is your only real risk on the ad side.

Target spin-offs to special-need segments of your audience. There is also a small but real risk that your spin-off's editorial will compete too directly with its progenitor. New publications that appeal too directly to your existing core readership can undermine your flagship's strength without providing enough profits to compensate. On the other hand, competition isn't always dangerous—especially if you target spin-offs to specific, narrow segments of your audience.

At G+J, we have just completed a special literacy-promoting magazine called *I Love to Read* for the StrideRite Corporation. It is being distributed directly to customers at stores where StrideRite shoes are sold, and its aim is twofold: to encourage mothers and fathers to read to their children as early and as often as possible, and to get parents to think of StrideRite as a family-information resource as well as a shoe manufacturer. Other than an introductory letter from Stride-Rite's president and a one-page ad, *I Love to Read* contains no commercial messages at all.

I often joke that *BabyCare* is *Parents'* "demographic edition," but it's true. Thanks to *BabyCare*, we can offer advertisers with highly specialized products an economical means of reaching young mothers at three-to six-month intervals during their babies' first two years. In fact, each of our *Parents* spin-offs serves specialized segments of the parenthood field that *Parents* dominates.

Spin-offs come in four 'flavors'— pick one. These relate, in general, to frequency, reach and duration.
• A "primary" or first-generation spin-off is an originally produced, free-standing publication that is designed to operate forever. *Expecting* fits that definition at Gruner + Jahr.
• A "second-generation" spin-off is slightly further removed from its source in concept and execution.

BabyCare, for example, was launched in partnership with Procter & Gamble, which wanted a way to bond consumers to its Pampers disposable diaper brand. During the years since we launched *BabyCare*, the magazine has evolved from its original incarnation as *Pampers BabyCare*, which accepted only P&G advertising, into *Parents BabyCare*, which is sold to many different advertisers (although it advertises only P&G diapers).

Not only does *BabyCare* benefit editorially from its association with *Parents* (many of its articles are condensed from pieces that have run in *Parents*), but *BabyCare* is a good way to introduce *Parents*, our Child Development Toy line, and our Read Aloud Book Club to demographically ideal potential customers.

• "Optionally transient" is the next spin-off tier. *Find The Real You*, a special one-time newsstand edition of *YM*, falls in this category. It could become a regular extra issue, or it might be the beginning of a long line of single-topic one-shots on different subjects. Time will tell.

• "Guaranteed one-timers" make up the final group. These are single-topic one-shots on highly specialized but relatively timeless subjects—like cholesterol primers or pasta recipes.

Be prepared to do some serious investigative study. Taking on a new project and/or attracting a partner to share the costs as well as the rewards requires careful study. You have to define, as nearly as possible, your potential partner's goals and compatibility with your own short- and long-term strategy.

For instance, if your partner is looking for new customers, do you happen to count those potential buyers among your readers? If not, do you think that you can reach them with a carefully targeted publication that is within your area of expertise?

You should also be very clear about whether your goals and your partner's are the same. It's okay to be accomplishing slightly different ends with the same product, but if your goals are incompatible, you may end up competing with yourself and undermining the very integrity and high standards that made you an attractive partner in the first place.

Ask yourself the six crucial questions. Let's say you have a partner for your spin-off or (lucky you!) you don't need one and are going to take on all the investment risk yourself. There are six crucial questions you should ask yourself before you begin.

1. Does my spin-off serve a distinct, underserved segment of my existing readership?

2. Can I reach these readers quickly and efficiently?

3. Does the niche I've spotted contain enough readers to give my project critical mass? Without a relatively large target group (or a small group that will pay an arm and a leg for your publication), you'll have trouble attracting advertisers, and even finding your customers.

4. Do I have the manpower to produce the spin-off? If your project won't be too elaborate or time-consuming, you may be able to create, market and deliver your spin-off using only existing staffers, although this may be optimistic at companies that have been downsized in this recession. Even if you don't add a single employee or freelancer to your team, it is essential that each project have its own internal structure: a business plan, clear editorial direction, and a project leader.

5. Will I be able to go outside for help? Projects that require extra hands are the norm, since it is unusual to find an efficiently managed staff that has an abundance of free time. Bringing in an outside art director, usually on a freelance basis, can make everyone else's life much simpler. Using freelance writers is almost inevitable, and well worth the cost. You may have to add one or two ad sales people if it's not possible to sell your new project in concert with your existing publications.

Although circulation and financial services can almost always stretch to accommodate an additional publication, you may need to sweeten the pot a bit if editorial staffers will have to do their share after hours or on weekends. For these employees, the chance to make some freelance income or a one-time bonus is likely to be welcome. What you want to avoid, however, is a situation in which employees shortchange their regular jobs to make additional money. For a long-term project, a permanent mini-staff of full-time editors, art directors and salespeople may be required.

6. Am I prepared to invest in this idea? If you are going it alone—even if you don't have to use outside staff—you will have to spend some money getting started. You would be wise to do some research to define your ideas and target your product properly.

You will inevitably incur promotional and manufacturing costs before you begin to make real money, but you will probably be able to get along on a budget that is just a fraction of the size of a regular monthly magazine's budget. If you haven't carefully anticipated your costs, however, you can easily end up in a hole.

If you have good answers to all the above questions, you're probably ready to get started on a spin-off. And if your experience is anything like ours, you'll be glad you did. □

Trade-Show Success Secrets

BY CARL S. PUGH

In hot pursuit of new revenue streams, many trade publishers are considering additions to their traditional, paper-based editorial products. Fax publishing, CD-ROM, online services and 900 numbers are all under the microscope. But trade show sponsorship, a decidedly low-tech option, may hold the greatest promise in the search for a healthier bottom line.

Trade shows have a well-documented track record, have earned some publishers millions, and do not rely on a new—and perhaps transitory—technology. Although most shows are feeling some effect from our current recession, the high margins typical of trade shows have allowed otherwise healthy events to remain solidly in the black.

The beauty of a magazine-sponsored trade show is its natural fit. Advertisers become exhibitors, readers become attendees, writers—or those written about—become speakers. Editorial topics become seminar topics, and your ad pages and lists form the basis of the marketing campaign.

Sizing up the market

The first step is to determine if the market your magazine serves needs a trade show and whether that need is already being met. If you are unsure of the trade show activity in your industry, *Tradeshow Week Data Book*, published by R.R. Bowker, is an excellent resource. If there are one or more shows, don't despair. An opportunity may still exist. For now, let's assume there is no show in your publication's market. The best way to determine your chances of success is to look at what's happening with your magazine. If you are struggling to attract advertisers, selling exhibit space will probably be no easier. You'll be relying on the same resources to close sales: your magazine's reach and reputation. On the other hand, if the professionals within your industry have embraced your editorial direction, then build the show and they will come.

Here's what induces people to go to a trade show:

They need knowledge and information that is not readily available from any other sources to grow their careers or businesses.

They use complex tools in the practice of their craft. For example, a manufacturer of kitchen cabinets uses a variety of sophisticated woodworking tools that can be better compared on a show floor than in a catalog.

They sell products made by other companies. Shoe stores stock their shelves with the latest Italian pumps from samples first examined at an importer's booth.

They need to make contact with peers, suppliers, experts, prospective employers or employees, new or current customers, etc.

The more of the above needs your readers possess, the more likely it is that your show will succeed. However, you will still need a quality promotional campaign to spread the word, an excellent educational component to capture their interest, and several key vendors as exhibitors to lend additional credibility and serve as yet another drawing card. The objective is to give prospective attendees many reasons to make the trip.

What if a show already exists?

In all likelihood, though, there are already one or more shows in your market. However, there still may be room for another. Your challenge is to find an angle that will allow you to capture all or part of the market. Here are six tried-and-true strategies you can use to get a piece of the pie:

Location. Almost every show is regional from an attendance standpoint. If your competition is running in Los Angeles, consider Atlanta.

Time. Larger industries can often support more than one show. If there's one in the fall, run yours in the spring.

Niche. Look for a vertical slice of a horizontal show, or a segment that is not being served. I started a very successful show for professional photographers in a market that already had a well-established show by targeting a fast-growing segment the competition was slow to recognize.

Quality. There are plenty of poorly run shows out there. Do yours better and knock them out of the box. I put a long-running show for graphic designers out of business in only two years by starting a competing event that was aesthetically more appealing and offered more amenities to exhibitors and attendees.

Mood. How are the attendees and exhibitors feeling? If either group is disgruntled, there may be an opportunity. Sometimes it's because of dissatisfaction with the sponsoring association or management company. Clues can often be found by talking to show participants, something you probably already do as a member of the press. I successfully launched a show for photo labs, for example, because they felt lost in the shuffle at the nation's largest show for camera-store owners.

Price. Occasionally you can carve out an opportunity through price cutting. However, this option is risky.

A trade show has two major components: the conference and exhibition. The conference, or educational portion, usually consists of seminars, workshops, roundtables and other interactive learning sessions that allow industry experts and participants to share their knowledge and experiences. Generally, those who attend either pay for each session on an ^ la carte basis or buy a package for the entire conference.

The exhibition provides a forum for manufacturers and suppliers to display their products and services. You generate revenue from this group by selling exhibit space. Some shows also charge an entry fee for exhibits-only attendees.

Maximizing your revenue
Whenever possible, include both a conference and exhibition in your plans. I've worked on several shows where the conference and exhibition each brought in $500,000. Yet, my incremental cost for having both was minimal. After all, with just one of the two you still have to secure a facility, promote the event, handle registration and manage the entire process. With both a conference and an exhibition, you get two revenue streams for (almost) the price of one.

Still, this may not always be possible. Some markets simply will not support both. Retailers making buying decisions for the coming season will spend hours at an exhibition poring over prospective purchases, but are often too preoccupied to attend seminars. Conversely, insurance brokers may flock to an educational event, but have little interest in an exhibition because they

don't use anything they can't find at their local stationery store. This is often the case when a group does not sell a tangible product or use special tools.

You can still make money with just an exhibition or conference; many events do. In fact, some of the largest shows in the country generate only a small percentage of their revenue from the conference side. Similarly, highly profitable conferences are not uncommon. Ultimately, your show's format will be dictated by the needs of the market you serve.

> The main reason for launching a trade show is the profit potential. Many return 50 percent of revenues or more to the bottom line.

Dates and locations
When and where you run your show are critically important decisions. It is always easier to take the show to the people than to get the people to come to the show. The effort and cost required to participate is significantly lower for the person who drives across town compared to the person who must hop a plane, reserve a hotel room and miss several days of work. Look at your circulation and see where you have the greatest concentration of readers. In most cases, that's where you should run the show. Also look at the desirability of the destination. More people will go to a show in San Francisco than one in Oklahoma City. And no one wants to go to Chicago in January or Miami in August.

If your exhibitors will have heavy freight and big booths, consider a right-to-work state such as Georgia or Florida. This means that their setup and teardown costs will be considerably lower, since use of union labor is optional. Hotel rates are another consideration. Figure around $175 per night for a room in Manhattan, versus $75 per night in Denver.

The "when" decision is affected by other industry events, buying seasons and traditional busy periods. Watch out for holidays, religious or otherwise. If you are planning an event in a major city, be prepared to have difficulty getting your preferred dates. This is especially true if your show will use lots of meeting rooms, but not a lot of sleeping rooms (i.e., mostly local attendees) or food functions. Hotels make their money on food and overnight guests.

The rest of the pie
The core of your marketing effort will be your own subscriber list and ad pages. Plan on mailing your pro-

gram brochure detailing the conference content, special events and exhibition about 12 weeks before the show. You should also consider tipping the same brochure into your magazine shortly thereafter. Also consider hitting association lists. Ads should start at least nine months out. In the beginning, they do more to support your exhibit sales effort than to attract attendee inquiries. Start with full pages and work up to spreads three or four months before show time. Remember that prior to your first event, all prospects have to go on is your magazine's reputation and the image you create in their minds through the show's promotion.

Enlist the support of as many industry associations as possible. (Prepare to strain your relationship with those that run shows, however, as they will feel you are treading on their turf.) The more groups, major suppliers and industry moguls you have in your camp early on, the greater your credibility with prospective exhibitors and conference attendees.

When you are selling booth space, reference-selling is king. Start with the industry leaders and work your way down. Mention to Apple that IBM bought a 20- by 30-foot island, and they'll demand one 20- by 40 foot. Then, armed with Apple and IBM, you can attract a host of companies that ride on the coattails of these biggies. If necessary, prime the pump by making a sweetheart deal with one of your major advertisers.

Don't chicken out on the booth price. The difference between charging $10 per square foot versus $20 on a 100-booth show is an extra $100,000 on your bottom line. In a survey conducted by the Trade Show Bureau on factors considered by exhibitors when choosing a trade show, price was low on the list. Up top were audience quality and quantity. Draw your floor plan with the largest spaces up front. Companies are often willing to take a bigger space to be near the main entrance.

Rounding out your trade show start-up chores are gearing up for the registration process, handling logistical concerns, putting the educational programs together, and whipping up some crowd-pleasing special events. Each is an undertaking in its own right with tricks and processes that are better learned through professional guidance than trial and error. Outside registration companies abound, as do show logistics con-

> Trade shows are a natural fit for a magazine, but they are a different kind of business and require specialized expertise.

sultants. As for the content of the educational program, your editorial staff is probably the best candidate.

Getting help

Okay, you've decided that an opportunity exists. What do you do next? As mentioned before, you probably already have the raw ingredients necessary. But, as any gastronome will attest, the secret is in how they are brought together. There are two options: Hire a chef or learn as you go. I strongly recommend the first option. Although trade shows are a natural fit for a magazine, they are also a very different kind of business and require specialized expertise. For this reason, it is best to acquire the services of a trade-show professional—at least until your staff has been through a couple of cycles and learned the ropes.

There are three ways to get help. You can hire one or more seasoned professionals into staff positions. They can be found by advertising in industry publications or through the National Association of Exposition Managers' job bank. You can also hire a consultant or show-management company. *Tradeshow Week Data Book* has a section listing dozens. Finally, you can form a joint venture with a show-management company.

Hiring staff or an outside company is initially more costly, of course, but you will own 100 percent of the show. Doing a joint venture may be the best option—unless you are certain that you have a hit on your hands and have the capital to hire outsiders. For starters, you will not have to pay salaries or a fee. The management company will make money only if you make money. Second, you are more likely to get a cautious appraisal of your show's prospects for success. No show-management company worth its salt will want to invest its time and money unless it can predict a favorable outcome.

Still, in a joint venture, if the show ends up making millions (and some do), you may well find yourself keeping 50 percent or less. Conversely, if the show loses money, you will have a partner to share the burden. It is even sometimes possible to get a show-management company to underwrite 10 percent of the start-up costs and assume all financial liability in return for a larger equity position.

My personal bias is toward the joint-venture route. It

served me well in 1983 when I was publisher of *Photo District News*, a fledgling trade journal for professional photographers. I was interested in starting a show for that market, but knew nothing about the process. I stumbled on a show-management company and we formed a joint venture. My staff provided industry-specific guidance, and the management company pulled the whole thing together. It was a perfect marriage. Ten years later, the resulting event has grown to 1,000 booths and 30,000 attendees from around the world.

The primary reason for launching a trade show, of course, is the profit potential. Many shows return 50 percent of their total revenues—or more—to the bottom line. But there are other good reasons. Before launching its show, *Photo District News* was having trouble attracting the attention of national advertisers. That changed very quickly after the first event demonstrated the quantity and quality of our audience. Today, *PDN* is the number-one book in its field—in part, I believe, because of its sponsorship of the industry's largest event.

Fringe benefits

Increased ad sales, circulation and marketplace visibility are all benefits of running a successful show. And, in putting your educational program together, your editorial staff will be forced to take a long, hard look at who and what is important in your market—a worthy exercise. Finally, there is the prestige and personal satisfaction that comes from creating and hosting a show that is embraced by the professionals you serve.

There is no guarantee that your show efforts will succeed. In fact, for every successful start-up, there are easily two failures. But with careful analysis and professional guidance, the downside can be minimized. When compared to the risks and costs associated with starting a new magazine, trade show launches are extremely tame. It is not uncommon for a trade show to turn a profit in its first year.

How many new magazines do you know that can make that claim?

Buyer's Guide Bonanza

BY STEVE WILSON

Few franchise extensions have as many beautiful contradictions as the buyer's guide: It's an issue dense with information, yet it's not a real issue. It's a showcase for several products, but it's not an advertisement. It can be much larger than a regular edition of the parent publication, yet oftentimes requires less work and money to produce.

A directory of the products and manufacturers serving a magazine's audience is a natural extension—and a potentially large source of revenue. If done properly, such a directory can also be a powerful marketing tool for attracting new advertisers and subscribers. Here, we examine successful guides from Hanley-Wood, Cahners Publishing Company, Wenner Media and Canoe America Associates, and uncover the secrets of their success: characteristics common to each that make the difference between profit and loss.

Guiding might

The best buyer's guides assume the role of publishing rainmaker: They bring in huge chunks of business and become one of a magazine's biggest issues of the year. *Builder*, from Washington, D.C.-based Hanley-Wood, Inc., and *Furniture Design & Manufacturing*, from Newton, Massachusetts-based Cahners, produce annual industry-guide issues as part of their monthly frequencies. Both are major money-makers.

Builder publisher Michael J. Tucker describes his directory, published as the April issue, as "a solid piece of business." The *1995 Buyer's Guide Issue* brought in 248 pages compared with the typical 120 to 125 ad pages in the 198,000-circulation (mostly controlled) magazine. Tucker says that of *Builder*'s total $20 million revenue, the 10-year-old guide (along with a CD-ROM version unveiled in 1994) generates $1.8 million, just below the January show issue in terms of profitability.

Although paper and printing costs are higher for the 412-page issue, which has a slightly increased print run, that cost is offset by money saved on decreased editorial expenses. Further savings are achieved by the sharing of the listings database with two other Hanley-Wood publications, *Remodeling* and *Pro Sales*, for their

own guides. The CD-ROM version is sent free to 30,000 readers with CD-ROM drives and sold through the magazine for $35. Having generated $175,000 in 1994, the disc is expected to make $750,000 in 1995.

Meanwhile, S.L. "Sandy" Berliner, publisher of *FDM*, says his 17-year-old guide—*The Source: Woodworking Industry Directory*—is less expensive to manufacture than other regular issues of the monthly *FDM*. He pays the same production costs, but the issue is 50 percent larger—412 pages instead of the usual 200—hence the savings. "You don't have to send editors on assignment," he says. "And you have no color separations—it's black and white."

Each May, the directory contributes more to *FDM*'s $5 million in total revenue than any other issue. (Like *Builder*, *FDM*'s show issue is more profitable, but it appears every other year.) In 1995, the guide produced over $700,000, compared with a regular issue's $400,000, according to Berliner. *FDM* has a controlled circulation, so most of that revenue came from advertising.

Canoe & Kayak, the 83,000-circulation Kirkland, Washington-based consumer bimonthly, has for the past 20 years made its comprehensive guide to products and manufacturers a section in the December issue. The 1995 edition, sporting 90 pages of directory, half of which were ads, won a 1995 Maggie Award in the Best Buyer's Guide category. The issue has also become profitable over the years, representing 21 percent of the magazine's annual ad revenues, says associate publisher Glen Bernard. Managing editor Dennis Stuhaug says the buyer's guide issue generates higher newsstand sales and has better sell-through.

The only cost difference involves going from saddle-stitch binding to perfect-bound, but the extra $1,500 is well worth it, Bernard says. "It gives the issue more of a quality feel. It's something people save and use all year."

Men's Journal, from New York City-based Wenner Media, also shells out extra money for the *Men's Journal Equipment Guide*—to the extent of making it a separate ancillary product independent of the magazine's frequency and available only on newsstands. "We don't include it in our subscription. We'd rather collect money for it," says *Men's Journal* group publisher Mark MacDonald. "For subscribers, it would be a nice value-added bonus, but you're hitting the same reader. With this, you try to bring in new subscribers."

How successful the guide has been in that role has not been tracked, MacDonald says. Introduced in November 1994 as an extended version of the monthly's equipment section, the guide breaks from the vertical approach of *Canoe & Kayak* and *Builder* by covering various consumer products of interest to 25- to 49-year-old active male readers, from bikes to footwear to electronics. On shelves from November to January to take advantage of the gift-giving season, the book had a sell-through of 41 percent last year, roughly 175,000 copies of its 400,000 distribution, according to MacDonald, garnering 71 ad pages and $835,315 in ad revenue. The guide is printed in a smaller trim size to fit better on magazine racks than the 300,000-circulation parent, saving money through lowered paper costs and, in theory, making it more accessible to newsstand consumers.

> The best buyer's guides assume the role of publishing rainmaker: They bring in huge chunks of business for the parent title.

Magnets for new business

No matter its size or marketing plan, a buyer's guide's uniqueness makes it a natural tool for drumming up new interest. "It's a good entry point for readers and advertisers," says *Builder's* Tucker. His directory averages between 20 and 25 new advertisers per edition. *FDM* usually reports 50, and MacDonald says *Men's Journal's* first guide hailed 10.

As publications so closely wedded to advertising, buyer's guides can offer advertisers more value-added options for their money. For example, the effectiveness of reader-service cards promising more product information is often heightened. Tucker says the *Builder* directory is the magazine's second-largest reader-service inquiry producer, generating 160,000 leads a year. "[Our advertisers] get leads all year long," he says. "That's why it's a good buy for all manufacturers."

Included in that figure are advertisers who opt for placement in special pages of new-product listings that run at the end of each section. For $1,200, a color photo of their product and a paragraph description of it appear on the page and the CD-ROM version, along with a mention on the card. In 1995 380 advertisers participated, and the special listings contributed $456,000 to revenues.

Canoe & Kayak makes a point to put reader-service surveys in the December issue. The response rate was up 47 percent over 1993, according to associate publisher Bernard.

The *FDM* guide also uses these cards, although they're not as effective as in a normal issue. Berliner attributes their lessened pull to the directory's "reader-service life" of one year instead of 90 days. "You use the directory in a different context," he says. "You look at it to find suppliers and call them up from the page. You don't need the card as much."

Neither is the guide a good tool for attracting subscribers, Berliner says. "The magazine reaches every known furniture and woodworking company, so the likelihood is strong that all who could use it are on the list to begin with," he explains. Still, he prints up several hundred extra copies to distribute at trade shows for free. The cover price for the issue outside its controlled circulation of 5,200 is $25, although Berliner points out that he receives no "brisk business" from sales. Nor does he pursue it.

But Jessica Raefsky, consumer marketing director at *Canoe & Kayak*, says the directory's powerful newsstand performance and year-long shelf life with dealers draw many subscribers. And Stuhaug extols the virtues of the guide as a promotion tool, which is why 10,000 extra copies of the book are printed for shows, boat shops, newsstands and recreational communities. It's left on most shelves for 14 weeks instead of eight. Raefsky says she also uses the issue as a premium, offering it free in promotions or to subscribers who seem wishy-washy about renewing.

Neither fish nor fowl: The ad:edit question

The relationship of advertising and editorial has always been tumultuous, and nowhere is that affair more confounding than in buyer's guides. Boundaries between what is editorial and what is advertising are sometimes vague, and editors and publishers must navigate carefully to preserve the integrity of their business.

Times Mirror's *TransWorld Snowboarding*, for example, stopped including advertising in its seven-year-old *Monster Buyer's Guide* in 1994. Instead, it produces a

54-page supplement polybagged with the September issue purely as a bonus to its readers and retailers. A portion of the cost is covered by adding seven ad pages in the magazine. "[The guide] was getting so big over the years, the editorial felt like advertising. Editorially, we felt it was a little tacky," says Brian Sellstrom, president of the 120,000-circulation title based in Oceanside, California. "There's already a bias toward the larger companies in the guide. How big they are and their distribution determines the space they get."

Others certainly don't share these moral qualms, although James Kaminsky, senior editor of *Men's Journal* and editor of the *Equipment Guide,* is careful to point out that the guide's existing format allows its writers to be critical of aspects of the products they recommend if they think it's necessary.

The guides produced by *Builder* and *Canoe & Kayak* offer little to no editorial comment, but list every known company and manufacturer for free in charts and let the advertisers do the talking for an extra fee. "There's no charge for content because we want the most complete information possible," Tucker says of the 2,100 companies his guide lists.

The *Canoe & Kayak* directory companies that take out ads one-sixth of a page or larger can have black-and-white photos of their products appear in the charts for free. Not only is this an added-value option for the customer, says Bernard, but from an editorial point of view it makes the pages look better.

FDM prints its information in list form as well, but it charges suppliers $45 for the service—unless they're advertisers, in which case their inclusion is free. "It's beneficial to readers," Berliner says. "They know they're looking at viable sources. We do get a couple of guys in the industry who think charging for this is reprehensible. But we're doing advertisers a favor. I could list any company free of charge and create competition [in a category]. I'm doing the guy who pays a favor by not listing his indirect competition."

MacDonald wanted the *Men's Journal Equipment Guide* to look like an expanded edition of the book's equipment section. The end result was a directory of color photos and short reviews of products listed under one of six categories. "The reader will hold on to [the *Equipment Guide*] longer, but not read any of it at any length," Kaminsky says. "He will look at it in little chunks, so it has to be written that way. We have more boxes of copy, more sidebars. We can't de-emphasize the user-friendliness of this."

"Shorter is better," seems to be the overriding philoso-

phy at work here, but that doesn't make the task of data collection any less crucial. Still, gathering information is one of the few labor-intensive jobs in producing a guide.

Builder contracts out most of that task and verifies the findings with phone calls. *FDM* collates information with Reed Technology and Information Services, a directory processing company in Ft. Washington, Pennsylvania.

"A mail-intensive documentation" is how Stuhaug describes the information gathering at *Canoe & Kayak.* He sends out 425 forms to every canoe and kayak manufacturer in North America, and averages an 80 percent response. From that point, a staff of seven (three editors, three salespeople and one clerical person) devotes half its time to preparing the section for a month and a half.

At *Men's Journal,* equipment is collected over the summer in a room that Kaminsky likens to "an explosion at a sporting goods store." After trends in the products are determined, two to 12 of the best items at different price points are written up. The project takes six months to complete, by Kaminsky's estimation, the last three reserved for the crunch time when an additional freelance staff of three editorial and four art people enter the fray.

"The only way to make it profitable is to wait as long as you can before using the whole staff," he says.

GUIDE boasts

The franchise is worth developing, MacDonald says. He plans to keep *Equipment Guide*'s distribution the same, but raise the cover price from $3.95 to $4.95.

With the help of the CD-ROM version, Tucker hopes to grow *Builder*'s guide into a $3 million to $4 million product in the next few years.

TransWorld Snowboarding also wants to make good from marrying the buyer's guide concept with a new-media venture by introducing a World Wide Web site in 1996, Sellstrom says.

"I don't think advertisers are willing to pay money for the value-added applications of a CD-ROM. Not in this market," he says. "I think it's more convenient for people to pick up a copy of the magazine and flip through it."

With no major plans in the works, the editors of *Canoe & Kayak* intend to grow and improve their guide at the same gradual pace they've taken over the past 20 years, the kind of strategy that garnered a Maggie Award, points out Peter Becker, advertising representative.

"It's pretty much a proven product over these past 20 years," he says. "It's not broken anyway." □

Take It to the Tube

BY MARGARET E. POPPER

Robert Johnson, founder of Washington, D.C.-based Black Entertainment Television (BET), wants his network to be the top black media company in the 1990s. So how is Johnson strengthening his firm's presence? He's expanding into print.

BET's latest move in this direction came in September 1991 with the company's investment in a start-up aimed at black teenagers. *Young Sisters and Brothers* (*YSB*) has a circulation of 80,000.

Nor is *YSB* Johnson's first foray into print. In 1990, with Time Warner as a partner, BET launched *Emerge*, a newsmagazine for black adults; it now has a circulation of 135,000. And Johnson is considering venturing even further into print territory with the introduction of a black women's magazine.

Why would a cable network invest time and effort in creating magazines? For the same reasons so many publishers are taking to the airwaves: "Providing a merchandising opportunity and added value to advertisers, public image-building, and profit," says Howard Friedberg, vice president and group publisher at Cahners Publishing.

In January 1992, Cahners' *Modern Bride* joined two other company publications—*American Baby* and *Healthy Kids*—on the Family Channel with "Getting Married," a one-hour special laced with six two-minute infomercials. Hosted by 1990 Miss America Debbie Turner and *Modern Bride*'s editor in chief Cele Lalli, the show focused on several brides as they prepared for their weddings. Shown four times in 1992, "Getting Married" generated much positive feedback among advertisers and viewers, says Friedberg. "We are committed to staying in cable TV," he says.

Publishers have increasingly been committing, in various degrees, to cable TV spin-offs:
• In September 1992, New York City-based Time Inc. began airing two- and three-minute consumer-service segments from *Money*, *Fortune* and *Entertainment Weekly* on Time Warner's four-month-old cable channel, New York 1 News.
• In a cross-media deal with ESPN's exercise program, "Bodyshaping," New York Times Magazine Co.'s

Fitness aired the first of 50 two-minute segments in December 1992.
• Emmaus, Pennsylvania-based Rodale Press' *Bicycling* coasted into cable in April 1992 with a monthly series of six half-hour segments covering bike races, personalities and other biking-related news.
• The cable medium is also serving Times Mirror well, according to in-house multimedia director George Bell. Beginning in March 1992, *Outdoor Life* and *Field & Stream* began a year-long cycle of four two-minute informational vignettes on ESPN. The company was so pleased with the results that it extended its agreement with the cable station for two more years.
• In addition, Times Mirror has developed cross-media deals with other networks for the majority of its titles, including *Popular Science* programming inside CNN's "Science and Technology Week."
• "A brilliant idea and an exciting concept," is how Asher Birnbaum, the editor and publisher of Chicago-based *North Shore*, describes cross-media packaging. Since the magazine launched a half-hour show in 1991 on seven regional cable stations, its paid subscribers have climbed 28 percent, to 48,000. Birnbaum attributes "at least part of that" to subscription pitches that are run during the program. "Cable does not diminish—it only enhances—a publication in every way," says Birnbaum.

Consider the dollar dynamics

Before undertaking a cable venture, the smart publisher must answer two questions: What is the audience I can deliver, and how can I enhance that delivery through cable TV?

"To go into this kind of a venture purely for leadership and image is a mistake," observes consultant Frank Cioffi, who heads The Media Link Group, a public relations and consulting firm in Marin County, California. "From what I have seen, a lot of magazines have gone into it purely for that reason—because it creates a lot of excitement. That's good if it's your third or fourth reason, but the dollar dynamics have to be there. The advertising base has to be there."

"A smart publisher looks to the market the magazine serves and asks how it can reach that market more efficiently on behalf of its advertisers," agrees Jay Campbell, president of Cable Ad Ventures, a Hillsdale, New Jersey-based multimedia programming company that produced "Getting Married," as well as the weekly "American Baby" and "Healthy Kids." "Cable represents an efficient way to reach out to a market."

Campbell advises would-be cross-media packagers to sit down and "decide what you want to accomplish" by getting involved in cable television. While most publishers list added value to advertisers among the top reasons they have crossed over, others cite circulation-building as a primary goal.

For Times Mirror's *Field & Stream*, for example, cable programming "is a legitimate circulation vehicle," says in-house multimedia director Bell. The magazine garnered a 15 percent higher response rate in subscriptions, he says, when it ran a 30-second circulation spot after an informational vignette, then when the circulation promotion ran alone.

Cahners' Friedberg, however, says that since *Modern Bride* is primarily a well-recognized newsstand publication, circulation as a top priority is "not desirable."

Once you've clarified your goals, says Campbell, be prepared to "put some muscle" behind your decision. "If you are serious, you have to be willing to open up your pocketbook—and your book—to promote your show."

Producers estimate that it costs $30,000 to $40,000 to produce an average half hour of TV. A one-hour special can cost $250,000 or more. Although the price tag can be high, it can amortize over the life of a show if the show can be syndicated, rerun or—as in the case of "Getting Married"—offset by the revenues from commercials.

Cable deals vary widely

Your options in structuring deals vary, from buying an entire show on which you sell all of the ad space, to splitting the sales of the ad space with the cable channel, to simply licensing your name and giving up any control over the ad sales or production. A licensing deal may be just right for a publisher who is interested exclusively in adding value to advertisers, says

consultant Campbell, but it's not the best choice for companies for whom profit tops the list.

Most magazines that have ventured onto the small screen have either hired a television consultant on retainer or an in-house media person. Someone with directing experience should be able to save you money in creating the show, but it is extremely important that the person you work with have TV production experience—which is invaluable in negotiating your contract with the network. "I would not have gotten into a television venture without someone who knows the ropes," says *North Shore*'s Birnbaum, who retains a producer's services. "Television is very different from print. Even figuring out the chain of command—who has ultimate authority—is a challenge."

To get the network interested in your programming, it's advisable to create a show demo to pitch the idea. The bottom-line cost of a 15- to 30-minute demo is $10,000, according to Times Mirror's Bell. "Be prepared to demonstrate to the network that you have something of real value," adds Birnbaum.

How to sell the package

If you want to exploit the synergies between magazines and cable, it helps to remember that advertisers employ ad agencies to help them decide how to get the most mileage from their media dollars. An ad execu-

> Before you undertake a cable venture, you must answer two questions: What is the audience I can deliver, and how can I enhance that delivery through cable TV?

tive is perfectly capable of buying print pages and cable spots without the help of a publisher. This means you have to think like an ad exec in creating your media package.

Richard Kostyra, executive vice president of media services at J. Walter Thompson in New York, demands media packaging that does more than his agency can do on its own. "We package [cable and magazines] ourselves right now," he points out. "If it happens that a magazine and a cable entity we want to use has a package that economically is better for us to buy that way than separately, we'll do it. The only interest we have in packaging is getting a better rate."

But there are exceptions to this rule, Kostyra notes.

"Time Inc. has developed a program that's terrific," he says. "They package an entire merchandising program. That's something we can't do on our own because we don't have access to all of their elements and the ability to tie them together. We can use their magazines and cable, but what we can't do is create a promotion using all of their vehicles."

A number of publishers are seeking to set themselves apart from the crowd by positioning themselves as the comprehensive source in their areas of expertise for all of an advertiser's needs. BET's Johnson says his goal is to be able to "go to an advertising agency and say, 'We are one-stop shopping to reach the black consumer.'"

Judith Princz, vice president and group publisher of Cahners' *American Baby* and *Healthy Kids*, says the company's approach is to "try to distinguish ourselves as *the* baby place, not just through cable and magazine, but through the use of sampling, custom publishing and couponing, too. By meeting all of an advertiser's marketing needs, we can position ourselves in a different league."

That's exactly the kind of comprehensive packaging Allen Banks looks for. The director of media planning at Saatchi & Saatchi in New York says he's willing to pay a premium for complete promotional packages that combine unique features of cable and magazines with some sort of contest, special issue or other targeted advertising exposure.

"The value of putting these things together is to have some sort of a hook," Banks says. "The hook might be that by buying the Lifetime cable channel, which is a health-oriented channel, with *Health*, we can develop some promotional ideas on both cable and magazines. It may be through couponing or whatever works in some way that gives greater value than the individual pieces can by themselves."

The pitfalls of going to video

Publishers are concerned—and rightly so—that the quality of the TV show that uses the name of their magazine not diminish the perception of the magazine's quality. Sometimes, however, they allow this concern to override sound creative judgment where the writing of the show is concerned. Yes, a high-quality magazine should spawn a TV show with high production standards, but that doesn't mean you can just lift your editorial lineup from an issue and present it to viewers with a bunch of talking heads. It's usually dull TV. "In the past, magazines missed the boat when they assumed that their titles had the same value in print and in television," says consultant Campbell.

Surfer Magazine, in San Juan Capistrano, California, ran up against this problem in developing the like-named show. Originally, the show had a "magazine" format. Each half-hour episode was divided into four or five segments on different topics: an athlete profile, an environmental piece on a surfing locale, a surfer movie review, a related sport segment, such as skateboarding, and a travel segment.

"We had to switch the format," says Surfer Publication Inc.'s in-house producer/director, Todd Lynch, who revamped the television shows for *Surfer Magazine* and *Powder* into a documentary style. "The original shows weren't interesting to the viewer. The advertisers and the surfers didn't like it."

"Surfer Magazine" now has five episodes, each of which focuses on a team of surfers taking a trip to a particular locale. The new format gives the show the continuity it had been lacking, while incorporating the environmental, travel and athletic profile elements that appear in the magazine.

At the same time, the revamping created a marketing opportunity, says Lynch. One of the major advertisers in the magazine sponsors the team that is featured in each show.

Common wisdom holds that sports and how-to magazines lend themselves to translation into television, since the active subject matter is usually enhanced by video presentation. How then to explain the success of the special "Getting Married" produced by *Modern Bride*, which is essentially a women's service magazine?

Once again, the concept for the program departed from the magazine's usual format: information for brides-to-be on where to find everything they need. While several infomercials were inserted for this purpose, also providing excellent opportunities for advertisers, the body of the show consisted of following real-life brides preparing for their weddings.

This format has the added benefit of allowing the show to be aired again with new infomercials, so it will appear completely fresh to new viewers, says Cahners' consultant Campbell.

Should your editors star?

Production quality is as much about the on-camera talent you use as is it about the writing and the number of cameras. Although putting your editors on camera is subtle promotion for the magazine, it can be a big risk if you are worried about the style of the show being slick enough to match the magazine's style.

"Getting Married" featured the magazine's editor, Cele Lalli, as one of the hosts. "I had no reservations about putting Cele on the show," says Campbell. "She is so passionate about the business, and she's been on camera. But the magazine shouldn't feel that it can make putting its editors on a condition of the show."

Obviously, using your editors on a show cuts costs, but they don't all have the polish or presence that makes for appealing TV. Some magazines hire a well-known personality or sports figure to offer cachet without the hefty price tag of a superstar. Cahners' "Healthy Kids," for example, is hosted by model Kim Alexis. Rodale's "Bicycling" uses professional athlete Greg Lewis as its broadcaster; cohost and *Bicycling* managing editor Tim Blumenthal provides the authority of the magazine. "Surfer Magazine" finds an effective combination in editors and surf celebrities,

> ## You can't just lift your editorial lineup and present it to viewers with a bunch of talking heads.

which pleases viewers and costs the magazine about $500 per show—down $2,000 since the show was reformatted and big-name hosts were cut.

Nor should editors necessarily have the last word in writing the show, says Rodale consultant Cioffi. "Writing for television is a completely different type of writing. Just because you can do one doesn't mean you can do the other."

"When I put my production hat on I play referee, making sure that we adhere to the editorial philosophy of the magazine while producing a show that is entertaining," says Campbell. "You shouldn't entrust an editor with the final say on the TV show. It's like putting an editor in charge of circulation."

Cahners' Friedberg concurs: "Make sure you are associated with professionals from conception to production. I am in total awe of the complexity of putting together a television show." ☐

Brands Across Borders

BY LAMBETH HOCHWALD

Expanding your franchise *overseas can be daunting. First, you must decide whether to syndicate your material, license it, create a joint venture or develop a wholly owned subsidiary. Then there's that little matter of establishing a global brand.*

Although targeting readers worldwide has always been an important potential source of revenue, industry analysts say that no more than 25 business-to-business publishers are currently tackling markets abroad (not counting multinationals), and only about 15 consumer-magazine companies have expanded overseas (again, not including multinationals). But the tide may be turning. Thanks to the reduction in trade barriers and breakthroughs in telecommunications, postal services and direct marketing, publishers may now find it easier to expand internationally. Following are examples of four publishers who have gone global, and the lessons they've learned.

Miller Freeman: Create a unified global brand

Miller Freeman, Inc., the 93-year-old trade publishing heavyweight, has long had an international presence as a wholly owned subsidiary of London-based United News & Media plc. (formerly United Newspapers) with such magazines as *Diagnostic Imaging Europe* and *Pulp & Paper International*, which was launched in 1959. Before this month, however, each business entity abroad had a different company header. To create a unified brand-consciousness, the San Francisco-based company extended the Miller Freeman name to all of its 220 business publications and 150 trade shows in 14 countries. Of those properties, 69 magazines and 73 trade shows are based in the United States.

The result: a global Miller Freeman magazine and exhibition division of United News & Media, with business-to-business titles and expos in the United Kingdom, United States and Asia. Because the divisions share a common name, advertisers and exhibitors doing business globally have a better understanding of the global nature of the Miller Freeman properties. This, in turn, makes it easier for them to use Miller Freeman to reach their markets—wherever they might be. The principal changes will be that Morgan-

Grampian plc., a long-time leader in business publishing and expos in Europe, will become Miller Freeman plc. United News & Media's Hong Kong International Trade Fair Division becomes Miller Freeman Asia Ltd., and Asian Business Press Pte. Ltd. in Singapore becomes Miller Freeman Pte. Ltd.

Miller Freeman, with total revenues in 1994 of $545 million in all three units, contributes almost one-third of United News & Media's worldwide revenue. (United News & Media last year reported an overall revenue of $1.5 billion. Asian trade shows and magazines account for £27 million, while U.K. and European properties account for £665 million.) The upshot of the corporate name change is that United News & Media, with 13,330 employees worldwide, has solidified its brand in response to increasing market globalization, says Marshall Freeman, president and CEO of Miller Freeman. The renaming comes along with a retooling as well. Miller Freeman has already set up market-focus coordinating groups in all the businesses where the company has global positions, including travel, jewelry and pulp and paper.

Managers of all global properties will now get together quarterly or more often to coordinate marketing efforts. "This way, when we present marketing vehicles to advertisers or exhibitors we will present the whole global package," Freeman says. "We're restructuring from a marketing perspective. We're not just marketing products in one geographic region, but telling customers how they fit into the worldwide market."

Don Pazour, senior vice president, says the international brand name is a way to establish dominance and keep the company running in an economical manner in all of its global markets. "We can present advertisers with a worldwide buy in areas that are international, like travel," he says. The company publishes several magazines for travel agents, including *Incentive Asia Planner* and *TTG (Travel Trade Gazette) Asia*, distributed both here and in Asia.

"We felt there was a marketing value first of all in having a common brand name," Freeman says. "Then we wanted to increase the coordination between the various divisions of United News & Media. Miller Freeman has sister operations in both Asia and Europe that do similar types of activities. It seemed unwise to not have those carry a common brand."

What's in a name? A lot, says Freeman. "There will be a massive extension of our name in Europe and the United Kingdom," he says. "It had been used in several parts of Asia, but there will be a substantial increase." This will be especially important when the company expands yet again, with Latin America and Mexico currently being considered as possible areas to enter within in the coming year.

Freeman says the move is in sync with international trends. "It's quite clear that as a general rule, industry in North America has got to become part of the global marketplace. As media providers, we are simply following that."

The *Elle Network:* Hachette Filipacchi's 'shining star'

With 25 editions published in 45 countries, the *Elle* franchise is Hachette Filipacchi Magazine's largest brand. In many ways, *Elle* was a trailblazer—one of the first Western publishers to enter the Asian market with a Japanese version licensed in 1969. In the two and a half decades since, the $2.2 billion company, a unit of

Paris-based Matra Hachette, has launched 10 more editions in Asia, Singapore, Argentina, Chile and Mexico. And, in April 1994, *Elle* launched a Czech edition. Earlier this year, *Elle* launched in China, and now the network reaches an estimated 14 million-plus readers, with over 16,100 ad pages annually.

Following a calculated international franchise expansion strategy, Hachette established a variety of agreements with international partners, including co-ventures with Telemedia in the Americas, Rizzoli in Europe and Bangkok Post in the Asia-Pacific region. In 1985, Hachette expanded its franchise into Spain and the United Kingdom. From 1987 to 1989, *Elle* moved further into Western Europe, Quebec and Brazil. From 1988 to 1993, Hachette targeted the Asia-Pacific market, and from 1993 to 1994, Eastern Europe and Latin America.

Five editions are wholly owned, including those in France, the United States, Japan, Hong Kong and Spain, says Paul DuCharme, Hachette's senior vice president of global advertising. The other 20 are co-ventures; editorial standards are set by Hachette, while selling, manufacturing and distribution are all handled locally.

From an advertising perspective, DuCharme adds, clients have to be sold on *Elle* as a global brand. "We're

---

■ Global guide

Here are 10 key factors in international expansion, according Herb Weikes, director of international sales at New York City-based Thomas IMG, a division of Thomas Publishing Co. Below, his comments:

Avoid product hybridization. "Never try to overlay so-called American expertise on foreigners. That will just blow up in your face. Many publishers think they can export an American magazine by changing words on the cover and adding foreign-language articles."

Beware of restricting overseas titles to English versions. "Readers think in their own language. Those readers aren't that interested in reading in English."

Keep up-to-date on changing tariffs. Customs charges shift constantly. "This is part of the learning curve."

Watch evolving local labor and tax laws. "A lot of American publishers don't know that you can't terminate people. There's a social safety net in a large partof the world."

Retool rate cards to reflect exchange rates. "When you're publishing abroad, make sure your rate cards reflect the different monetary systems."

Export publishing systems that have been tested here. "Map out a strategy before you find yourself with incompatible software or unusable technology."

Remember history. "When Europe was in shambles after World War II, Europeans looked to the U.S. to set the pace. Today, you can't create a magazine in Cleveland when it's being read in Dusseldorf."

Forge a mobile office. "Don't try to be the grand master and pull all the strings from the home office in New York."

Find out—early on—about censorship. "Some countries may have sanctions against articles and advertising relating to such topics as nudity, sex, feminine hygiene and abortion."

Respect local markets. "Look at the economics of the market you're going into. Don't just sit in a Hilton or Sheraton or walk the boulevards downtown. Tour the nation's plants and facilities. Find out whether people are buying cosmetics, and explore how those products are distributed. To set up a true franchise, do your research before you go in. You have to look at the whole region before you establish *Mademoiselle* in Vietnam."

into relationship marketing, global brand to global brand," he says, referring to global clients such as Nike, Lancaster and Elizabeth Arden. "Our clients want to know the advantage of advertising in *Elle,* so we have to establish some sort of brand benefit." That can't happen if local cultural factors run counter to the products' premise. DuCharme says that overcoming each country's quirks has become easier because the *Elle* editions are handled locally. And that's apparently a winning strategy: DuCharme says aggressive global marketing has produced a 500 percent increase in international ad revenue since 1993.

Keeping tabs is a challenge. "Now that the world is getting global in terms of branding, we can't offer a weak product," DuCharme says. "It's up to us to do the policing."

Finance & Development: Banking on a global presence

It would stand to reason that *Finance & Development*— a joint venture of the International Monetary Fund (IMF) and World Bank, specialized agencies of the United Nations—would be an international franchise from its inception. But when it made its debut in 1964, readers found only English, French and Spanish versions. Gradually, the magazine added German, Arabic and Portuguese editions in the 1970s, and a Chinese edition in the 1980s. Now, the push is to expand into the former Soviet Union by the first half of 1996, with a 15,000 circulation edition that will cost an estimated $80,000 to produce each year. Currently, the largest-circulation edition is the English version (50,000 readers) and the smallest is the Arabic edition (6,000).

"We need to provide information on what a market economy is and how to privatize," says Claire Liuksila, editor in chief. "There's such a dearth of information out there."

The cost of creating an international edition varies, depending on the available distribution channel and printer partner in each country. And the process can take anywhere from 18 months to two years, according to Liuksila. The Portuguese and German editions are the most pricey, while the Chinese edition is the least expensive to translate and produce. "We are constrained," she says. "Because we are an international organization, we try to print in the country where the language originates."

As a primarily members-only publication, the magazine's goal is "to reach as many people in our member countries as possible," Liuksila adds. "When the magazine started, there were 100 countries that were members of the IMF and World Bank. With the opening of former Communist countries, there are now 179 member countries. That's why we are publishing in seven languages."

The Washington, D.C.-based free quarterly now reaches 120,000 high-level government officials, academics, students, libraries and think-tanks, with the same content in all editions. Although the publication is distributed free by surface mail, with readers requalifying by mail every three years, those wishing to receive it by air mail are charged $20 a year. Liuksila would like the magazines to convert to paid circulation eventually. "We might end up with a sliding scale for subscribers. Readers from developing countries might pay less than those from industrial countries," she says.

And, with the World Bank and IMF facing tighter budgets, a new phase is being heralded for the magazine: adding paid advertising to the currently largely ad-free magazine, which to date has limited itself to house ads. *Finance & Development* is now targeting commercial banks and companies like AT&T that may want to bring in telephone systems or otherwise develop the infrastructure in developing countries, says Sylvia Chatfield, an ad sales consultant who specializes in international advertising. "We will crack something by September," she says. "It's an unusual sell. It's one of the few places where you can bring together public and private sectors. If you're building a toll road in Mexico, you need both private and public approval for the contracts."

"Advertising is an opportunity nobody had thought about," Liuksila admits. "We probably have one of the best mailing lists around. We have a list of every mover and shaker in the government and finance worlds that would appeal to major construction companies and financial institutions."

In spite of the magazine's support from its parent organizations, its executives believe the time is ripe to consider further developing the franchise's strength, even given its already established presence throughout the world. Future projects may include publishing via the Internet and spinning off articles into a book or a CD-ROM. "We're very strongly supported, and yet we don't have a commercial purpose," says Liuksila. "Still, that doesn't mean we don't think in commercial terms." □

So You Want to Sell Your Magazine?

BY BRUCE SHEIMAN

At some time or another, most owners grapple with the idea of selling their publishing company, or selling one or more titles. There are many reasons for contemplating a sale: retirement, death of a partner, a desire to cash out, estate planning, a change in personal or professional direction, and so on. And, indeed, now is a judicious time to consider a sale. There are more buyers in the marketplace today than at any time since the late 1980s. Most major publishing groups have spent the past few years digesting their previous acquisitions and fortifying themselves for future recessionary downturns, and are now on the prowl for strategic acquisitions—one of which could be your company.

What should you think about if you are considering a sale of your magazine publishing company? How should you prepare for a sale if you have decided that your company will be sold? Here are seven key considerations.

Valuation: There's an old saying that every company is for sale—at the right price. So valuation is a critical consideration. Although overall magazine valuations are not as high today as they were five or 10 years ago, it is still possible for a company to command a premium price. In general, valuations are expressed as a multiple of either revenue or profits, or both. Several factors determine the price that you could receive, only some of which are within your ability to influence in the short term. The more of the following that apply to your magazine, the higher will be its value:

- It serves a growing niche or market.
- The magazine has been benefiting from a growing marketshare.
- The magazine is primarily a paid-circulation publication from direct-to-publisher subscription sources.
- There is significant database marketing potential and/or the potential for ancillary product sales.
- The publication occupies a prestigious editorial position within its market.
- It is very profitable.
- The magazine has a strong management team in place.

Buyer expectations: Buyers naturally have high expectations. They want the best of both worlds—positive cash flow and growth potential; profits and long-term promise. The extent to which these considerations are absent will, naturally, affect your company's sale price. And there are obvious incompatibilities here. A company that has invested in a new property may have considerable growth prospects, but little or no profits to show for the investment. Another property may be very profitable, but mature with little room for additional growth. Properties in either phase are indeed salable, but at a relatively low multiple of revenues.

Regarding profitability, it is important to remember that private companies are structured with the major purpose of reducing income tax. Consequently, many private companies' bottom lines are low compared to those of public companies. For example, in private publishing firms, owner salaries are frequently inflated. There is nothing wrong with this. (After all, it's your company.) But in your effort to reduce Uncle Sam's take, you make your bottom line appear weak. For a sale of your company, it will be necessary to restate your bottom line to maximize profits.

Another consideration that is of crucial importance

> If you can, wait for an upcycle. The best time to sell is when you don't have to. You'll be able to command greater respect and a higher price.

to buyers is strategic fit and operational synergies. Today, few publishers will acquire a publication or group of magazines that does not in some way complement its current portfolio—no matter how much profit and/or promise it exhibits.

Management considerations: Management is a complicated issue that can significantly affect your company's salability. One common problem occurs when the "genius" of the company resides in one person. This problem is compounded if that person is the current owner—who, presumably, will not be staying very long with the company after it is sold—and there is no strong number-two manager who can take over.

A prospective buyer has to ask, "Without the owner, what are we buying over the long term?" If this scenario applies to your company, it is important to put in place strong editorial and marketing talent that contributes to the magazines' success in a meaningful way. In addition to a reader and advertiser franchise, a buyer wants to acquire managerial, creative and intellectual talent.

Timing: It pays to know when to sell. Most owners do not put enough planning into the process, and wait too long before they sell. Frequently, an owner considers selling when the magazines are facing growing competition and/or downward trends. It is incumbent upon the owner to be prescient. You should know your business well enough to see trouble long before anyone else. If the magazines and/or market trends are heading down, you will not be able to command a premium price.

The effect of timing is dramatically illustrated by the sale of *Ladies' Home Journal* by Charter Publishing in 1982. All women's service magazines are hit hard by a recession. (In fact, they could almost be considered leading indicators.) Charter, which is an oil company that wanted to get out of magazine publishing, sold at the end of a recession. Robert Riordan purchased the magazine for $12 million. Three years later, he sold it to Meredith Corp. for a reported $95 million. Much of the difference in value was due to timing. *Ladies' Home Journal*'s fortunes rose in the middle of the 1980s with the resurging economy.

If you can, wait for an upcycle. The best time to sell is when you don't have to. You will be able to command greater respect in the marketplace and a higher price, all other things being equal.

Role of the owner after the sale: Buyers come in two forms: those with a significant infrastructure already in place, and those without. Each scenario has profoundly different implications for your company. If you sell to a company that has little of its own management infrastructure, you (the owner) will need to stay on for at least a year, followed by a consulting contract that could last five years. Also, you can expect that your organization's status quo will usually be respected. In other words, you cannot just exit the business—which is fine in a majority of cases, since owners are often reluctant to give up control.

If, on the other hand, your acquirer has a significant infrastructure already in place, you may not be needed. Indeed, the new owner may very well not want you. And you can expect some consolidation; your organization could be reduced in the circulation, production and administration areas.

Selling to the competition: This is one of the most difficult possibilities you will have to face. The irony is that the most logical buyers are also the companies that an owner would least want to sell to. Also, the typical owner does not want the fact that the company is for sale to leak out—which it invariably does when competitors learn about it.

And selling to a competitor may not be good for your employees. When very similar operations are merged, there are many opportunities for consolidation of various functions. And I've seen new owners act vindictively toward employees. In one example, an employee who had switched from one company to another was abruptly dismissed when the former company acquired the latter. For these reasons, competitors are usually considered last as prospective buyers.

Transaction options: Besides seeking the highest price for your company, you should give thought to how the purchase price is to be paid. "Cash at closing" is the most highly desired. Other possible forms of compensation, determined by tax and risk considerations, are deferred payment, notes, non-compete agreements and consulting arrangements.

Another transaction consideration is whether you want to sell all or just part of your company. More buyers nowadays will consider a partial purchase, but always with the understanding that they can purchase the remainder at a mutually agreed-upon schedule, usually within three to five years.

A graduated sale is good for an owner skittish about giving up control immediately. It is also good for one who feels the company will be worth more in the future. If part of the company is sold now, the remainder can be sold at a multiple of future, presumably higher, earnings. Then it is up to the owner to deliver on those promised higher earnings. ☐

Mergers and
acquisitions

Reduce Risk with an Acquisition Screen

BY BARRIE J. ATKIN

Now that the economy appears to be improving, you may be thinking about acquisitions as a way to grow your company. Acquiring a new magazine—or a new business—can be risky. But there are ways to decrease that risk—especially if you are clear about what type of magazine you want to acquire, and why.

One way to foster such clarity is to create a set of guidelines—an acquisition screen—to help you evaluate whether a prospective magazine will be a good fit with your company. Such a screen can be a powerful tool. It will help you identify good candidates and eliminate inappropriate ones; provide a basis for comparison among the various targets; and identify key strengths and weaknesses of a potential acquisition. Here are some factors you might want to include in developing your acquisition screen:

Strategic fit: The strategic reason for this acquisition should be clear. For example, does it fit with your long-term goals and mission? Does this new business complement your existing businesses? Lack of strategic fit means that an acquisition will require more effort to evaluate and manage. This, in turn, creates inefficiencies and could divert resources away from more strategically important opportunities outside or within your company.

Knowledge of the field of coverage: Does this magazine or company cover an area you know well? If not, detailed research, due diligence and planning are advised to ensure that you know the trends and success factors involved. Companies often overpay for what they don't understand. The better you know the market, the easier it will be to establish reasonable prices and expectations.

It's especially important to learn where the magazine or company is in its growth cycle. Fast-growth magazines attract attention, but fast growth doesn't last forever. Is the magazine (or its industry) nearing its peak or about to consolidate? If so, you may be purchasing a "maturing" magazine—when your projections (and what you paid) were based on much greater future growth.

Corporate structure: This is especially important when you are merging the staff of an acquired company into your existing business. Do their values and work styles match yours? Or, at the very least, is there some overlap? Watch out for companies with very different approaches to compensation, corporate structure, and philosophy of risk-taking and decision-making. How do the salaries, benefits and working conditions that they are used to compare with those at your company? Is the environment significantly more laid back? more collegial? more aggressive?

If their culture is very different from yours, but the acquisition works in all other ways, it may be advantageous to keep it as a separate entity—perhaps even in a different city. This will minimize conflicts between opposing cultures.

Positioning and leadership: Will this title have at least the same level of market leadership as your current titles? If not, the revenue-to-expense ratios that you're used to may not apply. Is that level of leadership sufficient for its future success in its market? Declining markets may have room for only one or two books. An industry that could support three books in its boom years may have room for only one or two in its senescence.

Size: How large—and how small—an acquisition can you comfortably manage? With a first acquisition, or an entry into an entirely new field, it is often better to start small and learn from the experience. Remember, however, that a small acquisition takes almost as much analysis, due diligence and managerial oversight as a large one. Some businesses may be too small in terms of cash flow or net income to justify their purchase—especially if they come with large overhead costs.

> This process can help you identify acquisition candidates worthy of more evaluation and eliminate those that don't match.

Financial expectations: Can the new magazine or company be expected to meet the financial criteria and performance of your existing business? If the opportunity does not look as good as your current business, are there some other key strategic reasons, such as building marketshare, that make the acquisition worthwhile? How does this opportunity compare with your existing business in terms of cash flow, return on investment and prospects for future growth? How does investing in this magazine or business compare with other opportunities for investment?

One warning: Be sure you are comparing apples with apples. Do both companies (your existing business and the acquisition target) account the same way for subscription liability? for overhead costs? If not, have you adjusted their financials to match your methodology?

Editorial fit: Is there synergy between the editorial focus of the core business and the acquisition candidate? If so, you may be able to utilize some of your existing staff and other editorial resources. Is the editorial style (including design and costs) in keeping with the way you do business—or the way you want to do business?

Advertising fit: Does the new title complement your existing titles? Can you offer existing customers a logical combined buy? Can you build on the existing relationships of your salespeople? Will the acquisition give your salespeople entry into important new markets?

If the new business is too close to your existing business, the acquisition may cannibalize your core business. If the acquisition is far removed from your current business, be sure to invest sufficient resources to learn that business.

Circulation fit: What are the opportunities for cross-marketing? Will you be able to market this new business to your house lists? Will the new subscribers be interested in your existing products? Circulation fit can be too close as well, and can contribute to the cannibalization of your existing business.

Staffing: Will you gain from staff that complements your existing staff? Do you need additional staff/expertise to run the business? If so, do you have enough people—and if not, what are your options and the time frames for staffing up?

Give your screen a test run

These guidelines are suggestions. You'll want to develop your own list, and then weight the components according to their relative value to you. Then test your screen. Here's how:

Put your existing magazines through the screening process. Would they come out near the top? If they should, and don't (or vice versa), perhaps there are criteria that you need to change or add. Next, try this exercise with some acquisition prospects that you've considered in the past. Based on your knowledge of these magazines, where should they rate? If application of the screen doesn't give the answer you expect, are there ways to improve it?

This process of refinement is important: It helps achieve clarity of goals as well a validity of the criteria. Ultimately, this process can help you create a tool that can be used to identify acquisition candidates worthy of further evaluation, and help you eliminate ones that don't match the profile. ☐

The Buying and Selling of Small Magazines

By DAVID Z. ORLOW

The magazine-acquisition marketplace has roared back from the doldrums of the early nineties. Although several big-ticket transactions have made it into the news, many, many successful magazine transactions take place outside the limelight. In fact, as many as 200 magazine transactions take place each year that go unreported either because they are not perceived as newsworthy or because the participants desired confidentiality.

In the last few years, for instance, the following magazines were among those that changed hands: *Advances in Wound Care, Air Pollution Consultant, The Milepost, Bicycle Dealer Showcase, Blade Magazine, Casual Living, Learning, Signature, Nurse Practitioner, Pediatric Neurology, Plastics World, Popular Woodworking, Printing News East, Running Times, Solid Waste Technologies, Veterinary Product News* and *What's New in Family Fun Centers.* You get the point.

For smaller operations, buying and selling publications is like journeying to the Greek islands or traveling aboard the Orient Express—something one does too infrequently to become well versed in the terrain and local culture. So smaller magazines usually rely on outside help in completing a transaction.

My work in small-title transactions began more than 30 years ago with sales of my own small publications. For this article, I interviewed three other small-title transaction advisers, incorporating their observations along with mine. The other contributors are Peter Craig, Thomas Pecht and Katharin Norwood, all industry veterans.

We've divided the magazine-transaction process into four steps, outlined in this article, and for each, we offer both general principles and anecdotal material to illustrate our points.

The decision to buy or sell

It all begins with the goals of buyer and seller. And those goals, which will be different, are established by a magazine's strategic and tactical value. Strategic reasons for a transaction might include a desire to enter or exit a category, to buy market leaders, to acquire a fully oper-ational company or a single title, to enter or exit periodical publishing, or to add a new type of publication.

Katharin Norwood notes that when Seattle-based Vernon Publications, which publishes several regional construction magazines and directories, decided in 1993 to sell *Nurse Practitioner* to New York City-based Elsevier Science Inc., Vernon executives were keenly aware that *Nurse Practitioner*'s market was projected to experience continuing strong growth. The documentation they provided to the buyer made that fact crystal clear. But Vernon's larger strategy was to raise capital to complete financing of the acquisition of *The Milepost*, a drive directory for the Alcan Highway that produced a larger dollar volume and was in a market closer to Vernon's other holdings. In other words, Vernon's strategic intent was to form a more cohesive company through this buy-sell scenario.

Sometimes buyers base their decisions on perceived value, which can be abstract and difficult to quantify, rather than actual current performance. When William Ziff purchased *Travel Weekly* in 1967, he had already

> "It's not just the selling price that is important, it's what you end up with after taxes and other obligations are paid."

made the strategic decision to enter travel publishing, and to do it from the trade side rather than from the consumer side. The travel professional was seen as the funnel for booking of American tourism, which fueled the international travel boom of the seventies and eighties. Ziff's subsequent purchase (in 1968) of the *Hotel & Travel Index* directory for $1 million (20 times pretax profit) was an easy extension of the same strategy. The directory was doing about $1 million then. True to Ziff's vision of the market, the property these days grosses closer to $100 million than $1 million.

S.I. Newhouse's 1994 acquisition of a reported 15 to

25 percent stake in *Wired* for a rumored $3 million to $5 million was based on a similar motivation.

A slightly different take on perceived value involves a strategic plan for how a magazine might fit into an acquiring company's existing mix and culture. Transactions driven by this strategy include Ziff-Davis Publishing Co.'s acquisition of *Computer Shopper* from Titusville, Florida-based Patch Communications in the mid-eighties, and the Disney purchase of *FamilyFun* from Jake Winebaum in 1992.

Computer Shopper was a core piece of a major growth segment of consumer-computer publishing, and one of the only major positions that Ziff wasn't in. He pursued the title for several years, and his philosophy was not to worry about paying too high a multiple. When you foresee enormous growth for a title, or enormous synergy, "times earnings" becomes a lot less important in driving the sales price.

In the case of *FamilyFun*, Disney saw a magazine that not only fit its values perfectly but could be cross-marketed aggressively, even though it was a new magazine in a new, unproven category. The bet has paid off. Since the title's launch, ad pages and circulation have soared and the magazine has become a category leader.

Tactical considerations play a role, too

Tactical reasons for a transaction are much less often a driving force. And although the reasons may be unimportant to one participant, they may be quite significant to the other. Included among tactical motivations would be such things as the removal of a competitive title, the rounding out of a product line or the reallocation of overhead.

The reallocation of overhead often generates real value in a small transaction. Boston-based Fitness Publishing, which acquired *Running Times* in 1994 from Wilton, Connecticut-based Air Age Publishing, is an example. Its existing operation (publishing *Horticulture* under a separate corporation) had just enough underutilized management talent and work space to absorb *Running Times* with minimal incremental overhead. It wasn't a deal maker, but it saved $50,000 per year and helped to justify the transaction.

Establishing value

A magazine with a history of positive cashflow will make a transaction much easier because the buyer and seller can focus on the same basic data—which makes negotiations much simpler. Here, agreeing on an earnings multiple for the purposes of valuation is easiest.

Conversely, where the cashflow is erratic, nonexistent or negative, multiples cannot readily be applied, and other evaluation bases must be found—for example, the relative cost of an acquisition versus a start-up, or the minimum value of the assets plus the title's market momentum. When *Games* was sold by the former PSC Publications in 1990, it had already been demonstrated that the magazine was not profitable, although it had promise. The transaction price was based more on the magazine's perceived momentum, the value of its lists and the costs to duplicate its assets if one were going to start rather than buy. The buyer, Alan Segal of Boston-based Games Publishing Group, must surely have based his purchase price on assumptions about the value of the assets. In these cases, price, calculated as a percent of sales volume, tends to be much lower.

Taxing issues

Never negotiate price without understanding net after-tax yields and goals. Prior to entering a marketplace, small publishers should have a clear sense of the tax implications for such issues as stock versus asset sales, deferred-subscription-income liabilities, and other legal and accounting realities that may incur tax liabilities.

"The primary objective for the seller is to determine the take-home," says the Magazine Consulting Group's Peter Craig. "It's not just the selling price that is important, it's what you end up with after taxes and other obligations are paid." Craig says that under today's tax regulations, the amount the seller ultimately gets could vary by up to 30 percent, depending on whether the transaction is a stock sale, triggering one capital gains tax, or an asset sale, in which both company and individual income taxes must be paid by the seller.

The effect on the buyer, Craig says, could be even more dramatic: Some buyers may be able to write off most of the purchase price, while others may get no tax break at all. If you buy assets, you can amortize almost all of the purchase price over 15 years. If you buy stock, you get no tax benefits until you either sell it or, in a worst-case scenario, abandon it.

Finally, be aware that profitability and cash flow are calculated by an accounting system designed for uses other than the publication marketplace. The chances are good that the seller will therefore wish to make some adjustments based on the particulars of the business and the industry—such as the expensing of a start-up.

Sometimes such assertions are open and on the table. Sometimes the seller tries to wedge them in under the table, buried in the vagaries of corporate cost-accounting. For instance, let's say I start a second publication—a newsletter—and I lose $100,000 on it in the first year. The chances are that I'm going to expense that and take it as an offset against the profits of my main publication. But if in the second year I want to sell you my main publication, I'm going to insist that we make an adjustment on my last year's P&L, subtracting the start-up expense from the profitability—in effect, increasing the profitability—on the grounds that it is not an inherited cost of doing business for the main publication.

Should you sell at auction?

Another facet of a transaction involves the perceptions of fair market value and the minimum and maximum purchase prices of a publication. What is this publication really worth in the marketplace? How much of a range might one expect from the smallest to the largest bid? On the one hand, if the asking price is unrealistically high, it might scare off buyers. On the other hand, why leave money on the table?

In some deals, the seller will go to only one or two selected, logical buyers, while others are conducted through a bidding process. In some bidding processes, the minimum price is fixed, and in some it is open-ended. The question for each seller is this: Which way should I go? The answer will be based on some or all of the following: Are there large, identifiable bidders ready? Is a public process the only way to identify potential buyers? Is the seller better served by a premium-paying pre-emptive buyer? Do other related considerations absolutely require a rapid or silent transaction?

Projecting performance

As an owner begins to entertain the idea of a sale, there is ample opportunity for the inexperienced to overestimate the value of a publication. What's important here is to understand what's really for sale: people skills, momentum, market position, market growth, stability and other assets. Based on that type of understanding, value ranges and prices can be assigned realistically. Remember, it's not the buyer's concern that it took the seller 20 years of sweat equity to build the publication. Although such an effort is quite worthy of respect, sweat has no commercial value, and pricing a property beyond an objective, fair price range is unwise.

Craig advises that nothing substitutes for good, solid operations reviews. "You must find out what drives the numbers, not just the bottom line," Craig says. "As the buyer, it is important to determine your own bottom line from the acquisition, not just what the seller was earning. And you have to avoid surprises—the kind you get when you don't do your homework." For example, in circulation, a magazine's subscription revenue might check out very nicely, but that does not tell you whether there have been significant recent changes in source mix, pricing, term or promotional efforts in subscription marketing.

Conversely, there are times when the seller undervalues the potential of a publication. After all, they grew it as best they could and have now decided to sell, perhaps because they judge the profitability to be insufficient. What can it be worth? In the early nineties, buyers with differing visions of what to do next often came into these types of situations and acquired a title for as little as 25 percent of the sales volume, when it would typically sell for 50 to 90 percent of sales volume, assuming that it had good market potential but no significant current profitability.

If you're not profitable, chances are you'll command less than gross revenue. But 25 percent is down around a distress price level, or salvage, whatever you want to call it. And there are even some publishers whose basic acquisition strategy is to target such salvage situations.

Completing the deal

The most successful transactions are firmly based on win-win principles—which means that both buyer and seller achieve their goals. The recent purchase of *Bicycle Retailer* by San Francisco-based Miller Freeman is but one of many such instances. On the one hand, Miller Freeman was building a more integrated product line, and on the other hand, Santa Fe, New Mexico-based owner Bill Tanler and his associates wanted a capital gain while continuing to work on the magazine. Knowing the goals of the other party, whether there can be cash optimization, tax savings, product-line formation, face saving, trading up, trading out, or whatever, is usually critical to achieving a successful transaction.

Complex web of skills

Sellers should understand that for every transaction that takes place effortlessly, there are 50 that require a complex web of communications skills. To optimize a transaction, communications must be managed clearly, with buyer and seller each understanding the other's goals and obstacles. And buyers should know that a small publication serves a specific special-interest market. That market and its potential must be understood every bit as well as the publications in it. □

Welcome to the New World Of Multimedia

BY REED PHILLIPS III

Ever since Tom Wolfe redefined the term "Master of the Universe," we've had a new image to aspire to. Whether you were an investment banker on Wall Street or a small-town attorney, you could keep score by counting the perks of power you accumulated. Now that we've entered the multimedia age, however, the scoring system has changed—and almost overnight, a new system has taken its place.

Reading John Naisbitt's latest book, *Global Paradox*, helped me visualize this new world order. Naisbitt updated his prophecies from his earlier tome, *Megatrends*, for 1995 and beyond, succinctly subtitling *Global Paradox*, "The bigger the world economy, the more powerful its smallest players." Racing from one paradox to the next in Naisbitt's book, I was struck by how relevant his theme was to my own business experience.

For the past 15 years I have maneuvered within the media industry, holding various posts culminating in my present position as managing partner of my own investment banking firm, which specializes in media. My faith in my media knowledge has remained intact, until recently, when I have viewed my industry's metamorphosis into a multimedia amoeba. During this transition, I've observed a number of paradoxes about this new world order and, like Mr. Naisbitt, I've had the time to compile a list.

On the information superhighway, the typing I learned in high school is my most important skill. Just think about this for a moment and you'll realize the advantage anyone who can type adeptly will have in navigating the information superhighway. The paradox, of course, is that all those time-consuming, higher-education courses we took in college—like applied mathematics or computer science—may have taught us how to think, but did little to prepare us for communicating in the multimedia age. Fast typing is what counts because it means automatic efficiency. Who would have thought that the typing class I grudgingly took in high school would turn out to be so important in the new world order?

To some readers, this may seem ludicrous. At first blush, I thought so too—until I did a reality check: During a recent lunch with the president of a magazine publishing company, I asked my colleague to name the education course that had helped him most in his successful career. He thought for a minute, then, laughing to himself, answered: "Believe it or not, typing!"

Becoming more proficient in the age of new media means doing more on your own. For anyone who has ever complained about having to rely on others, your time has come. Cellular phones already force us to make our own calls and do our own dialing—and you can't very well have a secretary announce you when calling from your car. Other innovations increasing our independence from people—but increasing our dependence on technology—include personal computers, which make us do our own typing, and something called the Voice Organizer, a voice-activated, hand-held recording device that busy executives can use to keep their own calendars. At a recent media conference I attended, Barry Diller spoke about the coming multimedia revolution and chastised his audience of senior media executives for their lack of hands-on involvement. His message: Only by logging on to the Internet yourself will the secrets of this new medium be revealed.

Who needs a key to the executive washroom when the bathroom at home is just down the hall? Tomorrow's executives will gladly give up corporate perks for the convenience of home. Fax machines and modems have already made it easy to go to work without leaving home.

In the future, the UPS delivery man will know more about us than the IRS. So much for George Orwell's threat of Big Brother government. If Orwell were alive today, he would be warning us about marketers. They insidiously collect information about us in their computer databases to help them more precisely target their promotion efforts. And now with TV bringing retail shopping into our living rooms, we can just pick up the phone and order what we want. The next thing you know, the UPS man is knocking at the door with our latest purchase: He is our new conduit to the outside world.

We live in an age of increasing paradox. As the convergence of the media accelerates, individuals will become increasingly self-empowered. With each of us orbiting our own planets, the 1980s term "Master of the Universe" is in the 1990s likely to be replaced with "Master of Our Own Universe."

 New media

10 Reasons Why Magazines Are Leading the Race into Cyberspace

BY JIM GUTHRIE

Editor's note: *The position and strengths pf magazines on the information superhighway is discussed in the following remarks from a speech delivered by magazine executive Jim Guthrie at L.A. Magazine Day, November 16, 1994.*

It has often been pointed out that without advertising, the only publishers who make money on new media may be the ones who conduct conferences on the subject.

Yet, in what might be called the pre-dawn of digital advertising, hundreds of basically edit-driven magazines are leading the way in the cyberspace race. There are many good reasons why this is so. Here are my top 10:

1. Magazines are natural content providers.

"If you look at the future, you have to look at the historical patterns first to find the constants," says Roger Selbert, a futurist who edits and publishes "FutureScan," a newsletter that analyzes marketplace trends. "The constants are the only things you can be sure about in the future. And the magazine format is one of those constants. The electronic word is not going to replace the printed word. It will add to it, it will be another option, it may even displace some percentage of the market, but it's not going to replace [it]." For those who want reinforcement of Selbert's contention, consider that radio did not replace the newspaper and TV did not replace radio. But don't miss the point, either: Magazines are natural media content providers for online and CD-ROM products.

2. Magazines are digitally comfortable.

The editing and pre-production processes had been managed in digital form in magazines for several years prior to these new-media extensions.

3. Magazines can provide rich information archives.

And they are ideal for the initial text-driven digital

capabilities. Bill Ziff noted that people can absorb more complex information easily from a printed page than from any other medium. A single page of print contains more information than a typical nightly news program.

4. Magazines are a one-to-one medium.

As is the PC. But it's the content that counts, not the conduit. Television, by comparison, tends to be a shared experience.

5. Magazines create deep personal relationships.

Readers' personal involvement with magazine editorial and advertising has been confirmed in 12 years of research studies. Consumers rank magazines highest of all consumer media on providing a trusted authority, credibility and information, the qualities one seeks for an online relationship. Paul Saffo, executive director of the Institute for the Future, acknowledged the

> The reader/editor bond is inherently interactive. Futurists are trying to emulate the "congeniality" of magazines in the computer environment.

importance of magazines' authority with readers when he said, "It's the context, stupid."

6. Magazines are an interactive intellectual process.

They allow the reader to control a random-access experience.

7. Magazines are an interactive communication process.

The reader/editor bond is inherently interactive and becomes even stronger online. It is for this reason, notes Eric Hippeau, chairman of Ziff-Davis, that the Massachusetts Institute of Technology futurists are trying to emulate the "congeniality" of magazines in the computer environment.

8. Magazines' editorial core is ripe for enhancement.

Reader involvement creates the opportunity for hypertext, graphic and multimedia searches that enhance the value of the online magazine. As *Newsweek*'s Smith said, "no one wants to just read a magazine online"—it must be enhanced.

9. Magazines stimulate readers to share common interests.

This "virtual community" around shared values can stimulate a dialogue among readers that may or may not also involve editors.

10. Magazines are highly database-driven.

Their database targeting and tracking attributes make them a natural foundation to minimize the risk to advertisers considering interactive media.

According to the MIT futurists, it will be 20 years before interactive TV becomes computers that will respond to us. Others suggest that more rudimentary interactive TV will evolve within the next five years. According to Jim Clark, founder of Silicon Graphics, there will be more people online at the end of next year—whether through the Internet or commercial services like America Online, Prodigy, CompuServe, the new Microsoft Network or others—than there are households subscribing to cable TV. Ultimately, I believe, the debate over the medium will be academic.

Finally, a few educated guesses about selling in cyberspace.

Although in some cases it may be the result of a shared experience, the act of a commercial transaction is essentially an individual activity. Thus, it seems most natural that cyberspace sales should occur within the context of a personal dialogue, such as the one that is established by a magazine's content. The roles of the conduit(s) will vary according to their media strategy.

Just imagine: Television might be used to show big pictures that convey an image, and magazines will be used to close the sale.

Makes you think. ☐

Hiking Toward the Highway

BY CELINE SULLIVAN

Roaming about in search of the access ramp to the information superhighway, I'm overwhelmed by a certain *tristesse*. The signs posted by the builders warn that shortly we'll be seeing very little ink on paper as we opt instead for electronic alternatives.

Life without magazines is more than my techno-challenged mind can imagine. What of the redemption of the worst hair day by the arrival of the best magazine you've ever known? What of those moments when a really solid idea fairly leaps into your job performance from a brilliantly written article? What of the ease with which you can have a relationship with a magazine, and the rush that comes with that familiar look and editorial voice?

The highway developers suggest that, shortly, the magazine industry can concentrate its efforts exclusively on the gathering and digitizing of information. Our digits will then be dispatched to various stations along the highway, where users will interact with them in a rather deliberate, query-based manner that will have little or nothing to do with logos, cover blurbs, display racks or stamp-sheets.

The user may alter our digitized information product to his or her liking or purpose. The user may even embed it, in whole or in part, with or without attribution, in some new package—which in turn will be switched into the network. Some distribution agent will charge the user fees for access to the highway and for "hits" on our (formerly) magazine material. Via some contractual agreement, we'll be remitted a relatively small percentage of those revenues.

It's not likely that we'll know the names, addresses or Internet numbers of the users of our products, because that's being touted as an invasion-of-privacy issue. But it's quite likely that mastheads and bylines will be jettisoned as information moves around in cyberspace, presenting major intellectual property rights issues.

Not a happy scenario for those of us who like turn-ing pages—who'd rather have someone else package and present our media to us, who enjoy having questions answered that we never thought to ask, who actually use "intrusive" advertising in deciding what to buy and where.

Thankfully, we have a minute or two to figure out how we'll cope. There's comfort in the fact that you are *reading this book*. Magazines and newspapers have survived radio and television. Stone tablets, for that matter, remain our medium of choice for marking life's last major experience. But it's hard to argue the coffee-cup adage that "The future isn't what it used to be." The electronic future is being shaped by giants in giant steps, at least as measured in the general business press.

Maybe you work for one of the giants and are rocketing into cyberspace. But the law of averages and the *Folio:* subscription file suggest there's a good chance you're working for a small- or medium-size organization. So, for the more earthbound, here are some small steps we can all be taking toward destiny control in the electronic future:

Accept reality. The digital revolution is real. And we're all revolutionaries to some degree. Most of us word process our own stuff today, use modems and fax machines, send and receive e-mail and voicemail—and. more and more people have car phones. Desktop publishing is ubiquitous—our magazines are electronic at the core. Plenty of us subscribe to online services and/or have agreements with them to distribute our information products. So use as many of these new technologies as you can, even if it means doing it yourself with your own nickel. Happily, it's taking fewer and fewer nickels as the rewards multiply.

Be a sample of one as you adopt and use these tools. Monitor the ways the new technologies alter your workplace values, especially regarding information management: how much, how fast, how thoughtful,

> Media usage, including the emerging computer-based media, should be a routine inquiry in your reader research.

how excellent, how embellished, how personalized. Use those insights to engineer changes to your magazine that will enhance its value as nontraditional media come into play.

Read. (Now there's an idea!) Read the business press, science reportage, the interviews with the movers and shakers, their prognostications. If the jargon gives you hives, go to your local library (or get online) and master the *World Book* or junior-high science approach to the subject. Remember that no one really knows what's going to emerge as mass media options, although a lot of folks act like they do. Don't be intimidated. Jump right in and be part of the equation.

Go to the technology trade shows, particularly those dealing with consumer electronics. Make a list of vendors you might want to know better one day. Talk to them. Talk to the attendees. Go to the breakout sessions. Think how your magazine might work in any of the electronic variations you see. Don't leave until you've learned something new and made at least one follow-up plan. Then find out when the next show is coming to your neighborhood and make plans to attend that one.

Monitor your company's EQ (Electronic Quotient). Where are you versus the state-of-the-art in desktop? How about reader database marketing? ad sales systems support? human resource information systems? How organizationally broad and deep is access to the newer technologies? Think about the costs of neglecting these priorities and build yourself a continuous improvement workplan.

Stay as smart as your advertisers in harnessing electronic access to your markets. The integration of advertising and editorial is a powerful economic formula that may well require electronic weighting, but shouldn't fall apart when digitized.

Follow the ownership debate. We work today with rights agreements that defy control in electronic distribution of intellectual property. The "ownership" of original material is so fragile, once launched into cyberspace, and the rate of technological development so rapid, that even the sharpest legal minds have difficulty addressing worst-case eventualities before they worsen further. This issue is central to the success or failure of print as we know it, in traveling the electronic highway with its prestige and authority intact.

Where's your customer? At least as critical in your longer-range planning as demographics and lifestyle indicators is an index of customer involvement with technologies. Media usage, including the emerging computer-based media, should be a routine inquiry in your reader research.

Be a good corporate citizen. There's a real danger that use of the "highway" will be limited to those who have the great good fortune of being either linked to it at work, or able to afford and manage their own access. There's also the risk that workers who don't make the trip on the highway will end up in the unemployment office. Superimpose on this the declining literacy rate in America and the growing numbers of the economically disadvantaged. We can't do much with words—on paper or online—if people can't read them. And if you're reading FOLIO:, you're in a position to make a difference. It matters. □

 New media

Boost Profits and Credibility With Multimedia Marketing

BY STUART W. PARK

Major players in publishing—Hearst, Rodale, Time Warner and others—are committing heavily to multimedia exploration, striving to get ahead of the curve. Through a variety of multimedia offerings, including CD-ROMs and interactive television, these companies are attempting to create new vehicles and markets for core editorial content.

There's no doubt that emerging communications vehicles will spur massive changes in consumer markets. But for the immediate future, publishers must also overcome commoditization, restore rate stability and gain greater investment from advertisers in their core print businesses. Competition is squeezing advertising revenue from traditional print sources, while multimedia is calling for significant capital outlays.

At the same time, corporate America has raised the bar for sales professionals by implementing multimedia marketing programs of their own. It won't be long before advertisers expect the same from magazine salespeople.

The solution is multimedia marketing. Using it day in, day out, is the fastest way to raise the new media fluency of marketing, sales and editorial people. The more headway publishers make in multimedia product development, the more essential it will be to tell their marketing stories using the technology. This doesn't mean carrying, say, 16 *Road & Track* CDs into a sales call; it means opening a notebook computer, hooking up to a projector, and bringing the entire product story to life. Doing so empowers magazine sales forces, differentiates their franchises, and sells more ads. Moreover, it positions the publisher as a guide for advertisers who are striving to understand new media opportunities and establish sophisticated identities.

Magazine salespeople have a surplus of complex stories to tell, but their customers have no time to listen. The pressure intensifies to address a client's needs on the spot in an engaging and memorable way. Canned

> An interactive sales presentation is not a mere repositioning, it's a total transformation.

presentations—flip charts, transparencies, slides—simply cannot meet this challenge, no matter how expertly they're produced. Client questions about integrated marketing opportunities, in particular, force salespeople to stray from the script.

With a well-designed multimedia presentation, on the other hand, salespeople can customize pieces of the content and the order of the presentation without compromising the identity that corporate marketing has carefully crafted. These electronic presentations can be updated constantly at low cost without discarding an inventory of printed brochures, slides or videotapes.

Several major service providers are telling their entire corporate marketing stories via portable multimedia presentations. Rather than prolong the sales cycle by asking, "Can we schedule another meeting so I can present my other carousel of slides?" or "Let me send you the brochure on that," these salespeople marshal information immediately to overcome objections, answer questions and address concerns. Want to know more? Click on to a deeper level of detail. Need something else? Click into the subject of your choice. A hundred different presentations can be stored on the computer and called up as needed.

Marketing with interactive multimedia is a rapidly evolving discipline. Here are several of the lessons learned by companies who have moved aggressively into multimedia marketing solutions.

Don't go through the motions. Building a successful multimedia sales presentation isn't about a salesperson and a programmer working together in the media lab. It's a painstaking process that demands the attention of the company's top marketing minds. Publishers need to commit to it wholly, or not do it at all. Whether your solution involves a portable marketing presentation, a CD-ROM or a World Wide Web site, advertisers and/or readers will expect value in the form of timely, relevant and well-organized information.

Set a budget via corporate mandate. Launching a multimedia marketing program is a long-term strategic decision. The sophisticated identity it establishes tells the world what the company stands for. This is not a repositioning, it's a total transformation. To do everything right in an interactive presentation—to create tools that inform, excite and empower the way a beautifully executed magazine does—means spending $500,000 or more in the first year.

Stick with top designers. Don't trust your future to an unproven enthusiast. It's easy to fall into the trap of believing that computer whizzes automatically make good multimedia designers and programmers. They don't. What's more, they're not usually good marketers. Most have never prepared a marketing presentation or produced a corporate video. Effective multimedia design requires that content be presented in an intuitive fashion for easy access by the uninitiated, or that it be fashioned as speaker support for use by salespeople only. You need designers with 10 to 15 years of experience in high-end corporate design, and programmers who can demonstrate that they have worked effectively with video, digital audio and interactive multimedia.

Beware of Prototype Failure Syndrome. A narrowly scoped prototype that stays a prototype never fully demonstrates the value of multimedia marketing.

Multimedia presentations don't run on autopilot. The sales consultant should assume the role of navigator, customizing the presentation and solution for the advertiser. Use voice-over sparingly unless there is a reason for someone other than the sales consultant to provide an explanation or opinion. For example, although the *Forbes* CD-i presentation was a ground-breaking initiative, the program was conceived more as an interactive collection of self-running video clips rather than an interactive speaker-support tool.

Don't overload the sales staff. Use the same machine they use for word processing, e-mail and account management. Salespeople will be reluctant to carry any more than is absolutely necessary. Also, don't rely on equipment provided by clients or others unless it can be tested in advance of the presentation.

Don't be swept away by novelty. Focus on providing value through efficient, captivating communication.

Build effective programs through proper pre-production (flow-charts, scripts, storyboards).

Budget for heavy training costs. Mastering multimedia marketing is a learn-by-doing process, and everyone faces a learning curve with this new power tool. At the same time, managers must be careful not to focus their teams entirely on production, because in this fast-changing arena, designers, graphic artists and programmers become stale unless they get the training needed to keep their skills current.

Screen multimedia providers carefully. The field has more wanna-be outfits than proven providers. Take the time to examine a few key factors. First, has the team ever worked together on interactive multimedia projects? With what success? You don't want to waste time or money and risk failure on your first project by bankrolling someone else's first experiment in multimedia. Second, what process will they take you through, from day one through completion? Third, how will they keep the project in scope and on budget? If you're talking to an ad agency, you need to know two things: 1) Is their understanding of the creative possibility inherent in multimedia based on working in the medium? 2) Do they have the project-management experience needed to create a complex software program on time and on budget?

Build a leverage plan. Make each application one step toward a repertoire of mutually reinforcing communications. After all, multimedia is the most adaptable platform for repurposing core content. Literally dozens of marketing and communications applications can be created from one multimedia foundation.

Done right, what does a multimedia marketing program buy you? First, it lowers your cost per captivation while bolstering your image as a leader in multimedia. Customers who are merely made aware don't make buys—only customers who are captivated do. Second, it shortens the sales cycle. Third, it becomes an integrated system of consistent, powerful and up-to-date internal and external communications. Finally, it gives you a sophisticated identity in a flexible electronic format—a format that can be rapidly repositioned and redistributed, effectively cutting the time it takes to bring new information to market. ☐

Starter Tips for
New-Media Neophytes

BY BARRIE J. ATKIN

By the end of this decade, most households in the United States will have access via personal computer and/or interactive TV (whether through cable, phone lines, direct broadcast satellite, or a combination of these) to an electronic highway. Imagine virtually unlimited information and entertainment on demand—not just text, but audio, full-motion video, animation and magazine-quality graphics—when you want it and where you want it.

Non-print media are likely to offer significant threats to magazine franchises, but they also represent an opportunity to enter new markets and reach new audiences. You know your company should get moving on the information highway—perhaps your competitors are already revving their engines. Here are some driving tips to help you with your electronic media journey.

Use the new media. The best way to get started is to use the new media, play them, view them. If you are uncomfortable with computers, ask others (colleagues, friends, or computer-savvy children) to demo the CD-ROM titles and online services for you. Visit retailers that sell multimedia software. Talk with the sales staff about their perception of the market. Try out some CD-ROM titles whose content relates to your franchise. You should also explore the online services: CompuServe, Prodigy, America On-Line, Delphi, GEnie and ZiffNet—among others.

Finally, purchase one or more multimedia computers and some CD-ROM software to share with your colleagues and staff.

Find out what's happening. Read industry publications. There are many excellent magazines and newsletters covering multimedia developments. Attend conferences and trade shows such as the New Media Expo, CD-ROM World, Intermedia, New Media Summit, MacWorld, Multimedia Expo and the Consumer Electronics Show. If conferences aren't in your budget, purchase the tapes or transcripts of selected seminars.

Talk with other publishers, consultants and industry experts about what they're doing and their view of the future. Talk with software publishers such as Microsoft and Apple. What do they see as a market for your material?

Spread the knowledge. It's important to develop high levels of knowledge about, and comfort with, multimedia throughout your organization. Create an in-house, cross-department "New Media Watch" group. Because everyone is already pressed for time, members could each take responsibility for reading one or two publications, and then share key developments on a regular basis.

Take a similar approach for conferences and seminars. Spread attendance among key people. Encourage each to spell out the potential implications of what he or she learned for your market and your publications.

Track the competition. In reviewing the competition, be sure to include non-traditional publishers that are producing multimedia content in your fields. Microsoft, for example, is now a major publisher of consumer multimedia CD-ROMs and is developing online services. Software and entertainment companies (such as WordPerfect and LucasArts) and hundreds of

Not all magazine content lends itself to multimedia forms. But each of the new media has characteristics suited to certain types of editorial.

smaller start-ups are creating multimedia programs.

Keep in mind that when competitors produce new-media products, they're already ahead of you on the learning curve. And while you work on your first ventures, they are developing new titles as well as improved versions of their earlier works.

Look at the quality of the competition's product, its ease of use, and the relative value versus a print product. Look for titles and services that exploit the new technologies to offer the viewer a truly enhanced experience.

Pricing strategy also bears watching—especially since the cost to develop multimedia products is typically higher than the cost to develop magazines. As the multimedia market expands, price competition is likely to drive retail product prices lower. Consider what sales volume you need to break even at different price points.

Measure customers' multimedia purchases. How soon you get involved will be influenced by your customers' lifestyles. If your customer base is comfortable with technology (*e.g.*, upscale middle managers, college students), you may have a ready audience for new-media products. In contrast, if your customer base includes few computer owners, you will be under less immediate pressure to produce a product. Remember, however, that new media can reach new customers outside your current audience.

Talk to your advertisers about *their* level of interest in the new media. Ask them what types they're exploring, their levels of investment, and their expectations for interactive advertising.

Evaluate your editorial content. Magazines already have the advantages that the new media strive for—ease of access, portability, high-resolution graphics and a targeted audience—all at low cost to the reader. But many print publishers are creating electronic magazines, and some companies are creating CD-ROM periodicals with no print counterpart.

Certainly, not all magazine content lends itself to multimedia forms. However, each of the new media has characteristics well suited to publishing certain types of editorial. For example, CD-ROM, with its enormous storage capacity and searchability, lends itself to archives and reference material such as annuals, buyers' guides and interactive catalogs.

Online services can deliver time-sensitive information and provide more depth about a topic than what appears in a magazine article. In conjunction with a magazine, they can enhance the printed material.

Brainstorm new-media content ideas. Here are a few questions you can ask to brainstorm new-media product ideas: What content would be enhanced by video? by sound? by the reader's ability to conduct an interactive search?

Do we have historical content that still has value in

■ **Selected resources**

Magazines

Folio:, *Advertising Age*, *Publishers Weekly* and many computing titles offer regular sections on electronic publishing and interactive media. Some devoted exclusively to the new media are:

• *CD-ROM Professional:* six times a year plus six issues of CD-ROM News Extra, $98. 462 Danbury Road, Wilton, CT 06897-2126.

• *CD-ROM Today:* six times with discs, $29.95. P.O. Box 51478, Boulder, CO 80323-1478.

• *CD-ROM World:* 11 times a year, $19.97 charter sub. P.O. Box 3000, Denville, NJ 07834-9975.

• *Multimedia World:* 12 times a year, $9.97. P.O. Box 58690, Boulder, CO 80323-8690.

• *New Media:* 13 times a year, free to qualified new-media professionals; $48 for others. P.O. Box 1771, Riverton, NJ 08077-7371.

• *Wired:* 12 times a year, $40. P.O. Box 191826, San Francisco, CA 94119-9866.

Newsletters

The multimedia revolution has inspired many companies to launch newsletters. Here are some of the best known:

• "Consumer Multimedia Report," 24 times a year, $395. Warren Publishing, Inc., 2115 Ward Court NW, Washington, D.C. 20037. 202-872-9200.

• "Digital Media," 12 times a year, $395. Seybold Publications, Inc., P.O. Box 644, Media, PA 19063. 215-565-2480.

• "Multimedia Business Report," 24 times a year (going weekly later this year), $449. SIMBA, 213 Danbury Road, Wilton, CT 06897-7430. 203-834-0033.

• "Multimedia Monitor," 12 times a year, $295 introductory, P.O. Box 26, Falls Church, VA 22040. 800-323-3472.

Online services

Most of the online services offer forums on new media, as well as a free trial.

• Delphi: 800-695-4005

• GEnie: 800-638-9636

• Prodigy: 800-776-3449

• America Online: 800-827-6364, ext. 9216

• CompuServe: 800-848-8990.

online text or in a CD-ROM? Do we have unpublished information that readers would pay for?

Could our advertisers benefit by being part of a CD-ROM catalog or other new-media product?

What titles have been produced by others (in our areas) that we could do much better? What content do we have (or could we develop) that would expand our current audience?

Protect and prepare your editorial assets.

Rights: Traditionally, most publishing contracts covered print rights only. If you haven't already done so, update your contracts to include electronic rights or options. If you can't (or don't want to) purchase full rights up front, try to establish a pre-set purchase price should you decide to acquire the electronic rights later.

Digital storage: This allows you to access and modify your content as needed without rekeying or rescanning, and to reformat it into multiple products and services. Be sure that you also have clear archiving and easy access to final versions (along with rights information). As compression and scanning technologies improve, digital storage and archiving of photographs and video will become increasingly affordable.

Strengthen your leadership position. As the electronic marketplace becomes more crowded, leadership and name recognition will be necessary for market success. If you are not a market leader, look for ways to become one or to dominate a niche.

How easily could another company acquire your editorial strength or steal your franchise? Evaluate what you do well, and develop strategies to maintain and strengthen those skills.

Create a new-media plan. Now that you have lots of background, develop a plan for market entry. Consider these points:

• Your mission: Check if it's broad enough to hold up in a multimedia age. Become an information publisher, not just a magazine publisher.

• Entry strategy: Identify key factors that will influence when and how you enter the multimedia arena. What events will be trigger points?

• Potential partners: Increasingly, companies are forming strategic alliances. What will you look for in partners? What will you bring to the table?

Although the emergence of the electronic highway appears to be inevitable, its actual form is evolving—and the market is changing rapidly. Whether you get involved now or later, in small steps or a big way, be sure to review and update your assumptions frequently, and revise your strategy as needed. □

 New media

The CD-ROM Imperative

BY LORNE MANLY

Branching into CD-ROM can be treacherous for publishers. The mind-boggling technology, the different set of editorial skills necessary to create a product, the unfamiliar markets and distribution channels—not to mention the prospective costs—can all induce new-media vertigo when it comes to spinning off multimedia products.

So it's not surprising that publishers are treading gingerly, wondering whether they should be involved in CD-ROM publishing at all. Their dilemma is perfectly summed up by Eric Jacobson, director of acquisitions and divestitures at Intertec Publishing, the Overland Park, Kansas-based trade-magazine division of K-III Communications: "You want to know exactly what you're doing, but you don't want to be left behind."

But there is a growing consensus that magazine publishers can't sit back and wait until the dust settles and visibility on the so-called "information highway" is 100 percent. "Chairman Mao once said you learn to swim by swimming, and that's exactly what we're doing," says Rick Smith, president and editor in chief of *Newsweek*, which produces a quarterly, general-interest CD-ROM magazine called *Newsweek* InterActive. "We're not in a classroom looking at the chalkboard; we're in the pool."

Magazine publishers may just have to adopt a different business model—one that places a much higher premium on developing projects—if they want not only to reap part of the new-media bonanza, but also to keep their print franchises healthy.

"Traditional media have been spoiled because they haven't had to do R&D," says Al Sikes, president of Hearst New Media & Technology and former chairman of the Federal Communications Commission. "If you look at AT&T, Microsoft and Intel, these companies know their financial soundness will be based on what products they come up with for the future." Publishers, too, need to start building equity on the digital frontier.

CD-ROM—despite its technological limitations, supposedly imminent obsolescence, and development costs—can be an area where publishers learn the new skills that will be increasingly important in the multi-

media age. And, if done properly, heeding the CD-ROM imperative can prove a profitable course for those electronic publishing pioneers.

To help magazine publishers get a handle on how they should spin off CD-ROMs without hurting their magazines or losing their shirts, *Folio:* offers this guide to producing and marketing CD-ROMs.

How do you know it's for you?
First, publishers must determine if they should bother with CD-ROM products. Naysayers argue that CD-ROM is a transitional technology on the road to true interactive television and computer networks that will be able to transmit full-motion video at affordable prices. Others argue that CD-ROM is best utilized simply as an archive medium, and is a poor substitute for interactivity.

Louis Rossetto, editor and publisher of *Wired*, the San Francisco-based monthly covering the cultural implications of new media, prefers the online approach for providing interactivity, and views CD-ROM as an overhyped innovation. "CD-ROMs are dead, slow and you can't put a lot on them," says Rossetto, adding that *Wired* will limit its CD-ROM efforts to a non-multimedia reference work of the first year of the magazine. "CD-ROM is the Betamax of the nineties."

But executives from numerous magazine and multimedia companies disagree, pointing out that CD-ROM is a viable technology right now, unlike interactive television or multimedia online services, and will enjoy marketplace primacy until at least the end of the century, before coexisting with other media. Phil Hood, editor of San Mateo, California-based *NewMedia*, concedes that CD-ROMs are "klugey [flawed], slow and inelegant." But in a recent editor's note, Hood lambasted "CD-ROM whiners," calling them "the aristocrats aboard the Titanic, fretting that the rescue boats don't have leather seats."

The hardware hits critical mass
And for CD-ROM hardware, critical mass appears to be near. Tom McGrew, vice president of Compton's

■ What will you have to spend?

For most publishers, the single most pressing issue in CD-ROM development is the matter of cost.

Discussions with magazines and developers suggested a price range for multimedia CD-ROMs of $200,000 to $600,000, depending on the project's complexity and the price of acquiring rights to material that companies don't own. (Putting just text on disk—pure reference material—lowers the cost range to as little as tens of thousands of dollars to the low six figures.)

Gistics, Inc., estimates that development costs for the first two or three multimedia titles average $300,000; later issues cost an average of $125,000. Marketing and promotion add another $50,000 to $150,000 total. And manufacturing will add between $2 and $3 per disk, depending on how many are pressed and how fancy you want your packaging, say industry experts.

Save through licensing

Few publishers can or want to pay that kind of entry fee to an unproved market. For smaller publishers who can't afford new-media groups or bigger companies hedging their bets, licensing is probably the best route. According to multimedia developers, licensing fees range from 8 percent to 15 percent, and often publishers receive an advance against royalties. "We are somewhat new to the field, and [licensing] was the easiest and fastest way to get into the market," says Rich Fairfield, *Money*'s advertising business manager.

On the downside, publishers lose significant editorial control, gain little experience and do not profit as bountifully if the licensed product is a smash.

New Media, the Carlsbad, California-based developer of *The Sporting News* Multimedia Pro Football Guide 1993 and the upcoming Compton's Encyclopedia of Small Business, being done with *Entrepreneur*, points out that the software industry for the VCR didn't take off until the installed base reached 10 million machines, a level CD-ROM players are expected to hit by the end of this year.

The Software Publishers Association, a Washington, D.C.-based trade group representing 1,100 multimedia developers, says that during the latter part of 1993, the beginnings of a viable consumer software market for CD software began to appear. Software unit sales grew by 30 percent between the first three quarters of 1993 and the

comparable period in 1992, to 43.5 million units. But more important, a growing percentage of people bought their CD-ROMs separately rather than receiving them in hardware manufacturers' bundles, a less lucrative channel for publishers. Non-bundled sales—which averaged $45.81 per CD compared to $12.36 through the bundled channel—grew by 7 percent in the third quarter of 1993, to 46 percent of total sales, compared to the 39 percent for the first half of the year. And that means more money for software developers and the media companies that own the editorial content.

Shore up your marketshare

Jay Moses, director of multimedia projects at New York City-based Times Mirror Magazines, views the CD-ROM imperative partly in terms of shoring up marketshare. "If a CD-ROM company comes out with a product in your area, whether or not it's based on a rival magazine, you lose market share," says Moses. "That brand name has gained share in an area that you previously owned more of."

Adds *Newsweek*'s Smith: "If you're in a competitive market and the guy across the street is first with a successful electronic project, you'll have to scramble like hell to catch up, and you're going to be seen as a publisher who's not keeping up with change."

But such defensive—or what some may describe as paranoid—reasoning is not sufficient for taking the CD-ROM plunge. "The key skill is learning digital journalism, to deliver information and entertainment as a stream of bits," says *Newsweek* InterActive managing editor Michael Rogers. "Then you can fill any container that comes along," whether it's interactive TV, online, personal digital assistants (PDAs) or any other technological device. Dabbling in the online world is another valuable skill set to learn—particularly when the information you're providing is time-sensitive—but it's not enough. Currently, online services exercise a magazine's communications skills; CD-ROMs develop multimedia talents. "How are you learning how to do audio and video?" asks Rogers.

Adds Tom Lopez, co-chairman of Seattle-based Mammoth Micro Productions, which worked on the Sony MMCD version of *Newsweek* InterActive: "You can't be a screenwriter without knowing something about the movies."

What do your readers think?

But before publishers get too caught up in the multimedia hype and the whiz-bang gadgets technology can produce, multimedia developers proffer one word of advice: caution.

"Ignore all that technological crap," says Rich Bowers, executive director of the Columbus, Ohio-based Optical Publishers Association. "The first question you need to answer is, 'Are there any customers out there?'"

Certain magazines may decide to forgo the CD-ROM route, or place development on the back burner. For a magazine with an older-skewing readership, "CD-ROM may not be such a good idea, as there's not much of an installed base," says Paul Drexler, a principal in San Francisco-based developer Interworks and co-chairman of the International Interactive Communications Society. More reflective consumer magazines, such as *Commentary* or *Harper's Magazine*, don't work as well on CD-ROM, for which quickly consumed factoids are better suited.

> "The key skill is learning digital journalism, to deliver information and entertainment as a stream of bits," one editor says.

"Certain magazines are best read in a reading chair," says Michael Moon, the director of education at Gistics, a Larkspur, California-based research and consulting firm specializing in interactive telemedia—its term for multimedia—and a columnist for *Morph's Outpost on the Digital Frontier*, a technical magazine for multimedia developers.

And since most CD-ROM users are male, spinning off a Seven Sisters title may not hold much financial promise. Those findings have prompted publishers like Hachette Filipacchi Magazines and Hearst Magazines to concentrate their efforts on male-directed books such as *Car and Driver* and *Popular Mechanics*, respectively.

Then there are the pricing implications. "Without a high affinity [among your readers for CD-ROM] you can't charge the buyer a lot, so you have to rely on advertising," a riskier tack given interactive advertising's infancy status, says Jonathan Epstein, publisher of San Francisco-based *Multimedia World*.

Opportunity for trade titles

Publishers need to analyze their editorial resources to determine if CD-ROM is the best digital vehicle. If readers turn to your magazine for up-to-date information, go online. "But if they want rich media content, if the information has high requirements for visualization, online at this point can't do it," says Jay Eisenberg, director of sales and marketing at Ehrlich Associates, a Park Ridge, New Jersey-based multimedia developer specializing in education and reference that designed the Multimedia Business Week 1000 CD-ROM.

Certain subject matters lend themselves particularly well to CD-ROM. *NewMedia's* Hood believes trade publishers, particularly research and academic journals, have an advantage over the consumer side. "They already sell information that people won't mind accessing from a CD-ROM, and many in their audiences have CD-ROMs at their desks," says Hood. Byrd Press, in Richmond, Virginia, produces CD-ROMs for the American Society of Microbiology's *Journal of Bacteriology* and the Society of Exploration Geophysicists' *Geophysics*. K-III Magazines CEO Harry McQuillen—while "hesitant to push magazines into new forms until we see a clearly defined market"—does foresee business-to-business having the potential to become a lucrative field. Placing Intertec's repair manuals and trade-in guides for the boating and farm markets in an interactive format could prove a profitable ancillary revenue stream.

Other areas publishers and developers say translate well to CD-ROM are how-to, reference, education, personal finance and health. "There are a lot of complicated issues that would require a lot of time in print or other aids to come up with an answer," says Hearst's Sikes. "You can answer a lot of questions by letting the computer work for you."

You can't merely rehash back issues

But unlike on the trade side, consumer-magazine publishers can't just stick their material on a disk and expect people to clamor for it. When reading for pleasure, not work, comfort factors become paramount. "You can't assume that just putting back issues on disk will interest people," says Bob Ellis, publisher of Compact Publishing, a Washington, D.C-based developer that produces the *Time* Almanac and *Time* Almanac in the 20th Century. "You need a useful body of information that lends itself to interactivity and that you can't really lay your hands on in another place."

Multimedia elements are key. "Unless you take the extra step of making reading off the screen engaging in a multimedia way, I don't see why anyone would want it," says Doug Millison, the editor in chief of *Morph's*

Outpost on the Digital Frontier. "It's like looking at a lightbulb—it's beaming light at you."

Besides the fact that reading on-screen tires the reader's eyes more quickly, Gistics Inc. has found that people are four to five times less likely to remember what they read on-screen than what they read on a printed page.

A host of new products are designed to sidestep that pitfall by wrapping the text core in layers of video, audio and graphics. *Money*'s new product, *Money in the '90s*, from Laser Resources Inc. of Carson, California, includes the full text of *Money*'s regular issues from January 1990 through December '93, but adds video clips of its "Best Places to Live" feature, as well as worksheets. St. Louis-based *The Sporting News* put its football guides on CD-ROM, while adding footage from NFL Films (33 minutes worth that cost $33,000 to license) and other visuals from the Football Hall of Fame (free).

One-shots or periodicals?

Another issue publishers must face is whether to follow the *Newsweek* path and produce a recurring periodical, or the *Time* method of spinning off a one-shot or producing an annual. "You have to have a variety of information and big enough markets to justify doing multiple issues," *Newsweek*'s Smith says. "Some magazines keep coming back to the same stories every few years."

Despite competitors' jibes about a newsweekly producing a CD-ROM, *Newsweek* believes its approach will pay off. Not only will quarterly—or eventually monthly—issues prorate CD-ROM development costs, but advertisers are more likely to run ads in a periodical where readership can be measured rather than in a stand-alone CD-ROM. "We think that in the new media magazine, fundamentals will still apply— such as producing content on a repeating basis," says Rogers. "We're not essentially a company that does one-shots."

U.S. News & World Report, however, has no plans to follow in *Newsweek*'s digital footsteps. It expects to produce its college guides and career guides in CD-ROM form, allowing users to see the campus or easily calculate future student loan payments. "There is a

---

■ Finding partners for a CD-ROM venture

Once publishers determine which, if any, CD-ROM route they should take, the next step is to hook up with multimedia producers and distributors. Unfortunately, there is no simple way to find them. Trade groups are useful for obtaining lists of developers, but won't act as matchmaking services. As in much of the publishing business, word-of-mouth is a prime catalyst for producing alliances. Following is a list of some of the major developers and distributors.

Developers

Mammoth Micro Productions
Seattle, Washington
(206) 281-7500

The Software Toolworks
Novato, California
(415) 883-3000

Compton's New Media
Carlsbad, California
(619) 929-2500

Compact Publishing, Inc.
Washington, D.C.
(202) 244-4770

Ehrlich Associates, Inc.
Park Ridge, New Jersey
(201) 307-8866

Laser Resources Inc.
Carson, California
(310) 324-4444

IBM Multimedia Publishing Studio
Atlanta, Georgia
(404) 877-1300

Sony Electronic Publishing
New York, New York
(212) 371-5800

Trade Associations

Optical Publishers Association
Columbus, Ohio
(614) 442-8805

Software Publishers Association
Washington, D.C.
(202) 452-1600

International Interactive Communications Society
Portland, Oregon
(503) 579-4427

San Francisco Multimedia Developers Group
San Francisco, California
(415) 553-2300

market there—people are already buying [the guides] in book and software form," says Kathryn Bushkin, director of editorial administration at *U.S. News*. *Playboy* is also going the reference route, taking 30 years of its interviews and putting them on disk with the help of the Atlanta-based IBM Multimedia Publishing Studio. And *Inc.* is planning to release a series of small-business guides with partner Ikonic Interactive, a San Francisco-based multimedia developer, designing the CD-ROMs.

Attitude is the key

For those wanting to create a recurring franchise along the lines of *Newsweek* InterActive and CD-ROM-only magazines such as *Substance.digizine* and *NautilusCD*, attitude is key. Tossing a lot of content on a disk without an editorial point of view is unlikely to lead to financial success. "Mankind doesn't turn to magazines so much for the facts—which they can find in newspapers and almanacs and encyclopedias—as they do for truths," writes John Burks, a *Multimedia World* columnist and journalism professor at San Francisco State University, in the March 1994 issue of the IDG title. "We err when we confuse facts with truth, and that error is written large all over this first generation of multimedia magazines."

The same logic—the need for a voice—holds true for one-shots and almanacs as much as for periodicals. "A well-run magazine has a flavor to it, a personality, and that has to be adapted to the new media," no matter the frequency, says Keith Ferrell, editorial director of *Omni* and *Compute*. *Penthouse* Interactive, where the user becomes the photographer at a *Penthouse* Pet shoot and gets his work critiqued by company chairman Bob Guccione himself, definitely meets that standard. Wait too long to take a picture and a pouty-lipped *Penthouse* Pet appears, asking "What am I, a screen saver?"

Premiere hopes to avoid a personality crisis by not producing a multimedia translation of the magazine loaded with video and audio clips. Instead *Premiere*, working with developer Starwave of Bellevue, Washington, plans to release an interactive studio tour game. Users can essentially make a movie themselves as a studio would, calling the shots from the casting couches to the editing room. "We want to do something completely in keeping with *Premiere*'s concept—that makes them feel like partners in the industry, but that they

can't get in the magazine," says Susan Lyne, *Premiere*'s editorial director.

The advertising challenge

Many of the pioneering publishers hope to offset costs—and make money—from advertising. Hachette, considering a series of *Car and Driver* CD-ROMs, could, say, get one of the big accounting firms to sponsor a CD-ROM analyzing buying vs. leasing. But banking on those dollars now is foolhardy. "There is advertising there, but not enough that I'd base a business plan on," says *SI for Kids* publisher Cleary Simpson, who expects to release a CD-ROM in a few months.

The problem: "None of the [media companies] have quite figured out how to make interactive ads attractive to advertisers," says Kelly Black, associate media director of Apple Computer agency BBDO/LA. J. Walter Thompson Online has three criteria the media must meet to win their clients' business: ads must be tied into editorial; there must be room for real information, not just 30-second soundbites; and they must be truly interactive. No CD-ROM or online service has yet scaled those barriers.

Money in the '90s, however, may be a harbinger of the shape of advertising to come. The CD-ROM carries a paid ad from discount stockbroker Charles Schwab that is a demo of Schwab's StreetSmart software—allowing users to place stock trades, obtain real-time quotes and access 6,700 company reports. "It's interactive by definition," says Rich Fairfield, *Money*'s ad business manager.

Don't blow your lead

But despite all these hurdles, magazine publishers are well positioned to benefit from the coming multimedia explosion. After all, content is king for multimedia developers, and publishers own the goods. More than that, "magazine publishers have the market specialization and segmentation that lends itself to multimedia developers," says Mammoth Micro Productions' Lopez, who is also president of the Annapolis, Maryland-based Interactive Multimedia Association. "It's their business—to carve out a very specific niche and then support it with quality editorial." This characteristic provides magazine publishers with a head start toward staking a place in the multimedia world. It's a significant advantage at this stage of the game. Now, it's up to them to make sure they don't blow it. □

Secrets of a Money-Making CD-ROM

BY MATTHEW COHN

For many business-to-business publishers, new media is a source of millions of dollars in added revenue. Others pour money away without ever seeing dollar-one in profits. *The New York Times* recently reported that 40 percent of people who have CD-ROM drives with their computers never use them. And 54 percent don't ever plan to buy additional software. Still, despite statistics like these, some CD-ROM publishers are making millions.

How? What are the real secrets of success? It sounds simple: Develop a product that people will want to use, satisfy a real need, and always keep your customer in mind. All too often, however, CD-ROM developers get dazzled by the technology and forget the needs of the user. But by keeping a few important points in mind, you can create a new-media product that brings you multi-million-dollar results, and provides your subscribers and advertisers with new and improved services.

An effective tool

The best content for CD-ROM is information that people will use time and time again. Making this kind of information available on CD-ROM can be a cost-effective way to increase the range of services you offer your subscribers and advertisers. Buying guides or directories, for example, make ideal CD-ROM projects. For the subscriber, a big benefit is that they are searchable and sortable.

Your advertisers can feature key items in unique, interactive presentations to differentiate their products from others in the buying guide. Some products need more than a static printed image to be really appreciated. With CD-ROM, your advertisers can include more information, as well as animation, video, downloadable software and even interactive worksheets—all of which can add a great deal to the message.

Preparing a full-motion ad can cost an advertiser thousands of dollars, sometimes up to $10,000. The publisher's fees can often be equal to this expense, or more. Obviously, the CPM for reaching a given audience through some new media is much higher than for print media. However, the return can also be higher. And remember, when you involve the user, he or she will retain more information and use the product more frequently. Not only does CD-ROM hold more information than print (one CD-ROM holds about 350,000 single-spaced typed pages), it also holds the reader's attention better. One study shows that people spend only two to five minutes on print, but take about 20 minutes to a half-hour on new media. More important, only 20 percent of the paper product's content was recalled, as compared with 60 percent of the electronic material.

The first, most important considerations

Before you start, develop your idea around these principles. Your CD-ROM must meet the following criteria:
• Be need-driven: You should consider producing a CD-ROM only if it is truly need-driven. You should think, "What will my subscribers or advertisers get that they can't get elsewhere?"

• Have compelling content: Studies have shown that you have only three chances to get people hooked on your product. They have to find enough value to justify changing the way they're currently doing business.
• Be fast: One first-time developer of a CD-ROM created an application that took a full minute just to load. Most people would rather go to a printed resource than wait that long every time they want to look up some information.
• Be easy to use: Make it an easy and enjoyable experience. It's unrealistic to expect people to sift through volumes of training manuals just to learn how to use your product.
• Be compatible: Be aware of users' computer expertise and their hardware. Only half the computers out there

> The first investment in new media can be high, but after that, costs should drop dramatically.

run Windows, so you may want to consider a DOS-, Mac- or Unix-based system.

Another key consideration: Cost

A CD-ROM project can take anywhere from a few weeks to more than a year to complete. Projects like a CD-ROM directory or buying guide with complete search and print capabilities and multimedia ads take about six months.

The simplest CD-ROM project can be done for around $25,000, with the most complex jobs costing up to $1 million or more if original information must be gathered. Most fairly sophisticated projects range from $100,000 to $250,000. Some consultants advise taking what you think you will spend and doubling it. That number will be more realistic in the end.

If you're using a service organization to help do your project, ask them to give you a cost ceiling right at the beginning. This will help you avoid any big surprises at the end. Some will do joint ventures or even completely fund a project, claiming royalties from sales once the product is completed.

The initial investment in a new-media project can be quite substantial, but after that first-time expenditure, the costs drop dramatically. The cost of duplicating a CD-ROM is very low. Where you might spend $20 to $30 for each buying guide you print, it costs only about $1 to press each disc after the master has been created. And it can cost as little as one-tenth of the original cost to come out with a disc the second year.

Another cost savings is the addition of new information to the disc. Imagine that you had a 500-page directory that you wanted to increase to 800 pages. With paper, the costs are proportional, so adding this much information would add a considerable amount to your costs. However, on CD-ROM, the cost for space, whether it's editorial or advertising, is zero until you fill the disc.

Who you'll need

Whether you do a CD-ROM project in-house or decide to use an outside vendor, you must have a focused group dedicated to making your new-media venture a success. It should be the number-one priority. You can't expect your staff just to squeeze this project in and give it the attention it deserves.

Researchers: When starting a new project, the first thing you should do is speak with the end-users. Study how people currently use your publications.

Rely on what you observe, and not so much on what the end-users tell you in surveys. In surveys, people will often tell you what they want, not necessarily what they are willing to buy. For example, if you asked people if they would like a Ferrari, most would answer "yes." But if you asked, "Who's willing to pay more than $100,000 for a Ferrari?" you wouldn't get a lot of positive answers.

Production: You'll need programmers to make the system function as you wish; designers and artists to create the way your screens will look; writers for your "help" screens, training manuals and other technical copy; and others to make the product a reality.

Strong marketing and sales support: Your product is not going to sell itself. By introducing new media, you're asking people to change the way they do something. Most people don't like change. You need dedicated marketing and salespeople, as well as a compelling product, to convince them it's worth it.

Reliable support: There is a lot of hand-holding in new media. This goes from resolving technical problems to providing all the training that's necessary to make the user comfortable with your product. Because people are afraid of "messing things up," a patient support person can make all the difference in whether someone uses your product or not.

You don't have to do it all yourself

You don't have to know everything about the technology to be successful with new media. Most companies don't do their own printing, but rely on outside vendors—and the same is true now with electronic publishing. There are experts who can help you. Essentially, decide how much you can realistically handle in-house and let experts who have already done projects like yours help you with the rest.

Pricing your CD-ROM product

If you're providing real value, don't be afraid to charge for it. You shouldn't charge less for a CD-ROM than for a printed product just because the production costs may be lower. Charge for the quality and value of the service you are providing. □

How to Develop Great Editorial Content for a CD-ROM

BY TODD HARRIS

You're a top editor, but your head spins when those propeller-heads down the hall start talking bits, bytes and bandwidth. Unfortunately, that hasn't stopped your boss from dumping new-media development into your lap: "We gotta do something interactive, maybe a multimedia CD-ROM," she exclaims before disappearing into another meeting.

CD-ROM? I can't even format a floppy, you mutter to yourself.

Relax: You may be sweating bullets now, but working on a CD-ROM is not as mysterious as it sounds. With a little knowledge and a lot of enthusiasm, you can help shape your magazine's message for new distribution outlets and new readers.

Still feel like curling up into a potato bug? Don't. Your job description has just expanded, and it encompasses more than the printed page. There are some 20 million CD-ROM drives out there, and multimedia consumers are starved for good content that editors like you can deliver. Unlike book publishers, who began exploring CD-ROMs as early as the late eighties, most magazine publishers have only this year answered the call of the spinning disc and are in catch-up mode. Your publisher will probably want to explore a magazine on CD-ROM, a quarterly or annual CD supplement, or even a digital advertorial that's "bundled" with the magazine.

In any case, you need to be well informed and ready for the challenge because if editors don't manage the information flow into the digital domain, less knowledgeable people will—which could damage your magazine's reputation. Moreover, learning about new media could soon become your ticket to greater opportunities within your own company or elsewhere. CD-ROM is a hot commodity and it's too important to pass off because of time commitments or personal fears. (Remember what happened to those art directors who refused to learn desktop publishing.)

With that said, here's a basic primer that will help you speak intelligibly about this newfangled subject matter.

Get physical. The only way to understand CD-ROMs is to play with them, so get a multimedia computer for your home and office. (By the way, every good art director should have a drive in order to access clip art and stock photography, which is now best stored on CD-ROM.) By looking at a range of discs, from games to encyclopedias, you'll learn about different menu designs and search tools. Most titles are published for Windows-compatible computers, but there's enough to get you started on the Mac.

Learn the lingo. CD-ROM means Compact Disc Read Only Memory, and like its optical cousin, the audio CD, it can pick up data using a laser light. The difference is that CD-ROMs can "read" and integrate a range of information, such as video, text, animation, sound or whatever (hence the term "multimedia") and display it on your computer screen. Some CD-ROM drives, often called set-top players, can play CDs on your TV. One example is 3DO, a popular game format that has so far been incompatible with desktop CD players.

As you can tell, terms are used pretty loosely. "CD" can mean an audio CD or a CD-ROM; "multimedia" is often thrown around with the term "interactive," which refers to how much control the user has over the action. If you need help with the terminology, buy a beginner's book like *Byte Guide to CD-ROM* (Osborne McGraw-Hill; $39.95).

Keep up with the industry. There are hundreds of computer, gaming and multimedia newsletters and magazines, and new ones are being launched all the time. Because this industry is moving so quickly and in so many different directions, it's best to skim several publications.

For starters, read *Wired*. The editing is uneven and

> When you've mastered the basics, you'll know you've just begun. So put the phobias behind you and stay ahead of the competition.

you may have to squint to read the type, but its thought-provoking articles will help you tune into Silicon Valley's Zeitgeist. Next, check out some of the more niche-oriented consumer titles, such as *Interactive Age, Electronic Entertainment,* and *CD-ROM Today.* They'll give you an idea of what new titles and technologies are in the pipeline. Of course, it's a good idea to peruse some of the larger computer magazines, too, but their coverage of multimedia (read "CD-ROM") *is* not as extensive as the smaller upstarts' coverage. If you want developer or business-related information, try *New Media* and *CD-ROM Professional* magazines, respectively.

Don't forget the entertainment-industry trades, either. Get a subscription to *Billboard, Variety, The Hollywood Reporter* and *Publishers Weekly,* among others. They all track CD-ROM developments from their own unique vantage points, and their coverage is getting better. Red Herring will fill you in on the Valley's venture-capitalist trade. And if you've got the cash, newsletters like "Multimedia Business Report," ($479/year, 203-834-0033*);* "Multimedia Monitor," ($395, 703-241-1799*);* or Seybold's "Digital Media," ($395/year, 610-565-6864*)* are loaded with insider information.

Get an education. You need to make industry contacts and master the minutia. Every major computer trade show now has a multimedia pavilion where you can hobnob with developers who might be potential partners.

For a real boot-camp experience, enroll in a short multimedia course. These are held around the country at many of the large universities. In New York, contact the NYU Center for Digital Multimedia (212-998-3519), which runs intensive summer sessions. And in Los Angeles, UCLA Extension offers a mix of courses, depending on your skill level and interests (310-825-9064). Other good bets: Columbia University, Stanford University, San Francisco State University and UC Berkeley Extension.

You might also try networking with budding multimedia enthusiasts on an online forum within CompuServe or America Online. In addition, computer user groups, such as the Boston Computer Society (617-290-5700), offer meetings, seminars and workshops.

Go for it. Nobody has all the answers. If you don't understand something, be up front and say so. The ignorant are only those who ignore the new-media opportunities. By the way, if you're looking for clear firewalls between editorial and advertising in this realm, forget it. You'll have to make it up as you go along and trust your editorial instincts.

When you feel that you've mastered the basics, you know you've just begun. Depending on the business support within your company, you might be asked to structure a business relationship with a CD-ROM developer (hint: Be creative) or to set up an in-house project (hint: Recruit good programming talent). The important lesson is to familiarize yourself and your co-workers with the options. If you do, you'll put those computer phobias behind you and stay a step ahead of the competition. ☐

The 10 Commandments of Cyberspace

BY WILLIAM ALLMAN

Getting involved with new media is like a religious conversion. You must learn a host of arcane rituals, chants and evocations. You must struggle to glean an understanding of texts and codices known only to a few. You must endure the frenzied monologues of the true believers and suffer the cynical ridicule of the unconvinced. You commune with a vast, mysterious power that is beyond any one person's comprehension. Most of all, you must labor under the knowledge that Valhalla is but a distant vision—and might come only after you are gone.

U.S. News & World Report has been online for nearly three years, making our team the equivalent of Talmudic scholars among the typically tyro magazine editors and publishers in the online community. The learning curve has been more or less vertical. Before we went live on CompuServe, we set out a list of ideas we thought would apply to cyberspace. Almost every one of them has proven wrong. Now, older and wiser, I offer 10 commandments for your journey into the information revolution.

> The most important piece of equipment for venturing online is still the gray, squishy stuff between your ears.

1. Cyberspace is thy lord and master—thou shalt have no other gods before it.

There is no way to be partially committed to getting online. The process requires time, money and energy. Beware of false prophets from the online industry who promise a heavenly experience with little or no work. First, estimate the amount of resources you think you'll spend on the project—then double it.

2. Thou shalt not worship a (en)graven image.

Putting a magazine online does not simply mean putting a facsimile of the magazine online, nor is it merely a high-tech way for readers to send letters to the editor. Online services have three strengths: widespread, instant accessibility; near-infinite, easily-retrieved data storage; and speedy interactivity. Plan your online presence around these principles—not the pages of your magazine.

3. Thou shalt not take cyberspace in vain.

Well, okay, maybe a few times. Particularly when all the terminals go down at once, the online service loses all your files, or some nut pollutes your message areas with rantings written in all capital letters.

4. Remember to have a Sabbath day.

At regular intervals, take a break, take stock of how things are going, and readjust your plan. After all, this is publishing R&D. You must find new ways of taking advantage of what cyberspace has to offer. One of the biggest surprise successes of U.S. News Online, for instance, is our library, which is full of interview transcripts, public documents and other additional information that serves as "electronic sidebars" to our stories. When we recently did a story on how much money various members of Congress were taking from special-interest groups, for instance, we uploaded a huge database that showed a legislator-by-legislator breakdown of who was getting what—something that would have been too space-consuming to publish in print. The files were downloaded thousands of times.

5. Honor thy parent magazine.

It is good to remind people that your organization was an "information provider" before cyberspace was cool. Your printed magazine has a style, franchise and reputation that you should build on—not abandon—in the online world. *U.S. News* is known as one of the most fastidious of fact-checking organizations, for instance. No way are we going to put up "outtakes" from the magazine that have not gone through the same editing and fact-checking process as our print material.

6. Thou shalt not kill reader inputs.

Perhaps the part of cyberspace hardest to adjust to is that it talks back to you. By creating message areas inviting readers to air their views, you create an online community. The problem is, this online community has a mind of its own; you have to learn to give up some measure of control. The only recourse is to commit to being a full-time presence in this community, if only to make sure your forum members are not talking behind your back. Our writers and editors have engaged in lengthy online debates; we've set up new message areas in response to reader suggestions. Last year, U.S. News Online went one step further: We invited one of our online community regulars, a woman who lives in a small town in South Carolina, to visit the offices of *U.S. News* in Washington, D.C. She got a first-hand feel of what goes on in making a magazine, and became a goodwill ambassador online.

7. Thou shalt not adulterate your business model.

The American public does not now pay full price for its information stream, and people won't start doing so just because it is pouring out of a computer. Throwing out the money-changers from the gates of cyberspace might make one feel more holy, but there is no way such a business model will work in the long run.

Online services have only now, reluctantly, begun to let online magazines behave like magazines: U.S. News Online was the first information provider to run its own ads in its area on CompuServe. Ads are inevitable. The problem that now remains is waiting for the advertisers to come around. Ad agencies have always been the ones who have made the most innovative use of the features of any new medium, however, and it's only a matter of time before some smart ones realize how to make cyberspace pay. Advertisers also must seek out the smaller—but more focused—audience that is truly interested in the message.

8. Thou shalt not steal—only borrow.

In a world of tightening budgets and skeptical CEOs, one must look for disciples in every nook and cranny of a magazine staff. U.S. News Online is completely home-grown, with its staff drawn from writers, editors, librarians—just about anybody else who wants to participate. Hiring an army of consultants to produce your online edit is like hiring a caterer to cook Thanksgiving dinner: Sure, it tastes good, but it doesn't have a smidgen of your soul.

9. Thou shalt not bear false witness—nor shall those in your online community.

There is no cyberspace Leviticus, and no one knows exactly what the laws of cyberspace will be for publishers: Are you responsible if someone posts a libelous message in your forum? Are you responsible if some unknown slander published years ago still lurks in your online database of back issues? What if a member of your forum gives inaccurate investing advice? Worst of all, if information providers start weeding out those messages that seem undesirable, they run the risk of assuming responsibility for the entire contents of their forum, meaning they have just acquired a whole new staff of writers over whom they have no control. These questions don't make the online world impassable, but while you are traveling through this publishing frontier, it is definitely a good idea to have a lawyer riding on the dashboard.

10. Thou shalt not covet thy neighbor's cool technology.

Sure, your competitors are spending zillions of dollars to launch themselves into the information revolution. But the most important piece of equipment for venturing online is still the gray, squishy stuff between your ears. If you have something interesting to say, if you play to the strengths of the medium, and if you never lose sight of your user, you are going to do fabulously in cyberspace.

Many wise prophets caution that it is better to wait until it is clear which side of the swimming pool is the deep end before diving in headfirst. That may be so, but it is also true that when it finally comes time to take the plunge, those who already know how to swim are going to do much better than those who don't. ☐

The Character of Our Content

BY CRIS BEAM

How do you define an online magazine—by the medium or the message? Offering an electronic doppelganger of your print title won't draw new readers, but creating an entirely different online product means you lose the benefits of synergy. So, what do you do? Should you hire new writers and develop an independent business plan, or should you modify the print products you already have? While there are clearly more questions than answers, there are a few possible models.

Whodunit?

"The first question I ask whenever a company tells me they just went up on the Web is who did it—your marketing group or your editorial group?" says Andrew Anker, president and CEO of *Wired*'s electronic offspring, HotWired, which made its debut on the Web in October 1994. "You need to understand why you're doing it, and then make it a real business and give it the autonomy it needs."

And Anker should know about autonomy. HotWired, with its generalist approach to art and culture, news and entertainment, looks and feels nothing like the techno-centric *Wired*. The staff is different, the content is different, and even the approach to hiring differs from that of most print magazines. When Anker hires new employees, their interests take a back seat to the Internet. "The first step is you have to be Web-savvy. Then we ask, 'What are your interests?' and put you on that."

HotWired currently has a staff of more than 50, and the ranks are growing at a rate of one or two new employees a week. Unlike its print progenitor, which focuses exclusively on the digital arena, only one of HotWired's eight sections addresses technology. The rest focus on art, literature and entertainment, news, sports and interactive dialogues with its more than 235,000 subscribers. Ultimately, Anker says, HotWired plans to house a travel section with a version of *Rough Guides* travel books, and possibly a version of a

Reuters or AP feed—all fully searchable, of course. "Essentially, if you look at any consumer area—whether it's sports, entertainment, home and garden, travel—we think we can do something to serve our audience in each of these areas," says a confident Anker. "*Wired* talks about the digital revolution; HotWired *is* the digital revolution."

Down the garden path

Time Inc.'s Pathfinder Web site, which was launched in 1994 and rivals HotWired with more than 200,000 registered users, has an entirely different vision. While the staffs of HotWired and *Wired* are entirely separate, *Pathfinder* is extra work for roughly 130 regular Time Inc. employees who upload much of the exact texts and music from the 40-plus titles of parent company Time Warner. Although some might view this disdainfully as "shovelware"—a mere replication of existing editorial—Pathfinder editor James Kinsella claims digitized information is different from print because users can do so much more with it.

"Who cares what this material was like before it got digitized?" Kinsella asks rhetorically. "We need to

> Although the digital medium looks different, basic principles still hold: You need a clear editorial vision, a solid business plan and a talented staff.

think about how this is being ported out much more than how it came in." Kinsella says that Pathfinder has been "bluelined up the wazoo," providing readers with searching capability and background information not found in the print versions.

"We've turned Time into a highly explorable database, and suddenly we've got a powerful system," Kinsella says. "The reason we came up with the name Pathfinder is to help people find a path. It's really about personal empowerment."

Still, Pathfinder "is a weird idea for a magazine," says Jack Powers, director of the Graphics Research Laboratory in New York City and a publishing consultant on new media technology. Powers says it doesn't make sense to lump all the disparate products of a company together in one online magazine.

Home alone

But there may be a middle ground. HomeArts, a Web site from Hearst New Media & Technology Group, launched in August 1995, is a hybrid of HotWired and Pathfinder in its concept. Its staff (three full-time editors) works closely with the other Hearst magazines to choose material for online publication.

Kathryn Creech, vice president of Hearst New Media & Technology Group and general manager of Home-Arts, says that the site builds on the identities already established by titles such as *Good Housekeeping, Country Living, Redbook* and *Popular Mechanics* by providing home, garden, family and relationship advice. (Hearst also has separate Web sites for two of its publications, *Popular Mechanics* and *Esquire.*) Ultimately, Creech says, the site will also provide content from affiliates such as Books That Work or The Food & Drink Network, in addition to content from advertisers.

"Our job is to really serve the magazines," Creech says. "*Good Housekeeping* has five million subscribers, so they must be doing something right. We want to build on all of that knowledge and put it into new media."

But "long articles don't work because they're easier to read on paper," adds Creech. "For us, expert advice, exchange of information and interactivity are the things that work."

Opportunity knocks

"We don't have a revenue goal or profit goal; we have no stopping place," says Beth Vanderslice, vice president of marketing and strategy at HotWired. She adds that she will not reveal any specific financial information. "HotWired is not seen as a brand extension, it's seen as a once-in-a-lifetime opportunity," she explains. "We see the Internet as equally important as the paradigms of radio and TV, and that's why we're eager to get out there first."

Although not everyone has the revenues to follow HotWired's example, most will agree that Web sites aren't highly lucrative yet, but could prove to be so in the future. There are ways to make money online, but financial strategies are relatively vague, and actual fig-ures are hard to pin down. It's simply too soon to map out clear revenue generators, but there are a few starting places.

Who goes there?

One option is to charge readers registration fees. Many magazines currently require readers to identify themselves before entering sites. Although few sites collect any money, the mechanisms are in place as publications gather demographic information from Net surfers for themselves and their advertisers. But registration has its detractors: Scott Walker, director of The Utne Lens, the *Utne Reader's* Web site, claims registration screens may cause online magazines to lose readers. And HotWired's Anker recently eliminated the registration screen to simplify entry and gather more readers.

"I'm wary of registration right now because the important thing is to show up in the site," Walker says. "About 30 percent will bounce off that registration page because they've lost the password."

Zoom lens

A far cry from shovelware, The Utne Lens is created new by a full-time staff of six. Unlike the print version, which reprints articles from alternative media, The Lens contains two or three original "idea pieces" in each of the site's four areas: community and society; arts, travel and culture; body, mind and spirit; and media and technology. Although this online content may be different from the magazine's content, Walker says The Lens is building on the history of the *Utne Reader* as an information resource —especially since each online story will provide additional information sources.

"The meat of this is identifying key issues and ideas and giving people ways to get more information," Walker says. "I think [the *Utne Reader* and The Lens] share the same basic philosophy and values, but they're very different."

Even so, the two publications will "cross-benefit," each drawing readers to the other. Walker says that, as a single-title company, it's smart to have more than one product because of this potential for mutual benefit—both editorial and financial.

Walker suggests that instead of subscription or registration charges, companies should look into alternative revenue streams such as conferencing fees, or consider merchandising products over the Internet. For example, Walker says, the *Utne Reader* will soon have its own site, separate from The Lens, where readers

■ Where to find it

HotWired
http://www.hotwired.com

Pathfinder
http://pathfinder.com

The Utne Lens
http://www.utne.com

HomeArts
http://homearts.com

Popular Mechanics
http://popularmechanics.com

Esquire
http://www.esquireb2b.com

will pay between $1 and $3 to download an original story from a well-known author.

Profit motive

The most obvious revenue generator is advertising—a relatively new and uncharted territory online. Most of the larger sites have between five and 20 advertisers. With the format so new, rates are low and relatively unstandardized. HotWired, for example, charges advertisers $30,000 for an eight-week stint on the site, but many are so fresh to the game they won't reveal their rates.

"I think there is going to be an increased dollar amount attached to advertising online as it evolves," says Debbie Menfi, vice president and media director of the New York City-based advertising agency Deutsch, Inc. Menfi, who has worked with advertisers on HotWired in the past, says that, generally, products with higher price points like automobiles and financial services are advertised now because readers are willing to spend more time downloading information on these items. Still, she says, "People in publishing are getting out there just to get out there. Once there's a falling out of players, advertisers will be more willing to put more money into [online magazines]."

To each his own

To garner readers and advertisers, publishers have to offer something original. But what constitutes originality is subjective, and each publisher has to clarify his or her company's editorial mission, assess audience needs and weigh financial and staffing limitations. Although the digital medium looks different from the print medium, basic principles still hold true: You need a clear editorial vision, a captive audience, a solid business plan and a talented staff. And remember, today's struggles may engender surprising successes tomorrow. "What is interactive TV?" asks HotWired's Anker. "It very well could be this." □

New media

Get on the Web Now!

BY THOM FORBES

An assignment to compile a list of the top-50 places online had me cruising the nooks of the Internet for three solid weeks. As I reviewed my choices, I discovered one assumption I had made and one conclusion I had drawn. And each has direct bearing on how you build your online business in the cacophonous, competitive world of cyberspace.

My assumption: The World Wide Web is where the action is.

Wherever else you can afford to be in cyberspace, make sure you're on the Web. A few years ago, the Internet wasn't a viable or desirable option for publishers who wanted to develop an online business. However, thanks to the dazzling multimedia browsers based on the National Center for Supercomputing Application's Mosaic, the Internet has become the best option for online ventures.

There's certainly lots of valuable material, including some magazine brands, on the commercial services. I like *Business Week*'s site on America Online, *Newsweek* on Prodigy (when I'm near a non-Mac computer) and *New York Magazine* on CompuServe. But readers must subscribe to the individual services in order to see those digizines, while almost all the material on the Web is open to anyone.

The commercial services are easy onramps to cyberspace, but supportive Internet service providers are proliferating and getting less expensive. Even though the Web is now available through the commercial services' own browsers, most of their material is closed to non-subscriber traffic *from* the Web.

It would be great if you could afford to be on every service as well as the Web, but—trust me on this—you can't. Some services paid a few magazines a lot of money to lure their print readers online—but those deals are history.

The big bucks from now on will be for original concepts and content that exploit the capabilities of new media. AOL paid $11 million to acquire *Global Network Navigato*r, the first commercial digizine on the Web,

from Sebastopol, California-based O'Reilly & Associates. Not bad for a start-up.

My conclusion: Traditional magazines have a lot of catching up to do.

Because of my affection for print, I was surprised to find that so few newspapers and magazines were represented on my top-50 list. In fact, Reed Elsevier's *Travel Weekly* was the only traditional print publication with its own site among my top-25 choices, although *Paris Review* and *Publishers Weekly* were represented in other sites I admired (The Voyager Co., http:// www.voyagerco.com/, and BookWire, http://www.bookwire.com/, respectively).

I mention the sites ranked 25 to 50 in passing; Time-Warner's Pathfinder (http:// pathfinder.com), which includes all the Time Inc. magazines, was one. A lot of thought and resources are being poured into Pathfinder. It's notoriously slow and disjointed. However, I'm betting that Pathfinder will someday be mentioned with the same respect for tenacity that's usually reserved for the launch of *Sports Illustrated* 40 years ago.

I found that the better Web sites, whether they are by magazines or not, almost always have some elements in common. These may seem elementary to many of you at this stage of the game, but these guidelines bear repeating.

- Provide original content. Don't just shovel material from your print product.
- Be interactive. The main reason people go online is to communicate with others. Set up an address for feedback, and respond quickly. Better yet, set up an online forum where readers and editors can discuss the topics you cover.
- Maintain the site vigorously. Unless you freshen the content and keep the conversation relevant, viewers will not return.
- Exploit your multimedia capabilities. Graphics. Video. Sound. Hyperlinks. Incorporate all other media (as long as it doesn't take too long to download).
- Get management behind your Web effort, just as you would on any project.   □

Initial Web-site Costs Can Be Nearly Nil

BY THOM FORBES

The emerging business models for creating an effective online presence can seem daunting to publishers who remain doubters. Fears of squandering time and money are real. But Reed Travel Group's *Travel Weekly* ignored the fears, sidestepped the conventional approaches—and is nevertheless doing quite well.

Corporate indifference

In May 1995, the Secaucus, New Jersey-based twice-weekly magazine opened a World Wide Web site that has little original content, limited interactivity and no multimedia or graphics. It is updated just once a week, and got off the ground primarily because of corporate indifference. But the *Travel Weekly* experience illustrates an important concept as publishers venture online: Although costs will increase, and making money is not guaranteed, start-up costs can be low.

Guerrilla approach or not, *Travel Weekly* has one of the best magazine-based sites out there. And any magazine able to spare a clever, HTML-proficient staffer for 20 hours a week could do as well.

Seven months prior to the May launch, *Travel Weekly* had brought in a new technology editor, David Vis. Vis had access to the Web through a personal account with NovaLink Interactive Services (http://www.novalink.com/), an Internet service provider. He began to look for travel-related Web sites in his free time.

There were dozens of them, he quickly realized, but each had its own agenda. Some hyperlinked to a few other travel sites on the Internet, but none to all of them. Hyperlinks—if you click on highlighted words, you are transported to a new site—are the strands that form the "web." Sites welcome links from elsewhere because it's the prime way to build traffic, but an airline is not likely to link to its main competitors.

Vis, with the help of Orest Kinasevych, a *Travel Weekly* page-production person who knows the Web's Hypertext Markup Language (HTML), organized the existing Web travel sites into distinct categories and set up hyperlinks to them. All this went no further than Vis' own screen, however, until he demonstrated the new site (http://www.nova link.com/travel/) to Reed execu-

tives—who were impressed. NovaLink, which was eager for content, initially provided *Travel Weekly* with free space on its Web server; it now charges $1,000 a month.

Vis has divided the site into 12 logically arrayed areas, such as U.S. destinations, world destinations, travel agents and adventure. A news area is updated weekly with briefs gleaned from the group's magazines. Wry, informative one-liners describe the content within each area and the quality of the nearly 500 hotlinked sites. These pithy descriptions are the extent of the original editorial content, but they are as essential to Web travelers as traffic lights in midtown. In addition, the design is elegant but simple. The graphical icons load quickly; the viewer never feels lost.

Four months after the May launch, with almost no promotion, about 5,000 people were visiting the *Travel Weekly* home page each week. Vis was receiving about 30 pieces of e-mail—the only interactive component of the site—a day. Vis responded to all the messages personally.

Meanwhile, in July, Reed established a market development division under Jerry R. Landress, a former Ziff-Davis and CMP executive, to explore opportunities online and off. Landress says that industry advertisers want to know when they can advertise on the site, and when similar areas will be developed for other segments.

The site, Vis says, "was almost a wildcat project outside the normal chain of command." But expectations are now as high as its origins were modest. Some options being considered are registering viewers, adding a searchable editorial database (with, perhaps, a customized news service), and putting up advertisers.

"The next phase of the game is not cheap," Landress admits, but the first few innings were, as Vis says, "peanuts"—a couple of grand to NovaLink, three Internet access accounts at a combined $85 a month, and $99 for a modem.

The response to Travel Weekly Online offers clear lessons. Forget about paradigms and fears. Get a grip on your subject and your audience, link up with a techhead, and plunge ahead. If you address a need and deliver what you promise, the viewers will come—and you'll quickly learn a lot about where this business is heading. ☐

New media

Create a Winning Internet Version Of Your Magazine

BY STEFAN SHARKANSKY

Putting your magazine online doesn't have to mean joining CompuServe or America Online. Many publications that have launched Internet ventures have implemented their own systems, relying heavily on internal resources.

The World Wide Web

The most visible feature of the Internet is probably the World Wide Web. The Web is currently the best way to deliver text, graphics and some interactive capability.

To implement your own Web site, you'll need a high-end UNIX workstation, such as a Sun Microsystems SPARCstation 20. The list price for a SPARC 20 with minimal disk space is under $20,000. UNIX systems are not plug-and-play, however. You will need trained personnel to install and operate the system. Graphics-intensive Web sites are the most compelling, but demand a high-speed Internet connection; a T1 digital phone line is preferable. Start-up costs for a T1 line are $6,000 to $10,000, plus $1,500 or so a month in operating costs. MCI, Sprint and Alternet are among the companies that offer T1 Internet service.

The basic software for delivering Web data and answering user requests is a HyperText Transfer Protocol Daemon, or HTTPD. The most widely used HTTPDs are freely available from academic centers such as the University of Illinois. Additional software is required to perform special functions. Posting existing content and back-issues on the Web calls for filter software to convert documents into HTML, a standard language for Web data. Filters exist for popular formats such as FrameMaker and RTF, but if your magazine uses Quark you may need to write a custom filter. This isn't as bad as it sounds. Bear in mind that the most compelling Web content is not reformatted print articles, but interactive, original material created specifically for the Internet.

A simple Web site can store its data in ordinary files. If you have thousands of documents online, you'll want a relational database. Off-the-shelf Web servers, such as Netscape Communications' Netsite, are built on relational databases. You can also implement a custom solution using a commercial database such as Oracle or Sybase. A search engine integrated with your content database and HTTPD helps users locate information. Companies such as Personal Library Software, WAIS Inc. and Verity produce software that can perform sophisticated text searches of large bodies of documents.

Many online magazine sites feature a message board or newsgroup where users can send interactive letters to the editor and engage in discussions with magazine staff. To set one up, try Hypermail from Enterprise Integration Technologies. Keep track of who logs on.

> Don't limit yourself to one of the online services, or even just the Web. Build a site that encompasses the entire Internet.

Establishing a subscriber database lets you charge for content and restrict usage by password. It also enables you to offer your users personalized Web pages, which can be updated to send tailored information and advertising.

Once you've set up these basics, just turn the software on and let it do the work.

The problem now is letting people know you're there. One way to publicize a new online magazine is through The Electronic Newsstand.

Not the Web

A Web site is essentially a passive venture for the publisher, as interaction must be user-initiated. There are other, more active facets of the Internet. Electronic mail offers numerous possibilities. The number of people with e-mail access is estimated at 30 million worldwide, approximately 10 times the current Web audience. Plus, Web users can get information only when they proactively ask for it. With e-mail, the publisher can deliver information to subscribers. Mailing-list software, such as Listproc or Majordomo, is available on the Internet but may require customization for commercial use. (There is a Catch-22 here. Sending unsolicited marketing e-mail is a big taboo in cyberspace. Be careful to send e-mail only to those who have requested inclusion on your mailing list.)

Another form of Internet communications is chat, or real-time discussion groups. In chat, an editor can host an Internet version of a talk show, interviewing guests and fielding questions from users. Internet Chat software is widely available.

How do we make money from this? By advertising. If you sell goods online, you're faced with a plethora of competing payment schemes, none of which is widely adopted and most of which require special software. One payment plan without special software is First Virtual Holdings. Anyone with a credit card and e-mail can use First Virtual to buy information. Its main drawback is that it can be used to sell information only, not physical wares.

Although implementing an Internet site may seem intimidating, the problems are not insurmountable. Yes, costs are a big variable. A systems integrator might charge $500,000 to develop a complete system. But much of the basic software is available free, and some of the most successful sites owe their existence to college interns who can't yet legally drink beer. And, the Internet publisher's job will get easier as more magazine-oriented products come to market. □

 New media

Web Offers Many Resources
For Publishers

BY JEFF LAURIE

The Web is a great source for information retrieval, but surfing can eat up valuable time. Because it's easy to get distracted by the cornucopia of attractions at your fingertips, you must develop a strategic approach to finding what you need. One of the following Web-search engines will be useful.

Yahoo: This is a comprehensive catalog of the World Wide Web, organized by subject, at http://www.yahoo.com.

Lycos: The major advantages of Lycos, at http://www.lycos.com, are that it lets you perform searches by keyword, and gives you a short abstract of what's at the site.

OpenText: This keyword engine is known for its speed, at http://www.opentext.com.

URL-minder: Described as "Your Own Personal Web Robot," at http://www.netmind. com/URL-minder, this tool is an intelligent agent that sends you e-mail each time it detects a change in the Web pages you register with it. This allows you to keep up with a large number of sites without having to surf.

DejaNews Research Service: Located at http://www.deja news.com, this service does a keyword search of Usenet, the Internet's vast collection of discussion areas. (These areas are called forums, bulletin boards or special-interest groups in other online venues.) DejaNews lets you quickly home in on the latest talk on the specific topics you target.

Take action

In addition to offering search capabilities, the Web can assist you in daily tasks. One example comes from Webb Howell, president of Journalistic, Inc., a Durham, North Carolina, publisher. "I was in Montreal this summer and needed to see the art for an upcoming cover. We didn't have time to overnight a color proof, so we posted the comp on a Web page. I dialed into the page and got to look at it. It wasn't like seeing it in the flesh, but it was much better than faxing."

The Web is a particularly rich environment for design and production professionals. Boston freelance designer Dwight Ingram recommends visiting the Global Prepress Center at http://www.ledet.com/prepress. This excellent site has links to software, clip art, photography and more.

It's worth your time to look at font supplier Esselte Letraset's Ripper Web page located at http://www. esselte.com/letraset. In addition to visiting a showcase of fonts, clip art and background photography, you can type in sample text and see it displayed in any of Letraset's 300 Fontek fonts.

Seymour, located at http://www. pniltd.com, contains more than 300,000 high-quality, copyrighted photographs from 42 sources. In a single session, you can search and download low-res comp images, and price, license and accept delivery of high-resolution image files.

Something for everyone

Designers and production managers aren't the only magazine professionals who can take advantage of the Web. Here's a quick sampling of how some other departments might benefit from online resources.

Editorial: Editors can use the Web to make human connections; it can be a great source for new writers and new material. "We routinely scan forums, newsgroups and mailing lists for interesting topics and new people qualified to write about them," Howell notes.

Circulation: The Web currently has more promise than push in this area, but several resources are developing. The U.S. Postal Service has a site at http://www.usps.gov. It won't knock your socks off, but it contains a library of reference material that might answer a question or two. Standard Rate and Data has a site in development at http://www.srds.com, but it's not up as of this writing. And the Audit Bureau of Circulations has an informative site at http://www.access abc.com.

Marketing: Lew McCreary, editor in chief and publisher of IDG's *WebMaster*, pays close attention to competitors' and advertisers' Web sites to gain a marketing edge. "We use the Web to see what our competitors are doing,," he says. "And we look at potential advertisers' Web sites for insights that could be effective in sales presentations."

Magazine professionals can check out http://www. media central.com, from Cowles Business Media (*Folio:*'s parent company) to access a host of marketing and publishing services from *Folio:, Pre, Inside Media, Catalog Age* and other CBM titles. □

Seven Ways to Lure Readers
To Your Junction of Cyberspace

BY THOM FORBES

In real estate, value depends on location, location, location. Online, it's linking, linking, linking. There are nearly 200,000 sites on the Web, and new strands are being spun at a rate that even the most industrious of spiders would envy. Linking increases your profile and the chances that potential readers and customers will happen upon you as they cruise randomly through the Internet. Linking allows you to establish natural alliances with providers of related information. And linking usually costs nothing. The more sites there are that not only mention your site but also code the reference so that readers can get there with a click of the mouse, the more visitors you'll get. Here are the best ways to lure readers to your particular junction of cyberspace, through linking and other methods.

Get indexed. List your site on the various searchable metasites whose raison d'être is to categorize other sites. It's best to fill out each site's individual form. If you don't have the time, or just need a list of what they are, several Web sites allow you to fill out basic information about your pages and then transmit it to the metasites. Here are three: Pointer To Pointers; Submit It!; and Postmaster. (*See box below for URLs*). Post to each metasite only once.

Use cyber PR services. All metasites are not created equal, says Eric Ward, whose The Ward Group/NetPost service conducts "comprehensive Internet media-awareness campaigns." Ward tailors the information he sends to indices, editors and newsgroups that are individually selected for each client. Fees range from $395 to $895.

For a handy compilation of other free and fee-based posting services, see Web Diamonds #9, Marketing Your Web Site.

Link unto others. For many publishers, links to relevant pages at other sites are key editorial elements. It's not only courteous to inform the Webmasters at sites to which you link—it's also good business.

"I send a brief standard notice to the sites to which I have linked on my pages. This usually guarantees at least one visit and gives my site exposure to a Web professional who might in turn publicize my site," says Bob Poulsen, a Web-page designer who maintains a list of printed publications on the Web at Ecola's Newsstand.

Send e-mail updates. One way to keep surfers coming back is to let them know when you've updated your site. It's also a clever way to build a demographic database because recipients must register to receive the e-mail. Time Warner's Pathfinder, for example, sends out a weekly "Compass," with short descriptions of what has been added to all of its sites.

Participate in online discussions. There are probably dozens of newsgroups, forums, e-mail lists and live chats that discuss topics your title covers. Monitor groups before posting, keep your messages on-topic, and don't be too promotional.

> Links allow you to establish alliances with providers of related information. They provide editorial elements for your site. And they often cost nothing.

Search for relevant Usenet newsgroups at Deja News Research Service; for e-mail discussion groups, check out Inter-Links. Deja News also lets you search postings by key words.

Use your signature effectively. Include your site's URL—the ungainly address that begins with http://—in your signature and include a descriptive kicker ("Wyoming's Top Grunge Journal") to entice readers every time you post to an online discussion or send e-mail.

Remember ink and paper. Some magazines bury their online address in agate type in the masthead. This is definitely the wrong approach. Take a page from HotWired, which gets plenty of free publicity but relentlessly promotes its online address with house ads in *Wired*. You should also put your URL on business cards, rate cards and other material.

Write to other publications. Whenever *Iowa City's* managing editor reads a story about Web publishing, she writes a letter thanking the publication for educating the public about the new media. "I then describe what Iowa City Online is doing," says Nina Lentini. "Voilà, free publicity." (It obviously worked with us.)

The bottom line: If you build it, they will come at least once—but only if you give them explicit directions to the front door through a proactive PR policy and, especially, linking. □

■ **Sites mentioned**

Pointer To Pointers:
http://www.homecom.com/global/pointers.html

Submit It!:
http://www.submit-it.com/

Postmaster:
http://www.netcreations.com/postmaster/index.html

The Ward Group/NetPost:
http://www.netpost.com

Web Diamonds #9:
http://www.interlog.com/~bxi/diamonds.htm

Ecola's Newsstand:
http://www.ecola.com/ez/newshome.htm

Pathfinder:
http://pathfinder.com

Deja News Research Service:
http://www.dejanews.com/

Inter-Links:
http://www.nova.edu/Inter-Links/listserv.html

HotWired:
http://www.hotwired.com

Iowa City Online:
http://www.wcci.com/icmag/

Interactive Mags: Easy as 1-800

BY DAVID FRENKEL

Want to help your readers get follow-up information and sales support in minutes, and help advertisers quickly obtain and cheaply process pre-qualified leads? The technology for combining off-the-shelf, computer-based, touch-tone phone interactive voice response systems and fax-back services is here and proven.

Replacing the cost and slowness of bingo cards with an 800-number service significantly shortens the selling cycle and cuts costs for both publisher and advertiser. The reader gets better service and can begin to rely on your magazine as a first choice for assisting in important buying decisions.

The idea is simple: Using an 800 number, a reader can dial in and enter article or ad-based inquiry numbers via a touch-tone telephone. The system will ask a few lead-qualifying questions and fax back additional information to the reader immediately. The publisher can then provide these qualified leads to the advertiser.

Costs of interactive voice response (IVR) systems have dropped dramatically over the past few years following the introduction of a number of PC-based systems that, with the addition of IVR boards and software, can support close to 50 concurrent phone sessions on a single PC. Base hardware and software (before customizing expenses) for a four-phone-line input/single fax output system start at around $25,000. Such a system can conduct four concurrent phone sessions while simultaneously transmitting a fax.

A system based on a single PC can grow comfortably to as many as 48 phone lines and four fax outlets. A 48-line/four-fax system (before customizing) will cost $90,000. Multiple PCs can provide growth beyond this. Customizing and integration charges are highly variable, depending on what you want the system to do and where you want to connect it, but a full system, including software and customizing, can be set up for less than $100,000.

> An interactive voice response system based on a single PC can grow comfortably to as many as 48 phone lines and four fax outlets.

To help you assess the cost and the operational savings, a qualified systems integrator/consultant can work with you to define the current requirements and future direction. From there, a project plan, schedule and budget can be prepared and, after management approval, implemented. It is vital to establish clear objectives up front so that all parties will be able to agree on when the project has been completed. This may sound obvious, but it is frequently overlooked in new applications.

Not just a trade thing

Other IVR services can include a premium news summary fax service delivered on a more frequent basis than the regular publication's schedule. Each item in a one-page headline summary of important news and new products can be tagged with a number. Readers can call in and through IVR select the items about which they want more detail; the system then automatically faxes that information back. Select article reprints could be similarly provided.

In consumer magazines, advertisers can use the bulk of print space for their main message and implement a dealer-locating 800-number service attended by an IVR system. By entering a phone number and/or Zip Code, the reader can be directed to the closest dealer or store. The phone call can even be automatically directed to the store and the inquiry recorded in a database. This inquiry information will provide a rich database of response data, adding new demographic lead information to a publisher's market-research knowledge pool.

Other facets of IVR systems include the ability to offer materials in a variety of languages and the ability to link to existing systems such as subscription databases. Automated account status and renewal can also be engineered, as can text-to-speech conversion, where a computer reads out text. □

The Mysterious Business Of Web Sales

BY HANNA RUBIN

When New York City newsletter publisher WebTracks released its list of the top-10 Web publishers ranked by fourth-quarter 1995 ad revenues, you didn't need to be a statistician to interpret the numbers. The Web sites of only two print publishers made the cut: Time Inc.'s Pathfinder and *Wired's* breakaway Hot-Wired. Neither ranked above fifth place. The bottom line? Extending advertiser relationships from print products to the Web is a tough sell.

In spite of this challenge, magazine-based Web sites launch nearly every week. With the rules changing every day, there are no absolute answers about how to sell cyberspace, but at least the key issues are clear.

It's a hit!

The most hotly disputed question is how to measure your audience. Agencies used to buying readers on a cost-per-thousand (CPM) basis or buying viewers via Nielsen points expect equivalent measurement systems for a site's traffic.

Most advertisers make volume their main criterion, according to James Kennedy, managing editor of "InterAd Monthly," the WebTrack newsletter that created the top-10 list. "Right now, advertisers want sheer numbers," he says. "That's why Web search engines like Netscape [which nabbed first place on the WebTrack list] have the winning hand when it comes to advertisers who are looking for the safest way to experiment with a new medium." (Kennedy admits that his survey had to make "some big assumptions." Chief was that advertisers paid the full stated rate.)

Cyberspace technology has limitations when it comes to keeping tabs on the number of Net surfers, however. Although the file servers that host Web sites constantly gather information about hits, there are limits to their capabilities. If, for instance, entries to a site arrive via a proxy server (as do all that come through commercial online services such as America Online and CompuServe), they are recorded as one single entry in the course of a day—although in fact they represent thousands of individual users. Similarly, companies that have many personnel online may create a "firewall" that is designed to protect against unauthorized access. Dial-ups through the firewall then register on the server's log as one entry rather than dozens.

The medium's initial attempts at self-tracking, tainted by extravagant claims for the number of hits, backfired. The miscounts stemmed from file servers' logs totting up every element on a page as a hit, so that one request for a visually elaborate home page could score six or seven times. "Hits are less than useful," says Kate Delhagen, ad manager for Starwave, the Seattle company that creates and sells *Outside's* site. "Now people want to know 'pages viewed' or 'actual minutes spent.'"

Ad agencies burned by initial overcounts now seek the kind of ratebase assurances they get from magazines. "We want to know the number of impressions and if a company will guarantee them," says Hunter Madsen, director of J. Walter Thompson/ San Francisco's Interactive Enterprise unit. "There are few hard numbers and lots of chutzpah. A lot of people don't know how to price sites. We get every manner of price unconnected to CPM."

Although many Web publishers believe cyber ad space shouldn't be compared to the magazine model, some—including Delhagen—have signed with San Francisco-based Nielsen partner I/PRO or one of its competitors to "validate" logs. Television-viewer measurement can provide only a partial model for Web-surfer tallies, however. "Agencies are frustrated because the tools are not similar to what they've been used to," says I/PRO's director of sales Kevin Doerr. "The Web is a random medium. You get different people at different times of day. What we should be looking for is interactivity."

Once the numbers are in, how to evaluate them is another bear. "No one wants to devalue users or overvalue them," says Doerr. Lurking in the background, of course, is the issue of demographics. "What would you pay for a hard-to-reach audience?" Madsen asks. "The idea of targeting a site is important."

In the freewheeling cyberspace culture, however, some publishers fear that asking site visitors to sign up will inhibit activity. "To get user demos, you have to register people to your site, and that creates too many hassles for them," says Bill Congdon, marketing director for PM Zone, *Popular Mechanics'* site.

Some highly targeted magazine-based sites claim to have found a way around the demographics issue. "The Web is not really an eyeballs business, although right now it's being sold that way," says David Shnaider, vice president and general manager of Ziff-Davis Internet, a site created by Ziff-Davis, which publishes such magazines as *Computer Life* and *PCWeek*. Shnaider uses his audience's computer focus as a major selling point, relying partly on demographic information gathered from a percentage of the site's visitors who register for special features. He says, however, that the computer advertisers he woos are less interested in demographic information on Net surfers than other types of marketers. "They know people don't come to ZD Net for cheesecake pictures. We're a special-interest site."

ZD Net offers advertisers quarterly packages ranging from $4,475 to $39,975, depending on the degree of visibility. Current advertisers include IBM and AT&T; Shnaider says ZD Net's fourth-quarter ad revenues hit $800,000.

On the links

Figuring out what options to offer advertisers poses as much of a problem as what's being delivered. Should a site provide hotlinks to an advertiser's cyberspace address? Should site advertising be lumped into a value-added package with the magazine's print pages?

"Right now, most advertisers want traffic driven to their Web sites," says Congdon. He has a hotlink banner program that currently features Toyota. Although PM Zone's rate card requires $19,500 for two months of exposure, it's hard to pin down exactly what marketers are actually paying because even one page in *Popular Mechanics* immediately entitles them to a 15 percent discount.

Some site publishers see little value in links. "We don't want to become a link-o-rama," says Jim Cornick, publisher of Meredith Corp.'s *Successful Farming*. Cornick, who handles the business side of the magazine's Agriculture Online Web site, adds, "Once they're in your site, why send them someplace else?"

"There is real revenue out there. It may be small, but if you're not playing, you should be."

Not everyone agrees. "Advertising on the Web offers a unique opportunity to develop a relationship with a customer. If you don't let advertisers link to your site, you're going against what the Web is all about. If you have a good site, you're only losing the person temporarily," says Ziff's Shnaider.

"A lot of what advertisers are buying is the ability to jump our customer to their site," says Delhagen. Outside Online offers hotlinks in a two-tier package. Advertisers get what Delhagen dubs "a franchise position." Only that company's banner—including a hotlink—will appear on a page that receives a high traffic volume, such as the Table of Contents. The second part of the package comprises a "run-of-service" offer featuring the ad on a rotating basis throughout the site. "It means advertisers get a deep slice plus a broad swath," explains Delhagen. Although the structure sounds complex, the pricing is simple: $6,000 for three months. Current advertisers include Eastern Mountain Sports, Gatorade and Levi's.

Alternatives range from free space to free content. "Often, if we get a hotlink, we negotiate it for free with the link working both ways," explains Ingrid Ocanas, who is on Madsen's new-media team at J. Walter Thompson. "We've offered clients to Web sites, which the sites can carry for free to see if they generate traffic. We view it essentially as a test. Big-name ads enhance the impression that a site is a going concern."

Successful Farming's Agriculture Online offers a shrewd variation on this gambit. "We're trying to build partnerships with people who can provide content," says Cornick. His site features weather, news and market information vital to farmers, all bartered with companies that specialize in agricultural data. "They give us content; we give them space. We also give them an opportunity to sell added-value services like a newsletter." One such barter agreement is with Freese-Notis, a private Des Moines-based weather service that creates custom reports for agribusiness.

Cornick offers advertisers a version of Delhagen's two-tier package, with costlier slots on the Table of Contents page at $6,000 per month, and a lower rate for banners on less-popular pages. He has even created online classifieds, set to launch March 1. In the works are contracts with Cargill, a grain processor, and Agco, a machinery company.

Cornick plans eventually to charge membership fees for aspects of Agriculture Online that he deems premium services, such as weather updates. The site posts few articles from the magazine, focusing instead on hour-by-hour information that a monthly can't offer.

You talking to me?

While most publishers have mastered the art of making client presentations, the Web adds a new dimension: "If you log me on to your page, what you're showing me is the customer's experience, not what I need as a media professional," says Madsen.

Frustrated by inadequate online media kits, Madsen and Ocanas developed a checklist they send publishers pitching their sites. Key questions include, "How long has the site been up?" "How often do you refresh it?" "What do you do to bring people back?" and "How many levels is it?"

Few magazines' online media kits deliver this amount of detail, although some come close. PM Zone's kit, for instance, features a slick showing certain key pages with a description of how often each is updated, as well as a list of sponsorship opportunities and PC and Mac demo disks. PM Zone's Congdon still believes that logging someone on remains the most dramatic way to present the site. "To bring the medium to life, it's best to go live," he explains. This approach recently netted him the U.S. Army account as part of a package that included nine pages in *Popular Mechanics*.

Shnaider takes the process a step further with dummy creative. "We prepare creative treatments in advance showing advertisers what their banner could look like. It brings the situation to life," he says. ZD Net has its own sales force, although the site is also offered in a package with magazine pages.

With so many aspects of launching a magazine on the Web still uncertain, does it make sense to do it? "Online budgets at agencies are minimal if they exist at all," acknowledges Delhagen. "Still, there's real revenue out there. It may be small, but if you're not playing, you should be." ☐

Libel's Cold, Dark Shadow

BY SLADE METCALF

How often have you heard the expression that libel suits have "a chilling effect" on the ability of a magazine to cover the news? Libel suits come in all shapes and sizes. They can be serious, extraordinarily time-consuming—and very costly. At other times, they can be handled relatively quickly and inexpensively. But while a libel suit may be an irritating cost of doing business to a wealthy, large media conglomerate, it can be life threatening to the small, independently owned magazine.

Some smaller publishers have insurance that covers at least their legal fees for the duration of the suit. However, it is unusual for a small, independent publisher to have coverage in excess of $1,000,000. And that amount has to take care of both the costs of defending the case and any settlement or judgment. Under most insurance policies, as the attorneys' fees build up, the money left to cover settlements or judgments decreases. Publishers who have been through the unpleasantness of a libel suit know only too well that expenses for pretrial discovery, trial preparation, actual trial work and any appeals continue to mount and mount.

One libel suit involving a newsletter provides some insight into the lengthy—and costly—procedures sometimes needed before a case can finally be resolved. It involves a scientist who worked at the Frederick Cancer Research Center, which was performing experiments for the National Cancer Institute (NCI). The scientist, Melvin Reuber, had conducted experimental work during the 1970s on the carcinogenicity of certain chemicals, including pesticides. He apparently emphasized his ability to determine accurately the carcinogenicity of certain chemicals. In particular, he studied an insecticide known as malathion, and found it to be carcinogenic. This finding was in contrast to the official position of the National Cancer Institute, which had determined that malathion was not, in fact, carcinogenic.

Reuber prepared an unpublished manuscript that he apparently began to distribute to certain people at about the time (1980-81) of an infestation of the Mediterranean fruit fly in California. Reuber's manuscript, which was prepared independently of his regular work for the National Cancer Institute, was sent out with an address of "NCI, Frederick Cancer Research Center, Frederick, Maryland" below his name.

A letter of rebuke

On learning of the distribution of this manuscript, Reuber's supervisor at the research center sent Reuber a letter reprimanding him for supposed professional misconduct. The letter stated, "You have operated under the guise of the endorsement of both NCI and the . . . Frederick Cancer Research Center. These obstreperous actions have had a multimillion-dollar implication, giving the impression that the NCI may be administering programs of questionable competency."

Copies of the letter were somehow leaked to people outside the research center and NCI, and one copy ultimately reached the editor of "Pesticide and Toxic Chemical News" (PTCN), a Washington, D.C.-based newsletter with approximately 1,300 subscribers seeking information on pesticides and toxic chemicals, owned by Food Chemical News, Inc.

PTCN subsequently published an article about the letter (April 1981) and reprinted most of the letter's contents. Nine days later, Reuber resigned his job on the advice of his physician. He then sued the publisher of PTCN for libel, based on the newsletter's contents. The jury awarded him $625,000 in compensatory damages and $250,000 in punitive damages.

Thereafter the publisher appealed, but the award was upheld by the appellate court in 1990. However, there is a procedure in federal courts by which a party who loses the appeal before a three-judge panel can obtain a rehearing on a federal appellate court sitting in what is called *en banc*.

In October 1990, the publisher of PTCN argued the case before 11 judges in the federal appellate court in Richmond, Virginia, and in February 1991, the court, by a 7 to 4 vote, reversed the decision and dismissed the case.

The *en banc* court found that Mr. Reuber was a public figure under the libel law, since he had injected himself into the public controversy involving the carcinogenic nature of insecticides, and that the editorial staff at the newsletter did not have serious doubts about the truth of the allegations about Reuber contained in the letter from his supervisor.

Although the publisher of "Pesticide and Toxic Chemical News" was ultimately vindicated in performing his publication's First Amendment task of airing controversial issues, the costs must have been enormous, based on the fact that the case went to trial and through two separate appeals. (I would speculate that the legal fees alone probably were more than a half-million dollars.) Publishers with less capital or no insurance coverage would have been hard pressed to survive.

A unique protection

Smaller publishers who publish and are sued in New York are entitled to protection not available to publishers in most other states. New York has adopted a standard called "gross irresponsibility" that requires a libel plaintiff to show that a publisher acted in a "grossly irresponsible manner without due consideration for the standards of information gathering ordinarily followed by reasonable parties."

In other words, a publisher must have ignored certain obvious methods of verification or be placed on notice in advance of publication that certain articles were untrue. This standard becomes particularly helpful if the magazine relies on freelancers for preparation of its articles.

In one case, the magazine *Musician, Player & Listener* (at that time owned by Amordian Press of New York City), which had an editorial staff of fewer than five people, carried an article in its October 1980 issue titled "Jimi Hendrix—The Voodoo Lives On."

The freelancer, in discussing Hendrix's background, referred to Hendrix's manager by writing that Hendrix had "been forced to sign a $1 contract with an unbe-

Some observers have argued that corporations and trade groups have focused their libel litigation on smaller publishers.

lievably unscrupulous character [the manager], who later won 2 percent of his record royalties and the right to the *Band of Gypsies* live album in an out-of-court settlement because Hendrix's management-controlled lawyers weren't willing to mount a substantial fight."

The manager subsequently sued the freelancer and the magazine for libel. A court review of the contract that Hendrix had signed raised considerable question as to whether Hendrix would receive only $1.

The court refused to dismiss the case against the freelancer, but did dismiss the case against the magazine publisher on the grounds that there was no factual dispute that the publisher had complied with ordinary journalistic standards in relying wholly on the reputation and integrity of the freelancer regarding the accuracy of the information in the article. As it was, the magazine's small editorial staff relied extensively on freelancers for articles and the accuracy of those articles.

Making the choice

With the ever increasing size of jury awards, it is inevitable that publishers of small magazines and newsletters will be very concerned as to the contentiousness of certain articles. Some publishers and editors, when confronted with the choice of a multi-million-dollar libel suit or watering down certain sentences (or, even worse, not doing a story at all), may choose the easy and more financially secure way out.

Some commentators have even argued that some corporations and trade associations have focused their libel litigation strategies on the smaller publishers in the belief that it is easier to block legitimate discussion through intimidation and litigation.

It can only be hoped that this tactic will be resisted at every turn.   □

Publishing law

The Letters Page Is Not Risk-free

BY SLADE METCALF

Over the years, a number of editors have asked me, "Do I have to treat letters to the editor just like regular articles in my magazine?" The answer—which comes as a surprise to many—is an unequivocal yes. A publisher is not relieved of the need to follow basic, elementary rules to protect himself from legal claims just because it is a reader whose comments are being printed.

The most common area of concern involves potential libel claims. Many letters reflect a reader's heartfelt, yet often caustic, evaluation of another person's conduct, thoughts or products. Identifying these views as those of the reader does not protect a publisher from a successful libel suit brought by the person attacked in the letter. To avoid liability, the magazine must take the same steps to verify the accuracy of the statements in the letter that it would with any article.

For example, if a reader writes a letter about a recent article on drug use in the workplace, and states that a colleague in her office has been using cocaine for several months, the publisher is obliged to investigate the accuracy of the statement. Most responsible editors would know, without having to consult an attorney, that such a signed letter could not be published without some investigation.

How about a little more difficult example? Let's say the magazine prints an article about the growing ecological dangers posed by the timber industry. A reader sends in a letter that says, "In my opinion, the timber company my brother works for has caused untold damage to the streams in our state." In reading this sentence, an editor might think, "Well, the reader is expressing his opinion and the timber company is unnamed; we can publish it without any investigation."

Not so fast. First, just because the letter writer claims he is expressing his opinion does not make it so. The question of whether a sentence amounts to a statement of fact (that can be proven true or false) or is a supported expression of opinion (thus being protected) has recently become a more sensitive, intricate issue of law over which judges and lawyers fiercely disagree.

Second, although the timber company's name is not mentioned in the letter, it could still be identified. Many citizens in the town where the company is located may know that the writer's brother works for XYZ Timber Co., meaning the townspeople will be able to pinpoint that company as the alleged polluter.

Here are some guidelines to help magazine publishers satisfy their legal obligations, making it less likely that they will be successfully sued for libel.

Be wary of letters that attack persons or companies not regularly in the limelight. The amount of substantiation needed to support defamatory allegations is less when the letter relates to a public official or public figure than when a letter criticizes a private person. In the latter case, the publisher is generally obliged to conduct a reasonable investigation into the truth of the criticism.

Think beyond your local area. Remember that you can be sued in any state where your magazine is distributed. New York law is particularly hospitable to publishers, but the vast majority of states require publishers to undertake more investigation than New York requires.

Don't rely on opinion. Although a letter may sound like the writer's opinion (and we all believe that someone has a right to express his or her opinion), courts will generally examine the caustic statement to determine whether or not it can be proven true or false. If it can, then it is not protected opinion and must be investigated like any potentially libelous statement in an article.

Take steps to verify the truth of the critical statements. What can you do? First, it's a good idea to require letter writers to include their phone numbers. Have your researcher call the writer and go over the letter in detail. If there is an accusation of criminal—or even questionable—activity on the part of another person or company, ask the letter writer what his or her access was to the

> Once a letter is published, the magazine assumes an obligation to ensure its accuracy.

information. Did he or she read it in a newspaper? Does he or she have corporate documents to support the charge? Did he or she overhear it at a cocktail party?

Second, it is important to cross-check that the writer is actually who he or she says. Call directory assistance to confirm that the phone number is accurate. Call the writer's employer to verify that he or she works there. You might even consider calling a neighbor to check on the writer's bona fides.

Third, if you are determined to publish the letter, have your researcher undertake independent investigation. Check newspaper and magazine clips about charges in the letter. Call law enforcement authorities. Call the person or company identified in the letter to verify facts.

Fourth, you may want to contact the person attacked in the letter to solicit a response to be published in the same letters column. This approach became an integral aspect of a significant libel suit arising from a letter to the editor. In January 1983, the *Journal of Medical Primatology* received a letter to the editor written by Dr. Shirley McGreal, at that time the chairwoman of the International Primate Protection League, which advocates on behalf of primates—particularly those used for biomedical research.

The letter criticized a plan by Immuno A.G., an Austria-based company, to establish a facility in Sierra Leone for hepatitis research using chimpanzees. (Immuno A.G. manufactures biologic products derived from blood plasma.) The letter claimed that (a) the motivation for the plan was to avoid international policies or legal restrictions on the importation of chimpanzees, an endangered species; (b) that the plan could decimate the wild chimpanzee population; and (c) that returning the animals to the wild risked spreading hepatitis to the rest of the chimpanzee population.

The editor of *Journal of Medical Primatology*, Dr. J.

Moor-Jankowski, decided not to publish the letter immediately, and sent it to Immuno A.G. for comment or reply. Instead of a direct response, however, Immuno A.G.'s attorneys wrote back claiming the letter was inaccurate, demanding supporting documentation, and threatening legal action.

Moor-Jankowski referred the attorneys to McGreal for documentation and extended the time to reply by two months. When no further response from the attorneys was received, the *Journal* finally published the letter—almost a year after receiving it. One year later, Immuno A.G. sued the *Journal*, Moor-Jankowski, McGreal and five other defendants. All the defendants, except for the editor, Moor-Jankowski, settled out of the case, paying what the court described as "substantial sums."

Moor-Jankowski defended the suit up and down the judicial system. He twice went to the highest court in New York State and once to the United States Supreme Court. In the end, after more than six years of litigation, extensive pre-trial discovery (Moor-Jankowski's deposition was conducted over 14 days) and probably significant expense, Moor-Jankowski was successful and the suit was dismissed.

The New York Court of Appeals found that in portions of the letter, McGreal did not convey actual facts about Immuno A.G., but was "voicing no more than a highly partisan point of view." As to the remaining portions of the letter that were challenged, the court found that there was insufficient evidence that factual statements were false.

Letters to the editor cannot be treated as the sole responsibility of their authors. Once a letter is published, the magazine assumes an obligation to ensure its accuracy. A magazine ignores that responsibility at its peril. □

Libel in Cyberspace

BY JESSICA R. FRIEDMAN

Your technology editor has convinced you that you absolutely must put your magazine online to attract the millions of potential readers who hang out on the online services and on the Internet. She thinks that, at a minimum, you should consider uploading each issue and creating message boards with a view to publishing a separate online edition, and setting up your own site on the World Wide Web.

It sounds like a great way to increase your magazine's reach. But then you think you remember reading about a libel suit involving material published online. Could publishing online increase your potential libel exposure?

The short answer is yes, but exactly how much depends on what you're doing. If you're just uploading material that originates with you, you are not taking on any new kind of liability by publishing it electronically. What almost certainly will change, however, is the range of places where you might not only be sued for libel, but where you might be obligated to defend a libel suit to the end. The reason: Once you upload your material, it can be retransmitted to a location where you had no intention of publishing it.

The difference between just being sued somewhere and having to defend the suit on the merits derives from the concept of "personal jurisdiction." In this country, no one can be required to defend a lawsuit filed in another state (the "forum state") unless that person has certain "minimum contacts" with that state. Traditionally, the kinds of contacts that counted were things like having an office, retaining sales agents, and having a separate phone listing. Now, however, making your magazine available online in your home state, with the knowledge that it may be transmitted all over the country, may be deemed as giving you the requisite contacts with any state in the country.

If you make your material available online on a national basis, it is likely that any court anywhere in the country will have personal jurisdiction over your company. Obviously, if your magazine is already a national publication, this won't increase your exposure to suit. But if yours is a local or regional publication, publishing online could make a big difference in your legal bills.

Even more disturbing is the likelihood that your material will be transmitted to another country—for example, the United Kingdom. This is a particularly bad place to find oneself defending a libel suit because it is one of the countries where a libel plaintiff does not have to show any degree of fault on the defendant's part in order to win. Worse, the loser pays the winner's fees. If you fail to have someone appear in court there on your behalf, not only might you be found to be in contempt of court, which carries monetary penalties, but you will probably be hit with a default judgment—an award by the court to the plaintiff of everything that the plaintiff asked for in its complaint.

If you move from simply publishing online to running an interactive forum, your vulnerability to a libel suit increases because, in addition to having no control over where material may appear, you have no control over what material may appear under your name. If you set up bulletin boards, as *Time* has done, or create your own World Wide Web site with a chat site, and X uploads a potentially defamatory comment about Y, which is then read by or conveyed to Y, you might find yourself a defendant—or, worse, a losing defendant—in a libel suit.

How can you avoid this situation? There is little judicial guidance. Until recently, the sole reported court decision concerning liability in cyberspace was Cubby v. CompuServe (1991), which involved a libel claim against an online service provider. In that case, the court held that CompuServe could not be held liable for allegedly defamatory statements published in a newsletter on one of its bulletin boards because CompuServe didn't know, and had no reason to know, that the statements might be defamatory: The bulletin board was run by an independent contractor, the newsletter was published by a third party and CompuServe had no editorial control over it.

But in May 1994, in Stratton Oakmont et al v. Prodigy, a court held that Prodigy, another commercial online network, could be held liable for statements that had been published on its Money Talk bulletin board because Prodigy was a "publisher" and not merely a "distributor" of the material at issue. In contrast to CompuServe, Prodigy has asserted the right to review and edit material placed on its system, including any material that it considered "harmful" to other subscribers and to itself. Moreover, Prodigy had consistently implemented this policy by using "content guidelines" and "[Bulletin] Board Leaders" to enforce those guidelines, and by using a software program that screens postings for offensive words and warns their originators to erase the words or risk censorship of their messages. On top of that, Prodigy had publicly advertised and defended this policy.

The Stratton Oakmont decision is problematic. If you try to keep your more sensitive subscribers happy by pre-screening messages, not only will you force long delays in the transmission of messages, but you increase the risk that you will be treated as a "publisher" if you are sued for libel. (And a screening policy won't even work in real-time chat situations.) To run a successful online publishing business, you can't afford to close your eyes to what's happening on your network. If you do, you will be blindsided not only by litigation, but by consumer dissatisfaction. For example, if someone is regularly posting messages on your bulletin board that are likely to offend many readers, your print publication might lose subscribers or advertisers. The dilemma is compounded because advertisers and agencies are not yet sold on online advertising, so you can't count on making enough money to offset the increased risk.

One magazine that runs interactive bulletin boards on a commercial online network has tried to carve out a middle ground between having no editorial control and a publicized policy of editing. Its technology editor and bulletin board manager have the authority to delete any material they come across that they consider clearly obscene or libelous. However, this policy hasn't been tested by litigation, so it's hard to say how much protection it would offer if the magazine were sued for libel, especially after the Stratton Oakmont decision.

To sum up, there is no hard and fast way to avoid suit or limit liability for libel in cyberspace. But there are some steps you can take to try to lessen your exposure.

> There is no hard and fast way to avoid liability for libel in cyberspace. But there are steps you can take to limit your exposure.

• If you use a commercial online service, make sure its subscriber contract explicitly prohibits transmission of offensive material and requires individual subscribers to indemnify the online service for any violations of the rules and the subscriber contract.

• Limit access to your forum to people whose identities you have verified independently, and require them to use their real names so that you can track them down if they post problematic messages. If you're going through a commercial online service, the service may be doing this already.

• Train the people running your bulletin boards or chat sites to handle problems as they arise. For example, if someone claims to have been defamed by an article you published or a posting on your network, encourage this person to present his or her side of the story in the same forum as quickly as possible (so that the rebuttal will reach the people who saw the original message). If a manager wants to delete a posting, he or she should explain to the person who posted it why it should be deleted, and should encourage that person to rephrase the message in a way that minimizes the legal risk.

Such measures cannot eliminate the legal risks inherent in providing interactive services online, but they may prevent informal disputes from escalating into legal ones, thereby saving a lot of time and money. □

Copyright: Will It Do You Wrong?

BY LAMBETH HOCHWALD

Until recently, publishers needed to consider only print options, including syndication, reprints and microfilm, as they negotiated with freelancers. Now, many magazine executives are rewriting contracts in an effort to cover a broader range of media.

But it's not just publishers who are worried about the future: Contributors, including graphic artists, writers and photographers, are organizing efforts to control the re-use of their copyrighted material. The New York City-based Authors Guild and the American Society of Journalists and Authors (ASJA) has released an "Electronic Publishing Rights" statement demanding that if a publication includes an author's work either online or on a CD-ROM, the writer must receive additional compensation. A recent lawsuit filed by 10 freelance writers against three major publishing companies contended that the writers should have been paid for stories of theirs that had already appeared in electronic databases, including Mead Data Central Corp. and University Microfilms International (UMI).

Because images are an integral part of most digital media presentations, photographers' trade associations have also drafted position statements. The American Society of Media Photographers (ASMP) has formed the Media Photographers' Copyright Agency Inc. (MP©A), a licensing agency aimed at ensuring compensation for members if their photographs are used digitally.

David Korzenik, a media and intellectual-property attorney in New York City who has represented *Spy*, *Vibe* and *Emerge*, points out that the evolving media technologies create a new set of business issues, rather than legal ones. "It's not as if new laws are needed to deal with this," he says. "Copyright and trademark laws are all in place. The real problem is that there are no settled expectations about what the new technologies are."

Instead of trying to predict the form magazines of the future might take, many publishers are instead opting to amass whatever rights they can exploit short-term, in the hopes that they will be able to acquire the rest later on, if needed. "There's a lot of fear and trembling out there," Korzenik suggests. "Everyone is worried about whether their rights are adequate enough to justify investment in that technology."

Publishers interested in new media should first ascertain what rights they are buying from freelancers (*see box below*). "In a lot of cases, they are buying one-time rights for one magazine issue, but what rights are they acquiring the second time?" asks Bob Ellis, publisher of Washington, D.C.-based Compact Publishing, which produced the Time Almanac and Time Almanac in the 20th Century. "The magazine has to go back to the [picture] agency or writer and re-acquire the right from the copyright holder—a time-consuming and expensive process."

But should publishers expect to pay more to secure rights for projects that may be speculative or experimental? Absolutely, replies Judith Broadhurst, editor of "Freelance Success," a monthly New York City-based newsletter. "Online or CD-ROM magazines are another form of publishing and should be treated like any other spin-off," she says. "[Freelance] writers own the copyright, so if a publisher wants to use [the material] again, another fee must be negotiated.

"Publishers are trying to pretend that it's included as part of a blanket deal," adds Broadhurst. "We understand publishers want to do ancillary spin-offs and extend their franchises, but they need to pay a second fee for a second use of a story."

To address some of its freelance writers' concerns, *Mother Jones* developed a contract in conjunction with the National Writers Union nearly three years ago that guarantees the magazine's freelancers half of an online user's search fee once they pass $25. The agreement allows contributors to share some of the revenues from *Mother Jones'* participation in CompuServe and the Internet, says Jay Harris, publisher.

"The actual amount of money coming to publishers is quite small—a few pennies per access," Harris says. "But it's just like any royalty situation, and the amount can add up if we have a lot of people looking at our pieces. We feel we should get a share of the proceeds because we develop the piece, but the writers should get some of the proceeds, too. The electronic medium is just an extension of what has always been the truth in the print medium."

On behalf of writers, Broadhurst concurs: "We invest a lot of time and money in our pieces. Because of the economy, we need to make more money and do that as partners with publishers. We're in this together."

All rights means no hassles

Rodale Press, on the other hand, is testing a new copyright agreement intended to secure all rights, says Gary Pave, Rodale's corporate legal director. If contributors decline to sign it, the Emmaus, Pennsylvania-based publisher asks instead for a slightly narrower range of rights—and agrees, too, to pay an extra percentage to the creator should Rodale ever exploit those rights.

Let's go to the videotape!

Once a publisher adds video products to its lineup of offerings, rights and compensation issues become more complicated. Bob LaPointe, president of *Inc.* business resources, says that the magazine plans to release a CD-ROM on how to start a business using pieces of *Inc.*'s management videos. While most of *Inc.*'s printed content is produced by staffers—and therefore constitutes work for hire—*Inc.* still has to ensure that it has the

rights to re-use all the different elements involved in the videos in another medium. "We have to take a simplistic approach in trying to determine what—if anything—in this product constitutes a contribution by an author," explains LaPointe.

The complex part, in other words, involves trying to determine exactly how to compensate an author if a CD-ROM incorporates text, video footage and information based on a book. "If 10 percent of the information came from the author, and the CD-ROM retails for $100, we sit down with that author and determine that the author will receive a royalty of 10 percent of the 10 percent of the CD-ROM content, meaning $1 per unit sold," says LaPointe. Of course, the author isn't the only creative contributor. "It can become a bookkeeping nightmare. We try to keep our relationships aboveboard, but at the point where it becomes too much of a burden, we'll do the content ourselves."

Because multimedia involves highly visual components, publishers will have to start creating contracts that deal with video and images, says Tom McGrew, vice president of market development and product planning for Carlsbad, California-based Compton's NewMedia, developer of The Sporting News Multimedia Pro Football Guide. "If a checklist isn't in place to

---

■ What rights are you buying?

Below is a menu of terms commonly used in author contracts, as explained by David Korzenik, a media and intellectual-property attorney at Miller & Korzenik, and Jonathan D. Reichman, chairman of the copyright practice group at Kenyon & Kenyon, both based in New York City.

Exclusive first-time periodical rights: The publisher has the one-time right to print a work before it appears anywhere else. If the piece is not a work for hire (see below) and the author retains the copyright, then the author may sell the article to another publication after a certain period of time.

One-time exclusive rights: The publisher can use the piece one time in a particular issue. The use of that piece is limited to a particular period of time, e.g. 90 days from the date the magazine goes off-sale.

Non-exclusive rights: This is a fairly unusual provision that permits another magazine to publish the material concurrently.

North American serial rights: This provision grants a publisher the right to publish and distribute that material

anywhere in North America and to serialize excerpts from a book over a number of magazine issues.

Worldwide rights: Just as it sounds, the piece can be used anywhere in the world, in any language.

Sale of all rights: Covers electronic use, serialization and ancillary rights (see below) worldwide. Because it means losing the copyright, writers may balk at selling all rights.

Work for hire: A writer is either employed by a magazine or is a freelancer who has signed an agreement stating that he or she is creating a work for hire, meaning that the entire copyright is then owned by the publisher. CCNV v. Reid, a 1990 Supreme Court case, defined employee work for hire, meaning, among other things, that the publisher pays benefits and provides an office. For a freelancer's work to be work for hire, she must have a commitment to produce an anthology, translation, compilation, textbook or atlas for a publisher.

Ancillary rights: Frequently withheld by authors, this set of rights covers audiovisual products, that is, movie or television versions or taped readings of the work in question.

make sure everything is available for licensing, a project might not materialize," he says. The Sporting News Guide, for example, uses information from two books, as well as photographs and NFL videos. "If we own all the printed material but don't own the pictures, we have to get permission to use them."

Even when a company uses its own archived material, garnering new rights retroactively can involve a lot of research and paperwork. Tracking down ownership of photographs taken decades before can be next-to-impossible, says Jay Moses, multimedia projects director of Times Mirror Magazines, which relies primarily on freelance photographers and writers for its special-interest titles. "You need clearance on media that were never part of contracts. We're working on new language for our contracts because our existing contracts tended to be altered by contributors who would scratch out certain parts."

Photographers lobby for residuals

New media have the potential to give photographers more exposure than magazines alone ever could. The problem, again, is how to control and pay for re-use of those still images. "We're still feeling our way around on this, but we need our photographers," says Mark Rotenstreich, assistant counsel for *Newsweek*, which publishes a quarterly general-interest CD-ROM magazine, *Newsweek* InterActive. "It's to everyone's advantage to be mindful of copyright."

Richard Weisgrau, executive director of the American Society of Media Photographers, sees ASMP's licensing agency, resembling ASCAP and BMI, as the only way to police photo usage in the digital era. "You have to go back to the initial agreement between the photographer and the magazine," says Weisgrau. "These are usually oral agreements, not written ones, but the underlying principle of editorial use of photos is that it's a one-time right. The electronic format is considered another publication.

Be prepared to pay more to secure rights for speculative or experimental projects.

While it may bear the same masthead, the CD-ROM version is not the same thing as the magazine itself."

Weisgrau thinks photographers would accept a royalty system over receiving a flat re-use fee per picture. "We understand that, in the early years [of new media], publishers are in a high-risk, unprofitable venture. We feel photographers should share that risk and share the gains if they arise. We're looking for an even-steven approach."

Weisgrau says photographers share freelance writers' worries about the impact of forthcoming technology on their livelihood. "There isn't that trust that used to exist," he observes. "The photographers' perception is that magazines have been taken over by bean counters who don't care about photographers taking a bath on something. There's an underlying current of fear of magazines' management."

Beth Zarcone, director of Time Inc.'s picture collection, says that the company's plan to digitize its archives sometime in 1995, making it a dial-up image database, will be photographer-friendly. "We're going to ask permission to digitize," she says. "You lose your credibility if you don't honor copyright. We're not going to do anything individual photographers are going to be unhappy about."

Amid all this activity, some magazines are choosing to wait in the wings until they believe the moment is right to invest in electronic media. David Fishman, director of business development at *Discover*, says that while the magazine is looking into online and CD-ROM options, by the time it chooses an electronic course, its contract will be formulated with the contributors' needs in mind. "You have to have the mindset of the content provider," he says. "And, knowing that the magazine may be leveraged in CD-ROM, interactive TV or online, you have to give those contributors their fair share." ☐

Publishing law

Navigating the 'Fair Use' Privilege

BY HOWARD ZACHAROFF & BRENDA COTTER

Your features editor would like to run excerpts from the soon-to-be published memoirs of a celebrity in your next issue. Your art director has access to the book jacket and proposes reproducing the celebrity's profile on the cover of that issue as it appears on the jacket. Meanwhile, your marketing manager wants you to give approval for a new CD-ROM-based promotional campaign, which displays glimpses of photographs, art and text from competitive publications— all without permission, of course.

You can't reach your lawyer, and everyone needs to move quickly. You are concerned. Is there a risk in proceeding with any of these plans? The answer lies in the copyright law's "fair use" exception.

The Copyright Act gives authors the exclusive right to publish and reproduce their works. However, Section 107 of the Copyright Act permits the "fair use" of copyrighted works for purposes such as "criticism, comment, news reporting, teaching scholarship or research." When is a magazine's publication of copyrighted materials fair?

In general, the fair use doctrine requires a court to balance the public interest in disseminating information against the copyright holders' right to exploit their works. Section 107 of the Copyright Act lists four factors that must be considered in determining whether a use is fair:

• The purpose and character of the use, including whether such use is of a commercial nature or is for nonprofit educational purposes only.
• The nature of the copyrighted work.
• The amount and substantiality of the portion that is used in relation to the copyrighted work as a whole.
• The effect of the use upon the potential market for or value of the copyrighted work.

Let us examine these four factors to see how they are applied by the courts.

Purpose and character of use

Certain uses receive special protection, such as non-profit educational uses, non-commercial research, news reporting, comment and parody.

Commercial use of a copyrighted work generally weighs against a finding of fair use. However, that a magazine is sold for profit does not rule out fair use; rather, the inquiry is whether the use itself is directed to generating a profit. Thus, minor quoting from the *Jack the Ripper* diary before publication to analyze whether it is a hoax would probably be fair, while promoting the issue with the tagline, "Read it here first, excerpts from the *Jack the Ripper* diary," would hurt a fair use defense.

Courts also consider the user's conduct. For example, if the work was acquired by theft or trickery, the use is less likely to be considered fair. But note: Using a work despite the author's refusal to grant permission is generally irrelevant to a fair use analysis. Therefore, reporters should feel free to ask permission without concern that refusal will prevent a fair use finding.

The nature of the copyrighted work

Generally, works of fiction receive greater protection than works of fact. This makes sense in light of the principal purpose of the copyright laws: dissemination of information to the public. Still, quoting fiction for purposes of criticism or review is generally found to be fair use provided the other factors are satisfied.

Whether a work is unpublished is critical. Until recently, unpublished works were not subject to the fair use defense, given the strong policy favoring the author's right of first publication. Now, because of recent cases and a 1992 amendment to the Copyright Act, unpublished works can be subject to fair use. Nonetheless, magazine publishers should remain aware that unpublished works should be treated with extreme caution.

Amount of use

This factor refers to both the quality and quantity of the use. In some cases, courts have looked at the percentage of the work used. For example, in two cases, 1 percent and 4.3 percent were found acceptable.

The substantiality of the use must also be viewed qualitatively: If the user copies the critical heart of a work, for example, this is probably unfair even if the number of words copied is insignificant in relation to the whole. One case held that copying less than 1 percent of the copyrighted letters of Julius and Ethel Rosenberg could be substantial, particularly where the excerpts were featured prominently in promotional materials for the book, *The Implosion Conspiracy*. Thus, if a magazine published verbatim only the juiciest revelations in a celebrity biography, this would probably be unfair even if it was only a small percentage of the book.

Effect on the market

Most courts agree that the most critical factor in determining whether a use is fair is the extent to which it deprives the author of the commercial value of the work. For example, quoting substantial portions of a work (such as a poem), even for the purpose of legitimate criticism, provides people, in effect, with a copy of the work without payment to the author—generally not a fair use. On the other hand, creating a parody of the poem or other work will probably not diminish the market for it and so may be fair.

A finding against fair use is more likely to be handed down when the use is in a related medium or market and performs the same function as the copyrighted work. However, reasonable reproduction for comparative advertising is generally fair even though it harms the market for the copyrighted work, provided the harm derives from competition rather than infringement.

Strategies to ensure fair use

In considering the reproduction of copyrighted works, a reporter's or publisher's foremost consideration should be to avoid using the copyrighted work in ways that might diminish the market for the work. There are particular strategies that will help you avoid infringement:
• Where convenient, and particularly when you are in

doubt, ask permission from the author. Keep in mind, however, that denial of permission will not impair your fair use defense.
• Use only those particular portions of the work necessary for the criticism, comment or report.
• Do not reproduce that portion of the work likely to have the greatest commercial appeal (*i.e.*, the juiciest revelations in a celebrity biography).
• Do not create an article or story adapted from someone's copyrighted work.
• Use caution when reproducing fictional works, and extreme caution when reproducing unpublished works.
• Avoid any form of marketing or promotion, including cover references, that emphasizes that an article or story contains excerpts from a copyrighted work.

Given these guidelines, how should you respond to the problems posed at the beginning of this article? First, quoting more than insubstantial passages from the celebrity's book before publication could get you in trouble. To avoid a copyright claim, minimize quoting and paraphrasing: Tell the person's story, describe his or her revelations, but in your writer's own words.

Second, reproducing entire photos merely to promote your own magazine is almost surely an infringement: Don't do it without permission.

Similarly, the multimedia promotion is also a problem, particularly in light of the commercial nature of the use. However, if the promotion contains significant social commentary (and, ideally, reproduces only portions rather than the whole of these texts and photographs), you may have a shot at a fair use defense.

In considering whether a use is fair, consultation with an attorney is the safest course. However, everyday fair use questions can often be answered by conservative application of the above factors, and commonsense application of the Golden Rule. □

Protect Ownership of Your Title

BY JESSICA R. FRIEDMAN

Once you've chosen a title for your magazine and made sure that it doesn't infringe on anyone else's, you may think that you've done all you need do to assure permanent ownership of your magazine's moniker. Not so. You need to protect that title as carefully as you would any other valuable asset. The question is, how?

Apply for a trademark registration. A trademark registration in the United States Patent and Trademark Office will give you a big edge in protecting your title. A registration (and even an application for a registration) will show up in any search of the Patent and Trademark Office records—which should deter others from using that title or a confusingly similar one.

A trademark registration also creates a presumption that you are the owner of the title. This means that if anyone sues you (or if you sue someone else) for trademark infringement, the other person will have the burden of proving that you *don't* own the title—which is better than your having to prove that you do. Proving that you have the right to use a title, especially when that title is descriptive, can be very expensive.

A federal registration also entitles you to bring suit in federal court, as opposed to state court, which most lawyers will tell you is a definite advantage. It makes you eligible, under certain circumstances, to recover treble damages and attorney's fees, in addition to being eligible to recover damages, profits and costs.

You can apply for a federal registration even before you start to publish your magazine by filing an "intent to use" application in the Patent and Trademark Office. You cannot actually get a certificate of registration until you show the Patent and Trademark Office that you have, in fact, used the mark. But once you do that, the date on which you filed your application will be considered the date that you actually first used the title—which will give you priority over anyone who started to use it after that date.

It is advisable to have a trademark lawyer prepare the application and follow it through the Patent and Trade-

mark Office. The application examiners often raise technical objections. Usually, these objections can be overcome by someone experienced in these matters, but they can also result in the abandonment of your application if they are not handled properly.

Use your title continuously. If you stop using your title with the intent not to resume using it, you will be said to have abandoned the title. This means that you will not be able to stop anyone else from using it, and that if you want to start using it again, you won't be able to rely on your earlier use: You'll have to start building up goodwill and trademark rights from scratch.

Intent not to resume use of a trademark is inferred from the circumstances. If you have not only stopped publishing, but also fired your staff, moved out of your offices, assigned all rights in your magazine to someone else, and gone into the restaurant business, that indicates that you have no intention to resume use of your title. If you have stopped publishing temporarily because of cash-flow problems, a union strike or some other involuntary situation, that will not be said to be abandonment—as long as you start publishing again once the crisis has passed.

Courts are reluctant to find abandonment unless it's very clear, and a party claiming that you have aban-

> The costs of getting a registration and policing your mark are far less than having to throw out a title and building reader recognition all over again.

doned your title has a heavy burden of proving it. Under federal trademark law, however, non-use of a trademark for a period of two years creates a "presumption" that you have abandoned your mark. At that point, the burden shifts to you to prove that you have *not* abandoned the title. Continuous use can prevent this situation.

Continued use of your title is also necessary to maintain your federal registration. Between five and six years after the registration issues, you will have to show the Patent and Trademark Office that you are still using the mark. If at this point you can show that you have been using the title continuously for five years, your registration will become "incontestable," which makes it even harder for anyone to challenge your rights in the title. You will have to make a similar presentation to the Patent and Trademark Office at the end of 10 years, when your registration will be up for renewal.

Don't change the key elements of the title. If you alter the dominant features of your title so as to create a different commercial impression, you can lose your claim of priority to use of the original title. Dropping or adding a word, so that the title literally means something different, can have this result. For example, when the publisher of a former fitness magazine called *Shape Up* tried to re-enter the market after several years with a magazine called *Shape*, the Trademark Office held that those two titles were so different in meaning that the publisher couldn't rely on its original use of *Shape Up* to claim priority over a newsletter called "SHAPE Write-Up" that had been published in the interim.

Police your title. You can also be said to have abandoned your title if you do not take action against someone who uses your title or a similar title in a way that creates a likelihood of confusion.

Besides just keeping your ear to the ground (or your eye to e-mail), you should have your trademark attorney monitor the *Official Gazette* of the Patent and Trademark Office. Published each week, the *Gazette* shows all pending applications for federal registrations. If someone applies to register a title or a mark likely to cause confusion with your title, you can oppose the application. If the applicant is already using the mark, you may wish to sue the applicant for infringement, or at least sound out the applicant by having your attorney write a "cease and desist" letter—which sometimes is enough to solve the problem.

You can also be found to have abandoned your title if you license it to someone else without controlling how the other person uses it, or, in trademark terms, without controlling the quality of the goods or services sold under it. This would include licensing someone to do T-shirts with your title and failing to review samples, or licensing a company to put your magazines online and failing to supervise substantial changes in content or presentation. You should always have a formal license that sets out procedures for you to review proposed uses, but it's even more important actually to review such uses whether or not you have a license.

Following these steps costs money, but it's a sound investment in your magazine. The costs of getting a registration and policing your mark are far less than the costs of having to throw out a title and start building up reader recognition all over again. □

 Publishing law

Has a Competitor Gotten Hold of Your List?

BY JESSICA R. FRIEDMAN

Your fulfillment house gives a copy of your list to a competitor, whom we'll call X, without your consent. X does a mailing based on your list, which you find out about because you've seeded it. How can you stop X from using the list again?

Your first thought might be to instruct your lawyer to seek a preliminary injunction—a court order prohibiting X from continuing to use the list—on the ground of copyright infringement. You may be surprised to learn that this probably will not get you anywhere. No matter how much time and effort it took you to compile the list, and no matter how valuable it is in its current form, the list most likely is entitled to very little, if any, copyright protection. Why? Because the names, addresses and statistical data that appear on your list are merely facts. Copyright law does not protect facts per se, and the protection it gives to "compilations" of facts is, as the United States Supreme Court has said, "very thin."

A copyright registration for a "factual compilation" protects only any original "selection, coordination or arrangement" of the information in the list. If your list has one or more of these characteristics, you may be able to prevent someone else from duplicating those characteristics in his or her list. But it is *not* copyright infringement for someone who has been given a copy of your list to use the underlying actual information. Even if you have managed to obtain a copyright registration for your list, it will not enable you to stop X from using the data itself, which, obviously, is your main concern.

But don't despair. You may be able to get a court order that prohibits X from continuing to use the list on the ground that he has misappropriated a trade secret. The laws that govern trade secrets differ from state to state, but certain general principles apply:

• First, when X acquired the list, he must have known, or should have known, that the list was considered a trade secret.

• Second, X must have gotten the list as a result of a breach of a duty to you that arose out of a confidential relationship (*i.e.*, one in which the parties have special legal duties to each other, such as the duty that an agent owes to his principal or the duty that a trustee owes to the beneficiaries of the trust).

These conditions may sound obvious and easy to prove in a given case. In our hypothetical, for example, it seems reasonable to assume that anyone who gets a copy of a list from a fulfillment house—or from anyone other than the list's owner or broker—knows or should know that it is someone else's proprietary information. But it is possible (albeit unlikely) that X had a good reason to believe the fulfillment house was authorized to give him the list. If that's the case, and X made a substantial investment—such as a major direct-mail campaign—before being notified that the list was a trade secret, a court might not enjoin X from continuing to use the list or hold him liable for the use already made.

Treat your list as confidential information

More important, whether your list will be considered a trade secret will depend at least in part on whether you

> A key trade-secret misappropriation test is whether you had a confidential relationship with the party who gave your list to your competitor.

treated it as confidential information. Of course you do—or do you? In fact, owners of confidential information do not always take the precautions that entitle that information to such treatment.

What can you do to try to ensure that your list will be treated as a trade secret in this kind of situation? As our hypothetical indicates, whenever you share your list with third parties—such as your fulfillment house, your list broker or a company that is considering acquiring your company or entering into a joint venture with you—you need to identify the list as confidential. A written agreement should expressly state that the list is confidential and that the other party is not permitted to make copies of the list or to use it for any purpose other than the purpose for which you are giving it to them.

If you are not starting out with a list per se, you should provide that you will own the information contained in any list that may result from your joint efforts (and that such information is confidential). You should also provide that upon termination of the contract or discussions, the other party will immediately return all copies of the list in its possession and delete the list from its computers. An agreement with a list broker or list manager should also provide that you have the right to refuse rental of your list to any party at any time and to examine all material that will be mailed to any party renting the list.

It is just as important to take similar precautions in-house. Even if you don't keep a copy of your entire list in the office, there will be occasions when your staff uses it, or part of it, to do a telemarketing campaign or a direct mailing. All your employees, especially any who will be involved in compiling or using the list, should sign confidentiality agreements that refer to the list. Any part of your list that you keep or use, even temporarily, in any form, and any documents relating to it, should be clearly labeled "confidential." Access should be limited to people who absolutely need to use the list for any given project; and requests for the list from whoever has custody of it should be made only through a designated staff member, such as the circulation director or the fulfillment manager.

At the completion of any project that involves the list, anyone who has uploaded any part of it should be required to purge it, and anyone who has used a hard copy should be required to return it. The staff member in charge of access should confirm that this has been done.

You should take these steps not only with respect to your list(s), but with respect to all confidential information that may be generated in the course of your magazine company's operations. In fact, it is a good idea to develop a written trade-secret policy for all your confidential information and have it signed by all employees who have access to that information. It is also advisable to conduct periodic audits, and to destroy any extraneous copies of confidential documents and take back copies from people who don't need them anymore.

How you treated your list is not the only factor that a court will consider in deciding whether your list is a trade secret and whether X should be enjoined from continuing to use it. In New York, for example, some courts have been concerned primarily with how difficult it would be for someone else to duplicate the information at issue and the extent to which the information is known to people outside the company. A court that concentrates on these criteria is less likely to protect a straight list of names and addresses than a list that includes customer preference or other statistical information. Other factors include the amount of time and effort that a company put into developing the information, and the value of the information to the company's competitors.

Going back once more to our hypothetical, let's assume that you have followed the steps suggested earlier in this article and that your list is eligible for treatment as a trade secret. The next question for determining whether X can be held liable for misappropriation is whether you had a confidential relationship with the party who gave the list to X—in this case, your fulfillment house.

Even if you don't have a written contract with your fulfillment house, it probably can be assumed that the fulfillment house is your agent. This is also most likely true if you do have a contract but it doesn't contain a confidentiality provision—with one important caveat. Many boilerplate independent-contractor agreements provide, for tax purposes, that neither party is acting as agent for the other. If your fulfillment contract contains such a provision, you cannot meet the "confidential relationship" prong of the trade-secret misappropriation test. One way to correct this might be to insist on including a confidentiality provision when the contract is up for renewal. Or add it earlier, if the fulfillment house is willing.

You should consult a copyright attorney before coming to any conclusions about whether your list (or any other database) is protected by copyright and whether it is being infringed in a given situation. Similarly, you should consult legal counsel to determine whether you are in a position to claim misappropriation of trade secrets. But if you follow the precautions suggested above, you will be in a much better position if and when a list of yours ends up in a competitor's hands. ☐

Is It Predatory Pricing—or Not?

BY SLADE METCALF

"What is this world coming to? I try to reduce costs, provide better service, and lower prices to secure more advertisers—and then some small-time competitor starts screaming about antitrust violations." Sound familiar? With the increasing aggressiveness of the Antitrust Division of the United States Department of Justice, more of your colleagues on the advertising end of the magazine business may begin worrying whether conduct traditionally viewed as hard-nosed competition is in violation of federal or state antitrust laws.

The concept of "predatory pricing" is of growing concern to publishers and their advertising directors. When do special arrangements and discount pricing, at or below cost, become antitrust violations, as opposed to merely intense competition? First, the primary federal antitrust law—the Sherman Act—has a provision that prohibits companies from improperly becoming "monopolists" or attempting (or conspiring) to become monopolists. Without becoming too legalistic, it is necessary to give some meaning to these terms.

A monopolist is a company that, in a particular "relevant market," can control prices for a product and has a sizable share of that market for that product. A relevant market is the scope of suppliers in a particular geographic area whose products are reasonably interchangeable from the viewpoint of those products' consumers. In other words, if a particular advertiser chooses not to place an ad in your magazine because of your steep ad rates, what other vehicles are available for his advertisement?

For example, a manufacturer of specialty motorcycles may feel that the only economical way to advertise is to place his ads in magazines directed to motorcycle enthusiasts. There may be only two or three in that "niche market." Consequently, those three magazines comprise the relevant market for national advertising for specialty motorcycles. Continuing this analogy, if one of the three magazines has more than, say, 40 per-

cent of that relevant market (in terms of advertising and/or circulation revenue), that publisher could be considered a monopolist in that market.

Once a magazine becomes a monopolist in a particular relevant market, it is subject to greater scrutiny by the Justice Department and the courts. Certain acts that, in a market with numerous small competitors, might be ignored by antitrust regulators become magnified in a monopoly arena. One of those acts is known as "predatory pricing."

In an advertising market where the size of ad rates is important (which of course would be most ad markets), an ad director will usually want to undercut his or her competitor in order to close the sale. When does that lower price in a monopoly market become predatory?

Courts have repeatedly emphasized that the antitrust laws are designed to protect competition—not competitors. The theory is that increased competition makes the market more efficient and directly benefits the ultimate consumer. One court has written, "Rivalry is harsh, and consumers gain the most when firms slash costs to the bone and pare prices down to cost, all in pursuit of more business."

> Courts emphasize that antitrust laws are made to protect competition, not competitors.

Therefore, if a magazine dominates a market through hard work, efficiency and a superior editorial product, it is unlikely that it has committed an antitrust violation. However, if that dominant magazine undercuts its competitors by setting prices or providing special discounts that come out below its average marginal costs, a court may very well find a violation of the Sherman Antitrust Act.

Fortunately for those magazines that have gained substantial marketshare, courts have been extremely reluctant to upset the natural forces of the marketplace by finding a monopolization violation or an attempt to monopolize through predatory pricing. Again, aggressive price cutting does not automatically translate into predatory pricing. As another court has said, "Pricing is predatory only when the firm forgoes short-term profits in order to develop a market position such that the firm can later raise prices and recoup lost profits."

Civil suits under the federal antitrust laws may be instituted by either the federal government (the Justice Department or the Federal Trade Commission) or by competitors who can prove that they have been injured by the anti-competitive conduct. In either case, the party suing must prove that the price was not only below the average marginal (or non-fixed) costs, but also was set with the expectation that the short-term loss would be recouped down the road by raising prices after the competitor has been forced out of the market.

A few years ago, two small newspapers in a small town conducted an advertising battle to the death. The publisher who went out of business sued the surviving publisher for violation of the Sherman Antitrust Act and was awarded $230,000 by a local jury.

For over 100 years, Ripley County, Missouri, had been served by one weekly, paid subscription newspaper, the *Prospect-News*. In 1974, three individuals began to publish a weekly advertising shopper called the *Ozark Graphic Weekly Shopper*, which competed with the *Prospect News* for local advertising. Then, in 1980, the shopper's owners launched a weekly, paid subscription newspaper called the *Ozark Graphic*.

Faced with dual competition for the small base of local advertising, the *Prospect-News'* publishers produced their own weekly shopper, the *Prospector*.

In 1982, the *Ozark Graphic Weekly Shopper* ceased publication. The following year, the *Ozark Graphic* was sold; the new owners shut it down in 1985.

The owners of the *Ozark Graphic Weekly Shopper* sued the publishers of the *Prospect-News*, complaining that they were forced out of business by the predatory pricing practices of the *Prospect-News*. After the jury award in favor of the former publishers, the appellate court reversed and dismissed the case, primarily on the ground that the publishers of the *Ozark Graphic Weekly Shopper* never introduced sufficient financial infor-

mation to show that the *Prospect-News* priced its advertisements at below total cost, or below average variable cost. The court stated that predatory intent is not sufficient to prove predatory pricing.

As another court stated, "Competition is a ruthless process. A firm that reduces costs and expands sales injures rivals—sometimes fatally. The firm that slashes costs the most captures the greatest sales and inflicts the greatest injury. The deeper the injury to rivals, the greater the potential benefit. These injuries to rivals are by-products of vigorous competition, and the antitrust laws are not balm for rivals' wounds."

The appellate court found that statements by which the former owners may have exhorted their salespeople to "get" the competition at any price did not make up for the lack of financial information showing that the publishers of the *Prospect-News* charged some advertisers below their average variable costs.

An antitrust violation based on predatory pricing is neither particularly common nor easy to prove. The party suing must prove that the monopolist in the market has relinquished short-term profits in a particular product line in order to force competitors out of the market—with the underlying intention that, in the future, it can raise its prices (without fear of significant competition) in order to recoup those temporary losses.

To show that your competitor has, in fact, engaged in such a practice requires sophisticated financial analysis with significant approximation and guesswork as to your competitors' fixed and variable costs. Because of this guesswork, you will not have much idea of whether you will be victorious until after substantial discovery has been taken in the litigation. And unfortunately, that information may not be available until after you have spent thousands and thousands of dollars on legal fees.

Those of you who are already in a market with few competitors should be cautious about slashing prices below your total costs in order to avoid a viable claim of predatory pricing. □

The Name Game

BY JOHN BRADY

True Story: In August 1989, Douglas Dinsmoor, pigeon-holed as a circ nerd, happily switched hats and became associate publisher of *Bostonia*, a publication of Boston University. There, he managed, motivated and trained a staff of 15. Said the editor/publisher, who needed all the help he could get in advertising and business matters, "You're the publisher in everything but name."

As it would turn out, however, not having the title "in name" proved quite costly. Eighteen months after Dinsmoor took the job, the academic ax fell on budgets. "Hey, we already have a publisher," went the reasoning—"why do we need an *associate* publisher?" Wham. Dinsmoor was history.

The moral of this little tale is clear: You may be overseeing the troops and saving your boss's backside on a regular basis, but in the highly competitive environment of today's magazine world, what you are called is probably more important than what you do if push comes to shove at budget or salary/bonus time.

And so it goes. We are like animals in the wild, foraging for food and safety and survival. In an era of major restructuring on many mastheads, power and dominance are all part of the name game as players move about trying to establish turf that they can graze for sustenance. You need a scorecard to explain who's doing what—and to whom. Larry Burstein, for instance, recently moved from the position of publisher at Advance Publications' *The New Yorker* to publishing director of Hearst Magazines' *Esquire/Esquire Gentleman*, where Alan Stiles remains in residence as publisher of *Esquire*.

Nor is title-mania strictly a top-management obsession. Everyone is proactive about namesmanship nowadays. I have seen mastheads that list secretaries, receptionists, shipping clerks and interns. *Stuff Magazine*, a tabazine for the Boston art crowd, includes beauty tipster, publisher's urologist and revenue princess as staff titles. (The revenue princess, of course, is responsible for billing ads.) Meantime, fact checkers want to be *research editors*. Art directors want to be *design* directors. Editors want to be editors *in chief*.

Since the reincarnation of *Regardie's* in Washington,

D.C., owner/publisher William A. Regardie calls himself *Direttore Responsabile*. Meaning what? "It means he's the head honcho, the big cheese, the guy who signs the checks," says editor Richard Blow.

"It's my magazine," says the bombastic owner. "I can do anything I want."

Bill Regardie found the title in an Italian magazine several years ago and it fascinated him. Moreover, he wanted a new title for his role in the new version of *Regardie's*. "Publisher no longer fit because I have stepped away from the selling of advertising and the supervision of production," he explains. "And the whole idea is to build an idiosyncratic reputation in the marketplace. This title says immediately: 'Maverick publication straight ahead.'"

The only problem, of course, is that Regardie doesn't speak Italian and isn't sure how to pronounce his new title: "But most people who look at it don't know how to pronounce it either," he says. "So it's a standoff." Then, a bit insecurely, he asks: "Anybody else using it?"

Not yet. Even if *Direttore Responsabile* were to start appearing atop several of the glitzier fashion magazines, it would mean something different at each publication. The only constant in namesmanship is change. Ambiguity abounds. Consider the title managing editor, for instance. At some magazines, such as *New York* (owned by K-III Communications), the ME's job is heavy on coordination/production duties, "to make sure the trains are in on time," as a former staffer put it. At others, the ME job may be 95 percent administrative—overseeing budgets, developing schedules, making sure everything closes on time.

Then, of course, there is the Luce version of ME. At the Time Inc. publications, managing editor is four notches from the top, below editor in chief, editorial director and editor of new media. So who runs the magazine? "The title is a tradition from the old days of Henry Luce," explains *Life* managing editor Dan Okrent. "It goes back to the way newspapers were run in the twenties when he started *Time*. Newspapers were run by managing editors. Those who wrote editorials were called editors. Thus, Luce as editor in chief had managing editors at all his publications, and they reported to him. As late as the fifties, *Life* had a managing editor, followed by an editor, on the mast."

For the MEs at Time Inc., there is considerable autonomy. Each ME serves at the sufferance of the editor in chief, with the editorial director serving as an undersecretary of state. There are seven magazines, and Jason McManus, editor in chief, oversees four, while Henry Muller, editorial director, oversees three in a day-to-day sense. The general directive from on high is, "Let me see your covers, keep me posted if there's anything you think I need to know about—and go run your magazine."

"Each managing editor here has as much—or more—freedom as an editor in chief at Hearst or at Condé Nast," adds Okrent, "and a *lot* more than, say, the editor at *Boston Magazine.*"

'Anything short of God'

At *Men's Health*, Michael Lafavore has been atop the mast since this red-hot publication went from newsletter to magazine in 1986. His title: executive editor—which he explains as a corporate culture kind of thing: "I can call myself anything short of God," he says. "That's Rodale Press. I can call myself editor, which sounds kind of plain, or editor in chief, which sounds old and stuffy to me. But I have always preferred executive editor, which is just corporate enough—in boldface, of course."

Lafavore calls titles "an ego thing," and for someone who directs a staff of 18, there are more important considerations: "For one thing, dough. For another, autonomy and independence. On the edit side, I don't have a boss. I run the show. They can call me anything they want, as long as they let me do the job they pay me for. And they do."

Sometimes, of course, the title and salary do not move upward together. Elizabeth Crow, editor in chief at *Mademoiselle*, recalls her starting-out days at *New York,* where Clay Felker was legendary for developing star writers and editors on an earthbound budget. Felker regularly offered titles in lieu of salary increases, which were often minuscule or nonexistent. Crow started as an editorial assistant at 23. "By the time I was 29 I had gone from executive editor to editorial director, and I was barely making $30,000 a year," she laughs today. "I could then tell my parents, 'Guess what—I'm executive editor!' And they never asked what my salary was. What parents dine out on is the fact that their child is executive editor. Salary is something they never would have conveyed to a friend. Prestige," says Crow,

---

■ The upwardly mobile mast

Mastheads are like magazines—no two are exactly alike. Still, there is some consensus among editors as to who's on first and who reports to whom.

Editor in chief
Plans the magazine at large, manages and motivates staff, represents the publication in the community.

Executive editor
Works closely with the editor in chief to assign major pieces; works with high-level writers and helps plan the editorial well.

Managing editor
On the same level as the executive editor. Supervises the edit staff and oversees production of the magazine. Production and the copy staff report directly to this editor.

Senior editor
Someone who is knowledgeable and/or has longevity, but is not in line for a managerial post. Often has technical expertise. May edit articles that need rewriting.

Associate editor
Is likely to have department responsibilities, or editing of feature articles; may do some writing.

Features editor (a.k.a. articles editor)
Works with correspondents and outside contributors.

Assistant editor
Entry-level duties at large.

Editorial assistant
Entry-level editorial duties plus office, phone and scheduling responsibilities.

Contributing editors
Regular writers—for example, columnists. Sometimes listed individually according to their areas of expertise.

"rides on titles, not income."

Still, says Pam Fiori, a longtime editor at *Travel & Leisure*, and now editor in chief at *Town & Country*, "a new title should mean something. I have never understood giving someone a new title with inflated responsibility and no money. If it happens, it's a bad sign. Instead of changing titles, you should think of changing companies."

Consider Frank Finn, who is now editorial director at Tuff Stuff Publications Inc.—a Richmond, Virginia-based publisher of trading-card magazines. In 1978 he was hired as associate editor at the 13-30 Corporation in Knoxville, Tennessee (later to become Whittle Communications). He quickly moved up the ranks to senior editor, handling more than one publication; then to group editor overseeing five titles in the adult business group (*Moviegoer, Best of Business*, plus parenting titles); then to executive editor supervising group editors and reporting to the editor. Finally, he was offered the position of vice president and editor—a peculiar title blend that signified he headed all of editorial for the company and was also on the executive committee, which consisted of the CEO and all the executive-level vice presidents. Umm, there was one small catch: He was given the title, but no salary increase.

"I took it as a left-handed compliment," says Finn, who is right-handed. "It certainly wasn't a vote of confidence or any serious acknowledgment of my skills." He began to look at other job opportunities, and soon resigned to become editorial director at CommTek Publishing. "The president seemed surprised at my reaction," adds Finn. "But, while his words said one thing, his actions were saying something else."

"I think we have all taken raises that weren't big enough and struggled to keep our egos under control," says Fiori. "But at some point you have to draw the line. I think it's shameful when someone is offered a new title but no money."

So, what's in a name?

Quite possibly everything you have ever worked and hoped for in this business. Are you properly titled? suitably paid? sufficiently appreciated? To help you sort out any misgivings and to settle a few disputes at your next performance review, here are Brady's Top 10 Unwritten Laws of Title Management:

All titles are local. Titles vary from publication to publication, where there are myriad ways to do the same thing. Consequently, a magazine must be structured to meet its own needs.

Job descriptions are local, too. Creative director seems to have as many different definitions as there are magazines employing one. At Kalmbach Publishing Co. in Waukesha, Wisconsin, publisher Russ Larson created job descriptions for the six magazines he oversees by asking each staffer to write his or her own. The managers reviewed and amended them where appropriate. "Though the titles may be the same, each magazine has

> What's in a name? Quite possibly everything you ever worked and hoped for in this business.

its differences and each job description is customized," observes Larson. "The off-the-rack job description is an ideal; the reality, however, is lots of custom tailoring for a more comfortable fit all around."

Title inflation is demoralizing. In magazine publishing, talent is usually spotted early and rewarded quickly. Sometimes too quickly. "It's dangerous," says Elizabeth Crow. "If everyone is a senior editor or vice president or whatever, it's like everyone in class getting an A. After a while, grades mean nothing." The key is to develop a system where a title truly means something and defines a person's scope of responsibility.

Titles mean money. If you aren't offered a salary increase along with a new title, you are probably being abused. For the short term, there may be advantages for both sides; long term, this marriage cannot be saved. Taking a title without a pay increase is a good idea only if there is the assurance that somewhere down the line your salary and performance are going to be reviewed. Pay me now or pay me later should be the understanding.

Little things mean a lot. Like the difference between editor and editor in chief, for example. Editor is considered plain. "And when you think about it," says Michael Lafavore, "nearly everybody on the masthead is an *editor*." Associate editor, senior editor, assistant editor, yeah yeah yeah. "I've always liked editor in chief," says Pam Fiori. "No confusion with other editors, and the sound of it implies a leadership role." (When I left *Writer's Digest* a dozen years ago, the advertising director gave me a T-shirt saying "Editor & Chief," a version that I rather liked, but which has not caught on.)

Hyphens and slashes are dangerous. Show me an editor/associate publisher and I will show you a magazine that has asked the editor to oversee a little revenue stream on the side. This helps create the perception that the magazine is not altogether editorially upright. Moreover, the prefix "Associate" is like a tight leash attached to someone who has the real job and the real power in this particular office. Deputy (as in deputy editor) has some of the same quasi-ness (unless, of course, the job comes with a badge).

Titles mean self-esteem. They give staffers a morale boost that usually exceeds the kick from extra pay. It's important that a title make someone feel good about her or himself. One former service features editor at a city magazine told me that she was always trying to explain her title to people she called on for information or interviews. "Service writing meant nothing to outsiders. People were always asking me, 'What's that?' Still, I liked it better than my other title—lifestyle editor—because that made it sound like I was editing somebody's lifestyle."

Titles mean turf. To be effective, titles should be hierarchical so that everyone knows where he or she stands in relation to others on the mast. Turf battles are avoided when there is a direct line of reporting. Because the masthead does not truly reflect the internal chain of command at a magazine, an organization chart should be made available to all. Otherwise, there will be confusion and "end runs" around authority by ignorant or plotting souls.

Stroking may be hazardous to your health. If you have recently been told how wonderful you are—and then find yourself with a title that far exceeds your actual duties, you have been kicked upstairs and are expendable. Recent candidates for the hazardous-title category include director of new media or director of magazine development. Another high-risk title is director of special projects. Editor-at-large is also risky—similar to contributing editor, usually given to a staffer who has been let go with some pangs of conscience.

"It's been my experience that these titles are usually the last stop before updating your résumé and making multiple copies at the photocopier," observes one industry cynic.

The titles, they are a-changin'. The new technology has created some new titles, such as electronic production administrator—"Something that corporate dreamed up," explains Hearst Magazines' Fiori. "It used to be head of production." At Condé Nast, *Self*'s masthead now includes an interactive editor, presumably for the purpose of taking the magazine from here to interactivity. (Call 212-880-5555—and plan on 10 minutes just listening to all your many interactive options.)

Other titles are the result of more permanent changes in the way we do magazines today. "E-mail and voice mail and other forms of communication have eliminated many strictly secretarial tasks," says Larson of Kalmbach Publications. A few years ago, the company went through the ranks and changed the title editorial secretary to editorial assistant, meaning the job now includes editorial work along with handling phone calls, scheduling meetings and other tasks. There were salary adjustments as well. Now for the tough one: Who gets the coffee? "We all get our own at the coffee stations," says Larson. "And he—or she—who takes the last cup makes the next pot."

So what's in a name? For Douglas Dinsmoor, it was a happy landing and a new career direction (he's now marketing director at Cambridge, Massachusetts-based Sky Publishing Corp., which publishes *Sky & Telescope* and *CCD Astronomy*, as well as a line of books). And he has hopes of becoming a full-fledged publisher one day—without the prefix *associate* to stumble over.

"Yeah, I think it best that I stay clear of those second-banana titles. Of course," Dinsmoor reflects, "like most titles in this field, it all depends on whom you associate with." □

How to Hunt for a Headhunter

BY LORRAINE CALVACCA

Good help is getting harder and harder to find. In fact, as the publishing business model morphs, industry executives are commonly employing the "needle-in-a-haystack" cliché to describe their efforts to find the perfect person for a job. That pressing need is driving more managers to include professional matchmakers in their search.

So-called headhunters report that, for them, the result is a significant growth in business over the last few years. "There's more of an acceptance of retained executive search because good searches have been done and publishers are realizing the benefits," explains David Bentley, a partner at Nordeman Grimm, Inc., a mid-size generalist firm in New York City. According to Bentley, business increased 15 percent in 1995 over the previous year—much of it repeat clients.

"There has definitely been an increase in unsolicited inquiries in the past six months," says Gene Fixler, president of Ariel Recruitment, a small New York-based firm that specializes in publishing. "We are used more selectively as the market gets tighter and companies re-engineer and consolidate."

Jim Cornehlsen, a partner at New York City-based Lamalie Amrop International, who specializes in new media, says his company's growth reflects that ongoing trend. Lamalie's searches were up 20 percent in 1995 over the previous year as clients sought out well-rounded, multi-talented, topnotch professionals. "People are saying 'Help. We need someone with the skills and breadth to generate revenue.'"

Help needed—across all disciplines

Paul Kitzke, editorial director and vice president of Washington, D.C.-based HanleyWood, Inc., agrees. For key strategic positions, he says, it's not enough simply to call on people you know. The trade publisher used an executive search firm last year to fill an editor's position and two years ago to fill a marketing director slot. "In the old days, search firms were less important because we zeroed in on, for example, an editor who could get the book out. Now editors, and others, have to think well beyond that. They have to serve as mar-

keters and work on franchise extension, among other things." Kitzke also says using a headhunter offered a measure of objectivity about in-house contenders. Using the firm "allowed us to deal fairly and objectively with internal candidates. It eliminated emotion and subjectivity."

In fact, "a major trend," says Cornehlsen, is a growing number of requests for internal evaluations of existing staffers for immediate openings, especially in the area of succession. "Companies want to evaluate against an objective checklist of what they need in the future. Is the publishing model looking the same?"

A search firm also offers the advantage of anonymity and confidentiality, say users and recruiters alike. "Some people like the distance of a search firm," comments Martha Stephens, vice president of corporate human resources for Boston-based IDG, who assisted COO Jim Casella in employing recruiters at least five times last year to fill critical upper-level spots. "Sometimes we know people in the industry, but from an ethical standpoint, it's hard to go into other companies."

Recruiters add that, given the blurring of lines between publishing disciplines and the emphasis on marketing, technology and financial savvy, they are equipped to explore outside businesses to identify potential candidates not likely to be found within the traditional sphere. "A chief value of a search is to bring talented individuals from other industries," remarks David Lord, a Harrisville, New Hampshire, executive-search consultant. In fact, most sources agree, a search firm is best employed for jobs at a level that in some ways transcends disciplines—that is, positions with revenue and policy-making responsibility.

Manage the process

Hiring these gumshoes of the employment world takes some investigative work on the publisher's part. Before going with a firm, the publisher needs to figure out whether the job in question calls for the expertise of a search firm.

"Not every job requires a search," observes John Malcom, managing director at New York City-based

Accord Group Johnson, Smith & Knisely. "If, for example, you need an art director, that's usually the personal choice of the editor."

Once you've decided to use a search firm, "you've got to manage the process," cautions one industry executive, echoing a number of others. He attributes "poor results"—including one bad fit—at least in part to his taking a passive role working with the firm. Staying involved means providing the firm with a well-thought-out job description, making sure the service provider understands your company's culture, and making sure the search firm adequately spells out the search process, fee structure and time frame. It also means keeping the search moving once it's begun by being responsive to the recruiter's inquiries and recommendations. "Sometimes, an organization feels it has handed off a problem, and doesn't have to interact or return phone calls. Good talent gets away by the inability to act or to make a decision," says consultant Lord.

"There are no shortcuts," says Dan Mills, vice president and CFO of New York City-based trade publisher Lebhar-Friedman, who has successfully used headhunters several times to fill senior-level positions.

The experience of Starlight Publishing president and COO Lyndell Gooch is instructive—if atypical. He recounts hiring a national personnel agency on a retainer basis to find a sales manager for a new business-to-business publication. Although the Albuquerque-based company had been producing city publications for 10 years, executives had no contacts to fill a sales manager's job on a new publication. The agency promised three candidates in 30 days. The search stretched into four months and Gooch ended up placing a local ad and hiring a "capable" person with background in Yellow Pages ad sales. Even though the hire ultimately worked out, Gooch lost a significant amount of time and money in getting the person up to speed.

Gooch feels at least partly responsible. "I went in thinking that I would write a check and they would give me a sales manager. I was naive," he says in hindsight. As the search progressed, Gooch discovered that to attract out-of-state clients, the recruiters had inflated the compensation package by $10,000. The agency, too, he reflects, was remiss in not giving him an honest appraisal of the package he was offering. "They could have guided me and said, 'You can't afford it.'"

Like Gooch, a number of industry executives say they have learned the hard way the importance of staying involved with a search. "I'd say 'buyer beware,'" says IDG's Stephens, who strongly recommends shopping around and conducting reference checks on companies.

Who's doing the search?

It's important, too, that the search-agency point person visit your company. "Good search people will spend a fair amount of time to provide advice and counsel. If they are worth their salt, they will tell you if they are not the right outfit," asserts Dave Opton, founder of Exec-U-Net, a nationwide networking organization of executives and senior professionals headquartered in Norwalk, Connecticut.

Moreover, consumers of firms' services caution strongly that you make sure the point person who pitches you is the one who will actually head your search. "What's important to know about some large firms is that they send in this amazing person, but that's often not the person who does the research," says Marcie Jones, managing editor of "Executive Search Review," a monthly newsletter in Greenwich, Connecticut, that reports on the executive search industry. IDG's Stephens concurs. "It's important to have that person actively involved in the search—not delegate it to the back room."

When it comes to choosing a firm with a publishing-specific background versus a generalist one, industry executives and search principals agree that it depends on the job. "Generally," says Lebhar-Friedman's Mills, "I would look for someone with a publishing background. But if the search were for a CFO here, I might go to someone who is a financial specialist."

Stephens also tailors her choices to the position, not the discipline. "If I were seeking a human-resources person, I would go to a firm with that knowledge. For a publisher, I would go to a publishing background." She acknowledges, however, that what counts is the recruiter's insight. "I would use a person who does a wide range of searches if they really understood the needs and background of the company."

Cornehlsen argues that, with new employees sup-

> "Good people will spend a fair amount of time to provide advice and counsel. They will tell you if they are not the right outfit."

posed to possess the skills of the two or three people they replace, generalist firms offer publishers an advantage in that they can search the four or five industry segments in which any given candidate might be found. "What is happening is that media companies have very diverse interests. Ten years ago, we would have looked only in magazines. Now we are required to look in different areas."

Nordeman Grimm's Bentley says he believes that knowledge of an industry unquestionably strengthens any search. Yet, he allows, "a good recruiter can do a good search in any industry."

The contingency equation

In general, retainer search firms charge 30 to 33 percent of the candidate's total compensation, and tend to start

---

■ At a glance

With 2,893 firms nationwide, executive search is a $3 billion industry, according to *The Directory of Executive Recruiters 1995-96*. Following are a few retainer firms that conduct senior-level publishing searches.

Accord Group Johnson
Smith & Knisely
(212) 885-9100
Headquarters: New York City
Revenues: $12 million
Salary minimum: $75,000
Branches: Boston, San Francisco, L.A.
Industries include: Publishing, retail.

Ariel Recruitment Associates
(212) 765-8300
Headquarters: New York City
Revenues: appr. $300,000-$500,000
Salary minimum: $55,000
Industries include: Publishing, technology.

DeSilva & Partners, Inc.
(212) 686-2929
Headquarters: New York City
Revenues: $1 million-$2 million
Salary minimum: $100,000
Industries include: Publishing, PR, other media.

Heidrick & Struggles, Inc.
(312) 372-8811
Headquarters: Chicago
Revenues: $100 million-$150,000
Salary minimum: $100,000
Branches: 35 offices in 18 countries.
Industries include: All.

The Howard-Sloan-Koller Group
(212) 661-5250
Headquarters: New York City

Revenues: $2-5 million
Salary minimum: $50,000
Industries include: publishing, new media.

Korn/Ferry International
(212) 687-1834
Headquarters: New York City
Salary minimum: $100,000
Revenues: Over $100 million.
Branches: 61 offices in 35 countries.
Industries include: Publishing, technology, consumer goods, entertainment.

Lamalie Amrop International
(212) 953-7900
Headquarters: New York City
Salary minimum: $100,000
Revenues: $35 million (USA);
Branches: 66 offices in 40 countries.
Industries include: Publishing, technology, direct marketing, consumer products.

Nordeman Grimm, Inc.
(212) 935-1000
Headquarters: New York City
Revenues: $5 million-$10 million
Salary minimum: $150,000
Branches: Chicago and international.
Industries include: Publishing, financial services, nonprofit.

Sunny Bates Associates
(212) 932-0211
Headquarters: New York City
Revenues: $500,000-$750,000
Salary minimum: $70,000
Industries: Publishing, new media.
(All figures represent gross revenues in North America.)

searches at the $100,000 level and go as high as $500,000. While retainer firms are typically paid one-third of the fee upfront, and additional installments as the search progresses, contingency agencies—those that do searches largely on a non-exclusive basis in time-sensitive situations—with some exceptions aren't paid unless they make a placement.

Retainer searchers (who get paid in full whether they make a placement or not) of course, argue that you can't judge the price tag over the short term. Says Cornehlsen: "The cost of a search has to be measured over a two- or three-year basis, not after a month. Good people can add value, lead well, and grow the business, and that adds a huge amount" that is not always immediately quantifiable.

Retainer firms generally work on an exclusive basis, and routinely do the laborious weeding out of prospects, but contingency firms by all accounts have a definite place in the search process. "At the lower- and mid-levels we try to get someone on our own, but we will use a contingency," says Lebhar-Friedman's Mills. "While there are a lot of flesh peddlers, there are also a number of good firms out there."

"There's a role for contingency firms where volume is more important than quality and you're willing to do the sorting yourself," comments Roland DeSilva, founding partner of DeSilva & Partners, a mid-size, New York-based firm.

"Contingency can be useful" in that these firms provide a great number of names in a short period of time, agrees Sunny Bates, founder of boutique firm Sunny Bates Associates in New York, and a former publishing executive. But, she contends, a contingency search can compromise confidentiality because recruiters want to get the candidates into the company quickly. Also, if the publishing company is exploring prospects at the same time as the contingency firm or firms, the same candidate may receive multiple inquiries. "It begs the question if the candidate gets a lot of calls of 'What's wrong with this job?' and 'Why are they so desperate?' " comments Bates.

That, and other downsides of contingency may become less common as the search industry evolves, says Kennedy Publications publisher Jim Kennedy. Contingency firms, he notes, have grown in expertise and effectiveness, and many offer retainer services. "A new generation of quality contingency service is emerging and competing for senior management searches." Indeed, says Lamalie's Cornehlsen, there is "a lot of pressure from clients to offer the contingency pricing structure because of the pay-for-performance aspect."

What counts in any case, contends consultant Lord, is the publisher's diligence in learning about a firm's methodology and track record and—perhaps most important—a personal rapport. Says Lord, "Whether you are using contingency or retainer, it's important that you have good trust in the person" handling your account.

Pride and prejudice

Not all companies see an expanding role for search executives in their crystal balls. Instead, at least a few companies, including Elsevier Science Inc., say they plan to use them less, or not at all, in the coming year. At IDG, Stephens says the company is focusing on grooming existing staffers through a series of training programs to assure the best cultural fit in the long term. Linda Stone, Elsevier Science's director of human resources and organization, says search firms were used extensively last year because there was no human resources staff at that time, but her plans for this year don't necessarily include search firms. "I pride myself on being able to identify candidates," she says.

That doesn't mean they don't appreciate the particular advantages that a professional search can yield. "I would never say never," to hiring a search firm, says Stephens. And Stone says that while the executive-search approach would not be her first choice, "I couldn't live without them."

Personnel

10 Steps to the Right Candidate

BY JOHN W. MALCOM

Most publishing companies underestimate the stakes and shortchange the process when they search for a key executive. An effective search should fill an immediate need with someone who will not only cope with today's challenges, but also provide leadership within the organization over the long haul.

With advertising tougher to sell and technology changing the way readers want information, traditional jobs are being redefined, and emerging jobs are demanding new skills. To differentiate between stopgap hires and star performers who will propel your business forward without fomenting mutiny, you need to match a realistic vision of your company with a full picture of the talent, experience, ambition and personality of various candidates. Remember this: Even if a search consultant is involved, the ultimate decision is yours. You can go a long way toward ensuring that you hire the right candidate by adhering to these 10 principles.

1. Take a magnifying glass to your company.

Many searches turn up seemingly appropriate people who, in truth, aren't the right leaders for a changing business. The reason: Management didn't fully think through what they were looking for before starting the search. In this situation, the company loses in many ways—through severance costs, new search costs, opportunities lost and time wasted.

Worse, perhaps, is the chosen candidate who doesn't fail at the job, but who lacks the foresight and horsepower to pull the company into the future.

To prevent this, start your hiring process by taking a close-up, objective look at your company. Given the changing structure and character of the publishing business, do you really know your strengths and weaknesses, and how they apply to the position(s) in question? What about the management dynamics inside your company? Analyze the personalities of your key managers. Ask employees and managers alike what motivates them and they'll define the style that succeeds. Ask clients what needs the new executive will

have to meet. Evaluate the person this new executive will report to, and identify any ongoing internal conflicts that are relevant and will influence the new hire's career track. Now you're in a position to articulate the job completely, on paper and in direct contact with potential candidates.

2. Make sure your position description is complete.

Too many searches end up hiring the wrong "successful" candidate. The person you think you need may not be right for the job. The company and job profile in a position description need to reflect accurately how the company operates, and how the individual will need to operate to succeed in the job in question. The job profile should also set forth the skills that will be needed in the future. If you require all senior managers to sign off on the position description, you'll find out immediately if confusion exists internally over the candidate's role.

3. Set a realistic compensation range.

Pay ranges relate to four factors: the importance and difficulty of the job; the performance a candidate has demonstrated; the reward level qualified people expect;

> The best way for you to prepare for a fast-changing future is to fill your organization with very smart, multidimensional people.

and market supply. Determining the right compensation level is a balancing act: Don't be cheap, but don't overdo it. Many publishing companies unwittingly conspire against hiring stars, even from within publishing. They set the compensation range within limits that fit their existing pay structures but fall short of the job, the candidate's expectations and what is needed to attract a top performer.

Every manager says he does his homework; few actually do. It's critical to research the fair market value, especially if you are planning to import specialized talent from outside the magazine industry. It's also critical to do your homework ahead of time. Any time you contact a potential candidate or source, determine his or her compensation and keep the information on file. This will help you keep track of what people in different functional specialties and industries expect to be paid.

4. Let your needs dictate where you look.

Don't settle for yesterday's solutions when you have set out to solve tomorrow's problems. The more profoundly publishing changes, the more likely it is that the perfect candidates will hail from companies or business sectors that aren't immediately obvious. Contacting a short list or network of friends isn't enough anymore. You need to cast a wide net with the well-thought-out job definition in mind, looking deep within those businesses and functional areas that have developed the experience you've identified.

5. Assess the complete person.

The résumé and business experience add up to only one sign of a candidate's potential strengths. Most interviewers fail to determine what motivates an individual. Also, most interviewers fail to identify how candidates have succeeded or failed to perform in previous jobs—which goes a long way toward predicting that person's success within your company. There's only one way to find out what a candidate values most: Engage each one in dialogue about how and why he/she has made the choices that have shaped his/her career paths. Peel the onion by asking a follow-up question. Listen. Then ask another follow-up question. Let the candidate fill in any awkward silences. If you listen 80 percent of the time, you'll be surprised what people will say and how much you'll learn about how they really think and operate.

6. Challenge the résumé.

Did the candidate really do all this? In an interview, get the candidate to lead you through his/her accomplishments in detail—what he/she did to overcome specific hurdles, and what resulted, at each stage of the process. Concentrate on listening. Many very successful top managers, unpracticed or uncomfortable at interviewing, end up exalting their company or discussing business in general; they come away with the feeling that the candidate is "terrific," without knowing much at all about the candidate's approach to the job in question. If the candidate can lead you step by step through the accomplishments outlined on the résumé, you can begin to feel comfortable that he/she really does possess the knowledge and leadership capabilities you're looking for.

7. Get more references than you think you need.

There is no shortcut to checking out a candidate. Colleagues, bosses, subordinates and clients should all be contacted about the candidate's personal style, ambitions and work experiences. Many of these references won't tell you directly what you need to hear about a candidate, but they will give you subtle hints. Only after you've talked to a number of references will patterns of behavior and, perhaps, traceable problems start to become clear.

8. Pick people you can promote.

What a candidate actually achieves—often beyond the job he/she was hired for—is the ultimate measure of effective search. It's also a critical factor most publishing executives overlook when they're in the process of recruiting candidates. The clearer your vision of where your company is headed, the better able you will be to pick tomorrow's leaders from among today's candidates.

9. Don't be afraid to bet on the future.

Although none of us knows precisely what the future will bring, one thing's for sure: As magazine companies reinvent themselves, there will be a rising premium placed on agility. People at all levels of the organization will be called upon to adapt to changing situations that emphasize new combinations of skills. The best way to prepare for a fast-changing future is to fill your organization with very smart, multi-dimensional people.

10. Practice full disclosure.

This could be the smartest move you'll ever make. Nothing attracts smart, able people better than honesty. Tell candidates exactly where you're going, what your problems are and what your expectations are. Good people like challenges. Don't be afraid—you'll never cancel out a great candidate by being unabashedly honest. Rather, you'll increase your chances of finding the person who will fit both the job and the organization. Long-term, that's the person who will best serve your company. □

Personnel

Hidden Traps in Job Descriptions

BY ALLAN HALCROW

I'd be willing to wager that there's a potential legal nightmare lurking in your office. It's probably hiding where you'd least expect it, tucked away in a file folder or notebook you haven't opened in months or years. It's called a job description.

Most companies create job descriptions to give applicants a sense of available positions or, more commonly, to develop salary grades. In today's litigious climate, however, those seemingly innocuous documents can come back to haunt you on issues such as overtime, performance reviews and terminations. The risk is particularly acute as publishing companies cut back on staff and reassign tasks to get the work done.

The fundamental problem is that the job descriptions you may consider merely guidelines about work tasks and expectations may be seen as much more definitive by attorneys and the courts. There are several areas where management can take action to avoid costly personnel problems.

Overtime: All employers should be familiar with the exempt and nonexempt classifications applied to employees for the purpose of determining overtime liability. Exempt employees are generally those who supervise others or those who may be described as professionals; many publishers classify editors and designers as exempt.

You should know, however, that your overtime liability may be tied to an employee's duties as outlined in his or her job description, and not to what the employee actually does.

For example, suppose you decide that one of your supervisors should be moved to a larger office, or to one closer to the production department. If the employee comes in over the weekend to pack or move boxes, you may be liable for overtime—even if the employee is exempt—because packing and moving are not part of the employee's usual job activities. It doesn't take much imagination to see that if you decide to relocate the company, and therefore ask all employees to work late to help pack or

move, you could develop a significant overtime liability in a hurry. In such a case, it may actually be cheaper, in the long run, to hire a mover.

This principle applies to any tasks not normally performed by the employee, or to tasks that are not directly related to his or her normal job duties. Activities such as running to the post office or stuffing envelopes are other examples.

The important issue to consider isn't whether the activity is a one-time event, but whether the task relates to the employee's usual job duties. For example, the envelope stuffing would probably be considered related to the employee's usual duties if he or she is often involved in some other step of sending out mail. Similarly, proofreading would probably be seen as a task related to an editor's customary work, even if he or she didn't do it all the time.

Performance reviews: When conducting your annual performance reviews, evaluate employees primarily on the basis of the tasks described in their job descriptions. Consider this scenario: One of your editors left the company voluntarily and, because times are tough, you elected not to fill the open position. Instead, that person's tasks have been divided among the remaining editors. Everyone knows that "Joe" has assumed responsibility for editing the magazine's monthly events calendar. During Joe's review, you are careful to note that he is exemplary at most of his work, just as he has been since he was first hired. Unfortunately, you have observed that the most recent two issues of the magazine have included several errors in the calendar section. Worse, one of your biggest advertisers has called you to complain that the trade show she sponsors was identified with the wrong dates in the last issue.

If you find yourself in such a situation, be careful what action you take. If you deny Joe a raise he is expecting or put him on probation and threaten his job

> Each employee's job description should be amended when his or her duties are changed.

if the situation doesn't improve, you may be asking for trouble. If Joe responds, "It isn't even in my job description. How can it be that important?" you're in a difficult situation. Technically, Joe is right: You're at legal risk if you hold employees responsible for work that has not been defined in writing.

Of course, all employees occasionally do things beyond what's within the strict confines of their job descriptions. In such instances, you should feel comfortable commending an employee for going above and beyond the call of duty, or for saving you from disaster. You must also feel free to hold employees responsible for doing what they're supposed to do. The key is to be careful not to tie negative outcomes (such as discipline or denial of a raise) to duties outside the job description. You also should be careful not to focus during a review on duties not listed in the job description at the expense of duties that are listed.

Terminations: Consider this scenario: At the same time that Joe assumed responsibility for the calendar, "Sally," another editor, also took on other tasks. In addition to copy editing several stories each month, Sally is now writing the table of contents and has assumed some administrative tasks, such as returning original material to contributors.

When it comes time for Sally's review, you realize that her work has been mediocre all along. Although she gets her work done, she barely meets deadlines and her stories aren't as well crafted as those edited by others. Worse, the table of contents has been dull and you notice that in the last couple of issues, some page numbers have been wrong. The last straw was a call from a contributor complaining about lost material; it will cost the company $2,000 to replace it.

You conclude that, in tough times, you can't afford a mediocre editor, particularly one who isn't keeping pace with the other staff members. During Sally's review, you cite all these incidents and tell Sally that she is being let go. Two weeks later, you get a letter from Sally's attorney telling you that you are being sued for wrongful discharge. She argues that Sally's termination was based on incidents unrelated to tasks included in her job description. In this situation, the odds are that Sally will win, and that the case will cost you thousands of dollars.

Defensive strategies

As grim as these scenarios may be, they are far from foregone conclusions. There are several things you can do to protect yourself. First, each employee's job description should be amended when his or her duties change. Reas-

signing tasks or simply letting them drift until someone steps in to do them is not a good idea. It doesn't matter that everyone in the company knows who's doing the work, and that the situation is "understood."

If an employee leaves and you decide not to replace the person, sit down and go through the old job description. Reassign each task and add it to someone else's job description. As a rule, it's better to define additions as responsibilities, not tasks, because "responsibilities" is broader and therefore gives you more protection. For example, "The senior editor is responsible for the timely and accurate creation of the table of contents in accordance with the company quality standards" is better than "The senior editor writes the table of contents," which allows the employee to say, "But my job description doesn't say I'm responsible for the page numbers."

Be sure to go over the new job descriptions with employees. Review the new descriptions face to face; do not simply send a memo. Make it clear during the meeting what the new tasks are and that the employee will be held accountable. Be sure the employee is allowed to ask questions. You also should be sure to use the job description as the basis for each performance appraisal; refer to the appraisal beforehand and then address each area in your review.

The same techniques should be used if you promote an employee, add to an employee's responsibility or reassign tasks for any other reason. Do not assume everyone knows what is expected.

This process should be repeated each time a significant change is made. It's a time-consuming and onerous task (which is why it's often not done), but less onerous, ultimately, than legal problems.

You should allow yourself some maneuvering room in your job descriptions. One technique is to define responsibilities, as suggested above. Another is to include a line in each description that reads something like, "All other related duties." Such a sentence—and "related" is critical to include—accommodates unexpected tasks, one-time projects, temporary assignments because of co-worker absence and other situations. Of course, the phrase doesn't give you license to change the employee's job duties at will, but it does offer you more freedom than a rigid job description.

Finally, these suggestions are just that. Because laws vary from state to state and change often, it's always best to consult a labor attorney. Still, understanding the issues can go a long way toward protecting you from problems. □

How to Manage Technical People

BY ELAINE APPLETON

It is the rare publishing executive who doesn't see the potential advantage in all kinds of technology—from electronic prepress to wide-area networks. But most magazine executives lack technical training, nor do they have the time or the inclination to devote themselves to the step-by-step supervision of technology conversions. For expertise, they rely on in-house systems managers, MIS (management-information systems) departments, production heads and informal "gurus," or they talk with suppliers and call in consultants. But managing these technology experts can be akin to ordering a meal in a foreign land: Because you don't speak the language, you don't know what you're getting. And even then, you may not know whether the meal is overpriced—or if the chef is any good.

"It's always problematic dealing with technical people because the average user of a computer system understands the technology differently from the person who designs it and knows the inner workings of the machine," says David Laird, publisher of Boston-based *CFO*, who recently had a local-area network installed there, and connected that network to the wide-area network of its parent company, The Economist Group.

The chasm of understanding that exists between non-technical executives and technical professionals can lead to all sorts of problems, the most common of which is unfulfilled expectations on the part of the executive. "We tend to think everything is possible—it's just a matter of putting the right plug in the right machine. Sometimes there is no right plug," says Laird.

Not only does the average non-technical manager "assume wrongly that technology will take care of all problems," says Steve Paul, managing editor of *Datamation*, a Cahners Publishing Co. magazine for MIS managers, but most don't realize that introducing new technology also creates a host of new needs, problems and hidden costs.

Says consultant Bruce Campbell, president of the Caledon Group in New York City, if you implement a mission-critical electronic prepress system with the goal of never missing a publication deadline, "that leads you down to the issues that people never think about—

like back-up, redundancy and disaster planning. People put in these systems without thinking it all through."

For the uninitiated, overseeing the implementation of new pre-press systems, corporate databases and electronic sales tools can be frightening and confusing. Executives complain that technical staff members and consultants occasionally overwhelm managers with jargon; that consultants often recommend systems simply because they worked somewhere else, when in reality every magazine has different needs; that traditional MIS departments are experts on back-office business systems, but are often Macintosh-ignorant—and ignorant of editorial copy flow and magazine production processes.

Visionary planning

What's a beleaguered manager to do? The first and most critical element of any technology implementation is a visionary but feasible strategic plan, created by a committee of business and technical professionals.

John Sanders, director of production and manufacturing at Cahners Publishing, which owns 110 entertainment, computer, health and other magazines, says, "We have been in the process of examining just about every aspect of our operations and the technology that we use, from editorial systems to contracts and billing and ad production." A formal audit of existing information systems helps clarify where bottlenecks exist and how new technology can provide better or easier access to information.

Consultant Arthur Andersen & Co. audited Cahners' existing order-entry production system in an effort to understand how best to increase information access throughout the company. Says Cahners Boston Division vice president and general manager Mike Wisner: "They audited our system by taking an order and following it downstream."

While audits help determine the strengths and weaknesses of existing technology, small "pilot" projects can help determine whether major new plans will succeed or fail. Before rolling out a QuarkXPress-based production system to numerous magazines, Cahners piloted it at *Plastics World* and *EDN*. Arthur Andersen is auditing

---

■ 10 intelligent questions publishing execs should ask techies

Knowing what questions to ask technical professionals will help you uncover the potential problems and hidden expenses of new technology. Making the following inquiries should start technological change working for you—not against you.

1. What is the initial investment required to implement the new technology? What is the return on investment?
2. How will new technology change the organizational structure of this department or the company?
3. What new skills will existing staff need to learn?
4. What will training cost and how much time will staffers need to attend classes?
5. Will any new jobs appear or existing jobs disappear?
6. Do I have the in-house resources necessary to manage the new technology? If I use existing resources, will I be allocating them for the good of all concerned? (For instance, if the production manager must now manage desktop systems, will existing production efforts be shortchanged?)
7. Do the consultants bidding for my business demonstrate an in-depth understanding of my magazines?
8. Have I been offered viable alternatives to this new technology from which I may choose based on financial and managerial criteria?
9. Where a similar system has been implemented, has it achieved promised productivity increases?
10. Under normal circumstances, people resist change. How much resistance is there within the company to this new technology? How best can I "sell" the plan to those who will be affected by it?

---

the existing implementations, and Cahners will use the results to tune the new production system as it rolls out to more titles. Says Wisner: "We want to see electronically what happens. How many times do I fill out a piece of a paper and move that piece of paper? We want to look at efficiency levels."

Without strategic plans, executives have no way to evaluate the performance of technical professionals, or to know whether recommended systems will be appropriate for their needs.

To introduce desktop publishing to *Forbes,* says director of manufacturing and production John Romeo, "We have to come up with a strategic plan. Otherwise these consultants could go around in circles, tell you their systems worked at *Newsweek* or *Time.*

That's all well and good, but that's not our book."

A good technology plan forces executives to ask technicians the right questions (*see box*). "The question is never, 'What do the technicians know?' but, 'Where are we going with all of this?'" says Cahners' Wisner.

Plainspeak, please

Both during planning and after the plan is in place, directing techies to speak your language is important, says Laird. "Talk to me often, and in language I understand. Don't talk to me about megahertz and bits and bytes. Tell me where computers fit in terms of achieving the goals of the corporation. Tell me what the investment is, what the return on investment is, and what the opportunity cost is. Fit it into the overall strategic thinking for me, because at the end of the day that's what I'm qualified to do—I'm not qualified to say whether a Compaq system is better than a Dell."

At the same time, it's incumbent upon executives to learn technical concepts—to "move a foot in the direction of the techies, in order for the techies to move several yards in the direction of the senior manager," says Laird. Learning what technology can do today, how stable different technologies are and what new systems really cost—including the real price of learning curves, training and service—can help you avoid costly mistakes. Without "just enough knowledge to be dangerous," says Laird, executives are at a loss when evaluating the implications of technical recommendations.

"I can say things like 'relational databases,' and 'Oracle 7.0,' and 'Oh, it's going to be on OS/2? Why aren't we on UNIX?' Now I don't know what the hell that means, but I can ask because I know that UNIX is going to be here a long time," says Cahners' Wisner.

While he has a technical leg up on other publishing execs—he served for three years as publisher of *Datamation*—other senior managers, like Laird, are self-educated. Laird reads *PC Magazine* and his own title, which includes tutorials for the non-technical CFO.

Ultimately, says Wisner, a manager's job is to manage. "I don't worry about the day to day. What I look at is how we can do the right things from a structural point of view. Should we look at training so people get better information? Should we look at hiring quality people? Those are the buttons you push to increase efficiencies."

The payoff of exploiting technology has nothing to do with technical one-upmanship, but with making money through better information access, says Wisner. "I sell magazines, knowledge and lists, and if I can get my salespeople access to that stuff, I win." □

Need a Job? Think Like a Recruiter

BY TONY LEE

How's this for a great fantasy? You're toiling away at your job (or job search) and the phone rings. It's Ernie, the executive recruiter, and he wants to double your salary, boost your reputation in the publishing world, and provide you with lasting job security (or, at least, a sound employment contract) at a top-notch magazine publisher across town.

Sound too good to be true? Maybe not. More than 150,000 positions were filled by executive search firms in the United States and Canada in 1994, reports Kennedy Publications in Fitzwilliam, New Hampshire, which publishes the *Directory of Executive Recruiters*. But waiting for the phone to ring is about as productive as hoping that Ed McMahon will appear at your door with an oversize check in your name.

Instead, savvy magazine professionals should adopt the same tactics that successful executive recruiters and company hiring managers use to identify solid job prospects. By thinking like they do, you can anticipate recruitment needs and the best methods for becoming the primary candidate. That's the advice of David Richardson, co-founder and executive vice president of DHR International, a Chicago-based search firm.

"Job seekers need to stay current on the changing alternatives used by magazine publishing companies to identify their potential hires," says Richardson, who is based in the firm's Upper Montclair, New Jersey, office. "That way, they'll ensure that no stone is left unturned as they look for new job opportunities."

To this end, Richardson has identified eight methods being used most often these days by recruiters and publishers as they search for top candidates. By matching your efforts to these eight techniques, you'll enhance your visibility among hiring decision-makers, he says.

1. Start networking.
Inform your personal network of friends, business associates and colleagues of your job-changing interests, and give them a chance to help. Concentrate on meeting with contacts who are employed by publishing companies where you'd like to work, or who may have contacts of their own at those firms.

"A referral from an employee who feels good about his place of employment is the most cost-effective means a company can employ to secure new talent, since everybody wins," says Richardson.

"This is the way most jobs are filled," says Lew Levetown, a human resources vice president in New York. Adds Cathy Diamond, a New York staffing director, "My company welcomes and encourages employee referrals."

2. Participate in industry conferences.
Try to attend all magazine industry trade shows, particularly if companies that you've targeted are participating. Many headhunters attend with the sole purpose of identifying qualified, interested, mobile candidates. Being seen at conferences is especially helpful if you're from a lesser-known publication, or have recently graduated.

"There's always lots of networking going on, depending on the conference. Some are more amiable than others," says Marlene Kahan, executive director of the American Society of Magazine Editors in New York

> Inform your network of friends, business associates and colleagues of your job-changing interests and give them a chance to help.

City. "Formal, out-of-town conferences usually are attended more for educational reasons than for personal career advancement, although I'm always happy to accept résumés from our members and pass them along to the appropriate person if I hear of something," she says. Kahan notes that local gatherings—for example, luncheons and workshops—are usually better places to swap job leads.

In either case, don't rely on conferences and seminars as your main sources of leads. They simply don't occur often enough. And hiring managers who attend often use them only as screening events to separate applicants who are worth a second look from the rest of the field. That means you'll rarely leave a conference with a job offer in hand. At best, you may earn an invitation to interview, which means you'll have many more opportunities to wow them.

On the other hand, trade shows are perfect for learning the latest industry developments. "Magazines are looking at new means of distribution, such as CD-ROMs and online services, and unless you stay up to date, you'll be left behind," says headhunter Susan Bishop, president of Bishop Partners Ltd. in New York. "That's the real educational value of attending trade shows."

3. Join magazine industry associations, job clubs and career management groups.

Most publishing-related organizations, such as the Society of Professional Journalists and the Direct Marketing Association, have resources to help members locate job opportunities in person, online or through a phone-in service. In each case, success will be a reflection of your efforts to provide a precise self-description. Few publishers will approach your alumni relations office asking for a "smart, talented magazine executive." They may, however, seek a controller with 10 years' experience in trade association publishing. Use key words that will stand out to potential recruiters.

Associations also offer great networking opportunities. "Don't just join a trade group, but get involved," says Bishop. "Volunteer for or chair a committee. Then others will get to know you on a totally different level, not just professionally."

As you scan the horizon for opportunities, you might also contact past employers. "If you've left a job on good terms, it makes sense to stay in touch with former colleagues there" when you're looking for job leads, says Kahan. "Most people want to help if you let them."

4. Expand your use of help-wanted ads.

Look beyond your normal sources of recruitment advertising. Although the local Sunday paper is great (especially if you live and work in New York City, Chicago or Los Angeles), trade magazines and newsletters, as well as online job-listing services, are important too. "Follow up on as many help-wanted ads as you can handle," Richardson suggests.

Although surveys show that only 15 to 20 percent of all positions are filled through advertisements, they remain an important source of applicant leads, says Diamond. "Placing ads has been and is a successful, cost-effective approach to recruitment for us."

5. Be prepared to be telerecruited.

Given the improved equipment, widespread network coverage and more interested users, interviewing candidates by videophone is proving to be as popular a cost-saver as teleconferencing.

"Companies are close to being able to interview a group of prospects 3,000 miles away with the same realism as having them seated across the desk," explains Richardson. "With rising travel, accommodations and servicing costs," telerecruiting may become the next breakthrough technique in the search field.

Some large publishers already employ many of these practices for screening candidates, and it will soon be cost-effective for smaller businesses to use these tools and equipment as well.

In response, you'll need to practice your interviewing skills (which are different from the skills you've perfected as a reporter or editor) at every opportunity. Try answering typical interview questions with your spouse or a friend, and then videotape the results. Do you scratch your nose or say "uh" too often? Polish your style before you start scheduling real interviews.

6. Launch a direct-mail campaign and track your efforts.

With a targeted geographic area or specific job objective, such as art director or features editor, direct-mail campaigns have worked well for many candidates. Create a mailing list by reviewing the mastheads of publications you're targeting. It often pays to write to the person to whom you'd be reporting if you were hired, although some recruiters suggest targeting the publisher or editor so that your letter is filtered down from "on high" to the appropriate person.

Before spending big bucks on printing and postage, however, make sure that your correspondence is well written and sells your skills effectively. A great employer's name and address are worthless if your correspondence contains a blah, nothing-new letter and résumé.

Remember, too, that most publishers and search firms rely on databases to store candidate résumés. By computerizing your efforts as well, you'll gain an edge on the competition. "Through regular follow-up, you'll learn company requirements, and you'll make sure that your résumé is kept current in their files," says Richardson. Some candidates, for example, install automatic reminders in their systems that alert them when to follow up with each contact.

7. Use employment hotlines and faxes.

Stay alert to the methods and speed with which publishing companies want you to respond. Many firms have adopted 24-hour 800-numbers to record inquiries about job opportunities, allowing you to respond at off-hours regardless of where you're located geographically.

"Alert candidates make contact with potential employers as soon as possible, which could mean responding the same day an ad appears, contacting an employer at midnight to record an interest in an assignment, or simply faxing a résumé whenever it's ready," says Richardson.

8. Consider accepting a temporary position.

Many publishers have created supplemental workforces at the managerial level to avoid the expense of hiring more full-time employees. Faced with rising health costs, pension liabilities, absenteeism and reduced productivity when family concerns arise, more and more firms are developing trained, effective part-time professional staffs.

"Publishers have always used project-oriented people in circulation and marketing, but now it's happening more at higher levels," says recruiter Edward Koller Jr., president of Howard-Sloan-Koller Group in New York. "The more entrepreneurial the company, the more likely it is to happen," says Koller, who cites Chicago-based Crain Communications and Advanstar Communications in Cleveland as examples of companies more willing to hire interim managers.

Aside from helping you make mortgage payments and remain in the workforce, temporary positions can lead to permanent jobs. A major women's magazine in New York recently hired an associate marketing manager full time following her successful completion of a freelance project, which she researched and wrote at the magazine's offices.

"This process allows both the company and candidate an opportunity to get to know each other without the pressure of hiring deadlines," says Mike Kelly, a human resources director in northern New Jersey. "Such a process expands the universe of potential candidates well beyond those available at the time of a job opening, and allows the company to go directly to the most desirable candidate when there's a need." □

Who's Got the Skills to Succeed In an Overseas Assignment?

BY TONY LEE

Being chosen by your company to handle an overseas assignment, whether it's opening a new bureau or investigating foreign distribution channels, can be exciting and rewarding. Unless, of course, you get sent to the "wrong" country.

It takes more than technical expertise in your job and fluency in a foreign language to succeed abroad. Magazine expatriates swap horror stories about fellow editors and managers being groomed for the top who failed miserably in unfamiliar settings. Yet in many of these cases, it wasn't the person's fault. Their companies had failed to determine if they had the right personalities for the particular assignments.

One production manager for a major U.S. publisher is a good example of a bad match. At home, he was a modest, hard-working executive who made friends easily. But it didn't take long for problems to arise after he became the head of a printing plant in Indonesia.

In most developing countries, U.S. technical experts are respected and treated in a formal manner. In return, the experts are expected to solve problems as they arise. The production manager, however, was often unsure of what steps to take when a web press he hadn't worked with before needed attention. This prompted the manager to ask others for suggestions. In most cases, he eventually contacted a U.S. plant with a similar press for assistance. Yet his participatory approach and outward uncertainty caused the Indonesians to lose confidence in him. He was forced to leave after only a few months.

"If he had been more formal and said that he would provide the answer to each problem in a day or two, his expertise would not have been questioned," says Michael F. Tucker, Ph.D., an industrial psychologist and president of Tucker International Inc. in Boulder, Colorado, a relocation consulting firm. "This was a case of someone who was sent overseas [without regard to] his ability to adapt to a Third World factory environment.

"Many companies," Tucker continues, "mistakenly select people to go overseas using the same criteria they would use for domestic positions, instead of using a systematic approach to find out who will do well in a certain country and who won't." For example, an aggressive edi-

tor may succeed in Frankfurt or Berlin, where business assertiveness is valued. But that person would encounter great resistance among colleagues in Mexico or Japan, where personal relationships are developed before business is discussed, Tucker says.

A bad match usually creates two types of problems. The employee typically returns to the United States under a cloud of suspicion. Even though the person wasn't prepared for the foreign post, the fact that it didn't work out is enough to damage his or her self-confidence and reputation among colleagues. The other problem emerges when a company is unable to recognize its mistake. Instead of recalling the employee, the firm allows the person to serve out the assignment, even though the job isn't being handled effectively.

To help magazine publishers and other companies determine who's best suited for temporary overseas positions, Tucker has developed what he calls the 14 predictors of success. Each predictor covers an area where a transferee's personality can make the difference between success and failure. Before agreeing to become your magazine's newest foreign correspondent—or launching a job search with the aim of relocating abroad—review these predictors and compare them with your personality. You may be better suited for a post in New York than New Delhi.

Expectations: What do you expect life and work to be like in the new location? What are the probable difficulties and possible benefits? People who have positive expectations but are unrealistic about the challenges have a slim chance of succeeding.

Open-mindedness: You must be receptive to different beliefs and ideas without feeling as though your own are being threatened. People who suffer from ethnocentrism—the attitude that your country's way of doing things is inherently superior—can be expected to fail.

Respect for others' beliefs: Can you be nonjudgmental regarding other religions or political ideologies? Your willingness to demonstrate respect is important when trying to establish a meaningful intercultural relationship.

Trust in others: You need to believe that people in general are friendly and trustworthy. "This is a tough one in these days of terrorism, but despite what's going on, you must be able to trust the people you work and live with," says Tucker. Otherwise, personal and professional relationships will never develop.

Tolerance: Are you willing to endure the unfamiliar? This predictor concerns living conditions and your ability to leave the microwave and first-run movies—among other luxuries—at home. "The foreign city may be more crowded, hotter, colder or less developed than what you and your family can endure happily," says Tucker.

For example, one marketing manager with a New York magazine publisher was sent to China to investigate opening a new market. At home, he was accustomed to a lavish lifestyle and wasn't willing to accept inconveniences. "China offers a miserable lifestyle for most Americans," says Tucker. "The executive had to spend most of his time in the hotel where he lived, which wasn't as comfortable as he liked. He couldn't handle it and came home."

Personal control: Do you believe that you control your future? People who think things happen to them because of luck or fate won't easily adjust to a new environment. They will feel helpless and will adopt the attitude that, "It's out of my hands."

Flexibility: You must be willing to consider and respond to ideas and opinions that conflict with your own. "Flexibility is a way of approaching problems," Tucker explains. "It's the philosophy that there's always more than one way to handle the situation."

Patience: You can't become frustrated with unexpected delays. Understand the "sense of time" in the country where you are assigned.

Social adaptability: A loner or someone who feels most comfortable among a tight group of friends isn't suited for an overseas post. You must be able to socialize comfortably with new people in a new place.

A reporter in the Far East for a business magazine often complained she'd never meet a husband as long as she was stationed abroad. Finally, when she made the complaint directly to her boss, she was reassigned stateside.

Initiative: Self-starters tend to attain their goals and establish friendships quickly and with great ease. Without this initiative, you'll probably spend too much time waiting for others to put your plans into action.

Risk-taking: Exploring new ways of doing things and handling unusual challenges as they arise are critical abilities when overseas. But being good at taking risks isn't enough; you have to be better than the other guy to thrive in a foreign environment.

Sense of humor: "This is the most often overlooked ability," Tucker says. "Jokester-types aren't appreciated, but someone who takes things lightly and can inject humor

---

■ Would you be happy working abroad?

To determine how well you'd fare living and working abroad, check whether you agree or disagree with the following 10 statements by Dr. Michael Tucker:

1. In a group, I'm generally not one of the first to speak up and take charge.
2. When I'm in a new or unfamiliar situation, I feel uncomfortable.
3. Achieving my personal goals is a matter of being in the right place at the right time.
4. I cannot tolerate waiting in long lines.
5. I really don't know what to expect from living in a different country.
6. Sometimes I feel that I don't have enough control over the direction my life is taking.
7. I see no harm in trying to convince people that their political views need to change.
8. I dislike dealing with situations that involve unclear or complex issues.
9. The thought of going to a doctor in another country bothers me.
10. Getting used to different surroundings is something that doesn't come easily to me.

Score yourself: If you answered "disagree" seven or more times, you may be able to adapt well to a different culture, says Tucker.

---

into a difficult situation can ease tension and will facilitate further communications."

Interpersonal interest: A people-person who is genuinely interested in others will have a great advantage in adjusting to a new culture. This human element is critical when dealing with others for the first time, yet should come naturally to editors and managers who started their careers as reporters.

Spouse/family communications: There must be a great deal of communication among all family members before an assignment is accepted. "Troubled couples sometimes think a change of scene will help their marriages, but that never happens," says Tucker. "Pressures crash in on the family, often destroying it."

"The only way to assure a successful assignment is to discuss and examine each of these predictors before moving," says Tucker. "Even the best editor or circulation director at home can fail abroad, especially if he or she isn't prepared for what awaits."   □

Personnel

Help Wanted: Staffing a Start-up

BY FRANK FINN

Congratulations, you've been elected! You are the newly named editor of a soon-to-be-launched magazine. And like a newly elected U.S. president, the most critical decisions of your tenure must be made now.

Political pundits say the make-it or break-it stage of a presidency comes in the weeks between Election Day and the Inauguration, when the president-elect selects his cabinet. An editorship is no different: Choose the right people for your staff and you'll be well on your way to winning the battles that lie ahead.

You are probably fighting one battle already: the struggle to stretch your salary budget to cover the minimum number of bodies you feel you need to get your first issue out the door. Take heart: Few start-ups can fund a large editorial staff, but this is a situation where scarce resources are actually a virtue. Your magazine concept is a fledgling creature. The fewer hands that touch it, the better its chances of coming into the world intact.

As the keeper of the vision of what this new magazine will be, you have already devoted an inordinate amount of time to explaining it to people. You will be better off if you can assemble a small cadre of lieutenants and transmit your vision to them. The larger the launch staff, the more time you will spend explaining the vision instead of executing it.

Fill in your gaps

You can't build a good launch staff without a candid self-assessment. Most editors skew to one end or the other of the skill spectrum: Some are strong on ideas and must rely on others to fill in the details. Others are demons on planning and execution and could use help in striking that creative spark. So a good first step in your staffing is to hire your alter ego for the number-two editorial spot. If you're the steak, find someone who can supply the sizzle.

If you are an idea-a-minute person, find the organization man or woman who can sort through your brainstorms, fit the good ones into a coherent framework, and make them happen. Conversely, if you are the master planner who loves to build the structure and make the trains run on time, hire someone who can kick back and dream up an offbeat story approach, keep the writers' creative juices flowing, run free-wheeling brainstorming sessions with the designers, and otherwise keep everyone loose.

I learned the value of an alter ego some years ago when I got the nod as the lead editor of *Moviegoer*, a new monthly magazine for film buffs. Having never worked on an entertainment publication, I wasn't the obvious choice for the assignment. My strengths were in organization, line editing copy, and orchestrating an issue from start to finish. To compensate for my inexperience on entertainment titles, I teamed up with a colleague named David Epstein. He brought to the project a fan's encyclopedic knowledge of movies, experience working with the publicity agents who are critical to celebrity journalism, and a manic creative energy. Our combined skills and experiences made *Moviegoer* work.

■ Are all your bases covered?

An editorial staff must have a healthy balance of editorial skills. Use this matrix to see if your staff and the required job functions match.

Skill sets matrix	Editor	Managing Editor	Senior Editor	Associate Editor	Copy Editor
Vision					
Content expertise					
Organization					
Assigning					
Rewriting					
Prod. management					
Copy editing					
Story ideas					

Cover the critical functions

A successful magazine launch requires a staff of people with diverse skills. In your search for talent, make sure you have the following critical requirements covered:

Content expertise: This may seem an obvious point, but you can't waste time on a magazine launch waiting for your staff to learn about the subject of your new magazine. Most, if not all, of your editors should come to the project with at least some background in the field. Don't think that it is enough for you to know your subject cold. You can't afford to be giving seminars to the staff.

Story-idea development: Too many editors can't distinguish between a topic and a full-fledged concept for a magazine article. This can be fatal on a start-up, because there are no story proposals piling up in the in-basket from freelancers, and you are starting from scratch. You need at least one staffer besides yourself who knows how to research a topic, build a file of source material, and develop an angle appropriate to your new magazine.

Article assigning: To turn story proposals into publishable manuscripts, you must have editors who come to the launch with Rolodexes full of reliable freelance writers. They must have demonstrable skills in selecting the appropriate writer for a given assignment, providing guidance, and negotiating the fee and deadline. Bear in mind that your writers have no published issues to guide them, so it will take more time to give them direction. The percentage of stories that miss the mark will be high, so over-assigning is a must. All of that requires editorial horsepower.

Rewriting: As the deadline nears and the manuscripts flow in, you will inevitably find yourself with stories that need to be fixed on-staff rather than by the freelancer. You simply won't have time to return pieces to the writers for reworking. That's when a facile rewrite man or woman is invaluable on a launch.

Copy editing/fact-checking: A skilled hand on the copy desk is crucial to a successful launch. This editor will define the style of the magazine while simultaneously cleaning up errors of grammar, spelling and syntax. And if you don't have the luxury of hiring a fact-checker, the copy editor is usually best suited to verify critical facts and keep an eye out for libel trouble.

Deadline enforcement: Don't underestimate the importance of an organization man or woman who rides herd on copy flow, handles liaison with advertising and production, and generally enforces the schedule. But in a launch setting, you need someone with the experience to know that little will go according to plan—a pro who stays cool under fire and can remake a schedule in a heartbeat.

The leader of the pack

If, as you reviewed this list of critical functions, you kept thinking to yourself, "I'll do that," think again. As lead editor, you cannot do it all—the truth is that you can't even do half of it. You will have your hands full assembling your team, selling them on the vision, defining what fits that vision and what doesn't, making sure the design is right, helping your advertising and circulation people sell the concept, keeping costs under control, and keeping the investors or management team at bay. So decide early how you will apportion responsibility and then stick with that decision.

Another point: As you are interviewing for your staff, keep an open mind about hiring editors on a permanent basis versus putting them on a contract for a specified period. A contract allows you to try out staffers and offer permanent positions to those who prove themselves.

Whatever you do, find the best talent you can afford, people who share your passion for the magazine idea you are about to bring to life. Choose wisely and your launch could well be the most rewarding experience of your career. ☐

Personnel

Testing, Testing...

BY FRANK FINN

Nothing you do as an editor has a greater impact on the quality of your magazine than your hiring decisions. Your magazine is only as good as the staff you assemble to produce it, from the greenest editorial assistant to your seasoned second-in-command. So it behooves you to hire the best people you can find.

Easy to say, but difficult to do. Despite your best efforts to screen job candidates by scrutinizing their résumés and editing samples, checking recommendations, and putting them through a full day of interviews, you can still wind up with a dud. Is there anything else you can do? Yes. You can test them.

Make it a point to have serious candidates for editing jobs take a few relevant tests, and you'll have an objective measure of their knowledge and skills. Where do you find the tests? I recommend that you develop your own. At a minimum, you will need six: one each for proofreading, copy editing, writing, reporting, display copy writing, and story-idea generation. Use different combinations to screen candidates for different types of positions.

Prove they can proof

If there's one skill every editor needs, it's proofreading. So give all but the candidates for the most senior jobs a test that tells you whether they can spell, punctuate, capitalize and otherwise apply the rules of grammar and syntax. You'll also learn in a heartbeat whether an applicant knows the standard proofreading marks.

To put this drill together, just take a piece of copy from a back issue and fill it with every error you can think of—misspellings, uncapitalized words, omitted spaces, repeated words, bad punctuation and so on. If you include style mistakes—"fifty-six" instead of "56," for example—don't count it as an error if an applicant makes a choice you consider incorrect, but does so consistently.

Also, don't confuse applicants by planting clumsy phrases or other writing problems in this test. You will be asking them to copy edit in a separate test. Here, they are demonstrating strictly proofreading skills.

Can they copy edit?

What do editors do all day? Besides correcting errors of spelling, grammar and punctuation, they take awkward, disorganized copy and make it sing. Some call this line editing or top editing. I call it copy editing. You can test a person's copy-editing ability in at least two ways: Present a series of sentences that need to be fixed in a certain way (such as changing from the passive to the active voice), or reproduce part of an article fraught with problems and ask candidates to clean it up.

An editor who can't fix copy can only hurt a magazine, so I recommend using both approaches in a two-part exercise. In the "fix the sentences" section, test would-be staffers on their ability to recognize and correct passive constructions, wordiness, misplaced modifiers, and any other copy problems you find especially vexing. The second part should consist of three or four galley pages of text that suffers from typical writing problems—poor organization, bad sentence construction, weak or missing transitions, lapses in logic, unanswered questions, and so on. Unless you are blessed with an unusually talented and diligent stable of contributing writers, you shouldn't have to look too long for a piece of copy for this part of the test.

"Write," he said

A good writer doesn't always make a good editor, but no editor can function without sound writing skills. That's why I believe in asking candidates for editorial jobs to pen a one-page essay. You can let them choose any subject they like or give them a specific assignment. I've had reasonable success asking applicants to describe their most rewarding writing experiences. Often, their essays also provide insights into how they work.

Editors as reporters

At many magazines, staff editors must be able to function as reporters, generating some or all of the editorial content. If that's the case at your magazine, consider putting applicants through a reporting exercise. That's what they did at a trade magazine where I once interviewed for a job. After I met with the two top editors, they ushered me to a desk and handed me a package. Inside, I found a press release, several clippings for background, and instructions to write a four-paragraph news item. For additional information or a quote, I was to call one of the editors who posed as a company source. To make the test that much more real, I had 30 minutes to complete my story. (How did I do? Let's just say that after scanning my copy, the editor looked up and said, "You buried the lead.")

The art of assigning

At magazines that rely on freelance material, an editor's effectiveness hinges on the ability to help writers produce stories that suit the needs of the publication. A good way to test that ability is to have applicants compose an assignment letter giving guidance to a freelancer. Start with a query letter (a real one or one that you create) and ask each job prospect to write a response designed to elicit an article that will work well for your magazine. In the process, applicants will show how well they understand what you are trying to achieve, and will reveal their assigning styles as well.

Tailor this test so that it emphasizes the assigning skills that matter most to you. In its heyday, *Mother Earth News* was essentially written by its readers, people sharing tips on how to live off the land. Its editor gave job prospects an editing test designed to show how well they could rewrite instructions for amateurs. It consisted of a chaotic manuscript on ice fishing. "Show me how you would get a publishable story from this author," were his instructions. The results showed whether a prospect could reorganize the information and direct the ice fisherman to plug the manuscript's holes, but still leave him with a story he could recognize as his own.

Got any ideas?

The ultimate test of whether a candidate should work for your magazine is his or her ability to generate workable story ideas. Not only will you learn how well would-be staffers understand your publication and its readers, you'll also find out whether they know the difference between a topic for a story (nothing more than "what" it's about) and a well-developed idea complete with angle, format, suggestions for sources, and even approaches to illustrating the piece.

It takes a good deal of study and thought to develop story ideas, so you should save this exercise for the finalists in your search.

What if they object?

You may encounter job applicants who are reluctant to take a test of any kind. Here are some ways to defuse their objections:

- **I'm insulted.** Some applicants—especially more senior ones—may argue that, given their experience, they shouldn't have to take an editing test. "My qualifications should speak for themselves," they may say. Don't be a bureaucrat and say that "this is our standard procedure." Better to be open and say that you can't rely on published writing and editing samples because they may have been improved by others. You can also explain that testing makes the selection process more fair. A candidate who isn't as impressive on paper or in interviews may emerge as the best choice thanks to testing. Tests also make good tie-breakers, allowing you to distinguish fairly between equally attractive prospects for a job.

- **Your tests are biased.** Some candidates may raise the specter of job discrimination when asked to take editing tests. But you are on solid ground in using the tests described in this article to hire for editing positions. They meet the Uniform Guidelines on Employee Selection Practices set by the Equal Employment Opportunity Commission because they are job-related and do not unnecessarily invade an applicant's privacy. In fact, because they screen for skills and knowledge required to do the job, these tests are permissible even if they have a disparate impact on minorities, the disabled or other protected groups.

- **I'm not a good test-taker.** There are some who freeze when they sit down to take any kind of exam, and the pressure of facing a test with a job at stake may be too much for some people. That's no reason to abandon pre-employment testing. But you can reassure the test-panicked that you won't simply hire the candidate with the best score. The results of these tests should be considered in the context of each candidate's past experience, the results of a round of interviews, work samples and job references. If a person is right for the position, a weak performance on screening tests won't be enough by itself to eliminate that candidate from consideration.

- **This is work; I should be paid.** More experienced candidates for senior positions may raise this issue, especially if you ask them to spend substantial amounts of time editing copy or generating story ideas. To avoid being accused of trying to get free editorial labor, never ask job applicants to edit live copy that you have yet to publish. Always use old, unedited material.

For a sample package of editing tests, send a self-addressed, stamped envelope to Frank Finn, P.O. Box 1637, Glen Allen, VA 23060.

The Workforce Diversity Challenge

BY CHARLES F. WHITAKER

I'm pleased to complete *your survey even though our record of hiring minorities isn't impressive. However, I haven't hired anyone for eight years (extraordinary staff longevity in this business), so I won't claim to be embarrassed about it. I suspect that the industry is pretty monochromatic, but since I'm basing that assumption on nothing more than my own haphazard observations, I would be interested in the responses you receive.*
—John K. Manos, Editor in chief, *Consumers Digest*

For years, estimates of the number of minority staffers working in the magazine industry have been based on little more than the empirical observations of people with a vested interest in initiating such a head count—which generally has meant people of color concerned that so few of their colleagues were also people of color. Although many magazine publishers and editors have expressed embarrassment about what everyone admits is a dismal record of hiring and retaining minorities, efforts to prod the industry into undertaking a baseline survey that would establish some employment benchmarks and help in the development of hiring goals have been soundly rebuffed.

Minority hiring lags

When speaking on the record, industry executives base their reluctance to support or participate in such research on the proprietary nature of the information. "We're talking largely about privately held companies," says Vaughn P. Benjamin, director of the Workforce Diversity Council of the Magazine Publishers of America (MPA). "There is a strong belief that releasing information about employee numbers could provide an advantage to competitors."

Adds MPA president Donald Kummerfeld, publishers have dismissed data-gathering on minority hiring practices as a "statistical game of who is doing better or worse."

But the fact is, more than 70 percent of the magazines we polled had no minority employees at all. This included the bulk of the 32 regionals surveyed, many of the enthusiast and shelter publications, and three New York City-based magazines, each with a circulation of more than one million.

Our polling method was simple—and random. Focusing solely on consumer magazine editors, my research associate and I dispatched surveys to 625 publications. There were 211 responses, for a response rate of 34 percent, and they encompassed a broad range of magazines, from publications with more than eight million readers and 53 editorial employees to small operations catering to fewer than 20,000 readers. In the survey, each respondent was asked to identify the demographics of his or her staff, a process that produced data on 1,169 people.

Although only 3 percent of the editors who responded to the survey work for publications directed at minority audiences, their staffs accounted for about 19 percent of the 1,169 staff members covered by the study. Furthermore, of the 28 minority editors and managing editors identified in the survey, 20 (or 71 percent) work at minority publications.

Again, the 211 responses we tallied confirm what a glance at most magazine offices will tell you: The minority presence in the industry is indeed small. About 12.6 percent of the 1,169 employees in our pool of respondents are of Asian, African-American, Native-American or Hispanic descent. But on a positive note, we found several happy surprises in the numbers and in the anecdotal information collected in follow-up interviews. It turns out that the nineties may very well be a watershed period for American magazines in terms of staff diversity; in fact, the call to action on this front is perhaps louder these days than at any other time in industry history.

'A very incestuous business'

It's not just minority employees who are joining the crusade for nondiscriminatory hiring practices.

"I think we're seeing greater recognition in the industry that we haven't done well in terms of recruiting and retaining minorities, and that perhaps we need to cast our recruiting nets wider," says Marion Beale, director of financial planning for The New York Times

Sports/Leisure Magazines and chair of the Trumbull, Connecticut-based company's diversity steering committee. "This has been a very incestuous business. We've tended to just hire ourselves over and over again."

The survey supports the assertion that in the absence of any pressure to do otherwise, employers are content to hire only those who look like them.

"For all the complaining about affirmative action that you hear, I was really struck when I entered this business by how few minorities there really are."
—John Moore, associate reviews editor, *Home Office Computing*

African-American and Hispanic employment lags dramatically. While the U.S. Bureau of the Census, a unit of the Department of Commerce, shows that African-Americans currently make up 12 percent of the population, they represent only 4.7 percent of the editorial population in our survey. Americans of Hispanic origin, an estimated 10 percent of the population, made up 3.2 percent of the surveyed employees.

The survey suggests that some groups are better represented that others in the industry. For example, the percentages of Asian-American and Native-American editorial employees come much closer to mirroring overall U.S. population patterns. The Census Bureau estimates that Asian-Americans will represent about 4.4 percent of the population by the year 2000, and about 3.6 percent of the editorial employees working at the surveyed titles are of Asian descent. Native-Americans, who make up just under 1 percent of the U.S. population, also represent slightly less than 1 percent of the surveyed magazines' editorial staffs.

In general, though, the survey suggests a rise in minority hiring. Of the 290 employees hired at the responding magazines for full-time editorial jobs in 1994, 86 (or close to 30 percent) were minorities. Most joined the staffs of magazines that had circulations of 500,000 or more and were based in or near major metropolitan areas.

Even with those hires, concern remains that the industry has forged a quota system, pigeonholing minorities in certain jobs. When Stephanie Hamilton, now a senior editor at Time Inc. Ventures' *Parenting*, broke into the industry in 1978 as an assistant editor at *McCall's*, her predecessor was an African-American woman. "I think that made it easier for them to see that a black woman could do the job," she says.

Such seat-filling tactics explain why many minority professionals reject the quota concept entirely. "Quotas too often result in a very limited view of how many minorities should be in the industry and what they should be doing," says Jack E. White, a national correspondent, columnist and recruiter for *Time*, who throughout his 23-year tenure at Time Inc. has aggressively pushed management to diversify.

Racism not the issue, editors say

While many editors expressed concern about staff homogeneity, they attributed the lack of diversity more to their niche, location and size, rather than to racism. Micca Leffingwell Hutchins, editor of *Sailing*, a Port Washington, Wisconsin-based monthly published by Port Publications, Inc., offered this explanation for why her staff of 12 has no minority editors:

"Our [Wisconsin] community of 8,000 is 99 percent white. Nearly everyone is of German, Luxembourg, perhaps English descent. When we hire someone, we are happy simply to be able to fill the position, much less seek out a special race. A simple survey will never reveal this important background component, and, therefore, provides erroneous findings."

Another argument is that minority candidates don't appear to be out there, much as editors would like to diversify their teams. John Manos, editor in chief of Chicago-based *Consumers Digest,* says that on those rare occasions that staff openings occur, he simply doesn't see many résumés from minority candidates. "Journalism just doesn't seem to be attractive to minorities," he says. "But when we receive résumés that indicate the individuals are minority candidates, we do our best to interview them, if they're qualified."

Meanwhile, veteran minority journalists and industry observers bristle at the rationale that there are no qualified applicants to choose from. They say that magazines have long operated like country clubs with no membership options for minorities. "For too long, words like 'qualified' and 'best candidate' were used as exclusionary tools to keep minorities out of the industry," says Leo Harley, manager of staffing at Manhasset, New York-based CMP Publications, Inc., and a 28-year industry veteran who has done consulting work and headhunting for a number of publishing companies, including Time Inc. "The principles would be fine if the system were truly a meritocracy, but more often selection has been made based on trait characteristics, not job capability."

In turn, magazines—because of their special niches—

■ Methodology

Our one-page survey was limited to editorial staffers at 625 consumer magazines, culled from every seventh, then every fifth, consumer magazine listed in SRDS' September 1994 edition. Names were individually checked for accuracy, with contact names, addresses and circulation figures verified by phone from December 1994 to February 1995. Duplicates and now-defunct magazines were eliminated from the pool. Surveys were sent to managing editors and were coded for location to assure anonymity and to tally responses according to geographic location, staff size, circulation and the magazine's subject matter. By our April deadline, 211 magazines had responded, a response rate of 34 percent. The margin of sampling error is 6.5 percentage points.

In the Northeast—with 252 total publications responding—70 magazines (or 28 percent) responded; of those, 10 percent had either a Hispanic or an African-American editor. In the West, 39 percent responded, 11 percent of which had an Asian, African-American or Hispanic in the top post. In the Midwest, 40 percent responded, with 7 percent showing either an Asian, an African-American or a Native-American as editor. Of the 24 percent responding from the Southwest, no magazine had a minority editor, nor did the 31 percent responding from the Northwest. And, of the 37 percent responding from the Southeast, 6 percent had an African-American or Hispanic editor.

—Margaret Littman, research associate

have faced little internal or external pressure to broaden the workforce pool, also contributing significantly to the industry's relatively uniform complexion. "Magazines exist in this very insular world where everyone comes from the same place and has the same background," says *Time's* White. "There definitely is no welcome mat out for minorities in this industry, and for too long the levers of pressure didn't exist to force any kind of change."

It was pressure, after all, that forced other media to heed the diversity call. "If I may paraphrase from Frederick Douglass," says Jay Harris, author of the first newspaper industry employment report and now chairman and publisher of the *San Jose Mercury News*, "power concedes nothing without a demand."

That first census of newspaper employment, published in 1978 (and now done annually by the Ameri-

can Society of Newspaper Editors), helped "clear away the underbrush about how well or poorly newspapers were doing in terms of diversity," Harris says. "With the release of the report, we had a factual basis for challenging the industry to make progress."

That survey also enabled editors to gauge improvements on the hiring front, a practice the magazine industry could easily adopt. While the survey showed that in 1978, only 3.95 percent of daily newspaper employees were minorities, minority employment now hovers close to 11 percent. Although this is still far behind the overall minority population of 20 percent (according to Census Bureau figures), Harris asserts that ASNE would not have made significant gains without an annual reckoning: "It legitimized the notion that progress should be made each year."

The cumulative impact of the dramatically changing demographics of our society will have a profound impact on the magazine industry in the next century and, even more immediately, in the coming decade. Therefore, it's of bottom-line self-interest to any publisher to respond actively by investing in diversity.

—excerpt from the action plan of the MPA Workforce Diversity Council

In certain pockets of the magazine industry, executives have signed on to the notion that diversifying the workforce makes good business sense. As a result, companies such as The New York Times Sports/Leisure Magazines, CMP Publications and Time Warner have actively expanded their recruiting efforts. They are also focusing on making their corporate climate more hospitable to women and minorities. "From our standpoint, the goal is simply to do everything we can to put the best possible team on the street," says CMP's Harley. "That means a team that reflects the diversity of the culture in which we live. There's nothing all that altruistic about it. Diversifying our staffs means broadening our pool of readers and advertisers—no matter what niche you're in—and it increases the intellectual capital in the workforce."

Still, many expect that progress will be slow and halting, even as the companies remain committed to diversity. Says White, who is leading the charge at Time Inc.: "I want the corporate culture in magazines to change to the extent that when I walk into our offices, I can see the same broad spectrum of humanity that you see when you walk down the streets of New York City." □

section two

strategic focus

"Complacency, especially in the magazine business, **is death."**—p. 138

"The problem with custom publishing is that it **tends to be a feast-or-famine** proposition."—p. 148

"We just don't think that we should be **giving away online** what our members have to pay for."—p. 158

"Although European publishers are very open to ideas, **the host market always rules."**—p. 160

How to Get More Respect For Trade Magazines

BY RICHARD M. O'CONNOR

The problem with most trade magazines is that they accept mediocrity. Indeed, too many trade editors think that all they have to do is serve their industry and compete against their competitors— and they've done the job. Well, that's baloney.

Trade publications, like all publications, compete for a reader's time. Today's readers simply do not have the time to go through all the periodicals that come across their desks or arrive at their homes. If you want your book to be noticed, to grab a reader's attention and sustain that reader's loyalty, it must look and read as good as a top consumer book. Anything less is unacceptable.

When I became editor in chief of *Successful Meetings* some years ago, it was the leading magazine in the industry. I thought it was a quality magazine. But I also felt it could be better—much better. How I set about making it better illustrates several theories I have about publishing a successful trade magazine.

Complacency is death

First, I went to the publisher and discussed my plans for changes. I wanted to hire better writers, better photographers, better illustrators. I also wanted to redesign the entire book. Most of all, I wanted to add UV coating to the cover to give the magazine a polished, quality image.

The publisher looked at me as if I were nuts. "Are you kidding me?" he asked. "Why fix something that's not broken—especially when the costs would be high?"

My answer was simple. Complacency, especially in the magazine business, is death. Times change. Readers change. Tastes change. And it's the response to these changes that govern the rise and fall of a magazine's popularity. If a magazine isn't willing to adjust to ever-changing times, without sacrificing its essential philosophy, it will gradually become as dry as burnt toast.

The higher the quality, the more ads you will get

Since I clearly had my publisher's attention, I kept going. I want to create a magazine whose name is synonymous with editorial quality, I said. Indeed, I continued, the more quality you put into the book, the more advertising you will sell. I guarantee it.

The publisher rubbed his chin vigorously and thought a moment. Then he said, "Okay, fine. If we don't sell more ads, we can always get another editor."

Fair deal. We shook hands.

The cover must compel

The first thing to go was the logo. It was too small and outdated; it had as much appeal as a faded billboard. We tested over 80 logos and ultimately chose a typeface, called Didi, that gave us a look that was bolder, cleaner and richer, and that was infinitely more pleasing to the eye.

The next thing to be attacked was the cover itself. I told the staff that I wanted the cover to compete against *Esquire, GQ, Time, Fortune*, etc. It didn't matter that we weren't a newsstand publication. What mattered was that we thought like one. All I cared about was grabbing a reader's attention, either through a clever illustration or a strong photo.

I was prepared to spend to get what I wanted. Either original shots, or in some cases, stock photography. But only stock from the best: Scavullo, William Wegman, the best in the world. My feeling was—and always will be—that we live in a visual era. Therefore, the cover must be visually appealing. It must have a strong image. It must make a statement. It must provoke, stimulate, shock, motivate, excite, amuse, arouse. It must give the reader a sense of the magazine's spirit. And finally, it must compel—absolutely compel—the reader to pick up the magazine and read its contents.

Dramatize what's inside

Next, the table of contents was changed from one page to two pages. I wanted more white space, more visuals. Aside from making the table of contents more aesthetically pleasing, I wanted it to be an easier to use, easier to read directory of our editorial content.

I also wanted our layouts to be cleaner, bolder, more dramatic. I wanted more attention given to headline design and type. To accomplish this, I had story deadlines moved up. This gave the art department more time to prepare, to experiment, to come up with story presentations that really broadcast an editorial message.

Strive for lively, provocative editorial

The next change was critical. I didn't want the bland business reporting that is all too common among trade publications. I wanted stories with themes, with scenes, characterization and dialog. I wanted the writers to have more time and more freedom to pursue their stories. I didn't want them locked into a particular style. I wanted fresh, different voices. I wanted livelier, more provocative copy. I wanted humor, pictorials, satire, off-beat profiles. I wanted, in essence, an eclectic offering of information and entertainment. My goal was for the reader to expect the unexpected.

Readers have responded to this change. Our letters to the editor have more than doubled, averaging 25 to 40 per issue—the majority praising the new design and editorial approach.

Let me say here that the money we spent reworking and redesigning the magazine (which was not, by any means, astronomical) has been recouped many times over. Ad pages soared, up 131 for 1990 over 1989. Ad revenue for that period was up almost 8 percent—and we finished the year with the highest profits in history. But best of all, we created an exhilarating spirit among the staff—both editorial and sales—that we were on a roll, that we were hot—exciting! And if you don't think that motivates salespeople, you're crazier than Saddam Hussein.

Don't be afraid to antagonize advertisers

Why are so many editors of trade magazines afraid to give their magazines a point of view? Too many think their role is simply to report industry news. True, that's a large part of it. But I believe it's also the magazine's job to interpret the news—intelligently and fairly, yes,

The cover must provoke, stimulate, shock, motivate, excite, amuse and arouse.

but also at the expense, sometimes, of advertisers.

Too often, trade editors see their role as advocates for the industry they cover. They shy away from stories that might irritate a reader—especially if that reader is an advertiser. Yet by doing this, an editor cheapens his product. Readers are not dumb. They know who is producing puff, who has editorial integrity and who doesn't.

Here's a perfect example. Not long ago, a story emerged that put one of our largest advertisers in a bad light. The editors spent hours discussing the pros and cons of reporting the incident. Was it worth it? Would the advertiser get annoyed? Worse, would he pull his advertising?

Since at that time I was both editor in chief and publisher, the final decision was mine. I decided to pursue it. As it turned out, the story was terrific. It had all the elements: drama, characters, controversy, intrigue. It ran at length—and it made the advertisers who were covered pull their ads.

Yet, here's the irony. Readers loved the story. It caused so much discussion in the industry that a few weeks after the piece appeared, the angry advertisers came to see me. They said the story caused them great pain and substantial business losses. But they admitted it was a testimony to the validity of our magazine that so many responded so passionately.

I can't tell you how good that made me feel. I was elated by the power of journalism—good journalism, tough journalism. Not the kind of puff that too often characterizes the trades.

One final note. As long as I've been in trade publishing, I've heard trade writers and editors complain that trade publications never get the respect that consumer books do. Well, as far as I'm concerned, the reason is simple: Most don't deserve it. Yet it doesn't have to be that way. Boring and bland—or bright and biting? The choice is yours. ☐

Celebrating Service Magazines

BY PAMELA FIORI

Not much has been written about service magazines. There's no textbook that I am aware of (although there should be). You can look under "Journalism" in the *Encyclopaedia Britannica*—an 11-page entry in Volume 15—but what you'll find is just about every possible subhead *except* service journalism. That's pathetically little when you consider how important service magazines are and how far they have come in the 250-year history of magazines.

Service magazines are held in rather low esteem—not by readers, but by a number of journalism schools and even some editors and writers. It's as if the word "service" and the word "journalism" should not be spoken in the same breath—as incompatible a coupling as "corporate culture." Possibly that is because service magazines so often deal with the realities of everyday life, and not matters of cataclysmic importance. Earthquakes, wars, terrorism, global warming, drugs, poverty, homelessness. These are more the stuff of *Time* and *Harper's* than *Harper's Bazaar* or *HG*. And it is assumed that, if service magazines cover subjects of global significance, it's often with a limited approach.

A positive influence

Service magazines, detractors say, are more apt to be micro than macro; local as opposed to global; practical and directional; a bit flat-footed at their minimum and bordering on gimmicky when they try too hard. But at their best, they can have tremendous impact: They can change the way readers think or act, alter the way they spend time or money, influence style, eating habits and travel plans, improve relationships, diminish biases.

One of service magazines' most constant crusaders, James A. Autry, formerly Meredith's group president, defines them as "the delivery of ideas, information (and in some cases, inspiration) through words, illustrations, design and various formats."

He is talking here of the graphic devices of service magazines: lists, boxes, sidebars, boldfacing, charts, graphs, maps, calendars, recipes, Q&As, polls, step-by-steps, diagrams—anything that highlights the information for the reader in an accessible way.

"And," he continues, "it is intended to produce, on the part of the reader, a positive response. In other words, it goes beyond the journalism of pure information to include the expectation that the reader will do something as a result of the reading."

Do what?

Take action. Change behavior. Build something (a bookcase, a bank account, his or her confidence or upper arms). Find a better way (to talk to a child, a spouse, a boss, a contractor). Devise a smarter way (to eat, dress, argue, lose weight, entertain 12 people in a tiny apartment, dispose of garbage in a politically correct manner).

Service magazines help the reader cope—with aging parents or one's aging self, an alcoholic co-worker, a serious illness, unemployment, change of address or change of life. They might even inspire the reader to contribute to society—by volunteering his or her services, by writing to Congress, by joining a local environmental group. Or, closer to home, by spending more time with the kids.

A little history: Women's magazines were our first service publications. And the first of any note, *Ladies' Home Journal*, began life way back in 1883. Today, 113 years later, it is still with us, owned by Meredith. Two years later, in 1885, along came *Good Housekeeping*. In 1876, a magazine called *The Queen* made its debut and eventually became *McCall's*. In 1922, *Better Homes and Gardens*, another Meredith book, arrived on the scene (originally called *Fruit, Garden and Home*). *Family Circle* and *Woman's Day* followed.

Why so many women's books? Because—as if you didn't know—women were and still are the greatest buyers of consumer goods in America. Editors and

> At their best, service magazines can change the way readers think or act.

publishers caught on to this. So did advertisers. Before television, women's magazines were about the best way to reach this powerful audience.

For women only?

But what about men? There are plenty of men's magazines—*Esquire, GQ, Playboy, Details* (originally a very trendy female-oriented fashion book), *Sports Illustrated*. And there are male-oriented books on automobiles, stereo equipment and furniture making, as well as magazines like *Popular Science* and *Popular Mechanics*, to name a few. But there aren't any men's service books to speak of.

In 1990, there was an attempt to launch a service book called *Men's Life*, but it didn't live past a first issue. Maybe *Men's Health*, which is now up to an encouraging 500,000 able-bodied readers, could be the first men's service book to make it. But, is it possible that men don't *want* advice about how to conduct their personal lives? Or is it that they don't want the same prescription used in women's service books? Is there a "new man" or isn't there? And if there is, does he want a how-to book to call his own? Could it be that many men have problems with the very idea of service information, at least as it has been traditionally dispensed?

If so, it's understandable. The term "service journalism" sounds worthy, but isn't very tantalizing. Or, it can be gussied up to sound tantalizing but not very believable—"Thin Thighs in 30 Days," "The Only Diet You'll Ever Need," "Totally Change the Way You Look Without Plastic Surgery." Promises, promises.

But women's service magazines are changing. Some—not all—are bagging the silliness and getting smarter.

In 1991, *Glamour* won the National Magazine Award—its second—in the category of "General Excellence." It was described by the judges as a magazine "that radiates integrity and never condescends to its audience . . . all in all, a magazine for grown-ups."

Also last year, *Family Circle* won a National Magazine Award for a compelling investigation of a small southern town with a big toxic-waste problem. *Family Circle* pursued that story despite being warned by a local newspaper to "stay in the kitchen where it belongs." In sticking with its investigation, it performed a major service for its readers and for that town by exposing the attendant horrors of toxic waste.

Other kinds of magazines have made service their business—city magazines, for example. *New York*

■ The box of boxes: 10 tips on service

1. **Keep it simple.** Sidebars and boxes are intended to be great information, not great literature.
2. **Make it lively.** The tone and look of the material should, at the very least, be inviting. Just because it is straightforward information does not mean it should be dull.
3. **Be kind to the reader.** Maps and charts should be legible. The typeface should not require the use of a magnifying glass. Don't superimpose type over complicated backgrounds or use reverse type. This is the not the place to get fancy.
4. **Display the material prominently.** To relegate service information to runover is to diminish its importance.
5. **Be accurate.** Fact-check service information scrupulously. It is tedious, to be sure, but absolutely essential. If the information is proved wrong, readers won't trust you in the future.
6. **Avoid giving the reader too much.** Too much data weighs down the effort. The more selective the material, the better.
7. **Stick to one style.** This doesn't mean that all service material should look or read alike—that would be boring. Rather, develop a standard format that the reader (and the copy department) can follow.
8. **Coordinate with the art department.** Need I say more?
9. **Exercise restraint.** Too many graphic devices will confuse and irritate the reader.
10. **Don't fake it.** There must be a genuine reason to give service information. It's not the box, it's what is *in* the box that counts.

Magazine is foremost among them. Its secret is making sense out of the world's most nonsensical city, in good times and, even more, in bad times. It used to be said that the quintessential *New York* article in the 1970s would be titled "The 10 Most Powerful House Plants In Manhattan." Last year *New York Magazine* won two National Magazine Awards—one for "Personal Service" (on preventing child abuse) and the other, a buyer's guide to audio equipment, for "Special Interest."

The key: Be indispensable

Other city magazines have also done their part for their cities in the name of service journalism—sometimes effectively, sometimes comically, most modeling their coverage on *New York Magazine*.

A city magazine must be indispensable. In fact, being indispensable is the key to service journalism. If readers don't need the magazine, depend on it, use it, it is not—in effect—providing a necessary service.

All editors can apply the principles and devices of service journalism to their magazines, for their audiences, in a voice that their readers appreciate. When *Travel & Leisure* began in 1971, there were just so many destinations and just so many ways to get there. Today, the possibilities are staggering—not only the number of places to go, but ways to experience them. What we did with *T&L*—and what made it turn a sharp corner to profitability—was to give, sometimes even to make, choices for the reader. We did the essential (often costly) legwork, made the considered judgments, and then packaged what we had in a way that was manageable and interesting for the reader, and compatible with the magazine's style. It became—and still is—*T&L*'s job to figure it all out for its readers. But not without some consequences.

Every shred of advice a service magazine publishes is burdened with editorial accountability. So every recommendation counts. We are living in an era of the cynical consumer who is demanding more value and better service for his dollar. That sentiment translates directly to what readers expect from service magazines.

Creating a service magazine that matters doesn't mean creating mindless lists and vapid advice. Readers want intelligent choices and solid judgments delivered in a compelling way. If those judgments prove correct, you will keep your readers. If the magazine misses its aim, not just once but time and again, readers will move on and find another magazine they *can* trust. It is that simple. And that brutal.

To steer readers wrong is virtually to hand-deliver them to the competition—who's waiting with open arms and a subscription card. □

> Creating a service magazine that matters doesn't mean mindless lists and vapid advice. Readers want intelligent choices.

City and regionals

The Revival of City and Regional Magazines

BY HEIDI SCHULTZ

City and regional magazine publishers have learned the hard way that they are not immune to the ills of a down economy. Among the hardest hit during the recession, city and regional magazines are fighting back with creative, innovative programs to strengthen their advertising revenues and build upon their local franchises. Publishers have come to realize that, in order to survive, their magazines must parlay their assets in a way that will enhance the price-value relationship for both readers and advertisers.

Probably the greatest asset for city and regional magazines is their proximity to their readers. This proximity helps create a strong bond with readers that is based on an intimate understanding of local issues, interests and tastes. It also enables the magazines to assist advertisers in creating highly relevant local communications programs that often go beyond the printed page.

In truth, all markets are local. With the exception of catalogs and goods sold through 800 numbers, most sales eventually take place in a venue where the customer is physically present. Whether the transaction be in a retail store, a bank, a liquor store or a travel agent's office, almost all sales are, ultimately, local sales.

City and regional magazines have high concentrations of customers close to the point where a purchase can be made. To take advantage of this, publishers of city and regional magazines are thinking beyond selling ad space and learning to develop integrated marketing programs for their customers. As Mike O'Brien, publisher of *Sacramento Magazine*, puts it, "We have to tighten the feedback loop for advertisers."

Several techniques are being used to do just that and give advertisers tangible results beyond the walk-in traffic that is so difficult to measure even in good times. Reader-response programs—whether bingo cards or 800-number hotlines—are increasingly popular among city magazines and their advertisers. What is surprising is that these programs are generating response not only in categories where requests for information have traditionally been important (such as travel, financial planning and appliances), but in the more impulsive retail and restaurant categories as well.

Indianapolis Monthly, among others, is working on ways to counter the perception that city magazines are not appropriate vehicles for sale advertising. It ran an eight-page "January Sale" section on a lighter, newsprint-like stock that attracted advertisers who would normally use only the newspapers at that particular time of year. According to Deborah Paul, publisher, the section worked extremely well for the advertisers.

Event tie-ins

Another way city and regional magazines take advantage of their proximity to the marketplace is to tie in advertisers with highly visible events within their markets, often custom designing sections or inserts for the advertisers. In the fall of 1991, *Chicago* created a four-page, pull-out guide to the International Film Festival for an airline company. Taking a different tack, *Boston Magazine* worked with the city government to create a pull-out calendar of summer events and sold sponsorships to three non-competing advertisers whose products were incorporated in the various events.

Big ideas are great for big advertisers, but the core of any city or regional publication is made up of the small, local establishments in its service area. These advertisers are what give the magazines part of their special flavor and usefulness to readers. Since it is the smaller advertisers who are the most vulnerable during a recession, city and regional magazines have had to develop cost-efficient ways for them to advertise. Formatted ad pages, which are usually built around a theme such as "River North" or St. Patrick's Day, are increasingly popular as a way to go after limited ad budgets.

Learning from newspapers

Detroit Monthly has borrowed an idea from the newspaper industry by creating a micro-regional buy in upscale Oakland County. This special section, with editorial tailored to local interests, is bound into copies of *Detroit Monthly* distributed in the county, and is also overrun for distribution to nonsubscribers. The lower out-of-pocket cost combined with high penetration within Oakland County has made this an attractive product for small local establishments serving a limited geographical area.

Another way publishers try to give small advertisers greater benefit is to create additional exposure for them while maintaining the church-and-state editorial definition. For example, *Chicago* runs a merchandising page called "What's in Store" that is open to retail clients with a six-time or greater commitment. The section, which is marked as advertising, lists the in-store events going on during the month, such as beauty clinics, trunk shows, demonstrations and so forth. Other magazines have similar programs built around specific categories of business.

Multimedia advertising packages are a hot topic among national magazines, and city and regional magazine publishers are experimenting in this area as well. In some cases they are packaging buys in conjunction with local radio and television stations, even outdoor billboards. In others, they are using their knowledge of the area to provide programming on radio or TV.

Increasingly, city and regional publications are taking advantage of their position as the local authority on their markets and their readers and moving into projects beyond the confines of their monthly publications. This is what Ken Neill, publisher of *Memphis* and current president of the City and Regional Magazine Association, calls "the concept of the city magazine as the Mother Ship." The possibilities are endless, but here are a few examples of the creative endeavors going on around the country:

• Publishers are leveraging their local business contacts by producing custom-designed publications for both non-profit and for-profit organizations. These can be distributed either through the magazine's regular distribution system, or through retailers, hotels, the client organization or other innovative channels.

Honolulu Magazine produces 22 such publications on a regular basis for a wide variety of clients including shopping malls, car rental companies and visitor bureaus. Other city and regional magazines have built a significant business in custom publishing for chambers of commerce, regional airlines, retailers, cultural organizations and local businesses.

• Editorial assets are being leveraged as well to create additional newsstand revenue and incremental ad dollars. Several publishers supplement their monthly frequency with a 13th and even a 14th issue, typically a city guide or menu guide. Others are at work on stand-alone annual publications devoted to special interests such as home remodeling, weddings, newcomers and health-care. *Memphis* saw a need in its marketplace and developed an alternative weekly newspaper that has shown itself to be relatively recession-resistant.

Meeting the challenge

Most of the city and regional publishers I talk with know there is more to survival in the nineties than just the ability to do great merchandising and create special events, sections or publications. It must stem from a deep understanding of the marketplace, what their readers want, what advertisers hope to achieve, and what consumers are likely to respond to.

Expand your research

To meet this challenge, there is a need for even greater knowledge about readers and advertisers. In these tough times, it is hard to justify expanding research budgets, but the few who have made such a move have found the investment has paid off. *Connecticut* conducted an advertising perception/response study geared to retail buyers that gives clients insight into how their ads are received by readers. Although this type of study has been common in the business press for years, the application to consumers is innovative and should be carried further.

Underlying all this activity is a world view of the city or regional magazine as being at the center of an economic network of buyers and sellers. In this position, the magazine's role is to bring it all together. All publishers—not just those of city and regional magazines—are faced with the challenge of regaining the confidence of advertisers, and of adapting to the new imperatives of integrated marketing. Although everything begins with a strong local editorial franchise, this franchise can be parlayed into a wide variety of programs and products to help advertisers build traffic and sell products. □

> City and regional magazines are using new techniques to give advertisers tangible results.

Caught Between a Rock And A Database

BY LAMBETH HOCHWALD

Stephen Phillips, circulation director of *San Diego Magazine*, is more convinced than ever that, without a database, his monthly will soon lose its competitive edge. The time is right, he thinks, to create a multifaceted database so that the title can publish a bilingual edition geared to wealthy Mexicans who do their shopping over the border, who account for nearly half of the retail sales in certain areas of San Diego.

But it's hard to market subscriber names without a targeted database. For starters, there's the steep financial cost of overlaying outside demographic information, coordinating data retrieval with the fulfillment house, and then deciding how much additional customer information *San Diego* will need in the future. Then there's the expense of tapping into Mexican statistical records. "I've heard that it can cost $1.50 a name to get a useful database up and running," says Phillips. "That's a lot of money to convert our total file of over 40,000 names. We need to think about whether we can justify that $60,000 setup cost."

Phillips' cost consciousness is shared by many other regional circ directors. All, it seems, are coping with downsized budgets, overburdened staffs and upper management that wants to do database marketing but doesn't have the necessary circulation or ad revenue to foot the bill. Often, subscriber files are too small to justify appending reams of data, so it's the 100,000-circulation-plus regionals that have taken the lead in this area.

Even though the 39,000-circulation *San Diego* can offer syndicated reader-research information and general selects for list rentals, local advertisers still crave more. Like most other regionals, the 47-year-old magazine wants to keep tabs on the exact characteristics of its active circulation list, prospect file and expires. "If advertisers are interested in high-income shoppers, we have to be able to provide them with these names," Phillips says. "We want to sell people our entire list, but that's not always what they're interested in. We want to be able to give advertisers what they want. The market is too competitive for us to tell them what they want."

The numbers game

But database opportunities depend largely on a publication's size, says Pat Vander Meer, group circulation director of Birmingham, Alabama-based Southern Progress Corporation, which publishes *Southern Living* (with a ratebase of 2.3 million) and *Southern Accents* (275,000 ratebase). "Because *Southern Living* is more mass, we can find more reader information to target through a database," she says, adding that reader data is generated in-house as well as from outside sources. "If we want to target women with kids, we have a ready-made market. But if you've got a small-circulation magazine, an advertiser may not want to chop your audience up. At a larger magazine, advertisers might want to slice-and-dice the audience more."

Quality of readership matters a lot for regionals offering database access as a bonus to advertisers, says Joel Harnett, founder and publisher of the 43,000 paid-circulation monthly *Phoenix Home & Garden* and 15,000-distribution *AM Magazine;* his wife is publisher of the 135,000-circulation *Scottsdale Scene*, a bimonthly covering local events in that upscale city. "Using our database becomes an important selling point if someone wants to reach our upscale audience," he says. "Though regional databases are often too small to divide, Neiman Marcus and the Mayo Clinic will still segment our list to do mailings when they want to get the purest demographic cut. They want to reach extremely high-income pockets. So, for those clients, the efficiency they would achieve by targeting the whole list isn't high enough."

Depending on the nature of the data being requested, it *can* cost $1 to $1.50 a name to build the database, according to Toni Nevitt, president of Advantage Marketing, a Livingston, New Jersey-based strategic marketing firm that offers database marketing for publishers and information companies. On the plus side for smaller-circ magazines, it's more expensive to maintain one million names than 10,000 to 15,000. "You can build a 15,000-name database, and if you only want about three pieces of information, it may cost $1 a name. If you want 52 pieces of information for each subscriber, it will obviously cost a lot more."

Nancy Talmey, senior vice president of operations at Neodata, the Louisville, Colorado-based fulfillment company that works with such regionals as *Chicago*, says the company can overlay lifestyle, demographic and psychographic information or split out by Zip Code. "Regionals tend not to request detailed splits," she says. "Maybe there's enough wholeness in the region itself. Smaller publishing offices may not have the staff to do it, but the opportunities are no more limited than for larger magazines. In fact, smaller magazines may get more detailed information easier."

Robert A. Frankel, a Croton-on-Hudson, New York-based management consultant and former vice president of data processing and fulfillment at *Reader's Digest*, supposes that few regionals are taking the database plunge because they are driven by fulfillment. "Their lists are held by fulfillment houses," he says. "Their goal is to get those labels and bills out and do the customer service. They're not necessarily doing cutting-edge marketing databases."

Which brings up the point that, before getting started, check whether your fulfillment bureau is technologically capable of handling a growing database, says Jane Giles, vice president of The Giles Group, a Mamaroneck, New York-based circulation consulting firm. "What you can do depends on whether your fulfillment house has the ability to choose by demographics," she says. "For example, if you want to run a regional women-in-business seminar, you have to be sure your fulfillment house can break out the names of all your file's female readers."

Publishers should also check to see how good their data is. "A fulfillment system is not a database system," says Nevitt. "Database marketing is 'who are my customers, what do we know about them?' You need to look at what data you have and the system you have to capture or manipulate it."

Still, many fulfillment houses have eagerly pursued regionals to get a database up and running. Lorelei Calvert, senior vice president and general manager of *Texas Monthly*, says that for years Communications Data Services, Inc. (CDS), a Des Moines, Iowa-based fulfillment house, has pitched overlaying outside database information to their current 300,000-ratebase file.

> Database marketing can help a title build its franchise, find out more about its readers and become a source of advertiser tie-ins.

Partnering with CDS and another vendor, *Texas Monthly* can now offer advertisers information from state motor vehicle registration records from 1981 to 1994, which it has already overlaid with its own demographics. The setup will cost the magazine approximately $30,000 annually for overlays from Harte-Hanks, a data provider, as well as monthly charges from CDS, with the total investment ranging from $50,000 to $100,000.

"Now, if we go to Isuzu, we can have CDS pull how many married *Texas Monthly* readers live in Dallas-Fort Worth, earn a certain income and drive Isuzus," Calvert says. "We can also find out if a person in Dallas responds better to renewal efforts and price offers in order to make our circulation more profitable."

At Southern Progress, Vander Meer uses the database to do predictive modeling of responsiveness, test new-business-acquisition strategies and segment offers to the customers who tend to respond to them. "We look at a list that has a minimum of a million names and then pull a select off of it and mail our new-business offer. We'll take 50,000 names, mail to them and find out who pays, then model that to find out their buying characteristics. That opens up another huge database."

Regionals can use databases for a multitude of purposes beyond strategic planning in the circulation area. Database marketing can help a magazine franchise its name, find out more about its readers and become a source for advertiser tie-ins and ancillary product testing, Vander Meer says. "For a regional, database marketing works better because you have a larger penetration in a geographic area," she adds. "Because we have a big database, we can test to see what kinds of products people are interested in, including books and magazine launches. We can send mailings to a cross-section of our readers to find out what they think is the best idea."

Think long-term first

Before spending the big bucks, regionals should map out what they hope to gain from setting up a database, says Gary Johnson, group publisher of MSP Communications, which publishes *Mpls.St.Paul*, *Twin Cities Business Monthly*, *U.S. Art*, *ComputerUser* and several custom-published titles.

Consultant Nevitt agrees. "A lot of people say, 'build it and they will come.' I caution clients that there needs to be a solid, strategic reason for building it. The idea is to try to mirror the distribution pattern of your advertisers," she says. "In a regional book, if you're a retail jeweler, look at the customers' purchasing information, who comes into the store, and try to create a circulation story that mirrors that buying pattern."

To capture new audiences, *Mpls.St.Paul* also publishes an annual newcomers' guide using information on home buyers. In a one-time usage agreement, the magazine gets the names of people involved in local real-estate transactions from a company called Plat Systems and then mails nearly 1,000 copies of the guide to those newcomers each month. Johnson says about 2 percent of recipients subscribe, compared to the 4 percent who respond to direct-marketing offers. "The guide delivers new readers to advertisers and enables us to do circ promotion for *Mpls.St.Paul*," he says. "We get subscriptions back and, at the same time, we have a larger list of city newcomers than anyone else can deliver." This information can be used to promote newcomer events or establish online chatlines for newcomers.

Johnson is wary about divulging too much subscriber information, however. "We sell our list, but we're not into compromising our readers," he says. "We're trying hard to avoid deluging readers with information. We don't want them to think a subscription to *Mpls.St.Paul* is an invitation to a direct-marketing avalanche."

The best way for regionals to capture audience data is to offer their own retail events, trade shows, book lines and ancillary products. *Phoenix Home & Garden*, for example, runs three events each year—an interior design show, a landscape and flower show, and health and beauty show. For the last three years, rival *Phoenix Magazine* has run a two-day expo addressing women's issues. "Advertisers use the event to create databases of their own," says *Phoenix Magazine* general manager Win Holden of the expo, which is attended by nearly 40,000 women. "We also created a program with a window-shutter company where purchasers get a free annual subscription paid for by the advertiser."

Kristine Hoefer, publisher of *Atlanta Magazine*, says the 60,000-paid-circulation title does seminars involving advertisers. "We offer a free mailing-list rental once a year to regular advertisers," she says. "Usually they're after a certain Zip Code and feel that the bond we have with our readers makes it an attractive tie-in."

But when small-circulation regionals attempt to partner with local advertisers to set up a workable database, the advertisers may be hesitant to get involved. "There's a much lower level of sophistication locally than nationally about database marketing," says *Phoenix Home & Garden*'s Harnett. "Advertisers don't get it. We tell them we can cut out a section of our readership, but they don't understand it or believe it. It's not a big sales pitch for them."

It's the advertiser's mission that determines their interest. "To certain advertisers, a segmented list even at $15 per thousand is still a good value because they know they're getting targeted names," Holden says.

Another hurdle may be that publishers have to work directly with advertisers, showing them what works in promotional efforts. For certain audiences, polybagged product samples or coupons attached to the magazine might not appeal. "Upscale readers of regionals aren't looking for freebies, like a box of Rice Krispies that gets sent along with the magazine," says Jim Dowden, executive director of the City and Regional Magazine Association in Los Angeles.

Then, the magazine's salespeople need to meet with the circulation department to discuss the data package that's been compiled. "You have to get the account executives to know exactly what information is available before you pitch anything to potential advertisers," says Calvert of *Texas Monthly*. "It has to be a partnership between both departments."

Keep your file clean

Make it a habit to keep all your lists up-to-date, says circulation consultant Giles. That means constant updates. "Your circulation staff has to treat the database and list rental as they treat their own circulation file, by checking periodically to make sure what subscribers ordered is what they got," Giles adds. "When fulfillment is done off-premise, you lose a lot of control. Work closely with your outside list manager and make sure he or she understands your file. A list manager might say there are doctors on the file because there are a lot of Ph.D.s. Educate your list manager as to who your readers really are."

You've got to start somewhere, says Nevitt. "Let's say you want to create a Mexican edition: Find out what kind of information really has meaning to you. Then, go back to advertisers to find out what they're trying to accomplish. I don't believe in just gathering data for the purpose of getting it. The more you collect, the more complicated it gets. The more defined your needs are, the less expensive it becomes."

The Changing Face of Custom Publishing

BY DEBBY PATZ

If you're shopping for a new house in Cleveland and stop by Realty One, the agent will give you a copy of *Buying, Selling & Owning Your Home* as a gift. With Realty One's name on the cover and the agent's photo and personalized message inside, *Your Home* is 200 glossy pages of precisely the kind of information home buyers need. If you're thinking of relocating to Boston and contact Carlson Real Estate, you'll be sent a copy of *Your Home*, with Carlson's name on the cover and one of *its* realtor's pictures inside. Uncanny coincidence? No, custom publishing—with a twist.

Custom titles—marketing tools disguised as conventional magazines—are cropping up all over. The combination of more sophisticated database marketing and the slowing of traditional print advertising has prompted some major players to enter the field, including The New York Times Company and Hachette Filipacchi Magazines. Ironically, though, Knoxville, Tennessee-based Whittle Communications, which almost single-handedly put custom publishing on the map, has all but dropped out of the race.

As more and more businesses are discovering, commissioning custom magazines is not solely the province of large companies with highly developed marketing plans and deep pockets. Magazines are being produced in a variety of forms to suit a variety of budgets. And as more and more publishers are finding out, offering franchised custom publications—of which *Your Home* is a prime example—is the perfect way for those smaller marketers to reach customers in a high-quality, information-rich way.

"We're in a database craze. We've got lots of people with lots of data wondering what to do with it," says John Loughlin, MPS vice president and publicity director, based in Des Moines, Iowa. The turn to custom publishing, then, isn't so surprising. "Traditional revenue sources have gotten a lot thinner. Custom publishing affords another potential revenue stream for magazine publishers."

Indeed, The New York Times Company views its NYT Custom Publishing division as "a source of revenue and eventual profit by doing with a slightly different twist that which we were doing already," says general manager Dick Stockton.

Franchise custom publishers are well aware that sophisticated databases are their richest resource; it is what they have used to build their businesses, capitalizing on marketers' increasingly detailed knowledge of the consumers they wish to reach. Similar to a store franchise, franchised custom publications take a basic product—in this case, editorial—and re-create it in varying forms to suit the specific needs of its licensees. It's these variations that represent some of the most innovative thinking in custom publishing today.

But custom publishers' dependence on clients' marketing plans is a widely recognized drawback. Indeed, despite its much ballyhooed entry into that arena, American Express Publishing Corporation is choosing to redirect its energies elsewhere because, as president and CEO Dan Brewster states, "The problem with custom publishing is that it tends to be a feast-or-famine proposition."

A measure of continuity

Franchising ventures ensure some measure of continuity for a custom publisher. With a single-sponsor book, the publisher suffers a total loss when sponsors' marketing plans change, regardless of the magazine's quality or readership. But because franchised publications are licensed to numerous sponsors, the magazine remains viable even if one sponsor loses interest.

"We're not hamstrung by a weak player in any market," says Oliver Brown, co-founder and general manager of Englewood Cliffs, New Jersey-based ECV L.P., which publishes *Your Home*, licensed to agents in nearly 100 real estate brokerages. "All that holds our people together is their interest in consumer service." In fact, should one sponsor drop out, the publisher can offer the magazine—and area exclusivity—to another in that region.

Some industries lend themselves particularly well to franchise opportunities. "Certain product categories—such as health-care products and services and the whole financial category—generally require a lot more space to tell their stories and sell their services than you find in a single-page ad," says John Caldwell, president of four-year-old Marblehead Communications, based in Boston. "They need more than a 60-second commercial to deliver their message and deliver it effectively."

Richard Baumer, president of Los Angeles-based E.F. Baumer & Company and executive editor of *Dollar$ense*, a money-management magazine licensed to banks, agrees: "Typically, growth in the custom publishing area has been from very small companies, like ours, that have realized a need in a specific industry."

Adds Sondra Kurtin, publisher at New York City-based RKC!, whose 1994 spring launch, *Value,* is also licensed to banks, "Mail is so inundated. [Banks are] looking for a way to stand out and get their messages across."

Helping smaller businesses stand out in a regional marketplace is the main selling point of franchised publications. In the case of *Your Home,* "It's very difficult for real estate firms to differentiate themselves," says general manager Brown. "Our feeling was, if we offered them this book—the only mimic-proof marketing device that is truly consumer oriented—it would really give them an edge."

All feature standard covers onto which the sponsor's name is printed, with the inside and back covers available to be customized as the licensees wish. "Because it is tagged," says Brown, "it absolutely looks like their book. That's important." Most publishers offer more customization options, such as *Your Home*'s blown-in letter from a local real estate agent.

Fred Petrovsky, editor of Phoenix-based McMurry Publishing's 900,000-circulation *Vim & Vigor,* licensed by some 27 hospital groups representing 67 different hospitals across the country, likens the process to buying a car. It comes, he says, with a standard package, and you purchase options to suit your needs.

In the case of the 600,000-circulation quarterly *Dollar$ense,* 16 pages of money-management editorial are created by E.F. Baumer's staff; extra pages—either created by Baumer or provided camera-ready by the client—are stitched in according to licensees' specifications. Often, says Baumer, clients insert newsletters they would otherwise have sent separately, personalizing the magazine that much further as well as giving the newsletter additional clout. Costs for the magazine, which carries no ads other than those placed by the sponsor, range from 72 cents per unit for 10,000 copies to 36 cents per unit at 100,000 copies. The cost structure for inserts varies depending on the degree of E.F. Baumer's input.

And some licensees of *American Times*, Grote Publishing's 300,000-circulation general interest magazine that also goes to bank clients, are not always satisfied with having only eight of the magazine's 32 pages customized. According to Bill Lubing, publisher of the Madison, Wisconsin-based quarterly, "This is turning into a very modular thing. We are building signatures according to the bank," sometimes moving to larger signatures than originally planned.

Indeed, production on such segmented magazines can get complicated. In addition to customized editorial, many publishers offer bind-in response cards, which—while allowing sponsors to track the efficacy of their investments—make production that much more complex. "You've got to have a good relationship with your printer," advises Lubing, "and you've got to have a good printer. The traffic person at our printer sometimes gets a little nuts with us." *Vim & Vigor*'s Petrovsky, whose magazine customizes 22 of its pages and juggles bind-in and blow-in cards and segmented outserts for 27 different versions, agrees. "It has the potential to be a nightmare," he says.

But Marblehead's Caldwell insists that "it's not as complicated as it sounds," even though his company produces more than 50 versions of *Union Plus* for the AFL-CIO.

Many times, it is possible "to come up with a low-tech solution to a high-tech problem," adds Brown. *Your Home,* for example, simply slows down the printing process so the books can be immediately sorted by hand according to agent.

And Petrovsky, who claims *Vim & Vigor* has never misbound or misdirected an issue since it began in 1985, stresses organization and a partnership with the printer as key to production success. Think of your printer as an extension of your company, he advises: "We rely on them to make the magazine what it is."

The big payoff

Although custom publishing does require heightened vigilance, profitability is a definite payoff. Franchised custom-publishing houses are able to keep staff to a minimum, with much of the customized editorial coming from the sponsors themselves.

And while most franchised magazines don't carry advertising, books aren't produced unless they are paid for, a major difference from traditional publishing. "This year [*Your Home*] cost us $1.38 a copy, including all the customization," says Brown of the annual's 750,000 print run. Books are then re-sold to realtors for an average of $2.25 a copy, netting 87 cents per book—guaranteed income on top of the national advertising it does carry.

Newsstand sales are another potential source of revenue. A main distribution method for Hachette's custom titles, newsstand promotion also worked well for *Your Home*. With a cover price of $9.95, *Your Home* saw 98 percent sell-through of its first national newsstand trial of 16,000 copies sold through the Waldenbooks chain. Based on this success, a new shipment was authorized, with Barnes & Noble and B. Dalton also coming on as distributors.

Vim & Vigor has had less success with its single-copy sales venture—3,000 copies distributed on newsstands in Charleston, South Carolina, New Orleans and Phoenix. With only 10 percent sell-though, McMurry Publishing concluded that the markets were already saturated, since copies were being sent out by local licensees. It is now experimenting with distribution in markets with no hospital circulation; 5,000 copies of the latest issue are being tested on newsstands in Den-ver, Atlanta, San Francisco, Boston and Chicago. Even if this test doesn't fly, or if licensees have no interest in offering *Vim & Vigor* on the newsstands in their areas, the publisher suggests they still carry the $2.95 cover price. "It implies value," says director of marketing Chris McMurry, "and people keep things of value."

To increase the magazine's value to its licensees, franchise custom publishers tend to offer additional marketing programs built around the magazine. *Dollar$ense* sends study guides designed for staff training and a newsletter with community outreach ideas for building and keeping clientele to its banking clients. *Vim & Vigor*'s program includes a series of health-oriented radio spots onto which licensees tag their name. Similarly, *Your Home* has created television spots advertising the magazine, which realtors then personalize. This type of promotion ensures that the magazine is working for both client and publisher, enhancing the perceived value of the magazine to its recipients and further solidifying the relationship between sponsor and publisher.

■ Customer service

Below is a list of some of the major players in custom publishing. Titles and sponsor clients were accurate at press time.

American Express Publishing Corporation, New York City
Dan Brewster, president and CEO
Series of newsletters for American Express cards
No magazine contracts at present

ECV L.P., Englewood Cliffs, New Jersey
Oliver Brown and William Fried, co-founders
and managing directors
Buying, Selling & Owning Your Home, licensed to real estate agencies nationwide

E.F. Baumer & Company, Los Angeles
Edward F. Baumer, publisher
Dollar$ense, licensed to banks nationwide

Grote Publishing, Madison, Wisconsin
Russell Grote, president; Bill Lubing, publisher
American Times, licensed to banks nationwide
Life Today, licensed to banks nationwide, designed for larger corporations

Hachette Filipacchi Custom Publishing, New York City
Susan Buckley and Patrice Listfield, co-publishers
Know-How, General Motors Corporation
Jenny Craig's BodyHealth, Jenny Craig International
Beauty, Mary Kay Cosmetics
Wood Beautiful, Minwax Company, Inc.
tell, NBC
Sony Style, Sony Corp.
Sun, Ray Ban (a division of Bausch & Lomb, Inc.)
Contract signed with Tupperware

McMurry Publishing Inc., Phoenix
Preston V. McMurry Jr., publisher; Fred Petrovsky, editor
Vim & Vigor, licensed to health-care facilities nationwide

Marblehead Communications Incorporated, Boston
John Caldwell, president; Robert Benchley, editorial director
Profiles, Continental Airlines, Inc.
Union Plus, AFL-CIO
Professional Collector, Western Union
"Broadway Presents" (newsletter), League of American Theaters & Producers
Student Travels, Council on International Educational Exchange

ECV L.P. is taking the concept a step further, creating packets of national, home-oriented advertising that will be sent to confirmed home buyers, the net revenue of which will be split with the realtor. "Because we make it a profit center for them, they are much more likely to remain our customers on a long-term basis," says Brown.

Like all custom publications, franchised magazines face the accusation that they are more advertisement than editorial. "Anyone who tries to pass it off as objective reporting has spent too much time in the ozone layer," says John Brady, a partner in the Boston- and Fort Lauderdale-based consulting firm Brady and Paul Communications. "It is carefully directed editorial marketing, not straight journalistic information."

Dollar$ense's Baumer agrees that his product is a marketing device. But, he adds, "it's not advertorial. It has clearly delineated what's related to the banks and what's good solid editorial. And people are reading it."

Says Meredith's Loughlin, "These magazines are clear about where they're coming from. There's no obfuscation. Many custom publications contain much service journalism, and consumers are looking for more information."

Custom magazines are meant to create a positive selling environment for a sponsor's message, says Caldwell at Marblehead, and that alone does not preclude editorial integrity. "Those products that do respect the reader are the ones that will endure," says Loughlin.

Custom publishing itself promises to endure, despite its critics. "It's an avenue for advertisers that's really yet to be tapped," says John Heenan, senior advertising manager, print media at Sony Corp., which publishes *Sony Style* with Hachette. For franchisers, longevity means knowledge of and non-branded exclusivity within an industry that has plenty of information to disseminate." *Vim & Vigor* just entered its 10th year," says Petrovsky. "All the new twists have come from our customers making suggestions. Keep your ears open to new ideas and needs of people. Be responsive to what's going on in the industry you serve."   □

Massachusetts Tourism Guide, Massachusetts Office of Travel and Tourism
Boston Harbor Wine Festival, Boston Harbor Hotel
Winter Guide, Massachusetts Lodging Association
Private Screening, Continental Airlines

Meredith Publishing Services, Des Moines
Jack Fleisch, periodical publisher; Doug Holthaus, editor in chief
Friendly Exchange, Farmers Insurance Group
Mature Outlook, Sears Roebuck & Co.
Come Home, Andersen Windows
Poolife, Olin Chemical
Express Yourself, Tulip (a division of Polymerics Inc.)
Crayola Kids, Binney & Smith, Inc.

NYT Custom Publishing, New York City
Richard W. Stockton, publisher; Susan S. Peterson, editorial director
Four Seasons Hotels and Resorts Magazine, Four Seasons Hotels and Resorts
USAir Magazine, USAir Inc.
Profit, IBM
Beyond Computing, IBM

RKC!, New York City
Sondra Kurtin, publisher
Know How, Shawmut Bank
Dividends, Chemical Bank
Value, Making the Most of Your Money, to be licensed to banks nationally
Eight newsletters

The Publications Company, Detroit
Gary Deidrichs, president
Frontline and *DealerWorld*, Ford Motor Company
Performance, Detroit Symphony Orchestra
AS/400, IBM
Solutions, Unisys
Alpha and *Team USA*, NCR (a division of AT&T)
Place, Michigan Society of Architects
Inside GM, General Motors Corporation
Test Drive, advertiser- and newsstand-driven

Whittle Communications, Knoxville, Tennessee
Christopher Whittle, chairman
Special Report, distributed to medical reception areas nationwide, multi-sponsored

Five Myths of Association Publishing

BY LORRAINE CALVACCA

Association publications have long struggled with an image problem. But that's changing. Although some in the field concede that disparaging terms such as "second-rate" may have applied in the past, they insist that association titles have improved dramatically in recent years, and that a good number now rival their independent counterparts when it comes to editorial and economic vitality.

And yet, association magazines continue to labor under a broad shadow of doubt as advertisers, mainstream media and even their own kind raise questions about integrity, quality and overall viability. "People believe that association magazines are monolithic in quality and type," says Ian MacKenzie, a board member of the Society of National Association Publications (SNAP), and editor of *Life Association News*, the magazine for the National Association of Life Underwriters. "That's not true. There is a large range."

So how do association professionals attempt to dispel such entrenched notions? To find out, *Folio:* asked association editors and publishers to discuss, in their view, the five most common myths of association publishing. Here's what they have to say.

1. Association publications are strictly house organs.

"The myth is that associations can't publish credible, objective magazines," says Don Christiansen, editor emeritus of *IEEE Spectrum*, the flagship title of the Institute of Electrical and Electronics Engineers, which won a prestigious National Magazine Award for reporting. "There's a good reason for the myth. Many associations have historically used their magazines to deliver the party line." But that is less and less the case, he says, as publications realize they need to be "editorially vital" to compete for shrinking ad dollars.

Many titles are developing "arm's-length" agreements with their associations to ensure that the editorial is not just industry pabulum, according to Robert Rainier, former president of SNAP and editor of the 340,000-circulation monthly *Journal of Accountancy.* "Although the magazines may contain a lot of information about the associations, the good ones will also contain a lot of other information as well, and present both sides of a story."

IEEE Spectrum, which has been nominated for four National Magazine Awards and won two 1993 New York Business Press Awards, routinely provides news and stories that are "self-critical and self-analytical," says Christiansen. For example, one story focused on case histories of technical flops within the engineering industry. Despite initial objections by the association that readers would cancel their memberships and that subjects would not cooperate, the story was well documented and well received. "Members loved it," he recalls. "Readers are astute. They know when they are being given half the story."

Similarly, Kate Penn, editor and publisher of the Alexandria, Virginia-based *Floral Management,* the 15,000-circulation magazine of the Society of American Florists, found the sky did not fall when she ran a profile of a supermarket florist—which provides direct competition to *FM*'s readers. "The emergence of nontraditional outlets was upsetting to retailers—but they are here to stay, so we wrote about them."

There is a growing recognition among association titles that editorial integrity is attainable within the context of an association, says *ABA Journal* editor and publisher Gary Hengstler, who regularly runs articles critical of the law field.

IEEE's Christiansen concurs, saying there is a ripple effect: "When a couple of magazines [cover controversial subjects] and survive," he explains, "others say, 'Wait a minute. If they can do it and don't get advertiser criticism—and win awards—then we can do it.'"

2. Association publications do not make money.

"Many association publications make a substantial amount of money," says MacKenzie. "They are cash-flow centers. They are not viewed as profit centers, because they are usually run by nonprofit organizations and they cannot report profits. But these publications have to contribute to the bottom line."

More than a few titles have strong advertising bases and substantial subscription income, Rainier points out. In addition, "they have a solid base for ancillary products such as books and special reports that can be sponsored in the magazines' names."

Says Bill Otto, editor of the 500,000-circulation, Atlanta-based *Arthritis Today*, "We are extremely profitable. Last year we generated $6 million in circulation revenue and $1 million in advertising." That money, he notes, goes back to the Arthritis Foundation to fund research for a cure.

3. Association publications do not attract top talent.

"If there were a surplus of jobs chasing a limited number of people, that might be the case, but the reverse is true," says Lee Crumbaugh, president of Forrest Consulting in Glen Ellyn, Illinois. "There is definitely a trend toward a growing number of talented people at association publications. There is probably more job security, and the starting pay is no worse than at some independent magazines, and better than a few."

In fact, association titles are increasingly putting the hiring emphasis on publishing skills, rather than industry expertise. "We look for magazine professionals," says *Arthritis Today*'s Otto. "Many of the people we've hired happen to be from the for-profit sector."

When Hengstler was hired by the *ABA Journal*, "I had to have editorial experience *and* a law degree," he recalls. Under his direction, though, a law degree is no longer mandatory for potential job applicants. First and foremost, he says, is solid journalism experience, and then, preferably, knowledge of the law. "Magazine writing is not like brief writing," notes Hengstler, who joined *ABA Journal* from *Texas Lawyer*, a weekly newspaper he helped launch.

On the sales side, *ABA Journal*'s associate publisher, Susan Holland-Caamano, has culled her 18-person staff from major consumer magazine companies, including Times Mirror and Time Inc.

4. Association publications are disregarded by advertisers.

"This is an outdated view," says Crumbaugh. "If you talk to the media-buying community, they will look at the reach and frequency of the publication and the quality of the editorial before considering whether to advertise or not. Stereotypes will not keep them away."

In fact, because association magazines are often the leading periodicals in certain markets—or at least are nearly certain to reach key decision-makers—they may provide just the entree some advertisers are looking for. Such was the reasoning behind the decision of computer software-giant Microsoft to conduct a trial ad campaign for legal software in the April issue of *ABA Journal*. "We determined that decision-makers don't read general technical publications as we thought," says a Microsoft source. What's more, thanks to its 422,174 circulation and reputation for editorial excellence, *ABA Journal* was also chosen over such independent competitors as *American Lawyer* and *The National Law Journal*. "Media people are more willing to look at other ways to advertise," says *ABA Journal*'s Holland-Caamano. "They need to target other markets without waste."

Advertisers have also become more receptive to associations as the associations themselves have learned how better to sell their books, says Holly Townsend, an independent consultant and a sales rep for *Physical Therapy*, the publication of the American Physical Therapy Association. "Out of necessity, these titles have become more sophisticated at sales strategies, including putting together value-added packages."

5. Association publications lack authority.

Those in the profession argue that association magazines are, by their nature, authorities in their respective fields. "We have easy access to experts that consumer books don't have," MacKenzie contends.

"If the *Journal of Accountancy* isn't an authority in accounting, who is?" asks Crumbaugh rhetorically.

Some see this last myth as less an issue of credibility than one of visibility. "It's frustrating," says Pamela Baldinger, editor of *The China Business Review*, a 12,000-member title that focuses on U.S./ China commerce relations. "We get calls all the time from mass media for information. I know we get used by them and we don't get credited."

The ABA's Hengstler recalls the time *The Wall Street Journal* ran an article on the top-10 legal publications and never made mention of the *ABA Journal*. "They did list *The National Law Journal*, among others, which doesn't have half the circulation we have," Hengstler maintains. "We are *the* player. It just doesn't occur to the general press that we're out there."

Given the improving image of association titles, Hengstler hopes that's an omission that won't occur again.

How to Get the Most From Your Editorial Advisory Board

BY ANNE GRAHAM

For better or worse, editorial advisory panels are a fact of life for many association magazine staffs. Association members—who frequently bring limited publishing expertise and experience to their posts—can be involved in almost every aspect of association magazines.

"When I moved from a consumer to an association publication, no one told me I'd be inheriting an advisory panel that really wanted to run the magazine," retired editor Linda Pressman recalls. "During my first year, there were so many 'cooks in my kitchen,' it made the run-ins I'd had with my previous publisher seem like a marriage made in heaven."

To varying extents, advisory groups, variously called panels, boards or committees, affect the efforts of association magazines of all sizes and types. Whether these advisory panels represent rich resources or royal pains hinges on several factors. The trick for magazine staffs is to know how to capitalize on the knowledge of their volunteers, while keeping staff responsibilities clearly defined and separate.

Many association publications are highly specific and technical. Even in an ideal association-publishing situation, in which staff members combine solid magazine skills with direct knowledge of the business or industry, volunteers can be a critical asset. As practitioners, they have first-hand knowledge of the business or profession represented by the association. Their real-world insights and expertise enable them to contribute several valuable services:

Review articles. Association publishers and editors know that readers must be able to rely on the validity and usefulness of what they read in "their" publication, and screenings by competent, knowledgeable reviewers are a tremendous service. An editor knows when a manuscript is well written and intelligently organized, but a strong reviewer can say whether it was worth writing in the first place.

Assess the big picture. Board members can make informed suggestions regarding editorial direction and strategic plans. Their insights can help to keep the magazine's big picture rooted in reality.

Give useful feedback. Reader surveys are always helpful, but advisory panels will generally read the magazine more carefully and more analytically. Their evaluations of each issue can be invaluable.

Target advertisers and pinpoint leads. This kind of knowledge is especially important when the focus of a profession or industry shifts, or external forces create upheavals. When these changes occur, advertising bases are likely to veer in different directions. Practitioners are often the first to detect these permutations and their potential impact, both on advertising and editorial.

Enhance the credibility of the publication. When advisory panel members are highly visible, respected leaders of the profession or industry, the publication shares their stature. Readers assume these success stories would not lend their names to a magazine unless they believed in it.

Most association staffs openly acknowledge their dependence on volunteers. "Our publication has to do

> The trick for association-magazine managers is to know how to capitalize on the knowledge of volunteers while keeping staff responsibilities separate.

a lot," says Karin Quantrille, director of publications at the American Physical Therapy Association in Alexandria, Virginia. All the many disciplines within physical therapy need to be covered in the magazine, she says, but "our editors are not physical therapists; and, even if they were, no one person could know everything about all the aspects and sub-disciplines of physical therapy. The input from our board is critical."

In some cases, these positive contributions cancel out any negatives—but not always. Serious conflicts can occur between volunteers and staff, and the fallout can range from mild frustration on both sides to a magazine that misses its mark and loses its direction. There are four basic reasons why these problems develop:

• Volunteer members of an advisory panel may not fully understand that magazine publishing is a business, too, requiring as much specialized knowledge, experience and skill as their own work. Some of them are obviously convinced that they could easily edit and produce a magazine themselves—if they just had a few more hours to give to it.

• Advisory panels can be seduced, as magazine staffs are, by their connection to a project that combines so many creative processes and wields inherent power. Egos can incite volunteer forays into territory reserved for staff if roles have not been clearly defined.

• It's easy for volunteers to miss deadlines. Most people give first priority to their "real jobs." Association work doesn't pay the bills, but if an editor is waiting fruitlessly by the fax machine for a review or some other vital bit of information promised by a volunteer, frustration builds.

• Panel members may expect some preferential treatment—publication of an article that they or some friend has written, perhaps, or placement of an item about a particular new product. They may even suggest that staff adopt an editorial position that reflects their own interests or those of some other special-interest group.

Thoughtful planning and savvy management can help eliminate many sources of conflict between volunteers and magazine staffs. The best strategy is to zap potential problems before they develop. To this end, written guidelines can work wonders. In a simple pamphlet or packet of instructions and information, staff can explain and define the role of the volunteers, as well as their own responsibilities. If necessary, the guidelines can be formalized through a committee process. Making the guidelines part of the overall editorial mission statement or an extension of the group's association charter is also constructive.

Another management tactic staffs can employ is to keep the advisory groups focused on the big issues, such as editorial direction and strategic planning. Volunteers will be most likely to make critical contributions in these broad areas. Their strengths lie in the knowledge of their industry or profession, not in the details of magazine management.

Each member of the advisory group brings unique perspectives or experiences to the conference table. Staff may want to propose agenda items that aim at airing current developments within these areas. These discussions carry the potential to educate staff, but they also remind the volunteers that what they know about the profession or industry is their most valuable asset to the publication. Staff may encourage the volunteers to analyze and synthesize these trends and to consider if and how the information might be used in the publication.

Although most associations schedule at least one major meeting during the year, staff should communicate with members of the advisory panel as often as necessary. In fact, most volunteers like being consulted. It heightens their sense of participation and promotes the kind of involvement editorial staffs want. Communicating with volunteers also sends a signal to them that they are valued and that their contributions are appreciated.

Whenever possible, staff members should decide who will serve on their advisory panel. If the decision is made at an association executive level, magazine staff should at least be consulted. When panel members know that they serve at the discretion of the staff, they are likely to see themselves in a support or advisory capacity. They are more likely to perceive that, while their counsel and suggestions are solicited, not all their ideas will be used.

Staggered terms for advisory panels are a useful idea for most publications. Turnover in the make-up of the group allows staff to build a team that functions productively and positively and keeps new ideas coming. Of course, outstanding committee members can be kept on board, or terms can be extended.

No matter how supportive and helpful committee members may seem, staff should resist most impulses that would involve the volunteers in management issues and problems. If staff is struggling with an unsympathetic CEO, chafing under unreasonable budgetary constraints, or wrestling with other internal problems, it may be tempting to seek counsel or support among advisory panel members. Most often, this is a perilous path. Except in extraordinary circumstances, management issues should be discussed only in broad terms with members of the advisory panel, so that staff credibility and effectiveness within the association are not compromised, and the separation between staff and volunteer roles remains clearly defined. ☐

Find Success Through Benchmarking

BY ANNE GRAHAM

Benchmarking, in essence, is simply measuring a competitor's product according to certain criteria in order to improve your own product. Every association staff person who thumbs through the competition's latest issue is, in essence, benchmarking. Evaluating other publications and lifting or adapting choice elements is an obvious and essential aspect of magazine publishing.

Many major commercial publishers use sophisticated, complex measurements in their benchmarking efforts, but these are probably relevant only to the largest association staffs. But the underlying concept, appropriately adapted, can be of immense value to association staffs of any size. "Benchmarking isn't brain surgery," says Robert Boxwell Jr., author of *Benchmarking for Competitive Advantage.* "It's plain and simple learning from others. Identify [magazines you would like to benchmark against], study them, and improve based on what you have learned."

A benchmarking circle, made up of a half dozen or so association magazine staffs, is a good way to make that idea a reality. Such a circle can provide a systematic way to learn even more from others, not only in terms of evaluating a finished product—the association magazine—but in understanding how it was created, how problems were solved, and what organizational structures complement these processes.

Benchmarking may actually be a much more open, straightforward and useful process for association staffs than for others in the industry, partly because legalities and competitive risks that might worry commercial publishers aren't likely to be a major concern for association titles. Though association staffs must still be cautious about any "dancing with the enemy" issues, benchmarking can foster a spirit of openness and cooperation among participants. This sense of

> "It's plain and simple learning from others. Find titles you want to study and then improve based on what you have learned."

support can be especially meaningful to association staffs, who often feel an inherent sense of isolation in environments where the business of magazines is not always well understood. In fact, a key benchmarking area could focus on how staffs deal with some of these challenges.

Another positive aspect of the benchmarking process is that there is no mandate for the meetings to conform to any predetermined format, and no need to quantify findings. Although someone has to act as the initiator, the rules of the game can be as loose or as structured as participants wish.

Getting started

A prerequisite for successful benchmarking in association environments is buy-in from association leadership. This is a key step, because the organization may already be benchmarking in other areas. Thus, magazine benchmarking might simply be a matter of broadening these other efforts by pulling in the publication's dimension.

While association approval to proceed is being acquired, you should identify potential benchmarking partners. There are no formulas regarding the size of the group, but six seems to be a manageable number. If there are no "natural" alliances already established by your association, you may want to establish your own criteria—such as similarities in size, style or types of audiences. Identifying "best practices" is one of the fundamental precepts, and you may well want to seek out periodicals you admire and can learn from. Above all, each participant must have something to offer the others.

Prospective team members should be contacted by letter or memo, rather than by phone. Both the concept and the objectives need to be explained. Examples of the questions to be considered should be included, and the benefits should be described. Participants may need time to study the idea and to discuss it with their own organizational leadership. Others may elect to join on a "contingency basis," to see how the project plays out before making a commitment.

Your staff can feel comfortable in offering to design the initial benchmarking survey, and to compile the results and circulate them to everyone, because these processes don't have to be time consuming. The benchmarking instrument can be a simple questionnaire. Questions might focus on one issue or on several: how international circulation is handled; how the editorial mission statement was developed; staff size and structure; how manuscripts are solicited; what kinds of graphics software are used; or in-house versus outside advertising reps, for example.

It is important to have all circle members contribute questions. All participants can agree to withhold any information that might be compromising.

Deadlines for returning the questionnaires should be honored. Compile and circulate the results to everyone by an agreed-upon date. Once you have refined a computer format for reporting results, it can be used again and again.

Expand your contacts

After circle members have received your report, partners may want to pursue one-on-one contacts. For example, one association staff, noting that a problem they are wrestling with has been conquered by another, may want more direct information. Partners may also want to discuss future topics and explore other possibilities for exchanging information, such as conference calls or joint meetings.

Benchmarking surveys can be used on a regular or "as needed" basis. The responsibility for developing the topics and the questionnaires can rotate so that everyone has a chance to participate. It is conceivable that these benchmarking circles might be altered as some association titles change their focus or direction. New partners might join the group as others move on to new alliances.

Benchmarking can help association staffs to improve their processes and products, visualize their unique publishing issues in different ways, and forge valuable systems of support. □

Going Online? No, Just Looking.

BY ANNE GRAHAM

Most association magazines can be neatly assigned to one of three online publishing segments. Those with a quasi-independent presence on the Internet make up the smallest group. These magazines' connections to the parent associations are obvious, but in each case, the emphasis is on the publication. The second, much more common group is made up of association magazines that form one piece of an overall association presence online. Specific approaches, practices and products are almost as scattered as the Internet itself, but the focus is clearly on the organization and its mission, not the magazine. The third group—and by far the largest—includes all those association titles that are "just looking, thank you"—still equivocating, still unplugged.

Arthritis Today, the official magazine of the Arthritis Foundation, has been "out there" on The Electronic Newsstand for more than a year, supplementing the 500,000-circulation print version. As one of the association magazines with its own ID, *Arthritis Today* belongs in the first category of online publishers. The Foundation is also establishing a home page, which will be cross-linked to The Electronic Newsstand. "My feeling is that we're among the leaders of the charge," says William M. Otto, the Foundation's group vice president, publications. "When we started, we couldn't really find any appropriate models, so we've paved the way ourselves.

"We're actually positioned more as a consumer health magazine, rather than as an association publication," Otto observes. "On America Online, we're publishing our current table of contents, selected articles, our most popular departments and other special segments. We've had a very positive response and are planning to expand our efforts. We want to provide even more information and better service to the millions of people who want and need to be informed about arthritis."

For most association staffs, the issues related to online publishing are far less clear-cut than they might be for consumer titles. Although both must wrestle with the fundamental questions—such as how to turn a profit and protect copyrights and intellectual property—association staffs are also governed by their organizations' broader missions. Online communication is a vehicle for promoting the organization and all its programs—not just the magazine. As a result, it can be more difficult for the magazine's editor to convince management of the value of putting the magazine online. And the purpose and look of an association's online site will usually have little in common with a typical consumer magazine's online site.

Frequently, it's not even the magazine staff, but technical staff or others within the association, who assume responsibility for creating and developing the overall online presentation. Sometimes it is a team effort. "We're just a grab bag of folks working on our home page," says Brad Stratton, editor of *Quality Progress,* published by the American Society of Quality Control. "Actually," says Stratton, "it's our director of finance who heads it up."

Stratton says he believes in the future of online publishing but hasn't been swept into cyberspace just yet: "I'm convinced of the possibilities," he observes, "but I

> For most association magazines, the issues related to online publishing are far less clear-cut than they might be for consumer titles.

think you have to temper that potential with what makes good business sense. I don't think we should forget what business we're in."

Finally, notes Stratton, the numbers don't necessarily indicate a need to rush: "Our research shows that only about 10 to 15 percent of our members even have access to the Web right now. As a result, we are not panicking. There aren't that many people who can get to it yet. And quite frankly, another key issue for us is that, at this point, we don't want to put too much free information out there. We just don't think we should be giving away what our members, in essence, have to buy."

Some association professionals, including Mark Cheater, executive editor of *Nature Conservancy,* believe that online offerings must be substantially different from what is already being provided in the print product: "Users want fresh information and approaches, not the same things they can read in the magazine. We're working with a different media format, and we're looking for a kind of synergy between print and electronic media. To be effective," he adds, "the information provided online needs to be new and jazzy; and it has to be continually updated. It is actually quite easy to underestimate the amount of work, creativity and technical support that are involved in doing it right."

Concern about the amount of work and know-how required, not to mention pressing questions about money and fear of the unknown, probably account for the fact that many association staffs haven't committed to online publishing.

Peter Banks, editorial director at the American Diabetes Association, admits to the uncertainties, although his organization, with five professional and two consumer publications, is up and running on America Online. "This is a new way to deliver information," Banks observes. "In publishing, we've always been able to look to previous examples. We can easily see what others are doing. In this case, however, we can't—but we can't wait to get all the right answers. The early products are our research. Some of them will probably fail, but in failing, we will have gained knowledge that just couldn't have been acquired any other way—except maybe by watching—and then you're watching your market go by."

In almost every case, however, association staffs understand that the question is clearly not "if," but "when." Like smart shoppers, savvy magazine professionals need to do their homework. After acquiring as much information as possible, getting a clear fix on their own objectives and time frames, and finally staking an appropriate claim on their organization's online efforts, they need to stop looking and make the purchase.   □

■ Tips for association online publishers

"The first thing to do if you want to get started is to decide why you're doing it. You may have several reasons, but doing it for prestige alone could create problems. It's also important to recognize that your initiative should not hamper your other outreach efforts, especially since most people still don't have Web access."
John Merli, Senior director of communications
National Association of Broadcasters

"More than anything else, the value of online publishing is timeliness. But online success is highly dependent on print. No one can call attention to a site better than publishers who communicate regularly with large audiences."
Rafael Badagliacca, SpaceMaster, Inc.

"One of the things going online may do for us is bring in new members. We think we're going to find some people who have never heard of our association, or our magazine, but will find both of them of interest."
Brad Stratton, Editor, *Quality Progress*

"Have no fear. Online publishing doesn't have to be scary. You can control what you put out there. It depends on how much work you want to do. Costs can be controlled and managed so that they are consistent with the level of service you want to provide."
Frederick Bowes III, President, Cadmus Digital Solutions

"One thing online publishing can do for association magazines is help them create a database—'Here are 3,000 leads; this is where they came from; this is how long the user stayed at your site; this is what they viewed.' "
Rusty Speidel, Director, electronic publishing
Kluge Carden Jennings Publishing Co. Ltd.

"Electronic publishing is an important element of our overall publications strategy. It's a way for us to reach new members at relatively small cost—incredibly small when we compare it with direct mail. We've even acquired a full-time volunteer as a result of our online initiative!"
Mark Cheater, Executive editor, *Nature Conservancy*

International Insights—10 Steps to a Smoother Journey Overseas

BY JAMES C. MCCULLAGH

In 1994 I traveled about 120,000 air miles, mainly to Europe. It was rare for me *not* to bump into an American publisher heading east or a European publisher heading west. Recently, the American Magazine Conference has been dominated by international issues. No wonder: There's good money to be made in the international arena. Look at Reader's Digest Association and Hearst.

Interesting as the experiences of these powerhouses are, they don't speak to the organizational and financial realities of most smaller publishers. And equally important, most publishers don't have a stable of well-known titles that resonate from Moscow to Timbuktu.

But it is a good time for mid-size and smaller publishers to rethink the international market, particularly Europe, because according to such indices as gross domestic product, literacy rates and economic stability, Europe is still king.

Germany is undoubtedly the best market to enter these days because economic and political risks there are very low. The single-copy market is strong and the rate card is held in some esteem. Direct-mail payment rates rank high, and direct-mail sales are growing 15 percent annually, reaching $23.2 billion in 1992. Although data protection and privacy laws exist, few Germans appear opposed to receiving direct mail. Plus, Germany has the third most productive economy in the world, behind the United States and Japan.

After Germany, the United Kingdom, France, Italy and Switzerland remain powerful markets to tap. If we apply strict economic, financial and political yardsticks, few areas beyond Western Europe make the cut. Eastern Europe holds some promise, but it's limited at the moment. Russia is a huge market and will pay off for those who were in early and remain patient.

As in the United States, growth in new magazine titles in Europe is in the special-interest arena. Thus, small- to medium-size titles can seize major opportunities there.

1. Hot titles have wings.

If you have a hot title in the States, chances are it will work overseas. That's not carved in stone, but it's a decent yard-stick. The world gets smaller by the day, and strong titles and their images are highly exportable. We found this to be the case for *Men's Health*, which was named the hottest U.S. magazine by *Adweek* last year, with revenues up $11.2 million, ad pages up 55 percent and circulation up 37 percent. With a total paid circulation of nearly 1.3 million, *Men's Health* is well on its way to equaling the combined circulations of the U.S. editions of both *Esquire* and *GQ*, which total nearly 1.5 million.

Success at home almost compelled us to expand into the United Kingdom. That success was our banner and our caution. Experience had taught us that health is indeed an international franchise, and we had faith in that intuition. Our concern was about our particular angle on a savvy market. As *Esquire* discovered, one doesn't waltz into a new market, no matter how good the domestic product is.

2. Use your window of opportunity.

European publishers are nimble and move quickly to fill publishing niches. And, as mentioned above, niche publishing is where much of the game is being played these days. This means no one is waiting for Americans to fill a publishing slot. We sensed *Men's Health* would work in the U.K. market even though advertising agencies were cool in the early going. They had a point. As a Brit, I knew that the British male's sense of a healthy diet could mean shifting from drinking brandy to vodka and letting out a big sigh of healthy relief.

Meanwhile, when we arrived in London in July 1994, we found the men's category was already robust. We knew the men's lifestyle market would fill up quickly and pushed to get a publication out within six months of the launch decision. Three men's lifestyle magazines followed within months of our launch. If we had waited six months, the men's lifestyle category in the United Kingdom would have been filled and our chances for a quick success would have been reduced considerably.

3. All selling is local.

All publishers hope that ad sales for international editions can be made within an international arena, with clients signing up for schedules both here and abroad. Although this can happen, especially for the larger publishers, I've found that most of the advertising decisions are made locally for *Men's Health, Mountain Bike* and *Runner's World*. *Runner's World* has sold larger advertisers, such as Nike, into international editions, and the German edition of *Mountain Bike* has enjoyed some combination selling. But, as a rule, domestic sales teams are better utilized supporting the international effort, but focusing their energy on their own edition.

The British agencies we met with were impressed with the *Men's Health* success story in the States. But it was only when we had the U.K. version in hand that the agencies talked to us seriously about schedules. By then, the agencies were talking to their associates and counterparts in the States as well. Regardless of those discussions, most of the final advertising decisions continue to come from the U.K. offices of key advertisers. The home office can have some influence, but usually all selling is local.

> A brand name epitomizes a business and you should be slow to modify it. As a rule of thumb, fight for your brand.

4. Give your smaller titles a chance.
Sometimes the smaller-circulation title you're considering taking overseas ends up having more appeal than its larger-circulation counterpart. Rodale publishes both *Bicycling* (330,000 paid readers) and *Mountain Bike* (current paid circulation of 135,000), and when we expanded into Germany in 1993, it was natural that *Bicycling*, the larger-circulation title, would lead the way. As publisher of both titles, I agreed with that approach. And so did our joint-venture partner, Ringier. (Rodale has a joint venture with Ringier-Verlag, the Munich-based arm of the Swiss publisher and printing company, to produce both *Mountain Bike* and *Runner's World*.)

We were both wrong. The market and the editors argued for *Mountain Bike*, believing that mountain biking would grow activity. We opted to launch *Mountain Bike* with an emphasis on a niche product, rather than a broader sporting category. Quickly, we became the number-two title in a very competitive market.

5. Rely on your instincts—not the conventional wisdom.
We're all used to being told that certain things can't be done in certain markets. Don't believe everything you hear. I recall being told that subscription marketing would not work in Russia. At first, I believed our joint-

venture partner—at the time a post-Perestroika state publishing house that we're no longer affiliated with. We tried it anyway, and it worked. We now have a growing database of 100,000 names in Russia, and it is as valuable as the magazine we publish there, *Novii Fermer*.

In the early going, we got tens of thousands of names simply by placing ads in competing magazines. Now, as Russian marketers have become more knowledgeable about the value of lists, those glory days are over. But list building is still in its infancy and offers real prospects.

If I was told once, I was also told 100 times that subscription marketing wouldn't work in the U.K., despite the success *Reader's Digest* has had. We tried it, and it's worked to date. We received about 10,000 responses to blow-in cards in our first issue of *Men's Health*, about a 9 percent response. We believe we will soon be the circulation leader in the U.K. men's lifestyle category.

6. When in doubt, test.
Follow your nose, your instinct and the weathervane—but be sure to test, test, test. Our gut instinct told us *Men's Health* was ripe for the United Kingdom, but we still tested extensively.

We tested cover concepts until just minutes before we were due on press for the debut February/March 1995 issue. At the eleventh hour, we pulled a cover that had done well in the States in exchange for a more fanciful cover of a man with a bee buzzing by his head—rather more humorous than our typical American covers. It worked: We sold 112,000 copies and enjoyed a 72 percent sell-through, literally selling out in London.

One caution: A brand name epitomizes a business, and a publisher should be slow to modify it. U.K. advertising agencies and magazine distributors warned us that *Men's Health* was too American and, well, too healthy. I raised this issue at our focus groups and heard similar concerns. We felt the title was strong enough to carry the undecided. As a rule of thumb, fight for your brand. Modify it only as a last resort. English is pervasive in Europe, and that's to your advantage.

7. Make your content fit the market.
We all know content is king and if the editorial doesn't work, you can forget the business. That said, publishers

should not expect to use all American editorial in international editions. Because of time constraints, we used mostly Anglicized American editorial in the first issue of *Men's Health* in the United Kingdom. By next year, however, we'll cut the U.S. material to 30 percent.

Conversely, the German edition of *Mountain Bike* used very little editorial from either the U.S. edition of *Mountain Bike* or *Bicycling*. Because the magazine was oversize, the graphic package was different, as was its treatment of photos. Publishers should factor these costs into the total joint-venture expense.

The market, the competition and, to a degree, the sensibilities of the editors determine the ultimate package, unless the brand is so very strong it can dictate market terms. Although we have tried to stay with our basic American *Runner's World* editorial and graphic package in Germany, we've modified it by boosting the trim size to match other titles in the Ringier mix.

But what one exports, at the end of the day, is brand, influence, ideas, line-ups and as much editorial content as the market will embrace. So don't think for a minute that, just because you can't export every article, international editions won't work.

8. Let books lead the way.

If your company also publishes books, you might consider letting these products pave the way. Rodale's book division entered the United Kingdom, France and Germany in early 1993 with its health books, giving us some confidence that Europe's health interests were strong.

Compared to magazine joint ventures or wholly owned operations, book testing is very cost effective. As *Reader's Digest* has demonstrated, a small staff can enter a market, test lists and concepts, and make marketing decisions without absorbing a lot of upfront costs.

9. Beware of hidden costs.

If you're going to partner with a European publisher for your launch, expect payback in three years, especially if you're expanding into Germany and the United Kingdom. And while you can launch a magazine in a major European market for a fraction of what it costs in the States, keep in mind that the return is proportionately lower. A gross revenue of $5 million to $8 million would be very respectable for a mid-size title in Europe. That might translate to $1 million in profit if you own the title, or $500,000 for a joint-venture deal.

Publishers should consider structuring their businesses around prospective returns. This means analyzing the benefits of a wholly owned business, with all its

risks, located far from the main office. I know many successful joint ventures that net publishers in the $300,000 to $500,000 range. Below that, one might want to consider a licensing arrangement—unless you don't mind sailing uncomfortably close to the wind.

One lament I hear from even the most astute publishers is that they should have been more vigilant about how a partner figures infrastructure costs, which are high in Europe, especially Germany.

Total infrastructure costs of around 9 to 10 percent are reasonable. You might want a clause in your contract that allows you to invite bids on printing and other services to make sure the prices you are paying are competitive. Check on what costs are charged to the joint venture and how.

10. Check out licensing products.

If you are ready to sign a licensing agreement, figure you'll collect roughly 7 percent on circulation revenue and 10 percent on advertising revenue. You might want to negotiate a higher percentage on Scandinavian titles because circulation revenue there is proportionately higher. Whether you can also get a flat licensing fee for the title itself, however, will depend on your negotiating skills and the strength of the brand.

Generally speaking, there seem to be fewer risks in launching a strong title overseas these days. In part, this is because the business model has changed. Newsstand efficiencies are much higher in Europe, so that channel can be profitable from the first issue. And since single-copy revenue should more than cover printing and other costs, the decision to increase frequency, as we have already done with the U.K. *Men's Health,* doesn't have to be so heart-wrenching.

That European publishers as a rule don't invest heavily in direct marketing makes the financial model simpler and more manageable. And in Europe, one gets a sense of how single-copy sales are doing within a few weeks of the on-sale date. For example, I received trend reports from MarketForce, our London-based distributor, within seven to 10 days of *Men's Health*'s first issue on-sale date. This gave us ample opportunity to adjust draw, cover design and publicity plans.

One thing to keep in the front of your mind: Although European publishers are very open to ideas from American publishers, the host market always rules. On the other hand, you don't have to leave your skills or business plans at home. American publishers are known for their inventiveness and daring.

That, after all, is part of our charm. ☐

Publishing in Mexico After NAFTA

BY REED PHILLIPS III

Going global is certainly the thing to do in the 1990s. In fact, *The New York Times* predicted in January 1994 that "The corporate executive's mantra for the new year [will be] think globally, think globally, think globally."

For the past few years, the hot area for international expansion has been Eastern Europe. Not a week went by when I wasn't reading an announcement of a new venture to publish a U.S. magazine in one of those countries. U.S. publishers seemed to be climbing over one another in their haste to secure a foothold for their magazines. No one wanted to risk missing out.

Now it's Mexico's turn to be hot. In addition to being an emerging market, Mexico is the gateway to Latin America. Success in Mexico will open expansion opportunities for U.S. publishers in the Spanish-language countries throughout Central and South America. And now that the North American Free Trade Agreement (NAFTA) is in place, there has never been a better time to look south of the border for expansion.

For those U.S. magazine publishers who want to expand into Mexico, I recommend the following five steps:

Research the important macro trends. To understand your future in Mexico, you have to understand the trends affecting the future of Mexico itself. In the broadest terms, this means examining Mexico's economy, culture, politics, education levels and demographics to assess how these forces are shaping the country. One of the surprising discoveries you will make is that the median age of Mexico's population is just 19—considerably younger than the median age in the United States, which is 33. Another surprise: 70 percent of the population live in urban areas.

Once you have a picture of the future of Mexico, ask yourself how this future affects your magazine's chances of being published in that country. For example, does the existence of a youthful population improve or diminish your publishing prospects?

Learn how the Mexican magazine industry works. Probably the best way to learn how magazine publishing works in Mexico is to talk with the U.S. publishers who

are already publishing there—such as Hearst, *Newsweek*, *Playboy*, *Reader's Digest*, Time Inc. and Ziff Communications. They can explain both the similarities and differences. You will learn that although Mexico and the United States share a border, the two magazine industries are very different—certainly as different as the American and British magazine industries.

Size is the most significant variation. In number of titles, Mexico has only 10 to 15 percent of the volume that we have in the United States. In addition, most of the revenue comes from consumers rather than advertisers. Advertising budgets earmarked for Mexican magazines probably represent less than 5 percent of what advertisers spend in U.S. magazines. However, the passing of NAFTA makes it a good bet that this will increase substantially in the future.

One company, Mexico City-based Televisa, dominates magazine publishing in Mexico. It publishes more than 50 titles, and its marketshare is estimated at more than 70 percent. Televisa owns two magazine publishing arms: Corporacion Editorial, also based in Mexico City, and Editorial America, based in Miami. It also owns Mexico's largest national distributor, Mexico City-based Intermex. This is an important point because magazines in Mexico are sold predominantly on newsstands.

In fact, there is only one large consumer magazine in Mexico that is *not* sold predominantly on newsstands: *Reader's Digest*. Of a total circulation of approximately 670,000, roughly 90 percent are subscriptions. In a country that has almost no direct-marketing infrastructure, building up such a large subscriber base was an amazing feat.

Find your niche. Once you understand the trends that will determine Mexico's future and the dynamics of the Mexican magazine industry, you should be able to figure out what the opportunities are for your magazine. Here are some of the questions you should ask yourself:
• Do demographic trends suggest that there is a growing reader need for the information in my magazine?
• What editorial advantages do I have that give me an edge over other competitors in this market?

• Will the brand identity that my magazine has established in the United States carry any weight in Mexico?

Get another opinion. No one better understands the Mexican market than the publishers and advertisers already doing business there. Even if you are convinced that Mexico is the place you want to take your magazine, you should talk with these experts before you actually start to publish there. Publishers can tell you whether they think there is a market for your magazine and how best to reach that market. Advertisers can tell you whether they need to reach your market and how much they are willing to spend to do so. If you pass this last test, you are ready for the next step.

Decide the best way to publish your magazine in Mexico. There are three approaches for you to choose from: You can start your magazine on your own, without the help of a partner, or you can find a partner with whom you can either do a joint venture or negotiate a licensing agreement.

The riskiest way is to start on your own. Despite the research you will have done, you still won't know the country and its readers as well as a local partner will. Yes, *Reader's Digest* went it alone in Mexico years ago and today is the second largest circulation title in Mexico. But it would be difficult, if not impossible, to duplicate *Reader's Digest*'s success today.

As you interview publishers before making your final decision to publish, you will have the opportunity to see if any would make good partners for you. Having a Mexican partner can give you an important head start. The Hearst Corporation, for example, has been one of the most successful U.S. publishers in Mexico. For over 20 years, it has published with the Editorial America arm of Televisa, and recently converted the license to a 50:50 joint venture for some of its magazines, including *Cosmopolitan, Harper's Bazaar, Good Housekeeping* and *Popular Mechanics.*

NAFTA is expected to improve significantly the business fortunes of Mexico during the coming years. Now is the time for U.S. publishers to explore or re-examine the publishing opportunities waiting there for them. ☐

> Success in Mexico will open expansion opportunities in the Spanish-language countries throughout South and Central America.

Finding a Printer Over There

BY TIM BOGARDUS

For the average publisher, the prospect of printing a magazine in a foreign country is daunting, if not absolutely terrifying. The obstacles and issues to be faced—language barriers, currency-exchange dilemmas, printing-standards differences and the expense of sheer distance—can seem insurmountable if the process is not broken down into manageable parts.

Entry into Asian markets presents particularly burdensome linguistic and cultural barriers, although every country, regardless of its continent, has its quirky laws, restrictions and regulations. For example, according to Russell J. Melvin, director of international affairs for the Magazine Publishers of America, Brazil does not allow foreign ownership of communications companies. Neither does North Korea or China. European countries, at the moment, have the fewest restrictions, so it makes sense to explore them first.

Let's say you publish a small, technical magazine with a national distribution. You have determined that there is a market for your publication in Germany and, possibly, other European countries. You use a printer in Wisconsin for your domestic edition, but that printer has no European operations. Now what?

"Find a partner," says the MPA's Melvin. "It's the most practical way to do it." The majority of publishers in this situation find a licensee who pays to use the name of the magazine, but often takes very little of the content. It's essentially a franchise arrangement whereby the local publisher sells its own advertising, produces its own editorial content, and arranges its own distribution.

Print here, ship there

Another widely used strategy is to print in the United States, ship overseas, and use local distribution channels in the target country. According to Tom Nunziata, a spokesman at the New York City-based American Business Press, three-quarters of the U.S. magazines with international editions print domestically and ship abroad. In Europe, 80 percent of magazines reach readers through newsstands, according to Dave Bordewick, vice president of marketing at the Chicago-based R. R. Donnelley & Sons.

Like a start-up

The third strategy, and the most daunting, is to print your magazine in the target country. Working with a European printer partially solves distribution difficulties because a local printer is usually better able to facilitate distribution. Nonetheless, few small or mid-size American publishing companies print overseas as yet. "That is an uncommon experience," says Donnelley's Bordewick. "But the process is essentially the same as doing a new magazine start-up."

Rick Friedman, founder and president of New York City-based SIGS Publications, publisher of 13 specialized technology magazines, agrees. "There really aren't many publishers who venture into that arena," he says. "It's very risky."

But in 1994, Friedman decided the risk was worth

> "Keep the relationship very short-term. This is a new partnership—the printer needs to get to know the publisher and vice versa."

taking. SIGS, a privately held company with $10 million in revenues in 1994, had been sponsoring advanced-software conferences in Munich for several years when Friedman decided to launch a German-language version of his software programmers' publication, *Object Magazine.* He asked writers from other magazines and conference participants for advice. Through those references, he found a Munich-based design firm to handle the design and production of the magazine. In April 1994, with an initial $50,000 investment, SIGS launched *Objekt Spektrum.*

Friedman says the local designer was invaluable in

■ Getting started

Just finding the resources needed to begin to look for a European printer can be confounding. Neither the Magazine Publishers of America nor the American Business Press has printed resources about overseas publishing, although these organizations may be able to refer you to people who are knowledgeable about international production.

You can also try networking through U.S. printers and publishers on your own, advises Ziff-Davis Publishing's vice president of production, Roger Herrmann. Find your counterpart at a big publishing company that has international operations and ask that person for some names and advice.

Next, write or call the London-based International Federation of the Periodical Press (FIPP), which is the MPA's international counterpart. FIPP can put you in touch with its member publishers and suppliers, which may be a good source of referrals.

Finally, write to PIRA International, which publishes The Directory of Heatset Web Offset Printers in Western Europe, an annual guide.

Magazine Publishers of America (MPA)
919 Third Ave., New York, NY 10022
Tel: 212-872-3700; Fax: 212-888-4217

American Business Press (ABP)
675 Third Ave., Fourth Floor, New York, NY 10017
Tel: 212-661-6360; Fax: 212-370-0736

FIPP (International Federation of the Periodical Press)
Imperial House, 15-19 Kingsway
London WC2B 6UN, United Kingdom
Tel: +44 (171) 379-3822; Fax: +44 (171) 379-3866

PIRA International
Randalle Road, Leatherhead
Surrey KT22 7RU, United Kingdom
Tel: +44 (037) 237-6101; Fax: +44 (037)237-7526

15,000 paid circulation produced by a three-person staff in Munich. The magazine and SIGS's two German software conferences generated $2.5 million in revenues last year.

Research begins at home

If, like Friedman, you're sure there's a market for your title, a good way to begin the process of finding a European printer is to contact U.S. printers with overseas operations or affiliations. These include Ringier America (Ringier AG is its Swiss parent); Brown Printing (owned by German media giant Bertelsmann AG); Quebecor (the largest Canadian printer has operations in France, the United Kingdom and other countries); or R. R. Donnelley (which has plants in South America, Europe and Asia).

These printers may be able to provide referrals through their foreign operations. But after an American printer has provided contacts and referrals, its role in the process is finished. "We can take it to a certain point, and then the publication has to take it to the next level," says Bill Guthrie, vice president of sales and marketing for Brown Printing.

Roger Herrmann, vice president of production at New York City-based Ziff-Davis Publishing, says offshore paper suppliers are another good source of information: "They supply paper to many different printers in the European arena, and they can help you build a list." He also recommends contacting an international prepress operation. Finally, if you have no other contacts, Herrmann advises making cold calls to large publishers that have overseas operations. "If you have a non-competitive title, people will help you out as a professional courtesy," he says.

Herrmann should know, because he has been involved in the creation of several international editions of Ziff-Davis magazines, and he worked for Time Inc. in a similar capacity before moving to Ziff. In 1991, Herrmann was instrumental in starting Ziff's first foreign edition, *PC Professionell,* in Germany. Although Ziff-Davis is a large company (last year's pretax earnings for the publishing group were $150 million), Herrmann says its international experience nonetheless offers lessons for small- and medium-size publishers.

On-site visits

After you've networked to develop a "hit-list" of five to eight printers, Herrmann suggests that you conduct on-site visits, just as you would in the United States. "You're looking for the manufacturing platform, given

finding the printer. He and the design firm went with their choice of printer because the company was willing to help them navigate the complexities of obtaining the German equivalent of a second-class mail permit. "They really wanted to work with us," he says. "And they were willing to shepherd the magazine through the postal service."

Objekt Spektrum is now a 100-page monthly with

the particular specifications and requirements of your book and how it dovetails with the equipment they have," he says. Meeting the management, seeing the state of developments in new technology, and understanding their back-end systems are all important aspects of an on-site visit.

The distribution system in Germany, for example, is very different from the United States in that the production cycle is much more compressed. A six-week cycle (from ad close to on-sale date) in the United States is a three-and-a-half-week cycle in Germany. "They really have an ability to get magazines delivered in a hurry," Herrmann says.

When it comes time to choose your printer, there are several considerations beyond manufacturing compatibility and quality: Compare prices and costs with bids from other plants, and analyze all the variable factors (such as ink and paper prices). Publishers who are forward-thinking about technology need to look for a printer with a similar mindset.

Herrmann recommends creating a standard quote sheet for bids so that each printer will be providing data in the same format. This makes it easier for the financial staff to do an analysis. The bids should be submitted in the target country's currency, so that they can be recalculated in U.S. dollars as the currency fluctuates. And currencies fluctuate all the time, which Herrmann says is reason not to compare U.S. costs with costs in Europe. "You can take a snapshot today versus the European costs today at a certain exchange rate. But it's anybody's guess what the relationship will be a year from now," he notes.

Printer contracts in Europe are generally similar to those in the United States, varying primarily in what terms are considered "standard." But Herrmann emphasizes one significant difference: Many European printers do not have binding facilities, and they often subcontract that work. When you sign a contract with the printer, make sure you are clear on bindery issues.

And don't sign a five-year deal, he warns. "Keep the relationship very short-term. This is a new partnership—the printer needs to get to know the publisher and vice versa."

Intangible factors

Signing the contract is just the beginning, of course. The unexpected will occur, just as it does at home. For example, after the inaugural issue of Ziff's *PC Professionell* was printed, word leaked out that a German competitor had offered a DM 30,000 reward to any bindery employee who would spirit out an advance copy. Ziff had to post security guards at the bindery. "They were really playing hardball," Herrmann recalls.

In general, Herrmann recommends keeping an open mind. "As you look at your options in terms of printers, recognize that you're in a different market, and their emphasis may be in different areas." For example, inkjetting and selective-binding are not widely used in Europe, because there's not as much need to fractionalize the demographics as there is in the United States.

"If you go in with an open mind and flexibility, and you view it in that context," Herrmann says, "you can begin to rank the printers and their capabilities, and you will make a good choice." □

Publishing Opportunities in Russia

BY JAMES C. MCCULLAGH

Don't publish in Russia! The country is in economic and political turmoil. Inflation rages. The gross domestic product rivals that of Third World nations. And distribution across nine or 10 time zones remains problematic, if not impossible. Go to Mexico or Brazil—but please, please don't go to Russia.

Thus goes the conventional wisdom. Yes, Russia is a hard place to do business—hard, but not impossible. The business climate has improved markedly since perestroika opened Russia to the West. Today, American publishers are finding success there. Hearst Corp., Playboy Enterprises, Reader's Digest Association, Rodale Press and Hachette Filipacchi are all doing good business in a country that thwarted the first wave of publishers eight years ago.

First, some remarks about the general business climate. Then, some suggestions for publishers who want to have a presence in a country of 300 million consumers that is fast opening up to the West.

New day dawning

Rodale, Hearst and Reader's Digest went into Russia early, before a Western-style business structure existed and before enough Russians were "educated" in publishing and marketing techniques. Early entry meant dealing with the vestiges of the Communist apparatchiks. In 1989, the then-Soviet government imposed onerous conditions on joint ventures. For complex reasons, Rodale found itself investing in building a sausage factory that would earn hard currency to pay for publishing a farm magazine that would be printed in Helsinki. (Rodale got out of that business years ago.)

I don't know any media joint ventures that survived this initial love affair with Russia. Hearst dissolved its joint venture with a large Russian newspaper after investing big dollars. Rodale decided to go it alone after its joint venture partner did not live up to the terms of their agreement, a very common result of early pacts. It wasn't because these arrangements were not done well. Quite the contrary. Rodale had in its corner the Washington, D.C.-based law firm Arnold &

Porter, one of the best. The simple fact is that Russia was not ready for joint ventures when Gorbachev swung open the doors.

I am glad to report that all that has changed. Western advertising and marketing techniques no longer represent a foreign language. Hundreds of legitimate ad agencies have opened to meet the almost insatiable need for service. List rental is possible. Database management services proliferate, as do fulfillment houses.

The very face of Moscow has changed. Advertising lights up the broad, gray boulevards. Television channels are multiplying. Direct-response advertising is in its infancy, but growing fast. Direct marketing offers huge potential. Furthermore, the importance of database building has not been lost on the Russians. The days of renting lists, as Rodale did, for $20 per thousand are over.

Big Mac leads the attack

Publishers owe a debt to McDonald's, Pizza Hut and countless smaller enterprises for introducing to Russians the notions of service, value and fair prices. Not only did these companies condition the Russian psyche to accept new food served differently, they also trained a new generation of customer-friendly marketers. Anyone who was in the Soviet Union 10 years ago probably has a ripe collection of stories about horrendous restaurant service. That has changed—and not only in places that serve Westerners.

Make no mistake about it, the shift is generational. Men and women in their twenties and thirties are more open and resilient. The reason so many early joint ventures failed was that the older generation—in Russia, that's usually anyone over 35—simply did not have the imagination to embrace what the poet Auden called, "new styles of architecture, a change of heart." Western publishers, myself included, didn't pay enough attention to the psychology produced by 70 years of a command economy. The language of Russian magazines and newspapers was, and still is to a degree, paternalistic and autocratic.

But 10 years in Russia has been akin to a generation. The nation moved from the abacus to the computer in less than a decade. This is a nation on the move, with a growing army of marketers showing the way.

Hello, hello … ?

On my early trips to Russia, I told my family not to expect calls from me—communications were that bad. InTourist hotels had phones barely capable of connecting with the next room. I would wait hours, if not days, for a phone line.

That has all changed. New phone lines are being laid and the technology is often superior to much that we enjoy here. Educated Russians are computer-literate and use the Internet to transmit documents. Web sites abound.

There is little in the way of computer hardware and software that you can't buy in major Russian cities. Gone are the days when I and my colleagues had to carry all the office equipment from Pennsylvania to Moscow. *Byte*, *Macworld* and other U.S. computer titles keep Russians abreast of developments.

Rubles, dollars and credit cards

Although the Russian currency is pegged to the dollar, the days of the dual-currency carnival are over. Today, the ruble is the only accepted currency. In business circles, the credit card is the order of the day. It's no longer a hassle to transfer money out of the country.

On the other hand, Moscow is fast becoming an expensive city to do business in, although not yet on the order of Tokyo or London. Prices of consumer commodities, including magazines, reflect the real price of manufacturing, in stark contrast to the days when prices were controlled by the government. Consumers will pay $3 or $4 for one issue of a Western-style magazine. As Hearst found out, one can make money if Russian consumers see the relationship between price and quality.

Red (white and blue) tape

I can say flatly that it is easier to do business today in Russia compared to five years ago. Part of the problem was that the Russians didn't have a written legal code to embrace the new rhetoric of joint ventures. Not surprisingly, during Rodale's first Russian effort, the company spent more on legal fees than on production of *New Farmer*. The first wave of Westerners simply helped to write a legal code that would accommodate new ideas, structures and partnerships. But many publishers have found that the perfect agreement doesn't exist, no matter how much is spent on legal fees. In the end, the best protection is finding the right partners.

Bureaucracy still exists. Certain rules and regulations hinder business development. However, these are now more minor annoyances than real obstacles.

A 10-step program for success

The Russia projected into our living rooms nightly is one of border wars and dangerous politicians. The other world, inhabited by a growing middle class, is rarely seen. We read much about the new rich, but not about this middle class that represents both stability and a vast new market for American publishers. In that spirit, here are 10 suggestions for publishers interested in one of the world's remaining, relatively untouched, consumer markets.

1. Go it alone. The first Western publishers entering the Soviet Union were obliged to find partners because of government regulations and the Byzantine nature of the place. All that has changed. Both Reader's Digest and Rodale have wholly owned operations in Russia. Of course, Reader's Digest always operates that way internationally. Rodale also prefers this approach, but generally lets the market dictate the arrangement. That a reliable post office distribution system and workforce exist makes this option more compelling.

2. Find a partner. Joint ventures got a bad rap in the late 1980s when publishers—and many other businesses—hooked up with the first Russian who came along. One American publisher hired a KGB operative to run its Moscow office, convinced that he was born again in capitalist ways. When that venture failed, I hired him. The marriage lasted three months. I realized he still had Stalin in his heart. There wasn't much due diligence in those heady days.

The scene has changed. The Russian businesspeople I know want long-term relationships with their partners. Moreover, non-Russian alternatives now exist. After a false start with a Russian partner, Hearst returned with a Dutch partner, who is also working with Playboy and Hachette. *Cosmopolitan* is one of the hottest magazines in the country. Recent issues have closed with more than 100 ad pages. It's reasonable to expect the same reaction to *Elle*, *Top Model* and other women's titles that are joining Russia's fashion landscape.

Rodale decided to go it alone after its joint-venture partner failed to deliver and the contract was dissolved. That's ancient history. I would have absolutely no compunction about entering another joint-venture agreement in Russia, Ukraine and other republics.

3. Think special interest. When given the option, Russians will choose well-written, well-edited magazines over the long-winded Communist versions. Government-sponsored, mass-circulation magazines are in decline or already out of business. Today, the potential for women's, men's, health, fitness, business and computer titles seems great. Fashion magazines are showing the way. *Good Housekeeping* speaks to the emerging middle class. *Reader's Digest,* with a circulation of 120,000, has exploited a similar niche.

In conducting focus groups in Russia, I discovered just how keenly Russians are interested in American business practices, the latest health and fitness developments, and new technologies. Their bent for poetry aside, Russians are very practical, interested in process—which makes them very likely to embrace how-to magazines. Russian women hold the healthcare system together. Family health is a hot area and being defined, in part, by the massive influx of Western pharmacology.

Russians are extremely well-read, especially in the areas of culture, technology and literature. My short list of titles likely to find success in Russia includes *Prevention, Men's Health, Muscle & Fitness, Shape, Self* and *Wired.*

4. Use the mail. With the break-up of the Soviet Union, much of the economic infrastructure fell apart. That included the magazine distribution system, handled from a central warehouse in Moscow. Because of the subsequent inefficiencies (such as finding thousands of undelivered magazines in a warehouse), Rodale decided to build its circulation through the mail, learning from *Reader's Digest* in Moscow, which started database-building four years ago. Almost all the 70,000 circulation for Rodale's *New Gardener* (formerly *New Farmer*) was generated by mail. It was not uncommon to get a 25 percent response to early direct-mail efforts and, considering that money is sent in with subscription orders (through a debit system at the local post office), there is practically no bad debt.

Significant hikes in postage costs in the last year have forced publishers to offer short-term subscriptions (six months) to keep pace with price increases. Now that inflation has cooled and world paper prices have steadied, building circulation through direct mail will remain attractive. Nonetheless, it remains prudent for a publisher to have a balanced distribution mix, selling copies through retail and through the mail. Better still, if you can, sell newsstand copies on assignment, getting your money upfront.

5. Price aggressively. Russians constantly told me that consumers will not pay Western prices for magazines because titles there have long been considered—and

priced—as commodities. They're wrong. My experience has been quite the opposite. *Cosmo* sells at the kiosk for about 20,000 rubles. Magazines show no cover prices. And in Russia, there are no returns. Vendors who don't sell a monthly magazine reduce its cost when the new issue arrives. It is not uncommon to see four or five issues of *Cosmo* on the newsstand, all at different prices. If copies don't sell after five or six months, they find their way to other cities in the republic. Eventually, everything sells— or is bartered.

Subscription pricing is just as aggressive. *Reader's Digest* sells a four-issue subscription for about 100,000 rubles. Rodale's *New Gardener* is the same price. Keep in mind that is about $5 for one issue, a good price in any corner of the world. If you price it right, you can make money on the first subscription you sell.

6. Market your wares. One of the first remarks I heard on arriving in Russia was that American marketing techniques wouldn't work. My query about using response cards in magazines reduced my Russian friends to tears of laughter. Perhaps there was some truth to this belief then, but it's certainly not true now. I have successfully used insert cards, gift subscriptions, editorial premiums, sweepstakes and the like. Rodale developed a brisk back-issue business out of those thousands of undelivered magazines found in warehouses. Back issues containing practical, how-to information seem to hold their value for years.

7. Serve the reader. I recall discussions with Russian editors about serving the reader and editing the magazine to his or her needs. The response was either laughter or blank stares. Back then, the reader wasn't part of the equation. Such is publishing in a monopoly. Given the chance, however, Russian readers seem thrilled to correspond with a magazine. I've read hundreds of their letters and am struck by the value they place on magazines that serve them. Contrary to what one might expect in a former police state, magazine buyers are eager to share detailed information about their families, hopes and needs. Reader surveys, direct-mail efforts and new-magazine solicitations are accepted as first-class mail, in the very best sense of the word.

8. Think advertising. Eight years ago, magazine advertising was almost unheard of. No longer. From Ralph Lauren to John Deere, Russia is awash in display advertising. Few large agencies are not represented in Moscow. And homegrown, direct-response advertising—in print and broadcast media—is making great gains.

Rate cards are held in the same esteem as in the West. The new, hot magazines such as *Cosmo* seem to hold their rates reasonably well. I'm told by Hearst's Dutch partner that the magazine grosses more than a $1 million on a given issue. The other Hearst titles appear to be doing equally well.

9. Publisher beware. If one is careful, Russia offers great promise to American publishers. Nonetheless, obstacles remain. Let me name a few.

• Four-color, high-speed press capabilities are hard to come by and most full-color magazines are printed in Holland, Finland or Poland. (Reader's Digest and Rodale print in Russia because production requirements are less stringent for their titles.) That situation is changing. R.R. Donnelley & Sons expects to have modern press capabilities in Moscow within a year or so. They've been waiting for demand to catch up.

• Although the state's distribution monopoly has been broken, the smaller companies now in business can't deliver the services and efficiencies we are accustomed to in America. But that should change now that Hachette has entered a joint-venture agreement for distribution with the major newspaper, *Pravda*.

• As database-building becomes more important, many fulfillment houses have come on the scene, some with dubious business practices. Check them out carefully. In the early going, you might be better off doing the fulfillment work yourself. List management is still in its infancy.

10. Pick the right financial strategy. No one strategy will ensure financial success in Russia. Reader's Digest's first consideration is to build a database. Advertising comes second. Rodale is following a similar strategy.

Hearst's timing was right the second time. The company found a reliable partner and re-entered the market just when interest in high-gloss women's magazines was picking up. By every indication, *Cosmo* is profitable, even considering the initial investment. The other Hearst titles seem to be performing well.

If you're going into a high-risk/high-return category, a business model showing a three-year investment seems appropriate. In my opinion, the bigger the risk, the greater the need for a partner.

Obviously, a licensing agreement is the easiest to implement. A dozen American magazines are in Russia under licensing agreements. Details vary, but most reflect the standard licensing contract calling for a percentage of advertising and circulation revenues. Some pay a flat annual rate to the U.S. publisher.

Negotiating a joint-venture agreement is fairly straightforward. And you shouldn't have to outfit the office with new computer equipment. If that's on the top of the Russians' list, look for a new partner. In fact, one reason to find a partner is the relatively high cost of office space in Moscow.

If I were launching a global brand with a partner in a hot magazine market, I'd expect to invest at least $500,000. The partner provides office space and infrastructure. (I'm assuming that advertising already exists, as it does for fashion, automotive, cosmetics, pharmaceuticals and the like.) Keep in mind that for most publishers, there are no heavy direct-marketing costs. A strong title is likely to generate an upfront payment for single-copy sales. That significantly changes the financial equation.

But there are plenty of opportunities for less conspicuous brands, from *Soldier of Fortune* to *New Gardener*. Countless niches wait to be exploited.

My advice is to decide the nature of a publishing agreement on anticipated financial returns. If you expect a title, even under the best circumstances, to earn $100,000 to $200,000, you should seriously consider a licensing agreement. My caution is prompted by this fact: Licensing arrangements can be time consuming and therefore costly. Few publishers I know actually record and assign the true costs of managing licensing arrangements. Conversely, joint ventures always take longer and are more costly than budgeted.

If your title can earn more than $200,000, consider a joint venture. You could go it alone if your publication wasn't dependent on a partner to meet its financial goals. You can build a database without much outside support, but you cannot develop the advertising and marketing contacts needed to make an impact quickly.

Much of the hard work has been done in the Russian market. The "first wave" publishers helped establish a hospitable climate. American ideas are still embraced with great enthusiasm. So don't listen to the nay-sayers. You *can* do business there. ☐

section three

editorial

"At consumer magazines, young editors dare to believe that the **top job is to make magic."**—p. 176

"Editors will have to **schmooze the superhighway** like we work a social function."—p. 178

"To be an editorial bean counter is really **a step backwards."**—p. 181

"The editor's most **natural business-side ally** is the circulation director."—p. 204

Quality Pays

BY RICHARD M. O'CONNOR

I'm mad as hell and I'm not going to take it anymore.

No, I'm not mad at rate cutting or cost controls or even staff reductions. What's got me in a lather is the number of publishers and editors who pay lip service to the concept of producing a "quality magazine." Yet, the truth is, most of them wouldn't know a quality book if it sneaked up and bit them. And that's a shame, because publishing genuine quality not only serves the best interests of readers and advertisers, but your editorial staff and sales department as well.

Let me get down from my soapbox and explain why.

Quality as a motivator

An editor who emphasizes quality to his staff boosts morale. More than anything, editors and writers want to have a sense of significance and creativity about their work. Indeed, any writer who tells you that ego isn't the strongest factor in his or her drive is not to be believed.

Editors and writers don't make the kind of money that affords them much caviar and champagne. Their reward is having their copy given tender loving care and then seeing it stylishly displayed in the glossy pages of a magazine. And the better the quality of copy, the happier the editor/writer. And the happier the staff is, the longer they will work and the higher their standards.

A quick example. Not long after my magazine, *Successful Meetings*, underwent a major redesign, implementing UV coating, better photography, and higher editorial standards, one of our editors came across a street vendor selling back issues. There was *Life, Vogue, Esquire, GQ, Mirabella*—and, to her utter amazement, *Successful Meetings*. It was our special speakers issue with New York Knick coach Pat Riley on the cover—a clean, sophisticated photograph shot by portraitist Francesco Scavullo. There was no way you could tell the magazine was a trade book.

"Where did you get these?" the editor asked.

The vendor shrugged.

"But we don't sell our magazine," the editor said. "It's free."

The vendor put a finger to his lips. "Be quiet, will ya," he whispered. "I've already sold three today."

The editor beamed. She came back to the office and told the entire staff about the incident. God knows it made everybody feel good.

The point is, quality sells. The money invested in design and photography paid off. It even worked to catch the eyes of uninterested passersby and sold itself to people who otherwise would have had very little interest in the meetings business.

Sell your salespeople first

That kind of quality has an impact on your ad staff, too. If you want to convince media buyers of your magazine's quality, you must first convince your own salespeople. Salespeople want to sell quality. Indeed, if you give them a magazine with striking graphics, good reproduction and excellent editorial, I guarantee that it will be the first thing they whip out on a sales call. Why? Because a good salesperson knows that the thing that sells ads is your franchise, the magazine.

Before our redesign, I went out on a sales call with our best rep. During his presentation he talked (and talked and talked) about the magazine, its ad rates, its databases, its merchandising, its editorial. Yet not once did he show it. Afterwards, I asked why.

"Because I don't like the way it looks," he said. "Besides, I didn't need to. They were going to give us some business anyway."

I had to agree that the magazine didn't look as good as it could. Still, his words bothered me.

After the redesign I went with the same rep to the same account. This time he showed off the magazine the way a father shows off pictures of his new baby. He spoke of it with chest-swelling pride. In the end, he didn't get "some of their business." He got all of it.

'Gilt' by association

A quality product attracts (and keeps) quality people. That's what I call my "gilt by association" theory—the premise being that talented people want to be associated with something vital, something special.

After our redesign, I felt I needed a great writer to

cover a very specialized segment of our industry. I discovered that that writer was working for our strongest competitor. I called her. She said she liked where she was. Worse, I couldn't pay her more money. All I could sell her on was the quality of work she would be doing and the quality of the publication as a whole.

She had seen our changes and loved them. She agreed to take the job. Her writing has not only made the magazine better editorially, but also helped sell ads, insofar as her knowledge of the business has been invaluable in convincing advertisers to spend more in the sections in which her stories appear.

Reader affinity means ads

Just as quality attracts talent, it also attracts readers and advertisers. No one reads purely for recreation, simply to kill time. They don't want schlocky stories: They want magazines that will help them do their jobs and live their lives better.

In the end, they want you to deliver a product that combines literary quality with content of direct personal concern. If you accomplish that, you will earn the attention and respect of your readers. No doubt about it.

Now for the big question: Do advertisers perceive quality? Of course they do. Like readers, they look for good story presentations and relevant articles. Let's face it: Advertisers understand that reader responsiveness and affinity are generated by good editorial. So it follows that if readers are responding to a magazine's edit, they will also respond to a magazine's advertising.

Not long ago, I was on an important sales call. The rep and I had one hour to give a presentation, to be followed by one from our strongest competitor. At one point the client said, "Wait a second. Forget the rates and the merchandising. All I want to know is how your book differs editorially from your competition."

I knew I had a live one on my literary line; all I had to do now was reel him in. I told him to check the ad-edit ratio: We were much, much higher, almost 50-50. I showed him stories written by magazine industry publications heralding us for editorial integrity and uniqueness. I showed him an award we received for being the best travel trade magazine; *Conde Nast Traveler* had won it, I quickly added, on the consumer side.

Then I showed layouts and photographs and illustra-

tions and emphasized their excellence. I ended the presentation by saying that what meant most to me as publisher was communicating to readers that we are a quality publication and that I would spare no expense to maintain that standard.

Later, over lunch, the client informed us that we had won the business—all of it, exclusively. He said, "Your competitor cut their rates and, I gotta tell you, it was very tempting. But we decided to go with you because of your commitment to editorial. What we're seeing nowadays is too many books chintzing on their editorial and that cheats readers. Which in turn cheats us."

We raised our glasses. "Here's to the triumph of quality editorial," I toasted. We drank. And drank. Hell, why not? We earned it.

The bottom line is this: Quality triumphs. An editor who doesn't aspire to beat the graphic and editorial standards of the best magazine in his or her field—or any field, for that matter—is cheating readers, staff and advertisers alike. To strive to be anything less than the best is, to my way of thinking, a vulgarity and I wouldn't want to be associated with such a publication, no matter how profitable.

What I want—and what every publisher should want—is to create a magazine whose name stands for quality in thinking, in working, and in writing. It sounds simple. So why aren't more publishers doing it?

> Most editors and publishers wouldn't know a quality magazine if it sneaked up and bit them.

What about sponsored editorial?

Let's face it: Sponsored editorial and special advertising sections are often bastardized. But they don't have to be. Make it clear to advertisers that you control the section. Insist on quality edit—at least a 50-50 ad-edit ratio. There actually should be *more* editorial; don't agree to anything less because that would give the reader nothing more than puff and pap, in which case nobody benefits.

Explain to the advertisers that you want to form a partnership. Hey, we're in this thing together, right? So let them have a lot of input on photographs and editorial direction, but never—never, ever—let them have the right to edit copy. This not only compromises your editorial image, but creates a piece that is of no value to the reader and does nothing more than pander to advertisers.

The Erosion of Editorial Integrity

BY JOHN BRADY

Welcome to the Age of Editorial Erosion. It's an era when editors are under more pressure than ever before to bend, to accommodate, to acquiesce to the requests (read: *demands*) of people with various special interests—ranging from current or prospective advertisers, to people being profiled, to platoons of PR minions who must justify their salaries by interceding between editor and story for spin control. Editorial integrity—the notion that priority number-one is to make certain the magazine is honest and trustworthy—is on the ropes.

Increasingly, editors are expected to shake hands with every person who can do the magazine some good. Many consumer magazines stay away from reporting on topics that might rub advertisers the wrong way. Nor do city and regional magazines bite the advertising hand that feeds them in their annual "Best & Worst" awards, where "bests" are given out like media kits to prospective advertisers all over town, while "worsts" go to non-threatening establishments with low or no advertising budgets.

Sometimes the crossover between editorial coverage and advertising lust is even more apparent. *Esquire* featured a big "The Power of Armani" spread in its March 1993 issue, for instance, hoisted on the table of contents as though it were an editorial report "exploring the master's evolution of style." It ran, without byline, like an advertorial peek at the master's spring-summer collection, with the curious tagline, "For Store Information, see page 189." Hmmmm. The magazine for men is also the magazine for merchandising.

Women's books have long maintained a catalog-like look, with editorial that is strictly for atmosphere, filled with warmed-over press releases from many of the same clients to be found in ads elsewhere in the issue. Their editorial motto seems to be: Seldom is heard a discouraging word, ladies. Let's buy out the store here.

Money or magic?

Still, at consumer magazines, young editors dare to believe that the top job is to make magic. At business magazines, where the pressures to yield to an advertiser's demands are intense, the job is to make money—and advertisers often believe that the publication exists for *them*. Generally speaking, the customer does not come to the business magazine; rather, the magazine *goes to the customer* in order to make a sales call for the advertising sponsors therein. The dynamic is altogether different: no ads, no magazine.

Many business magazine editors consider their job not much different from the publisher's or the advertising director's. Why do editors end up forced to think like the ad-sales department? Because most of them report to a publisher who has come up the ladder from the ad-sales side, and who doesn't understand editorial very well, if at all. So they manage the publication like the advertising vehicle it has always been for them. There are a few exceptions, of course, but basically publishers with strong editorial leanings are rare nowadays.

Undoing the damage

I believe there are purely commercial reasons to bring back editorial integrity. The very survival of magazines as we know them is dependent on their being perceived as having value to the reader. If that value isn't there, a magazine is doomed. The days when advertising accounted for nearly 100 percent of business-magazine revenues are gone—and they aren't likely to return. The magazines of tomorrow will be in an editorial footrace to compete with other information-retrieval and delivery systems, including cable television and online publications. It is a race that will go to the source perceived as having the greatest credibility.

Where the ad slump has caused magazines to become more dependent on circulation for survival, the key to success is also a strong editorial product, one that caters to the readers' sense of self-interest. Ultimately, the question that readers ask of a magazine is, "What's in it for ME?" If there is no inherent editorial value—just valentine copy that is being run to buttress ads—you will lose that reader, and deservedly so. When the audience leaves, advertisers follow. Accordingly, if magazines are to survive as advertising vehicles, the greater their editorial integrity, the greater their market value

■ The 10 commandments of editorial integrity

1. Thou shalt do the right thing. Report the news without fear or favor. This means being fair, honest, open and careful to avoid even the appearance of conflicts of interest.

2. Thou shalt not make sales calls. Or host advertiser luncheons or perform similar marketing tasks. Such events create the impression that advertisers have special access to favorable editorial treatment. And in this business, perception is reality.

3. Thou shalt not covet perks and freebies. When someone offers free goods or travel, you are expected to pay with editorial coverage, which is far more credible—and cost-efficient—than taking ad pages in your magazine.

4. Remember to keep watch on advertising integrity. How can editorial integrity survive if a magazine's ad-sales system is virtually destroying its own environment? When you receive reader complaints about a devious advertiser, report your concerns to the publisher.

5. Keep holy the editorial pages. The narrower your ad base, the more corrupt your editorial is likely to be. But readers don't respect—or read—magazines written for advertisers. And as an audience abandons a publication, so too do advertisers.

6. Honor thy agreements. Check back with a source for an accuracy review of quotes obtained during an interview, if you promised to do so, but never give a subject the right of final review and approval of a manuscript. Your job is to play fair with a subject, not to be a rewrite department in the ego division.

7. Thou shalt not have false gods before thee. By making deals with PR reps or subjects to get their cooperation on interviews, stories, photo shoots and so on, you may be editing for your peers, not your audience. The reader, not the vested interests of the subject and assorted minions, is still boss.

8. Thou shalt set a good example. Ultimately, editorial integrity is people, not policies. The best magazines don't just talk about integrity; they live it. This means you.

9. Thou shalt edit from the heart. Editors know integrity when they see it. They also know a bad or biased or incomplete story that has a private agenda. When in doubt, the Golden Rule applies: Edit for others as you would have them edit for you.

10. Thou shalt quit if necessary. If you find yourself unhappy and professionally heartsick over the deals and demands made by your job, try pointing out that honesty is the best business policy. Bosses usually understand the rules that Sam Walton made zillions with at WalMart: "1. Stick to your business. 2. Take care of the customer." That's what editorial integrity is all about. If your boss still doesn't get it, try this test: Ask yourself, "Would I like an account of my magazine's practices in the pages of *Folio:*?" If not, consider looking for a job that measures up to your sense of pride in performance. Give a copy of these commandments to your replacement, and wish him or her luck.

---

will be. We need reforms. This can be done only if editors hang together—no easy task. In addition to being able to hold advertiser interests at bay, editors must ignore the deals and inducements that sources and PR reps are always clamoring for. *Just say no.* The issue here is one of fundamental trust, confidence and credibility—all of which are undermined when there is misconduct by the publisher, editor or ad director. By recognizing that a magazine is in the business of providing information first and selling ads second, a publication

stands to benefit in the long terms—even if there is some short-term pain. A prolonged battle between editorial and advertising in the publisher's office would only further tarnish the publication's reputation and almost certainly result in long-term damage.

In the end, it shall be apparent to all that no magazine in the history of humankind is ever remembered for its great advertising or circulation numbers. A great magazine is remembered only for its editorial content, and that is based upon its integrity. Amen. ☐

Six Steps to an Editor's Success In the Year 2000

BY LAMBETH HOCHWALD

In the not-too-distant future, customized evening news will be delivered to your television, and magazines will be downloaded to your personal, in-house color printer rather than bought on the newsstand. Publishing companies, meanwhile, are reworking editorial into a profit center, and are demanding far more versatile employees.

What does all this mean for the traditional magazine editor? Will editors become quaint symbols—like typesetters, telegraph operators or blacksmiths—of a time gone by? No. But it does mean that those developing the creative side of magazines must remain one step ahead.

The editor—trade or consumer—must become more than just the author of a print-based periodical to thrive in the business and media environment. He or she must rethink the editor's function and learn new skills. Editors need to master skills that today often apply only to incidental responsibilities. They'll have to be smart marketers, creative thinkers, financially conversant, comfortable and knowledgeable in the legal realm—and perhaps most important, technically savvy.

Following is a six-point guide for editors interested in assuring their continued relevance in an age of rapid change.

1. Understand the new media culture.

Editors are already beginning to anticipate the way sweeping shifts in technology will affect their future work. And with good reason, say some who feel that an aversion to new technology may dampen the chances of advancing to a chief editor position. In fact, editors may be even more essential in the digital age, many observers say. "Everyone is worried about what the 500-channel universe will look like," says Kevin Kelly, executive editor of San Francisco-based Wired. "In that world, the role and value of the editor become greater. What we're seeing is that the more information there is, the more valuable the editor is. Even our writers need to be e-mail and telecommunications savvy," he explains. "We're biased because our beat is the digital future. But it's not just logging on to a computer—

there's a culture and landscape that you have to be comfortable with."

To stay abreast of changes and contribute ideas for ancillary projects that will keep the titles cutting-edge, editors should closely watch the shifting marketplace, says John Andrews, editor of The New York Times Co.'s Custom Builder, based in Yarmouth, Maine. "We're all reacting to what technology is doing to our jobs and products," he says. "What we think we'll need by the year 2000 will be predicated on what technology ends up out there. We need to stay in command of technology as it progresses in leaps and bounds."

Other editors see the forthcoming information superhighway as a tremendous opportunity to have a one-on-one rapport with an audience. "Editors will have to schmooze the superhighway like we work a social function," says Roberta Myers, editor in chief of Tell, the Hachette Filipacchi teen quarterly. "We're going to have to work those electronic rooms, too."

And because new media formats will always need readers (or viewers, if the medium is screen-based), editors will still have to cultivate an audience. "While the editorial function may be clear-cut, the function of the magazine in society itself is changing," says Arnold Huberman, president of a New York City-based executive search and management firm specializing in communications. "The editor has to give readers information they still find relevant."

2. Follow media and employment law.

Editors are going to have to work harder to steer clear of legal troubles in the digital future, as original magazine material has already begun to reappear on online services and CD-ROMs. And because copyright laws are being continuously redefined through court decisions, editors must make sure that they do, in fact, have the legal right to reproduce material from their magazines in an electronic format. Editors must continue to fact-check thoroughly as material is translated into new formats; they need to be familiar with the variations in libel law from one medium to another, and remain sensitive to potentially problematic content.

"In the new media age, no one really knows exactly how much one can disseminate misinformation," declares Robert Nylen, editor in chief of "Media & the Law," a bimonthly newsletter based in Ashfield, Massachusetts.

Editors also need to pay a lot more attention to employment law and hiring policies. In the next few years, as more and more laws governing employment and the workplace are enacted or updated, companies are increasingly likely to turn up the heat on editorial departments to ensure compliance. For example, the Family and Medical Leave Act of 1993, which guarantees employees unpaid leave under certain circumstances, is very much an open question. "That act will cause a lot of procedural questions for companies and will impact on policies related to general absence and sickness," says Ruth D. Raisfeld, an attorney specializing in employment law in the New York City office of San Francisco-based Orrick, Herrington & Sutcliffe.

Another law, the Americans with Disabilities Act, which became effective in January 1994, is also a tricky statute in terms of coverage. "Editors should be aware that there are laws and regulations governing nearly every aspect of the employment relationship, from interviewing to advertising a position to affording benefits to terminating an employment relationship," adds Raisfeld.

The proactive approach here is to create an internal mechanism for dealing with complaints and grievances. "Issues editors will have to deal with over the course of the nineties include domestic partnerships and discrimination against homosexuals," says Raisfeld. "Editors need to create some kind of policy so that a situation can be dealt with before it becomes a real problem."

3. Know your way around the desktop.
Many editors say that understanding the basics of desktop publishing and maneuvering around computer sys8tems are skills that are becoming all but indispensable. Sally Koslow, editor in chief of The New York Times Company Women's Magazines' special-interest publications, says that although desktop software was once used solely by art departments, now editorial teams must be armed with those skills as well. "Editors need to learn QuarkXPress and know their way around

> "It's not just logging on to a computer— there's a culture and landscape that you have to be comfortable with."

the Mac," she says. "The more multiqualified you are, the more marketable you are."

Jim Meigs, editor of Wenner Media's *Us*, adds that although desktop publishing hasn't radically changed his hiring prerequisites, evolving desktop software has already blurred the distinction between art, editorial and production jobs. "I don't necessarily need an editor with tons of experience in Quark, but that person should have the tolerance to fix bad breaks," he says. "I need editors who are detail-oriented and aren't hung up on traditional job roles. If editors fix problems on the screen, it turns them into temporary typesetters."

4. Learn the art of number-crunching.
Also top-of-mind for everyone today is that there's no room at the top of the masthead for the spreadsheet-shy. While junior editors probably don't need MBAs to prepare to be editors, the fact is that today's editors are becoming more and more involved in their magazines' fiscal operations. This means editors may become increasingly sophisticated as they micro-budget for their department and beyond, says *Wired*'s Kelly.

And as staffs get leaner, editors will be less able to look at their jobs in a compartmental manner, adds Peg Moline, editorial director for Weider Publications Inc.'s *Shape*, based in Woodland Hills, California.

Editors will have to become more comfortable with spreadsheets and budgets in the near future, and, fundamentally, will have to see their jobs as a business as well as a craft, says NYT's Koslow. "It's important to learn how to read a balance sheet and put extra energy into not being dumb about numbers," she adds. "Editors should meet with their circulation directors, ad managers, publishers and support people to really learn how their companies work in a mega, not a micro, way."

And as editors continue to expand their accountability as business partners within the larger corporate structure, being able to document their departments' contribution to overall corporate health will be required more and more, says Al Samuels, head of the Rockland County, New York-based headhunting firm Davric Associates. "Editors have been forced by management to act like businesspeople," he says. "I have found that instead of editors' résumés showing the scoops their writers have chalked up, they show instead the ancillary products they introduced that helped them increase profit margins. Résumés are showing how editors are saving money without cutting output."

5. Be your magazine's envoy.

Only a handful of editors have broad public name recognition, although within their niches, good editors have always positioned themselves as knowledgeable authorities. But now, with the growth of online services such as America Online, Prodigy and CompuServe, observers say that leadership is expanding and becoming even more important.

In the digital age, communication between editors and their readers will be more immediate, more free-flowing and certainly more than the mainly one-way stream of information that has traditionally existed. Until recently, readers could send only letters to the editor (which were rarely answered personally), but now have the option to communicate directly with previously hard-to-reach editors.

This link will also make it tough for editors to duck inquiring readers, says *Wired*'s Kelly. "Editors of the future will have to have more of a public presence online," he says. "They will be more in front of a readership, and in a direct way." Again, it is important, observers say, for editors to take the extra steps to familiarize themselves with the mores of the new electronic forums and to make themselves available to answer their readers' questions.

Editors should also be prepared to be envoys in more conventional settings, too. In a tighter advertising environment, an editor's presence at a sales call might be an even greater incentive to buy an ad schedule than it is today. "Publishers will look more and more to editors to serve diplomatic functions and do more outreach work," says Andrews. "Shaking hands and helping publishers do business may leave the editor less time to edit, but editors are increasingly becoming spokespeople for their publications."

6. Read trends and adapt fast.

It's not only junior writers and editors who must hone their knowledge of a specific subject area, while at the same time maintaining a broad perspective on a particular market. The ability to be an expert in one area and remain conversant in others might make the difference when two people apply for the same job. "A shootings editor who can write her own copy is very marketable, as is a copywriter who can be sent out to style a photo shoot," observes NYT's Koslow.

Also important, when times change, as with the emerging new media, an editor will have to be versatile enough to develop creative editorial options to replace suddenly irrelevant topic areas, says Jim Burcke, editor of *Business Insurance*, a Crain Communications weekly. "Insurance is a very tight market, and many companies are failing," he says. "We also cover health insurance, and we're worried that President Clinton's national health-care plan will do away with the health-insurance industry. This, in turn, would do away with a major topic in our magazine. If part of the market disappears because of regulations or court decisions, you've got to find a new area to cover."

And, for that matter, if part of your job description disappears, find a new area to master. □

Editorial Benchmarking: Measure for Measure

BY TONY SILBER

Dealmakers and senior managers alike use benchmarks to determine magazines' editorial efficiency. The Magazine Publishers of America and the American Business Press, as well as groups like the Association of Area Business Publications, have long offered their members confidential benchmarking reports.

"Many publishers feel this is an invaluable yardstick for trying to measure their businesses," says John Emery, former president of the ABP and now a senior adviser at AdMedia Corporate Advisors, a magazine-industry investment bank and consulting firm based in New York City. "In a very recent situation, we were working with a client who was trying to buy a publishing firm, and were able to use these numbers to evaluate their performance. It's been an extraordinarily useful document over the years to me."

Editorial bean counting?

Newsweek editor Maynard Parker says that although he believes benchmarking to be a useful management tool, it should not be the primary factor in evaluating an editor's productivity. "In a news organization, there is an ebb and flow of events, and the consequence of that is that benchmarking doesn't tell the whole story," he observes.

Of more than 20 sources contacted for this story, including editors, publishers, CFOs, CEOs, and consultants, half felt some ambivalence about benchmarking. Their feelings could be summed up thus: There is some value to benchmarking, but it must be applied very judiciously. Some favor one aspect over another—say, measuring a staff against its competitors or other magazines in the same company, vs. measuring one editor against another. But the danger of benchmarking, most observers agree, lies in its potential to damage corporate culture. Because benchmarking measures what is measurable, it's easy for editors' focus to shift to quantity at the expense of reader service—or, in other words, quality. "It's a hazard," agrees Laurie Berger, editor in chief of Reed Travel Group's *Frequent Flyer*. "To be an editorial bean counter is really a step backwards."

And as Henry Muller, editorial director of Time Inc., points out, benchmarking is no substitute for a manager's involvement in leading and motivating his or her staff. "If you look at numbers carefully, you occasionally see some things that tell you something," he says. "But to the extent that we have this kind of information, it's not a substitute for managers doing their jobs."

Adds Ellen Levine, editor of Hearst Magazines' *Good Housekeeping* and president of the American Society of Magazine Editors: "Any editor in chief knows the real value of his or her employees. You can gauge that by instinct and intuition as an editor much better than you can with mathematical grids."

To illustrate why a feel for people, rather than numbers, may serve an editor better in the managerial role, Robert Burnham, editor of Waukesha, Wisconsin-based Kalmbach Publishing's *Astronomy*, tells the following story. For years, he monitored his staff's assignments, using a spreadsheet program to keep everyone's workload more or less equal. But recently, he says, "My thinking shifted toward giving story assignments based on editors' abilities to handle them," he says. Burnham now believes holding everyone to the same numerical benchmark may not result in the best possible magazine. And although he says it's too soon to declare his new practice a success, he adds, "I think it encourages [staffers to excel]."

> ■ **Common editorial benchmarks**
>
> **For comparing individual editors**
> 1. Inches produced
> 2. Bylines produced
> 3. Sources called
> 4. Story ideas proposed
> 5. Trade-show productivity
> 6. Travel
>
> **For measuring editorial staff efficiency**
> 1. Editorial as a percentage of total revenues
> 2. Revenue per editor
> 3. Average compensation per editor
> 4. Manuscript costs
> 5. Average pages per issue
> 6. Average pages per editor
> 7. Cost per editorial page

'What gets measured gets done'

The new emphasis on benchmarking stems from magazine companies' ongoing efforts to streamline editorial operations through cost cutting and, in many cases, staff downsizing. "Productivity and human-capital issues—those are big issues today," says Rita Stollman, a Brooklyn, New York-based editorial consultant. "But if you look only at quantity measurements, then you are going to be seriously eroding the quality of your magazine. I know people who produce only three articles a month, but the quality is such that they bring respect and win prizes for their magazines."

But for every critic of benchmarking, there's a true believer. At Atlanta-based Shore Communications, a fast-growing trade publisher, vice president and editorial director Karen Schaffner says her company is committed to fostering editorial excellence, and that means establishing standards and then measuring performance across its seven magazines and within the staffs of the individual magazines.

"Basically we have a quality range for each of the magazines," Schaffner says. "The editor's responsibility is to make sure the magazine falls within the range. We count up goofs at monthly postmortems. We want to get into things like what's an average time per page for an editor? What's a reasonable number of stories for an editor per month? We're asking editors to average two reader calls per day." Shore is even adapting ad-sales software to track editors' phone calls automatically.

The company has created a series of editorial awards that recognize progress, innovation, best article and best issue. Each award comes with a modest cash bonus. Every Shore magazine is expected to win at least three awards a year, either internally or from outside organizations. To Schaffner, the greatest benefit of the program has been the establishment of standards and goals. "Levi Strauss has a quality philosophy," she says. " 'What gets measured gets done.' We've made it really clear what our priorities are."

A short history of benchmarking

Schaffner and many other editors credit Howard Rauch, a former vice president/editorial director at Gralla Publications (now Miller Freeman), as editorial benchmarking's best-known proponent on the trade side. Rauch, now head of editorial consultancy Editorial Solutions in Tenafly, New Jersey, these days advocates measuring performance as a pre-emptive step. "Now is a terrific time for editors to bring the battle to top management as far as controls and performance," he says. "The editor's job is so diverse. We're working on advertorials, we're getting into conferences, CD-ROMs—we barely have the time to devote to our magazines. And the staffs are smaller. There's a case for delineating to top management all that we're doing and how long it takes us to do it."

Beyond that, Rauch encourages editors to measure column inches, quantify productivity of road trips, count bylines, calls to sources, errors per story, number of sources in a story, time in the field—*everything*. "Assuming that quality is comparable, why shouldn't the high performer be recognized?" he asks.

Still, others retort that the focus on numbers is a recipe for mediocrity. "You have to go for quality, not quantity. I'm a contrarian when it comes to that boxcar thinking," says John Brady, an editorial consultant based in Melrose, Massachusetts. "We're in a business where talent is recognized quickly, within six months, and that person is rewarded or punished accordingly."

And Berger, of *Frequent Flyer*, adds, "I know how I would feel if I were being clocked and logged and watched—it would affect me. You've got a business that is inherently creative and you're trying to impose

■ MPA benchmarks

Costs as a percentage of member magazines' total revenues, 1986-1993

Year	Editorial	Production	Circulation	Advertising
1986	8.78%	26.92%	30.57%	9.29%
1987	8.50	25.10	30.61	9.31
1988	8.52	25.94	30.06	9.01
1989	8.71	25.645	29.32	9.36
1990	9.14	25.11	30.92	9.53
1991	9.52	23.58	31.59	9.64
1992	9.69	22.77	31.25	10.20
1993	10.13	21.27	31.39	9.36

Source: Magazine Publishers of America. Survey responses varied year to year, from a low of 152 in 1987 to a high of 266 in 1992.

black-and-white economic principles on it—the whole thing just doesn't make any sense."

Benchmarking as a defensive weapon

Although benchmarking may be the scourge of lower- and mid-level editors, it can indeed be an ally to top editors. One editor in chief who used benchmarking to defend her turf exactly as Rauch describes is Marie Griffin of New York City-based Lebhar-Friedman's *Drug Store News*.

Griffin recalls: "Last fall, [my bosses] called me in and said, 'Okay, Marie, editorial-page numbers per editor are going down!' At one point we were producing more than 100 pages. We're hitting about 85 pages per editor now. I went to the other magazines in the company and saw what they were doing, and we were in line with them. I could tell my bosses it was too much, and we weren't getting the quality we wanted. I could say our people weren't whiners, they were killing themselves.

"Measuring things doesn't change the facts, so you may as well know what you're working with," she adds. "You've got to watch the assumption that your instinct about someone is right. In retail, buyers would always say, 'This is a gut-instinct business.' But the suppliers would invariably tell us the buyers were wrong. You need

> Editorial remains the least expensive of the major aspects of magazine publishing, while savings from desktop publishing appear to be reducing production costs.

to go beyond instinct because there is a bias in that."

The worst-case scenario, though, is when benchmarks function as a sentence without appeal. One large, New York City-based consumer publisher, for example, computes an anticipated cost-per-edit-page for each of its 20 magazines at budget time. However, in a cost-containment effort, the company has frozen that cost at 1993 levels, leaving the editors to contend with the consequences of negative inflation.

In that situation, as in all applications of benchmarking, it is not the benchmarks themselves that make editors' lives difficult, but how senior management applies them. Says Dennis Campagna, director of financial policies at Time Inc., "As long as things are consistently calculated, then it's fine. Some people, however, include benefits in figuring their cost-per-page, while others don't."

The ultimate benchmark

Perhaps one of the best benchmarks is an external one. As Gregory Jarboe, director of public relations at Ziff-Davis Publishing, says in response to our question about benchmarking, "We think the best measure of editorial—and we've used it for a long time—is paid circulation. If readers like what you do, they renew." □

Freelance Writers: How to Get What You Pay for

BY FRANK FINN

Even the best working relationships can run into trouble, and those between magazine editors and freelance writers are no exception to the rule. Sometimes, the relationship is so flawed that outright hostilities break out.

Some years ago, New York freelance writer Charles Kaiser took *Esquire* to small claims court over an assignment that had gone awry. *Esquire* had given Kaiser the green light on a profile of Robert Gottlieb, then editor of *The New Yorker*. But when Kaiser submitted the piece, *Esquire*'s editors decided against publishing it and sent Kaiser a kill fee of $1,000. Kaiser objected, arguing that his contract guaranteed him a chance to rewrite the article, assigned at $5,000, before it was killed. In the end, an arbitrator awarded the writer $2,000 plus $45 interest.

Here's what the combatants had to say to a *Washington Post* reporter about the dispute:

Kaiser: "I still don't have a serious idea about what their objections were, except a letter from their lawyer saying that it was 'entirely the wrong flavor.'"

Esquire articles editor David Hirshey: "I thought I was doing Charlie a favor—rather than go through the empty motions of having him revise a piece that the editors felt was unsalvageable. In hindsight I should have put him through a grueling rewrite process and then killed the piece."

Sound familiar? Is there an editor alive who hasn't assigned an ideal subject to the perfect writer—only to have the entire project turn sour? And is there an editor who, after reviewing a hopelessly flawed manuscript, hasn't wondered where to begin when the writer asks, "What, exactly, is wrong with my article?"

My own painful experiences with writers have made me a member of the "overkill" school of freelancer communications. The school motto is, "When in doubt, spell it out." Effective use of freelance writers depends on detailed communication of what you want at every step of the process—from the guidelines you issue to assignment letters and even to kill decisions.

You could simply instruct writers to "get the flavor" of your magazine by reading back issues and write their articles accordingly—and many editors do just that. But, in my experience, that approach leads to a low ratio of published articles to stories assigned. Few magazines can afford the time and the money it takes to go through those motions.

The overkill method of assigning consumes more time on the front end, and it doesn't guarantee that every writer will deliver. But it reduces the hours spent on extensive rewrite instructions, staff rewriting when time runs out, and acrimonious disputes over kills. By communicating in detail to writers what you want, you not only improve your odds of receiving every editor's dream—copy that can go into production after scant minutes of light editing—but you also build a solid case for killing a story if the writer fails to follow your explicit instructions.

I recommend the following step-by-step method for ensuring good communication.

1. Explain the magazine's mission.

The starting point for making successful assignments is a clear, concise statement of your magazine's mission. The mission statement gives you and your editorial staff a yardstick by which you can judge articles at every step—from query to manuscript. At the same time, the mission statement provides a reference point for writers, answering their questions about your magazine's purpose, its audience, and its attitude toward its subject.

When I took over as editor of *Country Journal* several years ago, I found that the staff was vague on two crucial points: the goals of the magazine and the target reader. Their confusion was understandable; I was the third chief editor in less than a year. But they were conveying their haziness to the freelancers, and the editorial was suffering.

To correct the problem, we sat down as a staff and drafted a mission statement that began, "*Country Journal* is a guide to the practical challenges and the intangible rewards of living in the country." Once we had that on paper, the confusion began to disappear. Everyone evaluating story proposals and manuscripts could judge whether or not they fulfilled the magazine's mission. And everyone communicating with freelancers could explain the criteria we used to make decisions about story ideas.

2. Define the 'architecture'.

The mission statement spells out "what" your magazine does for the reader, the issue architecture defines "how." Your list of regular departments is just the beginning of the structural plan. Go beyond that to organize your feature well, stating the kinds of features that should appear in every issue and those that you will publish less regularly.

At *Country Journal*, we created a blueprint for each issue's feature well that specified one "gear" story about country tools and equipment, one "growing" story on gardening, one profile of a country dweller, one issue piece, and so on. Beyond that, we also built in variety in story approaches, mandating a mix of straight narratives, profiles, how-tos, Q&As, and photo essays.

3. Writers' guidelines: Go public.

A mission statement and issue architecture scheme are invaluable tools for editorial planning and decision making. They also answer most of the key questions freelancers are likely to ask, giving them the background they need to write good copy for a magazine. Although many editors treat this information like state secrets, it makes more sense to share your magazine's goals with freelancers in writers' guidelines.

Be sure to include these points in your guidelines:
- **Audience:** Be specific about who your readers are, citing the demographic and psychographic details of age, sex, occupation, income, education and interests.
- **Subjects:** This is the place to make a statement about the content of your magazine as well as the topic categories you specified in your issue architecture. Pay special attention to the "cornerstones"—the essential article types that form the foundation of every issue.
- **Style:** Tell would-be contributors which stylebook you use, but go beyond that and tell them whether they should use an informal, conversational tone, whether they should avoid jargon, etc.
- **Length:** How many words do published articles run in your magazine? Cite a range both for your typical features and your departments.
- **Terms:** State the rights you buy and how much you pay. Many magazines quote a rate per word, when they actually set a total dollar limit for each department and feature. Why not state the base rate and word length for each article type? "$500 and up for departments/1,000 words. $750 and up for features of 1,500 words or more," for example.

4. Control the assignments.

Critical communication with freelance writers begins with the telephone call to discuss an assignment. The editor must be in control throughout the assignment process, or trouble is certain.

Never make an assignment without a research file. The assigning editor should build this file even in cases where a writer's query is the basis of the article. The file consists of news clippings and other published stories on the subject, lists of sources (both primary and secondary), and notes from discussions among the editors of how to approach the story. File-building is good discipline because it forces assigning editors to eliminate vagueness and unanswered questions.

The assigning editor should also write a paragraph summarizing the subject and angle of the article to top off the research file. This statement should be reviewed and approved by the chief editor, again ensuring that there is no vagueness lurking that will start the assignment off on the wrong course.

Use the article summary as a base to talk from during the phone call to the freelancer, and take notes on that sheet of paper. Detailed notes are important so that those casual understandings about the assignment aren't lost down the memory hole.

Once the article is assigned, the contract should go out with a cover letter restating the details of the assignment: who the writer will interview, what points must be covered in the story, what tone should be used, and so on. And give the writer the benefit of all the material you assembled to make the assignment.

Allow time for the package to reach the writer, and then make a follow-up call. Again review the assignment, the terms of the contract, the deadline and so on. This may seem compulsive, but it drives out vagueness.

Two weeks prior to the article deadline, make another phone call to the writer to check on his progress. This is the time to learn that the crucial source would not agree to an interview, or to make mid-course corrections because of what the writer has learned in the course of his research.

Finally, when the article arrives on deadline, review it promptly. Once a story is off his desk, the freelancer begins to put it behind him and move on to the next assignment. He can be more efficient at rewriting the story, or simply plugging holes, if you get back to him quickly with your reactions.

Before You Reposition...

BY RITA STOLLMAN

Not too long ago, a women's business magazine repositioned itself as a more upscale, lifestyle publication for successful women in their forties and older. Suddenly, on a July cover, there were cover lines touting original short stories. And the lead story, a profile of a "business woman," was an often snippy, tongue-in-cheek piece about a California real estate broker with "sequin-trimmed outfits and silicone-injected cheeks" who tooled around Beverly Hills selling million-dollar houses.

It was an abrupt shift for *Savvy Woman,* and it put the magazine in the middle of a crowded, highly competitive field. There it faced some formidable, established players and newer entries as well—all making claims to being upscale, arty and lifestyle-oriented.

A year and a half later, Family Media Inc. announced it was folding *Savvy.* Company executives cited the obvious, surface reasons: the tough publishing climate and a 31 percent drop in ad pages. But as a former devoted reader of the magazine, I'd add two other strategic elements that clearly fed into that ad decline. The magazine moved too far from the career and business interests of its core readership of executive and entrepreneurial women. And just as important, it went after some bigger, slicker players in an increasingly crowded niche—and in the midst of a general ad downturn.

Whatever the mix of reasons, one thing is clear: *Savvy* underestimated its competition. During the 1990s, this is a strategic mistake that no publisher or editor can afford to make. So, if you're rethinking your magazine's editorial positioning, be sure to weigh the competitive risks before you make a change.

There are three steps to conducting an in-depth analysis of your competitive environment. In a sense, the process is a bit like industrial espionage, except that the information you're after is all publicly available:

1. Identify all the direct and indirect competitors for your readers' time—and for your advertisers' dollars—since the more successful you are in your repositioning, the more likely that both your direct and indirect competitors will shift gears and go after your new market niche.

2. Evaluate the editorial strengths and weaknesses of each of your key competitors—not just now, but under different competitive scenarios. Try to predict what they're likely to do—and how successfully—once you change direction.

3. Chart this data on strategic positioning grids to locate your optimal editorial niche.

Identify your competition

Your direct competitors are usually easy to pinpoint. Any magazine that appeals to some or all of your magazine's readers and that covers the same or similar topics is a direct competitor.

But what about the magazines that appeal to some or all of your readers, but by covering very different topics? Or magazines that cover some or all of the same topics, but target a seemingly different group of readers?

Both those types are partial or indirect competitors, even though they're not currently filling the same market niche as your magazine. I say "currently" because some of them could suddenly become direct competitors should they begin broadening their coverage and/or readership bases.

For instance, say you produce a gourmet food-and-wine magazine for moderately upscale readers. Then, another publishing company decides to start up a travel magazine for fairly affluent (but still budget-conscious) travelers. The travel magazine's publisher and editor are so successful at attracting readers and ad dollars that they decide to broaden their coverage to include wine and restaurant reviews. Or, perhaps they decide to launch a spin-off publication targeted at readers who want a budget-conscious, gourmet, food-and-wine magazine. Uh, oh!

In other words, an indirect competitor can become a direct competitor rather swiftly.

Assess your competitors' strengths

An in-depth competitive analysis should include an editorial critique of one or two issues of each competitor magazine, as well as a review of each publication's media kit. In addition, you should look at any articles that have been written about your competitor and its parent company in the last two to three years.

The purpose is to determine the following: the editorial focus of the publication; its editorial mission; the topics it covers, both regularly and from time to time; and any areas of competitive overlap or potential overlap with your magazine.

In addition, you should analyze the overall editorial quality of the magazine now; the size and composition of its editorial, art and production staffs, as well as the source of all articles and artwork, so you can determine the publication's ability to upgrade or change the quality level rapidly; the magazine's overall editorial potential; and finally, the magazine's potential to compete with you and the likelihood of that happening either now or after you have successfully repositioned your publication.

Besides this, a good competitive analysis will also assess the quality of the design and artwork of each competitor magazine. It should also give you a wealth of ideas that you can adapt to your own refocusing plans. It also helps to compare the focus of a competitor's editorial content with the focus of its media kit pitch. If they're wildly different, the magazine may not be long for this world. But there's also the chance that a new publishing directive is pushing the competitor's editorial in the same direction you're thinking of going. A good competitive analysis can tell you an incredible amount about what's happening inside a magazine—long before anything appears in print.

Recalculate your market niche

Now that you know where your key competitors are headed, you can use a strategic positioning grid to determine your optimal market niche. The grid is a visual device to help you see where each of your competitors falls in targeting different sets of readers and different topics at different editorial quality levels.

To start, list the variables you're considering in repositioning your magazine. For instance, assume you're currently producing a regional magazine for small- to

> A good competitive analysis can tell you a huge amount about what's going on at a magazine— before anything appears in print.

mid-size companies that want to enter the international marketplace. You've decided that to grow your publication, you really need to transform it from a regional magazine into a national newsstand publication. But this involves going up against some pretty formidable players in business publishing.

Therefore, you need to make a decision. Are you better off going more upscale with your magazine by targeting the top executives at larger multinational firms? This would mean your editorial would have to be quite sophisticated. Or are you better off competitively if you continue to target the small- to mid-size companies that are just breaking into the international arena? Then you would have to keep the advice relatively basic, at the same time educating your readers about competing abroad.

To help reach a decision, create a strategic positioning grid that lists two sets of editorial variables: first, large multinationals vs. small- to mid-size newcomers to international trade, and second, sophisticated finance and other topics vs. relatively basic how-to tips. You can now look at each of the competitor publications on your list and place a dot to show where each one belongs on this grid.

Given the publications that currently exist in this particular market, you'll probably find that most of your real-world competitors are targeted at larger multinationals and offer highly sophisticated, technical advice to their readers. As a result, there is clearly an opening for your repositioned magazine in the niche that offers small- to mid-size companies more basic, how-to information.

You can then go through all the other variables you're considering in repositioning your magazine, such as whether your publication should focus more on exports vs. imports, or on contracting for production abroad vs. buying plants in other countries.

Once you've dealt with every possible variable that you're considering, you can determine the optimal market niche you should fill. ☐

Ad Sales Needs to Hear From Editorial

BY FRANK FINN

Was there ever a time when magazine editors could put all their energy into editing and trust their colleagues in advertising sales to read what they had produced and let everyone know how good it is? I doubt it. Nor do I believe that the world ever beat a path to the door of better-mousetrap builders.

You and your staff create a good editorial product, but that's not enough. Good products—whether they are magazines or mousetraps—need promoters to tell the world just how good they are. When it comes to advertising, it's the sales staff that does most of the promoting. But if their magazines are to succeed, editors must have enough carnival barker in them to convince their advertising sales staffs that they have a winner on their hands.

Management gurus call this process internal selling. Before salespeople can sell any product, they have to be sold themselves. Otherwise, they will lack the conviction and the information they need to overcome the objections of skeptical buyers.

So *you* have to sell the ad sales staff on the value of the editorial product and its superiority to the competing books in your market. No, they can't figure it out for themselves by reading the magazine. Good ad salespeople read every issue cover-to-cover to build an arsenal of examples of powerful, authoritative editorial. But they need to understand the editor's vision, the concept that ties everything in the magazine together into a coherent whole. Only you can provide them with the vocabulary they need to describe the wonderful things you and your staff are doing.

But how does an editor sell the value of editorial without opening the door to undue advertiser influence? The last thing most editors want is to engage in a dialogue with ad sales over the merits of their work. After all, too many ad salespeople define a good article as one that touts an advertiser's product so they can sell an ad. The answer is to restrict your contact with advertising to the person at the top, the publisher or advertising director. And make it clear from the start that your purpose is not to seek advertising's input on how to edit the magazine. You are out to help the ad sales staff sell more effectively by providing information about the logic behind the editorial product—how it serves the reader and why it is better than what the competition produces.

As for accepting feedback on the magazine or ideas for articles, I believe a strong editor should accept comments and ideas from any quarter—while making it crystal clear that only the editor decides what sees print.

The political environment at your magazine may make this approach unworkable. If so, make this a one-way communication channel. Pass along information through the publisher or ad director to help advertising sales do its job better, and decline to accept feedback or ideas.

What to communicate

You have a magazine to edit, so you don't have much time to spend writing memos to ad sales. I recommend giving advertising a monthly editorial briefing on paper or over E-mail. Stick to a schedule so the staff gets used to hearing from you at about the same time each month.

Start with background information. In your first briefing, review the underpinnings of your editorial strategy, the principles that guide your editorial decision-making. You should include the following:

1. The editorial mission statement: If your ad salespeople can't recite this by heart, they probably flounder when a prospective buyer asks, "Why do people read your magazine?" or "What's your magazine about?" So lead with the mission statement, the 25 words or less that explain your magazine's reason for being.

2. Editorial structure: This is essentially an elaboration of the editorial statement, explaining how the magazine fulfills its editorial mission, with a lineup of feature articles, regular departments, columns and so on.

3. Audience profile: Most magazines have a wealth of statistics on their readers' median age, household income, sex, education and other demographics, as well as their purchasing behavior. But it is important to go beyond the numbers and paint a portrait of the reader.

One effective way to create a vivid picture of the

reader is to write a composite biography of your mythical "typical reader." Fill in all the details, including how your magazine helps them in their work or their personal lives.

Tout the contents of the upcoming issue. Ad salespeople are always looking for another reason to contact a prospect, and the appearance of each issue fits the bill perfectly. Unfortunately, this opportunity is too often wasted because the sales staff didn't know what was going to be in the next issue until the office copies arrived from the printer.

That's why every briefing memo you write should include a rundown on the editorial highlights of the next issue. Approach this the way you do the contents page in the magazine—tease the ad sales staff to get them to read the articles. But go one step further: Briefly note how each major story advances the editorial mission of the magazine.

Finally, be sure to highlight the writers and the people profiled or interviewed in the issue, especially if they are well-known figures. Big names are coin of the realm to ad salespeople because they help them to show that your magazine features VIPs, industry leaders and deep thinkers—people whom advertisers like to be associated with.

Feature your staff. To the ad sales staff, the people on the editorial staff are probably faceless unknowns. Share with ad sales your staff's credentials and accomplishments. If one of your writers went to great lengths to get an exclusive story, tell the ad salespeople about it. When your staff wins an award, toot their horn.

Share your fan mail. There are few sales tools more powerful than testimonials, so when readers give you raves, include their letters in your briefing. Make copies of the letters themselves or compile the better excerpts into a "what our readers say about us" page.

Analyze the competition. A question that may be stumping your magazine's ad salespeople is, "How is our publication different from or better than its competitors?" You can help them by pointing out the editorial differences. Illustrate your points with specific examples whenever possible.

It's never a good idea to knock the competition, but don't be afraid to point out the ways in which your magazine is better. If you got the story first or told it better, let the sales staff know about it. Compare your readership surveys with the competition's (if they are published), and if readers spend more time with your magazine or rate your content more highly, note that, too.

Share your information and insights. You and your staff swim in a stream of information about your market, your industry and your subject. Some of the material you come across can be of great value to ad sales, especially research on trends in your market. Pass along this intelligence whenever you think it might buttress the case for advertising in your magazine. But share it with the publisher or ad director directly, rather than putting it in the briefing memo.

Answer objections about editorial. If you are on good terms with your advertising sales colleagues, ask them what objections their prospects raise that have to do with editorial. Any objection that goes unanswered can be death to a sale, so you'll be helping the cause no end by suggesting ways to respond. This is a sensitive area, however, since the ad sales staff may mistake your willingness to talk about objections as an invitation to bombard you with criticism.

Is this more trouble than it's worth—writing a monthly briefing to help ad sales do its job better? Shouldn't it be up to them or the advertising promotion manager to figure out how to explain the magazine's editorial? Maybe so, but consider this: The moment of truth in an ad sales call comes when the prospective buyer says, "Tell me about your magazine." If the ad sales staff can do nothing more than recite circulation figures and audience demographics, or if they spout ill-informed opinions about what the magazine is about editorially, they are in trouble—and so are you.

The more that ad salespeople can convey the excitement of your editorial, and the better they can demonstrate the powerful bond you establish with your readers, the more successful they will be. In the end, it's up to you, the editor, to make them believers in the value of your work. ☐

The Editor's Toolbox

BY FRANK FINN

How to edit a magazine? One school of thought holds that you edit to please yourself, choosing what to publish without regard to subscriber studies, newsstand sales or advertising interests. More pragmatic editors put the reader on a pedestal and devour every shred of information they can find on their markets. These editors systematically structure their magazines to appeal to the interests of a certain audience, setting themselves apart from the competition.

Some might call this approach editing without a soul. But I contend that as long as it is driven by a passion for the subject matter, it is the only way to go. Essentially, you are channeling your creative instincts, shaping your artistic inspiration with a craftsman's workmanship.

Three tools are essential equipment for the pragmatic editor.

1. The positioning map

Editing a magazine is like piloting a ship through treacherous waters: Unless you are guided by reliable charts, you will soon run aground. A positioning map sets out a clear course to follow.

To draw your positioning map, start with a square and divide it into four quadrants. Now you need to think about what it is that distinguishes your readers from other people with similar interests—their defining characteristics.

At *Tuff Stuff*, a title of Richmond, Virginia-based Cadmus Publishing Group that serves collectors of sports trading cards and memorabilia, we examined what separates one group of collectors from another. It soon became clear that age was a crucial factor—young collectors tend to focus on cards alone; older ones are more likely to buy both cards and memorabilia. The older collector is also more interested in the cards of players he followed in his youth, while most young collectors are interested only in today's athletes. So we had the label for the left side of the *Tuff Stuff* positioning map: "Age of collector." The top half of the map we labeled "Older" and the bottom half "Younger."

After more discussion, we concluded that "Item collected" was the appropriate label for the top of the positioning map. The left half we marked "Cards only" and the right side "Cards and memorabilia." So the four quadrants of our map were defined: upper left, older collectors of cards only; lower left, younger collectors of cards only; upper right, older collectors of cards and memorabilia; and lower right, younger collectors of cards and memorabilia.

With the map thus drawn, we marked *Tuff Stuff*'s position in the market in the upper-right quadrant because we cover both trading cards and memorabilia and attract a slightly older reader. Our primary competition—Beckett Baseball Card Monthly and its other single-sport trading card guides—falls in the lower-left quadrant, serving younger collectors of cards only.

What's the point of such a map? The editor of any magazine is often pressured to chase new readers (and advertisers) by running articles on related subjects. "If only you did stories on X," says the ad director, "I could sell ads to company Y." But with a map, you can show how changing the mix of articles can move your publication out of its niche and into direct competition with titles that make it their business to cover the field you are invading. That's called repositioning, and it should not be done casually.

2. The skill pyramid

Many magazine editors face the challenge of serving a diverse readership. Trade titles invariably span readers who work for huge corporations at one extreme, and mom-and-pop operations at the other. Special-interest magazines, especially those covering sports and hobbies, typically have audiences that include rank beginners and skilled veterans. The dilemma facing the editor: To whom do I address the editorial?

A useful tool for resolving this dilemma is the skill pyramid. When *Cross Country Skier* was owned by Rodale Press, executive editor John Viehman and his colleagues developed a pyramid to describe their readers. The great majority of people who own cross-country skis are beginners, or "back-door" skiers, as Viehman calls them. More often than not, they have bought a basic cross-country skiing outfit on sale, and pull it out of the closet only when it snows. Then they go out their back doors and ski in the neighborhood. These folks formed the bottom of Viehman's cross-country skiing pyramid. At the top were the "elite racers," the skiers who spend much of their spare time training for top cross-country skiing events.

Viehman faced the same problem that confronts every editor of a special-interest title. It was tempting to address the needs of the beginner. After all, that was the largest group with the greatest need for information. But if he aimed too low on the pyramid, he would lose the middle and certainly the top. Experienced skiers would quickly detect that the magazine was not for them.

So Viehman drew a line about two-thirds of the way up the pyramid. His target reader—the one he and his staff would bear in mind as they brainstormed story ideas and edited articles—would be the intermediate skier, someone dedicated to the sport, but who had yet to master all the skills. Beginners coming to *Cross Country Skier* wouldn't be entirely left out; jargon would always be clarified with explanatory phrases, and articles on equipment would always include basic gear for novices. But the overall tenor of the magazine would make it clear that you had to be pretty serious about the sport to read *Cross Country Skier*.

3. The planning matrix

This tool is essential for bringing organization to the content you choose to publish from one issue to the next. It's one that I found particularly useful when I was editing *Country Journal*. Formerly *Blair and Ketchum's Country Journal*, the title had been sold a few years prior to my arrival and was suffering from a loss of focus. Richard Ketchum, the founding editor, had created a magazine that addressed the broad-ranging interests of people who own country property in New England. It was definitely not about decorating your home with baskets and hanging dried herbs and wildflowers from the kitchen rafters. Instead, Ketchum ran stories about the practical concerns of maintaining

your land, such as building a fence or raising livestock. At the same time, he included pieces on the intangible joys and concerns that come with living in the country—articles on wildlife, conservation, pollution and threats to the rural way of life.

By the time I took over, *Country Journal* had become muddled to the point that one issue featured a piece on country inns, a story aimed at people who want to visit the country, not actually live there. So I worked with the staff to create a list of the subjects we would cover in each issue of the magazine. Our guiding principle was that we would concentrate on the abiding concerns and interests of people who own "a place in the country."

At the top of the list was a category we called "growing and harvesting." Every piece of reader research we had told us that *Country Journal* subscribers were serious vegetable gardeners who also improved their land by planting trees, shrubs and flowers. So every issue, we decided, would have a feature article on some aspect of growing and harvesting. The subject was so important that we also committed to continuing a popular column on the vegetable garden. Owning country property also meant that our readers were serious users of tools and equipment, so we made that a category for a feature every month.

Out of this exercise emerged our planning matrix. It can take many different forms, but at *Country Journal* we bought a white board ruled into boxes with magnetic cardholders. Down the left side we placed our categories, and across the top went the issue dates. Planning each issue, as well as evaluating freelancer queries and staff story ideas, became a matter of filling in the boxes to make sure we had our core subjects covered from issue to issue.

One risk of using these tools is that you can become their captive and plan the life out of your magazine. You still need oddball ideas that don't fit into the matrix to keep your publication lively and unpredictable. But, a plan executed with style and creativity is the surest route to a successful magazine.

> A planning matrix executed with style and creativity is the surest route to a successful magazine.

Extend Your Reach with Editorial Boards

BY ALLAN HALCROW

For the editor of a small national trade magazine (an editorial staff of four), reading the mastheads of large consumer magazines is a humbling experience. A recent issue of *Time* listed nearly 100 people with editorial titles on its masthead; *Fortune*'s editorial staff exceeded 40; and *Vogue* had approximately 30.

No four people, however intrepid, can hope to have the sort of editorial reach that a large staff has. However, they can compensate for their small number by using an editorial advisory board effectively. Such boards can be small or large, official or informal. They can meet regularly or not—but they all have one thing in common: They help the editors expand their coverage. In addition to verifying the accuracy of some stories (such as legal updates or highly technical material), they can facilitate important parts of the editorial process, such as evaluating ideas, establishing contacts and generating story topics.

Most advisory boards are made up of a representative sample of the magazine's audience. Thus, for example, human-resources executives sit on *Personnel Journal*'s board, and retail florists help out at *Flowers&*, a trade title for the retail floral industry. Because these people are working in their fields every day, they can provide the real-life context to a staff editor's hunches and brainstorms.

The feedback isn't always encouraging, however; what may seem like a great idea to an editor in search of a story or a fresh angle may not seem so great to a reader/board member. Still, the feedback can be invaluable.

"The real benefit of an advisory board is that you can start with them when you have a germ of an idea," says Jennifer Laabs, senior writer at *Personnel Journal*. "You may think you've identified a trend, for example, and they can confirm your observation or tell you that the trend isn't as pronounced as you thought it was. If you're on the right track, they can help you narrow the topic, and they can quickly identify other related issues.

Talking to advisory board members saves you both time and public embarrassment."

Sometimes story ideas spring from something already in print—and advisory boards are good sources for confirming or contradicting such issues. Editors at *Flowers&* regularly call advisory board members to solicit their feedback on articles already published. Members are asked to comment on everything from story content to covers.

Flowers& executive editor Bruce Wright says editors value the input, but notes that it isn't always easy to get useful comments: "We have to be very aggressive about getting feedback that's critical and specific," says Wright. "One woman on our board was unhappy with elements of a story we did on fall designs. She felt some of the designs showcased weren't good, but she couldn't tell me *why* they weren't good. Sometimes the input you get isn't easy to apply to day-to-day operations."

Getting in touch with board members at a time that's mutually convenient can also present challenges. "We don't call people at the beginning of May because of the Mother's Day rush," says Wright. "It's not a big deal, but it's something to think about when you're planning."

> Advisory board members are good sources of feedback on everything from story content to covers.

Establishing contacts

In many ways, editors are paid to network, and using an advisory board can make that part of the job much easier. You can call advisory board members to ask for referrals to their colleagues who might have expertise in a particular area. Doing so helps you avoid the trap of calling the same set of sources repeatedly as you research stories. Getting new contacts from advisory board members also helps expedite the process: People are usually flattered to be considered experts and are more willing to take the time to talk. When you call cold, they aren't as eager to help out.

Board members can help by working as amateur

"reporters." For example, they can work with editors to cover trade shows or conferences. This can happen in two ways. At large national conferences that you must attend, board members can introduce you to other attendees. They can also sit in on seminars if more are offered than the editors can attend. Of course, you can't depend exclusively on this sort of reporting, but it's better than missing the seminar entirely. A few calls before the conference are usually enough to find a board member who will be attending anyway and who would like to help.

There are also smaller conferences and regional meetings that smaller magazines don't always have the resources to attend. By contacting board members who live in the show's host city, you can sometimes have at least some presence at the event. In exchange for their time and a report on the meeting, you might offer to pay for parking and meals during the conference.

When board members participate in these ways, they get a better understanding of how you do your job—and that, in turn, makes them a more valuable resource.

Generating story ideas

Perhaps the most valuable contribution an editorial advisory board can make is to generate story ideas. As participants in the field a magazine addresses, they have a unique and valuable perspective on what readers really want to know.

For example, says Wright, "One of our board members suggested that readers want to see blueprints of shops. They want to see how stores are laid out and know more about the people who design them. We've started showing the blueprints when we can, and our readers have responded positively."

One of *California Lawyer*'s board members is especially good at coming up with story ideas. "We have a judge who presents ideas complete with headlines," says editor and publisher Ray Reynolds. "He has a real grasp of what makes the story."

In general, however, Reynolds says it's important to remember the editor's role. "We ask members to present what's going on, but not how to write about it," he says. "We figure out how to transform the information into a magazine article."

Story ideas may be solicited in several ways. *California Lawyer*'s board meets quarterly and members bring ideas to the table. They also write or call with suggestions. Reynolds tells of one member who forwarded a grocery receipt with an attorney's ad printed on the back; it inspired a story on advertising in the profession.

Another tactic is to ask board members to send clippings from local newspapers or general interest magazines that they found interesting or thought might be worth pursuing.

Finally, board members can be invaluable in helping you size up the competition. As much as editors don't like to admit that their competitors ever have good ideas, it's helpful to be reminded that they sometimes do. Board member reaction to articles in other magazines is one way of circumventing that natural prejudice.

Given all the benefits of using advisory boards, it's important to remember that the relationships are not one-sided: Board members benefit, too. "Recently I had to fill three seats on the board and received about a hundred applications," Reynolds says. "People *want* to help out."

Reynolds says the appeal of serving on an advisory board is almost irresistible. "It's an opportunity to help shape the magazine, and to shape the debate between members of the profession," he explains.

The real challenge

Other editors cite professional stature and credibility, the desire to give something back to the professional community, and even half-suppressed fantasies of working as journalists as reasons that people volunteer to serve. Whatever their initial reasons, the real challenge is to keep board members motivated.

"People are usually very excited about participating at the beginning," says Laabs. "We have the responsibility of keeping them involved and interested."

It helps if board members are recognized in some way for their participation. When one magazine co-sponsored the publication of an annual desk diary for the profession it covered, it sent board members copies with their names embossed on the cover. And to celebrate the launch of a redesign, board members were sent souvenir coffee mugs and T-shirts. These inexpensive items generated numerous telephone calls and a lot of good will.

Finally, editors must simply remember to ask for participation. Many board members surveyed consistently say they don't feel used enough. They want to be called and asked questions. Often the reason editors don't call them more frequently is the same reason they don't call editors: too many distractions. It's important not to confuse a busy schedule with apathy. In most cases, advisory board members are ready and willing. Says Laabs: "The more you ask, the more you will get." □

The Square Root of Roundtables

BY SCOTT BALTIC

Roundtable discussions are an effective way to explore a variety of viewpoints. That's why they're a staple of both trade and consumer magazines. But what if you're finding it tough to pull a roundtable together? People who are knowledgeable and visible enough to make good participants usually have hectic schedules, so assembling them in one spot can be difficult as well as expensive. Gathering a roundtable during a conference or trade show eliminates major travel expenses, but poses the problem of scheduling people when they're busiest.

One solution is to conduct your magazine's roundtable by mail. With a few rules of thumb to guide your planning, the process is fairly simple to implement and develop through to a finished article.

Pick the panelists. Once you've selected a general topic and the issue you want the roundtable to appear in, you must select your panelists. How many do you need? The ideal number is usually between five and eight. Fewer than five, and you might get too narrow a range of opinions. More than eight, and you're probably making additional work for yourself without improving the quality or diversity of responses.

Once you've determined the ideal size for your needs, think about adding one extra person to allow for attrition. Also, create a B-list in case one or more on the A-list declines to participate.

Beyond the known positions or viewpoints on the topic(s) to be covered, considerations for selecting your panel should include the following:

• Large versus small company or organization: Because their agendas are seldom the same, both big and small organizations should be represented on your panel.

• New versus established company or individual: Get both, since veterans and newcomers often see things differently.

• Geography: If you aren't looking out for this one, it's easy to realize belatedly that most of the participants are from, say, California or the East Coast.

• Race and gender: You presumably don't want a panel of eight to have seven or eight white males.

Develop the questionnaire. When you have your A-list

of panelists, call them to explain what you're doing and invite them to participate. As soon as any one gives you a yes, send out a letter confirming the arrangements and dates. If someone says no, go to your B-list.

In your letter, describe what the discussion will and will not include. Ask the participants for suggestions for specific questions. Also, ask for a recent head shot and a short bio. With fax machines and overnight delivery, two weeks should be ample time for this stage.

Allow yourself a day or two to put together the final questionnaire. Who should handle this important task? It can be a one-person job for the editor or managing editor, or a collaboration of two or more editors. The important point is that whoever works on the final questionnaire should know the subject matter as thoroughly as possible.

As a rule of thumb, a dozen questions should be plenty. More than 15 will be overkill in most situations.

As soon as it's ready, send out the questionnaire with a cover letter that again confirms deadlines. Tell your panelists whether you plan to give them an opportunity to review the material before it's published. If you don't want to incorporate review time in your schedule, politely explain that all material will be edited solely at the editor's discretion.

Assemble the responses. Should you fax or mail the questionnaire? A reason to mail is that you can enclose a microcassette onto which panelists can dictate their responses. A big plus to responses on tape is that people talking sound like people talking. Many people's writing sounds, unfortunately, like it has been generated by a committee, lawyer or PR person.

The major downside, of course, is the time and labor needed to transcribe a passel of tapes—although this is something support staff can help with. Keep the tapes handy for reference, however, because staffers who aren't familiar with specialized terminology can all too easily garble a transcription.

Another pitfall is that some people will talk forever. Yes, microcassettes get you better, punchier material, but can also leave you trudging through long deserts of stuff that's repetitious or off the topic.

And assume that at least one participant will ignore the tape and send in hard copy anyway—usually because he or she wanted (or had) to let the legal department or PR people review it first. If this happens, expect a big drop in quotability and a corresponding jump in buzzwords and other nonsense.

Edit the responses. Once all the responses are sitting in your word processor, get a mug of your favorite caffeinated beverage, close your office door, and prepare to spend some quality time organizing your panelists' observations. It will take you as long to edit this roundtable as it would to edit a feature of similar length, probably longer.

To organize the editing process, take a legal pad and draw in a grid of panelists versus questions. Read each response and score it for usefulness. A plus sign for above average, a zero for average and a minus sign for below average is as complicated as this needs to be. Unless one or two people are monopolizing the minus signs, you should be safe in deep-sixing all of them the first time through.

Then do whatever you need to present the material best. Combine two questions into one if that works better, or split a question if the responses seem to fit under radically different headings. But be careful not to misrepresent or distort a panelist's meaning by doing so.

Make sure the panelists don't fall in the same order all the time. Putting responses to the same question in a specific sequence based on content can give a sense of give-and-take, even though some of your panelists might never have met.

Use your judgment on how much of an oral flavor (*i.e.*, grammatical errors, slang, regional usages, etc.) to leave in. If you take it all out, you've defeated one purpose of a roundtable. On the other hand, the panelists are counting on your magazine to make them look good. Edit out anything that's potentially embarrassing, such as major verbal gaffes, and have someone else on your staff take a look if you have second thoughts. Just be consistent throughout the roundtable and from panelist to panelist.

Check any questionable facts or figures against the original tapes. If that doesn't resolve matters, a phone call to the source should take care of things.

Design a layout. You need a mug shot and short bio note for each participant, and a short introduction explaining the purpose of the roundtable, as well as its format. Be sure your readers understand that the panelists weren't all in the same room at the same time. To imply otherwise would be editorially dishonest.

Once the issue is out, send several copies to each panelist with a thank-you note. This is a simple courtesy that will put you in good standing with your panelists should you need to work with any of them again. □

Here's everything you'll need to know to economically and effectively pull together a really successful roundtable.

Perusing the Table of Contents

BY JOHN BRADY

The most important page in a magazine," a wise old circulation guru once told me, "is the cover." He then went on to explain how a newsstand browser makes a purchasing decision based on cover impact, "in a matter of seconds."

I disagree. My experiences as a magazine doctor and avid newsstand-goer tell me that today's browser is a different breed. Whether surveying a newsstand or shuffling through a stack of controlled-circulation magazines in the mail, he or she moves quickly from the cover to the table of contents—and then pauses for maybe 15 or 50 seconds. Whether he then makes a commitment to the magazine depends, mostly, on the table of contents (TOC).

Granted, the cover is the door-opener that gets the reader into the store; but it's the table of contents that motivates him or her to linger, to browse among the editorial and advertising aisles.

In short, the TOC is a marketing page. Ostensibly, its purpose is to spell out an issue's editorial particulars. Beyond that, however, it must sell the magazine, present it as something with both emotional and informational value—certainly worth the cover price, assuredly worth several hours of precious time in a crowded schedule, and possibly even worth keeping and referring to in the future, or telling like-minded souls about.

Despite its importance, most editors and art directors hate the TOC. And for good reason. After all, when you've been working on an issue for months and are about ready to ship, how can you love a page that comes through with all those tiny bits of artwork to be separated, the page numbers to be triple-checked against those 11th-hour changes, and on and on? You were planning on getting home on time for a change, and now it looks like you'll be in the office till 8:30 again, awash in TOC anxiety and nearly drowning in fatigue at the finish line. You wonder: How do other publications do it?

For its first 45 years, *The New Yorker* didn't. Not until

> The TOC must present your title as having both informational and emotional value.

1970 did the editors insert a table of contents. *Reader's Digest*, also founded in the 1920s, uses its cover, with minuscule typography, as a TOC. A colorful tip-on that highlights three features (the formula: family, sex, health/diet) is added to checkout/newsstand copies to provide impact—not to mention visibility. *Sports Illustrated*, the first magazine to use mini-photos as a preview of coming editorial attractions on the TOC, changes its look regularly. The magazine's distinctive, ground-breaking style continues today with the Big Picture look on a compelling spread. *Rolling Stone* commissions artwork that covers half the TOC—and appears nowhere else in the issue. *New York Magazine* employs a somewhat literary news-magazine tone, with lengthy summaries of key features, to give the reader a sense of what life in the city—and the magazine—is all about. *Washingtonian*, another great city book, uses a low-key textbook approach, listing hot contents matter-of-factly in chronological order. And *Spy* conveys a deliciously chatty attitude in teensy type on the TOC, contrary to prevailing design wisdom—but contrariness is *Spy*'s stock-in-trade.

How to annoy the reader

Indeed, there are probably as many ways to put the reader at ease with your publication as there are to put the reader off. Some of the biggest turn-offs for readers are TOCs that are design nightmares, with uncaptioned photos, no page numbers, and artwork that is placed haphazardly, seemingly for effect, rather than for clarity. Other magazines are given to puns and "cute" headlines that obscure the editorial message.

"A busy person who receives a new issue of a magazine turns to the TOC to get a quick summary of what is contained in the issue and to see what particular articles he or she wants to read immediately," writes one unhappy reader in a letter to the editor of a well-known computer magazine. Any editor who fails to meet that need puts his magazine unnecessarily at risk.

When cuteness strikes, make sure it lands some-where else in the magazine, because tables of contents must clarify. The browser is looking for a TOC that says: Here's what you need to know. The prospective buyer doesn't want to feel that it's his job to under-stand the magazine. That's the editor's task. Therefore, while it may seem necessary for an editor to use clever puns and oblique references to make subscribers feel they are part of an exclusive gathering of minds, it is more important for the magazine to win a steady influx of new readers—and this mission begins with the table of contents. Confuse a reader here and you have lost a sale, a potential subscriber and an emissary to like-minded readers.

Therefore, the TOC must walk an editorial fence, being neither too "inside" nor too obvious in describ-ing contents. It is probably best for the editor and art director to approach the page as a marketing job, all work and no glory. There may not be any awards at annual banquets for great TOCs, but make no mis-take—you will eventually find your reward in circula-tion heaven.

Here are five key yardsticks to use when measuring your own TOC and its impact on the audience you are endeavoring to serve.

Location: Front-of-book, right-hand side is best. Some old-style magazines insist on putting the TOC on the left, and seem to reserve all front-right pages for advertisers. This is an unfortunate marketing blunder. A left-hand TOC is consumer unfriendly. Subliminally, these magazines are saying to their readers: Our adver-tisers are more important than you are.

Length: Never less than one full page, devoid of mast-head, letter from the editor, or any other "front matter" that competes for the reader's attention. If space allows (or requires), a spread is exciting and provides visual impact. Another approach is a right-hand page jump-ing to a second TOC page. This conveys a "jam-packed," value-added feeling to the reader.

Logic: Copy should be organized either chronologi-cally or by editorial emphasis—feature stories first, then departments, columns and miscellany. The reader must be able to locate the cover story immediately (it can be boxed, labeled "cover story" or be highlighted on the page with a miniature version of the cover).

Heads should be identical to those used for features, but descriptive text for each article should be original. Don't merely regurgitate the heads and decks from the inside pages; instead, write fresh text that markets each story by emphasizing the benefits—insight, informa-tion, income—to be derived from reading on.

Linkage: The reader must be able to find all stories mentioned on the cover without having to use a decoder on the TOC. If the head for a story is "How to sell widgets in your spare time," that's the head that should appear on the TOC. The coverline should not be so cute or so remote ("The widget of ahs," "Confes-sions of a widgeteer," "Brother can you spare a time?") that the reader is unable to move quickly and logically from cover to TOC to story inside.

Look: The TOC must look designed, not pasted up. Full color is important, especially if the magazine uses it on inside editorial pages. The TOC must look signif-icant, like a great menu in a fine restaurant. The page must not look low-rent, as though it is picking up a process color by hitchhiking on an advertiser's quarter-page tail. Visually, the TOC should be enticing and informative, but not verbose and cramped. Photos and artwork should be strong hooks for the reader on this page. Use them.

When an issue ships, the table of contents may be the last page out the door, and a pesky one at that. But the wise editor makes sure it is the first page drafted the next day when a new issue begins to take form as a line-up sheet.

A good line-up sheet can be the organizing principle of a great table of contents. Along the way, it also serves as a litmus test for the punch and power of an editorial mix. Then, if all goes well, the table of contents tells us what the careful editor and art director have known all along: that the issue's whole is greater than the sum of its parts.

10 Ways to Revitalize the Editor's Page

BY JOHN CAMPBELL

As a judge of the Jesse H. Neal Awards Competition (sponsored by the American Business Press), I have been disappointed, year after year, by the quality of the editor's pages submitted. Of the entries I've seen, some lacked a clearly discernible point, or made their point only after forcing the reader to endure a long throat-clearing. Some that were written with a certain dash lacked intellectual rigor, while others that had an underlying rigor were dull. Some were much too long, and some suffered from poor typography or page design.

All of these shortcomings are easy enough to fix. But they are symptoms of a more basic problem: Many chief editors of business and trade magazines devote too little loving care to their editor's notes. And that's a shame because the editor's page can be the most important page in the book.

To put out a magazine that conveys the right substance with the right presentation, a chief editor must develop a deep understanding of his audience and its concerns. If the editor has the intellect that it usually takes to get that job, he or she can bring to bear on reader interests an informed, unbiased perspective difficult to find elsewhere.

That perspective, of course, should be implicit in the editorial plan as a whole. But nowhere can it be so explicit and so persuasive as on a well-crafted opinion page. And readers do respond to such a page. In my experience, a strong editorial page gets strong readership scores. And qualitative surveys show that some readers value such a page over any other in the book. The reason is clear: Most readers don't have the time, or perhaps the necessary information, to put their own industry in good perspective. Readers know that they need that perspective, however, and they value an honest, readable attempt to provide it.

It isn't only readers who benefit from a well-crafted editor's page: Editors benefit too. Writing is thinking. An editor who is forced to analyze problems and poten-

An editorial page must be well crafted and strongly reasoned.

tial solutions and to articulate them concisely necessarily improves his or her understanding of the readers' business and of the magazine's mission.

Not least, a good editorial page helps the chief editor build his stature among readers—and, yes, advertisers. Most publishers want their chief editors to be recognized as authorities in their magazines' fields. Personal contact and industry speeches can do a lot, but nothing beats a well-done editorial page.

To be good and to have impact, though, an editorial page must not only be well crafted, it must also be strongly reasoned. And for many magazines, there's the rub. A strong page is one that is unflinchingly honest about the business or profession the magazine covers. Inevitably, honesty means that you often have to gore someone's ox. And that "someone" may be a portion of your readers or advertisers. While most publishers profess the virtues of editorial integrity, many are loathe to extend it so far. The weaker a magazine, the more likely it is to pander to its readers and advertisers. Trying to run a strong editorial page under those circumstances is usually an exercise in futility.

If your magazine is a recognized presence in its industry, however, there's little excuse for a namby-pamby editorial page. Write knowledgeably, reasonably and with a clearly constructive purpose, and most of your audience will appreciate honesty—even when it hurts.

All this is not to say that the editorial page should always be critical. It's just as important, sometimes more important, to tell your readers what they are doing right. Furthermore, if you agree with an industry position on a controversial issue, say so. You might view this as "preaching to the converted." But if you have already established your independence, your careful presentation of the industry's position will not be seen as pandering. It can help you avoid being tagged as a carping critic. And even if your magazine is not read by the targets of an industry attack, for example, your editorial serves your readers by helping them articulate their own views.

Of course, not all editorials need take a position on an issue. The editor's page is a good place to reveal a trend. When you start to see an important pattern in recent developments, you'll want to develop a major story on it. But that takes time. Meanwhile, you can give your readers a short take on the editorial page. Stay ahead of the pack and get credit for your discernment.

So much for what an editorial page can be and ought to do. What does it take to make the page work hard for the magazine? Here are some suggestions:

• Solicit topics from the staff. That helps keep you from running out of good ideas, and it taps wells of expertise you may not have yourself.

• Devote at least a full half-day to writing a page. That's what it takes to think out a topic, do a brisk draft, and then rethink and polish. If needed, take a full day. The page is worth the time.

• Make your point in the first few sentences. Busy readers won't bother with leisurely copy and don't need to know everything that went on in your head.

• Keep the length to a page, except in cosmic cases. You are not writing a legal brief and needn't produce evidence for all your assertions. Much of the value of an editorial lies in its brevity.

• Tell readers what they ought to hear, not what they want to hear. Being the industry cheerleader may get you bouquets, but will seldom get you respect.

• Write strongly. Decide what you believe and say it simply and directly— without quibbling.

• Write thoughtfully. This doesn't mean waffling. It means using rigorous logic and supporting your major assertions just enough to show that there's ample knowledge behind them.

• Write crisply. Use short paragraphs, short sentences and simple words. This promotes readability and helps produce a tone of authority.

• Put the page through your copy desk or have it reviewed by your top staffer. Even if you are the staff's best writer, you need an in-house critic.

• Insist on a page designed for readability. If your art director wants a single-column page, make sure the column is not too wide and that the type is a readable font and not too small. Consider the possibility of presenting two (or more) shorter pieces instead of one longer one. Other things being equal, the shorter the piece, the more likely it is to be read—and, often, the more authoritative it will sound.

Much of what I have said here flies in the face of very different opinion formats that some magazines use. The format I have described need not be devoid of humor or similar humanizing elements. But it does imply a strong intellectual underpinning. Perhaps you use instead a highly personalized, informal approach. If so, consider the possibility that your page is just easier to produce or more satisfying to your ego than it is useful to your readers.

Then again, if your page works with your audience, who's to argue? □

How Do You Make a Story Great?

BY LEONARD WITT

You, as an editor, can make stories great—or at least you can help writers make them great. But to do so, you must be proactive from the moment a story idea is conceived. To wait until stories arrive on your desk means you will most often be talking damage control—not greatness. There's nothing mystical about fostering greatness. It's a logical process that starts at the beginning and works its way through to a finished product. The essential steps are as follows:

Find a great idea. Mediocre ideas do not make great stories. So your first job is to keep abreast of everything that interests your audience. Read, talk to experts, make connections, check the mailbag, go through the slush pile. When a strong idea comes along, you will know it from the excitement it generates in you and among your staff.

Test the idea. Few of us have the money, resources or time to assign stories that might go nowhere. So when an idea strikes, you must test it. Do research and get as much background information as possible. With computer resources like the Internet, you have the whole world of research at your fingertips. Even with a medium-size budget, you can get online with services like Viewtext or Datatimes, which will plug you into dozens of newspapers and magazines.

Today, many public libraries have local newspapers on CD-ROM. With CD-ROMs, you will be able to do a fairly complete search in less than an hour. And then you can download your finds onto a disk—all for free. And don't forget public relations agencies and agents. They are often happy to supply recent background articles relating to their clients.

If you are too busy to do this preliminary work, hire a local researcher to do it for you (usually at a cost of $10 to $15 an hour). The research will help you define the story. Plus, it will give you a mental picture of how it might unfold in the writing.

Define the story. Mentally, place your story idea on a continuum. That continuum starts with a straightforward news story on one end, moves to a features treatment in the middle, and at the far end becomes full-blown literary journalism complete with scene setting,

character development and the other fiction techniques often applied to the best nonfiction writing.

Where does your story fit? Is it going to be primarily a reported story, where facts alone will make it great? Or will it rely on stylistic writing? At my magazine, *Minnesota Monthly*, a great story for us is one that combines both reporting and style in literary nonfiction. Because we are a general-interest magazine, that makes sense for us. You have to decide what works for you.

Decide on the focus. Now that you have done your research and have a sense of the story's possibilities, give the story a focus. You should be able to define it in one sentence. I find that developing a working title for the story helps a lot. For example, a year after a boy was abducted in Minnesota, we decided to do a first-anniversary article on the abduction. The story could have gone in any of a hundred directions. But I knew, after doing the research, that the real story was about the boy's mother. The working title, "Patty Wetterling's Year without Jacob," told me and the writer exactly what the story was about.

Although stories may change in the reporting and writing, you will reduce the risk of failure by having a sense of where the story is going well before the actual writing begins.

Decide on a length. Next, determine a length. Part of this decision is mechanical—it depends on your page count and imposition. The other part is organic, a gut feeling based on experience. Take the organic measure tempered by the practical restraints, throw in the writing style—and you come up with an approximate length. It is a good starting point—and the writer will need a starting point.

Choose the best writer. By now, you will have a fairly clear image of what this story will look like and how you want it to read. The problem is, *you* are not going to write it. Someone else is. So how do you know you have the right person to do it? Study each prospect's clips. In my experience, what a writer has done in the past is an almost 100 percent predictor of what he or she is going to do in the future. If the clips indicate that a person is a reporter without much style, don't expect a story that is on the feature or literary journalism end of the continuum. If a writer is a beautiful stylist but hasn't shown an inclination to do much reporting, don't assign a story that requires reporting. To ask a writer to do a story without ever seeing his or her clips is asking for trouble.

Be specific in your assignment. Because you have done the research, you probably know more about the story's subject matter than the writer does. Take the time to write an in-depth description of how you see the story developing and what its elements might be. Tell the writer this is just a working outline and will, of course, be modified during his or her reporting and writing.

Decide on payment. Pay the writer an adequate fee. "Adequate" will mean something different to every magazine. You have to know what is fair in your field, geographic area, and so on. You should also pay for telephone and other research expenses—and let the writer know this up front. You don't want the writer to go light on research for fear of running up heavy phone bills.

Explain the rewriting rules. Because I have studied the clips, I know what the writer's potential is—that he or she can write the piece with all the life and information I want it to have, better than I could ever do it. Therefore, when it comes to rewriting, I ask the writers to do it, and I tell them up front that this is likely to happen. Yes, many freelancers, if given the chance, will take the money and run, even if the story does not meet their own expectations. But the best writers appreciate an editor who demands the best work from them, and who understands that great writing does not come easily.

Keep in touch. Once a story is assigned, the temptation is to forget about it and get on with more immediate problems. Don't succumb. Keep in touch with the writer. Talk about interviews. Ask about interesting facts. Pass on new information you may have come across. I have found that with long pieces, writers often begin to lose confidence. But if you have kept abreast of the story, you can remind the writer of the good parts, of the interesting anecdotes he or she told you, or about the information unearthed in the research. You can remind the writer of the shared vision you had when the story was assigned, and refire his or her enthusiasm.

Give yourself ample time to edit. The story arrives on your desk. If it is a short piece, chances are that it will be in very good shape. If it is a longer piece, it might have some structural problems. Read through it very carefully, making notes as you go along. A common problem is that writers want to tell rather than show. Or there may be an anecdote that you loved in your initial conversations with the writer that is missing, or an angle that needs sharpening. Look for the positive and try to build on what is working in the story.

Good editing takes time, and I refuse to talk to the writer about a story draft until I have thought about it extensively. I want to be prepared to defend my critique and, more important, I want to have constructive criticism ready to help the writer do a rewrite if it is needed.

Some writers are eager for criticism; others, judging from their facial expressions and body language, seethe. Putting your critique in writing not only helps clarify your thoughts, but also gives the frustrated writer an opportunity to cool off and reflect on your comments.

Be prepared to make fixes. Like most editors, I can't afford to kill stories. Usually, I don't even have to consider it because most of the problems have been resolved in the process. But in rare cases, the second draft isn't up to snuff. Then I take it from the writer and do what I can to improve it.

This holistic approach to editing is time-consuming. But when the kudos start coming from readers, the writers will be eager to do more stories because they know they are working with an editor who knows how to help them make a story great. □

Don't Forget to Write Tight

BY JOHN BRADY

The most influential magazine of the past 20 years, in my opinion, has been *People Weekly*. In addition to the endless fascination that people have for people, the magazine has another strong editorial feature: Everything in it is brief and browsable.

An average article is maybe 1,000 words, and that is usually quite enough. The pictures help, of course—easily worth another 1,000 words apiece—but it's the tight editing that makes the magazine really sizzle.

A friend who used to work at *People* once told me about a file the magazine had developed for a cover-length story on singer/actress Cher. "It ran on and on for thousands and thousands of words," he said. Then the pictures came in and a story was drafted, condensing the thousands of words down to an engaging 1,900. In a cover meeting, however, Cher was bumped when a celebrity died (Cary Grant, as I recall), and so the story was rewritten down to 1,000 words for the next issue.

Well, another story bumped it the following week, and this went on for several issues as other events overtook and overshadowed the Cher report. Finally, some space opened, and there it was in the front of the book, in the gossip section: one forlorn photo of Cher with a caption describing her outfit in maybe 35 words—or less.

"That was known as the $35,000 caption," said my friend, reflecting on the high cost of doing that particular piece of journalistic business.

But that was also good, tough editing at any price.

The editor's task today is to tighten, tighten, tighten. Readers don't have the time to curl up with the long read of yesteryear, and editors who defy this mindset do so at considerable professional risk. While it remains true that magazine columns are still written (not edited), it is even truer today that feature stories should be edited, not written. The prevailing attitude among many young readers is that magazines are long and life is short.

How, then, is an editor to turn those long, meandering manuscripts into quick, dynamic, straight-to-the-point pieces for his/her magazine?

In my travels as a magazine doctor, I frequently work with magazines in transition. My partner, Greg Paul, and I are often asked to develop a redesign that will make a magazine "more browsable," or "more open," and this often means creating a format that allows for more pictures and fewer words. (Thus the *People* influence, *cf.* above.)

Here are some guidelines that I have found helpful in working with editors whose intention is to achieve a "less is more" publication:

Plan ahead. Plan your lineups far enough in advance so that you know the exact lengths of the manuscripts and the quality of the photographs with plenty of time to trim, to revise, to repackage. You need to know what is likely to happen in the next six issues: The upcoming three issues should be planned and lineups should be available for review and discussion at staff meetings; the next three issues should be blocked out as tentative lineups, subject to the usual changes and revisions as manuscripts and materials are submitted.

Assign word lengths. Specific word-length maximums should be given to writers for all columns and features. When a manuscript comes in over the max, it should be returned to the author with instructions to tighten. If time (or temperament) do not permit such a return, give the manuscript to an in-house editor who can cut to fit.

Avoid lengthy and/or multi-part features. These are often slow, flabby and seemingly endless. They are out of sync with the new, dynamic editorial tempo we are trying to achieve. A feature should not run longer than four pages—five pages with photos and sidebars; longer only if it includes a signed confession by O.J. Simpson.

Think short. Tighten long pieces down to short

> The prevailing attitude among many young readers is that magazines are long and life is short.

ones—a difficult but necessary task that is best viewed as compressing coal in order to create artificial diamonds. You should have several one- , two- and three-page features for each issue. It is better to have a diverse mix of seven or 10 short articles than it is to have a limited mix of three lengthy pieces in an issue.

Keep evergreens handy. Because the ad count generally determines editorial space for each issue, there are likely to be some fluctuations at the last minute. Try to avoid "stretching" articles to fit additional space when it becomes available. Instead, keep evergreens on hand—timeless features that can be dropped in to fill one, two, three or four pages when opportunity knocks.

Use photo captions to inform. When writing captions for photos, make certain that the copy does not duplicate information already presented in the text. In addition to avoiding editorial overlap, you will save space and enhance the information value of each photo.

Show or tell. You can compact material by using an illustration, chart or graph—but don't show or tell anything twice. Instead of providing a narrative summary of the chart or graph, say, "Figure 3 illustrates how verbiage has soared," and move on. Charts and graphs save space only when allowed to do their share of the telling.

Kill your darlings. Take a look at the weakest photo in the layout. Toss it.

Use a dual-editing system. It's not unusual for editors to get too close to a manuscript. When this happens, they lose their perspective and are unable to edit a piece tightly. The solution is to have another editor go through the manuscript with strict instructions to tighten it to assigned word length. As H.G. Wells put it, "No passion in the world is equal to the passion to alter someone else's draft."

Bullets make a hit. Instead of long, rambling, serial paragraphs, use bulleted lists to make a series of points succinctly. Lists are easy for the reader to scan, and allow him or her to absorb a lot of information in just a little time.

Use the imperative. There's no subject, fewer words and more punch—especially for how-to articles. Just do it.

Delete the passive tense. The easiest way to avoid flabby paragraphs is to use the active, not the passive tense. It's also a good way to avoid putting your reader to sleep.

Leave your reader wanting more. Remember that good editing often requires that you not overstuff your reader. Leave the reader fulfilled, certainly, but also a wee bit hungry for more. That's the feeling that keeps the reader coming back for the next issue.

Deliver on your promise. Finally, if an article still runs long, you may have to cut on a grander scale by narrowing the focus of the piece. 'Tis better to promise less, but deliver all that you promise, than to go with the long-winded alternative. The latter choice may blow your reader away for good. ◻

Defending the Editorial Budget

BY FRANK FINN

The magazine budgeting process, never a courtly dance, has degenerated into a slugfest at many publishing companies. Hit by the double whammy of slumping ad revenues and the stiff postal rate hike, publishers are hunting for budget cuts. And all too often, the first office they visit is the editor's. Why? Simple. Publishers dread cutting expense dollars that may be tied to revenues. Cutting one dollar in advertising or circulation, only to lose one dollar in revenue, means that they haven't gained any ground on the bottom line.

Since editorial doesn't have a revenue line with its name on it, publishers persuade themselves that cuts in that budget won't endanger income, at least not in the short run. "The readers aren't going to notice," the publisher assures you (and himself or herself).

That leaves an editor between a rock and a hard place. On the one hand, you will be branded as out of touch with business realities if you climb on your high horse and insist that there isn't a penny of waste in your budget and that you actually need *more* money, not less. On the other, you won't do anyone a favor if you allow your editorial effort to be crippled for lack of funds. Readers and advertisers will sense the weakening of your magazine and, sooner or later, that will trigger declines in circulation and advertising revenue.

An editor's best response in difficult times is to go on the offensive and campaign for maintaining investment in editorial quality. Here are several strategies to use:

1. Stake out your position.
Start by determining the minimum amount of money you must have to do your job. This may seem like retreating before the battle begins, but you will forfeit your credibility if you don't make a serious effort to trim the fat from your budget. If you've already been through a round of cuts, don't assume that you won't be asked to come up with more savings. Be prepared with detailed justifications for every item.

Avoid being trapped by your assumptions—use zero-based budgeting. With this method, you start from scratch, throwing out last year's numbers and building up your expenses from nothing. Ask yourself how you would structure your staff if you were starting all over. Are you using a group of freelance contributors and paying them all your top rate? Could you recruit new ones for minor features, for example, and pay less?

Look beyond the core budget categories—salaries, manuscripts, art and photography—to find savings in areas like travel, telephone, subscriptions and air freight. The numbers are smaller, but add up quickly.

Once you've calculated the absolute minimum amount you need to produce a quality editorial product, you'll be on firmer ground when the publisher pushes you for cuts and you push back.

2. Dramatize competitive inferiority.
If you tell your business-side colleagues that cutting your budget will mean that you won't be able to afford the writers and photographers you want to use, you'll probably get blank stares. But you'll get their attention if you can demonstrate that reducing editorial quality could cost them ad sales or sub renewals.

You can best dramatize the damage cheapened editorial would cause by showing how your magazine will suffer in comparison with the competition. Are there departments that are popular with readers and distinguish you from your competitors that would have to be sacrificed? You may have well-known contributors who write exclusively for your magazine whom you would have to use less or drop entirely, further damaging your credibility with subscribers and advertisers.

Often the editorial that earns your magazine the greatest respect from readers and advertisers is the most expensive to produce. For example, features based on costly research—your version of the *Fortune 500*,

> If you have isolated yourself from your colleagues on the business side, you are in a poor position to ask for help.

perhaps—may have established your publication as the authority in your field. Magazines that weaken their market position by abandoning distinct editorial features may never regain their competitive advantage.

3. Promote the value of quality editorial.

You should *always* tout the quality of the editorial product. But even in the midst of a budget battle, you can score points by citing evidence of reader appreciation of your work.

Letters to the editor praising particular articles will buttress your argument for maintaining your budget. Look for more ammunition in readership surveys, particularly those that show which departments and features are read by the most people.

4. Tap business-side allies for support.

If you have isolated yourself from your colleagues on the business side, you are in a poor position to ask them for help in maintaining investment in quality editorial. But even if you aren't on the friendliest terms with them, campaign for their support.

Your most natural ally is the circulation director. His or her success in attracting and keeping readers on the subscription rolls depends on how well you do your job. So the circulation director will be concerned if budget cuts threaten to disrupt the quality and continuity of the editorial product. That concern may not motivate him or her to give up dollars in the circulation budget to protect yours, but you'll never know unless you ask.

Point out the specific changes that you would have to make in editorial to satisfy the budgeteers—changes that readers would notice. When sales are stable and the circulation model appears to be working, circ directors of paid circulation magazines dislike any change in the product that would affect their key statistics—subscription renewals, direct mail response and pay-up, and newsstand sales.

Editors and advertising directors often battle each other over such things as editorial mentions of advertisers and their products. But that doesn't mean the ad director won't support you in your fight to keep the editorial product strong. Set aside your differences and make your case, pointing out that a magazine that attracts strong readership is easier to sell to advertisers.

Making your appeal to both the circulation director and the advertising director will expose you to their criticisms of editorial. You need not adopt all their suggestions as gospel to win their support. Just hearing them out and taking their comments seriously will make them more willing to support you.

5. Find production efficiencies.

Your next best ally is the production director. You can take pressure off the editorial budget by working with him or her to minimize production costs. True, these expenses may not be in your budget, but many of them are driven by editorial and design decisions. And the publisher probably won't care if he gets more savings from production and less from editorial as long as he achieves his budget-cutting target.

The first place to look for production savings is in prepress charges. Schedule a session with your art director and the production director to review the prepress bill for your most recent issue. You may well find that elements of the design you can live without are driving up costs. For example, photography or type knocked out of full-bleed color screens that consist of several process colors make for complicated stripping at the prep house. Make sure your art director is aware of the cost of these design effects. If necessary, arrange for the prep house to brief the art director on less costly alternatives. If your art director balks, point out that the dollars saved in prepress will protect the budget for illustration and photography assignments.

The second place to find savings is in the typesetting bill, assuming you have your type set out of house. If you are paying a significant amount of money for author's alterations, institute a crash program to complete all editing and fact-check changes prior to the first type run. Bring discipline here, and you can wring wasted dollars out of the production budget and offer those savings to protect editorial.

The third place to look for production savings is color separations. Ask your production director to bring in the separator to review cost-cutting alternatives such as ganging separations. You'll find that the quality sacrifices are negligible.

Waging this campaign can consume untold hours. But is there a better use of your time than protecting the quality of your magazine? □

Budgeting: Facing Up to the Inevitable Battle

BY CAROL ADDESSI

Budgeting or forecasting: Say either word, and most editors break out into a cold sweat. As a financial manager, I have actually seen editors cry, heard them scream or watched their eyes glaze as they approached catatonia. It doesn't have to be this way. For all you budget-phobic editors, here are eight helpful hints to get you started on the process of pain-free budgeting. Although the examples assume you work for a monthly, the concepts can be applied no matter what your frequency.

1. It may seem obvious, but the first thing you should do is find out whether your company operates on a calendar or fiscal year. Whereas the calendar year is simply the predictable January through December, a fiscal year can be any 12 months, beginning with any month. Check with your finance manager to see which month is the beginning of your fiscal year, if indeed your company operates on a fiscal, rather than calendar, year.

Why? You may think that the fiscal year end means nothing more than wearing protective gear when boarding the elevator with your company controller, but there are other important things about this day as well. It advises you when to begin your budget. It also lets you know which issues are included in the next year's budget. If you run special issues, or are planning a big anniversary issue, or perhaps a big spring fashion issue with lots of four-color, you need to know where they fall in the fiscal year so that you can adapt the budget to accommodate them.

2. What about special articles you may be planning? It could be a show issue, with lots of articles covering the goings-on, or a special survey requiring up-front costs such as postage, or a travel article—again with lots of four-color and on-the-scene reporting. Whatever the types of special articles, the issues in which they will be running and the articles themselves need to be broken out. I suggest a two-step process. First, determine the number of articles per month, as well as the associated elements (photos, illustrations, etc.). Then, estimate a cost for each article and element, and total this for each month.

Another approach would be to determine your total monthly editorial page count and multiply it by the average cost per page from prior years' budgets (this information should come from your financial manager). However, this can be risky, which leads us directly to the next point.

3. You can't assume that next year will be the same as last year. Everything is going to cost a little—or a lot—more. And management's goals may have altered, as well. Make sure you are aware of any changes the company plans to make, and think about the changes *you* want to make. (If you think about changes you want to make only after your budget is accepted, your friends in the finance department will decrease.) And don't forget the little things. Has the price of a roll of film increased? What about kill fees? These items may seem minor, but many a budget has been broken by the small and unexpected.

4. Who budgets the fixed costs? A fixed cost is an amount that appears monthly, such as equipment service contract fees or payroll benefits. Don't try to balance your budget on these items, or they will come back to haunt you. In some companies, the fixed costs are budgeted by finance, so, again, find out from your friendly finance manager if you should cover these items or not. If you are told you must budget for them, lobby hard to have them moved onto the administration budget.

5. What about new equipment? Even if this is not a cost that will appear in the budget you are working on, you need to let the people in the finance department know what you need and what you are planning so *they* can include it in *their* budget.

To handle this type of expense, most companies will take proposals from department heads and factor them to a well-timed and researched purchase. The key is to make your proposals as early as possible so that your purchases are considered first. You may well be asked to prepare a cost-savings analysis to justify the purchase.

Include specific information about equipment type and usage in your proposal, and tie it into supplies that may have to be ordered for the equipment.

Finally, don't overlook service contracts for new equipment you may be considering. These can be tricky and as costly as the equipment itself.

6. Don't forget the people reporting to you. Certainly, their raises need to be included in your budget, but be mindful of the calendar. Raises can be allocated one of two ways, either at the employee's date-of-hire anniversary month, or on an annual date picked by finance. Be aware of when raises kick in and how that will affect monthly or quarterly reports. If finance gives you a predetermined percentage for your department, which you can later break out by person, be scrupulous about the amount you give each person, because finance doesn't have a supply of money to bail you out once you run out.

If someone leaves during the year, and you replace him or her with someone at a lower salary, inform finance that you want the difference to be held aside. Some organizations allow any extra money to be given as a bonus, which rewards a good employee and doesn't necessitate budgeting as part of future salary. The key lies in working with finance to reallocate any new-found funds. If you have performed well in the previous steps, finance will probably be more willing to indulge your department by being flexible about extra money—providing you don't keep it all for yourself!

7. And now, the Bermuda Triangle of budget categories: Supplies. If you're lucky, administration will handle this category for you; if not, you're stuck with it. The operating principle here is that supplies run short (vanish, if you will) in direct proportion to the increase in the supply budget. Although there is no way (short of rationing) to control this, you can work closely with administration to review past years' records and budget accordingly. Take note of items that vanish with predictable regularity, such as floppy disks, Post-it Notes, legal pads, pens and pencils, and requisition those in the future.

If administration is handling this category, keep them apprised of any future projects that might use more than the usual amount of supplies.

8. Finally, three budgeting myths not to live by.
• **If I overbudget, I'll look good.** This, from a finance standpoint, is like the boy who cried wolf. If you overbudget, you are only deceiving yourself as to your real operating costs, and the following year, you'll be asked to cut even more—regardless of whether your numbers now tell the truth or not.
• **If I save money each month, finance will keep it for me until the end of the year, when the company controller will gift-box it and put it under my pillow.** The fact is, if you save one month because you don't have all your fees in, tell your finance manager so he can accrue the related expenses. Remember, if you budget for a large expense that has been moved to a future date, keep your finance manager apprised so he can adjust the budget accordingly.
• **If I'm grossly underspending, I can use all that money for anything I want.** Yes, like printing up your resume. Need I say more?

Better Editorial for Less Money

BY FRANK FINN

Call it "The big squeeze." Magazine editors today find themselves caught between two inexorable forces. On one hand, they've had little or no relief from the budget crunch that came when the bottom fell out of ad revenues a few years ago. On the other, they are under pressure to deliver competitive editorial content that will keep renewals high, maintain good reader response, and convince advertisers they are buying a winner.

Just to make the challenge more interesting, editors have fewer editorial pages available to pull off this trick worthy of Houdini. Pick your metaphor: It's like trying to squeeze blood out of a turnip. Or pull a rabbit out of your hat. Or spin gold from straw.

The best strategy for meeting this challenge is to commit your editorial resources to content that will have the highest possible reader impact. Winnow out weak features and departments that don't "move the meter"— that is, do their part to make your magazine must-reading. Banish articles that find their way onto the editorial calendar only because "we do that every year."

To separate the strong from the weak, you should rely in part on editorial research that indicates which departments and features are most popular with your readers. Most magazines conduct surveys that ask readers whether they read a particular article, and if so, how interesting or valuable it was to them. If you have no such research, proceed with caution. A department that you are bored with and ready to deep-six just might be a reader favorite.

Don't let readership scores alone dictate what stays and what goes. Use the "authority" rule: If a feature or department doesn't reinforce your magazine's position as the authority in its field, drop it. Another valuable tool for separating the wheat from the chaff is the "need-to-know" versus "nice-to-know" standard. The logic here is that, with so many media options available, readers expect the time they devote to a magazine to yield information with genuine value. That could translate into current gossip or how-to

> You can emerge from tough times as the definitive and dominant title in your market.

material, financial data or recipes, depending on the audience.

What about editorial that is popular with the ad sales staff—for example, new-product departments? If you are convinced they do little to build readership, wasting pages you could be devoting to higher-impact material, you should at least cut them back. The fact is, however, that "what's new" product departments often top the list of best-read editorial in readership studies, particularly in trade magazines.

When you are done chopping the deadwood out of your editorial schedule, shift the dollars, pages and staff time you free up to high-impact, authority-building editorial. What kinds of articles pass the "authority" test? Editorial that conveys the message that your magazine is *the* source of essential information in your field or industry. Here are samples of powerful editorial concepts that can be executed without spending a fortune:

Take the pulse with an industry index. Magazines that serve a business audience should always answer the question that is foremost in their readers' minds: "How's business?" The best way to answer that question is to publish an industry index, a figure that expresses the state of your industry or field. An index can be as simple as a sales total, or be a more complicated compilation of different statistics. But whatever your methodology, establishing such an indicator is a sure way to assert your magazine's authority in its field.

Satellite Business News, a Washington-based trade title serving the satellite TV industry, publishes a chart on the front page of every issue showing current sales of satellite dishes. Editor Bob Scherman gathers figures from his network of equipment manufacturers and retailers, programmers and other sources to arrive at *SBN*'s estimate. Most companies are willing to share information so that a reliable barometer of industry sales is available to help them plan their business strategy.

Creating a meaningful industry index can be time-consuming. Often, obtaining the necessary statistics requires hours of research. Some magazines tap the academic community, commissioning an economist or demographer to compile the figures for a fee and a published credit. But the value of an industry index cannot be underestimated. It gives readers a specific reason to pick up every issue. And if your index wins recognition as a reliable statistic, it enhances your magazine's reputation as an authoritative source.

Publish list stories. They may be humorous (*Esquire*'s annual Dubious Achievement Awards), statistical (the *Fortune 500*), or contrived (every city magazine's "Best and Worst" issue), but list stories command reader attention. When James Seymore took over as managing editor of Time Warner's then-struggling *Entertainment Weekly*, he unleashed a barrage of list stories such as "The 100 funniest movies of all time." Seymore's strategy gave the magazine direction and boosted its fortunes.

Some statistical lists, like *Inc.*'s report of the 500 fastest-growing small businesses, can be budget-busters, requiring expensive original research and analysis. But it may be possible to adapt data already prepared by government agencies or industry groups to generate your own statistical list story.

But many list stories are much less expensive undertakings. Take the "Games 100," the list of the best games of the year published by the reborn magazine for lovers of every sort of brain-teaser. How does *Games* select the winners? The editors and their friends gather in the magazine's New York offices to "test play" the entries and vote for their favorites. While they're at it, the editors of *Games* choose the "Game of the Year" and name one or two classics to the "*Game*'s Hall of Fame."

Subjective and arbitrary? Perhaps, but the fact is that the *Games* editorial staff, indeed, the editors of any magazine, are as well qualified as anyone to make such judgments. The point of such lists, competitions and awards is to express the magazine's collective opinion and assert its authority. If some readers disagree with your choices and write a letter to the editor, so much the better.

Conduct definitive surveys. The readers of any magazine usually want to know what their peers or people who share their interests are doing, thinking and saying. That's why articles based on reader surveys—statistically reliable mail and telephone polls or unscientific bind-in surveys and fax polls—typically score well on readership studies. They also send the message that your magazine has its finger on the pulse of your audience.

Conducting a scientific survey of your readers can cost upwards of $10,000. But it can also generate enough powerful editorial material to fill an entire issue. *RN* conducted such a study several years ago, sending a four-page questionnaire on the ethics of nursing to a random sample of its subscribers. The editors devoted nearly all the pages of one issue to reporting the results. The special issue earned *RN* a nomination for a National Magazine Award. But more important, the survey firmly conveyed the magazine's commitment to discovering what was on its readers' minds.

Feature the big names. Whatever market you serve, people the pages of your magazine with the men and women who matter in your field. Interview them for reactions to news events, profile them, put them on roundtables and invite them to write guest editorials.

For a consumer magazine, celebrity profiles can be the most difficult and expensive articles to execute. But on the trade side, it's often possible and desirable for staffers to write profiles of leading industry figures. The magazine's editors can expand their source network by handling interview pieces. Travel costs can be minimized by conducting interviews at trade shows or other industry events.

Another device for involving high-profile people in your editorial effort is the advisory board. If industry bigwigs are commenting on the editorial direction of your magazine as well as reviewing the accuracy of technical content, you gain access to them for interviews and reaction quotes as well.

Tackle the burning issues. One measure of a magazine's authority is its coverage of controversies that matter to its readers. The format of the coverage is unimportant. What counts is the fact that the magazine is on top of the issues that concern its readers.

You can also build the authority of your magazine with the editor's column. Too often, this page is squandered on a bland recap of the table of contents. Make the most of the opportunity to write editorials that challenge conventional wisdom, sound the alarm, or otherwise stake out a strong position. In the process, the editor can give a magazine more personality by becoming its face and its voice.

Definitive, daring and dominant

Your natural tendency when beset by budget cuts and dwindling pages may be to pull in your horns and play it safe. But by allocating your editorial resources properly and taking an aggressive approach to covering your magazine's beat, you can emerge from tough times as the definitive, daring and dominant title. ☐

Double Your (Editorial) Money

BY TONY LEE

Finding and affording quality editorial has never been easy for magazine editors, but it's especially tough these days at small publications with limited budgets. Even small-circulation magazines published by major companies face tight budgetary restrictions in today's less than optimal economy.

For example, it's not unusual for a top freelance writer to call me with a great article idea, only to beg off nicely after I explain my publication's payment scale. And when I do assign a relatively expensive article, the next few freelancers who call hear the obligatory company line about keeping costs down in a poor economy (at least until I'm back on budget).

Yet the publications I oversee feature articles by some of the most respected authorities in the fields we cover, as well as articles by noted freelance writers who often appear in major consumer magazines. The trick is to devise unusual and methods to attract and pay for high-quality articles. What follows are 11 such tactics that can be duplicated by magazines of all sizes, but which can be most valuable to those forced to cope with tight editorial budgets.

Search your local bookstore every few weeks for new titles in your subject areas, and request review copies from the publishers for closer examination. Then ask the authors to adapt relevant chapters or sections for you. Most authors of new books are eager for publicity, and some will even agree to write original articles at no charge in exchange for a credit line that touts the book. At the very least, they'll contact their publishers on your behalf to request excerpting permission, minus any fees for subsidiary rights.

This reciprocal approach worked well for my magazines recently, as it garnered two articles (one original, the other excerpted) by best-selling author Harvey Mackay, in addition to a two-part series from the newly revised book, *What Color is Your Parachute?* by Richard Bowles—all at no cost.

As a side note, if your publication reaches a unique niche or is critical to the field you cover, book publishers should be approaching you to offer free excerpts. The publicity you'll provide is worth more than any rights fee you would pay, and more publishers are starting to realize this. Hopefully, subsidiary rights payments will soon become an anachronism.

Attend relevant trade shows and conferences, and ask speakers to adapt their presentations. Since 80 percent of the work is already done, most speakers will agree to turn their talks into articles for no more than a credit line. The result may need more than the usual amount of editing, but you'll be tapping into a group of talented people who probably don't write often (they tend to make much more money speaking).

Reprint articles from publications that are targeted to readers only marginally related to your audience. An author might adapt a piece for you for free (again, most of the work is already complete), or you might excerpt it from the other magazine at no cost, or in exchange for an article that you've previously published and own. We often reprint surveys from trade magazines such as *Research & Development*, or adapt articles on employment trends from general-interest business publications and women's magazines. In turn, these magazines often use material from us.

Increase non-monetary rewards to freelance writers. Offer free reprints, longer credit lines or a trade-off for advertising in a later issue. Also, invite your better writers to visit your magazine's offices at your expense, then use the occasion to explain your financial limitations and ask for their flexibility. Perhaps they have ideas about other ways they might be compensated that won't affect your bottom line.

Adapt one article for multiple uses. This works best if you are responsible for more than one publication, or for special issues produced for different audiences. My primary publication is targeted to middle- and senior-level business executives, but we also publish magazines directed to college and military readers. Well-written staff and freelance articles on trends, advice and profiles can often be adapted by the author or by your editorial staff for multiple audiences at a minimal expense. Make sure that you include a passage in your contracts with writers that allows you to use their articles again for reprint purposes—which includes reprinting in your other publications.

If you edit only one publication with one audience, create an informal alliance with another magazine that covers similar topics—but for a different readership. Agree to reprint each other's relevant articles on certain agreed-upon topics at no charge. Under this *quid pro quo* arrangement, one publication doesn't take advantage of the other. The trick is wording your contracts with writers to limit the expenses involved.

If you work for a large publishing company, contact the editors of other magazines under your corporate umbrella to create a similar arrangement.

Think of an expensive freelance article as a potential revenue generator. Package the piece as a reprint after it's been published and offer it at a premium price to readers through a stand-alone house ad. It's possible that you will recoup the cost of the article through the course of the year.

Assign in-depth articles that can appear as a series. If, for example, the average length of your features is 1,200 words, assign a 3,500-word article and divide it up. As long as you are not paying by the word, you will get much more for your money. Then apply the above tip and make the series a reprint for resale.

Create an opinion column that elicits reader submissions. Offer a token payment on publication. Although the quality of the articles will be mixed, you can expect some surprisingly good submissions and might uncover some promising contributors.

Launched about 18 months ago in one of my publications, this column has become a popular feature. It seems to build a closer tie with readers and creates a dialogue with them about our editorial coverage of important topics. The only drawback so far is that the column is so popular, the lag time between accepting a submission and publishing it is more than eight months (even though we are a weekly publication). Fortunately, most of the contributors are very understanding about this.

> Once editorial quality and integrity are compromised to save money, your title starts an inexorable slide down a slippery slope.

Conduct question-and-answer interviews with people who are just too expensive for first-person articles. Start this process by contacting their publicists or literary agents. To facilitate the process, make it clear that you will do all the work in exchange for a 30-minute phone conversation. Although you might end up with, for example, Sting's drummer instead of Sting, the range of potentially interesting articles using the Q&A format is endless and inexpensive.

Ask your two or three best freelance writers to become monthly or bimonthly columnists. The money-saver here is to offer flat annual fees that total less than what they would have received had they written a like number of articles for you. To combat any skepticism, argue that they'll benefit from the increased exposure and security of a steady payment. If necessary (and possible), bestow the title of contributing editor. But be sure to cover the frequency issue in detail in a contract before a column makes its debut.

Create a "Best of" issue that appears at the end of the year and in which you reprint the six, eight or 10 best articles of the previous 12 months, as decided by your editorial staff. Another payment isn't necessary, since you've already purchased the right to reprint—but send a plaque and letter of appreciation to each author. This technique won't work for every magazine, but where it does work, it works well. Readers seem to applaud the existence of an annual compendium of top articles, and writers strive to receive the honor.

While one or more of these 11 ideas may work well for you, none will have any credibility if you fail to maintain high editorial standards that are strictly enforced. Within this context, all the other strategies will work well. But once you compromise editorial quality and integrity to save money, your magazine starts down a slippery slope from which there is no return. □

section four

circulation

"You can have an excellent product, but if it isn't marketed well, **it can die."**—p. 216

"The inability to make decisions—**paralysis through analysis**—is a common malady of circulation directors."—p. 220

"If you allow **reader research to waste away** on a dusty shelf, you may soon find yourself and your magazine competing for space in the same place."—p. 235

A Circulator's Career Renewal Series

BY LAMBETH HOCHWALD

As a circulator, you can't ignore your responsibility for making sure consumers have a smooth ride through the ever evolving multimedia landscape. Cyberspace as a subscription and customer-service vehicle is sure to expand to encompass customer groups you may wish to target. And increasingly stylish online showcases for your magazine make it that much more likely that management will expect you to have a process that enables consumers to order subscriptions easily from the Internet—translating, potentially, to long-term circulation gains.

"Circulators are going to have to become Web savvy," says David Berger, a Charlotte, North Carolina-based senior circulation analyst for New York City-based Hearst Magazines, referring to the multimedia section of the Internet called the World Wide Web, which can already be accessed by nearly five million people. "The Web will work as a marketing tool, where the Internet isn't, because its graphic capabilities make it more usable. Consumers can see the product itself, as opposed to a description of the product."

Carol F. LePere, associate publisher and circulation director of the one million circulation, Washington, D.C.-based *Kiplinger's Personal Finance Magazine*, says that because the Internet invites consumers to sample copies before signing up for a subscription, issues should be shipped as quickly as possible. "The quicker you get the product to a person, the better off you are," she says. "You don't want to lose that already fragile connection." *Kiplinger's* recently joined The Electronic Newsstand and is working on creating its own Web site. The monthly is also negotiating to go online with CompuServe and America Online.

Circulators are also going to have to stay up-to-date on the audit implications of the new online universe. "If someone glances at an article, does that make him a reader? And is finding out [that he did] an invasion of privacy?" asks Karen Cheh, circulation manager of *Fine Homebuilding*, a seven-times-a-year title published by

Newtown, Connecticut-based The Taunton Press.

The evolution of the circulation discipline has also mandated a rise in computer literacy—not only in terms of the online universe, but also regarding supplier systems, including fulfillment data processing and database applications. "The big buzzword in circulation is reducing data entry and automating how we get reports from our fulfillment houses," says Hearst's Berger. "This eliminates us getting big reports from CDS and having to retype information into our system. We have more time to look at things that were previously left to accounting."

And if online fulfillment someday becomes commonplace, then the fulfillment sequence, which can currently take several weeks, may one day be concluded in one day or less. Circulators should investigate how expensive that scenario may be and then work with the publisher to determine who will shoulder the cost.

Be a customer-service junkie

Circulators aren't the only ones affected by sweeping industry advances. Readers will be, too. Although complaints about mangled covers might still be mailed to a

> "With new technology comes a lot of power for circulation people just starting out. But before you get there, you have to wear a lot of different hats."

publisher's office, now there are far quicker ways for readers to voice their concerns. By e-mail and fax, customers are not only complaining, but *demanding* better service—especially when it comes to delays in subscription starts. "Circulation departments are now divided between those who do the marketing and create catchy direct-mail packages, and those who respond to calls from outside," says Steven Koppelman, corporate circulation director at Morris Plains, New Jersey-based Gordon Publications. "Now that people are corresponding via computer, there's a demand that e-mail messages be responded to right away, versus the six-week grace period that used to exist."

But with faster communication, the goal of better service becomes an even tougher challenge. "It used to be that you'd send out a direct-mail piece, get responses back, count them and see how well you did," says Bill Coffman, director of marketing and sales at Mt. Morris, Illinois-based Kable Fulfillment Services. "Now responses are coming back via e-mail, interactive TV, 800-numbers and the Internet. It's going to be necessary to find out how many came back and how. You can track it and use it to your advantage when it comes to renewal time."

Make yourself a marketing maven

Although entry-level circulation positions historically have been low-pay, low-skill data-entry jobs, now the call is for even new hires to act as marketers who understand consumer buying patterns and needs. "We're hiring entry-level employees with marketing degrees," says Eric Schmierer, circulation director for Manhasset, New York-based CMP Publications, Inc. "These are people who are interested in the strategy of circulation versus the mechanics of just doing print orders, looking for duplicate subscribers and that kind of processing."

The days of circulators merely managing direct mail are over as well, with one goal now being a better understanding of the various methods for accessing the consumer and saving on mailing costs. This has become especially urgent in light of postal and paper increases.

Circulators of the future will also become participants in forging new markets based on shifting demographics. One example is the Hispanic market, which grew to 24.2 million people in 1992 from four million in 1950 and was expected to spend $206 billion in 1995.

Database marketing remains critical, too. "The less time you focus on the mechanics, the better," says Schmierer. "Our people are looking at circulation issues, not the technicalities."

Pitch circulation as a profit-maker

Over the course of the last 15 years, circulation has developed into a profit center for many publications. At most magazines, management no longer views circulation as a support department. "That change in mental-

ity means circulators must be more creative and marketing-oriented than ever," says Philip Whitney, *Money*'s consumer-marketing director.

It's also not enough to stay focused on the circulation department alone. "These days, there's much more of an emphasis on expanding the franchise and ancillary business, so we need to be thoroughly knowledgeable about what's going on in editorial and advertising," says Jerry Okabe, vice president and corporate circulation director at San Francisco-based Miller Freeman Inc. "We need to develop those relationships better."

Another ongoing challenge pressed on circulation from management is to raise prices. "Basically, we've been in a static inflationary environment for the last four years, with consumer price index increases of only 3 percent," says Whitney. "That makes it difficult for magazines to raise prices. And since price has an effect on response rates and profitability, your job may become a delicate tightrope."

Ride the managerial momentum

With their new importance as consumer marketers and product sales managers, more and more circulation professionals are rising to the ranks of publisher and CEO. "In the past, publishers were ex-ad salespeople who didn't know anything about circulation or manufacturing," says *Kiplinger*'s LePere. "Circulation people have found their way into publisher jobs because they have a better understanding of the bottom line—including printing and mailing costs and how much it costs to acquire a subscriber. They have a big piece of the puzzle already under control."

Publishers—right now—need staffers who not only know the intimate details about how a particular fulfillment system works, but who can also supervise a long list of printers, list vendors, lettershops, copywriters, designers and more. "We're looking for people with nimble minds who can sell things," says Whitney. "The sales orientation has to be there. We just do a different type of selling."

Deborah Winders, vice president of circulation at *Network World*, owned by Boston-based IDG, is optimistic. "We see circulators becoming publishers, opening up doors for ourselves and our colleagues," she says. "With new technology comes a lot of power for circulation people just starting out. But before you get there, you have to wear a lot of different hats." □

Circulation Secrets: Nine Steps to a Successful Launch Strategy

BY LAMBETH HOCHWALD

It's the moment of truth. You're working on your business plan, and you have more than a hunch that your editorial concept will appeal to a broad-based audience. The next step is to establish your circulation objectives, develop cost projections, and then find readers who are not only interested in your new title, but—if you're a paid-circulation title—will write you a check as well.

That's not so easy, say even the most optimistic experts already in the trenches. Today, with newsstand competition at its fiercest, direct-mail costs constantly on the rise and Internet publications proliferating, a traditional magazine rollout is no easy (or inexpensive) undertaking. "The big deal is to find a sustainable audience, understand your market, test it and have enough staying power to make sure the market accepts your editorial product," says Jack Ladd, managing director of Ladd Associates Inc., a San Francisco-based consulting firm.

No need to be discouraged. By following your business plan to the last detail, keeping circulation issues high on the agenda and making sure your readership is stable and committed, you might well someday see your title become a household name. Here, in roughly sequential order, are guidelines for executing a winning circulation plan.

1. Plan on a substantial investment in circulation.

With a subscription-based magazine, figure that circulation will be your third-biggest expense, after printing and paper, and personnel, says Bruce Sheiman, senior associate at the Jordan Edmiston Group, a New York City investment banking firm. In some cases, he adds, circulation outlays may even be greater than personnel.

2. Compile a list and check it twice.

Having said that, the official first step—especially for subscription-driven launches—is to find readers. The best way to do this is to hire a list broker who can direct you to those lists that best match your magazine's content. The best list broker for you can be found by using a consultant or by asking someone who knows the market you want to launch in—he or she can tell you

which are likely lists and which brokers specialize in your needs. The broker's fee is included in your cost-per-thousand names, which may run from $85 to $100. Typically, the broker gets about 20 percent of the total. One caveat, says Ed Fones, director of circulation at Emmaus, Pennsylvania-based Rodale Press: It's likely that the "big" audience you think will love your magazine may not be clustered on just one list. And, in some cases, your ideal list belongs to a prospective competitor, who may well refuse you access. Therefore, be sure to tap into multiple sources—and once you find a list that suits your audience, find out how it's maintained and how often it's updated. Contact other list users to make sure they're satisfied.

Be careful to use common sense during the list-acquisition phase, says Jan Edwards-Pullin, circulation director of *Sí*, an upscale lifestyle title that was launched in 1996 to cover the Hispanic market. "When I was at *Bon Appetit*, we thought it would make sense to launch a wine newsletter and mail it to *Bon Appetit* subscribers," says Edwards-Pullin, who has crunched circulation numbers for nine start-ups. "Unfortunately, we forgot that a large majority of wine enthusiasts are men, and *Bon Appetit's* subscribers are mostly women."

At *Sí*, Edwards-Pullin tested a total of 11 lists, with eight containing enough names for a one-million-name rollout. "Intense list selection is critical," she says. *Sí* tapped into magazine lists, databases, lifestyle-select lists and credit-card buyer lists. "What you're doing is dipping your toes in the waters, and if you don't cast your net wide enough, you may miss a very important list."

On the trade side, names might come from association or company rosters or a directory. Obviously, the goal is to get qualified readers—those who meet the criteria of your target audience—and get them to agree to receive your magazine.

3. Be realistic about acquisition costs.

As mentioned, list rental can range from $80 per thousand to $100 per thousand, and you'll probably want to start with at least a 200,000-name test, depending on your total projected circulation, says

David Obey, senior vice president and director of consumer marketing at Woodland Hills, California-based Weider Publications. At $100 per thousand, a 200,000-name test is $20,000, not including design, production and postal costs. And remember, a response rate is considered respectable if it's 5 or 6 percent—which for your 200,000-name test means 10,000 to 12,000 affirmative responses. "Make sure you have a contingency amount put away in your budget in case a list donor pulls a list off the market and you lose it—meaning you'll have to rent another," Obey says. Response patterns, unfortunately, have no predictive value for readers' willingness or ability to pay up when the invoice arrives: "If you base too much on too few lists, you can get burned," warns Rodale's Fones.

For trade magazines, acquisition costs vary over a wider range. Compiled lists (names culled from company rosters, association directories, etc.) rent for $65 to $75 per thousand. But paid lists, comprising people who have responded to a related product or a competing magazine, are premium priced, ranging from $90 to $110 per thousand.

4. The early bellwether: Your first direct-mail tests.
You've got your list compiled and you're confident you have the right group. Now it's time to test your title's viability. One way to do this is through a direct-mail offer, usually a "soft" offer, which means that readers who indicate they'd like to subscribe pay nothing up front. This approach is useful because publishers can gain a sense of how interested the target readership might be. But the overall cost of a test package can run from $500 to $700 per thousand pieces, depending on how elaborate it is, plus as much as $20,000 more for design.

A small sample of the list universe should be tested, including about 5,000 to 10,000 names from each list you've rented. "After the initial test, test again with five times the original amount," says Fones. So, if your first test reached 5,000 names, bump the universe to 25,000

■ Circulation resources

Publishers who want to try specialty distributors can start with this partial listing.

Armadillo & Co. Distributors
5795 Washington Blvd., Culver City, CA 90232
Desert Moon Periodicals
1226A Calle de Comercio, Sante Fe, NM 87505
International Periodical Distributors
674 Via dela Valle, Suite 200, Solana Beach, CA 92075
L-S Distributors
130 East Grand Ave., South San Francisco, CA 94080
Newsways Distributors
3700 Eagle Rock Blvd., Los Angeles, CA 90065-3623
Tower Magazines
2605 Del Monte, West Sacramento, CA 95691
Eastern News Distributors, Inc.
250 West 55th St., New York, NY 10019
Fine Print Distributors
500 Pampa Drive, Austin, TX 78752
InKo Book Company, Inc.
140 Commerce St., East Haven, CT 06512
Ubiquity Distributors
607 Degraw St., Brooklyn, NY 11217
Serendipity Couriers
470 Dubois Street, San Rafael, CA 94901

Speed Impex
1245 Forest Ave., Des Plaines, IL 60018
RPM Periodical, Inc.
52 Lonetown Rd., Redding, CT 06896
Anderson News
3601 East 46th Ave., Denver, CO 80216
Last Gasp
777 Florida, San Francisco, CA 94110
Book Tech
5961 East 39th Ave., Denver, CO 80207
Bernhard DeBoer
113 East Centre St., Nutley, NJ 07110
48 States News
1460 Williams Hwy., Grants Pass, OR 97526

—List compiled by Robert Sentinery

A source for national and specialty distributors is the Council for Periodical Distributors Associations (CPDA), at 60 East 42nd Street, New York, NY 10017. Phone: 212-818-0234.

Finally, another source is the *Folio: Special Sourcebook Issue.* Order it from *Folio:* subscription services, P.O. Box 4949, Stamford, CT 06907; or call 203-358-9900, x160. Price: $35.

names next, as you tap into different names from the same lists to see how those names respond.

That's exactly the tactic employed by Jim Forsythe, circulation director of New York City-based *Essence* and *Income Opportunities*, who is currently working on *Latina*, a bilingual women's title due to launch in May 1996. "We did a prepublication test mailing just to test the waters to see if people would buy it, and they did," he says. Next, the team created a prototype, mailed it to 70,000 names, and then refunded to potential readers the money they had sent in for a subscription. "Compared to doing market research, the prototype was a wise expenditure. It was worth doing the mailing to get these responses."

But test returns will never give you an exact picture of how the magazine will perform once you roll out, warns Michele Givens, consumer marketing director of Santa Fe, New Mexico-based *Outside* and *Outside Kids*. "The test itself will always give you the highest response that you're ever going to see," she says. "If you're dry-testing, meaning you've developed an idea but you don't have the product finished yet, typically you'll see response drop 20 percent between the test and the launch. Look at the test as a way to determine what the best lists are, how big the list universe is, the best creative approach and pricing structure." And don't be devastated by falloff, Givens adds. "Novice publishers are surprised when they see this," she says.

Although every would-be consumer-magazine publisher hopes for a double-digit percent response, that's not a very realistic scenario—nor is it necessary for success. "If you get a response that's over 5 percent, you've met your expectations," says one. On the trade side, however, response rates for a controlled-circulation test should be much higher because the recipient knows you won't be asking for money. A good list will produce a rate of 25 percent, says Cary Zel, president of ProCirc, a Miami-based circulation management services firm.

5. Gaze into the circulation crystal ball—with modeling software.

Judging from the excited responses to your direct-mail offer, you feel certain your audience is there. But will they pay, and will that revenue be enough? To find out, your circulation consultant can plug your numbers into several types of modeling software to help you determine that all-crucial pay-up percentage. And by comparing your response percentages to industry benchmarks based on your particular offer (whether it's hard or soft), consultants can also draw some conclusions about what payment patterns will be. Modeling accomplishes many things. It can project response rates for direct mail, renewal programs and insert cards. It can forecast and project the relationships between ad revenue, newsstand revenue and subscription revenue, along with the cost assumptions associated with each. Ultimately, modeling helps start-ups lower risk and boost profitability—quickly.

"Even if you get a good response to your soft offer and don't deliver the magazine because it doesn't exist, we have enough industry experience to predict pay-up that you can go to an investor with," says Rosalie Bruno, president of Circulation Specialists Inc. (CSI), a Westport, Connecticut-based consulting firm. Some numbers speak for themselves, however. "If you're getting 2 percent gross response on your soft offer, you're not in business," she adds.

Among firms offering modeling software: The Lighthouse Publishing Model, 800-999-8705; Media Services Group, 203-329-1170; Ladd Associates Inc., 415-921-1001; and PDC Business Systems, 619-456-6060.

6. Make a stand on the newsstand.

The true test of a publication's long-term survival lies in the performance of the second and third issue, not the first. "Don't rely on that first issue, especially if you're doing something unusual," says Givens. Newsstand success will ultimately vary by product, Fones says. "The first thing is to be very clear with your national distributor on product positioning and who your audience is," he says. "The distributors can help with placement, including the types of chains and the regional distribution that are best for you."

Definitely don't plan to publish your next issue one month after the first hits the stands, says Zel. "You need time to analyze your results," he adds. "Don't expect them until three months later and, even then, you're basing results on preliminary information."

Entrepreneurs usually are overly enthusiastic about newsstand sales, adds Susan Allyn, consumer marketing director of New York City-based Wenner Media. For that reason, they often forget to look at the pricing

> "If you get a response that's over 5 percent, you've met your expectations," says a circulation veteran.

and placement of other titles in the category they're entering. "New publishers tend to overprice their product on the newsstand," she says. "You should cut your price to get people to try the product so they'll come back. You can grab marketshare by coming in under."

At New York City-based *Sports Traveler*, a title launched last year, publishing director Polly Perkins decided to streamline her launch efforts, budgeting $24,000 for newsstand distribution and specialty retailers. In addition, the magazine—launched by Perkins with private backers—initiated a soft offer using two blow-in cards. *Sports Traveler* teamed with distributor Warner Publisher Services, placing 250,000 issues on newsstands nationwide (at a cost of $12,000). Then Perkins purchased supermarket pockets in two Midwestern supermarket chains and initiated a promotion with retailer Lady Foot Locker, passing out 5,000 issues free with purchase in selected stores. This year, Perkins' circulation plan includes a mail drop, distribution at health clubs and testing through Publishers Clearing House.

7. Is direct distribution worth a try?

If you have a niche title, you might find it worthwhile to look at direct distribution, keeping in mind that this takes a sizable investment of time and money. "To build up these accounts [in specialty retail outlets, usually, such as health-food or bicycle stores], you have to find and buy lists, do mailings and telemarketing, and create a system to bill people," says Fones. However, he adds, direct sales in vertical, specialty outlets often sell 20 percentage points higher than general newsstand distribution. (*See box below for distributors and other resources.*)

8. Set up fulfillment operations now!

As urgent as setting up your initial test is, it's equally important to establish some sort of fulfillment operation simultaneously, says Forsythe. "We have a track record and history [with *Essence*] at the firm we work with, but if you don't, ask around to find which fulfillment companies can best meet your needs," he says. "Fulfillment is one of the ducks you have to start lining up."

Tests have to keep the customer in mind. "Even if there's no money requested up front, people will still send it," says Givens. "You need a mechanism to return money right away and to make sure everyone on staff knows the mailing is only a test. If the launch is successful, you don't want charter subscribers ticked off because you've left them hanging."

9. Let your business plan and media kit evolve.

Because circulation is critical to making advertising and financials work, you have to keep evaluating sources and initiate modeling based on reader responses, especially in the early stages. And that means you should keep adjusting your business plan depending on the decisions you make. For example, in the case of frequency, Essence Communications Inc.'s *Latina* team is still deciding whether to go monthly or bimonthly. "That will have a lot to do with the decisions we end up making," says Forsythe. "If we go monthly, we'll start a mailing program right away. If we choose to go quarterly or bimonthly, we'll adopt a newsstand strategy until we find out if it's going to be viable."

Knowing when to readjust the strategy is important as well. "Early warning signs are low initial response, low pay-up and low conversion," says Ladd. "A lot of start-ups don't adequately model a five-year 'what if' matrix that assumes different conditions, response rates and pay-ups. A launch must pay attention to the economics of the entire enterprise on a timeline of multiple years."

In the end, the entire team must recognize circulation's vital role. Poor planning can lead to premature death, says Forsythe. "You can have an excellent product, but if it isn't marketed well, it can die." □

Paralysis Through Analysis

BY E. DANIEL CAPELL

It's been said that you can prove anything you want to prove in the consumer magazine circulation business. There are so many variables, so many numbers to analyze, that simply by changing a few assumptions here and there, you can create any analysis to prove your point.

Circulation is a computer nerd's heaven. What is that pay-up percentage on the third bill? How many people renew before expire—and on how many efforts? What does adding an additional blow-in card do to my overall return percentage? What will a change in the offer price do to my direct-mail-agent volume?

Assumptions built upon assumptions, endless computer-model runs—circulation directors all are guilty of hiding behind the "mystique" of circulation. In so doing, they frequently convince themselves that decision-making is dangerous to their health. In circulation, it is always possible to talk yourself out of taking almost any risk. Enough empirical "evidence" is always available to justify not taking any action. The more you know, the more you worry about what you don't know. The thought of taking a calculated risk (to raise a price, to change an offer) becomes frightening. What is my downside? Will I miss my ratebase? Will I lose my job? The inability to make decisions—paralysis through analysis—is a common malady of circulation directors.

> It helps to recognize that there are just too many numbers to be able to deal with all the information at once. The important ones are usually the same.

The numbers that count

So what's the cure? For starters, it helps to recognize that there are just too many numbers to be able to deal intelligently with all the information at once. But some of the numbers are a lot more important than others. For most magazines, the important variables are usually the same. Here are five you should focus on:

Subscription term sold: The length of term of your subscription offers is the critical variable in determining how much new business you have to sell every year to support your ratebase. Shorter term means more file "churn," and therefore more need to generate new business. This, in turn, means more new-business costs and a poorer circulation P&L.

Monitor the average term sold by source for every new and renewal subscription you sell. Do anything you can to lengthen that term. Not only will your new-business costs go down as term goes up, but a subscription sold with a longer term will also renew better. Circulation P&Ls rise and fall in direct proportion to how much annual new business a magazine must sell to replace subscribers who haven't renewed. The most money is spent on new business acquisition—and most of that on the last few thousand subs required to support a ratebase. Adding just two months of term to the average subscription for a monthly magazine can have a dramatic impact.

New business front-end response: If you can't get the front-end response up, it doesn't matter how good your pay-up is. This applies to all sources, from direct mail to television. Concentrate your promotional energies on producing the biggest front-end lift you can. Then, figure out how to get those people to pay a bill. Frequently, the key to gross response is not a free issue, sweepstakes and/or premium; it may be a lower dollar amount with a hard offer. Or, best of all, a longer-term hard offer at a lower per-copy price.

Test it. Often, you can improve your front-end response by spending more on new-business promotion, not less. Instead of saving money with that double postcard, try to drive up front-end response with a more elaborate package.

Insert-card returns: Many times, the best indicator of

the relative health of your magazine is the return percentage rate on bind-ins and blow-ins. You will typically see a higher figure on issues with above-average newsstand sale—because the issue is better read and the insert cards are used by more pass-along readers.

Strong insert-card response rates also provide you with the first indication that a price increase may be in order. And the insert card itself is the best place to test offers and prices. When the falloff to a higher price test is minimal, don't wait—raise the price and/or term of the offer.

Agent/direct source mix: Chart your direct-to-publisher versus your agent new-business source mix year to year. Has your P&L been affected by any dramatic source shifts? Weigh the impact of alternatives. What will longer-term, field-sold business do to your new-business requirement? If you rely more on direct-mail agents, renewals may suffer in the future. You need to determine if short-term savings on new-business costs will offset any future renewal losses.

A circulation P&L tends to be driven by the outlandish losses piled up by new-business direct mail. Source evaluation may tell you that it will take five years or more to make some portions of your new-business mail profitable. None of us can afford to wait that long. That's why longer-term, agent-sold business has benefits even if it sometimes renews poorly.

Advertising revenue/circulation revenue: Is your magazine driven by circulation or ad revenue? The answer should shape your circulation strategy. In an ad-driven environment, circulation acquisition costs are less important than increasing the number of subscriptions sold. The reverse is true at a circulation-driven magazine. Strategies can change over time. Be sure to understand the circulation/advertising dynamics of your magazine, and then plan and execute your circulation strategy accordingly.

No rocket science required

To understand these five leverage points is to manage your business profitably. All the planning in the world will not improve your circulation profit if you are spending your time worrying about the wrong things. The circulation director who agonizes over editing promotional copy, or analyzing the effectiveness of the seventh billing effort, or negotiating a 2 percent better remit from a subscription agent is wasting his or her time.

You must walk a fine line between hunch and reality. You must be willing to take calculated risks and, above all, be opportunistic. Circulation is the management of a constantly changing set of daily options. You have to be willing and able to make decisions and take risks within short time frames. Circulation is not nuclear science—even though some circulation directors would have you believe that it is. Circulation is a sales function, and there isn't a computer in the world that will replace a good salesperson. Keep it simple. □

Trim Your Way to Better Health

BY E. DANIEL CAPELL

It's become one of the more common circulation strategies for boosting magazine profitability: Over the past 10 years, almost half of all magazines audited by the Audit Bureau of Circulations that claim a ratebase have made at least one cut to their circulations. Of even greater note is that more than half of those cuts have occurred since 1990. (Roughly 55 percent of the 420 consumer members of the Audit Bureau of Circulations claim a specific ratebase on their publishers' statements.)

The trend reflects a decline in the success of magazines' new business efforts, including direct mail, and a decade-long slump in newsstand sales. Soft offers (premiums and free issues) now dominate the publishing industry. Declines in front-end response, coupled with poorer back-end pay-up, have become a major concern. At the same time, the ad sales climate has grown colder, meaning that the maintenance of higher, more costly circulation can no longer be justified the way it once was.

A ratebase cut, in tandem with other strategic circulation moves, can be a very attractive alternative—especially since the advertising community no longer automatically assumes such a reduction shows weakness (although, as the chart on the next page suggests, some of the titles that have made big cuts have had their share of problems). Even for those titles that don't make any ratebase claims, there are valuable circulation lessons to be learned from this approach. How do you know if a ratebase cut is right for your magazine? Here are some key issues to consider:

Advertising sales: If ad pages are on the decline and you see no immediate signs of recovery, then it doesn't do much good to keep chasing after those expensive, peripheral subscribers. Ad rate discounting, now a common industry practice, further erodes a magazine's profitability. The issue for circulation directors is to demand better forecasting of ad pages by the advertising department. If ad revenue can't justify circulation spending, then a reduction in ratebase is obviously the right alternative.

Circulation health: Cutting the ratebase provides a unique opportunity to improve the overall pricing strategy of your magazine. When you have the luxury of needing to attract less new business, circulation price increases—either newsstand, subscription, or both—are easier to pull off. In other words, you can maintain the same direct-mail volume as in the past, but still raise your prices and be able to afford the resulting fall-off in response.

Let's say you typically send out five million pieces of new-business direct mail per year and pull 1.5 percent net, or 75,000 orders. If you are cutting your ratebase by 25,000, you might still mail your normal five million pieces, but raise your introductory offer 15 or 20 percent, or perhaps lengthen the term of your offer. Or, instead of raising the price, you might want to try a harder new-business offer by getting rid of free copies or premiums. This should lead to better pay-up and, therefore, better net response for your mail. With a ratebase cut, you have more flexibility in the kinds of offers you can try.

Circulation expenses: Most publishers find that the best place to cut expenses in a ratebase reduction plan is in their own direct-mail program. Almost every magazine that uses direct mail in a significant way has a few hundred thousand pieces that lose a significant amount of money. It goes without saying, then, that you need to cut your most expensive—*i.e.*, poorest performing—lists right up front. You'll find that reductions in other new-business sources (television, agencies, and so forth) do not provide the same kind of cost savings as direct mail.

Audience quality: When making announcements

> Even for those titles that don't make ratebase claims, there are valuable lessons to be learned from this approach.

■ Ten largest ratebase cuts from 1984 to 1994

Magazine	High point	Jan. 1994	% change
Penthouse	4 million (1983)	1.1 million	-72.5
First For Women	3 million (1990)	1.2 million	-60.0
Family Circle	8 million (1983)	5 million	-35.5
Woman's Day	6.8 million (1983)	4.5 million	-33.8
National Enquirer	4.9 million (1983)	3.4 million	-30.6
McCall's	6.2 million (1985)	4.6 million	-25.8
Playboy	4.4 million (1983)	3.4 million	-22.7
TV Guide	17 million (1983)	14 million	-17.6
Reader's Digest	17.75 million (1985)	15 million	-15.5
National Geographic	10.48 million (1989)	9.15 million	-12.7

about ratebase cuts, most magazines are in the habit of saying that the goal is to improve the quality of their subscriber files. While this sounds good and gives the PR types something to work with, the explanation is actually more of a smoke-and-mirrors tactic—but one that Madison Avenue nonetheless seems to buy (*Time* is just one title that pulled it off). Cutting the ratebase is a way to improve a magazine's bottom line; it usually has no effect on the demographic make-up of your subscriber file. Your editorial product tends to be self-selecting regardless of the sub-scription sources you use.

That said, the "quality" argument will still be a big hit with the folks in your advertising department, so don't dismiss it—even if you know better.

Change in ownership: This is as good an opportunity as any for new management to make a ratebase cut and to blame all the magazine's mistakes and problems on the previous owner.

A ratebase cut need not be a permanent thing. A number of magazines—*Backpacker, Flower & Garden, Jet, Motorcyclist, New Republic, Runner's World, Workbench* and *YM*, to name just a few—have made temporary reductions in circulation at some point in the past decade (most within the past few years), improved their profitability, and then gone on to grow their circulations again.

Other titles—*Astronomy, Country Journal* and Canada's *Maclean's*—have used the reduction as part of the transition toward not making any specific ratebase claim at all.

In either case, the decision to reduce ratebase can open up a whole series of opportunities to improve a magazine's long-term health.   □

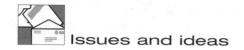

Try Fishing in a Controlled-Circ Stream

BY ROBERT COHEN

As the costs of acquiring and maintaining paid subscribers continue to rise, publishers of consumer magazines are turning to nonpaid controlled-circulation segments as a way to build circulation. Special-interest magazines, in particular, can often successfully position a controlled-circulation segment as a benefit to advertisers.

If you can identify a distinct group of readers who are not regularly promoted for paid subscriptions, but who are in some way affiliated with your paid reader base (and are therefore acceptable as a target for your current advertisers), you are in an ideal position to develop a controlled segment.

One of the clearest examples of the use of this strategy is *Parenting*, which sends 70,000 copies every issue to a controlled base of pediatricians, obstetricians and family practitioners. These copies, which are placed in doctors' waiting rooms, are read by pregnant women and new parents—key targets of many of the magazines' advertisers.

Eating Well sends a controlled stream of approximately 30,000 copies to physicians, dentists and dietitians. *Bicycling* sends nearly 8,000 copies every month on a controlled basis to owners and managers of bicycle shops. *Southern Accents* mails 18,000 copies per issue to members of the American Society of Interior Designers. And—the winner of the most precise use of the controlled-supplement strategy—*Sport Fishing*, which sends 9,000 copies to owners of power boats 40 to 70 feet in length.

The key to the successful use of the controlled-supplement strategy is advertiser acceptance. Because controlled copies generate no subscription income, you should not use controlled circulation unless advertisers will buy the idea of those copies being included in your ratebase. Most consumer advertisers are very wary of controlled circulation, however. Many consider "nonpaid" copies to be "unread" copies, and therefore of no value to them. Advertiser wariness, by the way, will usually be mirrored by your ad sales staff—so don't expect to be a hero when you bring up the subject of controlled in your next staff meeting.

It will be a lot easier to convince your sales staff that controlled circulation is a good idea if one or more of your direct competitors use it. But if that is not the case, you can build support for controlled through research. Look at the media-buying habits of your key advertisers and their agencies. If you can identify consumer magazines that have controlled segments in which your advertisers have already bought space, it will bolster your sales staff's confidence in the idea, and will provide them with sales ammunition to respond to potential advertiser objections.

■ ABC makes it easier with a rule change

For years, an obstacle to the use of controlled circulation was that the Audit Bureau of Circulations would not audit it or let publishers report it within the traditional Pink Sheet framework. A policy shift by ABC in 1990 changed the ground rules. Now, Pink Sheet consumer publishers can retain their Pink Sheet status by filing a Supplemental Data Report for the controlled portion of their distribution. The rules for what counts as qualified controlled are clearly laid out in the ABC rule book. The important features to know are these:

1. Publishers who claim a ratebase must make separate claims for the paid and controlled portions of the circulation.
2. Qualified recipients must be tightly defined by specific class (for example, occupation, industry, geography).
3. The source of the controlled circulation (e.g., lists, direct request, telemarketing) must be specified, and the age of the source document (one, two or three years) must be indicated.
4. Direct-request circulation must be requalified at least once every three years.
5. There are minimum issue service requirements, depending on the magazine's frequency. Monthly magazines, for instance, must serve at least six consecutive issues to controlled subscribers.

A final step before you consider a controlled segment is to run the numbers to see if the increased advertising revenue attributable to the ratebase impact will pay for the marginal service costs of these copies.

There are clear advantages to developing a controlled segment, depending on your particular needs. There are disadvantages as well, which I will address. On the positive side, many consumer magazines use controlled streams as part of a strategy to build public-place circulation—*i.e.*, distribution to waiting rooms, hotels, lobbies and other places where readers congregate. Copies distributed to public places tend to have many more readers per copy than do copies received at the home or the office, or those purchased at the newsstand.

Controlled streams to public places are also an excellent way to build total readership figures for magazines measured by Simmons or MRI. What's more, public-place subscriptions have the added benefit of generating much higher response rates from insert cards—two to three times the single-copy response rate would not be unusual. In fact, most circulation directors place additional insert cards in controlled copies of their magazines or use insert-card wrappers to take advantage of the high "velocity" of these particular copies.

The economics of controlled circulation almost always compare favorably with the costs of acquiring paid circulation through marginal direct-mail lists or other high-cost sources. Response rates to requester mailings are much higher than responses to paid mailings; package CPMs are generally lower for controlled versus paid efforts; and many publishers circumvent third-class mail altogether by using wrappers attached to free copies to generate direct requests. Of course, controlled copies themselves never generate renewal income, so use source-evaluation techniques to rank the long-term profitability of controlled before going forward with this source.

What about the downside? Besides the obvious problem of winning the support of advertisers and your sales staff, you will find that waiting-room circulation—a frequently used channel of controlled circulation for paid magazines—is becoming much more competitive. Doctors' offices are under media assault, and not just from magazines vying for limited display space. Cable TV, bulletin board programs and take-ones all compete for the precious waiting time of readers.

How to do it

Most publishers use two sources for developing qualified controlled subscriptions: direct-request promotions, and lists or directories. Many advertisers tend to judge the quality of the controlled circulation based on the proportion that is direct request, so you will usually start with this source when building your controlled file. The least expensive way to obtain requests is to use the wrappers attached to copies of the magazine that you send free to qualified recipients. This technique is almost identical to the renewal wrapper effort you probably already know. Consult the ABC rules for the specific format differences for the order form, since the requirements are quite strict.

Telemarketing is another method used to generate direct requests. Despite telemarketing's high up-front costs, you can qualify more than one name per call at a particular address—for example, a group medical or legal practice.

Lists and recognized directories are means also acceptable to ABC, provided they stand up to the bureau's audit standards. (For physicians, for example, try to find a list certified by the American Medical Association.)

Once you have obtained a legitimate list, you can begin sending magazines to individual recipients—and building your ratebase by counting them as qualified controlled subscriptions.

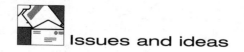

The Price Is Right

BY STEVEN BARBOZA

I'm willing to pay top dollar for a magazine: a buck ninety-five, no strings. But if the magazine has nice pictures, I'll splurge: $2.50 in cold cash. And if the cover art captures my heart, I'll lay out $3.50. Then again, I'll pay $27.95 for a subscription if each issue will occupy at least 20 minutes of my time—which averages 12 cents a minute. Not a bad price for a year's worth of intermittent entertainment.

I confess: I'm not sure what I would be willing to pay for a magazine. The "right" price—newsstand or otherwise—is, of course, subjective. Even for publishers with loads of circulation statistics and detailed demographics at their disposal, finding the maximum price that will still draw the maximum number of buyers remains a challenging game of calculation and chance.

Amid all the talk about needing to get more revenue from circulation, the bottom line is that consumer magazine prices have changed fairly little over the past two decades. It's still pretty easy to find offers of 12 months for $12—even for those upscale coffee-table titles whose readers could afford, ostensibly, to lay down much more. "As an industry, we haven't been as aggressive with pricing as we should be," says David Obey, the New York-based vice president and director of consumer marketing for Weider Publications.

John Klingel, a consultant and favorite keynote speaker at industry circulation events, takes every opportunity to remind publishers that circulation economics are in need of some serious repair. "We're in a business where the public does not perceive the value of the product in proportion to the cost," says Klingel, who also spends part of his time as director of new magazine development at Los Angeles-based Time Inc. Ventures. The cost of printing and mailing a typical monthly magazine, he points out, is $9 or $10—not much less than what many titles charge for their introductory offers. In order to make money from circulation, he says, "your subscription price should be about five to 10 times above the cost of production—because you need a big percentage for promotion."

And yet, so many of the larger publishers have grown so accustomed to subsidizing circulation with ad sales that they've created an atmosphere in which it's become very difficult to pursue aggressive pricing strategies and move away from premiums and the kind of "three issues free" soft offers that consumers have come to expect. "What's happening is that you're getting mass merchandise magazines that would like to work back to hard offers but can't," says Ken Chester, vice president/director of circulation for The New York Times Co. magazines, noting the industry's reliance on stamp-sheet agencies such as Publishers Clearing House and American Family Publishers as important sources for new business.

True, it's not as common as in the past to find a host of different offers and prices for the same publication. (Obey recalls an article from *Mad* about 20 years back that parodied *Time*'s renewal series by offering, among other enticements, dinner with Henry Luce and a date with his daughter.) Nonetheless, given the fact that some magazines still cost less than the price of a greeting card, the science/art of pricing is coming under more and more scrutiny as publishers attempt to shore up circulation's bottom line.

Even the old exhortation to "Test! Test! Test!" has lost some of its strength amid an ever-changing and often unpredictable marketplace. Newsstand consultant Ron Scott, for one, says he doesn't even bother to test cover prices anymore, claiming that by the time you gather the results, they're often useless. "I'm convinced that by the time you collect market information, the world has changed," says Scott. "People react much more rapidly than they ever did." In fact, he adds, testing with dated data probably can do more damage than good.

Others take an opposite view for precisely the same reason. "It's silly to go out with anything that you haven't tested," says Jack Shurman, senior vice president of publisher relations at Publishers Clearing House, "because the market is so volatile."

Fortunately, for those circulation professionals trying to make sense of all this, some basic rules of strategy have withstood the test of time:

10 percent up = 10 percent down. When it comes to raising prices, "the general rule of thumb hasn't changed much," says Dan Capell, editor of "Capell's Circulation Report" newsletter. "It's a one-to-one ratio: If you raise your subscription price 10 percent, you're going to get 10 percent drop off." The "10 percent rule" is an adage borne out by extensive testing. For those who raise their subscription prices by that amount, Capell notes, it usually takes three to six months to bring their circulations back up to par.

Per issue vs. total. Subscribers respond better to total price rather than per-issue pricing. As far as buyers are concerned, a $15 subscription for a monthly magazine translates to $15 spent over the course of the subscription—not $1.25 per issue. Weeklies provide the major exception to the rule. Prices sound less intimidating at, say, $1.19 per issue (for *Time*) than at $61.88 per year. (And even then, the newsweeklies try to soften the sticker shock by offering half-year rates as well.)

Inserts vs. direct mail. Insert cards are still the most effective and most profitable means to gain new business. "Basically it's a difference between need and want," says Robert Acquaye of *Black Enterprise*. "Someone who fills out an insert card is being active. Someone who gets a direct-mail piece—he's being solicited—that's passive, and that means you have to work harder to get him to renew. That person is more costly and more price sensitive."

Little leaps vs. big bounds. One quick way to make buyers balk is to convert at too high a price too fast. Testing has shown that converting at the introductory rate and renewing at successively higher rates, by smaller increments, works more effectively. (Business titles, on the other hand, can sometimes take more of a gamble. "*Directors & Boards* [a quarterly published by *Investment Dealers' Digest*] raised its price from $49 to $98 for a year, despite my hysterical warnings and much to my chagrin," says direct-marketing consultant Eliot Schein. "But they noticed no difference in their renewal rates."

■ The value of a magazine

The following is a sample of the various cover and basic subscription prices at either end of the spectrum. Keep in mind, however, that a good number of titles sell a substantial portion of their subscriptions at below basic rates.

Subscriptions
Highs:

	Basic price	# of subs	Frequency
The Economist*	$110.00	206,261	weekly
People Weekly	77.48	1,774,562	weekly
Harvard Business Review	75.00	209,497	bimonthly
The New Republic	69.97	94,888	weekly
Time	61.88	4,001,338	weekly

Lows:

Sassy	14.97	614,669	monthly
Redbook	14.97	2,632,923	monthly
Stereo Review	13.94	453,204	monthly
Ski	11.94	379,614	8x/year
Skiing	11.94	376,042	7x/year

Single-Copy
Highs:

	Cover price	# of sales	Frequency
The American Lawyer	$20.00	71	10x/year
Harvard Business Review	13.50	7,215	bimonthly
Foreign Affairs	7.95	15,797	5x/year
Unique Homes	6.95	36,573	bimonthly
Fine Homebuilding	5.95	50,163	7x/year

Lows:

Jet	1.25	141,977	weekly
Soap Opera Magazine	1.19	283,462	weekly
Soap Opera Weekly	1.09	522,739	weekly
Woman's Day	.99	3,414,750	17x/year
TV Guide	.89	5,889,364	weekly

*North American edition
Source: Audit Bureau of Circulations

Women and men. "Price resistance is higher with women's titles than with men's," says Obey, attributing the difference to the more mass-oriented approach of women's magazines and the incredibly competitive atmosphere at the checkouts, where even a 10-cent increase can cause havoc. "Seven Sisters titles like *Woman's Day* and *Family Circle* are so competitive," he explains. "They're locked into supermarket pricing."

While the above nuggets of wisdom were hardly gleaned overnight, one has to wonder how much it all means in a market that's changed drastically over the past 10 years, even if prices haven't. It's one thing for multi-million circulation titles like *Time* or *Redbook* to lop off hundreds of thousands of readers from their ratebases. But it's quite another to get the "core" subscribers to all of a sudden assign a much higher value to what they've already been getting.

"When you're in the circulation business," says Chester, "you're marketing subscriptions in concentric circles." After spending so much energy on building the outer circles—where the readers are the most expensive to obtain and keep—publishers now find themselves having to grow the center part of the circle. That becomes especially difficult for those magazines where the determining factor in setting price has been the need to maintain ratebase.

"Guaranteeing a ratebase on every issue is a very expensive habit we should probably do away with," says Klingel, a proponent of flexible rate bases. "It takes $5 of circulation revenue to equal $1 of ad revenue. We're going to have to find a way to give advertisers more value." And that leads back to the issue of pricing. "In general," says John Skipper, vice president of magazine publishing for WDPublications, "Advertisers feel that in years past they have picked up an unfair share of the burden. Why should readers pay 57 cents a copy and advertisers pay a high CPM?"

Skipper says that if magazines are going to raise prices, they should start at the newsstand, where he believes consumers are more likely to accept an increase (as opposed to subscription buyers, "who've been trained that they should save a lot of money.") Even if that's the case, though, the explosion of narrow-niche titles, combined with the impulse nature of the sale, makes newsstand pricing a more tricky endeavor than ever.

Don't discount experience

Sometimes, says Obey, the best pricing strategy is really no strategy at all. "I don't like to discount experience. You can test until you're blue in the face, but if you really know your audience, you know what to expect. When I was at *Rolling Stone*, we would just raise the price and then back test."

Obey admits that's a luxury he sometimes misses. But judging from the circulation challenges facing publishers today, it's becoming painfully more apparent that, maybe, the good old days weren't so good after all. While advertising sales have been declining since the late eighties, notes Klingel, circulation economics have actually been deteriorating for the past 10 to 15 years.

Still, old habits are hard to break. "The industry endlessly examines every little movement in ad sales," Obey observes, "but they only talk about circulation twice a year—when the ABC [Fas-Fax] reports come out."

When the talk will turn into real action, as far as pricing goes, is anybody's guess. "As long as the ad sales mentality holds sway," says Obey, "I don't see much change in pricing. But if ad pages continue to erode or stay flat, and printing, paper and postage continue to go up, publishers will be forced to raise circulation prices to get buyers to pay for what each magazine is really worth." □

> "It's a one-to-one ratio: If you raise your subscription price 10 percent, you're going to get 10 percent drop off."

Get More from Your Renewals

BY ROBERT COHEN

The single most important step you can take to increase circulation profitability is to reduce the number of new subscriptions you have to sell in any given year in order to achieve your magazine's circulation goals. Imagine if you could magically stop using your 10 most marginal direct-mail lists and still meet ratebase. You can do it, of course, by increasing direct-mail response and pay-up. But the surest route to lowering your new-business requirement fast is to improve your conversion and renewal rates.

Many publishers believe that there is very little that can be done to affect renewal response, since they assume that readers renew based on editorial or some other factor unrelated to circulation strategy. There is some truth to this argument—especially in the sense that breakthrough results, such as a 20 or 30 percent lift in response that we sometimes see with a successful direct-mail package, are unlikely in renewal promotion. Renewals is a game of inches in which a 3 or 4 percentage point gain in conversion response will have dramatic positive effects on the long-term profitability of any source. So it's always in a magazine's best interests to keep fine-tuning the creative, the offer, the timing and so forth to maximize renewal response.

Among the important factors affecting renewal response are three often overlooked tactics that represent fairly low-cost ways to get more impact from your renewal series. These are (1) mailing enough notices, (2) mailing early enough, and (3) mailing often enough. Here are ways to analyze and take action on these potential methods to increase renewal response.

How many efforts should I mail? Efforts analysis, in which we calculate the revenue, expense and profit of each renewal notice in the series, is an invaluable tool for determining the optimal number of efforts to mail. In renewal promotion, the basic idea is to continue to add marginal efforts until the net profit per sub produced by the last effort in the series is equal to the net

per sub from your least profitable source (usually your lowest response direct-mail list).

Let's look at an example: Soft-offer direct mail for our hypothetical Magazine X (*see chart*) receives an average 3.0 percent gross response and 30 percent pay-up from its low-response lists, and a 2.5 percent response, on average, from the sixth effort of the renewal series. Should the publisher add (or reduce) a renewal effort?

These computations derive from straightforward efforts analysis and show that, whereas the publisher *loses* $33 per net subscription from marginal direct mail, he *profits* $3 per net subscription from his sixth effort of the renewal series. The $36 spread between these two figures is a rough approximation of the profit leverage the publisher has if he increases the number of renewal efforts and decreases his direct mail to those marginal lists. A seventh renewal effort, for example, is more than likely to produce a net per sub at either a slight profit or a marginal loss—still far better than the minus $33 from direct mail. In fact, this analysis suggests that the publisher should test a seventh and even an eighth effort.

> The basic idea is to add marginal efforts until the net profit per sub produced by the last effort is equal to the net per sub from your least profitable source.

When should I start mailing? Depending on the source, sometimes immediately. This is especially true with business from direct-mail agents because you want the subscriber to renew with your offer before he has the opportunity to renew through the agent.

Most publishers wait too long. Four months prior to expire is the absolute latest, and many of our clients begin six or seven months prior. The logic behind an early start is that reader response declines dramatically after expire. Those of you who track response by effort can verify this from your own data. One reason is that your strongest selling point—renew now to avoid expiration—is no longer available once a subscriber expires.

Yes, some readers will complain about receiving notices so early. Human nature being what it is, however, I know of no publisher who has been successful with a single-notice system mailed out one month prior to expire. Readers need to be reminded to renew—again and again. And you will maximize renewal response by getting as many notices as possible into readers' hands prior to expire.

Keep in mind that renewal promotion does not always mean a conventional effort with order form, BRE, and so forth. Everything a publisher does to promote reader satisfaction and loyalty, from customer service procedures to a free gift sent to the reader prior to the start of renewal promotion (often called a cultivation effort), is part of the renewal process.

How frequently should I mail? Greater frequency equals higher response. It conveys a sense of urgency. Even publishers who start mailing six months prior to expire but wait two months between efforts to process returns are cheating themselves out of response.

Start early and maintain a tight 30-day (or four-week) interval between efforts. One successful exception I sometimes see is to increase the interval only between the first and second efforts. Since most responses come from your first effort, there may be some savings from this approach because it avoids

■ Should you mail another effort?

	Direct mail (low-response list)	Renewal: 6th effort
Annual mail volume (000)	40	30
Gross response	3.0%	2.5%
Cash with order	0.0%	25.0%
Credit pay-up	30%	70%
Net response	0.9%	1.94%
Sub revenue per order	$18	$21
Promotion cost per M	390	310
Reply costs/gross order	0.40	0.40
Billing cost/credit order	1	1
Bad debt cost/bad pay order	1	1
The analysis looks like this:		
Promotion costs	$15,600	$9,300
Reply costs	480	300
Billing costs	1,440	674
Bad-debt costs	840	169
Total costs	$18,360	$10,443
Net subscriptions	360	581
Cost per net sub	$51	$17.97
Revenue per order	18	21
Net profit (loss) per sub	$(33)	$3.03

duplicate mailings. But remember, it's worth it only if it does not depress overall response to the series.   □

Five Solutions to Your Database Problems

BY LAMBETH HOCHWALD

Face it: Your database is still your greatest marketing tool. Databases not only keep us connected to our customers, they also save us money and keep us steps ahead of our competitors as we tailor customized information to readers based on their demographic profiles. But what happens when the database you've honed for years starts to go stale? Or what if management has no interest in shoring up systems that are quickly becoming outdated? Here are five scenarios you may have already encountered, and some help in bringing your system up to date.

Your mainframe is a dinosaur.

Your subscriber database was created decades ago, and now it's obsolete compared with what's on the market today.

Not to worry, say experts. "Evaluate what you have before you decide it's outmoded," says Terry Nathan, executive vice president and co-owner of The Media Services Group, a Stamford, Connecticut-based provider of administrative software, services and consulting for publishers. "I've seen people take good technology and poor design and decide the whole system is outdated." Instead, Nathan recommends figuring out whether you have the internal resources to refuel your database in-house. If you don't, he suggests seeking companies that can help you modify your database or start from scratch.

John Woods, circulation and marketing director for Soundings Publications, Inc., an Essex, Connecticut-based publisher of four titles, realized six months ago that the company's subscription fulfillment software and database had passed their prime.

"Our old system was disintegrating and our system hardware was failing," says Woods. For that reason, Woods converted his subscription fulfillment files from a flat-file system, with data stored in discrete compartments, to a relational database. This change made it possible to access data in several different ways, which in turn made it easier to prospect customers and research their buying habits.

Updating the system was critical for the company's audience of more than 200,000 names, including readers of *Soundings*, a consumer boating title with 85,000 paid readers, and *Woodshop News* (circulation 90,000). "Since our hardware was no longer manufactured, we realized that we had to move quickly to salvage our applications," he says.

Even if you are forced to update, make sure you've examined all your options first, says Tom Rocco, vice president of marketing services of Emmaus, Pennsylvania-based Rodale Press. Rodale has used a marketing database for more than eight years. It might be just as important to focus on what your technology can still do for you, instead of isolating its limitations. "Remember that just because the technology isn't state-of-the-art doesn't mean you can't do business with it," he says. "There are probably a lot of cases where the technology may be obsolete, but still usable."

Tech costs are skyrocketing.

Whether your technology is outdated or not, your costs are rising—and you're worried that you may not be able to sustain the increase over the long term.

It may not be as bad as you think. "Anyone who has an open system and a database that uses open-system technology has bought insurance against outdated technology," says Nathan. "Software tools will allow you to move information easily from one environment to another."

Data transfers and data sharing are more complicated for those publishers who maintain their data in flat-file databases, rather than relational databases. Companies that have set up PC databases that aren't open systems may encounter difficulties and unanticipated expenses, says Nathan. "Without an open system, you're faced with an expensive and messy process to convert files."

If you have a flat-file setup, be prepared for six-figure expenditures to rehab or retool your database, including the possibility of investing in new system software and applications.

The boss is on your case.

You've spent so much time resolving database glitches and keeping systems integrity under control that you haven't kept management updated about the need to continue improving the database.

And now you're finding that management is less and less enthusiastic about your efforts—especially as budget time nears. "Give your database internal publicity," says Rocco. "We want our marketing people to use it most efficiently for cross-selling and promotions. We don't want them to forget to use it—especially since it will help them target mailings and ultimately keep costs down."

Jerry Okabe, vice president of circulation at San Francisco-based Miller Freeman, says that upper management is often the last group to hear about the need for a strong database. "They don't see the advantage of being proactive at making fulfillment and databases a resource," he says.

It may be a matter of demonstrating its efficiency once an integrated database is used regularly, says William Wright, vice president of circulation of Cincinnati-based ST Publications, publisher of seven trade titles, including 16,000-circulation *Screen Printing* and 21,000-circulation *Visual Merchandising & Store Design*. Four months ago, ST converted its circulation/reader service files to a unified system, eliminating a setup that had included four different platforms and 21 file structures. "The difficulty was researching the right platform, that the one we chose was big enough for us to grow into. Once management saw how efficient it was, they were sold."

You're stuck with dead-end data.
Your data is isolated by department, so resource sharing is impossible.

"Interdepartmental sharing increases efficiency because when you start building these isolated databases—one for circulation, one for reader service, one for ad sales—you've automatically severed your links," says Wright.

At some companies, however, the database is intended to be used for one function only—for example, subscription fulfillment. That's the case at Soundings. "Ideally, we'd have the subscriber base, classified advertisers and display ad accounts all on the same database," says Woods. "Advertising, ad traffic and receivables people were all out shopping for new applications that would best meet their needs. We didn't find application software that was compatible with our subscriber database."

In the near future, software that unifies a database across individual departments may come on the market. By the summer of 1996, The Media Services Group will introduce database software (now in testing) that will integrate circulation, reader service, advertising and accounting software systems into a single customer record.

"The basic concept would be to try to move toward an environment where all the databases the magazine uses are unified," says Nathan.

On the flip side, sometimes a company's database is too bulky to use efficiently. Breaking down the database into its various markets may be a viable idea. "Our pulp-and-paper magazine unit has developed its own database," says Miller Freeman's Okabe. "With the diversity of markets we have, maybe we don't need a corporate database as much as individual market databases."

The staff finds the system cumbersome.
Your equipment isn't user-friendly, so you're not getting the most out of it or your staff.

Case in point: Two years ago, Miller Freeman built a 2.5-million-name corporate marketing database, including subscribers, ancillary-product buyers, reader-service respondents and seminar attendees. The plan was to make it a marketing database, not a fulfillment database. Today, however, the company has a three-million-name database that's used occasionally. "I thought we'd do more cross-promotion among units, but it failed because it wasn't user-friendly," says Okabe. "Also, our staffers weren't told that the resource was available. In the end, management reconsidered the project because it was not returning on the investment."

If your database is the least popular resource at your office, figure out whether the problem lies in training, says Nathan. "I'd quickly try to get people more comfortable with the system," he says. "If it's built on old technology, you're working with your hands tied behind your back. Newer relational systems enable you to mold data, to get it into and out of the system more easily."

Ultimately, you can't dabble in database marketing, says Jed Lafferty, senior vice president of marketing at Farm Journal Inc., publisher of five agricultural titles including *Farm Journal*, which has a 675,000-name ratebase. The company has maintained an in-house database since 1982. "You have to make a huge commitment to data information systems—it's a lot more than a circulation file with a name and an address. You have to be ready to create data records on subscribers that may contain over 50 fields of information."

The database is the core of the company's commitment to serving readers, adds Lafferty. "Understanding more about who our customers are was an editorial mission that became a circulation strategy and then a competitive strategy," he says. "Everything we do is driven off our database." □

Expire Research Is No Dead End

BY CELINE SULLIVAN

When a subscriber fails to renew, we tend to forget that there's no friend as true—or as candid—as an old friend. Feedback from expires provides a wealth of insights that can be directly incorporated into your magazine's product and marketing strategies—which makes it well worth probing why the defection occurred.

Researching your expires needn't be a major undertaking. Focus groups, professionally moderated and objectively analyzed, are inexpensive and highly useful in shaping hypotheses. From there, you can move directly into strategy revisions and use market response to test the validity of those hypotheses, or (if your budget allows) detour via quantitative survey research into a risk-reduced market test. Renewal mailings present abundant opportunities to gather quantitative feedback from expires. Your telemarketing efforts can readily be put to this task.

As with any research undertaking, the more time and energy you invest in planning the study, the more reliable your findings will be. List and prioritize all your need-to-know items, and address as many as your budget permits. Spend time carefully shaping your survey questions. It's a good idea to write the table of contents for your research report first—then you can make sure that the questionnaire will yield the information necessary to build content behind those major headings.

Use your company's research professional as a resource in studying expires. If you don't have such a person on staff, it's worth retaining one for the project to protect your budget, select appropriate methodology and ensure the reliability of your survey results. You should also consult your staff freely in planning your research and analyzing the results. There's no intelligence quite as awesome as group intelligence—particularly in the magazine business, where the customer is never far removed from any departmental operations.

You probably already have some well-informed hunches to explore in your expire research, but here's a checklist of issues that merit examination in one way or another. The resulting data should help you target your magazine and its promotion more effectively, and identify new opportunities to expand your franchise.

Who left whom? Did the reader drop out of your market, or did you drop the reader somewhere along the way? You won't be doing your magazine or its advertisers any favors by re-enlisting the uninterested. But where have they gone, and why? Are they in good, growing company wherever they are? And is that a place you would like to take your title—or start a new one?

After all, you "know where these folks live," and that's a solid start in marketing new products and services.

When enough is really enough. Assuming the wayward subscriber is still in or hovering around your market, what has changed his or her information needs? Have you reached the end of a natural lifetime expectancy with the reader? Or is there a new editorial slant you can take to extend your relationship with the overexposed expire? Look at shifts in the expire's media (traditional and non-traditional) usage. Do these shifts suggest other products or services you should consider offering?

When less is more, or more is less. In our everything-on-demand world wherein information abounds,

> Some management gurus would categorize the expense of expire research as the cost of fixing mistakes. To an extent, that label is appropriate.

packaging, delivery, timing and access have become the points of *meaningful* media-product differentiation. Is your magazine as comprehensive as your expires need it to be? And is it as current, relevant, accessible and easy to use as it should be? If your grades are slipping on any point here, chances are good that other readers will soon be taking the same exit your expires have taken—so some remedial work is advisable.

The value of x. Start asking consumers why they stopped buying anything, and you're sure to hear that "it cost too much." Never stop there. Translate: The reader is having trouble solving the price:value equation. You need to think about any product changes that could punch up the value. What competitive thrusts might be eroding your title's perceived value? And what competitive response on your part is warranted? What has been the impact of the incentives and premiums you offer on the reader's perception of your magazine's value? How far from the optimal solution do you stand, and what would it take/cost to get you there?

Mistaken identity. Did your reader have realistic, informed expectations when he or she first subscribed to your magazine? (Some of the stamp-sheet promotions, for example, offer only the sketchiest of descriptions of the magazines they offer—sometimes only the title.) If your magazine on delivery paled against the subscriber's unrealistic expectations, is this a marriage you really want to save? Or do you need to take another look at your promotion strategies?

Time out. Is the reader "resting"? Recovering from what? Is there something you could be doing editorially to revive the expire? Becoming a parent, for instance, predictably alters one's participation in special interests. If yours is a lifestyle book, for example, do you have a sufficient number of new parents to warrant regular treatment of family, as opposed to individual, participation in activities of interest?

How are you doing? Compared to what? You know your best customers, and your worst—and you know where you found them, what you've sold them, what they paid and how quickly they paid it. You may even have overlays of other data to help you here. The question is, how do your expires compare to these two groups? Are you losing losers or winners?

Pink slippage. Have you made any changes to your magazine—a redesign, repositioning, or frequency change, for example—that may have disenfranchised the reader? And given that you can't win 'em all, is this the type of reader you intended to "fire"? In other words, are you winning more than you're losing?

Rehiring. You may have fixed the problems underlying certain expires' disaffections, or added genuine value to the original "contract" with the expire. But does your renewal promotion tout those changes? If the subscriber hasn't seen the last few issues or hasn't been prompted to pay attention to renewal notices, he or she probably hasn't noticed the change. What "re-trial" offers might be productive?

You show me your database, I'll show you mine. By the turn of the century, every company serious about doing business will have a database profiling its customers and prospects. You might as well start now to make your expire research useful and relevant to your organization's database development activities. At the very least, verify the expire's address. A commercial list compiler can be a very valuable resource in this task.

If your company is in a database-development mode, be sure to involve all concerned with the database initiative in planning your expire research. If not, design your project to maximize the database exploitation potential of the resultant data—that is, plan in the capability to qualify customers and prospects by measurable characteristics that can be correlated, positively or negatively, with customer lifetime value.

Some management gurus would categorize the expense of expire research as "failure cost," that is, the cost of fixing mistakes. And to the degree that your expire pool consists of disappointed readers whom you'd like to re-recruit, that label is appropriate.

Happily enough, though, the gurus advise that failure costs can be offset by more modest and highly respectable "prevention costs." These are the expenses involved in anticipating your readers' needs and expectations, and enriching all your efforts to satisfy them with heavy doses of customer input and feedback. Theoretically, at least, this timely and responsive dialogue with the customer produces only happy expires who spend their free moments sending volumes of new business your way.

It's just a matter of timing, of doing your expire research up front. ☐

Create Really Effective Readership Surveys

BY BRUCE L. KATCHER, PH.D.

You have urgent questions that need answers: Why are we losing circulation? How do readers feel about our format? What changes do our readers want? What issues are most important to our readers? How can we show a potential advertiser that a large segment of our readership values its products?

These are the types of questions that can be answered with readership surveys. But to get answers that are valid, that pass the credibility test, the survey must be properly conducted. Here are some important guidelines.

Choose the right survey method. There are four basic approaches to gathering the opinions of readers: focus groups, telephone surveys, mail surveys and in-magazine surveys. Each method is appropriate for a particular purpose.

• Focus groups are ideal for in-depth exploration of readers' opinions when the specific questions you want to ask are unclear. For example, the publisher of a retirement-related publication wanted a deeper understanding of how readers felt about the magazine. Several focus groups were held in which the participants read portions of the publication and were then asked their general opinions. The publishing team watched the groups from behind a one-way window and were able to gain valuable insights. For example, contrary to their expectations, they discovered that readers found the colorful graphics and illustrations entertaining but inappropriate for the seriousness of the articles' content. The editors responded by altering the format.

• Mail surveys are most appropriate when you want close control over who receives the survey. For example, if you have advertisers who want to know more about the purchasing patterns of a particular subset of your readers, a survey mailed to only that subset should do the trick. Because mail surveys are addressed to specific individuals, they generally yield better response rates than in-magazine surveys. And you can optimize the response rate by sending a pre-survey mailing to announce the survey, and a post-survey mailing to remind participants to complete the survey.

• Telephone surveys are often a good compromise

between a mail survey and a focus group. Interviewers can target specific individuals (whether they are current readers or not). And follow-up questions can be asked for further clarification. However, such surveys are very labor intensive and do not produce the quantifiable data obtained with either mail or in-magazine surveys.

• In-magazine surveys are an inexpensive and easy way to reach all your readers, but response rates are typically low, and the results are not statistically representative of your entire readership. Using the results for PR purposes, therefore, is usually not possible. On the other hand, this can be an ideal way to generate reader interest in a particular topic. Engineering News-Record, a national McGraw-Hill title, conducts periodic in-magazine surveys asking readers about career issues. The results are then printed in a special advertising section funded by recruiting firms. And women's magazines, fitness magazines, and health and lifestyle magazines all profit from editorial that is based on responses to in-magazine surveys on topics of high interest to their readers.

Keep it simple. Mailed surveys or in-magazine surveys should be kept to a single page. Questions should be closed-ended, since open-ended or fill-in-the-blanks questions are more difficult for readers to complete— and cumbersome to analyze. Rating scales, checklists or true-or-false questions work best. It is also important to use the same response scale throughout the survey. It is difficult, for example, for readers to alternate between a five-point rating scale and a ranking scale. For mailed surveys, readers should be provided with a self-addressed, postage-paid reply envelope.

Ask the interesting questions first. Studies have shown that asking the questions that readers find the most interesting at the beginning of the survey increases the chances that readers will complete the survey and return it to you.

Don't get too personal. Respondents are often understandably unwilling to give their names, addresses, phone numbers or incomes. However, if this information is vital to the purpose of the survey, ask for it at the end. Respondents are more likely to answer these questions once they have psychologically committed to the survey.

Offer an incentive. Respondent incentives can increase response rates. There are many different approaches to incentives for respondents. One publication we work with offers a copy of the survey results as well as a chance to win $500. Sometimes we offer to contribute $25 to a well-respected charity for each completed survey we receive. Placing a $1 bill in a mail survey can also improve the response rate.

Plan the data analysis ahead of time. If, for example, you want to know how three different subsets of your readers respond to a particular set of questions, print the survey in three different colors. That way, you will be able to analyze the data for each group without compromising the confidentiality of respondents. Or, if you plan to include any open-ended questions, make certain you have the available administrative resources to categorize or type the written comments.

Just as important as knowing what to do is knowing what *not* to do. In terms of reader research, there are three big pitfalls to be avoided.

Don't assume you have a statistically representative sample. Respondents to in-magazine surveys are self-selecting, and as such can bias results. Although there are some weighting strategies that can be used to correct for sampling bias, a mail survey is more likely to give you statistically valid results. In any event, plan ahead: Know who you want to sample—readers, readers and non-readers, specific subsets of your readers, and so on—and design your survey to reach them.

Don't allow readers to stuff the ballot box. Unless you take some precautions, the results of in-magazine readership surveys can be altered by readers. State clearly that photocopies of survey forms will not be accepted, and that each reader may submit only one survey. Consider the following potential problem: A popular consumer magazine published an annual survey to assess the attitudes of its readers toward different insurance companies. One company was consistently rated low on claim service. The company's CEO, who was fighting mad, asked his own research director how many magazines the company would have to buy to complete enough surveys to dramatically improve its claims rating. In the end, the CEO decided not to stuff the ballot box—but he could easily have done so.

Don't ignore reader feedback. If you ask your readers for their opinions about any aspect of your magazine, take what they say very seriously. Listen to them if they want change. If you allow your survey results to waste away on a dusty shelf, you may soon find yourself and your magazine competing for space on the same spot.

> If you ask your readers for their opinions about your magazine, listen to what they have to say very carefully.

 Lists

Choosing the Best List Broker

BY PAUL TAYBI

Choosing the right list broker can be complicated. There are more than 400 registered mailing list brokerage companies listed in the SRDS List Directory, plus thousands of advertising agencies and lettershops offering list brokerage services.

Unfortunately, many magazine publishers don't realize just how complicated it is to find the right broker. They base their decisions on the broker's size—the number of accounts a broker serves—or on a broker's general reputation. Certainly size and reputation are important, but they won't predict how well a broker will serve your magazine's long-range interests.

A more critical consideration is how a broker will contribute to your publication's profitability. It may seem like a lot to ask, but a mailing list broker can be expected to help your magazine maintain a healthy bottom line. At the very least, your broker should provide on-target list research and recommendations, and on-time delivery of labels and/or tapes to your mailing house. But there are other "behind-the-scenes" services a mailing list broker should provide to magazine publishers.

Narrowing the odds

To find the right broker for you, ask yourself these questions:

How well does the broker understand magazine publishing, or my specific readership? It makes no difference how many blue-chip accounts your broker serves if he or she is unfamiliar with magazine publishing, or with your particular audience. To recommend profitable lists for your circulation promotions, the broker must have a very clear idea of your magazine's marketplace positioning and its current and potential readership. If you publish an office-products trade magazine, for example, look for a broker who sees beyond office-products lists to new developments in the office-product industry—and how those developments can be addressed by innovative new list strategies.

Is the broker experienced in my field? There are list brokers who specialize in, for example, such vertical markets as high-tech office products and consumer catalogs, as well as brokers who focus almost exclusively on subscription mailings. These firms are on top of relevant new rental lists, new rental policies of established lists, etc. So it pays to find a broker with a built-in affinity to your marketplace, or better yet, to subscription mailings in your marketplace.

However, just because a broker specializes in your niche, there is no guarantee the firm will serve your publication's best interests. In fact, such a firm may send you the same tired collection of list recommendations it always sends to mailers in your field. Investigate the broker's willingness to seek out new lists and new approaches to your promotional needs.

Can the broker consult with me on my circulation marketing plans? One sure way to make the most of a talented list broker is to get him or her involved in your firm's market-planning process. Because lists are such an important factor in the subscription promotion process, it's a mistake to plan your promotional campaigns without considering the availability—and flexibility—of key lists. Look for a broker who can help you build list considerations into your firm's ongoing strategic planning activities.

Should I use a broker who is currently serving my competition? This is a ticklish question. On one hand, a broker who works with your competition will have insights into that firm's mailing strategies and will know which lists work best. This knowledge could be reflected in his or her recommendations to you. On the other hand, if the broker is recommending the same lists to you and your competitor, you may both deluge the same markets with promotions, thereby depressing response.

Most brokers have strict policies on client confidentiality, and would never divulge the mailing strategies of one competing mailer to another. Still, you can be sure your trust is not violated by refusing to work with brokers who handle direct competitors. If you have no choice, consider dividing your business among several brokers.

How can I be sure that the broker is keeping my mailing practices confidential? You must be satisfied that the broker will protect your publication's proprietary information. Check into the firm's employee agreements. How much confidentiality does the firm require of its employees? Does the brokerage company require employees to sign non-compete agreements? Always ask probing questions about how a list broker intends to safeguard proprietary information about your promotional practices.

Has the broker spent time on the mailer side? If you can find a broker with experience as a direct marketer—particularly as a subscription marketer—give that broker extra consideration. Chances are that broker will be more sensitive to your concerns about matching lists to campaign goals, structuring tests and rollouts, and meeting deadlines and budgets.

Can the broker advise me on analytical or computer processing technology? Because replicating positive test results is the key to successful subscription promotions, find a broker who can counsel you on structuring your mailings for ease of back-end analysis and rollouts. Also look for guidance on merge/purge, list hygiene, house file development, security and postal regulations.

What about research capabilities? Because list brokerage is a very specific form of marketing research, you should choose a broker with extensive research capabilities. Most established, reputable list brokers have complete libraries of mailing list data—often computerized and periodically updated for easy data retrieval and fast sorting by list subject, manager or by other relevant selections. A good brokerage firm will periodically distribute an updated list of all data cards in its current library. This gives you easy reference for future list selection, and for fast access to mailing lists of specific interest. An excellent list broker will also seek out mailing lists that aren't on data cards yet, or that aren't currently on the market.

So, check your prospective broker's willingness to go beyond the standard SRDS-published mailing lists. Sometimes those harder-to-find names can give your subscription promotions a competitive edge.

How responsible are the firm's accounting practices? Investigating this up front is not as intrusive as it may seem. A brokerage firm's track record in paying its bills can have a major impact on the quality of service your publication receives from the rest of the mailing-list industry. Some list brokerage firms engage in such deplorable practices as incorrect invoicing and slow payment, sometimes waiting more than 120 days to remit payments to the list owners/managers. Needless to say, the next time around, those same list owners/ managers will hesitate to extend quality service to such brokers.

Pick a broker who pays bills within five working days

of receipt of your payments. Make sure the firm has a history of timely, accurate invoicing (you can determine this by speaking with several of the list owners/managers with whom the broker works). And while you're at it, check into the broker's willingness to look out for your financial interests. For example, a broker should negotiate for volume or net discounts that satisfy both the mailer and the list owner/manager.

Does the broker's operational style match mine? The chemistry between both firms must work. Choose a broker whose office hours match yours. East Coast mailers can have real problems trying to work with brokers in Los Angeles simply because of the time difference. Service is the essential ingredient of the relationship. There's nothing more frustrating when working on deadline than to encounter constant busy signals or voice-mail messages, and to play endless games of telephone tag with your list broker. If you have to wait hours or even days for callbacks, consider taking your brokerage business elsewhere.

How many brokers?

Brokers differ in research methods, list libraries, subscription mailing experience and perspectives. Thus, two different brokers will approach your list research projects in completely different ways, and probably come up with different recommendations. By working with more than one broker, you'll learn many new angles to the list selection process.

But there are other reasons why it makes sense to work with more than one list broker. Sometimes two brokers will recommend the same lists at different prices. The higher price generally reflects a broker markup—the additional cost certain brokers tack on to lists to cover their own higher overhead, or to earn for themselves extra profit on your order. The only sure way to know if you're paying an extra markup is to work with different brokers.

There is also the issue of broker bias. Some brokers avoid perfectly good lists because the commission is only half the industry's standard 20 percent. Others refuse to work with certain list managers/owners because of a past problem. The more you divide your business, the less likely it is that your promotional performance will be affected by broker biases.

The most important reason to work with a list broker is to gain the perspective of a third-party direct-mail pro. But you should also look for a brokerage firm that fits your company's style of doing business. In the long run, the right broker can greatly improve your subscription-mailing response rates. □

Politically Correct Use of Lists

BY DONN RAPPAPORT

The moral question of environmental responsibility is one that all publishers must wrestle with. Certainly, adopting an environmentally responsible corporate philosophy and strategies for reducing both the volume and toxicity of the waste we produce are the right things to do. At the same time, however, the practical matter of cost must be taken into account. In many cases, what is environmentally sound is economically shaky.

One exception, however, is in the area of mailing lists. Where list maintenance and targeting are concerned, the right approach makes sense from *both* an economic and environmental point of view.

Wasted direct mail—that is, poorly targeted mail that has little or no chance of stimulating a positive response to your subscription offer—has become prohibitively expensive. Misdirected mail—mail that fails to relate to the recipient or to his or her lifestyle—can be particularly annoying to the recipient and a financial loss to the sender.

That both are also environmentally irresponsible should be the clincher in what is a compelling case for doing everything possible to target your direct mail as accurately as possible.

Industry estimates are that 10 to 30 percent of all wasted (or non-responding) mail is undeliverable as addressed—that is, addressed to people who have moved or died, or whose addresses, for one reason or another, do not match USPS standards for deliverability. Another 10 to 20 percent of wasted mail is the result of unintended duplication, and 30 to 40 percent stems from selecting individuals who have not been accurately targeted.

Let's take a look at each of these areas in terms of mailing list strategies and techniques you can use to reduce wasted mail.

I. Addressing: Clean is green

A clean house file is money in the bank and less solid waste for the landfill. Plus, it is the quickest and easiest part of the equation to fix. Here are some options to consider.

• The National Change of Address (NCOA) service has been offered by the USPS since 1986. NCOA is available through a group of non-exclusive licensees certified by the USPS as meeting an array of stringent matching requirements. New change of address information is provided to each licensee twice a month; the NCOA master file reflects the most recent 36 months. This information is compiled by the USPS from data provided by postal patrons when they move, and includes individual, family and business moves.

The main advantage of NCOA is that it lets you correct addresses *before* mailing. Thus, it helps expedite processing and saves the cost of mailing a piece that otherwise would not reach its proper destination.

• Deliverability is a function of the accuracy and completeness of an address. Always request complete address information on order forms. Capture address elements such as rural routes, box numbers, apartment numbers, street directionals and suffixes.

> Wasted direct mail has become too expensive. Misdirected mail can be annoying. The clincher is that both are environmentally irresponsible.

• Address enhancement (as opposed to list enhancement) comprises a variety of techniques and services. Two primary functions are Zip Code correction and address standardization. Accurate Zip Codes offer several benefits. They ensure timely deliverability and reduce the likelihood that the mail piece will be discarded as undeliverable. They lead to further postal discount opportunities through pre-sorting, carrier route coding, Zip + 4 coding and other automation and work-sharing procedures. They help standardize street addresses and cities, facilitate the unduplication process between and within mailing lists, and allow for higher match rates when overlaying census data with both demographic and psychographic information.

II. Unduplication: More is less

Merge/purge is the key to unduplication. The value of merge/purge lies in its results: Savings in unproductive duplicate mail; reduced postage through discounts; lower lettershop and list costs; increased marketing intelligence through unduplication; increased response; greater profit; and, of course, waste reduction.

Good merge/purge involves a fair number of judgment calls (or guesswork) in eliminating duplicates without losing unique names that "look like" dupes. In days gone by, mailers tended to err on the side of mailing to possible duplicates, rather than chance missing a unique name here and there. Today, the negative impact of mailing duplicates must be reconsidered.

Not only should duplicate records of individuals be eliminated, but family dupes should be combined into one household record for more efficient data management.

III. Targeting: More hit/less miss

Taking into account both economic and environmental considerations, the emphasis of every direct mailer—as well as the list brokers and managers who work for them—must shift from mailing more to mailing more efficiently. To do this, there are a number of segmentation strategies you may want to consider.

Test concepts before you test lists. When you test a list, you find out if a particular list will work for your offer or not. When you test a concept, you may discover a whole new category of lists, or list segments, that do or don't work.

Examples of concepts to test include such obvious ones as men versus women; senior citizens versus younger families; families with young children; hotline names, and so on.

Less obvious concepts to test might include women found on lists that are predominantly male; older names—13-month to 36-month names, for example, instead of hotline or 12-month names; population density—people living in less densely populated regions (Nielsen "D" counties) versus more densely populated areas (Nielsen "A" and "B" counties).

Test multiple segments of a file. Different segments of a file often perform in very different ways. *U.S. News* women, for example, may respond quite differently to a

particular offer than a general select of *U.S. News & World Report* subscribers.

The point is, many lists are *hetero*geneous conglomerations of a number of *homo*geneous cells. Don't assume you've adequately tested a file with a single list test. It might require two, three or four tests of various selections to determine which segments produce your optimum response and which result in more wasted mail than is justified for the orders they produce.

Eliminate non-responses. Test methods of eliminating potential non-responders. Test available data overlays and deliverability enhancements. Test mail residual addresses and Zip + 4 coded addresses. My experience is that these segments work better as negative screens to eliminate poor performing names than they do as selection criteria for identifying strong performing names.

Eliminate unlikely tests (pre-test). In its simplest form, pre-testing is a means of segregating your candidates for list testing into those that have a good chance of performing well versus those that have only a slim chance of being successful. In concept, you accomplish this by matching characteristics of the people on your test lists against characteristics of your active, paid subscribers. The higher the degree of similarity, the more likely it is that the test list will perform.

In practice, a mature publication— one with a relatively stable subscriber base and one that has been the beneficiary of a substantial amount of prospecting— lends itself to a fortuitous short-cut. Simply correlate the duplication factors between your test lists and your subscriber file with your response rates. You can back-test this on previous mailings or do it on a go-forward basis. But either way, you will soon discover the minimum duplication factor you need to predict success. You put into the mail only those lists that have a strong likelihood of success.

What about the others? Try negotiating to pay only run charges for those you choose not to mail. Or offer the list owner a 50 percent "kill fee." That way, you both win. You save 50 percent of the list rental cost, but more important, you avoid the printing, postage and mailing costs—and the waste—of mailing to a list not likely to perform. The list owner gets 50 percent of the rental rate, plus the chance to see how his or her list matches up with yours. If it does, he or she gets a test with good roll-out potential. But even if you end up paying the full list rental charge, you still come out ahead of the game. And so does the environment. □

Avoiding a Direct-Mail Disaster

BY ELAINE TYSON

I suspect almost every circulation marketer's career involves at least one direct-mail disaster. Using my own experience as an example, I can say without fear of contradiction that one direct-mail bomb is enough to last any circulator a lifetime. Many years ago, I responded to a combination of prospect price resistance, competitive pressure and ad sales woes by rolling out a short-term introductory offer without testing it. Do I need to tell you what happened? Unmitigated disaster!

Even as I did it, I was sure it was the wrong thing to do. Fortunately, I said so repeatedly—in writing—to everyone in the company. That's the only thing that saved me. Doing the wrong thing for all the right reasons cost us dearly. The campaign shortfall was 20,000 orders and about $200,000 in net revenue. We had a dismal year in circulation. And ad sales didn't break any records, either.

Insurance for disaster avoidance

I learned a valuable lesson from that experience. It is important to adhere faithfully to all guidelines for conducting statistically valid direct-mail tests. First, there are the five unbreakable rules for tests:

Test only one variable at a time. If you test a new offer and price at the same time on the same package, you won't know which caused the fluctuation in response. Variables worth testing one at a time include list, offers, prices, packages and seasonality.

Test only the important things. Concentrate on big issues, not paper stock or different color Johnson Box copy (*i.e.*, the boxed copy above the salutation used to bridge the gap between copy on the outer envelope and inside text).

Mail projectable samples. Usually, a 5,000-piece list test is adequate. This amount will give you a good feel for the responsiveness of the list. When you test other variables, mail enough pieces to ensure that you receive at least 50 to 100 orders from your test.

Base your roll-outs on net response. This means you have to wait long enough to know how credit orders are paying.

Don't overtest. Trying to test too many variables in the same campaign muddies the waters. It also jeopardizes overall response to the campaign. Don't use more than 10 percent to 20 percent of your outgoing volume for conducting tests. Send the balance of your volume the control package.

Use direct-mail techniques that have the best chance of success. Direct mail is a discipline founded on rules and formulas. Make sure you know the rules and practice the formulas in every subscription campaign.

Tried and tried and tried—and true

If you're not sure that you've got all the rules down pat, you can find examples of the formulas in almost every book on direct marketing. Basically, they all say pretty much the same thing:

- Get the prospect's attention.
- Keep the prospect interested in your promotion.
- Make the prospect want your magazine.
- Get the prospect to act immediately.

The ways in which your promotions accomplish

> The secret to avoiding a direct-mail disaster is this: *Follow the rules.* You know what they are—but just in case, here's a refresher course.

these objectives bring creativity to bear on the formulas—thus making direct mail both an art and a science.

Know your prospect. Learn as much about their wants, needs, aspirations and desires as you can from reader research. This knowledge tells you how to appeal most successfully to their emotions in your copy.

Learn the tried-and-true methods of getting your envelopes opened. There are different approaches to this job—and you should try them all as your test plans permit. Here's the list:

■ An offer they can't refuse

• Keep your subscription price as competitive as possible and test all price increases. Testing minor price variations—such as $9.97 versus $10 or $49.95 versus $50—may be more important than you think.
• Make payment terms painless. Extend credit to new subscribers—don't ask for payment with order. Test a "Send No Money Now" offer. A high subscription price is usually made more attractive by installment billing.
• Use a strong guarantee as part of your offer.
• Use response motivators and involvement techniques to enhance your offer. "Respond by" dates, devices that permit prospect participation, free issues and premiums can strengthen your offer.

Making a list; checking it twice

• 5,000 names are sufficient for a list test.
• Try to mail to other active subscriber files for your magazine's subscription offers and other mail-order buyers, membership lists and donors lists.
• Consider exchanging names with competitors. Make maximum use of any house lists.
• Use compiled lists carefully.
• Never mail to untested lists even though similar lists tested well.
• Don't test lists of less than 5,000 names—just mail them all.
• Don't let a few undeliverable names prevent you from continuing to mail an otherwise good list.
• Keep accurate, up-to-date list histories (gross and net response).

Promise the prospect something. Use a benefit to entice them inside your mailing.

Involve your prospects. Try using a device such as a lift-up flap or a short quiz.

Let prospects know who you are. If your magazine has instant name recognition, your name alone may make people open your mailing.

Make prospects curious. If you create some mystery about what's inside the envelope, they'll probably open it.

You can use these approaches alone or combine them. Odd sizes, extra die cuts, art, personalization and postage class also play a part in creating successful direct-mail packages.

Keep copy "you"-oriented and appeal to your prospect's self-interest. Nothing will make a prospect order faster than a compelling benefit.

Make your magazine desirable with lots of details about the editorial content. Be sure you've left no unanswered questions for prospects to dither over.

Figure out how to create credibility for your magazine and its offer. Testimonials, endorsements and guarantees are important to prospects being asked to purchase anything through the mail.

Don't expect creative work to compensate for a non-competitive offer.

Try to spell out exactly what your prospects will lose if your offer is *not* accepted.

Close the sale with a request that your prospect take action now, and make ordering easy.

Let your prospects have some fun with your promotion. Get them involved in it.

Mail your offer to the right prospects. Sounds easy, doesn't it? But some folks don't think much about anything but the cosmetic details.

Don't mail late or in a poor response period.

One final way to stay ahead of the game and avoid a campaign bomb is to keep up with the times. Mailbox clutter and constant bombardment of prospects by television and radio offers is forcing direct-mail marketers into some changes for the better. I'm seeing shorter, better written copy now in most subscription promotions. Very few four- or six-page rambling letters make it into the mail these days. No prospect has the time to read them.

Subscription packages are also much better designed now. There is acknowledgment that sometimes graphics can communicate even more powerfully than words. Consequently, direct-mail design has become the logical way to help improve communications with potential subscribers. Packages are more tastefully designed, which helps blast through clutter. The days of 10 typefaces on one page and no white space anywhere are over.

In addition to following the rules, instituting a test program that anticipates your magazine's future needs will help you avoid being pressured into a big mistake. You can show your management in black and white just what will happen if changes are made in your controls. That usually relieves a lot of pressure. □

 Direct mail

Decrease Your Direct-Mail Costs

BY LYNN CARLSON

Ad sales are off, postage is up—and suddenly circulation is "in." With circulation profitability becoming increasingly important to many publishers, now is the time to make your direct mail more cost-efficient, and to maximize other circulation sources. To that end, some suggestions:

Test less expensive versions of your direct-mail package. If you want to lower direct-mail printing and production costs, consider testing a double postcard against your regular package. This can be especially effective if you are using a free-issue offer, since the magazine sells itself— meaning you don't need much editorial sell-copy on the postcard. For the same reason, a double postcard works well if your magazine is well known or if the people on your mailing lists already have a good idea of what your magazine is about.

Another way to decrease the cost of your direct-mail package is to use your order form as the reply vehicle. By bulking up the stock (it must be at least 7 points thickness, such as 75# hi-bulk, to meet postal regulations) and printing the business reply card information on the reverse side, you'll save two ways: You'll avoid the cost of printing a return envelope, and you'll save 10 cents in business reply postage on every response.

A possible drawback to using the double postcard or converting your order form to a business reply card is that you will receive very few cash orders. However, if you are now using a free-issue offer, cash orders from direct mail probably make up less than 1 percent of your response anyway. Also, the ease of ordering with a postcard may encourage "samplers," subscribers who just want the free issue and have little intention of actually subscribing. With both these options, watch your pay-up!

Get creative with the premium. Another idea to help make direct mail more cost-effective and to encourage pay-up is to offer a premium in your billing efforts.

This might encourage samplers—who had been ready to use their option to cancel—to subscribe after all.

Decrease renewal price to increase response. A radical step to lower your dependence on direct mail is to decrease your renewal price—which should increase response. It might be difficult to convince your publisher that this is a good idea, since most have a preconceived idea of the dollar amount a subscriber should pay for the magazine. But the truth is that although you might lose some revenue with lower pricing, the direct-mail savings can be substantial and more than offset any lost revenue. And if you set your renewal pricing just "right," you may even boost renewals so high that you make more money than before.

How do you determine what renewal pricing might be more enticing? Take a look at where you are currently renewing your subscribers. Asking for a big increase from the original order (for example, bringing subscribers on for 12 months at $9.97 and then renewing them at 12 for $15), is not a good idea. Consider renewing them at the same rate/term as their original order, and then asking them for a few dollars

With the rise of postal rates and the decrease in advertising sales, publishers are looking to the circulation department to cut costs *and* become a profit center. Here are some tips.

more in subsequent years. This is particularly important for agent-sold orders, since you want to convert them with *your* renewal rather than sending them back to the stamp sheets for better pricing.

Extend the term. Testing a longer term (18 to 24 issues) will enable you to eliminate some mail campaigns or grow your rate base at a comparable direct-mail expense every fiscal year. This idea also allows lists to "rest" between mailings so that fall-off from list fatigue decreases.

Another way to work with the term is to offer multiple-year subscriptions on all renewal efforts and insert cards. A particularly attractive offer is three years for two times your one-year basic price. You can then promote this offer to your subscribers as "like getting an additional year free."

Add one or more renewal efforts. When analyzing the profitability of this technique, look at the additional gross response, pay-up, expense and revenue from the added effort only, not across the entire series. Although you may lose money on these additional renewals, they will probably still cost less than a direct-mail order. And if you need them to maintain your rate base, you might as well get them as inexpensively as you possibly can.

Put an additional insert card in the magazine. Use the same kind of formula as above to determine your incremental response, expense and revenue. Depending on the card stock and size of the additional insert, you may need to factor in additional second-class postage, since the additional card will make your magazine slightly heavier.

Include step-up offers (term extensions) on billing efforts to increase a subscriber's term up front. But make sure these offers are enticing—not simply a longer term at the original dollar-per-copy offer. For example, if the original offer was 12 issues for $12 (or $1 per copy), the step-up offer might be 18 issues for $16 (89 cents per copy). Although this will reduce your earned income on subscriptions, it will improve up-front cash flow and save money as well, since you won't need to promote these subscriptions for renewal for an additional six months.

Test a wrap with subscription cards on newsstand copies. But be careful: Newsstand wraps work when they add to insert response, not when they steal response from blow-in or bind-in cards. Also watch to make sure the wraps don't depress newsstand sales.

Get just a few of these ideas to work for you, and you'll not only save money and improve circulation efficiency, you'll become a hero in your publisher's eyes. ☐

Fulfillment Watch

BY CHRIS KALAMON

It was a circulation director's nightmare: 32,000 direct-mail respondents who had requested three free issues were sent a first-effort bill when they should have received an order acknowledgment. The phones were ringing off the hook. My head was spinning. How could this have happened?

It never fails. Whether or not you have a satisfactory relationship with your fulfillment service, mistakes of this magnitude can—and will—happen. Given the sheer number of people who handle a fulfillment account, someone is bound to overlook something, just when it matters the most.

What is surprising is that many publishers feel they have little or no control over the quality of certain services they receive from their fulfillment company, and often adopt a "what can you do?" attitude. Worse, many fall into the habit of waiting to hear the bad news from subscribers. This can have devastating results. "A small leak can sink a great ship." So said Benjamin Franklin. This is true, especially when subscribers are ill-treated. Fortunately, there is usually a chance to make repairs and redeem ourselves.

Most publishers already have some type of system in place to double-check fulfillment reports against the month's activities. However, there are some gray areas of the fulfillment operation that do not lend themselves to numbers and reports. They require greater commitment on the part of the publisher because it means becoming actively involved as a "subscriber." But the effort expended to monitor these areas can save you time, money and subscriber frustration down the line. And, it gives you some concrete information to present to your fulfillment house as proof that service needs to be improved.

Enter several regular subscriptions. Depending on your circulation mix, you should have valid subscriptions for paid (insert card), controlled and even gift orders—all in different names/addresses to help you monitor future mailings. If you offer a "bill me," option, enter a "bill me" subscription. If you don't offer "bill me," enter one anyway and track what happens.

Set up independent files for each subscription

entered, and collect any renewals, requalifications, bills, telephone and even new business solicitations that you receive. Analyze them for timeliness, package components, offer and term, and copy and design.

Test how smoothly your operation is running by responding to some of the above efforts. How long was the interruption in your service because you waited until the last renewal effort to renew? Is the renewal schedule being met? Did you receive all the premiums promised?

Seed all direct-mail tests so that you receive at least one package for each test. Enter a new order and set up a file. Track the different conversion and/or billing series to ensure that the correct follow-up efforts are being sent to direct-mail respondents.

Allow one of your subs to expire. Were you graced with the correct number of issues? Did you receive the last renewal effort in a timely fashion? Monitor the tele-marketing effort for politeness, timeliness and sales-manship. Did you receive a dead-expire mailing? Pay on the dead-expire mailing and start all over again.

Call in to the customer-service department several times a year. Monitor how you are treated when you complain about not receiving an issue; check on your expire date; order a back issue; request a refund; put your subscription on stop and hold; and complain about poor service.

Always get the name of the person with whom you speak. Note the time and date, and keep a checklist of items to assess: tone, personality, politeness, efficiency, speed, professionalism, etc. Monitor how effectively the representative processed the request: Was your order put on hold? Did you receive the issue you requested? Was the refund for the correct amount?

Write to the customer-service department several times a year. The correspondence can be similar to the approach you take when calling the customer-service department. But now you will be tracking written communication. How quickly did you receive a response? Was the response appropriate to your inquiry? Was it polite and professional?

Request live samples periodically. This is easily

accomplished, yet few publishers do it. Pulling a live sample means that while a particular mailing is in the lettershop being labeled, inserted and sealed, several samples are pulled off the line and sent to you. This gives you a chance to examine package components and source codes to ensure that the correct offer and package are being sent to the right individual. Only after you've approved the samples should the mailing be dropped. And, once you've started receiving orders back from the mailing, you can always put the live samples into clean envelopes and then stamp and mail them to the subscribers.

It is especially important to follow this procedure whenever a major change is being made—*e.g.*, a move from a hard offer to a soft, a significant change in renewal series, and so on.

Review all subscriber correspondence generated by the fulfillment service at least once a year. Are there form letters for the most common customer inquiries? How quickly does the fulfillment service respond to an inquiry or complaint? How are unusual inquiries handled? What kind of internal monitoring system does the fulfillment service have for quality control? How are you apprised of its performance?

Meet with your fulfillment service annually to review operational policies. Knowing these policies gives you the opportunity to have more control over your account. Areas of interest might include customer-ser-

> There are some gray areas of the fulfillment operation that do not lend themselves to numbers and reports.

vice procedures for refunds, back issues, bad credit/check, customer complaints, duplicate orders, and so on; merge/purge parameters; order processing of new business, renewals, agency orders, gift orders and group subscriptions; arrears policy; backstarting and supplemental issues; how complaints against, or burnout of, customer-service reps is handled; and the procedure to request a new account rep.

Show up at your own mailings to review live samples. Nothing is more effective than the presence of a client to guarantee quality service. If you or your staff can't do this, and/or your fulfillment service is out of state, hire part-time staff or a consultant to be your on-site representative. This can be especially effective if you feel you are the small fish in the big pond. Whether that person is used to review live samples hot off the line or to negotiate better service, an on-site watchdog guarantees you attention and immediate action.

It is imperative that you not allow your fulfillment operation to control you. Take responsibility—now— for the proper treatment of your subscribers, for monitoring service quality, and for ensuring that instructions are being followed. If you wait until you hear about a problem from a subscriber, you're too late. It might just mean your ship is sinking. ☐

Your Fulfillment Service: Resource Central

BY CHRIS KALAMON

I had a scare a few months ago. I was talking to a data-entry company that wanted to expand to include full-service fulfillment. During a discussion about double postcards, the president remarked that my comment about mailing them first class at 19 cents or less was incorrect. According to him, his clients were mailing postcards at the first-class letter rate, and he was certain that was the postal requirement.

For a nanosecond, my heart skipped a beat. Did the Postal Service really change the rate and forget to tell me and my fulfillment service? Visions of being shipped off to postal prison floated by. Then I realized that this company I was working with saw fulfillment as a one-dimensional service, and was in for a rude awakening.

Just to double-check, however, I immediately called my fulfillment company and spoke with their postal expert. He assured me that the rates hadn't changed (and then asked for the name of the above company so he could avoid doing business with them).

That's the kind of quick, accurate response I need to do my job effectively. I've come to rely on my fulfillment service for this kind of valuable information—and you should, too.

Circulation is now, more than ever, a revenue-producing department. And as this trend escalates, so will the need for fast and accurate information. Most circulation departments are understaffed and can barely handle the daily tasks of direct marketing, distribution, newsstand and fulfillment. That's why it is important that we take complete advantage of the resources available to us. One of these resources is the fulfillment company.

The following are some ways to access vital information through your fulfillment service and make your fulfillment company an extension of your circulation team.

Your personal postal expert: Your fulfillment company is a hotbed of postal information. Given the enormous volume of postal paperwork they generate annually, fulfillment services can't afford to lose touch with the permutations of the Postal Service. And their expertise includes first-, second- and third-class regulations. Call them first when you have a postal question, or would like another interpretation of a certain regulation. If they can't answer your question immediately, they usually know someone who can. And because they are familiar with the nuances of your file, they can personalize the answer to meet your particular needs.

For example, we have one publication that mails third class, and we didn't want to ruin the cover with the indicia. Our fulfillment service solved the problem by working with us and generating the indicia right on the label.

Remember, your fulfillment company is privy to the many creative ways that other publishers survive all the rules and regulations. This wealth of information can be a lifesaver when you have a problem to resolve.

A partner in promotion: Make your fulfillment company part of the process when you are designing your magazine's invoices, renewals and even its direct-mail promotions. An extra set of eyes reviewing the important parts of your promotional material is always welcome, and can prevent many headaches from developing later on in the process.

Your account representative can make sure that the correct amount of space is available for any computer-generated messages, for example, and that the postal information is correct and placed properly (thereby avoiding delivery delays and/or higher processing rates).

Once the design is completed and approved, ask your fulfillment company to bid on the printing, especially for bills and renewals. Fulfillment companies get print quotes quickly and easily, and usually at a good price. The volume of work that they handle gives them the power to negotiate costs. And sometimes they can

> It's important to take complete advantage of the resources available to you. One of those resources is the fulfillment company.

match you up with another client who is printing at the same time, giving you both access to even lower per-thousand costs. And wherever you print, be sure always to request that an extra set of bluelines be sent to your account representative for one final double-check.

Get assistance with your documentation: Fulfillment companies can prepare publisher's statements. And in most cases, it makes sense that the statement be prepared by the people who maintain and store your data. If you're currently preparing your publisher's statement in-house, find out if your company can do this for you. You'll still have the opportunity to review the statement and make changes and corrections. It's just a lot easier for the fulfillment company to access the data and generate the appropriate reports.

Taking it one step further, ask your audit company to conduct the audit at the site of the fulfillment company. The data and original orders stay in one place, minimizing confusion and risk of loss. And the auditor can call you if there are any questions and/or missing pieces in the audit trail.

There are many other ways that your fulfillment company can help you. For example, we currently have our fulfillment service handling our retail accounts for us. They generate labels, handle invoicing and account reconciliation, and set up new accounts through our toll-free number.

Fulfillment companies also know quite a lot about selective binding, building a database, up-selling subscriptions and much, much more.

An extension of your staff

It's important that you start thinking of your fulfillment company as an extension of your staff. Accord them all the courtesy and respect you give your staff, and keep them informed about your file's activity. Use them to help double-check your work, just as you double-check their work.

Finally, never be afraid to ask your fulfillment company for advice: They usually know more than you think. ☐

What's Behind the Newsstand Malaise

BY DIANE CYR

It takes a middle-aged woman wielding an understuffed wallet to bring an $800 million corporation to its knees. She's the woman K-III Communications was after when it launched its short-lived *True News* in November 1992. Backed by its own ample dollars, New York City-based K-III loaded checkout racks with the tabloid, then stood back to collect its $1.49 from an expected 300,000 targeted female buyers.

Target females, however, resisted—in astonishing numbers. At 391 Connecticut newsstands carrying 2,960 issues of *True News,* exactly 211 copies left the racks. The remaining 2,749 paid a visit to the shredder. And that's healthy compared to December, when only 151 readers coughed up the $1.49. K-III, after deducting costs for its national distributor, wholesaler and retailer, collected less than $200 for its 6,000-copy blitz.

An extreme incident, perhaps, but not isolated in the precarious world of newsstand sales. Even titles like *Time* and *Cosmopolitan* take wild rides at newsstands every month. For most of the rest of the 3,000 or so titles on 180,000 newsstands nationwide, sell-through is just three to five out of 10, hitting bigger numbers only with the occasional Charles-and-Di, swimsuit or "10 Best" hype.

Wasteful process

Beyond the economic problems associated with magazine newsstand distribution, poor sell-through means big waste. Even if the top 130 newsstand titles sell six out of 10 of their newsstand copies, they're still shredding an average of 52 million magazines per month, or nearly four billion pages. Add up a year's unsold newsstand copies nationwide, and it comes to about 600,000 tons, according to the Magazine Publishers of America.

This raises some obvious questions: If sell-through is dropping, why not just put fewer copies on the newsstand? Or, why not sell magazines as one would just about every other store commodity—on a non-returnable basis? Interesting ideas—but not too workable. For instance, if magazines were sold outright to retailers, there'd be no way to verify circulation—and your Audit Bureau of Circulations pink sheet would have about as much legitimacy as a Bazooka Joe gum wrapper. Second, putting out fewer copies, without analysis of store-by-store sales, is risky—and could lead to worse efficiency if your copies begin drowning under your competitors' titles.

The fact is, the average small-circulation title sells about two copies per month per retail outlet, and needs at least six or seven copies to maintain decent rack position. And not too many parties care about the waste: Retailers sell magazines on guaranteed return, meaning it's no risk to them to take too many titles. Distributors want the exposure for their titles, and so do publishers, for whom those tiny sales add up. "There are some publishers who can live on 15 to 20 percent sell-through and make money," says Frank Herrera, president of New York City-based Hearst/ICD, the distribution arm of the media conglomerate.

The good news is that most of the magazine bodies now carted off the racks end up recycled. A relatively new market has opened up for recycling coated paper into newsprint. About two dozen U.S. paper plants have begun using "flotation technology," which typically combines 30 percent coated magazine paper with 70 percent newsprint to generate recycled newsprint. Currently, wholesalers now truck about 75 to 85 percent of their shreddings directly to these processing centers, according to Nancy Risser, president of an environmental consulting group. But that's only a silver lining. The cloud remains: Industry-wide, newsstand sell-through continues to erode. "Twenty years ago," says David Maisel, partner, Publishing Management Services, a New York City-based newsstand consulting firm, "approximate sell-through [percentage] was somewhere in the mid 50s. Today I'm going to estimate it as somewhere in the mid to low 40s."

MPA is also concerned about newsstand erosion. "I don't want to say it's a crisis, but whenever there's a slow continual decline in sales, one has to be concerned," says Michael Pashby, MPA senior vice president. "For the last three or four years, cover prices haven't increased—and with unit sales declining, for the first time that means revenues are going down in the single-copy area. That alone has made people sit up and say we have do something."

All of this has more and more magazine-industry observers wondering again whether there's something seriously wrong with the magazine distribution business. The wasteful single-copy sales system needs to change its ways, many believe. There are no easy answers, and there probably is no radical solution. Following, however, is an exploration of the roots of the distribution woes, along with some ideas for improving things.

Roots of the decline in newsstand

The first thing that bears noting is what's hurting efficiency, and why. Here are the main culprits.

Too many magazines. Recession or no, magazine entrepreneurship continues unabated. In 1992, according to new-magazine maven Samir Husni, who produces *Samir Husni's Guide to New Consumer Magazines* (published by *Folio:*), 679 new consumer titles were launched, most landing on newsstands already bursting with hundreds of titles. "In the eighties, there were 1,700 titles handled by wholesalers," says John Harrington, president of the New York City-based Council for Periodical Distributors Association. "Today, it's 3,300."

Deteriorating relationships. For years, newsstand cover-price proceeds have been divided up using a fairly consistent formula: For each magazine sold, 5 to 7 percent of the cover price goes to the national distributor, which organizes distribution nationwide; 20 percent goes to the regional wholesaler, which trucks the titles and handles returns, and 20 percent goes to the retailer, who usually also collects an additional 10 percent retail display allowance (RDA) from the publisher after sale. That leaves the publisher with 43 to 53 percent of the cover price, depending on the RDA.

"Nobody's making the money they used to make," says George Lennox, operations director for Murdoch Magazines Distribution division. Publishers aren't raising cover prices, which hurts everyone's profits. Some, like Hachette Filipacchi's *Woman's Day* and Time Inc.'s *People,* have unilaterally lowered the wholesalers' discount; others, like the rest of the Time Inc. weeklies, have established a lower discount base with "incentive" points offered to wholesalers for on-time payments or special services.

At the same time, publishers anxious to make ratebase are pushing more copies onto wholesalers; overburdened wholesalers then withhold copies they believe won't sell—later filing a return for credit. Retailers, faced with bulging racks and their own cash binds, often return titles for credit weeks before the end-of-sale date.

Too many stores. Walk into your average mega-supermarket and you'll see 20, 30, even 40 checkout lanes—each, most likely, with its own magazine rack. That means in one store alone, Hachette Filipacchi's *Elle,* say, has to hold a pocket on dozens of racks. Multiply that by the number of recently emerged chain supermarkets, drugstores and discount stores, and you see falling efficiency. "It used to be that a famous title like *Cosmo* sold 90 percent every month," says Harrington. "Today, you've got about the same number of copies that sell, but the efficiency is in the 60s. To get coverage, they've had to put more copies in there."

Too many subscribers. The push for subscriptions "keeps taking more and more readers off the market," insists Derby, Connecticut-based newsstand consultant Ron Scott. "I sell one magazine in the United States with a 50 percent sell-through, and in the United Kingdom, which has no subscribers and just as many magazines, I sell 80 percent of the same magazine." The way Scott sees it, low-ball offers "convince people that newsstand prices are ridiculous," and discourage browsers who might otherwise buy eight or so single copies per year.

Too few field workers. When New York City-based General Media, publisher of, among others, *Penthouse,* whittled away its 16-member field force, the hope was that its national distributor "would pick up certain things our field force did," such as marketing to retailers, according to Joe Gallo, director of newsstand operations. The result? Sell-through has fallen monthly, according to one wholesaler who handles the titles. Despite everyone's good intentions, overburdened wholesalers and distributors aren't likely to keep up as financially strapped publishers increasingly drop their field workers.

Too many "phantoms." One month, a wholesaler's truck driver might decide to "tap" magazine bundles bound for retailers, shorting each one by a few copies that he then resells. Or, a new distributor might show up one day at a retailer with freshly bagged issues of a skin title—slipped off press by a crooked printer. A hefty 65 percent discount, he figures, will buy the retailer's silence.

Sales of these "phantom" magazines, according to one estimate, could account for a third of all magazine sales in the New York area—"but nobody really knows," says Lisa Scott, vice president, general manager, New York City-based Eastern News Distributors. Bundle-tapping is akin to stealing a stick of gum from every candy store in town; it's easy to hide, hard to prove, and quickly adds up. And by extension, each "phantom" sale pads the inefficiency rate. For instance, if a dealer receives 100 bona fide *Playboy*s and 25 stolen ones, then sells 50 and returns 75, *Playboy* sees only a 25 percent efficiency, even though actual sell-through was 40 percent.

Too little interest: Overall, the newsstand business presents a grim picture: overstuffed racks, over-wrought publishers, undersold magazines, outright corruption. Talk to experts in the field, though, and no one recommends radical surgery; unwieldy as it is, the system appears to make money for all parties.

Fixing the problem

Nevertheless, it's clear that the business could benefit from some tinkering, even if only store by store or title by title. Some suggestions follow:

Target your sales. At Danbury (Connecticut) Hospital's news-stand, *Yankee*'s sell-through hits 70 percent month after month, while elsewhere it's closer to 40 percent, says Andrea Bisson, customer relations manager, for Waterbury, Connecticut-based wholesaler Yankee News. The reason? Danbury insists on a restricted, authorized list of titles. Store clerks closely monitor what's selling and who's buying; they keep the shelves uncrowded and neatly arranged; and they tell the wholesaler exactly which magazines they want each month, and how many copies of each.

In 1993, additional data-collecting relief arrived in the form of PRIM (Periodical Retail Information Management), a service that collects chain-wide sales data among wholesalers. "It will help get low-level data in the hands of the right people," says Richard Lawton, president of Time Distribution Service (TDS). "PRIM is the best solution we've seen in a long time."

Tune your draw. One of the holy writs of the newsstand is that the smaller the draw, the lower the sell-through. Sounds contradictory, but consider: A mass-market title like New York City-based Condé Nast Publications' *Glamour* can count on a fairly large, predictable sale, meaning that a retailer can receive 100 copies, sell at a 50 to 70 percent efficiency, and still maintain good rack position with the remaining copies. But if the same retailer wants a 50 percent sell-through on *Walking*, which might sell three copies per month, a six-copy draw will quickly suffocate under the myriad other small titles on the mainline. Perhaps one copy of six will sell, per-haps two—and efficiency erodes.

Still, according to Susan Allyn, Time Inc.'s director

> Low-ball subscription offers "convince peo-ple that newsstand prices are ridiculous," says consultant Ron Scott.

of marketing information and finance for consumer marketing, even small publishers can tune the draw for better efficiency. While at *Bon Appetit* (then owned by Los Angeles-based Knapp Communications and now a property of Condé Nast), Allyn restricted and expanded draw according to seasonality studies, giving bigger draws to, say, November and December issues. She also continually analyzed sales information in top markets—collected by the magazine's national distributor—and eliminated weaker outlets during the magazine's slower sales months. As a result, she says, monthly sales increased from about 110,000 to 127,000, while sell-through surged from 36 percent to 47 percent in one year. "We printed fewer copies and sold more," she says. "What a concept!"

Push for more space. Say what you will about magazines' healthy profit margins—down at Avenue News in Greenwich, Connecticut, owner Nick Kurji says magazines take up half the real estate in his store, but bring in only 20 per-cent of the profits. So why does he continually fuss with the racks? "Magazines bring in a lot of traffic," he says. "People come in and then say, 'Oh, they have a deli.' Then they buy sandwiches and sodas." Armed with this and other tales of magazine benefits, publishers and wholesalers have been lobbying for bigger racks and an expansion of the periodical section that will conse-quently improve sales and efficiency.

Create incentives. Whenever there's a need to goose single-copy sales, Beverly Hills, California-based Flynt Distributing Company, for one, offers wholesalers boun-ties of up to $5 for each new dealer that takes on *Hustler*. Similarly, *Bon Appetit* twice created optional incentive programs for wholesalers who wanted to reach specific sales goals.

Improve editorial. Even the best display won't compen-sate for a poor magazine, as the *True News* fiasco amply demonstrates. On the other hand, a standout magazine will sell even on a crowded newsstand. In fact, consultant Scott claims, "We can show you how to design a maga-zine for just one-third of the cover showing." As Scott puts it, "A publisher will tell me, 'I have terrible sell-through.' I'll say, 'What was your best-selling issue?' He'll say, 'Well, we had one issue that sold 55 percent.'

"Now, whose fault is that?" Scott continues. "The sys-tem worked fine when the reader wanted to buy it!" □

Smart Distribution Tactics
For Small-Circulation Publishers

BY LAMBETH HOCHWALD

Roger Sandon, editor and publisher of Seattle-based *Café Olé*, is living the dream of every small-circulation magazine owner who ever wanted to take a magazine national. Five years ago he was publishing a Seattle-focused giveaway about coffee. Through a joint venture with Northbrook, Illinois-based ADS Publisher Services, his monthly title—still focused on human-interest stories about coffee and coffee-growing countries—will be targeting chain coffee shops like Starbucks and supermarkets beginning in May. It's likely that the magazine will soon appear at cafés in Borders and Barnes & Noble bookstores, as well.

As the coffee craze crests, ADS plans to distribute 110,000 copies of *Café Olé* on newsstands by the end of 1995—up from the paltry 10,000 issues once targeted to subscribers, local specialty bookstores and trade shows. As a distributor specializing in niche titles, ADS has invested in *Café Olé*'s future by paying for its mass-market presence, according to Harvey Wasserman, ADS' co-founder and CEO. ADS gives the coffee monthly an advance and pays to print the additional 100,000 copies, with the hope that sales of the $3.95 monthly will balance the printing cost.

Unfortunately, Sandon's experience is still more vain hope than reality for small publishers trying to make the mass-market leap. The large national distributors have been deluged with too many requests for too little newsstand space, and they've become more cautious about taking on untested titles.

But it's not all bad news for small-circulation titles. With readers' interests becoming more and more narrowly focused, strategically distributed specialty magazines are gaining a toehold in the retail market. Distributors that specialize in small magazines are fighting to get more exposure for smaller titles both in the traditional newsstand setting and in alternative retail outlets.

As for *Café Olé*, Sandon says that with ADS' support, total pages per issue will double from 48 to 96 on average in the coming months. "I'm very excited about this because the circulation increase is high," he says, adding that the monthly will place coffee or flavoring samples in polybags to further hype its newsstand debut. "With

ADS paying for the extra copies, I can now make the transition to newsstand sales without having to do it on the backs of our advertisers."

Rules for going retail

On a smaller scale, other independent publishers are exploring ways to take their titles into selected national locations, having already tested them regionally and gotten a strong response. For these small-circulation magazines, linking with an experienced distributor that treats their publications as extensions of its own business is often the best deal.

But first, special-interest titles must know exactly where they want to be, and belong, in the retail environment. This can be complicated, especially if a title is trailblazing an undefined category—like New Age topics—making it tough for distributors to know where it might belong on the racks.

"Try to figure out what's appropriate," says Martin Sadler, national sales director at Rider Circulation Services, Inc. (RCS), a three-year-old Los Angeles-based company with 40 magazine clients whose distribution numbers range from 3,000 to 330,000 copies. "Do you want to be in all 7-11s or is your magazine better suited to high-end bookstores?"

Finding a lucrative outpost hinges on the title's viability in terms of newsstand appeal and whether the editorial subject has already flooded the market. Successful placement also depends on the strength of sales volume in a particular region or local market. Without these results in hand, the publisher of a small-circulation title will have a hard time getting a distributor interested in marketing the title to a retailer—the first step in finding a place on the racks.

Other factors come into play, too. Some distributors have policies that prevent them from accepting any magazine with pornographic content, for example, while others are wary of working with tabloid-size or newsprint-based magazines. "We're solicited by 15 to 20 titles a week," says RCS' Sadler. Each is evaluated in terms of content, cover price and page count as it compares to competitors in the same category. "We'll take on two. We want to get magazines that will sell and have a strong financial base. We don't want to distribute one or two issues and then have it fall down."

Publishers also must know how many copies they want distributed, and keep their sell-through as high as possible. "Smaller magazines generally cost more to produce and have a higher cover price," says Lisa Scott, vice president and general manager of New York City-based Eastern News Distributors, a single-copy-sales distributor serving national and international markets. "It's best to put out three issues for every two you sell. You don't need to have 10 on hand to sell two. That way, waste is limited."

Then, a magazine has to be able to print enough pages to match its competitors. "New, underfinanced magazines don't have enough money to print enough pages to compete with existing ones," says ADS' Wasserman. "Say there are three competitors with over 200 pages and the new one can only afford to print 80 pages. It's very difficult to go on the newsstand, since ultimately the consumer doesn't know you're underfinanced. You have to charge enough and hope your cover tells the story."

Low volume, low leverage

Even with all the pieces in place, a distributor may still decline to work with a magazine. "We'll reject it if we don't believe this kind of magazine has had a good history with our customer base, or we can't get a certain quantity," says Fran Salamon, president of La Vergne, Tennessee-based Ingram Periodicals, Inc., a company that distributes over 1,100 special-interest titles. "At the turn of the century, there were 500 titles out there. Now there are 3,500 on the newsstand."

Low sales volume on the newsstand obviously means small-circulation titles have less leverage. They may be turned down by the large distributors—such as ICD/The Hearst Corporation, Kable News Company, Curtis Circulation Company and Warner Publisher Services—that are used to dealing with thousands of copies a month for the magazines they distribute. (Curtis distributes up to two million copies of *Ladies' Home Journal* each month.) "If you do $1 billion a year in billing, why would you want to handle a magazine that brings in $10,000 a year?" asks RCS' Sadler. "We're concerned about the survival of the magazine. If a small-circulation title goes to ICD/Hearst, there isn't the same concern. They're looking for magazines that can make an impact on their billing."

This means big bottom-line differences for distributors, adds Sadler. "When you go in as an independent publisher with a marginal title and the distributor takes 200 copies and sells half, the profit may be only $150 per month," he says. "Compare this to the income generated by 10,000 copies of a magazine with a $4.95 cover price. The wholesaler gets it at $1.98 and bills out at 99 cents. The distributor makes about $1 apiece, or $10,000 a month."

Small-circulation titles are likely to partner with distribution firms that can address their special needs, since the odds are already tough on the single-copy sales front. On average, only 35 percent of all magazines produced are actually sold, according to Sadler. "The top 100 magazines generate 80 percent of everybody's business," he says. "There are so many marginal titles that get eaten up on a national basis. Smaller national distributors like us can give these titles more attention."

Do-it-yourself distribution

Some publishers have brought the distribution function in-house, with some success. In 1993, W.H.

"Butch" Oxendine Jr., publisher and editor in chief of Gainesville, Florida-based *Student Leader,* decided to distribute his national college semiannual independently after the mailing firm he had hired stalled in sending out the October launch issue because of a dispute with United Parcel Service. Oxendine was unaware of the mailers' financial situation until the copies failed to arrive at the universities. Oxendine discovered the issues in boxes at the mailer's warehouse and ended up paying UPS to get the issues to the selected campuses. That's when he decided to handle things in-house.

Today, he sends 115,000 copies to nearly 800 college campuses nationwide. "Three people go to the printer twice a year and box and label the magazines before UPS comes to pick them up," says Oxendine. "It takes all day to get it done. Doing the distribution with another company is time-consuming and costly. We're saving at least $4,000 per shipment, and for a small magazine, that's a lot."

Although it's unlikely that magazines with higher frequencies and newsstand sales would have the time or inclination to manage their own distribution, it presents a big challenge. "Magazines can do their own distribution, but they're not going to be successful at it," says Ingram's Salamon. "I even know of a publisher of a national games magazine with over 100,000 copies per issue who tried to do it alone and then handed over their customer list to us. They told us they were messing up, that they're in the publishing business, not distribution."

Eastern's Scott agrees. "People always try to do it," she says. "The difficulty is the accounting side. The publication has to set up its own infrastructure. Getting people to take the magazine isn't that difficult, but at certain times of the year, the economy tightens and a publisher may find him- or herself devoting a lot of time to collecting money. Publishers usually come to us one year later. You need the distributor to keep your accounting straight."

> As readers' interests become more narrowly focused, strategically distributed specialty titles will gain a stronger foothold.

The added paperwork includes data entry as well as correcting shipping errors when the magazines don't get to the wholesaler. "Claims and tracers have to be filed and billing has to be adjusted," says RCS' Sadler. "The wholesaler has all the numbers in the computer and has to match that number with the national distributor. It gets very complicated, too, when publishers change cover prices, since barcode changes and billing percentages have to be adjusted."

Sadler says the best part of publishers handling their own distribution is the perspective it gives them about the distribution process. "This way, the publisher has empathy down the road for distributors," he says. "It gives the publisher a feel for why a magazine is turned down and an insight into what's going on in the market."

Distributors agree that special-interest magazines have gained clout on the newsstands, but should probably look into targeted retail locations or specialty shops for real sales volume.

"Small magazines don't need to be in the larger outlets. Historically, the waste factor in small-magazine distribution is higher," says Eastern's Scott. "When you negotiate printing contracts based on volume, you can get a better deal printing 500,000 copies than when you print 20,000. You want to sell more to avoid waste in the printing bill."

Keeping that hard-won clout will always be a challenge for small magazines, says Stephen Keen, cofounder and president of ADS. "There are 12 to 16 feet of magazines in supermarkets, and with such a limited amount of space, the toughest challenge is getting magazines to the right place," he says. "A lot are so specialized that they don't deserve to be in a large supermarket. Still, magazines have become more aggressive about marketing and we're getting more and more successful at getting space." □

The Phantom of the Newsstand

BY DIANE CYR

Sometimes, the color of money has flesh tones. Consider the 17 shrink-wrapped pallets of *Penthouse* just unloaded into the cavernous North Bergen, New Jersey, warehouse of Hudson County News, the nation's largest magazine wholesaler. Each pallet holds bundles of 25 copies stacked six wide, three long, six deep. Each copy carries a $4.95 price—which means a single bundle is worth $123.75, a pallet is worth $13,365, and the entire shipment amounts to $227,205 sitting on the warehouse floor.

And that's just a fraction of the nearly one million new copies handled by Hudson every day. Twice a week, Hudson's fleet of 100 trucks fans across New York and New Jersey, visiting 5,000 retailers and delivering and picking up anywhere from $2 million to $3 million worth of 2,000 different titles.

Back at the warehouse—where shifting piles of magazines lay strewn across the floor for 50 yards in any direction—every title is counted, numbered and tagged. "You *have* to be orderly," says Julian Garcia, Hudson's vice president of newsstand sales. He walks through the morass, pointing out alarm systems and scanning devices, tugging on padlocks and gesturing to ceiling-high gates that keep magazines from drifting into the wrong parts of the building or out into an employee's car. "If you don't have an orderly distribution system, how can you control something?"

You can't. Outside the warehouse, across the river in Manhattan, newsstands are rife with any number of "unauthorized" titles, from bagged copies of comic books to skin magazines that appear mysteriously before the on-sale date. How they get there is anybody's guess. Typically, a newsstand title passes through at least eight to 10 hands on its way to the racks: printer to binder to wholesaler to retailer. Any one of those hands can take a title off course, slip a bundle into a car trunk, "miscount" a stack, pull a few copies out of a pile.

It sounds petty, and in most cases, magazine thievery is. Isolated retailers somehow acquire magazines off the street or from bogus distributors, sell them, pocket the cover price and return the legitimate issues for full credit. "It's not a large problem," claims Larry Djerf, *Playboy*'s newsstand sales director. "One mis-sent bundle and one dealer is a pretty micro problem, and it usually happens for a short period of time."

But it's thievery that adds up. Djerf estimates that about 2 to 4 percent of *Playboy*'s returns—whether through error or fraud—"may actually be sales," meaning the dealers sold more than they claim. With newsstand sales of 700,000, and returns of about 50 percent, *Playboy*'s "micro problem" amounts to about $50,000 a month—or $600,000 a year—that the magazine never sees.

"Everybody forgets, these magazines have two- and three-dollar cover prices," says Frank Herrera, president of Manhattan-based ICD/Hearst. "That's like dollar bills just floating around on the street."

In the past, the big rip-offs mainly occupied the New York area, with its long history of corrupt union drivers. But as East Coast wholesalers have begun tuning up their systems, the theft has spread outward and the problem has turned national. "You're now finding this

> Where mistakes are the norm, rip-offs are tempting—and easy. "It doesn't take a genius to figure out that if one bundle gets pushed, that's a lot of money."

in Kansas and Montana," says Jim Gustafson, vice president, sales and marketing for LFP Inc., the Beverly Hills-based publisher of *Hustler*. "It's wherever there's a major metropolitan area."

Compared to other retail goods, magazines are a unique headache, drawing small-time crooks as pesky as gnats and just as hard to swat. "Is there a mass conspiracy going on?" asks newsstand consultant Ron Scott. "There isn't. Are there all kinds of little leaks in a business as big as this? Of course there are."

For one thing, magazines are returnable. Retailers who don't sell out a title can send it back for credit. In other words, 10 stolen copies of *People*, marked at, say, half price, make a tempting carrot to dangle in front of a retailer who can always return for full credit what isn't sold.

Moreover, mistakes do happen. Missing boxes of titles are "quite frequent" in shipments from printing plant to wholesaler, says Tony Murri, traffic manager for Warner Publisher Services in New York City. "Most of the time, we find that the [shipment] hasn't been shipped, or the trucking company lost the goods."

In the same way, shortages are the norm from wholesalers to dealers. In one Manhattan store, a retailer pulls out a note he made on the delivery form, claiming he was shorted 12 *Billboards* and 25 *Esquires*. In another, a manager busily amends his own form, showing five missing *Penthouses*. "Sometimes they credit you," he says, "sometimes they don't."

Garcia says that Hudson instructs all retailers to count and verify every delivery before signing the driver's form. But dealers say they can count only boxes, not individual titles. "The driver is never gonna give me a chance to look through this—he's backed up to the sidewalk," notes the manager of one downtown Manhattan store. Often, the wholesaler ends up paying credit for the shortage and passing it on to the publisher.

Weeklies are an even bigger headache because their tight delivery schedules force wholesalers to send them out loose, with the driver counting them out dealer by dealer. If there's a shortfall, the retailer eats the loss; in the case of an overcount, the publisher pays, since the retailer generally keeps quiet, sells the extra titles and pockets the price.

Where mistakes are the norm, rip-offs are tempting—and easy. As Gustafson notes, "It doesn't take a genius to figure out that if one bundle gets pushed aside, that's worth a lot of money."

Victims and culprits

So, who's ripping off whom? Big victims, naturally, are skin books, where the high price and timeless nature of

---

■ Fraud prevention: What publishers can do to plug the holes

Know if you're vulnerable. If you've got a low-priced title or one with few newsstand sales, consider yourself safe. It's much easier, and more profitable, to "tap" bundles of *Cosmo* than *Modern Drummer*.

Check your sell-through. Pay close attention to unusual patterns in returns, such as whether a retailer suddenly begins sending back more copies than usual, or more than nearby retailers. Some dealers will even try to return more copies than they received in the first place—a dead giveaway.

Visit wholesalers. Jim Gustafson, vice president, sales and marketing, for *Hustler* publisher LFP Inc., regularly drops in on large wholesalers, evaluating security systems and seeing firsthand how magazines are checked in, scanned, packed, returned and shredded. Visiting publishers should look for shredding on premises, proper supervision at entrances and exits, and reliable, consistent procedures for dealing with drivers' shortages, miscounts and suspect returns. Similarly, publishers should double-check printer security, although sources say printer theft and fraud is rare.

Get your national distributor involved. Your national distributors can act on your behalf with wholesalers in case of problems. In one instance of chronic shortages, *Newsweek* had its distributor follow a wholesaler's routes. Distributors will also audit shipments from printer to wholesaler, or gather information to help publishers prosecute cases of theft.

Code your titles. From time to time, *Hustler* instructs its printer to place a special code within certain copies to mark the originating wholesaler (at a cost of about $3,000 per 100,000 copies). Later, the magazine's field force spot-buys copies from retailers and sends them to *Hustler*'s attorneys, who check for the code. (Only the attorneys, the printer and Gustafson know where to find it.) "It's like random drug testing," Gustafson explains. *Playboy* also occasionally uses codes, and the title's field reps check retailers for bagged copies, early-sale issues, or whether, for instance, a New England advertising edition wrongly ends up in a New York store.

Close loopholes. *Newsweek*, for one, has begun creating small 10-copy bundles at its bindery in the hope of cleaning up counting errors during "loose" deliveries. Newsstand consultant Ron Scott tells how publishers eliminated one fraud ring simply by having certain wholesalers count actual bundles instead of pallets when magazine deliveries arrived. "When the driver knew he was going to get caught, he stopped. You take out the profit, and you put an end to the problem."

---

the editorial create a sizable black market, or "aftermarket," for out-of-date issues. Bogus distributors often bag stolen copies of recognizable titles, such as *Club* or *Hustler*, with less expensive books or foreign publications, selling them in "Valu-Paks" for $10 to $20. "It's a distribution subculture," says Gustafson. "I've heard stories of zealous businessmen who operate from the trunks of their automobiles."

Also ripe for the picking are titles with high sell-throughs. That's because a high sell-through usually means a big draw—and the bigger the draw, the more room there is to fool around with the numbers on the return form. For example, a dealer who usually sells 60 or 70 copies of *Cosmo* out of a 100-copy draw can easily pad the form with 10 phony returns.

Talk to just about anyone in the system, and he'll claim he's a victim of someone else's rip-off. Retailers complain about unfair shortages and unsympathetic wholesalers. "Today, I was one or two papers short," says one Manhattan retailer. "I called three times, and every time I got an answering machine. What are you gonna do?" Adds Michael Pashby, senior vice president, consumer marketing for the Magazine Publishers of America: "The retailer in the building I was in stopped carrying magazines because he was always shorted."

Wholesalers claim that dealers falsify return forms. "If somebody buys 10 copies of *Time* and sells out, then buys two on the street and returns them, it would be very difficult for me to enforce that," says James Cohen, executive vice president of Hudson County News.

Some say truck drivers are the usual cheats, putting aside copies or "tapping" bundles—that is, slipping one or two out—in order to supply certain customers on their routes. As one Manhattan retailer puts it, "Some dealers always ask [drivers], 'You got anything extra for me?' Let's say he's got 50 extra [copies of] *People* by the end of his route. The [dealer] will pay for 25, get the other 25 for free, and the driver pockets the money."

Other times, "it could be the guy who's supposed to destroy the product who puts it aside and at night throws it in his trunk," Herrera suggests. "Or it could be the guy who handles returns."

With so many players involved, it's nearly impossible to pin down the actual crime. "You can see it," says Herrera, "but finding where the magazines come from is the big problem."

In one case of stolen comics, Hearst followed a paper trail through four corporations, Herrera recalls. "We

found a trucking company in New Jersey that had since gone out of business, and a retailer in Maryland that had since gone out of business. We estimated losses in the millions of dollars, and we were never able to come back to the source of the product. It's like chasing a phantom."

The good news is that while prosecution hasn't worked, prevention is finally starting to have an effect. In recent years, wholesaler consolidation has led to "more consistent service and quality," says Richard Lawton, senior vice president for Manhattan-based Time Distribution Services. Generally, that means bigger wholesalers have the muscle to employ tighter security, have more disciplined drivers and more clout with errant retailers.

In addition, publishers ranging from *Hustler* to *Newsweek* are tightening controls on shortages and losses, using codes and other methods to track magazines. Meanwhile, wholesalers like Hudson have put in place computer systems that automatically reject suspect return claims. "Since we instituted the system, we've saved several million dollars," says Cohen, who estimates that losses now amount to about $15,000 on returns of $1.5 million to $2 million weekly.

The bad news is that rip-offs have spread to other titles. In the past, only skin books and comics got hurt. These days, as publishers like *Hustler* crack down, it's possible to find bagged issues of gardening titles, crossword puzzles and even computer books. "There are now more magazines dealt this way than there used to be," says Herrera.

The potential for mistakes has grown, too. "More wholesalers are loose-delivering more titles than they did before," Lawton points out. "A lot of new publications coming out are demanding on-time delivery and late printing schedules." That adds up to more counting errors—and more room for cheating.

Clearly, given the nature of the business, it's no place for an honor system. Some years back, *Playboy* tried putting copies in vending boxes in New York City parking garages, hoping to pick up sales from men waiting for their cars. Sure enough, all the copies in the prototype machine sold out in one day. "And when we opened up the box," Herrera recalls, "we had exactly one dollar and fifty cents inside."

Cohen, hearing the story, heaves a sigh. "Trust," he says, "is not something you work on in this business." □

What Premium on On-cover Premiums?

BY DAVID GARRATT

Cover-mounted publishing premiums have been around in the United Kingdom in a big way for some time, and in many ways have pre-empted editorial differentiation in the battle for readers' minds and money. Champions of editorial integrity have protested against such a cheapening of attitude, but they are fighting a losing battle.

Imagine, if you will, the creative and logistical challenges in cover-mounting the following, all of which have appeared as premiums on U.K. newsstand magazines in the recent past: golf balls, baby pampas grass, gardening gloves, a garden trowel, a can of regular-size dog food and a full-size garden seed tray. All these examples of "premium art" have been sourced and haggled down in price for one reason and one reason alone: to encourage potential readers to buy the magazines to which they are attached.

Today, the major users of cover premiums in the United Kingdom are the computer-title publishers. The explosion of magazines in this market sector has created a need for differentiation between titles with very similar names. Very quickly, the first enterprising publishers cover-mounted a free computer disk. The entire sector followed this lead in a matter of weeks. The situation then escalated to a point where two free disks became a standard premium—and some publishers even began cover-mounting three.

Launches are the other primary arena in which cover premiums have become key players. There has been a marked change in the United Kingdom away from heavyweight television advertising campaigns at a title's launch toward a much greater emphasis on "total packaging" at point of sale. For many years, the perceived wisdom when launching a new publication in the United Kingdom was to spend in excess of £500,000 on above-the-line promotion. Since the late eighties, however, publishers have devoted far more of their research and resources to creative "launch-package" strategies. Launches such as *Essentials, Me* and *Homes & Ideas,* for example, all published by IPC, part of the Reed Elsevier group, featured high-value launch gifts—either a binder, a clipboard or a relevant book.

Whilst this strategy caused some display problems in-store, the consensus has been that the high perceived added value that such gifts conferred had an immediate and beneficial effect on the sales of the launch issues. Moreover, the accountants were happier. As the old adage runs, "You know that half of your advertising budget is wasted— you just don't know which half." In the case of cover-premium marketing, however, you know the results directly from the shelf. And thanks to electronic point-of-sale information, you know it in real time. In other words, we are comparing a very focused reach with unfocused blasting—a rifle compared to a shotgun.

Words to the wise

However, there are as always the usual traps and pitfalls for the unwary. Sensible cover-premium marketers have followed a number of simple rules to maximize return:

The premium must have relevance. As with appropriate cover subjects and coverlines, the gift must be attractive to the "floating voter" purchaser. A premium that lacks perceived relevance to either the publication or purchaser can be a positive deterrent to purchase.

The premium must have perceived value. Any gift that will tip the balance in the potential prospect's mind must possess an intrinsic value worthy of consideration. Cheap and nasty premiums have a zero effect on peripheral sales and serve only to cheapen the host title's image.

The premium must have longevity. The gift will have to withstand a great deal of handling during its life to and from the shelf. It is vital that the manufacturing standards be up to the mark. One U.K. publisher who bought a cheap supply of hair shampoo sachets for cover-mounting purposes suffered the loss of the entire issue when the sachets burst during distribution. A low-cost deal is often best avoided.

Enclosed premiums need special attention. When the premium is enclosed with the publication—in a polybag, for example—particular care must be taken with the sell-copy promotion on the pack. A polybag, by definition, means that the premium cannot be examined without the package being torn open—an act that really commits the prospect to purchase. Consequently, the sell message on the bag itself must be of sufficient strength to do the job.

What lessons does all this hold for the American magazine publisher? Given the mirror-image make-up of the two countries' magazine markets, do on-cover premiums have a part to play in the promotion of U.S. consumer titles?

There is no question that the cover-mount concept is less widely practiced in the United States than in the United Kingdom—a result largely of the fundamental differences in the roots of the two marketplaces. However, there has to be a cogent argument in favor of testing the approach, either by wholesaler territory, retail chain or other relevant criterion.

There is increasing evidence in the United Kingdom that bind-in and blow-in cards are becoming detested by retailers because of the litter they cause in the stores. Rumor has it that retailers in the United States

U.S. publishers might consider relevant cover mounts as an alternative to ultra-discounted subscription blow-in cards.

feel the same way. American publishers might consider, then, relevant and well-attached cover mounts as an alternative to the ultra-discounted subscription offers on their blow-in and bind-in cards as a way to coax potential readers to sample their magazines.

There is one further—major—reason why American publishers may wish to experiment more with the cover-premium option. Indeed, it is a reason that is fast becoming an international concern: the rapidly rising costs of coated paper. The levels of newsstand waste in the United States have already reached proportions that few other countries' magazine industries could support. There are compelling commercial and environmental reasons to reduce these levels to more acceptable proportions. Sales efficiency on the U.S. newsstand has to be a priority. Why not consider printing less and promoting more in a controlled test environment to evaluate the options? The alternative is continued high waste and even higher waste-paper prices, which can only exacerbate the "deficit publishing" syndrome practiced by too many already.   □

Call Center Choices

BY LAMBETH HOCHWALD

Telemarketing is becoming more of a necessity than a luxury—more than 70 percent of publishers are tapping into it, according to DMA surveys. So your choice of call center is critical to the success of your campaign, and your magazine. "Our rising telemarketing efforts have everything to do with rising postal costs," says Sheila Sullivan, circulation manager of Fairchild Publications' *Supermarket News.* "We mail a double postcard, the cheapest thing you can put in the mail. Then we go the phones."

Dick Marzella, circulation director of Avcom Publishing Ltd., the Woodland Hills, California-based publisher of such titles as *Surfing, Car Audio and Electronics* and *Audio Video Interiors,* says telemarketing works well, especially for the more elusive renewals. "I skim off the cream with direct mail," he says. "Afterwards, when I've gotten the easy renewal, I start telemarketing. I wait for those numbers to come back in, and then I go back in with a final direct-mail effort."

To facilitate the process of finding a call center, some publishers (even those *with* telemarketing experience) partner with a broker to shop for the most cost-effective telemarketer. To set up a campaign is often double the cost of a direct-mail effort.

Supermarket News, a 52,000-circulation paid title, launches two annual efforts that involve 10,000 calls over a 10-week period. Sullivan says working with a consultant cuts down on the stress. "We know within the first few days of a campaign whether we're in the right place," she says. "That's the beauty of using a broker. If the campaign isn't working, we can switch locations."

Seek and ye shall find

Whatever path you take, plan on at least a full month of fact-finding. Be realistic about what each call center can do for you. "Look at the size of the telemarketing company," advises Gail Stone, president of New York City-based PTM Communications International, a firm that places and manages telemarketing campaigns (her firm counts Fairchild as a client). Some companies require a 100,000-call minimum, she explains. "If you're doing a huge program, you want a company that can handle the volume. If your program isn't big enough for DialAmerica or Neodata, you have to look for a smaller company."

Bob Lewis, vice president of sales and marketing at Peoria, Illinois-based Magazine Marketplace Telemarketing, which currently works with 150 magazine clients, says many publishers test a firm, at least initially: "Publishers will give us half of their list to test and half to another firm, to see whether one firm outperforms the other on a consistent basis. In certain cases, firms put their best people on a test. They'll run out of the best people once you sign on as an account."

Take a close look at the pool of telephone reps manning the lines—throughout the day. "A lot of companies hire part-time college students who come in when they can, which may not coincide with the time your program is going on," says Stone. "It's often hard to get that consistency."

The rest of the selection process comes down to the nitty-gritty details, like cross-referencing several companies and interviewing each one. "I also suggest looking into how the call center is set up, including the ratio of supervisors to telephone service reps and how long people have worked there. The longer they stay, the better they are at selling," Stone says. "It's important to check out whether the firm has any full-time people on staff at all."

The check is in the mail

Budgeting for a call center depends largely on your magazine's circulation. While consumer publishers aim to make as many calls as possible, business-to-business titles want to make contacts within a specified audience. "You will get more people turning you down in consumer titles than business-to-business," says Stone.

So plan your billing strategy before you sign any contracts. You have three choices: Pay your call center on an hourly basis; opt for a remit cost basis where the telemarketer makes the calls, sends out invoices and collects payment before remitting a portion back to the publisher; or pay on a commission basis, where the telemarketing firm makes the calls and mails the first invoice before turning collection over to the publisher. "Some of the bigger publishers prefer to be billed hourly because if the call center makes numerous calls, they will get a fair hourly rate for their work," Stone says.

Telemarketing costs are evaluated just like direct mail , says Lewis. "We're evaluated on a cost-per-net-order—meaning how well people pay up—and we're evaluated just like a mail campaign. If you do telemarketing in-house, you have phone number-look-up costs and other expenses to factor in—just as you would factor in postage and paper. The more sophisticated publishers just include it in their budgets."

The customer always rules

Every satellite service provider should act as an extension of the magazine's day-to-day business, say the experts. "Telephone service reps have to have extensive product knowledge to give the prospect the feeling that the rep knows the product and is part of the company," Stone says.

For in-bound calls, the phone rep is often the first person a customer reaches at the magazine. "If that person doesn't welcome the customer, you can lose business," adds Stone. "The reps need to help the prospect as much as possible, so look for a firm that offers sales incentives and contests to inspire its phone reps."

To ensure continuing improvement, monitor calls remotely. Lewis says his firm gets the phone reps and supervisors involved with overall product marketing, requesting that the publisher send promotional items, media kits and copies of the magazine. "We have a customer-service department, and if a reader has a problem or never ordered the magazine, we can go right back to the rep whose name is on the invoice or acknowledgment."

Service improvements can often be as simple as matching telemarketing reps with magazines that address some of their own hobbies. "If we have a hunting magazine and we assign phone reps to the account who like to hunt, we can get better returns."

> "Look for a firm that offers sales incentives and contests to inspire its phone reps."

Avcom's Marzella often places his own name in the phone pool to monitor reps. "When I connect with the telemarketer, sometimes I'll be contentious and see how the operator handles it. Other times I'll order the magazine and check the invoicing," he says. Ordinarily, Avcom uses telemarketing as the sixth effort. "There is a significant difference between outbound calls for renewals versus cold calls for new subscribers. Renewals lend themselves to a more agreeable audience because they're more familiar with the magazine. It's not like trying to explain the product to new customers."

Raise the red flag

Your best bet is to insist on a clause that lets you opt out of any arrangement. "Sign a contract to make sure the testing doesn't continue," says Stone. "It's a problem if you're not getting reports from your service bureau. Telemarketing companies tend not to call if things aren't going well. So, just because you aren't hearing from the firm doesn't mean things are going well."

Check the telemarketer's track record, says Lewis. "If you'd like to get a campaign up and running quickly, make sure your telemarketer isn't going to get around to it a month later," he says. "If it takes one telemarketer three months to call the names another could reach in three weeks, you might not get renewals or make rate-base."

Andrew Smith, president of Boulder, Colorado-based Aspen Media Research Ltd., a research company specializing in telemarketing for controlled titles, points to financial issues as the biggest underlying concern for any publisher, large or small. "The biggest red flag to look at is total numbers and the bottom line," he says. "Advertisers don't want subscribers who have been forced to say yes. So find a call center that takes a more holistic approach. Business depends on the magazine doing well in total, not getting through the next audit. You have to keep quality up year-round." □

Script Your Way to a Successful Guerrilla Campaign

BY LAMBETH HOCHWALD

1. Find a specialist.

Consult with outside telemarketing experts and choose the vendor with the experience and price you can afford. "Get references from the vendor you'd like to work with," says Mark Facey, president of Mark Facey & Company, a Bristol, Connecticut-based telemarketing firm that works with more than 200 controlled-circulation titles. "Telemarketing is an easy business to get into—and therein lie the pitfalls. If you've got a phone and a voice, you can put a business together."

Be sure the company makes an effort to understand your markets, he adds. "We ask for a media kit from every client. We train our interviewers. We try to speak the language of the reader and make the magazine of interest to him."

Of course, it's even better if you already have an existing relationship with certain vendors, says Tim Twerdahl, *Time*'s associate marketing manager. *Time* works with five vendors and has 300 in-house calling stations located in Ocala, Florida. "You need connections, people you can trust," he says.

Finally, make sure the vendor is equipped to deal with your circumstances. "Talk with other clients to make sure that what the telemarketing company tells you is the real world," advises Norma Clousner, director of subscriptions at Woodland Hills, California-based Weider Publications. For Clousner, this meant looking for a firm that could handle a large volume of inbound calls in response to a TV commercial for *Shape* and *Men's Fitness*. "You may feel a telemarketing company has a large staff, but it may not be large enough to handle a huge campaign," she notes.

2. Put your fulfillment house on the team.

Your campaign's success depends on constant, clear communication between your fulfillment house and telemarketer. The fulfillment house generates the subscriber tape and sends it to a company that enhances that list by adding phone numbers. The vendor loads the numbers and starts dialing.

"The strength of the vendor relationship is key," says Twerdahl. "Fulfillment centers may not be used to working with a vendor, and the tape layout might be all wrong. If I were starting a campaign, I would arrange a conference call between the vendor, fulfillment center and myself to make sure things don't fall through the cracks."

It's also a good idea to check regularly with the fulfillment house about the condition of the file and the accuracy of the appended phone numbers.

3. Strategize on your script.

Although some telemarketers offer scripts or dialogue plans in a package deal, campaign veterans prefer to write their own. "We are the best marketers to our customers. I know what works on the phones, and we can do it better," says Weider's Clousner.

> Campaign veterans prefer to write their own scripts. "We are the best marketers to our customers. I know what works, and we can do it better."

The publisher can decide when and if additional subscription savings or premiums should be offered once a person is reached. "When a person calls off a TV ad, we capture that information and try to upsell an additional year of the magazine for a lower rate, or we add a premium," Clousner says.

Review the script with everyone involved. "The vendor should be an expert on legal ramifications, but make sure you're contractually protected in terms of do-not-call regulations," warns Twerdahl. This means running all scripts by your legal counsel and making sure any offer meets Audit Bureau of Circulations requirements.

If you do leave script development up to the service

bureau, ask to see the result. "Publishers should want to see those scripts," says Facey. "They have the right and an obligation to their subscribers to look at them. They should listen in on conversations, too, if it's legal within that state."

4. Insist on testing prior to rollout.

Both publishers and telemarketers stress the necessity of testing a portion of former subscribers or new business prior to calling the entire list. A few days' testing enables publishers to change course quickly if the response level lags or the scripts are ineffective. "You need a pretty good chunk of names, at least 5,000, to test," says Bob Lewis, vice president of sales and marketing for Magazine Marketplace Telemarketing, a Peoria, Illinois-based outbound telemarketing firm. "Out of those 5,000 names, you'll find phone numbers for only about 2,500, and you'll reach only 90 percent. Of those customers, you'll probably sell to only 20 percent."

For smaller circulation titles, about 500 names would make a viable test, since it's likely that the callers would reach only 250, advises Facey.

5. Beware of billing traps.

Telemarketing firms have varying price structures and policies. Try to get the best rate, playing one vendor against another, if necessary, says Twerdahl.

But, warns telemarketer Lewis, "Publishers have to be careful in terms of cost." His firm charges per successful call rather than per hour, or per call itself. "We include everything, but telemarketing firms can charge separately to look up phone numbers, do computer reports, process invoices and write scripts."

Adds Twerdahl: "Some work on commission, others work for about $30 per hour. With after-expire calls, commission makes more sense because you're not going to get high conversion rates. We use our in-house vendor for the most profitable segments to keep money in-house."

Facey believes that telemarketing sales representatives should be paid on a salary basis. "Don't be fooled by low hourly rates," he says. "The real acid test is to ask how employees are paid. Anything other than salary, and you don't want to work with them."

6. Make the offer salable.

Premiums and bonus items must be closely related to the magazine's subject. "A couple of our titles sell 13th issues or similar publications along with subscriptions," says Lewis. "You can't go into any long explanation of a complicated product. So *Gourmet* might have no problem selling signature salt-and-pepper shakers, but might have trouble selling garden items."

Hopefully, an inspiring product will lead the customer to pay for it promptly. "The most important thing is pay-up," says Facey. "If you get a lot of orders and not a lot of pay-up, it could be a money pit for small publishers."

7. If all else fails, set up your own.

You may consider creating an in-house call center. Beverly Hall set one up in 1991 at Stevens Publishing Corporation, a Waco, Texas-based publisher of such titles as *Occupational Health & Safety* and *Environmental Protection*. "Our reps make a minimum of 75 attempts a day, following sales goals based on renewals projected a year in advance," she says. The initial $500,000 investment included equipment, hiring and training. The call center employs six full-time staffers and expects to have 23 permanent phone reps. The company now has an inbound 800-number, as well.

Bringing telemarketing in-house means the telephone sales reps can talk with the editors and ad salespeople. "If a customer has a specific question about the magazine, reps working for an outside vendor might not know the answer," Hall says. "Our publisher and editors are right here. Would you want to outsource articles to freelancers who don't understand the mission statement of the magazine?" □

section five

ad sales

" For the most part, advertisers and agencies **don't fully understand the information** so painstakingly gathered by the audit bureaus."—p. 270

" The realities of the marketplace **ultimately prevail over the fantasies** of internal politics."—p. 272

" You can make automated voice-mail systems an ally instead of having them **be an impediment."**—p. 274

" Every word in your media kit must be aimed at **generating sales."**—p. 276

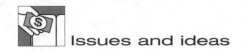

How to Make a Sales Presentation Work

BY JOSH GORDON

Has this ever happened to you? You are in a media director's office pulling out a prepared presentation that your publisher has been hounding you to use. The media director reaches across the table, touches you on the arm, and with a strained smile says, "Look, I don't have a lot of time right now. Can't you just explain it to me in your own words?"

Having seen many of the presentations given in the name of magazines, I can't say that I blame those media directors. To read some how-to books on presentations, you would think that a successful presentation has the salesperson starting at the beginning, overcoming objections from the prospect, managing distractions along the way, and then closing at the end. But the true purpose of a prepared sales presentation is not to give an uninterrupted lecture, but rather to intensify and deepen the selling dialogue.

Think about how much actual face-to-face selling time you get with most clients. Aside from your top accounts, it's possible that you don't get more than a few hours a year. If you can arrive at that call with a well-thought-out presentation, you can focus the dialogue, add proof to the points you make, and cover more ground than if you just showed up and had a spontaneous conversation.

Preparation is the key. Before you put your next presentation together, ask yourself these questions:

Will this presentation encourage communication? Bill Slapin, publisher of *Presentation Products Magazine*, offers this advice about good presentations: "Don't create a presentation just to make a presentation. Create it to help the communication process. A presentation is a communication, and the media used should reflect this. If you are presenting to a group at an agency, a slide presentation could be extremely effective, but if you were to show up at a one-on-one lunch with the same presentation, it would be overkill."

Does the presentation encourage two-way dialogue? If your publisher gives you the option, pick a presentation format that will maximize interaction. Overhead transparencies, color slides, flip charts and notebook-size presentations allow you to control timing. Should you

miscalculate where your client's interest lies, you can instantly refocus the direction of the presentation.

Video or film presentations can be terrific dialogue starters when they are brief and focused, but if they are long, they can inhibit dialogue.

Whose business is my presentation about? Chances are pretty good that your client is not in the magazine business. This means that if your presentation is all about circulation, rate structure, editorial focus and so on, you are talking about *your* business, not the client's. And you will have great difficulty involving your client in that kind of conversation.

If you are selling ad space to a company that sells gumballs, present your information in terms of how it will help sell more gumballs. Talk about gumballs first, and sweep your magazine's story in behind it.

If you get a canned pitch from the home office, customize it. Chances are there are some parts that are relevant to what you want to say to a particular client, and some that are not. Every one of your clients is unique. Each has different products, markets, distribution channels, pricing strategies, and marketing communications needs. To be effective, your presentation should reflect this.

Am I talking about the right things to the right person? Different people you call on will want different information. An agency media person may want to know about the numerical side of your magazine's story. But to a marketing VP or company president, the details of your audit statement and CPM will probably be a bore. They will want to know how advertising in your magazine will help them sell more of their product.

Has my client heard all this before? If you are just beginning a new territory, chances are that the rep who had the territory before you has given the basic pitch to most of your clients. Reinforcement is always a good thing, but if it is the central focus of your visit, your client may think twice about making time for you on the next occasion.

Can I prove the points I am making? It may well be that you can present a brilliant case for your publication to be added to a schedule, but so can every other space rep who calls from other magazines and competitive media. After all the pitches and dialogues are done, the question is, which stories stick? Often the story that sticks is the one that offers proof.

Proof can mean different things to different clients. For some, solid independent research is "proof," whereas other clients will believe what you say only if they hear it from some of their key customers.

Once you have answered these questions, start thinking about your specific presentation. Here are some points to keep in mind:

Start by asking questions. Has the situation changed since you prepared for the visit? Is it possible that the presentation you've so carefully put together is now obsolete? Is the selling problem you are trying to overcome still relevant?

Use a hook. You need something to get your client interested in what you have to say right from the beginning.

• Let your client help set the agenda. A week before you show up, call your client and ask what he or she wants to talk about. Then open with that topic.

• Start with an attention-getter, a relevant joke, a personal anecdote, something specific to the client.

Encourage feedback and objections. Ask, "Do you agree with what I just said?" or "Is this consistent with what your perception is?" Without feedback, you are flying blind.

Prepare to chase the selling problem wherever it goes. Sometimes as you overcome one objection, another, unanticipated objection emerges. If it's important, stop and take a side trip to answer it. If you are truly pursuing a selling dialogue (and not a one-way uninterrupted flow of information), you cannot completely predict the direction or outcome. You need to be flexible. Remember, you are there to make a sale first, and a presentation second. The presentation should follow the direction of the sale—not the other way around.

Stay flexible. It is important to maintain enough control to keep the conversation focused on getting a commitment for ad space, or more ad space. But gaining complete control can be a mistake. Your client is the only one who can tell you why he or she isn't buying, or what opportunities would make him want to buy more. Therefore, it's up to you to make certain your client has the opportunity to do just that.

Know what to ask for. Before you leave, you need to ask for two things. Of course you need to ask for an order, but you also need to ask for another visit. If you didn't make a sale, but your presentation was successful, chances are good that some points were raised that you could follow up on. While you are there, define how you will keep the selling dialogue going.

If you did close the sale, you still need to keep the dialogue going. Ask for an opportunity to discuss how the ad worked, whether goals were met, and so on. This will give you a chance not only to maintain your relationship with this client, but to upgrade the sale as well.

In 600 B.C., Plato wrote, "I hear and I forget. I see and I remember. I do and I understand." A prepared presentation helps you visualize points for greater impact, but it is Plato's "do" part that lets you achieve the greatest impact.

A well-constructed presentation helps you turn a sales visit into a "doing" laboratory where your client works through a new sales idea. □

> A well-constructed presentation will help steer your client through a new sales idea.

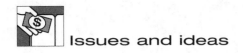

Give Your Media Kit More Muscle

BY JULIE A. LAITIN

Every word in your media kit must be aimed at generating sales. This means your kit must target eight key sales areas effectively and persuasively. The more facts you can offer to demonstrate your strengths in these areas, the more likely you are to sell your customers.

Your market: Nothing is more important to advertisers than market facts. Even large advertisers seek additional information on the markets they serve. Agencies, too, are hungry for facts that educate them about their clients' products and customers. The information you provide will enhance your stature as an expert in your field and as a resource for your advertisers. If possible, you should show market size, components, levels of distribution, history, potential and future growth areas. This will give advertisers confidence in your ability to help them market their products effectively and productively.

Circulation: Don't rely on your audit statement to spell out the facts about your readers. Because many agency personnel start in media—often without sufficient training or understanding of how to read audit statements—relying exclusively on your audit statement to explain your circulation benefits can be a grave oversight. Provide a simple and clear explanation, in words and/or charts, of what your circulation advantages are: more readers, more decision-making executives, more influential purchasers, more readers in specific areas of importance to advertisers, and so on.

Demographic study: Too often, publishers simply reprint information about reader demographics provided by a research firm, thinking that the facts will speak for themselves. This is what I call "telling"—not "selling"—the results. Instead, provide a headline that will highlight the benefit contained in each chart.

Example 1: Use a headline such as "Our readers are seasoned professionals" for a chart showing your readers' years in the business or profession.

Example 2: Try "Our readers are heavy buyers of electronic equipment" as a headline for a chart showing the percentage of readers who buy various types of equipment.

Advertisers should be able to understand, just by reading the headlines, exactly what the final research has uncovered. More detail is provided by looking at the charts. Headlines make it easier for your customers to quickly absorb and retain the major benefits of your magazine and audience.

Editorial: Of all the sections included in media kits, by far the most neglected is the editorial area. Perhaps this is because most magazines assume—wrongly—that advertisers and agencies already know what their publications are about. In fact, few agency buyers know the specifics of your editorial, especially in the trade area. For this reason, it is vital to underscore exactly what your magazine brings to your readers—and, by extension, to your advertisers. Among the items to include in this section are the following:

An editorial profile explaining your magazine, its reason for being, and how it helps readers enhance their lives—personally and/or professionally. The editorial profile has another important function: It should explain how your magazine differs from its competitors so that advertisers will have a clear idea of your magazine's position in the marketplace.

An editorial calendar outlining everything your magazine offers each month, including value-added services and benefits. This will help advertisers select the months in which they want to run. This calendar should work as a sales tool, not just as an editorial rundown of major features. It should help bring in new categories, generate schedules, and trade up existing clients.

Additional fact sheets, which might include the linage or number of editorial pages you ran last year in specific advertising categories, linage comparisons with your competition, bios of well-known columnists or authors, and lists of editorial awards.

Remember that the importance of your editorial to advertisers is not that it be interesting or informative, but that it bring readers into your magazine—and into contact with their ads.

Readership: That a certain number of people receive your magazine is not proof, from an advertiser's standpoint, that they read it. Proof of reader interest and involvement—in your editorial and your advertisements—comes from research surveys. These studies offer qualitative distinctions that set your publication and its audience apart from its competitors as a marketing vehicle. Among the facts that can be demonstrated are the following: how many issues your subscribers read; how much of each issue they read; the time they devote to an average issue; where they read it; what they do with the issue after reading it; and to how many other people they pass it.

Advertising: This section should show advertising success and advertiser results. Increased ad pages are third-party endorsements that your magazine works for your clients. Showing your competitive advantages in graphic form (bar charts) offers immediate accessibility.

Even if you can't show more ad pages than your competitors, you may have a significant jump in ad pages or in marketshare over the previous year. If so, show your percentage growth. Many agencies place greater importance on percentage growth than on total pages because growth implies that the market is turning to you.

If you have neither of the above, don't give up. Do you have more exclusive advertisers? more new advertisers? more advertisers in a specific industry (travel/auto/liquor) than your competitors? Any of these can show leadership strength and should be included as fact sheets in your media kit.

Finally, because advertisers like to know that they're in good company, it is always helpful to include a list of happy clients. Ordinarily, this should be done alphabetically, by category. However, if you have too few advertisers to make this work, or too few in important and/or growing categories, then list all advertisers together, alphabetically.

Value-added services: Merchandising is taking on an ever-greater role in advertising buys. Consumer magazines thrive on merchandising services—but business and trade magazines, with their smaller budgets, often worry that such programs will be too costly for them to manage. What many overlook is that they are already providing such services—free!

It is important to recognize that (1) merchandising doesn't have to be funded exclusively by the publication; it can be shared or even underwritten exclusively by the advertiser. And (2) value-added services can tip the balance in favor of your magazine over a competitor.

Moreover, merchandising benefits both you and your clients: Advertisers benefit from their association with your magazine and its image, which adds cachet to your advertisers' names and products. And you will receive additional image-building benefits and visibility from the services you provide—for example, signage, publicity and exposure.

For all these reasons, it is important to include a list of some of the free value-added services you offer (for example, advertising research studies and bonus distribution), as well as customized programs in which you provide the coordination and planning, while your advertiser provides some funds.

The important point to remember is that offering value-added services results in a "win-win" situation for you and for your customers.

Rates and mechanical specifications: Media buyers remove rate cards from media kit folders and file them separately. To help media buyers make their evaluations more quickly and easily, include both your editorial profile and your circulation on the card itself. This reinforces your editorial positioning and helps buyers work out your cost per thousand without going back to their files.

Also keep in mind that your rate card is as much a selling tool as the rest of your kit. As such, it should include items of special significance that will help sell your magazine. Special programs or unique benefits can—and should—be featured. Among them are your editorial calendar; closing dates; reader-service programs; insert rates and specifications; graphic representation of ad sizes; selected highlights from your subscriber surveys; and merchandising services and programs. □

> What you've got to do is prove your editorial brings readers into the magazine—and into contact with the ads.

Make Your Circ Statement A Better Ad-Sales Tool

BY LAMBETH HOCHWALD

When publishers get together to swap horror stories, the one about the junior media planner who controls a multimillion-dollar ad budget and who makes decisions based solely on a magazine's circ numbers is sure to arise. Yet, for the most part, advertisers and their agencies don't fully understand the implications of the data so painstakingly gathered by the Audit Bureau of Circulations (ABC) and BPA International.

"Every magazine attempts to use circulation statements to sell, but they don't get enough interest from agencies and advertisers," says E. Daniel Capell, managing director of Vos, Gruppo & Capell in New York City. "Trying to educate media departments is a tough sell. They're not schooled in circulation."

But Jim Tricarico, eastern sales manager of *Tennis*, thinks that market shifts will force agencies to look harder at circ statements. "As money gets tighter, agencies and clients tend to stay away from the 'creative sell' or going on a good feeling," he says. "Agencies start with price and editorial content, and then the distinguishing factor between two books might come down to the [audit] statement."

Reliance on circ statements could also be strengthened by the release in 1994 of a confidential draft report from a Magazine Publishers of America (MPA) committee that questioned some audience-measurement methods used by the largest syndicated research firms, Simmons Market Research Bureau and Mediamark Research, Inc. The dispute had been building ever since Simmons changed its research methods in 1990, causing a steep decline in casual readers in later surveys.

Up until now, media buyers have given more weight to the readers-per-copy or total audience figures supplied by syndicated research rather than the sworn circulation information. "The controversy over measurement might make ABC statements more vital for larger-circulation magazines," says Capell. "If there's anything to these problems, it might lead to more use of the [audit] statements."

Most agencies don't need convincing. "Readership and subscriber studies provide demographics about lifestyle and the health of the readership. ABC and BPA statements show the strength of circulation and the health of the magazine itself. And, you can look at the statement to see if the magazine is going to be around much longer," says Susan Carey, vice president and media director of Ogilvy & Mather's Detroit office.

Susan Allyn, consumer marketing director at Wenner Media Inc., publisher of *Rolling Stone, Men's Journal, Us* and *Family Life*, admits that there has always been some skepticism about syndicated research. "Circulators have felt more comfortable with audit numbers and direct audience research versus syndicated research," she says. "A lot of consumer marketing people feel more comfortable with real live data."

Rule changes and audit upgrades

But the audit bureaus haven't been waiting for others' misfortunes to bring in new members. ABC—which audits 712 consumer, 284 business and 52 farm magazines—and BPA—which currently audits 1,290 business and 256 consumer titles—have recently made rules changes that enable applicants to qualify for audits more easily. Other rules, pertaining to qualified circulation, have been amended. For example, in July 1994, ABC's board of directors did away with the stipulation that business publications have at least 70 percent paid circulation. In late 1993, BPA agreed to include pass-along copies as part of a magazine's average nonqualified circulation total. BPA also urged members to report documented delivery of copies to trade shows and conventions, as part of the average nonqualified section of the circulation statement.

Both audit bureaus have made their statements more user-friendly by including maps to illustrate geographic distribution and bar graphs and pie charts that reflect five-year circulation trends or qualifications by source. Both repackaged information to make it more accessible to scaled-down agency staffs. ACCESS ABC:Periodicals is a CD-ROM that includes publisher's statements for all business, consumer and farm publications members, as well as four years worth of data on consumer title members. According to ABC, nearly 80 agencies and publishers now use the CD-ROM product.

Stephen Sullivan, president of Mintz & Hoke, a Boston advertising agency, likes the product. "Providing information electronically will help a media buyer manipulate audience and demographic data without having to lay out the audit statements side by side," he notes.

Mark Wachowicz, vice president of publisher marketing at Schaumburg, Illinois-based ABC, says that no electronic presentation of audited data can replace circ sheets. "You'll never get away from hard copy as part of a media kit," he says. "Publishers like to demonstrate things on their own."

What media buyers are looking for

On paper or on-screen, pink sheets help media buyers to sort through such factors as the number of copies in arrears or the number of subscriptions bought at a discount or with a premium. Each is a telling indication of a magazine's vitality.

"A good media planner has to know how to completely dissect ABC or BPA statements. You look to see not only if a magazine is making its ratebase, but you also look at year-to-year trends and how the book is distributed. For example, sometimes national books have a definite regional skew," says O&M's Carey.

David Leckey, vice president and circulation director of Hachette Filipacchi Magazines, says audited circulation serves as the basis for more in-depth analysis. "I'm hearing as many, if not more, media buyers putting pressure on magazines to carry more information on average price paid, to clean up the number of subscription prices cluttering up a pink sheet and to include more detailed description of sources," he says.

The statements are becoming more complex as more data becomes available, says Sullivan. "On the consumer side, people can now use split-run publications to segment out distinct audiences. Media planners will be able to look at a *TV Guide* and not just segment out 18- to 24-year-olds, for example, but also those people within that age group who are dedicated bike riders and live in college towns."

"Some smart agencies are beginning to look more closely at the information underlying the numbers," adds Wenner Media's Allyn. "The audit statement contains quantitative data—it isn't intended to be qualitative. If you look only at the numbers, you're not seeing the whole picture. There has to be a balance where the

---

■ Key rules changes in 1994

ABC
- Farm publications: March. Amendment allowing all farm publications to be audited regardless of their percentage of paid, nonpaid direct-request or telecommunications circulation.
- Channels of subscription sales: March. Amendment allowing subscriptions resulting from publisher-initiated telemarketing renewal efforts to be classified as direct-request subscriptions.
- Business publications: July. Amendment allowing all business publications to be audited by ABC, regardless of their percentage of paid or nonpaid direct-request circulation.

BPA International
- Passalong rules: January. Rule adopted to allow magazines to report their passalong or extended circulation.
- Overseas circulation: June. Rule adopted that allows publishers to offer and report different basic subscription rates by country. Circulation statement rules had previously required publishers to report only one basic worldwide subscription rate.

---

story the numbers tell is looked at to see whether that matches what an advertiser wants."

Joseph DiMarino, associate publisher/advertising director of *Caribbean Travel and Life*, is more critical. "Agencies don't use the statements enough as they should," he says. "Advertisers use them to verify circulation and to look at the mix between nonpaid circulation and subscribers, but they don't have the time to look at growth trends in circulation or do geographic analysis. A lot of information can be garnered from these statements about where the magazine is going internally. Agencies can learn a lot about whether the magazine is dumping a lot of stamp-sheet subscribers."

Michael Tucker, publisher of Washington, D.C.-based Hanley-Wood's *Builder*, says: "In the age of database marketing, it's the key to selling advertising," especially when selling editorial sections with overlays or selective binding. "For example, we can show advertisers exactly how many of our readers are in those states with the highest housing starts." □

The Case of the Missing Client

BY JOSH GORDON

At some organizations, media-buying decisions are decided by politics rather than based on marketing needs. A high-up person may have delegated decision-making for media buys, but when media are bought, he or she descends briefly from on high, rewrites the media plan, then vanishes. Over time, the people on the media-buying front-line learn to base their decisions not on the opportunities that exist in the marketplace, but on what their superior thinks is right.

In extreme cases, the true decision-makers are so out of touch with fast-changing details that the media buys they dictate seem to have little or no connection to reality. Over the years I have seen a book kicked off a schedule because a company president's wife didn't like it; a company president buying media from people he knew from "the good 'ol days," even though things "today" were very different; and a major contract bought according to the company CEO's personal reading preferences, even though his preferences ran contrary to those of the company's customers.

These extreme cases make little sense, but pointing that out to the people involved is a formula for disaster. Political buys are personal. If you attack the buy, you are attacking the person who made it—usually someone high up in the organization. Other times, the person making the buy knows it makes no sense, but views his buying as a way to advance his career—not as a way to advance the company's sales and marketing objectives.

Navigating internal politics is difficult, especially if you are flying blind. If you find yourself in such a situation, here are some pointers that might help you out.

Remember, everybody has a boss. Because politically motivated media buys are based more on upper management's perception of your magazine than on its true merits, make sure your client's management's perception is positive. Get your publisher to meet with the higher-ups. Join an association in the industry or category in your area so you can meet them yourself. And add top management to your comp list.

I once sold an account by getting a copy of the company's annual report and adding the members of its board of directors to my comp list. When our annual issue that focused on this company's product came out with no ad from them, the company president got a few phone calls.

Make the person you call on a no-risk proposal. Sometimes the political buy persists because the person who knows better doesn't have the courage to fight upper management for the better buy. But even if this person is a fighter, putting your book on the buy list can be too much of a risk for him personally. After all, it's his neck on the block. If you can find a way to take his neck off the block, you could make both a friend and a sale.

For example, once while working on a magazine that pulled sales leads well, I told a media planner that placing an ad in my book would cost a certain number of dollars per lead generated, up to the cost of the ad. If the ad didn't pull, he wouldn't pay much for it. Another version of the same technique: Run the ad in an issue studied by an advertising performance study (like Harvey's Ad-Q Study). If the ad doesn't generate a certain level of readership, the client doesn't pay.

Create an event. Political buys have momentum; to derail them often requires an event beyond the ordinary. You need to figure out a way to get the various layers in the organization you are selling to focus their attention on your magazine and reach agreement. For example, I once turned around an account by conducting a booth survey that included a readership question at a major industry trade show. Secretaries from the company handed out survey cards, company salespeople saw that the cards were filled out, and the company president tabulated the results in his

Sure-fire tips for how to navigate an advertiser's hierarchy and internal politics and reach the real decision makers.

hotel room after the show closed every night. It was an event in which everyone in the company participated.

Another time, my associate and I hosted a spectacular dinner. My associate discovered that the company CEO had a favorite Manhattan restaurant. By securing the CEO's presence there, we were able to get the company president and all the product marketing managers to join us. The dinner took on a life of its own. Even our publisher flew in for the event (a detail we were grateful for when the check arrived). There were no sales pitches at the table. The guests showed up, had a great time, and went home happy. Soon we were doing more business with them than ever before.

Play to the corporate culture. Maybe you can't meet with the CEO or the president who influences your media buys, but you can position your magazine so it sells to the company the CEO is shaping. A corporate culture is that hidden body of rules and values that affects how individuals within a company interact with one another and are rewarded. It is no surprise that corporate culture also affects how the company treats and buys from vendors like you. So, play to your audience. If, for example, you are dealing with a "nuts and bolts" kind of company, present your book as a practical marketing tool. If you are calling on an image-conscious company, sell quality. Of course, it gets much more complicated than this, but suffice it to say, sell the person you are calling on as if he or she were the president of the company.

Sell reality. Internal politics and perceptions often take on a life of their own, especially at large accounts. But ad space is a tool for reaching target customers on the outside, where the realities of the marketplace ultimately prevail over the fantasies of internal politics. The ultimate boss of everyone in the company you are calling on is that company's customers—your readers. Said Woody Allen, "I'm not crazy about reality, but it's the only place I know where I can get a good steak."

Put it in writing. In a large, political company, you will never be able to meet with all the people who influence the media plan. So put all your selling points in a letter and aggressively circulate it. A follow-up letter that you "cc" to appropriate others is a good way to tell your story the way you want it told. But to get your correspondence beyond the person you actually called on, you must add something new—some news that affects the company's business, research your magazine has done, or an idea that you have come up with. Without this addition, your letter is likely to go no further than your contact's desk.

Toot your horn. If the political wind is blowing in your direction, invent ways to remind the organization that you are so favored. High-level schmoozing is a great way to do this. If you can't meet with the top people yourself, make sure your publisher sees them when they are in town.

Political influence on the media buy is a fact of life in space sales, and can be a serious impediment if you don't learn to control the situation. But it can also be put to your advantage—if you know how. □

Telephone Tag—and You're It Again

BY DENNIS MILAN

The ad close is fast approaching. Your clammy hand pounds the phone once again, dialing for dollars in the last few hours before the impending deadline kills your last chance for late ads and crucial quota dollars. The phone rings at the other end of the line:

"*Hi, it's Mary. I ...* "

"*Hi, Mary.*" You're confident that Mary remembers the conversation at the trade show two months ago, when she semi-promised an ad in this issue.

" *... I'm away from my desk right now and unable to take your call.*"

Your heart hits the floor with an audible thud.

"*Please leave your name and number at the tone, and I'll call you back. Beep!*"

Call you back? Not likely. You've communicated with Mary regularly during the past year, but have never had a live conversation. Your voice-mail messages—detailed, congenial, one-way—have never been returned, and you've gotten nowhere.

Today's business people are shielded by the electronic advances of the age. Through the miracles of digital recording techniques, call screening and fax, print-media purchasers are becoming harder and harder to reach by phone. Voice mail is just another tool—but no matter how irksome it might seem at times, the ad salesperson who uses it properly will have success with it.

Correct use of tools usually involves little tricks to make them work better. Here are a few designed to make voice-mail systems work better for you.

Make every call count. One thing a media planner probably hates worse than a boring telephone conversation is shuffling through all those lifeless—and vague—voice-mail messages.

"*Hi, Jerry. This is Phil from* Hackneyed Journal. *Please give me a call today about our September '93 issue. Thanks, Jerry, and have a nice day.*"

Jerry has probably heard a thousand messages like that this year. Worse, there's no compelling explanation

of why he should call you back. He's probably forgotten that he said he'd run in the September issue with special editorial focus. Why not make it easy for him? Be direct. And to expedite a response, create a sense of immediacy:

"*Jerry, it's Phil from the* Journal. *I'm leaving this voice-mail message because I know you're busy. At lunch last month, you indicated that you wanted to run the half-page ABA Manufacturing ad in the September directory issue. We're closing the issue this week, so I've got the production manager alerted to your need for a good position. Just need to speak with you and confirm the rate. Please give me a call today at ...* "

Jerry did indicate he wanted to be in the issue, but you need to get the official okay. His return call should be with an insertion order. But even if he doesn't call back today, you've gotten some important information: He probably won't be in the issue.

Don't be a 'breather.' Most ad sales people need a strong, confident voice to conduct their business. When leaving your message, maintain good posture, support your upper body with plenty of breath, and speak in clear, confident tones. Inhale before the recording tone sounds. Inhaling after the tone creates an obnoxious hissing sound. Any breathy speech will sound bad, so keep the wind out of your telephone receiver with solid voice tones.

Use the touchtone as your key. When the person you are calling can be trusted to return a call, a concise, to-the-point message works well—voice-mail nirvana. However, when your prospect is using voice-mail to screen calls, more creative approaches are needed. When you're closing an issue on a tight deadline, you need to be able to use the system to your advantage, eliminating time-consuming games of telephone tag. Here are a few field-tested tips.

• **Help!** Remember that most voice-mail systems have built-in Help menus that you can use to your advantage

> You've left seven messages. You need to talk to your contact now, but his voice mail answers. What to do?

by working the keys on your touchtone phone. This can get you to your source.

While listening to your prospect's recorded message, try pressing "H" for "Help," or "*H" on the touchtone keypads. You'll be transferred to a nice-sounding voice that will politely explain combinations of symbols and numbers for you to tap into your phone keypad. These combinations can be used to work through the voice-mail system, and can connect you to other phone extensions.

If you're not going to get through to your prospect anyway, it's probably a good idea to try working with the help matrix. You're venturing nothing, and you may find some key information that will make better use of your time. (It's a good idea to write down the commands you find useful for future calls to this number.)

• **Transfer to operator:** You've left seven messages, some returned, some not. You need to talk to your contact now, but his voice mail answers. What to do? Dial "0" during the message (usually before the beep). In most cases, you'll be transferred to a switchboard operator, who is in a position to be your saving grace. Be nice, be friendly, be funny. If your situation is urgent, tell the operator. Ask to have your party paged.

If you still don't get an answer, ask for someone in ad production, the traffic department, or anybody you may know at the company. The key is to keep your call alive, hoping to find someone who can bring your party to the phone. Very important: Each time you ask for another department (or other new contact) ask the operator for the name and extension number to which you're being sent. It will come in handy during future calls.

• **Transfer to another extension:** If you know someone else who may help you, or who may have a line on your contact, you can usually press "*T" or "T" for transfer to that number (you may also be required to press the "#" sign as well). Then dial the extension number. However, don't get caught napping should this person's voice mail answer. Transfer to another number, or back to your new-found friend at the switchboard. A convincing story and a pleasant demeanor can really get this person involved in your cause.

• **Use the "2-3" and/or "*-#" combination:** Okay. You've

transferred in and out of several departments, talked to everyone breathing, and your prospect is still not available. You must leave a message, and you want to make sure it's the right one. You know that the difference between a sloppy message and a crisp one can mean the difference between being called back and being ignored. What to do? Edit your message using the keypads.

You'll have to experiment because all systems are not the same. But there exists an option to let you listen to the message you've just recorded. Usually, pressing the keypad digit "2" will rewind your message, and "3" will play it back. If you've left a confusing message that may embarrass you and your magazine (not a top career move), you may erase and re-record. There's time to get it right, so don't panic. When it's the way you want it, you can approve the message and hang up.

Use voice mail to reinforce a fax message. If you've tried everything and you still have to leave a voice-mail message, don't despair. Use it to reinforce a fax message. Stress that the fax is crucial to the success of an important business opportunity—an ad in the issue you're closing, perhaps. Make the message succinct, with a sense of urgency:

"Hi, Jerry. I know you're too busy to talk right now, but I'm calling about the ad we discussed for the September issue. I'm sending a two-page fax right now with the details. We're closing the issue tomorrow and need your confirmation. Call me, etc."

Of course, this is less preferable than talking to Jerry, so make certain the fax contains what you promise—and that you send it when you say you're going to send it. You'll lose Jerry forever by not following through. There's another reason always to tell the truth on a voice-mail message. Most voice-mail systems offer users the ability to keep and file messages. They can be played back at any time, and sent to other voice-mail boxes. If you must fabricate a reason for your prospect to call you back, for example, you've got bigger problems than dealing with voice mail.

Voice mail is here to stay. It can be exasperating and stress-inducing. But it can also be an effective ad-sales tool when used creatively and efficiently. □

Media Kit Design: Techniques That Bring Results

BY JULIE A. LAITIN

Media kits: the single most important tool your sales staff has, and one that fulfills many needs. Think of the different things media kits can do:

• Presell your customers and convince them to see your reps, in person, to hear more about how your magazine can help them market their products.

• Strengthen your personal sales calls, providing fact sheets that clarify and expand on critical issues and sales points.

• Overcome objections by framing difficult issues in a positive light.

• Help you trade up current advertisers and bring in new categories through effective presentation of research facts.

• Help media buyers sell—and justify—their decisions to top management.

• Increase the effectiveness of your sales letters and direct-mail efforts by providing fact sheets that illuminate and reinforce your sales points.

When to update

To remain effective, however, a media kit needs to be updated every couple of years. The extent of both copy and design changes will depend on what has happened in the marketplace, and in your magazine. At the very least, you should change the color of your kit and the accompanying inserts. If possible, revise the design to provide a fresh, contemporary look. Must-change features include your editorial calendar, your rate card, and fact sheets highlighting changes in your marketshare (including ad linage, ad growth by pages and/or percentage, and current advertisers). The same goes for your circulation numbers if they have changed significantly.

If you're happy with your present kit, and if your magazine and market have remained stable, you may be able to pick up much of its copy, devoting most of your promotional dollars to a new design and graphics.

To remain effective, a media kit needs to be updated every couple of years. Revise the design to give it a fresh, contemporary look.

One overriding rule to remember, however, is this: Keep it simple. When promotion staffs start designing media kits, visions of sugarplums—not to mention die cuts, gatefolds and elaborate artwork—dance in their heads. Tempting though it might be to go with an unusual design, remember what the kit will be used for. Design it with the needs of the users (both your sales force and clients) in mind. Don't go with something too far out unless it's clearly better.

One publication I worked with showed me a basic media kit folder that contained seven smaller individual folders, one for each category. Although it was pretty to look at, it was time-consuming to open and awkward to work with. Neither the media buyer nor the salesperson was able to grab any particular sheet without an elaborate fuss. While you may want to consider something out of the ordinary, don't lose sight of the main purpose of the kit: to sell quickly and effectively.

To make your media kit work for you, think in terms of objectives, structuring the format, presentation and content to meet the specific goals you want to achieve. If, for example, you want to bring in a new category—say, widgets— you will probably need to do research showing that your readers are heavy buyers (and future buyers) of widgets. This means your media kit will require maximum flexibility in order to add fact sheets customized for widget manufacturers.

If you've decided to revamp your media kit folder, here's a list of available format options, their advantages and drawbacks:

A traditional folder: With pockets on the inside to hold the magazine and fact sheets, this is the most common and cost-effective format for media kits. It's also the easiest to file and update: Simply replace outdated sheets or add new material as needed.

Drawbacks: Because the sheets are loose, they can fall

out at any time or be replaced in the wrong order. Also, the traditional folder is limited in how much it can hold.

A looseleaf binder: Information such as fact sheets and audit statements are bound inside. In addition to its image-building appeal, looseleafs guarantee that fact sheets will stay in place. They are also likely to be placed on executives' bookshelves if they contain useful reference information.

Drawbacks: These binders are more expensive, and mailing costs are higher. Also, they are difficult to file because of their shape, have no tabs to call attention to themselves in a file cabinet, and often lack pockets on both inside covers. Pockets can be ordered, but add to your cost.

A saddle-stitched booklet: Used to explain facts about the market and other timeless information. They are image-building presentations that keep pages intact and in order. Because they usually serve as reference sources, they also have greater shelf life than other formats.

Drawbacks: Booklets are more expensive to produce than standard folders and lack flexibility in terms of updating. Hint: To update material without reprinting the entire booklet, design the kit with pockets on various pages so you can change any outdated sheets.

A clear, plastic pocket or jacket cover: Holds fact sheets of different colors and sizes, but has a more limited capacity than traditional folders. This see-through fea-ture will spotlight your magazine cover if you place it inside the front section.

Drawbacks: Because this is a see-through format, your magazine cover alone has to do your selling. There's no place to print a design element or theme line.

An expandable folder: This is a good format for magazines that require substantial numbers of fact sheets and booklets. While it's more expensive than traditional folders, it will keep your reference materials showcased in a neat, adaptable form.

Drawbacks: Because the folder can be expanded, publishers tend to include too much (often disorganized) information. This makes it unwieldy for the user. If a media buyer wants to file it in a drawer, it also lacks a tab for instant visibility.

Separate your selling categories

Organize your kit exactly the way your best salespeople sell the magazine to a new advertiser. If they sell the market first, put this section up front. If they sell your editorial content first, make this the first order of the day.

While media kits are probably your most expensive tool, they also have greater impact and potential than your other aids. Investing your promotional dollars skillfully in effective, revenue-producing media kits can give you the returns you seek—many times over. □

Issues and ideas

Peg Your Ad-Sales Pay
To Performance

BY TIM BOGARDUS

Since the advertising bonanza of the 1980s evaporated, ad salespeople have found themselves either treading water or fighting hard just to maintain their territories—if they still have jobs at all. In many page-driven compensation systems, rate-cutting has contributed to the drop in net incomes and the disappearance of third- and fourth-ranked magazines in certain categories.

Today, revenues from ad sales are once again on the rise, but industry analysts agree they will never reach the frenzied levels of the mid-1980s. "I don't hear anyone predicting a burst in ad sales in the near future," says Hal Jaffe, senior consultant at Los Angeles-based Magazine Consulting Group. Ad pages in consumer magazines were up a scant 1.2 percent, to 167,917, in 1993, and advertising revenues gained a modest 6.1 percent, to $7.6 billion, according to the Publishers Information Bureau. Those numbers are a far cry from the 10 to 15 percent annual gains of the 1980s.

Also, the nature of the game has changed. Publishers have reduced their sales staffs, restructured compensation packages and extended their franchises with ancillary products. Many ad salespeople must now be prepared to sell TV air time, trade show and retailer promotions, and other value-added products to supplement ad page income.

"The biggest trend, causally, is not new products, but rather the tepid state of advertising sales over the last five years," says David Orlow, president of New York City-based Periodical Studies Service. Compensation, he says, was "disproportionally accelerated" in the late 1980s. Salaries became inflated and incentives were based on bringing in new business. "Now," says Orlow, "management realizes that saving ground is as valuable as gaining ground."

Orlow adds that when ad sales went sour at the turn of the decade, publishers began to ask themselves what their salespeople were really worth, and adjusted accordingly. The result: Base salaries, which used to be 60 to 70 percent of the entire compensation package, dropped to about 50 percent, and incentives became a larger part of the package. Total compensation is down compared to where it was five to seven years ago.

Dan McNamee, president of the McNamee Consulting Company in New York City, agrees: "Publishers are finally catching up to modern compensation theory," he says. "Companies are paying for performance, and that performance is based on the economics of the company." Thus, the shift has been away from commissions based on a percentage of total billings and toward a bonus system based on meeting defined goals.

Caveat vendor

But Orlow and McNamee offer a caveat: No one compensation system works for every magazine. In fact, the systems can vary even within multi-title publishing companies. "There is no way on earth an intelligent sales incentive plan can be developed by using a formula," says Orlow. The most important thing is that an incentive plan meet a magazine's specific needs.

At Cleveland-based Penton Publishing, for instance, management gave the sales force a voice in developing a fair compensation plan. In 1991, a committee composed entirely of salespeople reviewed existing compensation plans. They proposed raising commissions from 5 percent with a quota to 10 percent with no prescribed quota because the sales force felt that the management-imposed quotas, or bogeys, limited their earning potential. Management accepted the proposal, but reserved the right to set quotas for the largest territories.

But that's not as simple as it sounds. Penton publishes 32 industrial trade magazines, including *Industry Week*, *Electronic Design* and *American Machinist*, that vary greatly in size and revenue. Penton's magazines base their compensation packages on the plan, but because of the disparity in earning potential among the publications, several plans are actually in effect. Some salespeople with smaller territories are on a standard base-plus-commission plan with a flat 10 percent commission. Those with large territories begin earning a commission after they achieve the bogey for that territory. The bogey and commission are adjusted for the size and earning potential that goes with the territory.

"It's very tailored to the territory, the magazine and

the individual," explains Penton CEO and president Sal Marino. "We have a philosophy that if a salesperson has X amount of billing, he should be able to earn X amount on that billing." Recently, Penton increased the size of certain territories, but each is structured so that salespeople have the potential to earn between $70,000 and $80,000 for every $1 million of business. Marino notes that there is always the potential to earn more.

In addition, the company places no cap on commissions if a salesperson grows the territory, and individual compensation packages and territories are re-evaluated annually and adjusted according to fluctuations in the market and the territory. "I think our people are very satisfied and paid competitively," says Marino.

As for ancillary products, Penton pays a flat percentage or a bonus for sales of card decks and annuals, but Marino doesn't want his salespeople to become distracted. "Our salespeople concentrate mainly on ad sales," he says. Since the new plan was implemented, yields per page are up 4 percent.

Staying put

Still, some publishers have found no need to switch systems. The basic compensation structure at Wenner Media Inc., publisher of *Rolling Stone, Us, Family Life* and *Men's Journal*, hasn't changed in 10 years. "Our philosophy has been to pay people a competitive base salary and then pay them a very, very, very lucrative commission plan that is totally pegged to performance," says Wenner senior vice president Kent Brownridge. "There's no safety net and no guarantees, but there's no cap. The sky's the limit."

Wenner's compensation plan is based on page goals and linked to net revenues. Base salaries, ranging from $40,000 to $70,000, are low, but the potential to earn on commission is great, according to Brownridge, who adds that a couple of salespeople have earned as much as $150,000 on commissions. "Ours is a totally formulated commission plan so that any salesperson at any time can tell you how much they have earned that year to the day," Brownridge says. "That really motivates people."

Because the plan is page-driven, Brownridge admits the temptation to deal off the rate card can be "irresistible." All rate-cutting deals must be approved by him, however.

> The aim is to align motivational tactics with realistic financial goals—and remember that no plan is the universal solution.

Still, Wenner Media *has* had to rework its definition of a successful salesperson. There used to be greater rewards for bringing in new business, but that policy was amended in 1992. "We finally decided there ought to be equal rewards for a salesperson who has a mature group of accounts and can maintain them in tough times," Brownridge says. "That person should be rewarded as well as those who bring in new business."

Tying into TV

At Times Mirror Magazines, ancillary products, special events and broadcast programming occupy so much of the sales teams' time that upper-level management formed a committee to study how to adjust compensation plans at its 12 publications, including *Golf Magazine, Field & Stream, Outdoor Life* and *Home Mechanix.* Its salespeople work with the standard quota-plus-commission format tied to net revenues, but the burgeoning role of alternative revenue sources necessitated the review.

For example, *Golf Magazine* garners ancillary revenue from its annual sponsorship of the Big Apple Classic golf tournament in Westchester County, New York. Besides selling ad pages, the sales team sells corporate sponsorships, television time, ad pages in the on-site magazine and even exhibitor tent space. Other Times Mirror Magazines, such as *Salt Water Sportsman, Yachting, Ski* and *Skiing,* offer a palette of products and events that the ad salespeople must sell. A source at Times Mirror says that magazine-related broadcast programming last year brought in more than $1 million in revenues.

"The question is, how do we compensate the salesperson for the television time as opposed to the ad pages as opposed to the sponsorships?" asks executive vice president Jim Kopper, adding, "We know one thing: We don't have the formula. But we *will* have a formula." Each magazine, he says, will adapt its own compensation structure to whatever the committee recommends. "There have to be different programs at each magazine," Kopper says.

Ancillary products are not as prevalent at smaller companies, notes Magazine Consulting Group's Jaffe, whose clients are primarily trade magazines with less than $10 million in revenues. But even in smaller publishing companies, Jaffe says the trend is to offer a lower base salary with a greater emphasis on commissions or profit sharing. "Most publications are running leaner these days," he observes.

KC Publishing in Kansas City, Missouri, is certainly one of them. When president and publisher John Prebich bought the company, which publishes *Flower & Garden, Workbench, WorkBasket* and *Easy Does It,* in 1990, he eliminated the in-house sales staff altogether. Then he offered them the opportunity to form their own companies and represent KC as independent representatives. Four years later, Prebich says the strategy has worked. By paying independent reps the standard 15 to 20 percent commission plus bonuses as incentives, Prebich eliminated heavy travel and entertainment costs as well as expensive benefit programs. "I would not consider hiring in-house employees to sell advertising," Prebich says now.

By contrast, Doug Edgell of Randolph, New Jersey-based Edgell Communications, works very closely with his salespeople and insists that they specialize in the market their magazine serves. Each of Edgell's three trade magazines—*RIS News, Consumer Goods Manufacturer* and *Retail Systems Reseller*—has a separate sales team that is paid a base salary and a commission on a sliding scale, based on net revenues. As a salesperson's net revenues reach certain increments, the commission's percentage rises. "As they get into the big money, share it with them disproportionately, and that motivates them," Edgell counsels.

Edgell and his wife, Gabrielle, are part of each magazine's sales team. But each salesperson is compensated for every piece of business, no matter who makes the sale. There are no house accounts and no exclusives. Everything is shared. "I don't care if the client is my long-time friend and I go fishing with him every year," Edgell says. "[My salesperson] is coming with me on the sales call. I'm encouraging my people to come in and constantly take my turf away from me."

Sharing Edgell's commitment to the team approach to sales, John Miller, president and publisher of Equal Opportunity Publishing in Hauppauge, New York, says it is important to make every sale "a cause for celebration." At EOP, most sales are made over the telephone, and a bell is rung every time a sale is made—an act that Miller says "energizes the whole staff." But bell-ringing doesn't put food on the table. EOP salespeople are paid a base salary plus commission, and extra incentives are given for bringing in new business. Each time the account is renewed, the salesperson gets an additional bonus, like insurance salespeople. "That encourages salesmen to stay on top of new accounts," says Miller, who happily reports that ad sales are up 8.5 percent over last year's figures.

The aim is to align motivational tactics with realistic financial goals—and remember that no compensation plan is the universal solution. Publishers need to develop compensation structures that dovetail with their own corporate philosophies and financial priorities. Says Wenner Media's Brownridge: "The purpose of the compensation plan is to clarify, crystallize, focus and motivate the sales force." When someone suggests a change, he adds, "If the language is right, we'll do it. If it muddies the water, then the plan stays as it is." □

The State of Church and State

BY LORRAINE CALVACCA

Magazines are increasingly *charging one person with the classically adversarial roles of editor and publisher. Are two heads still better than one when it comes to producing a book with editorial integrity? Here, some industry veterans offer their views.*

John Brady, consultant, Brady & Paul Communications: I really feel it is a marriage that doesn't work. Show me someone who has the title of editor/publisher, and I'll show you a publisher in sheep's clothing. Someone who carries both titles has to be first and foremost a publisher, and the title of editor comes with it either to save money and create the illusion that there is someone who can do both jobs on one salary, or it's to express the rather apparent attitude from on high that this is a magazine that is not editorially driven. It is in the hands of the commercial side of the enterprise and therefore its editorial integrity is, at the very least, suspect.

Ed Kosner, editor in chief, *Esquire*: It depends on the magazine. Business magazines couldn't have an editor/publisher because most stories are written about advertisers. An advertiser who was unhappy would complain to someone who is responsible for advertising *and* editorial, and that's not a good position to be in. Otherwise, it can be a good thing, depending on the skills of the person. Being both editor and publisher worked well for me at *New York*. From one standpoint, you can make damned sure that the editorial department gets the support it needs and making sure the reproduction is good. It can also be good if you have one vision or sensibility about the magazine.

Gary Hengstler, editor/publisher, *ABA Journal*: Your first priority is to stay in business. The biggest problem is how much do you need to bend to stay in business? You can have editorial parity, but if you lack in advertising and the magazine folds, what do you gain? There can't be a complete separation of church and state. When we prepare the editorial calendar, we consult with the sales reps and the associate publisher and we ask what advertisers are looking for in edit. Just because an idea comes from outside the edit department does not mean it's not legitimate. We then see if there is a legitimate editorial fit. For example, a lot of our advertisers are legal software publishers. They would like to see articles about legal technology. Lawyers want to know more about it, so rather than focus on court cases we have increased the number of stories on law practice management and technology. Readers benefit from the information and advertisers from the environment. It comes down to this, when it comes to integrity: When I'm dead and gone, people can say many things, but I will maintain a good reputation as a journalist who ran a good magazine and didn't sell out.

Michael Levy, publisher, *Texas Monthly*: We believe in church and state. I own the candy store, but Greg Curtis [editor] owns the magazine. The only thing I can do is fire the editor. Short of that, everything is subject to Greg's purview. My job is to pay for it all. He doesn't tell me how to sell ads. I don't tell him how to do the editorial. In selling ads, we are constantly hit with advertisers who say, "Write about us." I say, "If you deserve a story, you will get it whether you spend one dime or not." We've seen a number of magazines go out of business in Texas. One reason is that they had rubber rate cards. The other is they wrote about advertisers. Everyone thought that they were whores. Advertisers love when the magazines write about them, but they don't respect them the next day.

Mark Mulvoy, editor, *Sports Illustrated*: I don't know how you'd find the time to serve two masters. It's emotionally, physically and professionally impossible. I found the six months as editor and publisher at *Sports Illustrated* very wearying. First you're closing the magazine, the next thing, you're in a circ strategy meeting. You don't spend as much time figuring out the stories and working with the writers. The best magazines are hands-on, but how can you be hands-on if your time is fractionalized? You're talking about the rare person who can make the hard sell and edit the book. Not many editors have an instinct for the business world. If you try to do both, it's inevitable that one or the other or both will suffer. If you sell out either side, suddenly half of the business is your enemy. There's no question that it's a major balancing act.

Create Power Testimonials

BY JULIE A. LAITIN

Testimonials can be enormously useful in convincing your audience of the benefits of your magazine. They are objective, third-party endorsements from credible, authoritative speakers who are willing to put their names and reputations on the line. All participants enjoy shared benefits and mutual advantages from a testimonial program, which can turn complimentary statements into bottom-line profits.

Testimonials must be strong, attention-getting and concrete. The more specific they are, the more of an impression they will make on others—and on your circulation numbers and ad sales. Every word should reinforce your magazine's benefits and advantages. Statements by people who simply "like" your magazine or think it is "a fine publication" will not convince anyone of anything. Although this sounds straightforward, it takes planning and skill to get people to voice strong statements of benefit that will convince a skeptical audience.

When you are planning a testimonial program, think about the results that your readers and advertisers get from reading or advertising in your magazine, and then work backwards. Put together a wish list of statements you would like to have as testimonials. For readers, this might include statements that your magazine offers valuable information and advice; provides insights into their relationships, families, professions and special interests; or helps them improve or advance in their jobs, professions or outside activities.

For advertisers, your wish list might include statements that your magazine creates awareness, visibility and exposure for their names, products and services; reaches lucrative new and/or existing markets; brings in sales (usually for direct-mail advertisers); generates response; and paves the way for their sales staffs.

With your wish list firmly in mind, your next step is to contact prospective endorsees. Generally speaking,

> A good testimonial program can turn complimentary statements into bottom-line profits for your magazine.

the better known the endorsers are, the more likely readers are to sit up and take notice. Ideally, they should be people who are well known and well respected in their fields, authoritative speakers whose approval carries weight. But where do you find them?

Ask your co-workers

Your editor can be one source of help in finding readers like this. Editorial board members might also fit the bill. On the advertising side, your sales staff should be able to give you superb leads. In fact, asking for advertisers' participation gives your staff a wonderful reason to contact important customers.

Ideally, your editor or sales staff will contact participants and tell them to expect your call. If your staff can't do this, then you will simply have to call cold. Here, presentation is everything. First, let people know who you are, why you are calling, and what you are planning. Second, tell them they will be among the "select group of readers (or advertisers)" who will be participating. This reinforces their sense of being part of a small, elite group. Then ask for their agreement.

Once you have their agreement, participants will usually ask if you want a verbatim taken over the phone or would prefer a letter. I have found that personal interviews conducted then and there give you the best results. They allow you to guide the speakers' comments and frame them into strong, direct statements of benefit. Through your questions and suggestions, you can encourage each participant to focus on a different benefit. This ensures that all the benefits on your wish list will be featured, and that no two participants will say the same thing in the same way. And telephone interviews give you the statements you need immediately.

Getting your testimonials via letter can take time, sometimes months. And often once you get them, they are so watered down that they are virtually useless. If you have been promised a testimonial that fails to come, you might consider writing a testimonial yourself and sending it with a letter offering it as a sample. Be sure to emphasize that the person can, of course, use his or her own words and statements in place of yours.

Organize your material

Feature the strongest statement from each testimonial as the headline. The body copy can follow up with additional comments that reinforce or expand this statement. Keep the copy brief, deleting extraneous material.

When you are editing testimonials, it is permissible to take creative liberties as long as you keep the integrity of the original thought. Such liberties might include shortening the headline or deleting words and phrases to simplify and strengthen the statements. Participants do not mind improvements in style, and even find it acceptable to include additional benefits that coincide with their own statements. They do not, however, appreciate vastly altered thoughts or inflated numbers.

Once you have your material assembled and edited, you need to get approval from the endorsees. Send two copies of every proposed endorsement to each participant, and ask that it be approved and signed, with one copy returned to you. This protects you against any errors in their statements. And because companies sometimes decide to switch their spokespeople at the last minute, it helps you avoid political blunders.

Some endorsees, once they see their statements in black and white, alter or even dilute their statements for fear of giving too much away to competitors. Recognize that it is far worse to have an angry reader or advertiser than it is to display a positive endorsement that has less vitality than it once had.

A bevy of bonuses

Testimonials can support your promotional efforts in a variety of ways.

• As media kit inserts, testimonials can show both advertiser and reader support. However, don't mix tes-timonials from both groups. Create separate inserts for placement in your editorial and advertising sections. You can do this by combining the statements into one insert, for each group, of one, two or even four pages. This is more manageable and has more impact than a dozen separate sheets, all on different stationery, each from a different respondent.

• As in-house advertisements, testimonial ads can be designed in a variety of sizes and inserted on an as-needed basis. Each ad should spotlight a major benefit from each participant and be run with the others on a rotating basis. Advertiser testimonials can be organized one to a page, or several to a page, with spokespeople all from the same category-specific industry.

Put power into your testimonials

Remember that when you are designing reader testimonials, visuals should show the speakers doing something that relates to your magazine: They might be bicycling, playing with their children, or instructing their staffs. Pictures of people in action get more attention than pictures that are posed.

Advertiser testimonials, on the other hand, can show either the company's ad or its spokesperson. Showing your customers' ads is far more powerful than showing their portraits. First, advertisements are considerably more interesting to see and read, and readers are curious to see the kind of ad that generated results. Second, testimonials that show successful ads are more likely to encourage the participation of advertisers who know that their ads will be showcased free of charge—even if it is in the interests of promoting your magazine.

Finally, a campaign theme will strengthen your program immeasurably. This calls for a theme line at the top of every ad, with the headline in quotes beneath it. *People* used the theme *"People* Performs," for example; *Business Facilities* used "Set Your Sites on Success with *Business Facilities."*

Remember, well-planned testimonials pay dividends, strengthening your circulation and sales promotion efforts. They require time and thoughtful planning, but the bottom-line benefits justify the effort. ☐

Neutralize Your Rate-Cutting Competitors

BY JAMES PARKER

Astute publishers and sales managers accept that long-term client relationships are the key to continuous sales growth. But given the extraordinary amount of competition in virtually every market segment, there will always be second- or third-tier competitors willing to cut rates to snatch away your hard-won business. And other things being equal, your clients wouldn't be human if they didn't go with the lower-priced option—or at least pressure you to match the lower price.

But there is a way to eliminate these price-cutters once and for all: Ensure that other things never are equal. In short, the day a client believes you are acting in his or her interests rather than your own is the day price ceases to be the dominant factor in media-buying decisions.

Achieving such a relationship takes time and patience, but is actually not that difficult. Here are some tips:

1. Improve your editorial.

This doesn't mean splashing on more color or doubling the number of pages. Rather, it is a matter of making sure that editorial content accurately meets the needs of your target audience. In the business press, this invariably means slicing out as much advertorial as possible and replacing it with reports on specific threats to and opportunities in each particular market. In consumer magazines, it's more a matter of staying close to your readers, and constantly brainstorming for ideas and trends that affect them.

Once you've achieved superior editorial, it's crucial to ensure that your clients understand that the better the editorial quality, the more time readers will spend studying the adjoining ads. You need to keep hammering that point home: Very few advertisers will make the connection on their own.

The long-term aim should be to create an editorial product so good that you could confidently ask adver-

Turn your customers into partners and in the process it's harder for them to be swayed by something as "irrelevant" as price.

tisers to poll their major clients to find out which title they read and respect. Even if you know that most won't bother, the fact that you're prepared to issue such a challenge is sure to impress them.

2. Offer service, service, service.

The first marketing tip I ever learned was the old maxim that "Success comes not from the sale, but from the re-sale." As soon as a new client's ad appears in your magazine, competitors will start swarming around in an attempt to get your client to switch the business to them—usually offering generous discounts in the process. The only way to repeat or better that first schedule at card rates is to convince the advertiser that you're not just a media rep, but a business partner as well.

Last year, for example, one of our titles picked up a new client that has subsequently become the magazine's second largest advertiser. Today this client advertises exclusively through us (in a very crowded market) because we offered their marketing managers service every step of the way. In the process, we've convinced them that our fortunes are tied to theirs—which in a sense is not far from the truth.

As sales guru Tom Hopkins is fond of pointing out, clients can't realistically expect to enjoy the best quality product with the finest back-up service, yet pay the cheapest price. Convince advertisers that "price" and "value" are entirely different concepts, then provide that value through superior service.

3. Be pro-active.

Call up clients to offer possible editorial ideas for ad-related features or product surveys. Your clients may not have the time to write press releases themselves, so keep a list of reliable freelance PR writers and photographers that you can pass on when the need arises.

Obviously, it's important not to make any promises, and not to compromise the magazine's editorial credibility. But for those advertisers without their own PR strategy or agency, your thoughtfulness will definitely be appreciated.

4. Help clients find new business opportunities.

One of my clients once mentioned that he was seeking a new distributor for a cheaper line of glue guns. By coincidence, I knew of another advertiser who wanted to extend his range of packaging products. So I introduced the two to each other.

Keep your eyes open for these sorts of opportunities: Whether or not a deal is consummated, such assistance helps convince advertisers that you have their concerns at heart. A sales rep's industry network is often bigger than that enjoyed by his or her advertisers. Don't be afraid to use these contacts to your—and their—advantage.

5. Get them involved.

Guide your biggest clients around your office, introduce them to production and editorial staffs, and show them how the process of putting a magazine together works. Make them feel valued, and—more important—make them feel a part of your business.

6. Become a friend.

If necessary, even seek out other media that may help them. One of our advertisers wanted to expand his client universe beyond the particular segment our mag-azine serves. But because he didn't use an ad agency, he wasn't sure where to start. We advised on suitable magazines within each new sector that he wanted to attack, even when these new titles didn't fall within our stable.

Some may argue that such a strategy is counterproductive. But in this case, the client was so impressed that we'd looked beyond our own immediate self-interests that he switched his entire business for our segment to us—and out of our much less expensive competitor's magazines.

7. Assist with creative.

Even if you have your own creative department, or the client uses an agency, don't be afraid to brainstorm ideas that you think might work. This shows clients that you understand their business and are as concerned as they are that their ad dollars are effectively spent. And don't be afraid to criticize a client's concept constructively (or even, in extreme circumstances, the agency's) if you think their advertisement will not generate the desired response.

The effect of such strategies will be to turn customers into partners, making it much harder for them to be swayed by something as "irrelevant" as price.

Obviously, this is a time-consuming process. And given the need to find new business, you can't lavish such attention on all your clients. But if you value the business of, say, your 20 largest spenders and want to make sure they maintain or increase their business at card rates, you are going to have to go that extra mile. But isn't that what characterizes the best sales reps, anyway? ☐

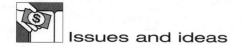

The Pariah Factor

BY MICHAEL KAPLAN

Selling magazine pages is tough under the best of circumstances. But what happens when the readers your magazine attracts repel mainstream advertisers?

Then the task of selling advertising is Herculean. *Mother Jones, High Times, Poz* and *Soldier of Fortune* have few editorial commonalties, but they share surprisingly similar ad-sales challenges. In spite of strong editorial focuses, decent to excellent demographics, devoted readers and sound operations, these four titles are not exactly first-choice venues for America's major advertisers.

Herewith, a glimpse into the ongoing resistance these magazines face and the strategies they've employed in selling around media-buyers' fears.

■ Mother Jones

Like many products of the sixties and seventies, leftist political bimonthly *Mother Jones* (which in fact was launched in 1976, but has the soul of a sixties baby) has come to seem a little stale to potential advertisers. "The magazine got stamped as this vintage-seventies left-wing rag," publisher Jay Harris acknowledges, recalling a ground-breaking story on exploding Ford Pintos. "Now, in the 1990s, the fact that we deal with politics is not a problem. [The problem] is the perception that we dote on the politics of another era. The perception is that this magazine is for over-the-hill baby boomers."

In the early 1980s, *Rolling Stone* faced a similar problem. The Wenner Media title resolved it by sinking loads of money into its now-famous perception/reality ad campaign. As a nonprofit organization, though, *Mother Jones* is ill-equipped for such a costly undertaking. Instead, the magazine—which Harris admits had been in maintenance mode until last year—is working slowly but cheaply toward changing its image.

One step in the process has been to establish a site on the World Wide Web. "It has generated a very strong response on the college and grad-school level, which we had specifically targeted," says Harris. The payoff can be seen in new ads that grace the magazine's pages. "We've tripled our music advertising," Harris continues,

adding that the bands in its ad well are surprisingly contemporary. "The Cranberries, Joan Osborne and various world music artists are being advertised. PolyGram Records has put in a couple of ads," he says. "And A&M Records and Sony Music Entertainment will have space in the next issue."

Harris and his three-person sales staff have concentrated their efforts on traditionally receptive categories: socially responsible investment firms, record labels and books. Still, he admits the really major advertisers have yet to come around. "[Our] audience should be square in the sights of Saturn and Saab," says Harris. "But the problem tends to be that our numbers—circulation of 120,000—are not big enough." Pressed on whether this is really the only issue, he admits, "We have a qualitative argument—a lot of our readers are opinion leaders and early adopters—but we have thus far been unable to make it stick," Harris says. This in spite of the fact that he can show that 50 percent of *Mother Jones* readers regularly purchase new Japanese cars.

Harris' combined opinion-leader/youthful-reader positioning has worked with smaller advertisers, however, which has helped raise the magazine's ad pages by 25 percent this year. "We are at fault for not being as aggressive as this product can handle," allows Harris. "We need to turn up the heat, to go after national consumer accounts in a really big way. For an awful lot of advertisers, *Mother Jones* [could] represent a very positive, liberal, engaged part of society. I mean, it's not like we're very far out of the mainstream. Hell, we're your neighbors."

■ High Times

Serving as a poster child for the First Amendment will cost you. The founders of the 200,000-circulation, marijuana-connoisseur title *High Times* know it, and so does the Drug Enforcement Administration. When the magazine's exhortations to flout the law proved impossible to stifle, DEA agents went after its advertisers of ganja-growing/consuming equipment.

"The government went into advertisers' offices with ongoing investigation warrants and asked to see sales records from the last five years," recalls advertising director Harry Crossfield Jr. "They said, 'If we find any of your customers using these lights for growing marijuana, you will be arrested as an accessory.'"

Suddenly *High Times* was a total pariah, even with those advertisers who couldn't get ads accepted elsewhere. Robbed of his endemic base, Crossfield bulked up his book with page after page of 900-number phone-sex ads. He knew that it cheapened the magazine and further reduced its likelihood of getting national advertising, but he was desperate. Now, however, with ad sales back on an even keel, he hopes to phase out the sex sponsors. "We currently have the music industry behind us," says Crossfield. "Companies like Sony, Warner and Atlantic represent one-fifth of our revenue."

Another new revenue source is Hollywood. Aggressively pushing the magazine's youthful demographics, Crossfield has attracted ads by DDB Needham Los Angeles for its movie clients. It began with *Dazed and Confused* (a film about high-school pot-heads in the seventies—a perfect fit) and continues with less obvious films such as *Kiss of Death*. "I went after movie people for a long time," says Crossfield, whose sheer persistence has finally paid off.

Although Crossfield has managed to attract a few spirits producers by co-sponsoring events, he has had no luck in wooing cigarette companies. This is in spite of the fact that R.J. Reynolds Tobacco has been running an ad that depicts people selling cigarettes as if they were contraband.

The point, of course, is that further government crackdowns on tobacco may end with it becoming illegal. "I called RJR and told them that they have the same problem we had in 1937," recounts Crossfield, referring to the year in which marijuana was banned. "They said, 'No. It will never be the same thing.' I said, 'Really? just wait.' Our readers are not all cigarette smokers, but they definitely are sympathetic to the issue." No matter, cigarette ads still do not appear in the pages of *High Times*.

Crossfield's next target category is fashion. He has managed to land a few fashion accounts (albeit, companies that make clothing from hemp), and he's looking hopefully toward Adidas USA, which is about to release a sneaker made from hemp called The Chronic—drug slang for really good pot. "Donna Karan has announced that she is doing hemp and Calvin Klein is going to start working with it as well," says an opti-

mistic Crossfield. "The hope is that I can convince them to advertise hemp clothing in here. Eventually that may lead to ads for their regular clothing."

Does Crossfield believe that the magazine will ever be part of a major advertiser's media schedule? "Most agencies won't even sit down and talk to me," he admits. "And I accept that for now. But once marijuana is legalized, they will all flock to us."

■ *Poz*

Forget the demographics and spending patterns; certain advertisers just won't place ads in gay publications. Period. Now try selling them on a magazine aimed at the HIV-positive community. When Sean O'Brien Strub decided to launch the bimonthly *Poz*, he faced daunting opposition.

"We have a real problem with agencies recommending the magazine to clients," admits the publisher/executive editor, who is HIV-positive himself. "We are new, our circulation has not been audited, and we're about AIDS. People get weird." However, Strub adds, he has found a way of working around the fear factor: "We go directly to clients and create safe spaces where agencies can recommend us."

An example of how badly agencies may misjudge clients' receptivity to advertising in "problematic" publications is exemplified by a recent encounter between *Poz* and Tanqueray gin. The distiller helped sponsor a bike-a-thon to raise money for AIDS research; the 100,000-circulation *Poz* was a co-sponsor of the event. Yet Tanqueray's ads promoting the race (which seemed to be everywhere else this summer) were conspicuously absent from *Poz*. Ultimately, Tanqueray apologized to Strub, characterizing the seeming snub as a mix-up.

Strub acknowledges that the question of carrying alcohol ads—considering that substance abuse is recognized as a conduit to risky sex—is a difficult one. But he has devised a resourceful way of working around it: "I pitched a liquor company, which has been very responsive to the gay community, to center a series of ads around responsible drinking. The idea is that you drink responsibly so that you do not risk your life with irresponsible sexual behavior. They were intrigued, and now I am waiting to hear back." Already in the magazine, Miller Brewing has created special ads that rally support for AIDS research charities.

> What happens when the readers your magazine attracts repel mainstream advertisers?

By approaching agencies and advertisers one-on-one, Strub himself has managed to change some perceptions about the HIV-positive community. When his magazine first launched, its advertising centered around gloom and death. Strub has since managed to convince some advertisers—such as travel agents who serve the gay community—that people with HIV want to live their remaining time to the fullest. They want to go on dream vacations and enjoy peak experiences.

Poz's sales staff has also targeted medical advertisers, some of whom now target ads explicitly at readers who are HIV-positive. "Nizoral shampoo is a great example of that," Strub says, pointing out that scalp flaking can be acute among those infected with HIV. "I had been having that problem and nothing seemed to help. Nizoral cleared it right up. I wrote to the manufacturer and told them that I liked the shampoo and wanted it in the magazine. My salespeople and I drove to their headquarters in New Jersey and had a meeting. By the time we returned to the office, they had faxed us a contract for a nine-times insertion order."

Strub is on his way to convincing advertisers that his readers represent viable consumers—only half of the *Poz* audience is actually HIV-positive—and many advertisers are responding favorably. "The ultimate statement of support would be for a car company to advertise in *Poz*," says Strub, adding that Subaru has expressed tentative interest. "Look at me," says Strub. "I have zero T-cells, and I bought a new Jeep Cherokee just three weeks ago."

■ *Soldier of Fortune*

Monthly mercenary handbook *Soldier of Fortune* had always been a hard sell to anyone other than manufacturers of weapons or espionage gear. But after news broke in 1985 that a reader had hired a hit man through an *SOF* classified to rub out his wife, advertisers became exceedingly skittish.

Augment that with magazine founder Robert K. Brown's distaste for cigarette ads, and you get an idea of what kind of job associate publisher T. "Lefty" Wilson (he begged us not to publish his real first name, for fear that it would sound too prissy) faces every day.

But he tries. "We don't have the money for our people to be out there, beating the bushes on Madison Avenue," says Wilson. "We have pitched the large agencies. We sent out media kits and got a couple of phone calls back. But they didn't generate anything in terms of pages; the military is not very popular right now. We'd love to get automobiles and liquor into the magazine. We came close to getting a Humvee ad—after all, it's military related—but then people advised them to stay away from [us]. They backed off."

Citing a circulation of 100,000 and an average median household income of $50,000 for its readers, Wilson insists his problem is primarily image. He understands why Anheuser-Busch and Chrysler are spooked by *SOF's* politics, but expresses surprise that some of the likelier prospects get cold feet. "When people have high-ticket items—like night-vision goggles—they get nervous about *Soldier of Fortune*," he admits. "They think our readers are riding around in pick-up trucks with $200 to their name." Wilson tries to correct that impression. "We try positioning ourselves as a newsmagazine that reports on wars ignored by the mainstream media. Also, we've been very active with gun rights and the Waco situation. Our politics are very conservative, and they will remain that way. We've been around for 20 years, and we don't want to go out and say that we will let the advertisers direct our editorial content." (Wilson's pitch eventually won over the night-vision goggle-maker.)

Although Wilson would like mainstream ads, he insists that he already sells out his ad pages each month and seems relatively content to fill *SOF* with paid messages from the NRA, Military Book of the Month Club and Wesson Firearms and Glock, Inc. (The last two, he points out, are the Cadillac and BMW of *SOF's* world.)

Indeed, *Soldier of Fortune's* most successful advertiser promotion may be its annual convention in Las Vegas. "We have 700 tables and 300 booths and 12,000 walk-through visitors," he says. "Some of the exhibitors participate in the convention before becoming comfortable enough to take out an ad. We have a three-gun shooting match, a banquet, canine demonstrations and self-defense courses. We [also] hold what we call the Mad Minute—actually about two-and-a-half minutes—with machine guns going off and blowing up dynamite targets. It's very awesome." □

Ad Sales Must Wise Up About Circulation

BY BRUCE SHEIMAN

With the current emphasis on circulation revenue, circulators are becoming the new heroes of magazine publishing. And as a former circulation director, I applaud this long-overdue recognition. However, circulation still has quite a long way to go before it becomes the equal of advertising sales. The traditional view prevails that circulation, although growing in importance, remains a function subordinated to advertising.

Despite this, there is no question that circulation is gaining in importance, recognition and respect. To help set the stage for the continued ascendancy of circulation management, I want to address what many circulators over the years have identified as the misconceptions and faulty expectations that advertising people—and by extension, many publishers—have regarding circulation.

Circulation is not a faucet. Hard as it is to believe, many ad salespeople continually beseech their circulation counterparts to grow circulation to demonstrate their magazine's editorial vitality to the advertising community. True, being able to demonstrate circulation growth and leadership gives an ad salesperson a powerful competitive advantage. What they need to understand, however, is that a magazine's circulation cannot be increased indefinitely. According to circulation consultant Ron Scott, there is such a thing as a "natural" circulation level—a level at which both subscription and newsstand sales are profitable on their own merits, and based on which advertisers pay a cost per thousand that does not require them to subsidize circulation. Some publishers, of course, have already come to this realization. *Time, McCall's* and *Reader's Digest* have all lowered their ratebases in the past several years.

If the circulation department is to be run more as a profit center, then serious consideration must be given to the cost of acquiring circulation. The days are over when escalating ad rates and increasing volume more than compensated for increased circulation expenses.

The circulation department can't significantly alter a magazine's demographic profile. Many magazine publishers and advertising directors wish their publications had different readership profiles. But this is like a person wanting a different eye color. Just as a person's eye color is genetically determined, a magazine's readership composition is editorially determined: It is almost entirely the result of the magazine's editorial content. Some magazines are destined to have older than desirable readerships (such as the women's service magazines), or predominantly female readerships (such as health magazines), despite an advertising director's wish to the contrary.

The circulation department can try to nudge readership in one direction or another by selecting different circulation sources or different direct-mail lists. But it is impossible to change a magazine's readership profile significantly without changing its editorial content—and, even then, the desired change could take several years.

Renewals are not an absolute. Every circulation manager dreads being asked about a magazine's renewal rate—an inquiry usually prompted by an advertiser. The reason, simply, is that there really is no such thing as *a* renewal rate. Every magazine has several renewal rates—conversions, first-time renewals, second-time

> It's important that advertising people become more familiar with the circulation side so that they better understand what they're selling.

renewals, renewals at birth, identified renewals and unidentified renewals, as well as rates for each distinct source of subscriptions.

More important, every magazine is characterized by such different market dynamics that making a generalization beyond the frame of reference for that particular magazine is difficult—if not hazardous. If I were to tell you, for example, that a particular title's conversion rate (*i.e.*, the percentage of new subscribers who choose to subscribe for a second term) is 25 percent, you would probably quickly assume that the magazine is in serious trouble. But if I then told you that this is the figure for a bridal magazine to which people subscribe, quite naturally, for a short period, then 25 percent suddenly looks rather good.

Direct-mail agents are okay—really. One of the reasons that one cannot identify a magazine's agent-sold subscriptions on an ABC statement is that they are viewed by some advertisers—and, by extension, some ad salespeople—in a negative light. But the reality is that Publishers Clearing House and American Family Publishers subscriptions are essentially no different demographically or psychographically from a magazine's direct-to-publisher derived subscribers.

PCH and AFP mail to just about everyone with a mailbox. In a typical mailing, they offer more than 100 different magazines. And while the majority of sweepstakes promotions appeal to middle America, this is not exclusively the case. Everyone in America knows that PCH and AFP offer the best prices. And with more than 100 magazines to choose from, respondents select only those magazines that they are most interested in.

Customized subscription sources are frequently unproductive. Every circulation manager has a similar story. The publisher or ad director or even the editor has a bright idea to reach a magazine's purest, most on-target prospective readers. If it's a parenting magazine, they ask that subscription offers be distributed through daycare centers. If it's a business magazine, they suggest distribution of offers through corporations. If it's a health magazine, they recommend distribution of offers through hospitals. These are all good ideas. But, at best, these customized programs can be no more than supplementary sources of paid subscriptions. They should be pursued only after a circulation department has worked through the more traditional, ostensibly less targeted, sources—such as direct mail, insert cards, newsstand, and so on.

Customized sources of circulation may not be very expensive in terms of a magazine's investment in materials, but they typically are very labor intensive. If a magazine's ratebase is 500,000, a customized program that "costs" a magazine five hours per month in man-agement time and generates just 300 net subscriptions per month is a very inefficient use of a circulation department's resources.

Moreover, contrary to the hope of ad directors and editors, these sources rarely generate many subscriptions. This is in large part because prospective subscribers have not been pre-qualified as mail buyers. Let's take the parenting magazine example. It may sound counter-intuitive, but knowing that someone has subscribed to other, compatible magazines is a better predictor of whether a person will subscribe to a parenting magazine than knowing that a person has three children.

Readership numbers and subscriber numbers can't be compared. Usually included in a magazine's media kit are demographic comparisons of the magazine and its various competitors. And often what is compared is the magazine's subscriber information and the competitor's syndicated readership information generated by MRI or SMRB. And guess what? The competition will be shown to have comparatively inferior demographic profiles.

Why? Subscribers (made up of buyers only) and readers (which includes buyers as well as pass-along readers) are like the proverbial apples and oranges: They can't be compared. Proof of this incomparability comes from taking a look at the differences between subscribers and readers for the same magazine. Almost always, subscribers are more affluent. And this makes sense: Those who paid for the magazine have more money than those who are content to read a pass-along copy.

Pass-along readers are the great modulators, diminishing the strength of any particular characteristic. For example, if a magazine's subscribers tend to skew female, readership figures will show a more balanced proportion of men and women (resulting from men in the household being counted as "readers"). If subscribers tend to be older, readership will show a younger age. And so on.

It's important that advertising people become more familiar with the nuances of the circulation side of the business—less for academic or intellectual reasons and more so that they—and their publishers—will better understand what they are selling. □

promotion

"Most trade magazines are gold mines of information that the consumer media could and would use **if the information were properly packaged** and presented."—p. 294

"Before you decide which television shows you think your article will work for, make sure **you've actually watched them.**"—p. 298

"It's remarkable how **few publishers seem to recognize a good ad.** As proof, we point to publishers' own house ads."—p. 300

How to Get PR Without a PR Pro

BY GEORGE SIMPSON

Often, when editors and/or publishers see news stories that favorably position a competitive magazine, they grumble about how effective the competition's PR is—and lament that they haven't the resources to gain the same kind of exposure for themselves. Putting aside the debate about just how effective PR people can be "getting ink" where none is deserved, the fact is that publishers can do quite a bit on their own to get publicity for their magazines.

There are something like 13,000 magazines published in North America, 9,500 classified as trade or professional journals. Most trade books are gold mines of information that the consumer media could and would use if the information were properly packaged and presented in a timely fashion.

That leaves 3,500 consumer titles battling for the attention of bookers on "Good Morning America" and the other news and TV talk shows, and for the interest of high-profile reporters at *The New York Times, The Wall Street Journal* and *USA Today*. Your chances of turning up in their stories are greatly enhanced if your name is Tina; if you are partnering with Time Inc. Magazines; if you have exclusive rights to the private diaries of Princess Di; or if your circulation has shot from 25,000 to two million in 14 months. Nevertheless, you can raise the profile of your magazine—business or consumer—through a variety of resources listed herein, most of which don't require the help of a PR professional.

First, separate your "consumer" PR—that is, editorial content directed toward prospective newsstand buyers and subscribers (you may even catch an advertiser or two in the same net)—from your "trade" PR—which covers the business side and is designed to affect potential and current advertisers.

Consumer PR Rule #1 is to determine, "Is it news?" or "Is there enough human interest here to push some buttons?" It is extremely difficult for most editors to step far enough away from their work to be objective. (I recall an editor who, at the end of each month's editorial meeting, would conclude that he had at least 35 stories worthy of national publicity!) But failing to be relentlessly honest about the newsworthiness or human interest of what you decide to promote will only result in wasted time and effort, whereas a clear-headed approach can bring you spectacular results.

So if you have an article worthy of some media attention, where do you start?

Pick-up by the printed word

"Nothing can help your cause better than pick-up by the printed word," says Drew Kerr, president of New York City-based Four Corners Communications, "because all news sources—newspapers, television and radio—borrow from what they read. And the most effective way to get your words into black-and-white is via one of the major newswire services, The Associated Press or Reuters."

Timing is important, says Kerr: "The wires turn around stories pretty quickly, so a few days before your Big Story hits the newsstands, call the nearest wire service office, ask for the news desk, and tell whoever answers what your story is in no more than two or three sentences. If you've piqued their interest, they may ask you to fax or messenger it over. Ideally, you should staple a one-page, smartly-written, straight-to-the-point press release to the cover of your magazine. Always put an embargo date on the top in bold letters and highlight it. This is the date that you want your story to break in the news. One good wire story can snowball into a ton of coverage."

If you want to get your Big Story on TV, timing is again critical, says Kerr. Producers of the televised national morning shows and daytime talk shows work on a very advanced schedule—so start your PR efforts in the galley stage.

"Targeting a story to the right reporter is not difficult," says Kerr. "If there is a local newscaster who covers health, and your Big Story comes under that category, call up the station and ask who the producer is for that reporter. If your story doesn't fall under a particular reporter's beat, ask for the assignment, planning or futures desk and ask who is in charge."

Next, says Kerr, "Write that producer a one-page cover letter explaining the article, which issue of the magazine it will be in, and what the newsstand date is. Suggest who would represent the magazine, as well as what visuals could be provided for the segment."

Kerr stresses the importance of the visual aspect: "For example," he says, "if you are a food magazine ranking the five best hamburgers in the country, your proposal should be more than talking about grilled meat—it should suggest colorful chefs who could artfully demonstrate how to cook these classic burgers."

Finally, says Kerr, "Attach your letter to the story's galleys and send it to your targeted producer at least three weeks before the issue on-sale date. One week later, make a follow-up call to establish contact with the producer and perhaps flesh out the idea. Your enthusiasm and creativity will always carry the day."

Trade-side PR

The list of national reporters interested in the business success of magazines is remarkably short. But because they stand between you and the advertising community (both agency and client), they take on a disproportionate importance. The most significant trend in their coverage has been away from features to reporting news. So, just as with the consumer PR side, your first consideration must be, "Is it newsworthy?" The second should be, "Is it trendy?" Third: "Is it truly innovative?"

News can be as seemingly insignificant as a ratebase increase or as major as a start-up; in either case, a media release is appropriate. A news release should contain just that—news. Leave out all promotional phrases such as "landmark," "exciting" and "innovative." Also omit extraneous commentary such as, "We are pleased and excited to ... ". Try to keep it to a single page—and, most important, be totally accurate.

Research studies are always of interest to the media, particularly if they reveal something about consumer behavior that had been unknown. Those studies should be sent not only to ad trades, but also to the vertical trades read in the industries serving those consumers. For example, if a survey you sponsor reveals that women buy 95 percent of the neckties men wear, a half-dozen trades serving the garment industry and retail stores would love to see your data. Trade publishers should also keep in mind that their editors are marketable experts. For example, when PepsiCo realigned its marketing operation, the editor of *Beverage Digest* was quoted by *The New York Times* as an expert.

Foster closer relationships with key trade reporters by calling them with tips about news that is breaking elsewhere in the industry. Information is indeed power in the PR business. If you go on to pitch an idea, don't get frustrated if reporters don't share your enthusiasm about your magazine. Remember, they are bombarded by hundreds of publications—and what *you* think is innovative, *they* have already seen a time or two before.

All is not lost, however: Even if the reporter declines, you have brought yourself to his or her attention—which could result in coverage later.

Probably the single most important thing you can do is to start a media comp list to those who write about publishing for the ad and publishing trades, and to the handful of columnists around the country who highlight interesting editorial stories. Out-of-sight is indeed out-of-mind for those who are already on hundreds of comp lists.

If you are based outside New York City and plan a visit there, call reporters to arrange a meeting. The premise is simply to get acquainted, but you are better served by having a list of talking points rather than just shooting the breeze. Most important, never try to give reporters a sales presentation. They hate them, and you could be banishing your name from their Rolodexes for all time.

Now that you have the basics, review the resource guide supplied here for those listings that apply to your needs.

MAGAZINE PUBLIC-RELATIONS RESOURCES*

■ MEDIA DIRECTORIES
Sources for developing targeted mailings to appropriate reporters.
Bacon's: 800-621-0561
Newspaper/Magazine Directory: Annual, published in two volumes. Includes one mid-year update in print and a toll-free number for subscribers for updates: $275.
International Checker: Western Europe: $275.
Radio/TV Directory: $275.
Business/Financial Directory: All media, $275.
Can provide top editors' names on labels/diskettes.
Broadcast Interview Source: 202-333-4904
Power Media Selects: 2,300 of the most influential media in the country at 840 publications and broadcast operations. Overview of 17 different media segments. No updates: $166.50. Will provide mailing lists on label and discs.
Talk Show Selects: 750 leading radio and television shows in the country. Based on audience share/influence. No other media book has this information. Focuses on news talk programs. No updates: $185. Will provide mailing lists on labels and discs.

Yearbook of experts, authorities, spokespersons, 15th edition: Sourcebook for interviews, sent to 15,000 working members of the press, including wire services, magazines. You pay to list yourself as an expert in certain topics. One half-page ad, $695 ($50 to typeset); full page, $1,195 ($100 to typeset); reference listing, $425.

Burrelles Media Directory: 212-227-5570

Annual, published in November, with quarterly updates. Includes print: 1,800 dailies, 9,300 non-daily, 12,000 magazines; all major TV, radio and cable outlets.

Newspapers: Two books, $200.

Magazines: One book, $200.

Radio/TV/cable: Two books, $250.

Also sold on CD-ROM, $795.

Gebbie Press: 914-255-7560

Directory of all daily and weekly newspapers, TV stations, radio stations, magazines, trade publications, business papers. Black and Hispanic media and farm publications broken out separately. Annual. No updates: $85, $90 if billed. Also available on diskette. Prices vary depending on breakout.

Hudson's Directory: 914-876-2081

Washington News Media: Directory of all print and broadcast correspondents, foreign and domestic, who are located in the Washington, D.C., area. Listed geographically and by subject matter. Updated quarterly: $185.

New York Publicity Outlets: 203-354-9361

Published twice a year (July 1 and at the end of the year) by Public Relations Plus, Inc. All local and national print and broadcast (radio and TV) consumer media based within a 50-mile radius of New York City. Includes a national magazine editorial guide: $165 plus $7.50 shipping.

Metro California Media: All media throughout the entire state, published twice yearly: $165 plus $7.50 shipping.

■ MASS MAILING HOUSES

Companies that will reproduce your releases and mail or fax them to targeted mailing lists you design.

Bacon's: 800-621-0561

Mailing service: Full service includes printing release, photo reproduction, inserting release with magazine, mailing to selected targets provided by a variety of target options. (Example: one page to 100 contacts, $73 plus postage.)

Media Distribution Services: 800-637-3282

Maintains list by category, such as "science editors" and "science magazines." Pay per 100 names. One-time use of labels. Will also photocopy, collate, stuff, etc. Largest

distributor of media material to 165,000 dailies, weeklies, consumer, trade, broadcast, syndicates, Congress, security analysts. Updated daily by 25 researchers.

• Fast-fax: Simultaneous broadcast fax to editors including a personalized cover page—$1 per page up to 100, then prices drop.

• Targeter: PC-based package of media systems. Software available for $495, daily updates are additional $75 per month, plus fee for usage per label or name.

PIMS: 212-645-5112

Thirteen-year-old British company, in the United States eleven years. Maintains media lists. Also photocopies, collates, stuffs, etc. Reproduces and distributes color and b/w photos, slides, audio and videotapes. Produces kit covers, letterhead, etc.

PR Newswire: 212-832-9400

Affiliated with mailing house. Can do all PR and promotion mailings. Largest fax broadcast service (over 100 dedicated lines); $0.65 per page per news point (overnight). Higher rates for business hours.

■ PR WIRE SERVICES

Companies that will write your release and distribute it directly into the newsrooms of thousands of media outlets.

Business Wire: 212-575-8822

2,100 news points, $100 annual membership. National: $435 for the first 465 words, $115 each additional 100 words. Special targeted circuits: High-tech trade publications, $45; Entertainment, $395 per 100 words; Health, $450/400; Sports, $350; Automotive, $450; African-American media, $250; Hispanic, $250; Asian, $250. Overseas, cost varies.

PR Newswire: 212-832-9400

2,000 news points. $100 annual membership. National, $450 first 400 words; $110 each additional 100 words. Similar targeted circuits and costs.

Feature News Service: $230/400 words, $60 each additional 100. Numerous overseas services including Russia and China, translated into local languages.

■ CLIPPING SERVICES

Companies that clip publications and monitor broadcast to assemble a record of where you got play.

Bacon's: 800-621-0561

Clipping service: $219 per month (three-month minimum) plus $1.19 per clip. Full U.S. coverage, except newspapers under 3,000 circulation. Does not include broadcast coverage.

Burrelles Press Clipping Service: 212-227-5570

Print coverage: 17,900 publications (includes Canada). $246 per month plus $1.35 per clip. Television: 170 cities, 450 stations. Radio: 65 stations in 25 cities. $58 monthly, transcripts only, plus every 10 words $1.25.

"News Express": 50 largest newspapers/major business publications/network television—$2,050 per month includes 40 clips per day; over that, $1.25 per clip.

TV transcripts: $4 to $7 for full show.

Luce Press Clipping Service: 212-889-6711

Print media: 500 readers scan 16,000 publications, including every daily published in the United States; 7,000 weekly newspapers; 6,300 trade and consumer magazines; 200 English-language foreign publications; all major wire services: $245 monthly, plus $1.35 per clip.

"AM Newsbreak" scans 20 dailies/business publications. $45 per month, $5 per page per fax.

TV: covers 33 major markets, plus networks, PBS, some cable—$55 per month (first three months are free). Transcripts: each 10 words equals one clip ($1.35). Videotapes: $95 up to one hour.

"Impact" is a monthly or quarterly computer analysis of clipping tailored to clients. Price varies according to customer requirements. Can provide foreign coverage.

■ SERVICES TO REACH BROADCASTERS
Media Link: 212-682-8300

Photographic Service: Cover or inside photo sent via satellite to more than 700 stations, with repeated notification to station about the feed. No guarantees that it will be picked up. Doesn't monitor, usually. $750.

Satellite Media Tour: From New York or Los Angeles. Two hour 12- to 15-city tour includes booking, press kits, B-roll, on-site coordinator, satellite time, crew, monitoring. $11,200 to $12,000.

■ MAT SERVICES

Companies that help you write stories about your products or services, then distribute them in camera-ready format to thousands of newspapers. Local editors elect to run your story or not. Pick-up is generally good, but the market coverage is usually weak.

North American Precis Syndicate Inc.: 212-867-9000

• Suburban newspapers (3,800): Camera-ready, one-newspaper column. Writes column for you. One to 400 placements, $2,000.

• Television: Four slides (you provide, they duplicate) and script sent to 325 news and talk show/stations. Forty to 80 placements, $2650.

• Radio: 5,000 stations will result in two to 300 pick-ups/$1,850.

For all three services combined, the discount is $1,700. Costs include pick-up reports.

News USA: 800-355-9500

• Syndicated to 10,000 newspapers: Writes stories, production, distribution, follow-up reports with clips that include comparable ad-space values. $2,700 for a one-column feature of 200 words. Guarantees one to 400 newspapers and one-million circulation. Frequency discounts, even with changed content.

• 6,600 broadcast stations, documents results with airchecks. $3,400 for 60-second script (written). Script includes opportunity to be interviewed by user stations. Frequency discounts. Guaranteed 4,000 airplays.

■ PUBLICITY/MEDIA INFORMATION

Publications that identify upcoming publicity opportunities and/or explain how to pitch certain reporters.

Partyline: 212-755-3487

Identifies editorial needs of shows and publications. Weekly, two-sided page: $160 a year.

Bacon's: 800-621-0561

Media Calendar Directory: annual; editorial profiles/calendars: $275.

Note that prices and services listed in this compilation may vary. □

How to Get Yourself—
And Your Magazine—on TV

BY DREW REID KERR

For almost every magazine, there is a TV show that wants to use the editorial or editors as expert sources. In fact, television is more reliant on magazines as an idea pool than ever before because budget cuts have depleted the TV staffs that would normally come up with segment concepts in-house.

Although the merits of TV exposure are difficult to track in terms of circulation gains, TV will definitely boost the image of the magazine in the advertising community. Regardless of the perceived benefits of getting on television, everyone agrees that just about any TV publicity is good publicity—as long as they get the magazine's name right.

The objective, therefore, is to get the cover of your magazine shown on screen, to be interviewed on TV—or both. How do you start? You first have to decide what you want to get on TV—an article from your magazine or an editor. Then you must determine which show could use your material. And finally, you have to promote your material to the show's producers.

To get an article publicized on television, look at the table of contents of an upcoming issue and ask yourself these questions about any article you think might be appropriate for TV:

• Does it work visually? Put yourself in the shoes of the viewer. Is there action? An unusual backdrop? Does the article inform or tell a story in *visual* terms? Can the story be done with more than just talking heads— perhaps slides or video?

• Will the article appeal to the audience of the TV show you want it to appear on? For example, baby-boomer women are the primary viewers of shows like "The Joan Rivers Show," "The Home Show," and "Oprah." Their producers will be looking for unusual and interesting stories on issues that affect their viewers, such as health, sex, love and relationships, and celebrity matters.

• Does the article have a human interest angle, or does it reflect what's happening in the news? Good television

means an interesting story with real people. If your article makes its point with actual case studies or describes a trend that reflects things that are happening right now, it's an ideal candidate for publicity.

An important rule to remember is this: Not every article merits publicity, so go with the one, two or three stories that work best. There's no point sending out press releases on every single story just because they are in your magazine. Imagine you're a baseball pitcher who knows how to throw a fastball, a curveball, a spitball and a slider—but you throw fastballs and curveballs best. Just stick to those two pitches!

What does TV want?

Ironically, getting the attention of and working with television producers and talent bookers will force you to reverse the traditional role; you get to play the part of freelance writer pitching "the editor." You have to choose the appropriate TV programs likely to be receptive to your ideas, and you may have to tinker with your ideas a little to make them fly.

One of my favorite tricks for figuring out the right TV shows is to look at a magazine's table of contents and play a round of mental "Jeopardy." If the article is the answer, what is the question?

For example, if a magazine featured an article on how to control business health care costs, the question would be, "Can business lower its health insurance costs and still provide good benefits?" Then I ask myself, "What television shows would have audiences asking this very question?" Several come to mind, such as network business reports and news segments. The national morning network shows have more time than most shows to cover just about anything, and they welcome all submissions.

Trade publications are encouraged to work with business programs, no matter where they are located. "The more obscure, the better," says a reporter/producer for CNBC-TV. "Everyone grabs the stories from the

> Just about any TV publicity is good publicity—as long as they get the magazine's name right.

big magazines right away. But the small magazines know their industries better than anybody else, so they carry a lot of weight here."

Because trade editors are held in such high regard, they are often perfect candidates for 10- to 15-second sound bites on current business events. If, for example, there's a controversy in the steel industry that has caused government hearings, CNN and others will be looking for unbiased sources immediately—like the editors from *Iron Age, American Machinist* or *Journal of Metals.*

Another trick is to think of your readership (and your potential readership) and ask, "What television would they be watching?" Magazines about pharmaceuticals, jewelry appraisal, life insurance or personnel would be useless to the audiences of daytime shows like "Geraldo," but perfect for CNN or CNBC-TV. Then, there are topics that are hot on every TV program because of their newsworthiness: health, money, gadgets, the environment, women's issues, older Americans and family life.

A word of warning, however: Before you decide what shows you think your article will work for, make sure you have actually watched them. Take the time to set your VCR and tape your targeted programs. If you are targeting talk shows, pay particular attention to the personalities of the hosts, what kinds of guests they book, and what kind of relationship exists between them. If you suspect a personality clash, you may want to rethink your choice of program—or prepare yourself to deal with an adversarial situation.

Once you've mentally matched your article with a particular program, the next step is to get it on the show. Every TV producer has his own style of dealing with magazine material. As a rule of thumb, material should be sent out two to three weeks before the newsstand date for monthlies and quarterlies, and one to two days for weeklies. There are two ways to do it:

1. Send the magazine with one cover sheet of highlights and/or a press release. Take your best stories, synopsize them in one pithy paragraph each, and put your name and phone number on the bottom.

2. Send a galley or clipping of the article with a one-page note. Producers *will* read galleys—as long as they

are clear. In your note, describe the article's newsworthiness, summarize it succinctly, and suggest visuals that might be used.

If you have a publicist or use a PR firm, be sure they are as focused on your audience and the article as you are. Ideally, publicists should have long-established relationships with producers, which will get your foot in the door of most TV shows.

Once you're booked on a show, prepare to do some work. If you saw the film "Broadcast News," you know what a mess TV is behind the scenes. In real life, it can be even worse. Here's how you can help:
• Send them at least three copies of the magazine. Producers tend to lose things, and you want to make sure all the people involved in your segment have the material.
• Make it clear that you want the cover of the issue to be displayed on the air. You want your current and potential readers to know exactly what issue has the article.
• Make sure you and your producer are in sync in presenting the material. Go over your segment thoroughly: What questions will be asked? What props do you need to give them? How long will you be on? Who else will be on the show?

Have story, will travel

One last point. It's a myth that you must be located in New York or Los Angeles to be interviewed for television. Every national talk show has a sizable budget to provide travel, hotel and transfer accommodations to and from the TV studio. A few shows even share travel expenses if they are all featuring the same guest.

On the other hand, CNN has bureaus around the country and uses them all the time for live and taped interviews. The morning shows have affiliates in every major city that send their local reporters to tape stories and satellite them back to New York. Some shows have been known to send crews out nationwide for important stories.

If you are rejected, remember the old adage editors hand to freelancers: Try, try again! You will always have articles to publicize as long as another issue is just around the corner. □

Improving your Ad-itude

BY JOHN HANC & JACK SHERIN

Considering that publishers make a good part of their living by selling ads, it's remarkable how few seem to recognize a good one. As proof, we point to publishers' own house ads. Whether they're soliciting subscriptions, spotlighting upcoming special issues or promoting ancillary products, many publishers betray a lack of understanding of some of the most basic principles of ad copywriting and design.

Granted, there are few absolute rules in advertising copy and design. After all, advertising is not a hard science, it's a craft. And just as you can't teach cabinet-making in a day, we wouldn't presume to try to teach anyone to be an advertising creative in 1,500 words or less. But to help you further your own selling efforts through your house ads, we offer some tried-and-true guidelines on how to write and produce ads that are more likely to get read—and get results.

Let's begin with a headline that illustrates the guiding principles of copywriting as espoused by the great David Ogilvy. He urged us to flag the prospect, appeal to the reader's self interests, and respect long headlines. As early as the 1950s, Ogilvy could cite research showing that people are more likely to read headlines of six to 12 words—as long as the headline says something that's relevant to them. Presumably, this one is relevant to you:

Publishers: Want to create more effective house ads for your magazine? Follow these nine steps.

1. Before you write, think!

This IBM-like advice is entirely appropriate in advertising, too. Before you write, think—about what you are promoting, about the target audience and—often overlooked—about what, exactly, you are trying to communicate. You can't say everything about a special issue or an ancillary product in one ad, so concentrate on one important selling point.

2. Ask the right questions.

To avoid overlooking what might be important information when creating an ad for your magazine or any of its derivative products, keep in mind the advice that Keith Hafer and Gordon White offer in their textbook,

Advertising Writing. The authors recalled a veteran New York agency copywriter who began every project by propping up a hand-lettered card on her desk. On it were these lines: What is it? What does it do? How does it do it? Where can I get it? How much does it cost?

3. White space has its place.

A sure sign that an ad has been designed by an amateur is when every inch of white space has been filled up with type or art—as if the designer were getting a day's docked pay for each inch of space not crammed with something. This is a mistake. A quick perusal of ads created by the best designers will confirm that white space is good. It helps an ad breathe, and makes it more inviting to readers.

4. Let coupons breathe.

Can your house advertisements pass the coupon-crunch test? Try to fill out the coupon in one of your own magazine's subscription ads. If all the letters in your name begin to take on the shape of little fire hydrants—short and squat—it's time to give your coupons some air. Cramming the coupon into a tiny corner defeats the purpose of the ad. If you make it too difficult for respondents to fill out the coupon, they might just put down their pens, shake out the writer's cramp—and turn the page.

5. Don't trivialize the body copy.

That advice comes from Ken Roman and Jane Maas, two Ogilvy disciples whose *How to Advertise* is a fine handbook for both advertisers and publishers. People will read body copy, but only if you serve up plenty of information—and hold the hype. Here's a good test of the reader-interest quotient of your house advertisement: More nouns in the body copy usually mean more information about your own product; more adjectives usually mean more self-serving blather about the advertiser.

6. Use reader-friendly type.

With the rise of desktop publishing, there's a tendency to get type-happy. But in ad design, less is usually more.

The fewer typefaces you use, the more likely you are to have a neat, clean ad that's easy on the eyes. Try to limit the size of the type as well, and the number of type elements. Typically, there are three: the headline, the text block and a logo/sign-off. To make the sum total easy to read, we offer the following type tips: Set your copy block in 10- or 12-point type; make your line length no more than 35 or 40 characters; and if you increase the length of the line, increase the leading (the space between the lines).

Readers are willing to plow through long, densely packed blocks of copy if they are reading an exciting novel—or a letter from the Internal Revenue Service. But not your house ad.

7. All-type ads are not a punishable offense.

Some folks think advertisements must have an illustration or photograph to be read. Not so. In advertising, art is not ornamental—it's functional. And a strong, benefit-oriented headline can catch the eye just as effectively as an illustration or a photograph.

8. Write as you speak.

Language that is concise, casual and conversational is extremely important in advertising copy. People will pay to read your cover stories, but nobody will pay to read your advertisements. One of the best source books for ad wordsmiths is *The Copywriter's Handbook*, by Robert W. Bly. In it, writers are urged to put a little "you" in the copy. Not "you" the writer, but "you" the reader. Bly also reminds us to avoid technical jargon, to use short words and short sentences, and to remember to break up copy like this with ellipses, boldface type, underlines or subheads.

9. Loosen up.

Any good copywriting coach will tell you that you will just have to forget some of what you learned in your high-school English class. For example, sentence fragments are okay in advertising. Really. They are. And so are sentences that begin with "and" or "but." Why? Because, whether you like it or not, that is the way people speak. And communicating with people visually and verbally, in ways that they understand, about a magazine or its products and how those products can help make their lives and jobs easier or better—well, that's the essence of good advertising.

Don't Penny-Pinch Promotion

BY DONALD J. AUSTERMANN

For the past 10 years or so, ad sales promotion budgets have been taking it on the chin. Although budget cuts are happening in every area of our business, that's small consolation for salespeople who depend on advertising and promotion support to help them connect with their prospects and clients.

Although the days of glitzy, costly presentations and high-profile direct-mail campaigns are little more than a memory for many (if not most) publishers, that does not mean the support should be turned off altogether. There are inexpensive techniques that can be used to inform, persuade and remind customers, prospects and their agencies of your magazine's unique value. And there are some painless ways to save dollars in areas that have been eating your promotion budget alive. Here are some things to consider:

Letters: As promotion vehicles, letters have always been important to magazine sales staffs. And at 32 cents to mail, a letter is still quite a bargain. Letters are especially effective when speed is essential. And this is true now more than ever with the availability of the fax machine, a welcome substitute for costly messenger and/or overnight delivery services.

For letters to maintain their cost-effectiveness, however, word processors are a must. Few ad sales departments can afford the secretarial backup of yesteryear—which means ad salespeople must generate much of their own correspondence. Many computer-smart salespeople now do their own letters on computers at home, while commuting, or in the office. One salesperson I know did all her follow-up letters in the air between Minneapolis and New York City at the end of a sales trip.

Of course, to be effective, letters must be done right. Imagination, flair and a clear presentation of benefits will get your message read. To take full advantage of the sales (and savings) potential of letters, ad salespeople should hone their letter-writing skills. Most salespeople are, or can become, better writers and more creative

> Here are some painless ways to save money in areas that have been eating into your budget.

than they might think. All they need is a little guidance, encouragement and the application of their powerful selling skills to written communication.

Presentations: This has always been a vital activity, but also a costly one. New-business proposals, proposals to hold on to business, and mailings that get favorable research results out to your clients are ongoing and necessary. And again, the in-office computer may be the answer. Your promotion staff, working with a computer and any of the currently available desktop software (such as QuarkXPress, Aldus Freehand, Aldus PageMaker, Adobe PhotoShop or Adobe Illustrator), can turn out very effective presentations to be used in specific selling situations. If your promotion people are highly skilled, you may be able to bypass the graphic design department for further savings in time and money.

Inside or outside promotion help: Whether to use in-house promotion help or outside sources has long been a dilemma for publication management. In-house staffs require major expense outlays—training, salaries, benefits, office space, equipment, and so on. The advantages are accessibility and working knowledge of the magazine. There is also some volume-buying clout in terms of printing and paper buying.

Using outside help offers strategic and tactical opportunities to get quality thinking and objective insights on campaigns or special projects. Often this makes for highly original, lower-cost promotion, especially in the areas of presentations and direct mail when you have important statements to make.

If you have an advertising agency working for you, however, be wary. Even though the agency may offer collateral work along with advertising production and placement, its direct mail and presentation capabilities often do not measure up. Additionally, they can be very costly.

When assessing the pros and cons of inside vs. outside, think of small, in-house staffs making full use of computer capabilities for your immediate promotion needs (and use your company's buying leverage for printing and paper purchases). Use outside help for idea generation, imaginative sales-oriented thinking and the latest creative techniques.

Clean up your act

Promotion lists: Not that long ago, it was commonplace for magazines to have promotion lists well into five figures. Anyone with even a remote chance of being a media influence was put on the list, there to languish long after he or she changed jobs, quit, was fired, retired or died. Today, any magazine that does not regularly prune its promotion list is making an expensive mistake. Figure it out: Using a cost of $1 per promotion piece (inexpensive), mailing to a list of 10,000 (probably too many) that is only 75 percent effective (generous) costs a magazine (or wastes) $2,500 each time a mailing goes out.

So clean your lists regularly—at least twice a year. Another way to make promotion dollars go further is to segment your promotion list by advertising categories. This could mean, for example, automotive, financial, management or influence level on the company side, and media, creative and account management on the agency side. Segmenting enables you to make highly selective, category-specific mailings. Which means you don't waste money sending promotions to non-involved or non-influential people.

Complimentary copies: Like your promotion list, your comp list should be reviewed and cleaned regularly. You know what your production costs are. You know your mailing costs. Multiply that by the frequency of mailing and you get quite a lot of money. And chances are that you have too many copies going to the wrong people—including relatives and old college buddies. The bottom line: Make sure Aunt Minnie is a media supervisor at Bates before she makes the list.

Merchandising: Long a perplexing activity for magazine management, merchandising has assumed many roles. Publishers have variously considered it a valuable promotion activity, a necessary evil, a way to get a jump on the competition or a way for advertisers to play one magazine against the other.

It is difficult to offer ways to save money here—except to say that merchandising should *not* be a promotion expense. Merchandising (or value-added) activities are *sales* expenses, a cost of doing business. If you haven't already, take "value-added" out of the promotion budget and shift it to sales, where it belongs.

Some of the ideas presented here are easy to implement now. Others will require a little planning and adjustment. What should be uppermost in your thinking, however, is your sales force. What is the best way to give them the selling tools they need, while keeping a close eye on your budget? Salespeople are important revenue producers. You can treat them right and still not kill your budget. □

Trade-Show Secrets

BY HELEN BERMAN

Trade shows offer ad sales people more face-to-face contacts per hour than any other sales vehicle. If you know what you're doing, you can accomplish several weeks' worth of selling in a few days on the trade show floor. The secret is pre-show organization and preparation. The following checklists will help you develop an effective strategy for prospecting new accounts and selling current advertisers.

Laying the groundwork

Discuss your expectations, objectives and strategies with your team before you leave your office. Review the exhibitor list and decide, by prospect, what you want to achieve. For instance, your goal with one prospect might be to solidify your relationship; with another, it might be to close a specific ad sales contract.

Set up meetings with clients ahead of the show. As you talk with clients in the weeks before the show, make appointments with the most important—and send confirmation notes or faxes. Set up a breakfast (or two) plus some lunch, coffee, cocktail-hour and dinner dates. One West Coast sales manager requires his ad salespeople to schedule eight to 10 appointments a day at the show. In order to spend time with his most important clients, he also gets a dozen tickets to a major evening sporting event. In fact, you may decide to sponsor an advertiser/ exhibitor breakfast.

Clients too busy to make specific appointments will probably invite you to "come by the booth." Although this may be a genuine invitation, it could also be a polite brush-off—so be prepared to handle a cool reception with good grace.

Get a floor plan from the show producers. Then, organize your time and notes by exhibitor-booth numbers so that you can work the hall by aisles. Consider color-coding the floor plan or exhibitor list to indicate your A, B and C prospects. At especially large shows, you may want to visit with A prospects on the first round, circle a second time for B prospects, and so forth. Remember, top executives in bigger companies often leave the show after the first day. With this strategy, you ensure that you meet with the most important advertisers before they leave.

Keep track

Make notes about what you want to accomplish. You may want to write reminders to yourself next to your clients' booth numbers on the exhibitor list or floor plan. Is this to be just a friendly public relations call? a prospecting and fact-finding mission? or a time to recommend an ad program and close the sale?

Schedule time for special events. These include opening night receptions and exhibitor cocktail parties. But remember—you're still working. These are not times to let off steam or hang out with your buddies—no matter how great the temptation.

Walk the trade show hall with the publisher, editor or even the circulation director. Because these individuals may have relationships with people at higher levels within your prospects' companies, they can introduce you to key decision-makers. They can also add different points of view for the advertiser. Shows are also a perfect time to bring a new ad salesperson into the territory, or to "pass the baton" from one ad salesperson to another.

Develop your networking skills. Learn to work a room, and you'll find yourself making contacts with top executives and industry leaders you might not otherwise meet.

Stay physically and emotionally fit. Working the trade show floor is an athletic event that demands enormous stamina. Your physical fitness and nutrition program can be as important to your success as pre-call planning or presentation skills. When you get to the show, don't fall prey to the temptations of high-fat junk foods and liquor—they may take the nervous edge off, but they'll slow you down. Some people are night-owls, and some of us need a full night's sleep to function in top form. Respect your particular needs and pace yourself.

Wear appropriate business dress for your market or industry. Although in most cases that will mean a business suit, some of the ad salespeople in the sports market wear sweats with their publication's logo. Make sure you wear comfortable shoes—even tennis shoes if you must. For women, high heels may make your legs look more shapely, but you may not make it to lunchtime walking the aisles. I prefer dresses or suits with pockets for business cards.

Carry as little as possible. Try to limit yourself to a clipboard, floor plan, note paper, and whatever you need in terms of media material or research. After you leave a prospect, make notes about your conversation or use a microcassette recorder. If your publication has its own booth, use it as a storage and message center. Don't, however, sit idly in the booth and fool yourself into thinking that this is working the show.

Remember that you are "on" the entire time. When does the show start? When you register at the hotel, if not before. Keep your badge on at all times, worn on your right side (if possible) to best catch your prospect's eye as he shakes your hand. Your face may crack, but keep smiling.

Prospecting for new accounts

Be alert. When you work a trade show, the only certainty is that there is no certainty. So make your plans—but be ready to switch gears and be spontaneous. Clients forget appointments, or simply get distracted by their customers. As you walk the hall, keep your opportunity antennae up and follow your instincts—some of the best contacts and results may be a pleasant surprise.

Be sensitive to your clients' schedules, moods and needs. Keep in mind, however, that your prospects—the exhibitors—are there to sell, not to buy. Small-booth exhibitors, for instance, may not have the backup personnel to relieve them so that they can chat with you. Exhibitors need to trust that you are there to help support their success—not to impede or distract them. So be courteous and use good judgment.

Remember that the most important business asset you have is your reputation. In many industries, ad salespeople are viewed as aggressive hustlers. When I first started selling, I was kicked out of a trade show booth by a grumpy exhibitor who was convinced that all ad salespeople were piranhas. Be careful that your behavior doesn't fit the "space peddler" stereotype, or your prospects will shut you out.

Avoid starting conversations with the hackneyed question, "How's the show going?" If it isn't going well for the exhibitors, your prospect may pound you with all that is wrong with the show and the world. If your company produces the show, you've invited attack. Although it might be tempting to knock a competitor's show, or

shows in general, you don't want to begin your conversation on a negative note.

When talking, make sure you stay clear of the hard sell. Approach your prospects as a marketing consultant, and let them guide the sale. They'll let you know how far into the selling process they are willing to go.

Give your prospect something to get his attention. You might prepare advertising lead evaluation reports from reader response cards that are geared for a specific prospect. Since exhibitors and advertisers are obsessed with leads, you'll hit their hot button immediately. Perhaps you have a market tidbit to pass along. One salesperson I know scores lots of points with advertisers by bringing potential buyers to their booths.

If your prospect doesn't have time to talk to you, ask if you can watch him in action for a while. Even a few moments of eavesdropping on a sales conversation can yield precious information. For instance, you might hear what major benefits the salesperson emphasizes or how he handles his prospect's objections.

In the worst case—when you can't even get your prospect's attention long enough to ask if you can observe him—write a note on your business card and slip it to him or one of his associates. A simple "came by to say hi—glad to see you so busy with prospects" can put you in good stead. I remember the frustration of going by an exhibitor's booth a dozen times, unable to make contact. Later, on the phone, the client complained that I never came to see him. Sometimes you just can't win!

Follow up immediately. At the show's conclusion, cut and paste your handwritten notes into alphabetical order and read your report into a tape recorder. Send the tape overnight to the office, or take it with you for immediate transcription. Presumably, you've assigned someone to collect exhibitor brochures and factsheets for later use. They are valuable fact-finding tools and can help you recommend product ad copy. With your show report and sales literature in hand, you are ready immediately to follow up on leads from the show.

Trade shows are an ad salesperson's dream. Your prospects and clients are captive under one roof, riding an adrenaline high of excitement and anticipation. If you're properly prepared and organized, working a trade show can be, as one East Coast advertising director said, "like shooting ducks in a barrel." ☐

section seven

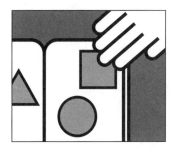

design and production

"At a magazine on the verge of a technology overhaul, **fear confronts many.** And while the fear may be irrational, it has a rational foundation."—p. 310

"Art directors and editors should focus on making the product the best it can be, but the production director's job is to **bring them back to reality.**"—p. 313

"You should **begin planning now** for the day when your publishing-production operation spans more than one medium."—p. 320

Scanning the Horizon

BY TIM BOGARDUS

Imagine being able to sign off on a completed editorial layout that has been color-corrected and proofed to everyone's satisfaction, but has never left the premises. Now imagine dragging the file for those pages across your desktop to an icon marked "Printer" and watching it disappear as it is automatically downloaded to a fiber-optic line. At the printer, it will be fed directly to a digital press and printed in 100 separate versions. No proofs, no film, no plates. No worries. Total fantasy, right? Not exactly.

Although the production workflow hasn't quite achieved the icon-on-the-desktop level, advanced imaging and transmission technologies are transforming long-standing job descriptions of production professionals, altering the traditional workflow, and redefining the business relationships between magazines, printers and service bureaus. If these changes haven't already affected you, they will soon.

"The technology is going to continue to put power into the hands of the creators," predicts Mary Lee Schneider, director of marketing at R.R. Donnelley & Sons' new Digital Division in Memphis. "We're seeing a natural migration of processes upstream," she says, referring to digital photography, desktop scanning and in-house color management and proofing.

Leading the way in high-tech imaging and transmission technologies are Time Inc.'s New York City-based weeklies: *Time, People, Entertainment Weekly* and *Sports Illustrated*. At *Sports Illustrated*, for example, all imaging is performed in *SI*'s imaging department, which is essentially a high-tech, in-house prepress operation.

The imaging department digitizes photographic transparencies it receives from the photo department using sophisticated drum and flatbed scanners. The scanners create high-resolution images, which are imported into Scitex workstations. There they are color-corrected and proofed using Iris digital color proofers. Final editorial pages are imported to the Scitex workstations from Macintoshes, and the low-res images (used only for placement in layouts) are replaced by the imaging department's high-res images using automatic picture replacement (APR). The final

page, complete with text, graphics and photos, is proofed again on the Iris and then sent to the transmission department on a local area network (LAN).

In the transmission department, the file goes into a queue, where it awaits its trip to the printer. First, the file travels via a dedicated T-1 line to Time Inc.'s satellite uplink on Long Island, where it is then beamed to one of seven U.S. printing plants (including Donnelley, Quebecor USA, Brown Printing, Perry Printing and Quad/Graphics) and to five countries in various parts of the world.

It's a very efficient and very sophisticated production and transmission system that cost hundreds of thousands of dollars. But for time-sensitive weekly publications such as *Sports Illustrated* and *Time*, it makes a lot of sense. And because Time Inc. is part of the world's largest media and entertainment company, there are economies of scale that justify big investments in technology, equipment and staff.

Frank Scott, Time Inc.'s director of prepress development, takes a lot of pride in the system, which he helped devise. But he knows it's not for everyone: What works for the high-volume weeklies may not yet be the right approach for monthlies. "Many publishers don't want to do [color management and proofing]. They say, 'I'm a publisher, not a service bureau,'" Scott says.

Time Inc. installed its Scitex systems and top-of-the-line scanners some time in 1990. But Scott says that with the latest expensive equipment on the market, there are ways to bring imaging and file transmission tasks in-house for a more limited cost.

Steve Romeo, editorial/art production manager at New York City-based *Business Week*, already knows this. At McGraw-Hill's offices, just down the street from Time Inc., Romeo and his staff process half the magazine's color images each week. And they do it with just three people and off-the-shelf equipment representing a fraction of Time Inc.'s investment. Using Macs, Adobe Photoshop, two scanners and an Iris proofer, Romeo and staff scan, color-correct, resize, sharpen, retouch and proof about 45 images a week.

First, they scan transparencies to produce high-resolution images. These are imported into Photoshop where they are color-corrected, sized and retouched. Two or three color proofs are generated on the Iris proofer until a final match is determined. The color-corrected high-res images are sent to the service bureau via a dedicated T-1 line, and a low-res image is put on the network for placement in the layout. When a page is finalized at the magazine, it is sent to the service bureau on the T-1 line, where the high-res image is swapped for the low-res image. The page with the high-res image is then RIPped, compressed and sent to the printer via satellite.

In the two years that Romeo and company have been managing color imaging, they have never missed a deadline. The key to the operation is the color proofer. "The Iris is the body of this department," Romeo says, because it allows him to achieve the color he and the art director want. An Iris costs about $50,000, but Romeo says the purchase paid off quickly. The annual savings from going in-house, he says, was about $600,000, and the quality of the finished product is undiminished.

"Considering the equipment we use, the results we get are pretty amazing," Romeo says. The tradeoff is that Romeo and his staff work long, hard hours under a lot of pressure. And a certain level of expertise is mandatory: "You have to have an eye for color," says Romeo, who has been working with color for eight years. "It's a trade, a skill," he says.

Like Scott, Romeo cautions that bringing color-correction in-house may not be for everyone. It requires an ongoing commitment of both training time and money for upgrades. Many publishers may find that it's just as cost-effective to continue using a service bureau or prepress house. In fact, *Business Week* itself still relies on its service bureau to process half its color images.

As relationships between publishers and service bureaus evolve toward a completely digital workflow, the role of the production manager is changing. The new digital technologies present opportunities to streamline production workflows and gain more control of the process at the same time. "The industry has rapidly educated itself," says R.R. Donnelley's Schneider. "But the best thing you can be is educated about what you don't know," she advises. □

Advanced imaging and transmission technologies are revolutionizing the production process.

Technophobia

BY LYNN CRIMANDO

Since 1983, *Lynn Crimando has helped* Sports Illustrated *evolve from a magazine whose stories were sent away to a typesetting department for fit, to one where editors now fit their stories on-screen at their desks. As director of editorial operations, Crimando has experienced first-hand the effects that technological change can have on a magazine's staff and management. Here she shares her insights with* Folio: *readers. She was assisted by Nancy Hutchens, an organization and human resources consultant in Ossining, New York.*

If only overhauling a publishing system were as simple as renovating a restaurant. Imagine hanging a sign on the newsstand reading, "Closed for technology upgrade. Watch for our new improved magazine." You'd have the luxury of uninterrupted time to dismantle the old system, install the new one and get back into print. Sounds too good to be true?

Well, it is.

In the real world you've got a publication to produce while upgrading. Forget about uninterrupted time; installations are usually squeezed into limited windows of opportunity in the schedule. This means phasing in the new stuff, temporary work-arounds and confusion among staffers trying to learn new skills on deadline.

It gets worse when you realize that nobody is at his or her best during transitions. When comfortable patterns are changed and people are not sure what the future holds, the atmosphere can become polluted with high anxiety, low tolerance and a rumor mill that won't quit. Why?

All transitions imply danger

Although there are those few individuals who thrive on change, most of us find uncertainty discomforting. All transitions, even the "good" ones (getting married, taking a new job, etc.) imply an element of danger. Fear of the unknown, fear of loss or failure, and fear of losing control are all part of the experience.

If it's difficult to assimilate the changes we bring upon ourselves, what of the ones that we can't control—changes that affect something as fundamental as our jobs? At a magazine on the verge of a technology overhaul, fear is confronting many. And while the fear itself may be irrational, it has a rational foundation.

As soon as you start fiddling with the computer system, the natural tendency is to adjust the rest of the process accordingly. After all, why replace the production tools without making operational improvements? But while you're envisioning a smoother system, individuals who are disturbed by a changing environment are apt to feel less interested in big-picture benefits and more concerned about their own situations. To them, a major change in operation may represent nothing so much as a big intrusion, maybe even a threat to their jobs.

Production managers are by no means exempt from this whole business. Suppose you're asked to make operational changes that you don't personally support. The apparent ease of desktop publishing—especially on the Mac platform—makes everyone an expert. Consequently, it is not uncommon for production changes to be mandated from above. Nevertheless, as a manager it's your responsibility to shepherd change through in an orderly way.

Make communication part of the plan

Organization and human resources consultant Nancy Hutchens points out that while some people handle transitions better than others, there are common reactions likely to surface at each stage of your project (*see box on next page*). Knowing what to expect can help you minimize the stress level.

During the design phase you'll determine how best to utilize the new technology. Now is the time to examine the whole process step by step, looking for ways to streamline. Items such as workflow, page and staffing costs, deadlines, and so forth should all be analyzed. But that "clean slate" approach that results in a better system also raises the anxiety level. Your ultimate goal may be better production methods, but staffers will be justifiably apprehensive about the effect your work will have on their jobs.

You may find it difficult to get necessary information from people who feel threatened. You'll probably also get plenty of arguments about why things should stay the way they are. And don't be surprised if you are repeatedly delivering the same message. Anxious people don't absorb information well. They may misconstrue your words or even fail to hear them the first few times around.

"Communicate and inspire," Hutchens advises. "Enable them to get involved and help them understand that these changes are inevitable."

Maintain a chain of command

A major equipment installation brings with it an element of chaos. If you're establishing the new system in stages, as is often the case, you'll need parallel processes, interim procedures and extra quality checks. Somewhere around mid-way through the changeover, you could be producing pages via three different routes: old, new and interim.

While some staffers will let you know in no uncertain terms that they don't want to be left alone with new equipment, others will quietly worry about their ability to adapt to new production methods. Those nagging fears of loss of control experienced during the planning phases can evolve into full-blown anxiety attacks once the new equipment is in place.

These do not make for optimal training conditions. In addition to learning a new system while maintaining the schedule, staff members will be making decisions on the fly about procedures that may be unfamiliar to them. Frustration will be on the rise. To preserve sanity, make sure the chain of command is clear. If you've included enough people in the planning process, you should have help during this phase. Make sure you've got at least one person on site who can make decisions

■ Animal House

Though each person shows the strain differently, unproductive responses to change fall into four broad groupings. To make these behavior patterns easier to understand, consultant Nancy Hutchens uses animal imagery to describe each type. Although people tend to act out just one of these responses, many adopt a second when the going gets really tough. Recognizing these traits (in yourself as well as others) can be the first step toward mastering the real beast—change.

Having an awareness of these unproductive tendencies may help you to see when the conversation is out of control and should be diplomatically terminated. Later, when tempers have cooled, the employee should be taken aside. Explain in a clear, firm and nonthreatening way that, while you understand that the process is difficult, employees are still expected to perform their jobs and maintain professional demeanor.

Be aware of your own unproductive responses, or you'll undermine your effectiveness as well as authority. You might even want to "practice" your approach with someone you trust first.

The most important thing to remember is that the channels for communication must stay open, and that people feel that their concerns are being heard.

The Sparrow ('Why me?')
The Sparrow is a chronic victim. Sparrows internalize change and assume that it will hurt no matter what. This individual has difficulty believing that there could actually be some positive result. The Sparrow may also use self-defense as an excuse to subvert the project in subtle ways. When you start hearing about work slowdowns, look for the nearest Sparrow.

The Ostrich ('You'll have to find me first.')
Avoidance is the Ostrich's most common trait. This is the manager who is chronically unavailable for meetings, or the worker who is conveniently indisposed whenever it's time to learn the new system. The Ostrich really doesn't believe the change will happen. When it does, it can be a real trauma.

The Monkey ('Whatever it is, it'll never work.')
The Monkey alleviates anxiety by acting out. Here's a person who doesn't need facts in order to spread the word about what's happening. This person will gossip, complain and bad-mouth the project to anyone who will listen—except you.

The Pit Bull ('Just try it.')
Pit Bulls are hostile and aggressive about making their feelings known. They are confrontational and abrasive, and usually won't be interested in hearing anyone else's opinions. You'll be wasting your time if you try to reason with a Pit Bull who's on the offensive.

and who understands the big picture. Good hand-holding skills won't hurt either.

Don't oversell the notion of how easy everything will be. Be careful not to inflate the expectation level. "Let them know that it might be confusing," says Hutchens. "Be clear that you don't expect perfection. And remember to recognize the personal cost. Tell people that you appreciate how difficult things might be."

Celebrate achievements along the way

Once the new system is installed, procedures, job descriptions, schedules, even copy flow, must be adjusted. Interdepartmental relationships and dependencies will shift, resulting in a realigned power structure. In other words, it's renegotiation time.

No matter what people have been thinking or hoping about the new structure, it's now here. There will be some mourning for the past as that reality sinks in. There might also be some residual resentment on the part of folks who liked things better the way they were.

These are issues that are best dealt with directly. Don't try sneaking change in through a side door. Be straightforward about what must be done. And don't be afraid to have lots of meetings to clarify who's doing what. Although they may not like the new order, your colleagues will appreciate the chance to participate in the changes.

Consultants like Hutchens advise that you set benchmarks, key points that allow you to acknowledge that things are different now. Set up goals and celebrate when you achieve them. Perhaps it's a first issue, or even a first page, produced using the new system. While you're celebrating, be sure to acknowledge what people have been through to get to that point. Don't be surprised, however, if you or others intensely involved with the project feel some "postpartum" depression. You have all been through a lot to get to this point. Don't forget to acknowledge and appreciate your own achievement.

Help!

Maintaining your cool despite conflicting feelings—both yours and others'—is tricky. If you're embarking on a big change and you haven't anticipated negative reactions from the staff, you can either do so now or wait till the phone calls start coming in the middle of the night.

So how can you prepare for what's coming? You might spend some time in the business section of your public library. The librarian should be able to point you in the direction of some books on change management. Two I recommend are *Changing Ways: A practical tool for implementing change within organizations*, by Murray M. Dalziel and Stephen H. Schoonover; and *The Flexibility Factor*, by Jacquelyn Wonder and Priscilla Donovan. Articles to look up include "Why change programs don't produce change" in the November/December 1990 issue of *Harvard Business Review*" and "Cost cutting: How to do it right" in the April 9, 1990, issue of *Fortune.*

Depending on your individual situation, you may want to get some professional help. If your company has a human resources department, there's probably someone in it who can help you, or at least point you in the right direction. If there's no help available in-house, ask colleagues to recommend consultants they've used. ☐

Production Primer

BY TIM BOGARDUS

This is it. Your dream of publishing a magazine is finally becoming a reality. The Muse inspired you with a brilliant idea, you raised a bundle of money, hired some great editorial talent, and found the perfect office space. What are you forgetting? Psst! It's the "p-word"—PRODUCTION.

Often overlooked or put off until the last minute, production decisions are critical to the success of your launch. Costs for production and distribution—including prepress, printing and paper—account for 40 to 60 percent of the average magazine's operating expenses, according to experts. And with that comes choosing a printer, negotiating a contract, finding a prepress house, selecting a paper grade, and myriad other details to worry about.

So we have put together the following primer to help you navigate the complicated process of building a strategy. Here's how to find the right printer for your needs, what to watch out for in negotiating a printing contract, what to look for when selecting paper, and some tips about other production-related issues. This is not intended to be a comprehensive guide. Whole books have been written on the subject (*see box on next page*). But we hope this will get you started on the right path and help you avoid some of the most common mistakes.

Go pro

First, consider hiring an experienced production manager. If you've invested in qualified staff for your editorial, art and sales departments, it makes sense to hire someone to oversee an area that will consume about half of your budget. Laura Reed, production director at New York City-based *Worth*, says it is critical to hire someone with experience or at least to get a consultant to guide you. "If you don't know anything, get someone who does," she advises.

The production manager must be knowledgeable about desktop publishing and prepress processes such as scanning and color separation. In addition, he or she should have an idea of how much services and supplies should cost, and know how to set up schedules, work with prepress vendors and printers, and troubleshoot

in general. Mark Abraham, production director at *Natural History*, based in New York City, says a good production professional can help turn a great idea into a living, breathing magazine. "Art directors and editors should focus on making the product the best that it can be, but a production manager's job is to bring them back to reality," he says. The savings realized by avoiding the costly mistakes of inexperience should more than offset the cost of a production manager's salary.

Define your needs

Next, you need a solid plan. Go beyond your broad objectives to define the specific parameters of your magazine—this is where the production professional will earn his or her first-year's salary.

Start with your operation's financial requirements. How much money do you have? How much can you spend? What options will save money at various stages of the manufacturing and distribution processes? Then, outline specifics:

• What is the magazine's frequency?
• What should the trim size be? (Remember, trim size affects both paper and postage costs.)
• Who are your competitors?
• What kind of paper are they using?
• What kind of deadline schedule will there be? Is it a late-closing book?
• What is the target circulation and the length of run on the press?
• Should it be printed on offset press (preferred for its flexibility and faster makeready) or gravure press (preferred for longer runs because of its faster press speed and more stable print quality)?
• Will it be perfect-bound (glued spine) or saddle-stitched (stapled spine)?

The answers will help you define your objectives and narrow the field of printer candidates. Laying out detailed specifications also helps you articulate your needs to vendors. Those parameters will dictate budgetary requirements and force you to look realistically at the financial picture.

The biggest reason for failure of magazine start-ups,

says Janet Mannheimer, president of Publishing Experts, a New York City-based consulting firm, is funding. "The reason they aren't funded properly is that the people who are starting them don't really know how much they cost to produce," she says. As a general rule of thumb, therefore, allocate about 50 percent of operating expenses to production and distribution.

Find a printer

This looks like the easy part. Printers want your business. "Everybody can find the names of printers. They hear when there's a start-up, and they're probably at the door before somebody has a chance to call them," says Mannheimer.

Ask for recommendations from other publishers. Check out whom your competition uses. Consult printer directories. From these sources, develop a list of names and then make some calls to screen likely candidates. "The first thing we look at," says Angela Calitri, a sales representative at Brown Printing Company, "is whether their specifications match our equipment and schedule." Printers who don't have the equipment or press time to handle your magazine are easy to whittle from your list.

Your distribution plan may narrow the field even more. Most printers are based in the Midwest, which makes national distribution more cost-effective. However, this isn't always an advantage. If you're planning a regional magazine with heavy newsstand distribution, look for a local printer. If your magazine is subscription-driven, it may not matter where it's printed because most copies will be mailed (although postage costs come into play here).

The Request for Proposal (RFP)

After narrowing the list to six or seven candidates, you're ready to create a Request for Proposal (RFP), sometimes called a Request for Quotation (RFQ). The RFP communicates your needs to the printer and provides space for them to communicate their prices, capabilities and requirements. "Printers are smart people," Mannheimer says. "They can tell very quickly whether you have experience or know what you're doing. You want to put your best foot forward because you want the best pricing and the best schedule." In other words, make the RFP as professional-looking as possible. You want them to know you are serious.

Design your RFP so that you receive information in a

■ Getting started: Three handy resources

It's impossible to describe the entire production process in a short magazine piece. But there are books written on the subject, and they dig much more deeply into the nuances of the graphic arts industry. Directories, glossaries and how-to advice are abundant. Here are three resources we find useful.

Pocket Pal, A Graphic Arts Production Handbook: This digest-size, nuts-and-bolts classic is in its 16th edition, and has been the authoritative introduction to the graphic arts for 61 years. From the Egyptians to Gutenberg to current digital print-making technology, Pocket Pal covers it all. It includes chapters on typographic imaging, photography, color separation, film assembly and imposition, electronic prepress systems, platemaking, printing, paper, ink and more, including a glossary of terms. $7.25. Published by International Paper. Distributed by Print Resource, P.O. Box 770067, Memphis, TN 38177-0067. 800-854-3212.

Directory of Printers: As the title indicates, this is a directory featuring listings for more than 700 printers of books, catalogs, magazines and other printed materials. The first few chapters give advice on how to choose a printer, construct an RFP (RFQ) and how to save money on your printing bill. Especially useful are the indexes, which categorize printers by state, binding capability, equipment (offset/gravure), and additional services such as fulfillment, prepress and list maintenance. Includes an extensive list of magazine printers. $14.95. By Marie Kiefer. Published by Ad-Lib Publications, 51 West Adams, P.O. Box 1102, Fairfield, IA 52556. 800-669-0773.

You Want It When?! A Conversation With Your Friendly Printing Production Operator: Written by Jack Parker in layman's terms as a conversation with someone in the trade, and not as a textbook, this book takes the reader through the print production process. From concept and design to color balancing and proofing, it is a simple and straightforward read and a good counterbalance to the more jargon-heavy handbooks. The book is pricey at $29.95, but it could be helpful. Published by the Printing Industry of Illinois/Indiana Association, 70 East Lake St., Suite 300, Chicago, Illinois 60601. 312-704-5000.

standard format, which makes it easier to compare the candidates.

Specifically, the RFP should contain the following basic information:

- Title of the magazine
- Circulation/print run
- Book size (estimated number of pages)
- Frequency
- Trim size
- Insert and binding specs (saddle-stitched? perfect-bound?)
- Paper (cover and body stock)
- Color availability (e.g., all four-color?)
- Mail and shipping requirements

In response to the RFP, the printer should be asked to provide the following:

- A quotation of their best price to do the job
- A price list of services
- A sample schedule
- Sample publication (examples of other magazines)
- Equipment list and floor plan
- Sample contract
- Client list and references
- An annual report

Before you look at the price quotations you've received, examine each RFP. Was it submitted on time? Is it complete? Does it follow the structure you requested? You'll gain early insight into whether these are people you want to work with.

Think about the future. Does the company demonstrate that it is capable of handling your publication a year from now? "You want to find a partner who's going to be flexible with your growth, especially if you're a launch," says *Worth*'s Reed. What will happen, for example, if your print run doubles in the first year? Will this printer be able to handle it? "Make sure you're not going to be left without press time," she cautions.

Price is important, of course, but don't automatically choose the low-ball bidder. "The printer who comes in at rock-bottom prices may have something wrong," Reed cautions. If the printer you like best comes in with a significantly higher bid than the rest, ask why. Find out if they can negotiate a better price, and ask them to submit a lower bid to bring it into the range of the other bidders.

In addition, all candidates should provide a list of their other magazine clients. Call those publishers and ask them about their experiences with their printer. How does the printer respond to problems? Are they flexible when deadlines can't be met? Do they treat their customers like partners?

Make the choice: It's about 'fit'

Your list is narrowed to two or three printers. Now you conduct on-site visits to meet the customer-service representatives, plant managers and staff with whom you will be working. This is an opportunity to do a little snooping. Does the plant have the right kind of equipment, the right number of presses, the right bindery? Is it up to date? Finally, look at some of the material coming off the presses. How is the quality?

There are intangibles to consider as well. How was the tour organized? How did the equipment operators treat you? Does the customer service rep or plant manager give straightforward answers to your questions?

In the end, let instinct govern: "Go with your gut," says Reed. "Numbers are important, but they will probably fall in line. The most important thing is matching the personality of the printer and the magazine. Make sure the printer you choose sees you as a person and not just a number."

Mannheimer agrees. "The reality is that the fit needs to be right—it has to be right for cost, for quality and for the culture of the vendor and the magazine. You want a printer who wants to be part of your team."

Printers say they approach the deal in the same way. "We like to look at the long-term relationship," says Richard Dean, a sales representative at American Signature's Memphis printing plant. "It is a partnership arrangement."

The contract

Once you've picked a winner, it's time to draw up a contract. Hire an attorney. Do *not* try to do it yourself. Most printers will supply a boilerplate contract. You can work from this, but it is imperative to have a lawyer examine it and guide the negotiations.

"A contract is something that you hope never to have to use once it is signed," says Mannheimer. But if a dispute arises, the contract will decide the outcome. The idea is to cover all the bases and protect yourself against every possible scenario, before it occurs. Contracts cover prices and price changes, terms of payment, paper, variations in quality, schedules, liability, confidentiality, acts of God, insurance and many other details that require the attention of an attorney to ensure thorough coverage.

The typical printer contract is good for one to three years, but be aware that many contain an evergreen clause that automatically renews the contract if 90 days' notice of termination is not given.

Be realistic about paper

Paper pulp is a commodity, just like oil or pork bellies. Its price will fluctuate—sometimes dramatically—based on supply and demand, and this in turn drives the prices on finished paper.

Most paper transactions involve at least three parties: the paper manufacturer, a broker and a buyer. The more paper a buyer can purchase, the better the price that buyer can negotiate. If you're just starting out, it's unlikely that you will have the buying power to get the best prices, and paper is expensive right now. Since July 1994, the average price for 40-lb., #5 coated groundwood paper, the grade used by most magazines, increased 53 percent, from $830 a ton to $1,270 a ton. Analysts predict prices will edge upward for at least the next two years.

> A general rule of thumb: Allocate about 50 percent of operating expenses to production and distribution.

Most printers buy paper in large quantities and will purchase and store it for customers. Because of the volume involved, they can get a better price than you can. What you need to focus on is the grade of your paper. The first thing to do is check out your prospective competition:

• What kind of paper are the publications in your target niche using?
• Is it coated or uncoated?
• What weight is the stock?
• Are they printing on recycled paper?

Get samples of likely grades from the paper manufacturers or your printer. Ask the printer to price the job with several paper types. Although it's tempting to go with a higher grade to try to outdo the competition, be realistic: This is an area where money can be saved, and it could ultimately save your publication.

Natural History's Abraham recalls working with an art magazine called *Portfolio* in the early 1980s. The magazine eventually failed, he says, not only because it was insufficiently funded, but because production costs were way out of line. The publishers insisted on using an expensive glossy, heavy, top-of-the-line paper. "They did-

n't buy as efficiently as they could," says Abraham. "No one was focusing on how much this was costing." It's good to be aware of what other publishers are using, but it's not necessary to match it. "Is it really going to make or break it if you go down one grade? There's a point when you have to say, 'This is good enough,'" he adds.

What printers look for in a customer

Most printers prefer to work with established companies because, above all else, they want to be sure they'll get paid. However, most will work with start-ups too, provided they have confidence in the project. The printer's own analysts will measure the risk of taking you on as a client based on economic evaluations of your publication's niche and its potential for growth.

"We do take risks and start-ups are risky," says Brown Printing's Calitri. For example, Brown worked with *Staten Island Monthly* on an issue-by-issue basis, even though the title was struggling financially. "We were willing to work with them because they were really committed to the idea," she explains.

Every printer requires a letter of credit that details your financial arrangements. Most require some payment up front, and some want full payment before starting the job. "We need to know something about their ability to pay," says American Signature's Dean. "Ultimately, the bean-counters make the decision."

But keep in mind that the printer-publisher relationship goes beyond money—it's about working together to achieve a common goal. "Being the best customer doesn't necessarily mean you have the most money, but that you live up to what you promise," says Mannheimer. "If you say your book is going to close on a certain day, then it closes on that day."

No production process is without problems, so identify where the potential trouble spots are early and alert your vendors about them promptly. Be realistic and straightforward. "Printers are afraid of the unknown, not the known," Mannheimer says. "And they may be your best resource to help you fix it, or to support you while you're going through it." □

10 Commandments of Production

BY HELENE ECKSTEIN

Magazines are started by editors and sales-people, but the greatest costs are in production. To exist and prosper, every magazine must control printing and related expenditures. How do you do this in an atmosphere of rising postage and paper costs? By following the 10 Commandments of Production:

1. Communicate, communicate, communicate.
Whenever you request a quote or a change, confirm everything in writing. Spoken instructions are often forgotten or misunderstood, and can lead to disasters. And disasters usually mean added costs to you. Protect your bottom line: Get it in writing.

2. Always quote apples to apples.
And include *all* services in your proposal requests. Additional charges and unexpected costs arise if you don't specify exactly what you need. Involve your suppliers in preparing requests. That way, you can be sure that all services are covered in their quotes and they are all bidding on the same project.

3. Proof with care.
Proofing is the most important part of the production process. It's your chance to catch errors early and keep costs under control. Reserve time to proof and emphasize to your staff that proofing takes precedence.

4. Decide what you want early and reserve last-minute changes for true emergencies.
Modern technology allows you to make changes constantly. But don't be fooled into thinking that just because you can, you should. Save the crisis mentality for a true crisis (which will occur), and you can avoid mistakes and maintain the quality of your magazine.

5. Make technology decisions on the leading edge/bleeding edge principle.
Yes, technology has drastically improved the way we produce our magazines, but when suppliers suggest a new approach, question them carefully. Have other clients used this new technique? How much experience does the supplier have using it? Don't do R&D for your suppliers. Technology for technology's sake is not progress.

6. Ask questions.
There's never been a dumb question—only a good question that was never asked. Make sure your supplier explains all processes to you. Visit printers and prepress houses to get a first-hand understanding of their work systems. And be sure to clarify the terms and conditions common in the printing industry. Graphic arts is not an exact science. Get a full understanding of your and your suppliers' obligations.

7. Test, test , test.
Before trying any new technique or even engaging a new supplier, have him send you a test showing exactly what he can do for you. It's far better to be surprised on a test than to get the devastating disappointments and cost overruns during live production.

8. Establish good relationships with your suppliers.
Respect your suppliers for their years of experience. Count on them to help you through even the most difficult production problems. Certainly call them to task when they're wrong, but be sure to thank them when they do an outstanding job.

9. Plan a realistic production schedule and stick to it.
Creative people want more time to finesse their writing or artwork. Salespeople want additional time to bring in the ads. You have to control both of them so you're sure of getting your book out on time without costly errors and disasters. Balance the creative and ad needs with your need to control production costs.

10. Show a healthy respect for the god of printing and realize that everything that can happen, will happen.
The perfect magazine has probably never been printed, but beautiful books are produced each day that fulfill their purpose and make a profit. By following the commandments listed here, you'll be well on your way to being a successful publisher. ☐

Five Ways to Save Money At the Printer

BY MIKE CUENCA

Face it. Unless you're the Rockefeller of the publishing industry, you have only so much money to spend in the production of your magazine. And it's likely that someone who does have such deep pockets didn't get them by being a spendthrift. If you're the publisher, you have to worry about staying in business; if you're the production manager, you have to worry about keeping your job. Careful spending is a primary concern for all of us.

You may feel that you've cut all the corners you can on things like printing, paper, ink, binding and shipping, and you've also reviewed your invoices to make sure you're not being overcharged for anything. But there may be more you can do to lower your manufacturing costs—without compromising your magazine's print quality.

1. Take a look at how you buy your paper.

If you currently buy paper from your printer, buying your own could make a big difference in your costs. Printers charge a markup for the paper they sell, and the percentages range from friendly to downright hostile. In addition, many printers charge a handling or insurance fee. Carefully review your printing invoice to determine what you're being charged per hundredweight (cwt). Then call some paper brokers, merchants and mills. You'd have to buy extremely large amounts of paper to make buying directly from a mill cost-effective. But even if buying from a mill is not for you, a mill can still often refer you to a suitable broker.

The difference between merchants and brokers is that merchants are large retailers, while a broker acts, in a sense, as the mill's sales force. Merchants will often have very low prices, but their supply for a particular stock may be limited, forcing you to choose another paper. Brokers are going to charge a markup (though often not as high as print-

> There may be a lot more you can do to lower your manufacturing costs without compromising your title's quality.

ers), but provide more stability in terms of supply.

Each source has its advantages; you have to decide which is more appropriate for your paper needs. You can do this by asking for quotes on the paper you're using and for papers of comparable quality. When you find one that you like, try to negotiate an even better price. When I first arrived at *Mothering* magazine, we were paying our printer nearly $46/cwt for 70,000 pounds of paper. After considerable comparison of suppliers, papers and prices, we chose a paper with similar characteristics from a paper broker for $39.50/cwt. We love the look of our book on the new paper and are now saving $4,800 per issue.

2. Review your imposition.

The general rule for saving money on the press is to keep your forms as large as possible, while paying to print only as many colors in one form as you absolutely must. If, for example, you're printing three multi-color pages in a 32-page color form, you're definitely wasting money.

Let's say you print a book with mostly black-and-white pages, sprinkled with a few multi-color advertising pages. If you're printing a 32-page color form to accommodate those few color pages, you may save by printing the form four colors over one color (4/1), or three colors over one color (3/1), instead of four colors over four (4/4). That translates into fewer plates and less ink, which means less makeready—and that means less expense. Another option would be to print a short color form and have it split-delivered to the bindery. For example, print a 16-page 4/c and have it delivered as two eight-page forms that will bind into different areas of the magazine.

Similarly, if you're dividing up a 32-page form to accommodate placement of a bind-in card, you may be throwing money away. By compromising on that bind-in position, you could save money on the press—and later at the bindery. For instance, at *Mothering* we were running a reader-response bind-in card within a catalog section of our book in a place where the forms didn't divide naturally. Because of that, we were splitting up what could have been one 32-page 3/3 form into one 16-page 1/1 form and two eight-page 3/3 forms. By moving the section and the card, we saved almost $5,000 on press charges.

Your printer representative should be able to help you rearrange your imposition to maximize your savings. With luck, you won't also have to rearrange your pages within the book—but if you're open to this, you can save some real money throughout the course of a year.

3. Reduce the number of forms delivered to the bindery.

This goes hand-in-hand with your printing imposition. Once your book is printed and delivered to the bindery, you'll pay for every form. If you've accommodated that bind-in card by dividing up one large form into several smaller forms, you'll be paying for it not only at the press, but also at the binder. Just by moving that catalog section and its bind-in card described above, we saved over $700.

Bindery charges are based on the number of pockets and stops. A pocket is each form or insert that is placed in the binder. Stops are just that—stops to change a form within a pocket. Obviously, if you have five pockets and no stops, you'll pay less than if you have 10 pockets and stop to change one or more of the forms several times.

4. Consider changing your trim size.

This might seem like a drastic measure—and one that could require at least minimal redesign of your book—but if you're currently trimming to larger than 10-1/2 inches in height and you need to make significant cost-cutting measures, this could be the way.

Trimming the size of your book from a long cutoff length of 10-7/8 inches to the short cutoff length of 10-1/2 inches can decrease your paper needs by 4.5 percent. The 3/8 of an inch that you'll lose is a relatively small price to pay compared to what you can save. If you're spending $30,000 per issue 12 times a year for paper, that can mean a savings of over $16,000 per year. On top of that, you'll realize a minimal savings in ink.

5. Don't stop the presses.

There's no valid reason to stop a press run voluntarily. If you do, it means you're either not taking the time to proof your publication adequately, or that you're not being flexible enough about the mistakes you may miss.

Build in more time to check your bluelines. Add more eyes to the proofing process. Make sure that when those plates are made, they are perfect. Stop thinking of the press run as another step in the proofing process. If the press breaks down, however, that's not your fault—or your cost. But if you stop it to replace a lost comma, you're making a huge financial mistake. At our printer, the total cost for plate change, press makeready and paper stop is over $300. That adds up quickly if you do it a few times.

Even if you are stopping the press to change versions or to print regionals, make sure your investment in the plate change and press delay is matched by your return. It may be more cost-effective to combine those versions. Also, check with your printer about new technology that allows some types of pre-planned version changes without stopping the press. ☐

SGML: A Solution to Content Portability

BY JOHN L. CLEVELAND

Many traditional publishers are understandably skittish about the electronic-delivery era. Each day brings news of alliances among traditional publishers and telecommunications, computer and entertainment companies. But take heart: Electronic media have voracious appetites for useful, well-presented content—yours included.

You should begin planning now for the day when your publishing operation spans more than one medium. Authoring software tools like SGML (Structured General Markup Language) offer long-term protection from any surprises technology holds, allowing you to move your content with relative ease to any media, platform and output device. They let you integrate sound, video, animation and hypertext linking into information developed within traditional pre-press systems.

SGML vs. PDL

The term "authoring" is applied loosely to a variety of software applications. However, authoring properly refers to document tagging applications supporting the SGML ISO standard 8879. Adopted in 1986 and promoted heavily by the United States Department of Defense, SGML has moved beyond its niche in government as a document tagging scheme for mission-critical, often-updated technical manuals. Increasingly, SGML is embraced by private enterprise as a comprehensive, long-term solution to the content portability problem.

It's important to understand the difference between tagging schemes like SGML and page description languages (PDL) such as Adobe System's PostScript. Each offers a different solution to similar problems. PostScript preserves the *visual* integrity of documents on any computer platform or output device. Adobe's Portable Document Format (PDF), built around PostScript, includes the hyperlinking and application customization features needed to publish visually rich documents on electronic media, such as CD-ROM and online services.

Rather than visual integrity, SGML has evolved to preserve a document's *structural* integrity. The power of SGML is needed in situations requiring the long-term storage of thousands of pages for transfer to any media, or the sharing of documents across a network linked to different platforms and devices.

In effect, SGML separates content and formatting from structure and transforms documents into specialized databases, searchable on almost any criteria, with nearly infinite possibilities for linking and reconfiguring elements across media. You could, for example, easily search an appropriately tagged SGML file for all addresses and phone numbers scattered randomly throughout a lengthy document, and then extract and sort them for publication in a directory.

The power is in the tag

The power of SGML-compliant software comes from its ability to recognize document elements (headlines, subheads etc.) by their purpose and relationship to other elements. The SGML file itself is an ASCII text file in which various elements of documents have been tagged with embedded codes according to their purpose and/or relationship to other document elements. A file's Document Type Definition (DTD) sets rules for how other SGML-compliant applications will handle its various elements. The Tag Description Table (TDT) describes the meaning of each tag in the DTD and the specifications for how it is used.

SGML's rich tagging and annotating features let developers spin complex webs of interrelated information throughout documents, facilitating hypertext-linking transferable to any media. In fact, Hypertext Markup Language (HTML), used widely on the Internet to help users navigate between related topics with a click of the mouse, shares similar ancestry with SGML. SGML's built-in ability to recognize document components can also be used to make sweeping changes that would be extremely difficult on a standard desktop system. Suppose you want every headline directly below a cutline on a right-hand page to print in boldface type. In SGML, the DTD could be modified to filter the document—with the changes you desire—into style sheets readable by your desktop publishing software.

Content stored in almost any form (including paper) is ultimately SGML taggable, but electronic material is faster and cheaper to convert. If typographic codes have been used consistently (all subheads in 10-point Times Roman, for example), filters can be written to translate the formatting codes to SGML tags. Inconsistent formatting, especially documents from a variety of desktop systems, will make the translation more difficult.

New software tools continue to bring SGML tagging within the resource range of smaller publishers. Microsoft's new SGML Author for Word saves SGML-compatible files from within a standard word processor. Boulder, Colorado-based Avalanche, Inc.'s FastTag filters word-processing files into preset style sheets and generates hypertext links in either HTML- or SGML-compatible format.

Incorporating SGML tags doesn't mean giving up

You need SGML's power for long-term storage of thousands of pages for transfer to any media.

your current desktop publishing system. Rather, think of the SGML file as the master document on which versions in other applications are based. What will change is the way you process documents. SGML requires a significant organizational commitment in the form of personnel training, DTD and TDT creation, as well as the discipline to work within rules established in the DTDs. Considerable preplanning in creating DTDs and TDTs will be required, involving writers, editors and typographic personnel.

You may want to consider outsourcing portions of authoring projects, including the SGML tagging. Rarely will a publisher have all the in-house creative talent necessary to produce superb electronic media products that fully integrate text, graphics, animation, video and sound. Still, don't lose control of your content or its presentation. In all the confusion over media and mergers, superior content is the one bellwether of success or failure. □

The Production Poker Game

BY ROBERT SENTINERY

The growth and diversity of independent publishing operations have given us a bounty of new titles during the last few years. And they're all vying for shelf space with magazines from major publishing houses. Walk into a well-stocked newsstand and expect to be overwhelmed by the plethora of unusual and interesting publications in a diversity of shapes, sizes, styles and colors. It's become an obsession of mine, as a publisher, to pick up these newborn magazines and analyze how they were produced and why their publishers made the choices they did.

Starting up a magazine involves more than defining an editorial focus or zeroing in on a specific readership or advertising market. One of the things publishers often overlook is how a magazine is actually put together. What type of printing press will be used? What kind of paper? How much color? How will the publication be bound and trimmed?

Your mission drives production values

Every magazine has a unique purpose that in itself will outline various production options. For example, a local weekly alternative publication like *The Village Voice* doesn't require high-quality paper and printing; it's just not necessary for the way that particular title functions. Readers don't expect it and wouldn't be willing to pay for it. *The New Yorker,* on the other hand, also a New York City-based weekly, has a significantly different attitude about printing techniques and paper choices.

Perhaps it's the "alternative" status of *The Voice* that allows it to avoid the costly production methods of its counterpart. *The Voice* at its inception capitalized on a grassroots philosophy that viewed content as being far more important than the package it comes in. Alternative weeklies have become a big business around the country; jam-packed with local advertising, they combine printing technologies adopted from daily newspapers with a concern for high volume, low cost and quick turnaround.

However, *The New Yorker,* to carry my example further, utilizes the latest four-color, heatset web printing technology, the same technology that any premium monthly would use. This is expensive and requires a volume of four-color national advertising to pay for it. *The New Yorker*'s approach is based on its original genteel readership, which appreciated literature and the arts. The magazine continues to reflect this with its current audience.

The coated-paper *Zone*

My current operation straddles both sides of this fence. I publish *Zone,* which is a glossy, high-dollar, quality-oriented publication, distributed internationally through bookstores and on newsstands. I also publish *Java Monthly,* a low-cost, local newsprint publication that's free to the public. There are completely different sets of standards and considerations that affect these titles. *Java* costs about 10 cents a unit to produce, whereas *Zone* runs over $1.50. It takes about an hour to print the full 20,000 run of *Java Monthly* on a newspaper press, while *Zone*'s 30,000 printrun ties up two sheetfed Heidelberg presses for an entire day.

You as publisher must choose a method appropriate to your audience's expectations of your magazine.

Most free publications are printed on newsprint, for obvious reasons. Publishers of these "freebies" will often add upgraded color covers to encourage higher circulation, while the interior usually remains low-grade porous newsprint. My advice for free publications is to start out on the low end and add upgrades as your advertising base grows.

Magazines for sale on the newsstand have an additional revenue source based on their cover price. This

> Figure out what your readers really want and what your advertisers will pay for, and then give it your best shot.

should allow for better paper, higher-quality printing, and color. However, these publications must compete in the heated and ever-growing world of newsstand titles. A publisher must consider types of paper used not only on the inside, but also on the cover; whether or not to varnish a cover for ultra-high gloss; the amount of full color inside; the choice between saddle-stitched or perfect-bound; and trim size.

Size is one of the more visible gimmicks used to attract readers. Magazines with unusual sizes—like *Interview*, which towers above the crowd, or *Bikini*, with its funky square format designed to appeal to Generation Xers, or even the unconventional *Wired*—grab attention on the newsstand and generally increase sales.

But remember that anything more than standard size costs more money. So, although a unique look may attract more readers, it may not be cost-effective unless you have the budget to ensure staying power and format consistency.

Some of the most interesting success stories are those publications that started out at the low end and gradually upgraded. *Interview* and *Rolling Stone* are examples. However, while upgrading is a natural progression, downgrading because of cost constraints can seriously damage a publication's reputation. One title comes to mind—*Wet*, which became Los Angeles' new-wave culture bible in the late seventies, but then went from a glossy coated stock inside to newsprint inside with an outrageous glossy full-color cover. The publication was never the same after this, and it didn't last much longer either.

The newsstand game is like poker, only with much higher stakes. Publishers should consider test marketing a new title on newsprint in a local area, and if that is successful, taking an upgraded version to the national newsstand. But remember, there are a lot of options out there. Figure out what your readers want and what your advertisers will pay for, and then give it your best shot. □

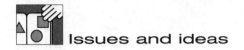

Self Test: Do You Design For Your Readers?

BY JAN WHITE

We publication-makers think our stuff is great. We are sure it is. So we fall into a trap: We cannot understand why our readers sometimes fail to see it our way, and why they don't clamor for our products.

The answer is that they don't clamor because we don't pay enough attention to showing off what we feel is excellent from their point of view. Oh, yes, we scream with stunning graphics. But too often the graphics are superficial efflorescences whose purpose is to startle (and display the brilliant prowess of our art direction). But readers don't care about that. They buy our product for its meat, not its skin. Why do we do it? Because we don't think of our readers, and we don't think *like* our readers.

Publications are complex products. We are always juggling the need for creating a product that has its own recognizable character (using unity and repetition) and the need to create excitement (using material differently). Here's a self test to help you decide whether your magazine is designed with your readers' best interests in mind.

Does your publication have a sense of self? It must be recognizable and unique. Its character is defined by the underlying styling system, which is a subtle mix of headlines, logos, slugs, display type, body-copy type, spacing, columns and color. Its success depends on disciplined self-control of the patterning, which causes the reader to say, "Of course, it couldn't be any other way."

Is your publication handled as a continuum? A magazine is a sequence of impressions. The best opportunity for outstanding magazine-making lies in the deliberate use of consistent flow, coordinated with planned, unexpected surprise. Pacing the issue is more valuable than clever illustrations here and there.

Is the presentation self-conscious or invisible? The best presentation is so natural and obvious that the readers are aware only of the wonders of the information they are reading. If they are tempted to notice the design, then that design has interposed itself and is therefore a failure—no matter how exciting or pretty. The medium is not the message. The message is the message.

Does each item have first-glance value for the reader? Are the meaningful words noticeable and visually irresistible? Do the words and images reinforce one another's meaning? Are the readers encouraged to dip in wherever there is something interesting?

Do headlines promise a benefit? Short and snappy is fine for a newspaper, but magazine headlines must be long enough to persuade readers of the value of the story to them—and should use as many words as necessary.

Is there a starting point that will get the viewer involved on every page? Is there a dominant image or other element that is supported by minor images or elements, creating visual contrast and intellectual interest?

Are captions exploited as the primary entry point? Pictures are the first elements that readers look at on the page. They arouse curiosity. Their explanations are opportunities to draw readers into the text, so they must do more than simply describe the picture.

Does the display type attract or repel the reader? The most user-friendly type is invisible, transparent. It must not be so self-consciously designed that it attracts attention to itself. Lower-case type is essential for ease of comprehension and reading smoothness. Flush-left is kinetic; centering is dignified but deadening.

Does the design make readers aware of your excellence? Do you use design to expose the marvels of the piece? You know how great it is, so you assume that it will speak for itself. It won't. We must clue the readers and make it all obvious with written and visual techniques.

Is everything that can be told visually turned into visuals? Statistics that are boring in words can be fascinating as charts. Locations are clearer with maps. Diagrams make relationships, structures and flow more comprehensible.

Is white space used to separate information units? Can the viewer recognize the elements, their relationships to one another and the length of each item at first glance?

Is audience participation encouraged by self tests, summaries and checklists? People love to get involved with hands-on activities. These devices facilitate a relationship between the reader and the magazine.

Does the magazine leave your readers with several strong impressions that they will remember? Did they notice the service that you provided? Will they feel good, fulfilled, amused and helped? The publication that gives the best service will win. □

Edit Is from Mars, Art Is From Venus

BY JOHN JOHANEK

Although publishing is a communication-based business, many insiders note that internal communication, or the lack of it, is a problem. When editors and art directors are out of sync, the ensuing frustration becomes a divisive wedge that makes the relationship less productive. Left unresolved, confrontations can take on the character of sibling quarrels.

When the art directors and editors feel hopelessly out of touch with one another, it's time for some positive action. Start by improving communication. Here are a few tips to help improve the way design decisions are discussed and resolved.

Note problems, not solutions. Some editors believe that communicating design preferences to their art directors means spelling out exactly what needs to be done. "Add some color to this page," or worse, "Add some blue to this headline." Although this may give editors what they want in the short run, it could be undermining team spirit. You'll serve yourself better if you simply identify the problem: "The page is too boring," or "The design lacks pizzazz."

Art people thrive on solving design problems. Give them the parameters and let them find the solution. This allows the designer to be more than just a tool to implement your idea. It also prevents you from forming any preconceptions.

On the other hand, avoid situations that leave room for too much interpretation. How much blue is "some blue"? If you have a mental picture of what you want, try to keep an open mind. Demanding the exact solution you envisioned can cloud your ability to look at another perfectly acceptable—or even better—option.

At the same time, don't be vague or completely dismiss a design without some concrete feedback about its shortcomings. "That's not what I wanted" or "It doesn't do anything for me" tells the art director nothing about what needs to be changed.

Use reader research. Does your art director seem to be designing for another magazine? Not all design suits all occasions. Some art directors get so infatuated with a style, they lose sight of the design elements that are appropriate for the magazine's readership.

If you and your art director aren't seeing eye to eye editorially, chances are the design will also be askew. Make sure the art department is kept apprised of reader research. Pass along copies of the results from reader surveys. Invite your art director to focus groups. The more you and your art director can keep abreast of reader sentiment, the more you'll be able to agree on how material should be presented.

Sketch it out. Art people are visual people. They typically communicate best with a pad and pencil. Not surprisingly, art folks are comfortable receiving information that way too. Even the crudest sketch will be more readily interpreted than your most eloquently composed memo. In fact, many such scribble sessions can become a two-way communication that results in an effective approach.

No copycats. Editors have an understandable tendency to use stories or pages from other magazines to make a design point. Although the photo treatment or page layout may work well in one magazine, it may not be right for yours. And most art directors will be turned off by any suggestion that they "lift" a design—and rightly so. Each magazine has its own personality, which is an extension of the art director's personality. Attempts to influence the design sensibilities of your art director by forcing him or her to copy someone else's work will cause resistance and alienation.

Include everybody. Larger magazines fall into the trap of discussing story ideas only with the art director, who relays the information to an assistant designer for execution. The assistant then interprets the concept again. By the time the editor sees the story art, it may be totally different. Instead, invite the hands-on designer to the initial meeting to avoid confusion.

When assigning art, arrange a meeting where critical details are discussed by everyone involved. As the creative process develops, everyone will be working with the same input, and surprises will be minimal.

Design will always be a subjective thing. As such, the design process will always include improving the way it is discussed, finding ways to remove the ambiguity, and minimizing the emotions with which it is associated. □

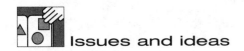

Great Design on a Slashed Budget

BY VERA STEINER

As the design members of the publication team, many art directors are facing their greatest challenge in nearly a decade. Publishers of trade, consumer and association magazines are cutting art and production budgets to the bone, while mandating that art directors produce the same well-designed publications as before.

Impossible? No. But some basic steps have to be taken to establish an environment conducive to low-cost, high-quality art. To begin, the art director must make the effort to learn about production methods and their relative costs. Art directors who have been happily designing in a vacuum of creativity, giving little thought to the production aspects of their projects, must change their approach. They must develop open, clear and friendly communications with their production departments, bringing the production people into the loop *before* they start designing—not when they are ready to hand over mechanicals, disks or film.

A production person can tell a designer when a format or element will cost too much or slow things down. The designer can then decide if the time and/or cost is worth it—or, if not, can come up with alternatives that do not compromise the appearance of the magazine.

Working together, having open access to one another, and (if you'll excuse the expression) communicating, creates the best environment for achieving mutual goals of cost-efficient, creative and exciting design.

Unfortunately, the next step is to realize that some of your favorite design elements (the ones that drive costs up) might have to be reduced or eliminated—at least for the duration of this economic downturn. Here is the "short" list of the most obvious and expensive: die cuts, embossing, hot stamping, metallic inks, varnish effects, special papers, unusual sizes, and anything done by hand. Not everything has to go, of course, but more careful consider-

ation has to be given to costly techniques.

These days, though, steering clear of the obvious is not enough. You may have to consider reducing the number of those familiar design devices that immediately added graphic interest—and cost—to layouts. These include silhouetted photos, full bleeds, multiple color screens, colors butting up against other colors, knock-outs, fifth color in a four-color book, critical trapping situations, and original commissioned illustrations and photography, especially on-location work.

If all this sounds too draconian, keep in mind that, as a magazine art director, you are not creating "art for art's sake," but are engaged in what used to be called "commercial art." That term has gone out of fashion and is considered crass, but it is exactly what you do. The object of the magazine publishing game is to make a profit—and that's commerce. True, the art department is not a profit center, but by keeping costs down, an art director can make a direct contribution to his or her magazine's financial health.

Furthermore, cutting back on the expensive elements does not leave you without options. One production manager suggests using bright colors over large areas, and heavier coverage to keep the colors true and stable. She also suggests avoiding overpowering a page with too many color photos, using one large photo for dramatic effect instead. This cuts down the cost of multiple color separations and stripping. I second it for better visual effect as well as cost savings.

Typography-as-design is another way to go. Strong, bold typographic effects (or delicate, soft ones, if the subject matter so dictates) can take the place of costly photos or illustrations and their associated color separation, stripping and printing costs. In these cases, it is important to get headline copy from the editor early in the design stage, since that headline will be the major design element. Because many editors like to leave the

> "Keep in mind that, as a magazine art director, you are not creating 'art for art's sake' but are engaged in 'commercial art.'"

writing of the headline for last, there may be some resistance to this idea. But it is a practical approach that saves money.

Strong type design can also be tied to a smaller (less expensive) spot illustration or an existing photo.

Here are four more tips on ways to save without cutting quality:

• **Learn to bargain.** In more prosperous times, we figured that a commissioned cover illustration for a trade publication, for instance, would cost between $1,000 and $2,000. We'd just call our choice of illustrator and make the assignment. Now it's a little different. We call the same first-choice artist—but now we haggle. We state, truthfully, that our budgets are lower this year than last, but we need the same quality art. Nobody likes this, of course—not the haggler or the hagglee— but it's a fact of current business life, and most illustrators understand. Unfortunately for them, business may have dropped off, too— meaning they need to take the job even at the lower price. A good, ongoing relationship really helps in these situations.

• **Look for discount opportunities.** You might want to consider an agreement in which you promise to give a particular artist a specific number of assignments per issue or per year for a reduced "quantity discount." This idea can apply to photographers, too.

• **Try the untried.** New, young artists—perhaps recent art school graduates—are often willing to work for a lower fee in exchange for the opportunity and exposure. This is not exploitative, since it helps both parties: You get good, inexpensive art and the young artists get exposure.

How do you find this new talent? Go to art school gallery exhibits, look at lots of portfolios, and ask your industry peers for recommendations.

• **Use stock art.** Stock art and photography services are another alternative. These services are almost always less expensive than commissioned art. And today, a wide range of stock work is available—which means you won't see your image all over the place. Some stock houses offer special pricing for regular clients, working with your budget, and some even have "specials," such as waiving the research fee for a certain period of time for their priority customers.

Good design at a good price

A strong black-and-white or two-color page can look smashing if it is well designed. The challenge now is to get back to basic design precepts, to give up design gimmicks and special printing techniques that we've been using as a crutch for so long. Let's start looking at shapes again, at good typography, at judicious cropping of photos, to make the editorial page a pure visual composition that will clearly and pleasingly convey the information our readers want and need—at a price we can afford. □

How to Review a Portfolio

BY JOHN JOHANEK

A photographer friend of mine was recently lamenting the slowness of his business, despite an increased number of requests to view his portfolio. He speculated that novices were doing the initial screening and, being novices, probably didn't know the first thing about what to look for.

He has a point. There's no Portfolio 101 in art schools. People faced with reviewing a portfolio for the first time are usually on their own, seldom able to call on a veteran designer who could show them the ropes. In some cases, even experienced art directors are at a loss when it comes to an art or photo portfolio review. And at many magazines, acquiring art or photos is the responsibility of the editor, which can mean that quality work is occasionally by-passed.

For some, the solution is simply to hire a "name." Although this may allow the hirer to eliminate the review process with some degree of security, not all of us have the luxury of hefty budgets. Others try to side-step portfolio reviews by delegating the initial screening to assistants. But unless you as hirer are an experienced and educated photo editor who understands exactly what to look for, you could come up short.

Finding the right vendor for art or photography requires two steps: The first is to solicit portfolios—lots of portfolios. Get them from a variety of sources. If your intention is to build a file of available, qualified suppliers, you may want to look at two dozen or more portfolios. If your need is more immediate and you have a specific project in mind, six to 10 might be enough. In addition to contacting rep firms that handle the kind of visuals you're looking for, you'll also want to call some creatives directly. If you've seen something in print somewhere that strikes your interest, track down the source. And don't hesitate to contact other art directors for recommendations.

So, there you sit with stacks of portfolios. Now what? Don't look only for examples of work that pertain to your immediate assignment. Instead, check all the examples in several key areas, including the following:

Composition: Does the artist understand basic design? In still lifes, are the objects arranged in a pleasing man-ner? Do scenics show an understanding of balance and proportion? Is there an effective use of color? Has the artist created satisfactory eye movement for the viewer? Are the images compelling and evocative?

Variety: Is this person versatile, or does the portfolio show the same basic approach to problem solving? For instance, has the photographer lighted each subject differently? Is there variety—things shot in natural light, dramatic light, and with a high-tech approach? Are tabletop objects photographed at the same angle, or does each piece appear to be shot from the most interesting or informational angle? Is the illustrator limited to a narrow scope of subject matter, such as wildlife or airplanes?

Competence: Is there a mastery of techniques, or does it appear that there's only one safe style that's used repeatedly? Look beyond the content of each sample and determine whether there is an underlying ability to deliver a quality product. Are there techniques employed that are transferable to your subject matter?

Unfortunately, this is where most people end their search for a vendor. In reality, you're just halfway through the process.

Set up appointments

The second step, often ignored, is the most important: Meet with the artist or photographer. When dealing through a rep, don't be surprised if he or she insists on accompanying the artist. In fact, you may even want to suggest it. Procedural questions could arise that the rep is expected to handle. But don't agree to having the rep as a substitute. There are some specific things you'll want to find out from the artist that the portfolio review alone won't uncover.

For example, you need to know exactly what the artist's or photographer's actual contribution was to each piece in the portfolio—especially those that really impressed you. If the piece expressed a unique creative approach, how much of the credit belongs to the artist? Did the artist/photographer participate in the creative development, or was he or she responsible merely for clicking the shutter or executing someone else's idea?

Was there an art director or other creative person involved during the photo shoot? How closely did the final piece match the original concept?

Ask about time frames. Did the photographer have two weeks to finesse the set and lighting? Did the shot involve numerous film tests before the final frames were clicked off? Can you afford the same amount of time and money that some of these pieces may have required, or can the vendor deliver the same level of quality within your particular financial constraints?

Was the piece actually created for print, or is it just a portfolio sample? Frequently, illustrators and photographers are willing to put a great deal of their time and energy into getting a portfolio to "sing"—time and energy you may not be able to afford on your projects. This is often true of portfolios from recent college graduates whose entire books might be made up of student work. Carefully worded questions can elicit details about a piece that will influence your opinion of the vendor's capabilities.

If the photos you've reviewed reveal a variety of styles, from still lifes to portraits to fashion to science, ask the photographers which area they enjoy shooting most. Not surprisingly, creative people will spend the most time and take extra care with techniques that provide them the greatest pleasure. The same is true of subject matter. If, for example, a photographer's favorite pastime is camping, he or she is likely to put more effort and care into assignments related to backpacking or camping gear. Frequently, the person's intimacy with the subject matter will result in a sharper eye for editorial correctness.

Take note of repeat work for the same client. Continuing work with a particular client demonstrates satisfaction. Also, don't hesitate to inquire about how current a specific piece may be. Too many old samples could indicate that this person lacks a willingness to experiment, or is unfamiliar with new techniques. Or worse, it could reflect the person's own dissatisfaction with the caliber of his or her current output.

Don't look only for examples of work that pertain to your immediate assignment.

Spend some time talking about your publication and your problems. Have several samples of your magazine on hand. Review a story or two from past issues that you believe could have been handled better. Solicit input and feedback. Get a sense of the artist's abilities for brainstorming and problem solving. Chances are, an artist not willing to take the time to understand your problems now won't take the time when it comes to a real project, either.

Be sure to talk about budgets. Ask how much specific portfolio pieces cost to produce. You may find that the samples you admire represent $1,500 budgets—and you are typically limited to $550. If your budget won't purchase the same level of quality, where would the compromise be? Some artists are willing to trade a reduced rate for more lead time without a loss of quality. Take this opportunity to lay some groundwork.

Finally, one of the best reasons to bring the artist in for a personal meeting is to check the chemistry. Samples alone won't reveal egos or arrogance. Get a feel for his or her attitudes about your magazine's subject matter. Does this person harbor strong sentiments in areas that could hamper his or her performance on your projects? In short order, you'll know if this is someone you can (or care to) work with.

A personal meeting won't tell you everything, but there is one more thing you can do. Most candidates will leave behind some sort of client list. It may even be a résumé. Frequently, it's accompanied by a printed sample or two. That's not enough. Ask for specific references. Get the names and phone numbers of the people involved with some of the memorable samples you admired. Call them and discuss their working relationship with the illustrator/photographer in question.

There's more to an effective portfolio review than just simply admiring nifty art or ogling cool photographs. By investing a bit more time up front to find the best person to do the job, you'll save time, money and aggravation later. But it all starts with knowing exactly what to look for. □

The Thrust and Parry of Fee Negotiations

BY VERA STEINER

The question I'm most frequently asked by editors, publishers and artists alike is not, "How do you keep coming up with fresh, new ideas?" not "What are the new trends in design and typography?" and not even, "How has the computer changed publication design?" It's "How are fees negotiated?"

As the principal of a design studio, I have to deal with both sides of this question on a daily basis—first negotiating my own design and production fees with my clients who are editors, publishers and art directors, and then becoming the client and negotiating fees with illustrators and photographers whom I commission for my clients' projects.

This is probably the toughest part of the job, with the possible exception of dodging bike messengers in New York City. The process falls into three basic parts: deciding what you are willing to pay for a job; determining what your negotiating strengths are; and finally, commissioning the job and negotiating the fee with the artist.

What is the job worth?

Flexibility and a willingness to approach each project individually are important in determining what you think is a fair price for a job. We quote a flat per-project fee that we feel is appropriate for a specific project. However, we have a general "laundry list" of prices for jobs that are similar. We customize that price based on many factors: size and complexity of the job, number of pages, usage rights, color, circulation of the publication, whether it is consumer or business, standard or tabloid format, and so on. We also factor in how much time is allotted for the project and how many design variations the client wants to see. Then we add on estimated costs and expenses, which we guarantee within 15 percent.

There is another aspect of determining price that is not openly discussed, but everyone figures it in—or should. We call it the nuisance factor, and it's just what it sounds like. Early on, an astute designer might discern that a client is going to be difficult or fickle—or

worse, just doesn't know what he wants. Or it may become apparent that the artist is a prima donna who will be difficult to work with. Either situation translates into more work and more time spent on the project than normal—which you must factor into the price you're willing to pay.

To enhance your skills at coming up with payment quotes to offer an artist that are both within your budget and fair, consider the following steps:

• Shop around. See several artists (in person, not just their portfolios).

• Get recommendations from others who have had similar projects.

• Compare apples to apples. If your project is a publication redesign, don't get quotes from a designer who specializes in annual reports. If your photo shoot is of a company executive, don't get quotes from a still-life photographer.

• Look at lots of portfolios, even when you don't have a specific project.

• Compare prices between artists who have similar amounts of experience in your type of project. A hot young talent fresh out of art school may not yet grasp the concepts of budgets and deadlines. This doesn't

> "First, guarantee that the artist will be paid on delivery or within seven days of submitting the finished work. That is always attractive."

mean you shouldn't use him; it just means you shouldn't compare his fees to a more experienced artist's fees.

• Go to art school exhibits to discover new talent who may be more eager for exposure and printed samples than a big dollar figure.

• Even if you don't think you can afford a particularly well-known talent, ask. If she is between projects, or likes you, your project or your magazine, she will often do the job at your lower price.

• Don't be too proud to beg and grovel. I often tell high-priced illustrators and photographers (truthfully) that I know they are used to getting more for their work than we can afford to pay, but if they can find it in their hearts to do this for us at this price, we will be sure to make it up to them in the future. This has really worked for us, and there is nothing unsavory about it. If you don't ask, you don't get.

Once you have determined what you think is a fair price for a job, it's time to start negotiating with the artist. David Goldman of the David Goldman Agency says, "There are a couple of aspects that can enhance your negotiating stance. First, guarantee that the artist will be paid on delivery or within seven days of submitting the finished artwork. This is always attractive to an artist in need of money, in lieu of the extra $100 or $200, in these tough times. Second, offer the artist numerous reprints—25, 50, 100 or even 200. This will give the artist the ability to do a direct-mail promotion while saving him printing costs."

Wendy Tiefenbacher, who as photo editor of *Meetings & Conventions* commissions a large amount of photography each month, says, "My rates [budget] are low, compared to the rest of the industry, but I still want to use the best photographers. So I'll gang up shoots, give the photographer more than one assignment."

And, Goldman adds, "The prestige of working with a certain art director or designer, or for a very prestigious publication, is an important factor to many artists" and may help in negotiating the price downward.

The negotiation dance

The artists or photographers with whom you discuss assignments are likely to start the negotiations with the highest figure they feel they may get, but will have in mind a figure they can live with. The purchaser should set a figure he'd like to pay, but have a maximum figure in mind that he could come up to, if necessary. When we commission an illustration or photograph, this is how the negotiating "dance" usually goes:

We first ask the artist what he wants to charge for our project. More often than not, he will turn it around on us and say, "Well, what's your budget and we'll see if we can work with it." Since we already have a good idea of what we can pay, we'll come up with a figure slightly below that, to give ourselves room to negotiate. These are the most common response scenarios:

A. *"That sounds great. When can we start?"* This usu-

ally means you quoted a higher fee than the artist expected. Everyone should be pleased.

B. *"That's less than I had in mind, but I'd like to work with you, so I'll do it."* You quoted a price he expected, more or less. You can do business if he seems eager to do the project. But if he seems to say "yes" because he is desperate and his attitude is bitter, you might not get his best effort. In that case, we'd say, "Perhaps this is not the right project for you."

C. *"That's quite a bit less than I expected. Can you do any better on the price?"* If I think the artist's work is worth more, and I think I can get more money, I'll fight for it. If I can't get a higher budget, I'll say, "I'm really sorry we can't work together on this, but the next job that's right for you, with a higher budget, is yours!"

D. *"You must be kidding. That price is outrageous and insulting!"* To something like that, I'll say, "I'm sorry you feel that way, but there are a great many artists as talented as you looking for work, and I'm sure I'll find one who will not only work within my budget, but who will also be more pleasant and professional to deal with." And I never call that person again.

Another variation on pricing style, which lends itself mostly to designers, is the hourly rate. This is usually used by artists, designers and production people who work on computers. Most of the freelancers we hire for a day or a week are hourly workers. Experienced computer artists make between $25 and $38 an hour. But some will charge as much as $200 an hour. If you decide on an hourly rate, be sure to set maximum boundaries—and put it in writing.

In fact, any arrangement you make with an artist should be formalized and put in writing. As David Goldman says, "A purchase order is a contract that protects both parties equally. A negotiation must be documented in writing before an assignment begins, and should be signed by both parties."

To sum up, the best way to get the best work for the best price is to be clear, honest, friendly and knowledgeable. Give value for value, and ask lots of questions—both of your peers and the artists you work with.

Have some set budget in mind before you start negotiating. Trade off generous time allotments, creative freedom, extra reprints, additional future work and a great working relationship for a better price for top-notch work.

And remember: Get it in writing. ☐

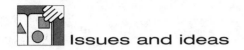

Reduce the Risk in a Redesign

BY VERA STEINER

Redesigning a magazine can be as exciting and exhilarating as discovering and exploring a new world—and fraught with just as many perils. At each step, questions must be asked. The wrong answers—even the wrong questions—can create serious problems. To help ensure that your redesign runs as smoothly as possible, here are 10 areas to watch carefully.

Why ask why? There are as many reasons to redesign a magazine as there are magazines: to keep a publication visually contemporary; to boost readership generally or within a certain group; to make a magazine more competitive; to facilitate a change in editorial focus; or to show advertisers and prospects that the magazine is on top of things and always improving. It may even be a last-ditch effort to revitalize a failing product, or make it more salable.

The point is that if you don't redesign for the right reasons, your expectations may not be met. Not only will you be disappointed in the results, you will also be out a great deal of time and money.

The "tweak" vs. the "total": Some magazines need only an in-office facial; others, a surgical face-lift. Perhaps it's time to update the logo or contents page, or add more color, just to give the magazine a fresher look. In such cases, a total redesign is not called for. Perhaps this magazine has a long-term historical identity that should be left alone. Major changes could upset or even anger loyal readers.

On the other hand, many magazines do need a totally new look, yet their publishers hesitate because they fear change and/or worry about the cost. It is true that a magazine should not be redesigned too often. If it is, it risks losing its identity and direction. But a careful redesign every five to seven years, on average, will maintain reader loyalty and keep the publication from looking outdated.

How did all these people get in my room? In most of the redesigns we work on, a major problem is whom to please. We've been in planning meetings that included the publisher, the editors, the production and salespeople, the in-house art people, the marketing/promotion person and a couple of folks from the mail room and

reception. This is very democratic, but not conducive to a good outcome. It is far better to get pointed direction from the publisher and editor only—after they have done their own research and gotten input from whomever they choose.

Go it alone, or go for help? The age-old question is, "Should we do it in-house, or hire an outside redesign specialist?" The age-old answer is, "It depends." If your on-staff art director has had redesign experience and is not simply an art/production/computer person, but a true editorial designer; if the production schedule permits this person the time (probably a couple of months of concentrating on nothing but the redesign while someone else puts out the regular issues), then, yes, your in-house person is right for the job. Otherwise, the right choice is an outside editorial designer with experience in redesigning, not just art directing, magazines of great variety.

Clash of the titan egos: If you decide to use an outside designer, you will have to deal with possible ego conflicts between that person and your in-house staff—especially if the staffers wanted to do the redesign but were overruled. Let the designer know that he or she must work with your staff. After all, there is a great deal of practical information that they will need to exchange. This working relationship is sometimes fabulous, sometimes a nightmare. But the major consideration in making your decision should be the outcome of the redesign, not the health of delicate egos.

Who am I? Steer clear of the following scenarios: "We want to look just like *Business Week*, even though we are a monthly." "We want to look like our competition." "We want to look scholarly, yet cutting-edge; conservative, yet fun; business-like, yet funky; edgy, yet classic." Don't try to look "just like" another magazine. Create your own identity to serve your special readers.

Timing is everything: Too often, the decision to redesign is made too late to meet the best launch date. Give yourself three to six months to redesign your magazine. Have a mock-up ready for the sales force well before your relaunch date, and time that date for maximum effect. A healthy magazine with a good sales story can launch a redesign at any time of the year. But for a book that is third or fourth in its field, pre-planning, promotion and selling at the right time are imperative.

It'll cost you: If you think a redesign is something you can squeeze into your expenses under promotion or office supplies, you won't get the job done right. It's always best to budget ahead for this type of project, but if you haven't and your magazine urgently needs to be redesigned, you must bite the bullet.

If you go with an in-house redesign, you will have to pay free-lancers to carry on the day-to-day design and production. If you've decided to hire an outside designer, first look at redesign samples, befores and afters, and then narrow your choice of designers to three. Be sure to compare them on the same scale in terms of experience and specialization. When you solicit bids, ask for written estimates, guaranteed to within 10 percent. One of the major pitfalls of a redesign is the added expense you incur when the designer's bills far exceed the original estimate.

Did I just buy the Brooklyn Bridge? In planning and budgeting for your redesign, you must be clear on the costs that will be incurred—especially if you are using an outside designer, who will probably be using his or her own sources and equipment. But whether the job is done outside or in-house, there are lots of extras. Some possibilities: color output (like Fiery or Iris prints), new fonts, scanning of photos or art, photostats, typesetting, type design/hand-lettering, messengers, overnight delivery services, long-distance phone/fax, additional staff, computer training for in-house staff, new software programs, and so on.

Have the outside designer specify what is included in his or her fee, and what is charged as extra. Ask if you will be given computer templates, mechanicals (if you still work conventionally), style sheets, a mocked-up book for style, fine-tuning after the first issue is out, ongoing or limited-time consultation services to make sure the new design is properly implemented, and so on. All this needs to be discussed and negotiated at the beginning. And again, get it in writing.

Beauty and the Beast: If you choose an outside designer, it's most important that the technology he or she uses mesh with your in-house equipment and software. Even if initially it doesn't, prior planning can overcome the obstacle. We've redesigned publications on our Macs in Quark for clients who use PCs and Ventura. Because we knew the incompatibilities in advance, we were able to make provisions to overcome them. It can be done, but first you must factor in some additional time and expense. If yours is not a computerized operation, this can be a good time to convert—but again, time, money and training must be planned for—well in advance. □

> A careful redesign every five to seven years, on average, will maintain reader loyalty and keep the book from looking outdated.

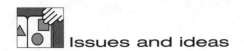

Define Your Redesign

BY TIM BOGARDUS

Publishers often turn to design to solve problems that can't be solved by design. For example, while a redesign can be used as a sales tool, it can't turn your sales staff into better salespeople. And even though a redesign can be used to generate a buzz at the newsstand, a declining newsstand presence may have nothing to do with the design of the magazine. Sales could be flat because of poor placement, increased competition, or any number of other reasons. And nothing, including design, can gloss over a mediocre editorial product.

Redesign is not a panacea to be used whenever business goes sour. There are perils: Most people don't like change. And change just for the sake of change doesn't play well in a business environment. Solid brand identities and winning formulas require hard work and take years to develop. As the old cliché says: If it ain't broke, don't fix it.

But redesigning a magazine can be a powerful tool for improving the bottom line if you enter the process with clearly defined goals and realistic ideas about how it can be most effective. What are you trying to accomplish? Who are you trying to please? Readers? Advertisers? A new editor or publisher? If a redesign is structured not just from an aesthetic perspective, but also with solid business objectives in mind, the result can be doubly effective.

Below, we profile five magazines that have recently undergone some form of redesign. We asked the principals involved about their business reasons for redesigning. The responses were as disparate as the markets the magazines serve. And each editor, publisher or president had his or her own redesign philosophy. We can learn something from each of their examples.

> *Individual Investor* aimed to eliminate a newspapery feel with better stock and more color.

■ Individual Investor

When Jonathan Steinberg bought the *Penny Stock Journal* in 1988, he envisioned something much more than the financial title's existing mission of chronicling the ups and downs of the stock market. The dream was to create a magazine that not only tracked the markets, but also conducted proprietary research and offered real investment advice and insight. The dream was realized quickly. Competing with the likes of *Money, Worth* and *Kiplinger's Personal Finance, Individual Investor* (circulation 175,000), based in New York City and published by the Individual Investor Group, has carved a secure niche in the highly competitive financial-magazine market.

Once the magazine had established a loyal following among the investment-minded and achieved its raison d'être of providing savvy investment information, Steinberg, who serves as editor in chief, CEO and chairman, and Robert Schmidt, who has been president since 1994, turned their attention to the form of the magazine itself. Data-intensive and printed on low-quality uncoated paper, *II* was hard to read and too newspapery. And because of the paper stock and the mostly black-and-white pages, it was difficult to attract advertisers outside of the financial services sector. In addition, the magazine's oversize format caused problems on the newsstand.

With the clearly defined goals of making *II* more readable, attracting new subscribers and advertisers, and improving newsstand sales, Steinberg and Schmidt hired New York City-based Morris Studios to help them remake the magazine. *Individual Investor*'s average reader is an affluent, 50-year-old white male, and the objective was to make the magazine cleaner, crisper and more attractive, while continuing to fulfill its mission of being a no-nonsense investment tool.

The newly designed version was introduced in July 1995 to enthusiastic reader and advertiser response (Schmidt says he had a half dozen calls during the first week from interested advertisers). The new incarnation was reduced to standard size. It was upgraded to a coated stock with two-color and four-color pages throughout. For readability, the type size was increased, color was added to the charts, and new graphic devices enhanced the organization of the data. At the same time, Steinberg used the redesign as an opportunity to add new sections.

"The main reason for all this is to create a more effective magazine for readers," says Steinberg in his editor's note. "But I'd be lying if I didn't acknowledge economic incentives." Schmidt says the redesign cost about $75,000, but that the new look will help draw consumer-product advertisers and achieve his goal of adding 125 new ad pages to the 765 the magazine carried last year.

■ Men's Fitness

"It is necessary to remarket your magazine every two to three years," contends Michael Carr, president and CEO of Woodland Hills, California-based Weider Publications. "But I believe in evolution, not revolution. Revolution shows some contempt for the reader," he says. "A magazine's relationship to the reader is like that of a friend," says Carr, and radical changes can hurt a relationship.

Weider's fitness titles—*Shape, Flex, Muscle & Fitness, Prime, Living Fit, Men's Fitness* and others—are targeted to specific demographic groups. Carr says design should cater to the demographic of each magazine. *Flex*, for example, is aimed at 18- to 25-year-olds, and the design is flashier and more frenetic than *Men's Fitness*, which is targeted to men in their thirties. *Men's Fitness*, Carr says, requires a cleaner, more subtle design than *Flex*. "Design is about relating to people in the images they understand," Carr says.

One reason for redesigning, or "refining," as Carr prefers to call it, is to create excitement at the newsstand. Because 65 percent of Weider's titles are sold through single-copy sales, newsstand presence is particularly important. "We need retail energy," Carr says.

When *Men's Fitness* was hovering at 165,000 circulation in 1991, Carr says the magazine underwent a "redefinition," which helped grow the circulation to 185,000 over the next two years. Then in early 1994, when the title had reached a circulation of 200,000, *Men's Fitness* redesigned again, seeking a cleaner, more contemporary look. This month's issue offers a sharper logo and the tagline, "Your Guide To Healthy Living." The work was done by Weider's in-house staff.

In 1996, Carr says, *Men's Fitness* will raise its ratebase to 300,000, a 50 percent gain in two years. Carr attrib-

utes about one-third of that increase to the evolutionary refinements, but advises that a redesign must be supported by promotion, marketing and editorial quality. "You have to fulfill the promise," he says. "Anybody can do something once, but our business is about relationships. Art sells, but editorial renews."

■ Soap Opera Update

Like sands through the hourglass, so go the issues of *Soap Opera Update*, the biweekly Bauer Magazine L.P. title published in Englewood Cliffs, New Jersey. Photographs, gossip and sneak previews are the bread and butter of a market that requires comprehensive coverage of daytime television's continuing sagas—and the more the better.

In late 1989, about a year and a half into *Soap Opera Update*'s life, Angela Shapiro, editor in chief, decided to add a digest-size supplement to the magazine. The purpose of the digest was to give the impression that the 370,000 circulation title contained extra news and gossip: It was a gimmick to boost newsstand sales, and a way to take on *Soap Opera Digest*, a more established, 1.4 million circulation title owned by K-III Magazines that Shapiro had founded in 1975. According to Shapiro, the ploy worked and sales increased, although she wouldn't say by how much.

But the digest caused problems, too. Because it was bound around the outside of the book, it obscured two-thirds of the cover, which limited choices for cover art. And the digest was printed at one printer and then shipped to the magazine's printer, where the two were bound together. This, of course, added time to the production cycle. Finally, the digest looked as if it did not belong to the magazine, and it didn't draw advertising.

So starting in 1994, Shapiro and her staff—working without an outside designer or consultant—designed test issues that incorporated the digest's content into the front of the book. "We felt very positive after looking at the test results and talking to subscribers that this was the way to go," Shapiro says, and the redesigned book was introduced with the June 27, 1995, issue. The move gave *Soap Opera Update* a more cohesive appearance, cut a week from the production cycle, and created more full-size color pages for advertising. Shapiro says reader response has been overwhelmingly positive.

■ Utne Reader

"A magazine is a work in progress," proclaims Eric Utne, president and editor in chief of the Minneapolis-based *Utne Reader*, published bimonthly by Lens Publishing. "A redesign seems to be an opportunity to nudge people and get them to take another look at us." After 10 years of billing itself as "The best of the alternative press," the *Utne Reader* (circulation 300,000) changed course in January. The magazine was updated for a cleaner, less cluttered, slicker look. More important, the focus was broadened. The title now carries the tagline, "The best of the alternative media," recognizing the diversification during the last decade and the increased range of sources, such as the Internet, public radio and zines.

And though *Utne Reader* intends to continue in its role of "the alternative Reader's Digest," the magazine will also begin publishing more original articles. In addition to the redesign—which was executed by Minneapolis designer Jan Jancourt and new art director Andrew Henderson—Utne announced new ventures in book publishing, Utne Online and community salons in bookstores and libraries—all of which are intended to extend a new "activist" agenda.

These changes were not made for business reasons, Utne claims, adding that the "reinvention" was not based on reader research at all. Utne recalls a conversation he had with Margaret Mead, who told him there was a difference between entertaining readers, which she defined as giving them what they wanted, and delighting readers, which she said was giving them what they didn't know they wanted.

But Utne acknowledges that the redesign was not without a business motivation. "We wanted old readers to take a look at us again," he says.

> *New York* used its redesign to revitalize itself and break through the media clutter.

■ *New York Magazine*

When a 26-year-old regional magazine gets tired, one way to pep it up is to hire new blood. In February 1994, Kurt Andersen took over as *New York Magazine*'s editor in chief. Charged with the task of revitalizing a weekly with flat circulation and advertising numbers, Andersen began renovating New York City-based K-III Magazines' 400,000 circulation title.

"There is definitely a business argument for doing a redesign," Andersen says. "It's a way to grab attention in the cluttered New York newsstand world." The changes started during the first week of his arrival, beginning with the 26-year-old typeface and extending into major overhauls of each section, a retrofitting of the New York logo, the use of bigger pictures and the creation of a design that was "more flexible and modern" than the old design.

"Most magazines take the same wine and put it in a new bottle," Andersen notes. "We actually made new wine." He says the redesign was a combination of trying to please readers, advertisers, himself and his staff. It was conducted with designer Michael Bierut of the New York City firm Pentagram, and cost in the "low five figures," Andersen says. Readers' reactions were mixed. "People don't like change," he explains. "With a weekly, it's much more intense. It's like you snuck into their house and rearranged their furniture."

Publisher Amy Churgin, who came on board in August 1994, before the redesign was introduced in October, says bottom-line results have been strong. By mid-1995, ad pages were up 9 percent, compared with the first half of 1994, and newsstand sales had increased about 12 percent. □

Give Your Readers What They Want—In the Form They Want It

BY EVE ASBURY

The magazine industry is no stranger to target marketing. Titles as disparate as *Newsweek, Child* and *Farm Journal* have taken advantage of selective binding to reach segments of their audiences. But increased production costs, database limitations, complex fulfillment logistics and philosophical concerns mean this option isn't for everyone. So what do you do if you want to fashion a highly targeted version of your publication for specific readers? Can it be done? What options are there?

Real options do exist, thanks mainly to recent advances in technology. Publishers are using different types of technology to fit their needs. For example, Ticketmaster, a marketing company, is getting into the publishing game with the aid of sophisticated desktop publishing technology. CMP Publications is using the World Wide Web to reach certain readers and boost its core technology-oriented magazines. And *TV Guide,* the nation's largest-circulation weekly, has digitized its workflow to produce over 100 separate versions.

Digital *TV Guide*

For a magazine like Radnor, Pennsylvania-based *TV Guide,* targeted editions are more than a marketing ploy—they are essential to the publication's existence. The 14-million-circulation, 42-year-old title, published by News Corp., used sophisticated database technology to set up a customized, database-driven workflow system that replaces its "paste-up and repro" production process. The move brings the production of all 119 editions in-house. With the help of many different vendors, *TV Guide* has created an unparalleled fusion of technology and versioning.

"We're nearing completion of a project that began over four years ago," says Gary Melara, chief information officer, information technology, for *TV Guide. Because* of the unusually complex nature of the magazine, extensive planning was necessary. *TV Guide* editions generally share a common four-color cover

and feature well, but the black-and-white features and listing sections are specific for each individual market. The listing grids comprise scheduling information (show name, time, channel); explanatory listings (what episode); and features, such as the kids' section, close-ups and the crossword. Because this information is unique to each version, the listing section is in a constant state of flux.

Says David Bessen, vice president, operations, Management Process Integrators, Inc.—a Scottsdale, Arizona-based consultancy working with *TV Guide:* "We were shocked at the deep complexity of the magazine. There's a lot of artificial intelligence built in to accommodate editorial rules."

With this powerful technology, *TV Guide* can now create final, digitally imposed pages ready for output. The process begins in the editorial department, where powerful database engines—running on Silicon Graphics and Intergraph servers with PCs running in terminal emulation and PC applications—capture the two major types of editorial content, scheduling information and listing information. Ads, which also change from region to region, are managed separately by a proprietary advertising production system.

Once all the individual components have been

> "Look, here's a model that works: People subscribe to a magazine and it gets delivered to their mailbox. Why shouldn't that happen electronically?"

processed (listings, ads and features), the system creates the edition by performing an Edition Build, which is initiated automatically by a workflow management system (WMS). Developed in-house and running on Sun workstations, the WMS tracks the different components, ensuring sequential processing of all the specified tasks. Over 10,000 elements are managed by the WMS to get 119 weekly versions.

The Edition Build then feeds into the Intelligent Layout software, which is driven by an expert system engine running on an Intergraph workstation. There, WYSIWYG editions are composed on screen. Once the editions are signed off, the customized imposition software creates imposed flats of 16 pages, two-up. The flats are imaged on an Optronics ColorSetter filmsetter at six different locations using a WAN (wide area network) with frame relay connections. High-speed RIPs can process a flat in just eight minutes. With 22,000 to 25,000 new pages being created each week, and a close of just two days, the technology has to be robust enough to support the information.

The conversion process began in July 1995 and, at press time, *TV Guide* was producing 82 editions using the new system. Although publishers may marvel at the power of this setup, at a low-ball figure of $7 million for technology development alone, most will not be quick to follow suit.

TV Guide has created an unparalleled fusion of technology and versioning.

Ticket to publish

Marketing and technology have not been strangers to Ticketmaster, the Los Angeles-based ticket-sales giant, but magazine publishing is less familiar ground. Thanks to the desktop revolution, many marketers—such as Ticketmaster—believe they can create their own magazines, and are entering the publishing arena with Macintosh-based design departments and off-the-shelf software.

For the past five years, Ticketmaster has contracted with JSA Publishing in Santa Monica, California, to produce the 35 versions of its regionally segmented, monthly entertainment guides. Now, the company will incorporate those guides into a self-published monthly magazine, *Live!*, set to be launched in February 1996.

Live! will have 19 regional editions, each with a different 10- to 12-page listings-guide insert that will be bound in using selective binding. Marc Barrington, director of production for *Live!*, says it will be produced with Quark's QPS (Quark Publishing System).

In addition to hardware and software costs, the company has added 40 staffers to work on the project. "Having the system [in house] has streamlined the process considerably and increased efficiency by seven days," Barrington estimates. "We are looking at options for personalized information to be ink-jetted onto the guide cover, such as late-breaking concerts."

Executives declined to reveal specific switchover-related costs.

Direct e-mail

One of the main deterrents to traditional versioning has been the high cost and complex nature of distribution and fulfillment. With the flexible nature of the World Wide Web, and the ease with which dynamic, interactive documents can be created, the electronic variety of editorial versioning becomes a less costly and a more manageable proposition. Although many publishers are considering joining the Web stampede, uncertainties about how to offer readers value and make the project financially viable remain.

CMP Publications, based in Manhasset, New York, has addressed the problem of delivery. The company unveiled the beta version of TechWeb Direct at the giant Comdex computer show in Las Vegas in November 1995. TechWeb Direct is a digital delivery service that sits on a user's desktop and searches the vast TechWeb Web site (home to all 16 of CMP's technology publications) for articles that match the specified interests of that registered TechWeb user. After the user has downloaded a piece of software and filled out an interest profile, the service automatically retrieves articles from the Web and places them into folders on the hard drive, alerting the user when new information has been found.

Users don't have to log on to the Web or disrupt their daily work. "It's a pipeline directly into a reader's desktop," says Jeff Pundyk, one of the directors of CMP's Interactive Media Group in charge of TechWeb Direct. Unlike e-mail or listserve newsletters, TechWeb Direct delivers articles in their original format with all the graphic elements intact, he adds.

The technology that makes all this possible was developed by New York City-based Digital Delivery, Inc., which is currently beta-testing several versions of Delivery Manager (product name at press time) with other publishers. Director of marketing Mark Friedler says the company hopes to offer the package commercially in early 1996 for between $2,000 and $5,000. Delivery Manager, which requires no additional hardware, includes the software to create electronic documents, as well as an unlimited number of delivery agents (distributed for free to end-users), and sophisticated statistical tracking software to obtain valuable subscriber information. Publishers would pay a fee to Digital Delivery of "pennies per megabyte" for each transmission. (Rates will depend on the size of the document, the frequency of delivery and the transport mechanism used—TCP/IP or dial-up line.) Friedler compares the company to a virtual FedEx.

The service is currently being offered free to TechWeb users, but CMP plans to monitor reader feedback to refine and reintroduce the product in several months. "We have to determine if people think this is worthwhile," says Pundyk.

Pundyk explains that, in some ways, this digital experience mimics that of the real-life reader at a newsstand. "When you go to a magazine stand, you are bombarded by magazines, but you really read only about three. In the future, you could subscribe to Digital Delivery versions of those [titles]. With custom versions, you will get less information, but more of the information that's important to you."

Digital Delivery's Friedler comments: "Everyone's saying, 'Come to my Web site,' but no one cares about the Web site. Look, here's a model that works: People subscribe to a [print] magazine and it gets delivered to their mailbox. Why shouldn't that happen electronically?"

At the end of the day, for today and the future, publishers who are eager to begin the versioning process have many choices. A customized, database-driven setup such as the system employed by *TV Guide* is probably too costly for most, although there are as many approaches as there are magazines. And fortunately, the ease of implementation and lower cost point for versioning on the Web may attract publishers who want to add value through targeting specialized reader interests. □

Prepress in the House

BY STEVE WILSON

In 1986, Alan Dalfen, then president of Weider Health and Fitness, had a good idea. Tired of rising prepress costs, Dalfen decided to bring the task of prepress in-house and created Dynamic Color Inc. With an investment of $1.2 million, Dalfen acquired the imaging, scanning and proofing equipment needed to handle Weider Publishing's four magazines, as well as attract other clients.

Eight years later, in 1994, he was forced to dissolve the company. It had become a drain on Weider's coffers, never evolving into the profit center Dalfen had anticipated. Trusting the advice of consultants who were out of touch with the company's production needs, Dalfen wasted an additional $1 million on proprietary equipment that soon became obsolete. The workload was overwhelming, and the staff of 30 was not proficient enough with the machinery to handle running out 800 pages of film each month for the magazines, as well as the company's in-house advertising, posters and food-packaging labels. In the end, Weider was forced to hand prepress operations to its printer, Quad/Graphics, Inc.

The project became "economically stupid," in the words of Steve Weprin, Weider's production manager. He says the root of the problem was that Dynamic failed to live up to the impossible standards the Woodland Hills, California-based company set for it. "[Dalfen] mistakenly thought we could do everything," Weprin laments.

Despite Weider's ill-fated experience, more and more publishers have brought prepress functions in-house, inspired by a decrease in imagesetter prices and the promise of greater time flexibility and reduced production costs. But what many magazines don't consider is that the savings inherent in doing it themselves do not always equal long-term cost-effectiveness. A publisher must weigh both the obvious and hidden costs of taking prepress functions in-house against what it stands to gain.

Size counts

If you're considering acquiring an imagesetter, first determine whether your operation is large enough to benefit from owning the equipment. Robert Holt, former director of industry markets publishing at Scitex America Corp. in Bedford, Massachusetts, says publications with editorial staffs of 10 people or more could find the investment worthwhile. Be sure to take into account the actual size of your publication as well. "The smaller the format, the smaller the imagesetter you need," Holt says. "There are high-quality imagesetters for below $30,000."

Dan Segal, general manager of Cambridge Prepress Services in Cambridge, Massachusetts, contends that magazines demand the quality and speed that only $70,000 imagesetters can provide. He recommends such a purchase for group publishers, basing his model for cost-effectiveness on the number of pages to be separated into film. Segal says a $70,000 imagesetter, plus RIP and processor, will cost about $125,000. Factoring in 6.5 percent interest over three years, Segal estimates that roughly 1,000 pages must be separated per month for a company to break even on that investment.

Savings accounts

Some publishers might consider this figure extravagant. Willis Caster, prepress director of New York City's Wenner Media, says the *Rolling Stone* publisher finds it economical to separate 500 pages per month with a high-end Barco Graphics Commercial Printing and Publishing system. He says he saves 30 percent off what he used to pay an outside vendor. The setup—operated by a staff of eight—links three workstations, two Barco 3700M imagesetters and two Linotype 3500 drum scanners.

CMP Publications of Manhasset, New York, produces a minimum of 1,200 pages of film each month for five of its titles, including *NetGuide* and *HomePC*. The company began to bring prepress in-house in 1989, when it purchased a Linotronic L300 imagesetter and a Fuji Color Art proofer. In 1993, it added an Agfa 1000. The most recent addition is an Agfa Select Set 7000. Brian Holland, manager of operations and prepress, says he also saves 30 percent off what he would pay an outside service bureau.

Burlington, Ontario-based Town Publishing used to shell out $17,000 a month in prepress expenses for *Hamilton This Month*. Two years ago, the Canadian publisher opened a prepress branch, Eclipse Color Ontario, Ltd. Now it bills back the magazine at $12,000, according to general manager Angelo Antoniadis. Armed with a Linotype-Hell Company scanner and Linotype 560 imagesetter, a staff of eight produces the 96 pages of *Hamilton This Month* and the 64 pages of bimonthly *Hamilton Business*, and caters to outside clients as well.

Under one roof

Although running your own film can be significantly less expensive than sending it out to a service bureau or printer, those savings may be offset or lost if an in-house department fails to keep up with the competitive edge vendors will always have. "If I'm a vendor, when a client tells me 'We need this in 24 hours,' I'll figure out how to do it," Segal explains. "If I'm an in-house department, I may say 'I can't get that to you until 72 hours from now,' and they'll have to work around it."

Says Weider's Weprin: "We failed to establish a proper vendor/client relationship." Because of limited training and time constraints, Dynamic Color's staff was unable to take care of special requests the way an outside vendor can. "We worked too intimately," says Weprin.

However, that level of intimacy is the reason *Playboy* in Chicago owns two imagesetters (an Agfa Avantra and Varityper 4500) and an Enco proofing system. For the past six years, *Playboy* has been output almost entirely in-house (about 100 pages per month), except for the covers and centerfolds, which are farmed out to a veteran vendor. The staff of 12 works with the art department to make last-minute corrections or changes. According to graphics technology manager Chester Kiernicki, these last-minute changes often result in extra work hours. The time savings *Playboy* would otherwise gain from having an in-house setup are sometimes diminished because "art directors tend to be fussy."

For CMP's Holland, time is money. When he compares his prepress fees and performance to a vendor's,

---

■ Behind the prepress curtain

Before opening Eclipse Color Ontario, Ltd., Town Publishing in Burlington, Ontario, used to pay up to $120 for separations. Now, their cost is $45. Savings like these can be achieved by taking prepress in-house, but other expenses—initial investment and equipment upkeep—play a big part.

Dave Flanagan, president, and Dan Segal, general manager, Cambridge, Massachusetts-based Cambridge Prepress Services, break down the costs as follows:

The obvious costs

The imagesetter: A $35,000 to $70,000 machine is suitable for most magazines. Quality doesn't vary with the price tag, but speed does. The RIP device, which processes the data to be imaged, is typically priced at $35,000.

The film: The total cost of film, plus the chemistry needed to process it, is about $1.64 per page.

The chemistry: Developer and fixer usually cost around $300 to $350 a month.

The film processor: This device is about $20,000.

Proofing: In addition to $25,000 for a proofer, the contact frame costs $2,000. Each proofed page can cost from $40 to $70.

Scanning: The minimum price of an adequate color scan-

ner, be it flatbed or drum, runs between $50,000 and $70,000.

Staffing: Expect to pay between $14 and $25 an hour for skilled prepress technicians.

The hidden costs

Spoilage: Even experienced imagers encounter a 5 percent spoilage rate. A self-run operation, with a less experienced staff, could easily run that figure up to 20 percent.

Upgrades: Upgrading software and equipment can cost at least 10 percent of the total setup price every 18 months.

Silver recovery system: A device to capture leftover silver from the film can cost from $400 to $5,000, depending on the environmental regulations of the state where the magazine is based.

Densitometer: Film must be dense enough to transfer an image to the printing plate. Densitometers, which take this measurement, cost from $1,000 to $2,000.

Space: You'll need "at least the size of an efficient kitchen" in order to set up shop, plus a darkroom, says Segal.

Downtime: To determine the amount of money lost when an imagesetter isn't running, amortize these costs over the number of operating hours.

---

turnaround time is just as important as cost per page. "We routinely turn around a page in three hours," he says. "For vendors, 24 hours is the norm." As long as Holland can keep this edge, he will continue to run film in-house.

Keeping up with the competition

At the very least, keeping up with vendor expertise requires a lot of training. The learning curve is high, so don't expect a truly seamless production process immediately. Bill Benway, film technician at *Playboy,* says that while the production department was getting used to its first imagesetter, it experienced some hard times. "Our color would be approved, but the film would go haywire," he says. After a few issues, the process was under control.

When a magazine-owned prepress department mimics the functions of an outside vendor, it has to spend like one, too. Equipment maintenance and the need to replenish consumables, such as chemicals and film, require an ongoing investment. Proofing isn't cheap, either. Town Publishing's Antoniadis says proofing runs him about $70 a page. Caster of Wenner says he pays $100 for each proof. To cut those charges, Wenner wants to install digital proofing devices soon.

Finally, an idle imagesetter isn't a profitable one. Wenner and Playboy Enterprises run their machines only during regular business hours, unless their staffs are working overtime. Holland, on the other hand, wrings all he can from CMP's setup. His department of 13 works two shifts, from 7 A.M. to 1 A.M. This January, he initiated a third shift, from 12 A.M. to 8 A.M.

Cultivating customers

Although it's possible to achieve a cost-effective in-house setup to serve your own magazines, some publishers have gone further, achieving what Dalfen of Weider once envisioned: turning the prepress department into a profit center with outside customers.

Carmel Color Graphics produces *Homes & Land,* a 48-page real estate guide that comes out every five weeks. The Carmel, California, publisher uses a Varityper 6000 imagesetter and Fuji proofing equipment to run 100 pages of film over the span of two-and-a-half weeks. During downtime, Carmel prints brochures and catalogs for local businesses. Gregg Underdown, the production manager, estimates that the side business constitutes 40 percent of the workload.

Meanwhile, Wayne Narciso, Town Publishing's owner, was a veteran of the prepress industry when he opened Eclipse Color Ontario, Ltd., in 1993 to help amortize the production costs of *Hamilton This Month and Hamilton Business.* His experience and reputable staff attracted enough other clients that his magazines now represent only 15 percent of Eclipse's business. "If we'd just set this up for the magazines, we'd be broke," says Eclipse general manager Antoniadis. Instead, Eclipse has staffed up from two to eight, and is in the market for another scanner and imagesetter.

A filmless future

There is one very large caveat to all this: Although prepress equipment is cheaper and more accessible to publishers than ever before, a filmless future is on the horizon. Film-based imagesetting will eventually be replaced by the computer-to-plate solution and digital data delivery. CTP technology has already kept some publishers who do their own prepress from buying machines that they fear will soon be obsolete. A study in the October 23, 1995, "Seybold Special Report" found that 40 percent of large printers say they will buy CTP technology in the next few years.

Tim Nickel, imaging systems manager of Horsham, Pennsylvania-based TVSM Inc., says the company started producing *Total TV* using CTP last November. With 21 versions and a lot of last-minute updates to manage, CTP makes economic sense for the 1,000,000-circulation magazine. "You open your production window while maintaining your press window," Nickel says.

Nevertheless, because many printers and publishers believe a CTP solution is still cost-prohibitive, film-based imagesetters should be around for some time. But no matter what technology is used, taking prepress in-house will still be rife with hidden costs and hassles for the unsuspecting publisher. Yet, with caution and research, the investment can be a wise one. □

section eight

resource directory

■ Advertising/Databases/Marketing/Fulfillment

American List Counsel
88 Orchard Road CN-5219
Princeton, NJ 08543
Phone: (908) 874-4300
Fax: (908) 874-4433
List Brokers; List Compilers; List Managers

Communications Data Services, Inc.
1901 Bell Avenue
Des Moines, IA 50315-1099
Phone: (515) 246-6920
Fax: (515) 246-6882
*Computer Modeling; Database Marketing;
Fulfillment: Circulation/Product/Book & Premium/
On-Line; List Maintenance*

Cowles Event Management
911 Hope Street
PO Box 4232
Stamford, CT 06907-0232
Phone: (203) 358-9900 ext. 701
Fax: (203) 961-8399
Trade Show Management

Database America Companies
100 Paragon Drive
Montvale, NJ 07645-0416
Phone: (201) 476-2300
Fax: (201) 476-2405
*Database Management; Data Entry & Conversion;
Direct Mail Consultants*

Direct Media, Inc.
200 Pemberwick Road
Greenwich, CT 06830
Phone: (203) 532-1000
*List Brokers; List Managers; List Brokers/Managers,
Canada/International*

Electronic Data Systems Corporation (EDS)
1251 Avenue of the Americas, 41st Floor
New York, NY 10021
Phone: (800) 324-3245
or (212) 403-6000
*Circulation Promotion; Consultants/Management,
Marketing & Editorial; Databases: On-Line; Data
Processing; Electronic Editing Systems & Pagination;
Interactive Media*

Mark Facey & Company
225 North Main Street
Bristol, CT 06010
Phone: (800) 28-FACEY
or (203) 589-0221
Fax: (203) 589-9128
Telephone Marketing, Inbound/Outbound; Research

Fulfillment Corporation of America (FCA)
205 West Center Street
Marion, OH 43302-3707
Phone: (614) 383-5231
Fax: (614) 383-2875
Direct Mail: Full Service Direct Marketing;
Fulfillment: Circulation

Gillespie Magazine Marketing
191 Clarksville Road
Lawrenceville, NJ 08648
Phone: (609) 452-1633
Fax: (609) 520-1633
Consultants/Circulation; Direct Mail and Promotion
Specialists

Julie A. Laitin Enterprises, Inc.
19 W. 44th Street, 9th Floor
New York, NY 10036
Phone: (212) 840-1270
Fax: (212) 840-1676
Consultants/Management, Marketing & Editorial;
Direct Mail and Promotion Specialists;
Media Kits/Rate Cards/Advertising Promotions

Marketing Information Network (MIN)
9401 Cedar Lake Avenue
Oklahoma City, OK 73113-0960
Phone: (405) 475-1050
Fax: (405) 475-1055
List Research

Omeda Communications, Inc.
3005 MacArthur Blvd.
Northbrook, IL 60062
Phone: (708) 564-8900
Fax: (708) 564-9154
Custom Database Design; Databases: On-Line;
Fulfillment: Circulation

Rider Circulation Services
550 N. Brand Blvd., Suite 700
Glendale, CA 91203
Phone: (213) 344-1200
Fax: (213) 256-9999
Distribution: National

TAI Tyson Associates Inc.
440 Main Street
Ridgefield, CT 06877
Phone: (203) 431-8905
Fax: (203) 438-8232
Direct Mail Consultants, National/International;
Promotion Services

■ Art/Design

Ayers/Johanek Publication Design
2003 31st Street, S.W.
Allentown, PA 18103
Phone: (610) 797-8253 or
4750 Rolling Hills Drive
Bozeman, MT 59715
Phone: (406) 585-8826

Brady & Paul Communications Inc.
62 Hillside Avenue
Melrose, MA 02176
Phone: (617) 665-4941 or
120 East Oakland Park Blvd., No. 105
Fort Lauderdale, FL 33334
Phone: (305) 537-9040

David Merrill Design
4 North Pasture Road
Westport, CT 06880
Phone: (203) 222-1781

Vera Steiner Design
110 W. 40th Street
New York, NY 10018
Phone: (212) 768-8075

■ Executive Search Firms

Association of Executive Search Consultants
500 Fifth Avenue, Suite 930
New York, NY 10110
Phone: (212) 398-9556
Fax: (212) 398-9560

Bert Davis Associates
400 Madison Avenue, Suite 1401
New York, NY 10017
Phone: (212) 838-4000
Fax: (212) 935-3291

The Howard-Sloan-Koller Group
1140 Avenue of the Americas
New York, NY 10036
Phone: (212) 704-0444
Fax: (212) 869-7999

Korn/Ferry International
237 Park Avenue
New York, NY 10017
Phone: (212) 687-1834
Fax: (212) 986-5684

■ Magazine Management

Editorial Management Strategies
795 East 19th Street
Brooklyn, NY 11230
Phone: (718) 434-1100

The Jordan, Edmiston Group, Inc.
885 Third Avenue
New York, NY 10022
Phone: (212) 754-0710

Magazine Capital
457 North Harrison Street
Princeton, NJ 08540
Phone: (609) 924-9394
Fax: (609) 924-3935

Magazine Consulting Group
11845 Olympic Blvd., Suite 845
Los Angeles, CA 90064
Phone: (310) 477-2232
Fax: (310) 479-0720

Venture Funding Group International
49 W. 12th Street
Executive Suite
New York, NY 10011
Phone: (212) 691-9895

■ New Media Consultants/Developers

FaxBack, Inc.
1100 NW Compton Drive, Suite 200
Beaverton, OR 97006
Phone: (800) 873-8353
For demonstration call:
(800) FAXBACK (329-2225)

Fry Multimedia
5340 Plymouth Road, Suite 202
Ann Arbor, MI 48105
Phone: (800) FRY-MULTI
Fax: (313) 741-0906
E-mail: fry@msen.com

Gotham Interactive
99 Hudson Street
New York, NY 10013
Phone: (212) 376-6063
Fax: (212) 376-6067
E-mail: sepso@gothamcity.com

Inlet
Magazine Publishing on the Web
222 Third Avenue S.E., Suite 20
Cedar Rapids, IA 52403
Phone: (319) 369-0096
E-mail: inlet@inlet.com
Web: http://www.inlet.com

Integrated Data Concepts
PO Box 93428
Los Angeles, CA 90093
Phone: (213) 469-3380
Fax: (213) 962-9040

Interactive Media Associates
11 Eagle Nest Road
Morristown, NJ 07960
Phone: (201) 539-5255
Fax: (201) 539-5255

Media Conversion Corp.
800 Roosevelt Road, Bldg. D, Suite 106
Glen Ellyn, IL 60137
Phone: (708) 858-4566
Fax: (708) 469-1277

Metatec New Media Solutions
Metatec Corporation
7001 Metatec Blvd.
Dublin, OH 43017
Web: http://www.metatec.com

Millstar Electronic Publishing
1170 Wheeler Way
Langhorne, PA 19047
Phone: (800) 628-4623 or (215) 752-2900
Web: http://www.millstar.com

Reed Technology and Information Services
20251 Century Blvd.
Germantown, MD 20874
Phone: (800) 922-9204 or (301) 428-3700
Fax: (301) 428-0224

Sprint TeleMedia
6666 W. 110th Street
Overland Park, KS 66211
Phone: (800) 735-5900 or (913) 661-8000

Wickham & Associates, Inc.
1700 K Street N.W., Suite 1202
Washington, DC 20006
Phone: (202) 296-4860
Web: http//www.wickham.com

■ Online Vendors

America Online, Inc.
8619 Westwood Center Drive
Vienna, VA 22182
Phone: (800) 827-6364 or (703) 448-8700
Fax: (703) 883-1509

CompuServe, Inc.
5000 Arlington Center Blvd.
PO Box 20212
Columbus, OH 43220
Phone: (800) 848-8199 or (614) 457-8600

LEXIS/NEXIS
PO Box 933
Dayton, OH 45401
Phone: (800) 227-9597 or (513) 865-6800

NewsNet, Inc.
945 Haverford Road
Bryn Mawr, PA 19010
Phone: (800) 345-1301 or (215) 527-8030
Fax: (215) 527-0338

Prodigy Services Company
445 Hamilton Avenue
White Plains, NY 10601
Phone: (914) 448-8000
Fax: (914) 993-8093

■ Organizations/Associations

American Business Press
675 Third Avenue
Fourth Floor
New York, NY 10017
Phone: (212) 661-6360
Fax: (212) 370-0736

American Federation of Television and Radio Artists
(AFTRA)
260 Madison Avenue
New York, NY 10016
Phone: (212) 532-0800
Fax: (212) 545-1238

American Library Association
50 E. Huron Street
Chicago, IL 60611
Phone: (800) 545-2433 or (312) 944-6780
Fax: (312) 440-9374

American Management Association
135 West 50th Street
New York, NY 10020
Phone: (212) 586-8100
Fax: (212) 903-8168

American Marketing Association
250 S. Wacker Drive, Suite 200
Chicago, IL 60606
Phone: (312) 648-0536
Fax: (312) 993-7542

American Society of Journalists and Authors
1501 Broadway, Suite 1907
New York, NY 10036
Phone: (212) 997-0947
Fax: (212) 768-7414

American Society of Magazine Editors
575 Lexington Avenue
New York, NY 10022
Phone: (212) 752-0055
Fax: (212) 888-4217

American Society of Newspaper Editors
PO Box 4090
Reston, VA 22090-1700
Phone: (703) 648-1144
Fax: (703) 476-6125

American Telemarketing Association
4605 Lankershim Blvd., Suite 824
North Hollywood, CA 91602
Phone: (818) 766-5324
Fax: (818) 766-8168

Audit Bureau of Circulations
900 N. Meacham Road
Schaumberg, IL 60173-4968
Phone: (708) 605-0909
Fax: (708) 605-0483

Bureau of Electronic Publishing
141 New Road
Parsippany, NJ 07054
Phone: (201) 808-2700
Fax: (201) 808-2676

Business Publications Audit (BPA) International
270 Madison Avenue
New York, NY 10016-0699
Phone: (212) 779-3200
Fax: (212) 725-1721

City and Regional Magazine Association
5820 Wilshire Blvd., Suite 500
Los Angeles, CA 90036
Phone: (213) 937-5514
Fax: (213) 937-0959

Direct Marketing Association
1120 Avenue of the Americas
New York, NY 10036-6700
Phone: (212) 768-7277
Fax: (212) 398-6725

Editorial Freelancers Association
Madison Square Station
PO Box 2050
New York, NY 10159
Phone: (212) 677-3357

Fulfillment Management Association
60 East 42nd Street, Suite 1146
New York, NY 10165
Phone: (212) 661-1410
Fax: (212) 661-1412

Information Industry Association
555 New Jersey Avenue, N.W., Suite 800
Washington, DC 20001
Phone: (202) 639-8262
Fax: (202) 638-4403

International Association of Business Communicators
One Hallidie Plaza, Suite 600
San Francisco, CA 94102
Phone: (415) 433-3400
Fax: (415) 362-8762

International Intellectual Property Alliance
1718 Connecticut Avenue, N.W.
7th Floor
Washington, DC 20009
Phone: (202) 833-4198
Fax: (202) 872-0546

Magazine Publishers of America
919 Third Avenue, 22nd Floor
New York, NY 10022
Phone: (212) 872-3700
Fax: (212) 888-4217

Resource directory

National Association of Broadcasters
1771 N Street, N.W.
Washington, DC 20036
Phone: (202) 429-5300
Fax: (202) 429-5343

National Association of Desktop Publishers
1260 Boylston Street
Boston, MA 02210
Phone: (800) 874-4113 or (617) 426-2885
Fax: (617) 437-0014

National Association of Printers and Lithographers
780 Palisade Avenue
Teaneck, NJ 07666
Phone: (800) 642-NAPL or (201) 342-0700
Fax: (201) 692-0286

National Small Business United
1155 15th Street, N.W., Suite 710
Washington, DC 20005
Phone: (800) 345-6728 or (202) 293-8830

The Newsletter Association
1401 Wilson Blvd.
Suite 403
Arlington, VA 22209
Phone: (800) 356-9032 or (703) 527-2333

Public Relations Society of America
33 Irving Place, 3rd Floor
New York, NY 10003-2376
Phone: (212) 995-2230
Fax: (212) 995-0757

Society of National Association
Publications (SNAP)
1650 Tyson Blvd.
McLean, VA 22102
Phone: (703) 506-3285
Fax: (703) 506-3266

Society of Professional Journalists
PO Box 77
16 South Jackson Street
Greencastle, IN 46135
Phone: (317) 653-3333
Fax: (317) 653-4631

Society of Publication Designers
60 E. 42nd Street, Suite 1416
New York, NY 10165
Phone: (212) 983-8585

Society for Technical Communication
901 N. Stuart Street, Suite 904
Arlington, VA 22203-1854
Phone: (703) 522-4114
Fax: (703) 522-2075

■ Paper Suppliers

Bowater Incorporated
PO Box 1028
55 East Camperdown Way
Greenville, SC 29602
Phone: (800) 271-7733/282-9387
Fax: (803) 282-9562

Georgia-Pacific Papers
Communication Papers Division
55 Park Place, 15th Floor
Atlanta, GA 30303
Customer Service: (800) 727-3738
Sample Dept.: (800) 635-6672

Niagara of Wisconsin Paper Corporation
1101 Mill Street
Niagara, WI 54151
Phone: (800) 826-0431

Paper Resource Group
800 E. Ross Avenue
Cincinnati, OH 45217
Phone: (800) 436-4100 or (513) 242-3600
Fax: (513) 242-3604

■ Production Services

Automated Graphic Systems
4590 Graphics Drive, Box 188
White Plains, MD 20695-0188
Phone: (800) 678-8760 or (301) 843-1800
Fax: (301) 843-6339

The William Byrd Press, Inc./
Specialty Publications Division
2901 Byrdhill Road
Richmond, VA 23228
Phone: (800) 234-BYRD (2973)

Dartmouth Printing Company
69 Lyme Road
Hanover, NH 03755
Phone: (603) 643-2220

Judd's, Incorporated
Route 55E, Box 777
Strasburg, VA 22657
Phone: (800) 368-3492
Fax: (703) 465-6506

The Mack Printing Group
1991 Northampton Street
Easton, PA 18042-8189
Phone: (610) 258-9111
Fax: (610) 250-7202
E-mail: sales@mpg.com

Quad/Graphics, Inc.
Duplainville Road
Pewaukee, WI 53072-4195
Information Hotline: (414) 246-2800
Fax: (800) 888-9010, Program 888

Trade & Technology Press
26 Sixth Street, Suite 262
Stamford, CT 06905
Phone: (203) 323-3385/(800) 275-7107
Fax: (203) 323-0606

■ Publishing Institutes

Denver Publishing Institute
2075 University Blvd.
D 114
Denver, CO 80210
Phone: (303) 871-2570
Fax: (303) 871-2501

New York University
Center for Publishing
48 Cooper Square
New York, NY 10003
Phone: (212) 998-7219
Fax: (212) 995-3060

Radcliffe Publishing Course
Radcliffe College
77 Brattle Street
Cambridge, MA 02138
Phone: (617) 495-8678
Fax: (617) 496-2333

Rice University Publishing Program
Office of Continuing Studies
Rice University
Mail Stop 550
6100 Main Street
Houston, TX 77005-1892
Phone: (713) 520-6022
Fax: (713) 285-5213

Stanford Professional Publishing Course
Stanford Alumni Association
Bowman Alumni House
Stanford, CA 94305-4005
Phone: (415) 725-0544
Fax: (415) 725-7510
E-mail: publishing.courses@leland.stanford.edu

■ Reprint Services

FosteReprints
4295 South Ohio Street
Michigan City, IN 46360
Phone: (800) 382-0808
Fax: (219) 874-2849

Reprint Management Services
147 West Airport Road
PO Box 5363
Lancaster, PA 17606-5363
Phone: (717) 560-2001
Fax: (717) 560-2063

Resource directory

■ Research/Information Services

Bureau of National Affairs, Inc.
1231 25th Street, N.W.
Washington, DC 20037
Phone: (800) 372-1033 or (202) 452-4200
Fax: (202) 822-8092

The Conference Board, Inc.
845 Third Avenue
New York, NY 10022
Phone: (212) 759-0900
Fax: (212) 980-7014

FIND/SVP, Inc.
625 Avenue of the Americas
New York, NY 10011
Phone: (800) 346-3787 or (212) 645-4500
Fax: (212) 645-7681

Gale Research Inc.
835 Penobscot Bldg.
Detroit, MI 48226-4094
Phone: (800) 877-GALE (4253) or (313) 961-2242
Fax: (313) 961-6815

Minority Business Information Institute
130 Fifth Avenue, 10th Floor
New York, NY 10011
Phone: (212) 242-8000
Fax: (212) 989-8410

National Technical Information Service
5285 Port Royal Road
Springfield, VA 22161
Phone: (800) 336-4700 or (703) 487-4600
Fax: (703) 321-8547

Roper Starch Worldwide, Inc.
205 E. 42nd Street
New York, NY 10017
Phone: (212) 599-0700
Fax: (212) 867-7008

SIMBA Information Inc.
213 Danbury Road
PO Box 7430
Wilton, CT 06897
Phone: (203) 834-0033
Fax: (203) 834-1771
E-mail: SIMBA99@aol.com

Simmons Market Research Bureau, Inc.
309 W. 49th Street
New York, NY 10019
Phone: (212) 373-8900
Fax: (212) 373-8918

Standard Rate & Data Service, Inc.
1700 E. Higgins Road
Des Plaines, IL 60018-5605
Phone: (847) 375-5000
Fax: (847) 375-5001

U.S. Department of Commerce
Bureau of Economic Analysis, BE-53
Washington, DC 20230
Phone/U.S.D.C.: (202) 482-2000
Phone/BEA: (202) 606-9900

section nine

contributors

Carol Addessi is vice president and general manager of Avenue Magazine, Inc.

William F. Allman is assistant managing editor for new media at *U.S. News & World Report.* He developed its CompuServe site and launched the USNEWS Online Web site.

Elaine Appleton is co-owner of Fresh Air Communications, a Newburyport, Massachusetts-based freelance writing partnership. She has written extensively about magazine production.

Eve Asbury is a partner in the New York City-based pre-press consultancy Asbury-Bristow Communications.

Barrie J. Atkin is executive director, consumer marketing, *TV Guide.* She has been director of new business development, the Miami Herald Publishing Company, and president of Atkin Associates, a management consulting firm.

Donald J. Austermann is president of Somers, New York-based Austermann & Co. He had been a promotion specialist for McGraw-Hill and director of communications, *Business Week.*

Scott Baltic is the editor of *Fire Chief* and the former editor of *Midwest Real Estate News,* both publications of Argus Business.

Stephen Barboza is a New York City-based freelance writer who has explored such diverse topics as dance, religion and travel. Doubleday will be releasing his fourth book in Winter 1997.

Stephen Barr, a Metuchen, New Jersey-based freelance writer, covers the newspaper and magazine industries.

Helen Berman is president of Helen Berman and Associates, a Los Angeles-based publishing sales training and marketing consulting firm.

John Brady is a partner at Boston-based Brady & Paul Communications, a magazine consultancy, and head of John Brady Seminars, which provides on-site training for publishing professionals.

John Campbell is a magazine editorial consultant. He has been editorial director, Hearst Business Publishing Group, and is a former senior editor of *Business Week.*

Contributors

Patricia G. Campbell is executive vice president, brand development group, Times Mirror Magazines.

E. Daniel Capell is president of Direct Marketing Data Corp. and managing director of Vos, Gruppo & Capell, an investment banking and consulting firm based in New York City.

Lynn Carlson is vice president, circulation director, *Harper's Magazine.*

John L. Cleveland is president of St. Louis, Missouri-based POS Sytems and Consulting, specialists in SGML tagging and document imaging.

Robert Cohen is president of Miami, Florida-based Robert Cohen Associates, Inc., specialists in start-ups and creating strategies and business plans for existing titles.

Matthew Cohn is president of Millstar Electronic Publishing Group in Langhorne, Pennsylvania, which specializes in digital directories and catalogs.

Peter Craig has been in the publishing industry since 1967, first as a partner in the accounting firms Deloitte & Touche and J.K. Lasser & Company, and later as president of his own firm, the Magazine Consulting Group in Los Angeles.

Lynn Crimando is assistant managing editor of *Money.*

Elizabeth Crow is editor in chief of *Mademoiselle* and was previously president, CEO and editorial director of Gruner + Jahr USA Publishing.

Mike Cuenca is a professor of journalism at the University of Kansas, and was previously director of production at *Mothering.*

Helene Eckstein is vice president, sales and marketing for PrepSAT, a national color pre-press firm headquartered in Franklin, Kentucky.

Frank Finn, president of Cadmus Consumer Publishing in Richmond, Virginia, has survived numerous magazine start-ups, large and small, in the course of more than 20 years in the business.

Pamela Fiori is editor in chief of *Town & Country* magazine.

Thom Forbes, former editor of Adweek Magazines, covers media and marketing from Hastings-on-Hudson, New York.

Catherine Fredman is a New York City-based freelance writer and editor. She currently edits Power the Vote (http://www.lhj-lwv.com), a Web site sponsored by *Ladies' Home Journal* and the League of Women Voters that is covering the 1996 election. She collaborated with Andrew S. Grove on *Only the Paranoid Survive,* a book on management strategy to be published by Doubleday in August 1996.

David Frenkel is president and CEO of Management Process Integrators, Inc.

Jessica R. Friedman is a New York City-based attorney who specializes in copyright, trademark and publishing law.

Richard P. Friedman is president and CEO of SIGS Publications, Inc., publisher of 12 computer magazines. He spent over a decade in publishing, honing his skills at *Signature, Parade,* ACM Publications and John Wiley & Sons.

David Garratt is managing director of COMAG Magazine Marketing, the largest independent British magazine distributor.

Anne Graham is executive editor of *Internal Auditor,* published by the Institute of Internal Auditors in Altamonte Springs, Florida.

Josh Gordon is president of Gordon & Associates, a publishers' rep firm located in Brooklyn, New York, and is the author of the book *Competitive Selling.*

Jim Guthrie is executive vice president of marketing development at Magazine Publishers of America.

Allan Halcrow is editor of *Personnel Journal.*

Todd Harris, former editor in chief of *CD-ROM World,* is a new-media consultant based in New York City.

John Johanek, a regular speaker at FOLIO: conferences, is founding partner of Allentown, Pennsylvania-based Publication Design, and works out of the firm's Bozeman, Montana, branch office.

Chris Kalamon is president of CEK Associates, a circulation consulting firm in Evergreen, Colorado.

Bruce L. Katcher, Ph.D., is president of Sharon, Massachusetts-based The Discovery Group, which specializes in readership, employee opinion and customer satisfaction surveys.

Drew Reid Kerr is president of Four Corners Communications, a public relations firm in New York City.

Julie A. Laitin is president of Julie A. Laitin Enterprises, Inc., a New York City-based consulting and marketing firm specializing in publications.

Jeff Laurie is a marketing consultant to the Village Group, an interactive service based in Cambridge, Massachusetts.

Tony Lee is editor, *National Business Employment Weekly* and *Managing Your Career*, publications of Dow Jones & Co. Inc., Princeton, New Jersey.

John W. Malcom is a managing director in charge of publishing at The Accord Group, Johnson Smith & Knisely, a New York City-based executive search firm.

James C. McCullagh is a magazine and media consultant, based in Hellertown, Pennsylvania and specializing in international publishing.

Slade Metcalf is a partner in the New York law firm of Squadron, Ellenoff, Plesent & Lehrer, where he specializes in media law and general litigation.

Dennis Milan is director of marketing for the National Systems Contractors Association, a trade association for electronic systems integrators.

Katharin Norwood, president of The Norwood Group, Inc., of Rowayton, Connecticut, has been working exclusively on magazine transactions for the past few years. Prior to that she was a publisher of specialized magazines.

Richard M. O'Connor is publisher of *Successful Meetings,* published by New York City-based Bill Communications.

David Z. Orlow is the founder and president of Periodical Studies Service, a New York City-based consulting

group specializing in small-magazine transactions and ad-sales growth. He was formerly a vice president at Ziff-Davis Publishing.

Stuart W. Park is president of i3 Information & Imagination Inc., a Westport, Connecticut-based interactive multimedia firm devoted exclusively to the marketing and sales needs of businesses.

James Parker publishes several business and consumer titles for Sydney, Australia-based Yaffa Publishing Group.

Thomas Pecht is the president of Publishers Network, Inc., of Buford, Georgia. He previously ran a print-media investment banking group.

Reed Phillips III is a managing partner at DeSilva & Phillips, Inc. in New York City.

Margaret E. Popper is the U.K.-based editor of "European Media, Business & Finance," a newsletter published by Phillips Business Information Inc. She was previously features editor of "Mergers & Acquisitions Report."

Carl S. Pugh is president and COO of the trade show/seminar group at Mecklermedia Corporation in Westport, Connecticut.

Donn Rappaport is chairman of American List Counsel, Inc., a full-service mailing list and database broker, manager and compiler located in Princeton, New Jersey.

Hanna Rubin is executive editor at *Travel Holiday*, published by Hachette Filipacchi Magazines. She was formerly editor of the online edition of *Boating*.

Heidi Schultz is executive vice president of Agora Consulting, a marketing communications consultancy in Evanston, Illinois.

Robert Sentinery is the founder and publisher of *Zone* and *Java Monthly*. He is also a consultant for independent publishing projects.

Stefan Sharkansky is a technical editor at Quarterdeck Corporation in San Francisco.

Bruce Sheiman is managing director, The Jordan Edmiston Group, Inc., New York City.

Contributors

Jack Sherin is president of Jack Sherin Design, a New York City-based graphic design firm specializing in corporate communications projects. John Hanc is assistant professor of communication arts at the New York Institute of Technology in Old Westbury, New York. He has written presentations for *People, Entertainment Weekly, Fortune, Health* and *Audubon*.

George Simpson is president of New York City-based George H. Simpson Communications, which specializes in PR, promotions and special events for magazines.

Stephen A. Socha is president of Paramus, New Jersey-based American Equities Group Inc., a full-service financial-services firm catering to the publishing industry.

Vera Steiner is president of Vera Steiner Design, a New York City-based studio specializing in editorial design, redesign and start-ups.

Rita Stollman is president of Editorial Management Strategies, a Brooklyn, New York-based consulting firm that specializes in starting up and repositioning magazines.

L. Mark Stone is a managing director of Broadview Associates in Fort Lee, New Jersey.

Celine Sullivan is vice president, market development, Cowles Media Company.

Paul Taybi is owner of Taybi Direct, a list brokerage and management firm in El Cerrito, California, specializing in business-to-business.

Elaine Tyson is president of Tyson Associates, Inc., a Ridgefield, Connecticut-based direct response advertising agency and consulting firm.

Charles F. Whitaker is an assistant professor at Northwestern University's Medill School of Journalism. Before joining Medill, he served as a senior editor at *Ebony*.

Jan V. White is a communication design consultant. His most recent book is *Color for the Electronic Age* (Watson-Guptill, New York).

Leonard Witt is executive director of the Civic Journalism Initiative at Minnesota Public Radio. He was formerly editor of *Minnesota Monthly* and *The Complete Book of Feature Writing* (Writer's Digest, 1991).

Howard Zacharoff and Brenda Cotter are members of the Media and Publishing Law Group of Brown, Rudnick, Freed & Gesmer, in Boston. □